Film Style and Technology:
History and Analysis

Barry Salt

Second Edition

* STARWORD *

This book is dedicated to the National Film Archive, without whom ...

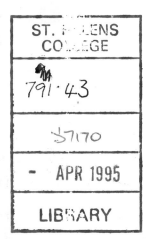

Notice to librarians

This book is a work of film history; and in the first place specifically a history of film style. It is *not* primarily about film technology.

Catalogue records relating to it may be obtained from the British Library and the Library of Congress.

Distributed in North America by **SAMUEL FRENCH**

7623 Sunset Boulevard, Hollywood, CA 90046

First Edition published 1983, this Second Edition 1992

Typeset in Adobe Garamond
by Oxford University Computing Service

Printed by Hobbs the Printers, Southampton

Published by Starword, 5 Tadmor Street, London W12 8AH
Copyright © 1983, 1992 by Barry Salt

Made in England

ISBN 0 9509066 2 x

CONTENTS

PREFACE

The main body of this book is made up of an exposition of the history of the development of the formal features of film style, and also of those developments in film technology that might have some connection with stylistic developments. Although the main events in the history of film technology are covered, it is not intended to be an exhaustive treatment of that subject, and I omit all those technical ideas that had no success in the film industry, not to mention the pre-history of film technology. My consideration of the major trends in film style and technology is based on the examination of several thousand films whose production dates spread fairly evenly over the years from 1895 to 1970, and on the comparison of those films with information about film-making and technology derived from the sources listed in the Bibliography of this book, and also from my own film-making experience.

This book is basically concerned with mainstream fictional cinema, and most truly avant-garde films are excluded from consideration in it. This is because there is a very real separation between these two bodies of cinema, with avant-garde films being influenced mostly by other avant-garde films and other contemporary advanced art, and not by mainstream cinema, and vice-versa. My failure to treat avant-garde cinema does not mean that I consider it to be unimportant: on the contrary, following the principles I set forth in Chapter 4, I believe that on the whole its works are of at least equal value to those of mainstream cinema. Japanese cinema is also excluded for rather similar reasons. Until fairly recently there have been influences on Japanese cinema from Western cinema, but no influences going the other way. Also, the large number of films that are necessary to get a clear and accurate picture of overall developments within which individual films are placed has not been available to me in the case of Japanese cinema, nor has a complete knowledge of the very different social and cultural background to Japanese films.

The main work in this book extends naturally in several directions, and some of these are exemplified in the consideration of the films of Max Ophuls at the end of it. In that final section some of the stylistic information from earlier in the book is put to work in combination with the analytical and aesthetic principles I develop at its beginning. In their turn, my analytical and aesthetic principles are justified in both positive and negative ways by the critical material in Chapters 1 to 3. Although it is possible to understand everything that follows Chapter 3 without reading these first three chapters, there are further good reasons for their presence in this book. Ideally, the critical material in these early chapters should have been published long ago in one of the serious film journals, but in fact *Sight & Sound*, *Movie*, and *Screen* in England, and *Film Quarterly* and *The Quarterly Review of Film Studies* in the United States have all refused to publish all, or part, of various earlier versions of these first three chapters, with no reasons given. As well as this, quite a number of American film academics have tried to prevent these chapters being published in book form, so I have drawn the obvious conclusion that all of these people have no answers to my criticisms of various previous forms of film theory that they happen to believe in. Adding the fact that a recently published book on film history uses novel information taken from the manuscript of this book without acknowledgement, it is clear that I had to get all of this book published by the only means left to me. However, I am very glad to acknowledge that there were two people, namely John Ellis and Ben Brewster, who though they do not agree with many of my ideas, were broad-minded enough to advocate its publication, though without success.

My work was supported for some years by the Slade School of University College, London, headed by Sir William Coldstream, where the prime mover of the beginning of my researches was the head of the Slade Film Unit, James Leahy. James Leahy has given me massive support ever since, and it is difficult to be sufficiently grateful to him for this. Pieces of useful information about past film practices have been generously provided by Kevin Brownlow, Byron Haskin, Vic Margutti, Mark Pytel, Noël Burch, Charles Musser, André Gaudreault, Tom Gunning and Tim Dean, and a special acknowledgement goes to Ben Brewster for pointing out to me an important stylistic trend that I had overlooked. I have another important debt to Richard Abel for his descriptions of four films by Louis Delluc and Jean Epstein that I have so far been unable to see. I also owe a lot to Laurence Baxter and Valerie Isham for their help with the analysis of the statistics of shot length distributions, and Wai Ling Chan for her calculations on those same distributions. Other people whose help I want to acknowledge on the production side of this book are Frances Thorpe and Peter Miller for their advice, Cathy Grant for doing the typing in the early stages of the writing of it, Nick Collins for proof-reading, Yossi Balanescu for the jacket design, and Tom Graves of *Wordsmiths* for his mastery of typesetting from microcomputer disks.

The large amounts of film viewing that lie behind my work in this book depended on the help and facilities provided by a number of film organizations and the people who work in them, and I tender my appreciation to Eileen Bowser and the staff at the Museum of Modern Art film archive, the American Film Institute Archive at the Library of Congress, the Danish Film Museum and Ib Monty and Karen Jones, the Cinémathèque Royale Belgique and Jacques Ledoux, the Cinema Studies Department of New York University, and the film archive at Eastman House, Rochester, under John Kuiper. By far the largest part of part of my viewing has been done in London, and here my thanks go to the National Film Theatre and its staff, and the British Film Institute Distribution Division under Colin McArthur, where I especially thank Nigel Algar and the Film & Video Library. But my major debt is to the National Film Archive of Great Britain and its staff under David Francis. My special personal thanks go to Jeremy Boulton, Elaine Burrows, David Meeker, Clive Truman, and Tim Cotter who do their all to keep researching viewers happy, not to mention Roger Holman and the staff of the Cataloguing Department, particularly Don Swift and James Patterson. Without them nothing could have been done, and for this reason this book is dedicated to the National Film Archive and all who sail in her.

London, June 1983

PREFACE TO THE 2ND. EDITION

Many things have happened since the first edition of this book, some of them good, some of them bad. One of the good things was that I sold all the 2000 copies of it that I had printed, and it has made a certain impression, at least in Europe. On the other hand, the printers destroyed the film from which a reprint could have been made. But even this has its good side, as I have taken the opportunity to revise the book and include the latest discoveries I have made about the development of film style. I have also extended the treatment up to the present, with full chapters on the 'seventies and 'eighties.

Another piece of bad news is that even after I had successfully published the first edition of this book, many American academics have continued to oppose its distribution in the United States, and have used their power as advisers to American publishers to prevent them distributing it or making a co-publication deal with me for the second edition. Proper distribution in America is impossible for very small publishers like myself without either a co-publication deal with an American publisher, or alternatively by paying out a lot of money to a commercial book distributing firm. The reason for this academic opposition is that the opening chapters of this book criticize various forms of film theory and interpretation that they happen to believe in, and in particular those derived from Marxism and psychoanalysis. Psychoanalysis is apparently an area of blind faith for most American academics in the humanities departments of universities, and their closed minds are shown by their inability to produce any rebuttal of criticism of its validity. In fact there has been no attempt whatever to produce an intellectual defence of any of the forms of film theorizing and interpretation that I criticized in the first edition of this book, which is just what I expected. All this has continued, despite the admission by Althusser and Lacan towards the ends of their lives, that they were indeed charlatans, as was obvious twenty years ago to any intelligent and informed person. Yet Lacan's version of psychoanalysis is *still* being taught as received truth in film departments in universities around the world, and new 'theoretical' nonsense of similar kind has continued to appear, so the early chapters on film theory in this book still have to stay there. I do what I can, though those academics who oppose the truth being told know they can continue to rely quite successfully on their institutional power, which grows ever stronger, to protect their inadequacy.

However, another good thing that has happened is that there has been an increasing amount of research into silent cinema over the last nine years, immensely helped by the appearance of new yearly festivals of silent film, and also by single conferences on aspects of the subject. The most important of the festivals is the *Giornate del cinema muto* at Pordenone, but there are others which include silent film sections, such as the *Mostra del cinema libero* at Bologna. I have not been present at all of these, but like everyone else interested in the subject, I am profoundly grateful for their existence. The people who have begun researching early cinema in the last decade are mostly eager to collaborate in the production of knowledge, though there are unfortunately a few Americans who are more dishonest and careerist about what they do.

On the good side again, Ben Brewster has shared a number of viewings and ideas with me, and most importantly, let me see his frame enlargements of some of the copyright fragments of early Vitagraph films in the Library of Congress. His work on this, together with frame enlargements, can be seen in *Vitagraph Co. of America* (ed. Paolo Cherchi Usai, Studio Tesi, 1987). Much of the other contributions to film history during the last nine years are valuable too, but nothing that has appeared removes the need for this book in a second edition, even though some works, like the new series 'History of the

American Cinema' that has started appearing might be thought to cover a lot of the same ground. Although the volumes on the silent period written by Charles Musser, Eileen Bowser, and Richard Koszarski are packed with good stuff, there are major aspects of the evolution and nature of American mainstream continuity cinema (or 'classical cinema', if you prefer) during the silent years that they do not properly cover.

My work has also continued to depend on all the films from various times and places that continue to come into the National Film Theatre in London. There Waltraud Loges and Helen Deeble, and also the other staff, have been very helpful, as always, with my detailed studies. Nevertheless, most of my viewing has continued to be done in the National Film Archive, where the preservation programme has produced thousands more viewing copies of silent films in the last several years. I have now seen nearly all of these new viewing copies, and although there has not been anything comparable to the revelations that came from the first several hundred, many points have been further clarified. At the National Film Archive, the Viewing Service, run by Elaine Burrows, assisted by Jacqui Morris, and more recently Julie Rigg, have done all they could to help me, as they do other researchers. And Clive Truman is still the helpful man in charge of the machines in the basement. I also have to thank those reviewers of the first edition who picked up some errors, though not a couple who invented a large number of errors which were not there. During the last five years there has also been a further enlargement of my knowledge of professional film practice through working with my fellow teachers at the London International Film School, and I am grateful to all of them for this, and particularly to Roy Pointer.

With this new edition I have tried to keep the cost down, both to myself, and to the purchaser, by changing the format, with a larger page, double column setting, and a different typeface. This means that, although the actual content has increased by one third, the number of pages has decreased. I have also rearranged the order of some sections within chapters, to make the treatment of topics follow more consistently, thus aiding anyone wishing to follow any single major technical topic all the way through. To this end there is also, as before, the index in the technical glossary to aid such a longitudinal search. There are a more frame enlargements than before, but having the even larger number that I would like is still prevented by the high cost of half-tones, not to mention colour plates to illustrate topics in the last couple of decades. On the production side, this time I give special thanks to Stephen Miller for his help with the typesetting.

I suppose what anyone who has bought the first edition of this book will want to know about is the additional material in this edition. Inevitably, given the thousands more silent films I have seen from the pre-1915 period, it is the chapters dealing with this area that have changed most. In particular, the chapter on 1907-1913 is more than twice as long as it was before, and contains many new insights on various topics. The other major additions are full chapters on style and technology through the last two decades. There has been a great enlargement in my database of formal statistics, and this clarifies the descriptions of various stylisitic trends. Besides all this there are various additions and corrections elsewhere, so although I got the *major* developments pretty right in general the first time, it is probably necessary for anyone interested in the history of film style to buy this new edition. For instance, since I considered that it did not need me to point out the basic features of the large-scale construction of film scripts, I did not say much about this in the first edition, though I did briefly indicate some of the important points in this area. Now that some people have attempted to deal with this topic, and have not managed to get it right, I felt that I should spell out the obvious in a couple of places. So, although you could try xeroxing sections of this new edition from a library copy, if you just do that you are bound to miss something significant that wasn't in it before.

London, October 1992

1. INTRODUCTION

Although there has been hardly any extended writing about the historical development of film style, with or without its relation to film technology, there are some people who will say, and indeed have said already, that what I have written on the subject is false and worthless because I do not have the correct theoretical approach. Because of this, and because it is a good thing to have one's conceptual frameworks clear to oneself and others, it is essential that I show why their claims on your time and attention are unjustified, and why my approach to the matters with which this book deals is the correct one. Some of what I have to say is simple and some is not, for although simple arguments can often be conclusive, and simple analyses and demonstrations will take us much further in the study of films than has been realized, recent developments in this field force me to deal with some apparently difficult matters on their own level. And because I am forced to deal with some very fundamental matters in the course of these explanations and demonstrations, I will very briefly sketch my biography to indicate why what I have to say should be taken seriously.

Although I first became interested in and involved with film more than forty years ago as a member of a film society that screened everything from Méliès to Maya Deren, by way of the usual 'Film Society Classics', and whose members also indulged in amateur film-making, I later had a rather varied career that included dancing in a few ballet companies in Australia and England, and doing research in theoretical physics. For the latter work on the theory of superfluid helium done under Professor David Bohm I gained a Ph.D. from the University of London, and then went on to do a year as a lecturer in physics and mathematics at one of the colleges of that University. I had retained an interest in what was going on in the cinema during those years, and when it became clear to me that I was not another Einstein, I returned to film-making, doing a course at the London School of Film Technique for which, in a Diploma thesis written in 1968, I proposed the methods of stylistic analysis that you can see carried out in later chapters of this book. I worked professionally as a lighting cameraman on a number of small films of one kind or another, including an independent feature, before declining into the teaching of film-making and film history at various institutions in London, including the Slade School at University College London, and the Royal College of Art. At present I teach at the London International Film School, where, amongst other things, I supervise the 35 mm. studio production exercises, to a total of something like 4 hours of finished film a year. In the past I have also directed a few films, including a 35 mm. feature.

The intellectual position that I take from this background could be described as Scientific Realism, and this can be crudely summarized as the view that there is a real world, and that this real world is described by the established natural sciences. Scientific Realism is a development of commonsense realism (or 'naive realism' as some would have it), and the relation between Scientific Realism, commonsense realism, and the real world is a kind of parallel to the relation that exists between science, technology, and the real world. The rest is just words, some of which have some sort of correspondence to the real world as described by the natural sciences, and some of which do not. Perhaps I should make it clear that amongst those working in the sciences it is recognized that what constitutes an established or mature science is, amongst other things, that there should be agreement amongst its practitioners as to what are its basic concepts, and also the general way research should be carried on. Disciplines such as biochemistry and astronomy meet these requirements, whilst others such as sociology do not. Linguistics and psychology are in a marginal state, but making some progress towards maturity. One of the essential and characteristic features of the way the natural sciences approach the world is through thinking and reasoning in terms of strict causal relationships, and indeed this is the source of our present and increasing power to control the natural world, and also of the benefits enjoyed by *everyone* to some degree in the industrialized world. All our technology, including the components of the cinema, could not exist without the kind of rational, causal thinking central to the real sciences, and even the economic and other organization of all countries East and West is attempted using the same principles. Procedures based on other kinds of subjective, semi-arbitrary, irrational, associational, relativistic, or magical thinking have no power to produce results with any certainty, and if everyone restricted themselves to such thinking the average person would have to live a short and unpleasant life in a mediaeval hut. Before the advent of science and technology the average person had the benefit of stuffy, dark, cramped dwellings, butcher-type surgery, and a very good chance of dying in an epidemic or famine, and this is the alternative that a specially favoured minority of the population in the very richest parts of the world has managed to forget or never learn about.

The other essential component of real science is the continual interaction between theory on the one hand, and experiment and observation on the other, and this too is necessary for the useful application of the products of science. It is because of the features I have just mentioned that the natural sciences present the paradigm of objective knowledge, and because they are the same everywhere – in Russia and China, Britain and America – they demonstrate that objective knowledge is possible, whatever some ill-informed literary intellectuals may happen to believe. For the unfortunate truth is that many people have great difficulty in thinking rationally, logically, and causally, and are limited to purely verbal manipulations. They tend to conceive of the world as being totally describable by words only, and to think of words as the labels over discrete pigeonholes into which everything in the world fits. But just as there are not three distinct categories of heights of people corresponding to the words we use to describe them – tall, short, and average – but a distribution of heights over a continuous range for the population, so many other phenomena exist in a fairly continuous range that defies exact description by words alone, however precisely defined. Just so with objectivity: it is not an absolute quality, but something one can have more or less of, and the way to get as much objectivity as possible is by adopting the general attitude to their subjects (*not* necessarily copying any particular methods) that workers in the natural sciences take. As I said before, this entails the critical use of rational and logical thinking in inspecting one's theories, and also the careful comparison of those theories with the real world. I have purposefully put these essential characteristics of real science in a form sufficiently general to accommodate all the major attitudes in the philosophy of science that are acceptable to actual scientists as being in accord with their practice: for instance those of Kuhn, Lakatos, and Popper. The importance of these requirements for real science is that they are what ensure that it will 'work', and that we can be as sure as possible of its results. A large proportion of the psychologists, linguists, and anthropologists in the English-speaking world, and even some of the sociologists, wish their disciplines to meet these requirements. But there are people, without exception uneducated and inexperienced in the real sciences, who desire to attach the name of science to what they call the 'human sciences', which apparently include no more than Marxism, psychoanalysis, and perhaps the French schools of linguistics and structural anthropology. Their motives for doing this are not clear, but it is natural to conjecture that they desire to appropriate some of the prestige and trust that are attached to the real sciences, even though their activities lack the precise characteristics that have given rise to that prestige and trust.

So there has recently arisen the remarkable phenomenon of what is claimed to be a scientific theory of film created by people calling themselves theorists, who yet know very little, and apparently have no interest in learning, about what the films that exist are actually like, as I shall show in subsequent chapters. I call this a remarkable phenomenon because it is only fairly recently, after several hundred years of its existence, that just one of the established sciences, namely physics, has reached the point of having quite separate groups of theoreticians and experimentalists, who nevertheless continuously depend on each others' work. On the other hand, in biology, despite its vast achievements in this century, there is still little real separation into experimental and theoretical branches. So the idea that a few people can, by sitting in a chair and

spinning a web of words, create a 'science' of film can only seem grotesque to anyone with any close acquaintance with the real sciences.

There are other subsidiary features of these unfortunate attitudes that need commenting on here, the most serious of which is the belief that it is only necessary to cite one feature of one or two films to support vast generalizations about the nature of all films, without bothering to note that there may be hundreds of films that contradict those generalizations. Such procedures have always been endemic in writing about the arts, but never before has a claim to 'scientific truth' been made on that basis. Again, I shall give examples in succeeding chapters.

Although it is not necessary for the acceptance of what I have to say in this book, I will add that in its entirety my philosophical position goes beyond Scientific Realism to the most tough-minded form of Physicalism, which is the most recent and sophisticated variety of philosophical materialism. I mention this to point out to Marxist film 'theorists' who always coyly use 'materialism' as a euphemism for Marxism that there are forms of materialism prior and subsequent to the historical and dialectical variety.

Many people whose behaviour shows that they accept the truth of scientific realism, in that they expect that transistor radios will produce sound (rather than say paint the room blue), or that modern drugs will cure their ills, and so on, indulge in a form of 'double-think' in coming to irrational and arbitrary conclusions in less essential areas of their lives, and refuse to recognize that it is possible to arrive at sounder knowledge. To do this one only needs enough theory to do the job in hand: in this particular case to produce new information about film style and its determinants that is not only true now, but will always be true to the greatest possible extent. This extent is limited by the essential uniqueness and idiosyncrasy of individual art objects, in our case, films; and of course that idiosyncrasy and uniqueness is what makes some films art rather than craft. It is in the nature of artists to defeat the expectations of everyone about what they are going to do next, as I, and I think other interested observers, found out during the last three decades. Around 1960, having reached the minimal extremes of abstract painting, there seemed to be nowhere left for artists to go, but then there was Pop Art. And several years later the same kind of impasse looked as though it might have been reached, but Conceptual Art was in the egg. And who could have anticipated New Image painting twenty years ago?

So the study of film can never completely be a real science, although it can use the scientific approach in the general sense described earlier. In fact this is largely what has been done in Art History as it has successfully developed in this century, and this should provide the model for the development of Film History. (When I speak of Art History, I mean Art History proper, and not the occasionally entertaining but always dubious business that is variously called 'cultural history' or 'culture critique'.) Some younger workers are proceeding in the sound direction of Film History, but this development has been impeded by the attitude that a correct total theory explaining everything about films is necessary to do any valid research.

2. OLD FILM THEORY, NEW FILM THEORY

Before proceeding to my main task, it is necessary to present the general theoretical framework within which my descriptions and analyses are conducted, and before doing *that* I will clear the ground of unsatisfactory previous theories about film. My criticisms will have two prongs: I shall demonstrate the fundamental flaws in the various attempts at theorizing of the last two decades, and I shall also deal with the errors in one attempted application of each of these theories. I will not bother to discuss theories that pre-date the *auteur* theory, since the shortcomings of the previous major efforts by Kracauer, Bazin, etc. are adequately dealt with by Victor Perkins in *Film as Film* (Penguin Books, 1972). More recently Noël Carroll has gone over the same ground in much greater, even excessive, detail in *Philosophical Problems of Classical Film Theory* (Princeton University Press, 1988). In his book, Perkins also presents theoretical proposals for dealing with most, but not all, commercial feature films, though he himself admits that his proposals are both restricted and restrictive. Since his ideas have strong connections with some aspects of the *auteur* theory, I will not deal with them in themselves, but instead discuss the more influential form of that theory given by Andrew Sarris in *The American Cinema* (E.P. Dutton and Co., 1968).

The Auteur Theory

The *auteur* theory in its Anglo-Saxon form derives from the *auteur* policy operated by film critics on the French magazine *Cahiers du Cinéma* in the nineteen-fifties. This policy was to value all the films by certain film-makers whom they considered to be the controlling creative forces behind the films in question, and to dismiss the work of all the others. However Andrew Sarris gave these ideas a slightly different form in what he called the 'auteur theory', and although his presentation is neither complete nor consistent, it is still worth discussing since it could well have been expanded into a complete and consistent critical approach to film.

The central tenet of the Sarris auteur theory is that the aesthetic value of the films made by any director depends on the degree to which he succeeds in expressing his personality in at least some of them, and that if he does this to any detectable extent he becomes an *auteur*. Then all of his films, even those in which his personality is not evident, become of more value than those of a non-*auteur*. The central part of the criterion of excellence in this theory, which is that value resides in expressing the maker's personality, is certainly fairly definite, and although Andrew Sarris does not outline in his theoretical presentation how one establishes if a film-maker is expressing his personality in a film, he does demonstrate it in practice. But it can be considered a weakness of this criterion

that it will, if strictly applied, rate a film-maker with a commonplace personality as highly as one with a unique personality, provided he gets as much of it as possible into some of his films as does a more original figure. For instance, there were quite a number of directors such as Tay Garnett, Mervyn Le Roy, and George Sidney in Hollywood in the 1930-1950 period who had the kind of vulgar extraverted personality that usually goes with a background in the popular theatre, and whose films, although reflecting their makers' personalities, can be rather difficult to distinguish one from another on any grounds connected with those personalities. Although Sarris does not rate them as highly as for instance John Ford, he presents no reason why they should not be so rated.

This may be because Sarris' presentation of his theory is far from consistent, even though what he is saying is quite clear at any point in his exposition, and this lack of consistency may have escaped his attention. For instance, Sarris says at a point subsequent to the introduction of his main criterion that a good director is one who makes good films, but he does not define what determines whether a film is good or not. If we are meant to suppose that a good film is just one that expresses the maker's personality, then this is simply a restatement of the original criterion, and the objection I have made above stands. But in his discussion of the films of Billy Wilder, Sarris implicitly introduces the criterion that a good film must be a 'coherent comment on the human condition', though nowhere else does he refer to this necessity, so it may be that this is a hidden basic criterion for quality in his critical practice. If this is so, it is regrettable, for the requirement that all works of art be coherent comments on the human condition is a most pernicious one, as it immediately rates most avant-garde and fantastic art, including films, as worthless, and it has appealed to the stupider critics of the past and present for precisely that reason. Certainly Sarris has a low opinion of the value of avant-garde films, though he justifies this by the quite specious argument that they have made no contribution to the subject matter or forms of commercial cinema. Imagine the reaction in serious music circles to the claim that Anton Webern's music was valueless because his techniques had no effect on popular music! In fact the points I have made above about the deficiencies of the auteur theory can be graphically illustrated by imagining an attempt to apply an equivalent of the auteur theory to the other arts, for instance assigning values to paintings of this century according to how much of the artist's personality they express.

The instance of Billy Wilder also seems to be an attempt by Sarris to satisfy his personal prejudices by introducing yet another unacknowledged criterion for value, namely that a sentimental view of life is truer ('more profound' as he has it) than a cynical view, and hence that works which promote such a view are more valuable. It may well be that sentimentality is more attractive to the mass audience, but those who are not eager to make the Box Office the final arbiter of aesthetic value may agree that cynicism is at least an equally possible attitude for the artist to take to human behaviour.

Finally, Sarris admits that his theory has exceptions in the form of films that are better than the theory will strictly allow, and also in the form of good films which have no *auteur* at all. One example he gives is *Casablanca*, and whatever one thinks about the value of that particular film, the fact that the theory does have exceptions means that it is to some extent unsatisfactory.

So taking this last point together with the imperfections listed above, there is no doubt that the *auteur* theory as expressed by Andrew Sarris leaves a lot to be desired. A more modest formulation that went no further than to claim that those films in which a director had succeeded in expressing a *distinctive* personality were especially valuable would be much less vulnerable to objection. But it would still omit films without an *auteur* as defined, but which every interested person would insist on finding valuable. An obvious example is *Das Cabinet des Dr. Caligari*.

The *auteur* theory is basically an evaluative theory having implicit subsidiary analytical and interpretative components that are only demonstrated in practice, and this has usually been the case with film theories until fairly recently. But now it is necessary to deal with new theorizing about film that has been developed in France, and which has no evaluative component whatever, but which is only meant to be interpretative and analytical.

New French Film Theory

To fully understand the development of French theorizing about film since the middle nineteen-sixties it is necessary for me to explain what seem to be little-known features of French education and intellectual life, and in particular the peculiar position of the natural sciences in France.

Until fairly recently, science has been taught in French state secondary schools in a very strange way. It has been presented to the students as abstract systems of theories, and the idea of the comparison of scientific theories with the real world has not been brought home to the students by their carrying out experiments, or by them learning anything much about experimentation at all. Those few French students who went on to do physics and chemistry and biology at university level eventually discovered that science essentially involves a checking of theories against reality by experiment and observation, and that all engaged in the natural sciences are agreed on this, even though some may differ about the finer details of the process.

One should also know that philosophy forms a compulsory part of the French secondary school curriculum for those students going on to university, but again students get a very inadequate and strange idea of that subject. The philosophy course is directed towards the German nineteenth-century tradition of system building after the manner of Hegel, which is quite unable to deal with the nature of modern science. For Hegel was the first, but not the last, in that tradition to claim to have built a complete philosophical system providing a framework for all possible knowledge, despite his total lack of understanding of contemporary mathematics and science, as was pointed out at the time by one of the major creators of that mathematics and science, Carl Friedrich Gauss. This philosophic tradition has been rejected in the English-speaking world precisely because it is incompatible with scientific and technological thinking, a fundamental point which is invisible to the French for the educational reasons I have just mentioned.

In France the philosophic fashion of the decade or two before automatically becomes part of the secondary school philosophy curriculum: in the 'thirties and 'forties Henri Bergson's vitalism was taught, then next phenomenology, and subsequently Marxism. All of these philosophies have arrogated to themselves the right to decide what shall be believed in the natural sciences: Bergson was so foolish as to decree that Einstein's relativity theory could not possibly be true because it conflicted with his own philosophy; then the phenomenologists tried to dictate to scientific psychologists like Jean Piaget whether their experimental observations were correct or not, purely on the basis of the phenomenologists' own introspections (see *Insights and Illusions of Philosophy*, Jean Piaget, Routledge and Kegan Paul, 1972); and since then similar situations have arisen yet again, as I shall relate.

Another very relevant peculiarity of French education is that anyone who has passed the graduating examination (Baccalaureat) has the right to attend university, without acceptance standards and numbers being under the control of the universities themselves. The result of this is that at any particular time there are more than 800,000 university students in France, about twice the number there are in Great Britain, even though the population of the two countries is roughly the same. Obviously a large proportion of these students would be considered unfitted for university study in Britain, and possibly even in America, and not very surprisingly more than 90% of them choose the easy option of studying arts and humanities subjects. Although a large proportion of them have failed or dropped out before the end of their courses, the fact that they have been to university, and so consider themselves educated, means that they form part of the undiscriminating audience for the endless series of literary intellectual fashions that emerge from France.

This whole unfortunate educational situation has produced the weakness in the French natural sciences during this century that is well-known to scientists, and which is measured by the relatively small number of references to French scientific work in the international literature, and by the Nobel prize statistics, and so on. Its other result is that French literary intellectuals, including would-be film theorists, so-called social scientists, and 'philosophers', have not the slightest idea of what science is really about: that thinking in terms of causal chains, interaction of theory and experiment, and certain standards of demonstration and proof are what distinguish all the established sciences from disciplines (if they are disciplines) of lesser certainty. This is just as true of biology as of physics and chemistry, as a top biologist relates in P.B.S. Medawar's *The Art of the Soluble* (Methuen, 1967, p.99 et seq.). A striking illustration of the ignorance of French literary intellectuals in this area is provided by Michel Foucault, whose name is often invoked by English devotees of French film theorizing, in his book *Les Mots et les Choses* (Gallimard, 1966, translated as *The Order of Things*, Tavistock, 1970). He repeatedly describes mathematics, physics, and chemistry as together being purely deductive sciences, in opposition to biology, economics, and linguistics, which alone he characterizes as empirical sciences (op. cit. p.246 and p.347), and repeatedly states that mathematization is the only essential element of the natural sciences.

Such fundamental misconceptions based on ignorance also surface in the writings of Louis Althusser, who equalled Bergson's folly by proclaiming that the biochemical theory of genetic transmission could not be correct because it conflicts with Marxism- Leninism. So it is no surprise that Althusser repeatedly advanced the notion that all that is necessary to constitute a science is that it have a distinct object, and also that it have a theory and technique (*Lenin and Philosophy*, New Left Books, 1971, p.184). By this criterion innumerable activities such as witchcraft, palmistry, repairing motor cars, playing football, etc., etc., which all have quite definite objects, theories, and techniques, would all be sciences with the same standing as physics, neurophysiology, and botany. It is clear that Althusser has no conception of the simple logical distinction between the necessary conditions that such and such be the case, and the necessary and *sufficient* conditions that it be so; for although his criteria are indeed necessary for the existence of an established science, they are not sufficient to guarantee its standing. As mentioned before, logical reasoning, causal thinking, comparison of theory with experiment and observation, and the maintenance of certain standards of demonstration are also necessary for real science, though sadly lacking in the theorizing of Foucault, Althusser, Lacan, Greimas, and other Parisian Left Bank favourites whom I will come to presently.

Let me make it quite clear before I proceed that most aspects of the modern industrialized world, from the U.S.A. to China, including its communication systems, its industries, its economic planning, (yea even unto the cinematographic apparatus and the film stock that runs through it) are designed, or produced, or organized in large part by the kind of logical, causal, experimental, dynamic thinking that is used just because such thinking is the best guarantee of the most certain and most usable knowledge that we can have. Those who have no access to this sort of thinking are cut off from a large part of modern culture, and are in no position to pontificate about its general nature.

But all this means nothing to the massive audience formed by the people who have been to university in France, for they are much more impressed by meaningless rhetorical flourishes like 'Desire is the desire for desire' (Lacan), and only too ready to take in any novel system of ideas that contains nothing more than a few new words with a few vague connections between them. Anything containing mathematical and logical difficulties beyond the limited comprehension of this audience never becomes fashionable, as is the case with Jean Piaget's work in psychology during the nineteen-forties. This last is a very interesting case, for there are definite indications that Piaget's publications on the logical organization of concepts in the development of children's thinking (particularly in *Traité de Logique*, Colin, Paris, 1949) influenced features of the ideas of more recent and fashionable figures, though they make no acknowledgement of this. It is to these latter writers that I now turn, though only after remarking that unlike them, Piaget demonstrates his understanding of the logic and mathematics to which he appeals. Claude Levi- Strauss, Jacques Lacan, and A.J. Greimas do not, as I shall show.

Linguistics and Film

The interest of French literary intellectuals a decade ago in the linguistic systems of the schools of Saussure and Hjelmslev has now entirely evaporated, and all that is left are a few pieces of terminology that are occasionally brandished to impress the ignorant. This is despite the incessant claims that were made at the time that these systems were going to solve all the problems of investigating not only language, but also other forms of communication. Since the failure of these pretensions is fairly obvious to most interested people, and in some respects is demonstrated in readily available books such as Jonathan Culler's *Structuralist Poetics*, I shall not examine them in detail. However, the important points that should have occurred to any thoughtful person at the time are that firstly, then as now, linguistics is not a well-enough founded science to base anything else on, as no agreement has been reached among its practitioners as to the validity of the several irreconcilable theoretical systems that are current in the subject, and that secondly the mechanisms that lie behind our perception seem to differ too much between our different senses to allow our understanding of things by means of them to be described by a unified system. As pointers to this, note that we learn to speak our language with much greater ease and speed than we learn to write and read it, and also that we have visually and mathematically formalized understanding of things for which we have no verbal understanding. And contrariwise. This situation seems to be a consequence of the processing of visual and verbal information separately in the two halves of the brain, as has been shown by neurophysiological investigation.

Within its own area it has become clear that French structural linguistics has only had a very limited success in the area of phonology, and has achieved nothing whatever concrete and practical in syntax and semantics. As an instance of this failure it is worth examining the work of A.J. Greimas, because this has often been referred to by the English disciples of French theorizing, and also because it is one of the few instances of the actual attempted application of that theorizing to the meaning of film narratives.

In a paper written with F. Rastier and included in his *Du Sens* (1970), which has been translated in *Yale French Studies* No. 41, 1968, Greimas produces a model on page 161 which is represented by the following diagram:-

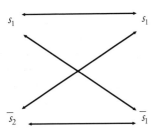

which he claims represents the elementary structure of meaning. Now although Greimas does not define the relations between s_1, s_2, $\overline{s_1}$, and $\overline{s_2}$, he claims that this diagram is a representation of the Klein (or Piaget) group. (Both Greimas and I are using 'group' and 'representation' in the mathematical sense here.) Now this is certainly not the case, for a representation of the Klein group requires two more relations to be added to such a diagram, and also that the relations be defined in a certain way. This would produce a diagram like this one:-

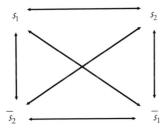

What seems to have happened is that Greimas has borrowed, without understanding the mathematics involved, a diagram of Piaget's like that I have just illustrated, which had the relations between the elements properly defined, and has tried to combine it with a much older diagram often used to illustrate the relationships between the four propositional forms of the classical logic of the syllogism. In the case of the logic of the syllogism the element s_1 is a statement of the form 'All S is P', s_2 is a statement of the form 'Some S is P', $\overline{s_2}$ is the form 'No S is P', and $\overline{s_1}$ is the form 'Some S is not-P'. Now for the particular case of these logical forms we can define the relations between them of 'contrary', 'contradiction', and 'implication' which are represented by the arrows (though the relation of implication is not reversible as is necessary for them to form a group), but unfortunately these relations cannot be generalized to cover the cases when the elements '*s*' are some-

thing other than the logical forms of the syllogism. But this is just what Greimas tries to do in his model. This fundamental misunderstanding becomes quite apparent when he applies his model to the particular case of the possible sexual relations in traditional French society, when his diagram becomes:-

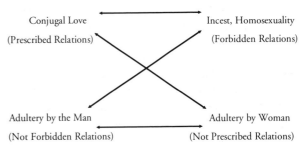

We can see that he is positing that conjugal love is the contrary (or opposite) of incest and homosexuality in the same way that male adultery is the contrary (or opposite) of female adultery, which is ridiculous. Further than that, it is obvious that the sexual relations which are 'not prescribed' include adultery by the man, and incest and homosexuality, as well as adultery by the woman, and a similar situation holds for the relations that are 'not forbidden'. The source of Greimas' error here is a failure to understand that although one can always find the contradictory for any term (i.e. for any P there is always a not-P), there is not in general an opposite or contrary to every possible term. There would not be a great deal of point in going into this matter but for the fact that there have been a number of published attempts in English-language film journals to use the above kind of approach in the interpretation of films. Besides the particular method I have just discussed, many other aspects of Greimas' work are based on this kind of faulty thinking, and in particular his so-called transformational model of narrative, which has been applied to a television play by Roger Silverstone, without any recognition of its basic falsity. I shall return to this.

Eco and the Idea of General Semiotics

At that time around 1970 when there began to be some kind of dim recognition of the lack of success of a science of communication by signs (semiotics) which was directly based on the model of French structural linguistics, there was an attempt to create another theory of this putative science which did not depend so heavily on the linguistic model. The most clearly written example of this development was Umberto Eco's *A Theory of Semiotics* (Indiana University Press, 1976). In Eco's treatment the sought-after generality was obtained by defining a sign as something that can *possibly* be interpreted as standing for something else by a *possible* interpreter. This hypothetical process of signification is taken to define codes that could be used in anything that might be taken to be a communication process. These codes are a set of relations between one system made up of elements of *expression* (for instance whether the indicator lights on a motor car instrument panel are on or off), and another system made up of elements of *content* (whether the battery is charging or discharging, etc.). When we are concerned with such simple examples there is no problem about the concept of 'code' being used, for in such a case the system of the elements of expression is fixed, as is the system of the elements of content, and also the relation between the two systems. In fact the usage in the case of the indicator light example corresponds to the way the word 'code' has been used, not only in the past, but also in more recently developed mathematical communication theory. But Eco stretches the concept to extend very much further, as is indicated by his general definition, given above, of the signs (or strictly 'sign functions') that make up the codes. To give a specific example from the cinema, if a dissolve in a film always meant that a time lapse had taken place, it would be part of a code of shot transitions functioning in the same general manner as the battery indicator light. And indeed functioning as the word 'code' has been ordinarily understood. But as I shall show later in this book, for most of film history the meaning of the dissolve has been ambiguous, and there have even been periods when it did not mean a time lapse at all. The same applies to every other feature of film form, even down to such classic examples as who wears the dark clothes and who wears the light clothes in a Western.

It is quite definite that in Umberto Eco's theory of semiotics such vague and transient relations are still described as 'codes', and in fact Eco quite explicitly extends his 'codes' to the point where a unique feature of some communication medium, which might possibly be interpreted by someone as having some meaning, falls under a 'code'. An example might be that someone decides that one of the dissolves in a commonplace film such as *From Russia With Love* represents a transition to a mystical higher state of being for the characters. Obviously this use of the concept 'code' to refer to private interpretations takes us even further away from the way the word 'code' has been used in the past.   In fact what Eco and other would-be semioticians have done is to replace an existing set of descriptive terms – codes, conventions, and interpretations – which made distinctions between fixed relations of meaning, transient relations of meaning, and arbitrary relations of meaning, with a vastly extended use of one term which fails to make these distinctions. This would not be a valid criticism if such a greatly extended use of the concept of 'code' had produced new knowledge of any kind, but the effect on people who have taken up the idea of semiotic theory has been quite the opposite, particularly as far as film is concerned. The use of the word 'code' with something like the incredibly wide meaning given to it by Eco, but without any recognition of the true nature of this use, has led people to think that whenever they use the word 'code', they understand everything about the 'code' to which they are referring, or at any rate could with ease if it would not compromise their standing as pure 'theorists'. So this thoughtless adoption of such a notion of codes has nearly totally inhibited the investigation of the actual forms of films past and present in England and France, and also to some extent elsewhere. If everyone had

been content with the already existing concepts of 'stylistic conventions' and 'stylistic rules' they would have had adequate terms for the formal analysis of films, and none of these difficulties would have arisen.

After establishing the basics of his theory in *A Theory of Semiotics*, which he does in a clear and consistent manner, whatever its fundamental flaws, Eco then adopts an excessively eclectic approach, and tries to include as many as possible of the previous ideas of others working in this area. For instance, he uncritically accepts the theory of Greimas that I have discussed above, not to mention others similarly deficient. As far as film is concerned, Eco's own idea, which was much discussed at one time, is that it forms a triply articulated code. This idea rests on a failure to make a distinction between the film strip which has separate images on it, and the image on the screen, which can be continuously present without any obvious transitions between images under certain conditions of projection, as happens in the best contemporary viewing tables, such as the Magnasync Moviola. When it comes to trying to incorporate a semantic theory into his general semiotic theory, Eco returns to a model based on verbal language, as everyone else has had to do.

The general approach of other would-be semioticians has rested, though less explicitly, on exactly the same sort of assumptions about 'codes' as Umberto Eco makes, and in particular this is the case with the much more confused and contradictory writings of Christian Metz.

Metz and Cinema Semiotics

The theoretical writings by Christian Metz on his proposed semiotics of film have made only one practical proposal for the analysis of films, and otherwise, on the rare occasions when Metz deals with actual films, he can only reproduce the old critical clichés about the same old 'Film Society Classics', as happens on pages 112-114 in his *Language and Cinema* (Mouton, 1974)

One of Metz's last statements of his position on straightforward film semiotics before he abandoned the subject to pursue that new Left Bank will o'the wisp, psychoanalysis, can be found in his lecture of 1971, *On the Notion of Cinematographic Language*. This is readily available in translation in *Movies and Methods* (University of California Press, 1976). A large part of this lecture is Metz's usual mixture of truisms, error, and contradictions, such as his repeated initial assertion that there is no 'cinematographic language system' and then his final claim that the notion of a cinematographic language system is useful. Metz also asserts that the cinema is not a communication system because 'it does not permit immediate bilateral exchange between a sender and receiver', which shows that he is not aware of the simple fact that all that is necessary for a communication system is that there exist a sender, a method of encoding, and then transmission followed by decoding by a recipient. If these conditions are satisfied, then the *potentiality* for inverse transmission exists, and that is all that is necessary. In fact the average member of the cinema audience could, if given all the appropriate facilities and support, make another film that conveyed a narrative with almost equal probability of having it understood by a film-maker. What such a film would *not* have is the technical smoothness and individual artistic qualities that make commercial films interesting beyond being the bare transmission of a narrative. Incidentally, if Metz does not believe the cinema is a communication system it is rather strange that he should always refer to its conventions as 'codes'.

Such contradictory statements run right through Metz's earlier writings on film semiotics, and although he does not realize it, they are forced on him by the ambiguities and inconsistencies of all film construction, which increases in rough proportion to the artistic interest of the films under consideration. Even in the most banal films of any period the constructional and other features which appear with some consistency are so few and limited that no coherent way of classifying them into a useful system can be created. Metz's sole concrete proposal in this direction, his 'grande syntag-matique', suffers from a basic difficulty in how the segments he uses are to be precisely separated from one another in an actual film. This crops up immediately at the beginning of his sole published analysis, that of the film *Adieu Phillipine*. Metz assigns shot number 8 to two successive segments simultaneously, and this means that a segmentation and attribution of categories different to the one he actually gives would be possible within his system. Similar alternative possibilities of analysis under his system occur later in the film, and are half-recognized by Metz, but what he fails to recognize is that these ambiguities remove the point of the creation of his new terminology. They were quite apparent with the already existing system of segmentation into scenes, sequences, and so on, and the 'grande syntagmatique' does not resolve them. Not only is Metz's system no improvement on the existing terminology of film analysis on this level, but when we look at its deeper basis we find even more unsatisfactory features. Metz lays out the classification of his fundamental units of film narrative or 'syntagms' as shown below.

The most striking of the many unsatisfactory features of this classification is the wide separation, by several dichotomies (or branchings), of the continuous scene done in one shot (the *plan séquence*) from the continuous scene done in a number of shots. The former falls under Metz's category 'autonomous shot', and is classified by him with Inserts of various kinds, and the latter exists alone in the category 'scene'. But as far as the presentation of narrative is concerned, both the scene shot in one continuous take, and the same scene broken down into a number of shots with temporal and action continuity fulfil exactly the same function. This means that these two out of Metz's set of syntagmatic categories can be interchanged without altering the meaning of the film, and this is contrary to his claim that the 'commutation test' of theoretical linguistics, which does not permit this, can be applied to distinguish his categories of narrative units one from another. As a matter of fact this point also applies to some of his other categories under certain conditions, so that it seems that Metz's often repeated claim that the applicability of the commutation test is one of the things that demonstrates that he has discovered a codified filmic system is also false. To put it another way, even in the films of the 1933-1955 period the sequence and scene construction is so little codified that analytical concepts borrowed from linguistics are of no use whatsoever.

But Metz's major claim that he has identified and described one of the language systems of the cinema is returned to in the course of the lecture I am considering with a new example. He calls this narrative unit 'durative montage', and presents an imaginary example of it as follows:

"Here is a film that shows two men walking painfully over a vast expanse. We see, alternated, tight shots of their socks falling into pieces, close-ups of their faces, little by little overgrown by hairy beards, medium shots where we understand the immense expanse they have to travel across and where they appear on foot with their somnambulistic and abrupt gait. The successive images are connected one to another by dissolves and also by a unitary musical motif. The dissolves and the music stop when the two men, for example, reach a water hole and rest in the shade of a tree, exchanging a few words: it is then another sequence that begins, dominated by another principle of montage.

On the plane of the signifier, this configuration involves three relevant characteristics: 1. cyclical and narrow mixing of several motifs taken from the same space; 2. Systematic recourse to an optical effect and to one alone; 3. Chronological co-incidence between a musical motif (a single one) and the iconic series under consideration.

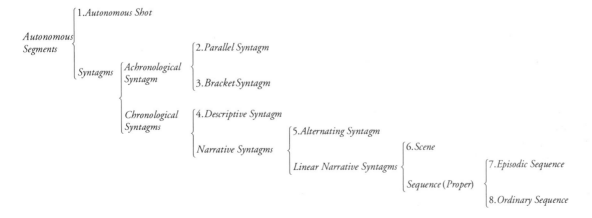

Why do these traits deserve to be considered pertinent? On the one hand, because they do not appear – or their exact combination does not appear – in the other types of montage in usage in the same period. On the other hand, because they appear, in return, in all the 'durative montages' of this period, beyond the diversity of the filmed objects and actions (which are not pertinent here). This figure therefore does not correspond to an occurrence, but to a class of occurrences; it is a code unit (in the code of classical montage in this case).

On the plane of the signified, three pertinent traits are shown to us...

1. The semantic trait of *simultaneity, while* the beard grows, *while* the socks are worn out, the expanse of the desert is gradually crossed.

2. The 'durative' semantic trait. In other sequences of the classical cinema, temporality is strongly vectoral: actions succeed each other, and are added to each other. Here, time is organized in a vast, immobile, and slack synchrony. The single action (that of 'proceeding painfully') is interminable and does not advance: it is the protagonists that advance and not the plot.

3. A semantic trait that concerns the modality of enunciation. Ordinarily, the film is fully assertive; it affirms that events unfolded down to their smallest details, exactly as we see it on the screen. Here, the modality becomes, so to speak, sub-assertive; the sequence does not pretend to present to us the heroes' long walk with all the factuality of the upheaval of events, but rather to offer us a *plausible illustration* of it, to give us an idea of it, a convincing sample. This method of affirmation is no longer 'It was thus', but 'It must have been something like this'."

Leaving aside the obvious point that no-one moderately knowledgeable about film has the slightest difficulty recognizing without the help of Metz's semiotics what is, or is not, a montage sequence indicating passing time in films of the 1933-1955 period, his discussion contains a number of errors, both major and minor. Specifically, montage sequences indicating the passing of time are not restricted to cyclical and narrow mixing of motifs, but can be made up of a totally diverse collection of shots, their shots can be joined together by various sorts of wipes as well as dissolves (i.e. by recourse to more than one sort of optical effect), and the mood music accompanying them does not necessarily begin and end with the first and last dissolves of the sequence, but usually continues into the beginning of the next scene. Incidentally, this last point connects with other uncertainties about where sequences start and end, and these Metz is both unable to recognize and unable to deal with. The sort of situation I have in mind can be demonstrated by an example from *Only Angels Have Wings* (Howard Hawks, 1939), in which a cross-cut sequence of a radio conversation between Cary Grant and one of the pilots ends in the middle of a shot with an abrupt transition to an ordinary sequence of a dramatically quite different nature involving Cary Grant and one of the women. This sort of thing can occur from time to time in the films of lesser directors too, but Metz's definition of his syntagms requires that they end where a shot ends.

Returning to the matter of montage sequences, all that truly characterizes them is that they be made up of a series of *short* shots whose images represent features in scenes associated in some way with the action of the surrounding film, and that they be joined together by *any* sort of optical transition. This is so obvious that it is scarcely surprising that no-one has bothered to say it before, and even if Metz had seen enough films to be capable of recognizing it, he would have no way of being more precise about it. As for his statement: 'On the plane of the signified, three pertinent traits are shown to us ...', this could be replaced with equal accuracy by 'Three pertinent traits of meaning are shown to us ...', and again he is wrong in what he says about these traits, for:

1. Simultaneity is not unique to such montage sequences, but occurs in the same sort of way in cross-cut sequences.

2. In the sequence described, actions succeed each other and are added to each other just as in other types of sequence: the shots of the same feet walking with socks that are more worn-out are clearly successive in time, and can in no way be described as synchronous.

3. The attempted distinction as to different modalities of enunciation is also mistaken, as ordinary sequences also often elide small and insignificant parts of the action between cuts, and in the case of cross-cut sequences quite large amounts of action are elided. The only distinction in the example described is that very large amounts of insignificant action are omitted. However, Metz would have a point here if he had described the kind of montage sequence in which the dissolves between shots are butted up against each other, so that there are no single shots in the sequence, but only a continually changing sequence of superimposed shots. In this case the superimpositions make it impossible to recognize all the details in each shot, and we could say 'It was roughly like this' (not 'It must have been like this'). Metz is unable to make this distinction, and I have shown how his subsequent claim that terms from linguisitics like 'signified', 'commutation', and 'syntagm' are necessary to such observations as can be truly made about such a sequence is false as well. Some of the more knowledgeable and intelligent people who have long been concerned with film have intuitively recognized the emptiness of Metz's writings, but unfortunately they have not properly demonstrated these failings in print. Metz himself seems to have some sense of the inadequacy of his attempts at theorizing, for Raymond Bellour has very obliquely reported a private admission that Metz made to him that his 'grande syntagmatique' does not work. This admission can be read in Bellour's article 'Segmenting/Analysing' in *The Quarterly Review of Film Studies* Vol.1, No.3. Nevertheless, some people are still busy republishing Metz's articles and talking about 'syntagms', and some of Metz's authorized disciples are still teaching his theories as received truth at various places around Paris, which must say something about the integrity of French literary intellectuals.

Marxism and Althusser

The very limited additions made to Marxist theory by the

'philosopher' Louis Althusser have led to claims, which are still being repeated, that his ideas justify some of the more recent developments in French film theory, so it is appropriate that I should examine a typical example of his thinking from his essay *Lenin and Philosophy* (New Left Books, 1971). This piece contains some incredibly ignorant statements about the history of philosophy, most particularly Althusser's assertion that Ernst Mach's work had no importance whatsoever for subsequent developments in philosophy, when in fact the Viennese Logical Positivists explicitly acknowledged him as an immediate predecessor, and other interested parties detected a strong influence from his ideas on Russell, Wittgenstein, and William James. That Althusser should know nothing about these matters is no surprise, but that he was happy to make dogmatic statements about them to an audience of French philosophers should be.

The nub of the first part of the essay under discussion can be found on p.42 et seq. as follows:

"Marx founds a new science, i.e. he elaborates a system of new scientific concepts where previously there had prevailed only the manipulation of ideo logical notions. Marx founds the science of history where there were pre viously only philosophies of history ..."

Notice here again the assumption that all that is necessary for a science to exist is the existence of a system of concepts; there is no realization that this system needs to be checked against reality in any way. Further than this, Althusser's assertion that what composed Marx's system were scientific concepts, whereas his predecessors were only dealing with ideological notions, is nowhere demonstrated, nor does he show any awareness of the necessity of this, if our belief in Marx's alleged science is to rest on anything other than blind faith.

Althusser continues:

"... before Marx, two continents (of theory) *only* had been opened up to scientific knowledge by sustained epistemological breaks; the *continent of mathematics* with the Greeks and the *continent of physics* by Galileo and his successors ... A science like biology which came to the end of the first phase of its epistemological break, inaugurated by Darwin and Mendel, only a decade ago by the integration with molecular chemistry ..."

Here we have demonstrated a total ignorance of the history of science and mathematics; an ignorance that Babylonian and Egyptian mathematics existed before that of Greece, that Galileo's astronomical theory and observation were preceded by those of Ptolemy, and that there was a science of biology before Darwin. It also becomes clear that Althusser's 'epistemological break' is a very strange sort of 'break' indeed, since one phase of it can cover a hundred years and generations of scientists, from Darwin till a decade ago. I say that the evolution of the sciences needs an analysis better than this simple-minded crudity, even though it might seem impressive to those who know nothing about science.

As everyone knows, Marxists have been very unsuccessful indeed in predicting the course of history over the last hun-

dred years, so if they have been working by a science of history, it is a totally unsatisfactory one when compared to the real sciences, which can tell us what is going to happen (or be observed) with better than chance probability, given a set of initial conditions. And as far as social organization goes, the last seventy years have provided conclusive proof that Marxism always leads at the the best to bureaucratic totalitarianism, not to mention what it leads to at the worst. There is no such thing as Socialism with a human face.

A major contributory factor to the inadequacy of Marxism is that, particularly in its Leninist form, it is only made up of a limited number of indeterminate concepts like 'class struggle', 'ideology', 'petty bourgeoisie', and a very few others, which is not much with which to confront the complexities of modern society. One of Althusser's main claims to fame was to have invented a new concept, that of the 'Ideological State Apparatus', which according to him is made up of the systems formed by the churches, the educational system, the trade unions, the political system, the legal system, etc., and which he alleges is distinguishable from the (repressive) State Apparatuses, which include amongst other things the Government, the Administration, the Police, and the Courts. One might ask how the man who has repeatedly demanded rigour in analysis can so easily separate the Government from the political system, and the Courts from the legal system, particularly when he goes on to claim that what distinguishes the two Apparatuses from each other is whether they function by repression or ideology, though at the same time maintaining that both Apparatuses function by both means to some extent. (See page 138 of *Lenin and Philosophy*).

But it may be that the true-believing Marxist is immune to argument of any sort. Page 8 of the Foreword to *Lenin and Philosophy* may be claiming this immunity with the statement "... it is only from the point of view of class exploitation that it is possible to *see* and analyse the mechanisms of a class society and therefore to produce scientific knowledge of it." This is exactly equivalent to saying that one has to be a Marxist to see the truth of Marxism, or even more concisely, Marxism is true because it is true. This is demanding a purity of blind faith equal to that of the most primitive Christian.

Psychoanalysis and Lacan

The claims of traditional psychoanalysis and its validity can be dealt with quite quickly. Psychoanalysts in the English-speaking world sensibly do not claim that psychoanalysis is a science, and so the only reason for believing in its validity is its success as a treatment for mental illness. Unfortunately, surveys of the effectiveness of psychoanalytical therapy show that the cure rate for patients with neurotic symptoms who have been selected for treatment by psychoanalysis is about two-thirds after two years of treatment. This is just equal to the rate of spontaneous remission of neurotic illness occurring in patients who are not given any special psychological treatment at all. So it seems that psychoanalysis has no curative effect. Even worse, other forms of individual and analytical therapy give just the same results, or lack of them, as psycho-analysis. All the evidence on these points is presented and discussed in S. Rachmann's *The Effects of Psychotherapy* (Pergamon Press, 1971), and H.J Eysenck & G.D. Wilson's *The Effects of Psychological Therapy*, (Methuen, 1973) and as far as I am aware there has been no reply from the apologists for psychoanalysis. So if the therapy based on the theory does not work, there is no reason to believe in the correctness of the theory.

Let me make it clear that I am not saying that there is no such thing as the unconscious mind, the existence of which had been noted by scientists such as Sir Francis Galton before Freud, but just that Freud's theories about it are patently unsatisfactory. And I am not denying that elements of 'kitchen-Freud' have been intentionally put into Hollywood films by writers such as Niven Busch and Ben Hecht from the nineteen-forties onwards, and even sometimes by directors. For this last reason it is as well to know something about psychoanalysis, but it does not follow that it can serve as a sound general basis for interpreting all films, as its disciples claim. I will also admit that traditional psychoanalytical interpretation of films can be a lot of fun when practised by someone with imagination and wit, as the writings of Parker Tyler, for instance, demonstrate. But this is not the case with the new variety of psychoanalysis which was preached by Jacques Lacan.

Jacques Lacan was the guru of a schismatic sect of French psychoanalysts, and he claimed to be the only guardian of the True Faith of psychoanalysis through a return to Freud's original teachings, which, he would have us believe, had been perverted by everyone else. However, Lacan's version of what Freud was really saying radically transforms his source. The stimulus for this revised version of Freud can be detected on page 73 of Lacan's *Function and Field of Speech and Language* in his *Écrits* (English translation, Tavistock 1977). There one can see that his psychoanalytic pretensions to provide a complete explanation of mental functioning were being threatened by Claude Levi-Strauss' claim to have discovered the basic method of operation of the human mind through his theories of savage myth and kinship systems. Since Levi-Strauss' ideas were guided in part by the French variety of structural linguistics, Lacan immediately advanced the idea that "... psychiatric systems are structured like a language ...". Of course the fundamental shortcomings of Levi-Strauss' theories, which stem from their failure to take account of myths and kinship systems which do not fit them (see Edmund Leach's book *Levi-Strauss* (Collins, 1970) particularly page 117), do not trouble Lacan, or for that matter other French literary intellectuals in the slightest.

The evidence presented to support Lacan's reformulation of Freud is rather difficult to disentangle from the wilfully increasing obscurantism of his writing after the secession of his school from the main body of psychoanalysis in 1953, but it seems to depend on a few slight odds and ends of doubtful anecdotal evidence like Freud's observation of one instance of preliminary language behaviour in one German-speaking child. Lacan does not even bother to inquire what some, let alone most, children speaking other languages start out doing when co-ordinating pre-language with their actions, and whether it supports the inverted pyramid of interpretation Freud constructed on it.

Eventually we come to the usual French allegation that what will guarantee the status of psychoanalysis as a science is its formalization, and nothing else (see page 72 of *Function and Field of Speech and Language*). The necessity of some sort of experimental testing of psychoanalytic theories is explicitly rejected in this essay with the astonishing assertion that the experimental sciences have no more relation to nature than does pure mathematics (page 74). How Lacan then accounts for the way we act on nature with devices based on our knowledge of physics, chemistry, biology, etc. must be beyond the comprehension of anyone with any real acquaintance with the natural sciences.

Lacan next describes psychoanalysis as a potential 'conjectural' science, like mathematics. He does not realize that part of the significance of mathematics for us resides in the fact that it grew out of applied mathematics in real situations in the first place, and that since then parts of it keep turning out to have applications in the natural sciences. If this were not so, the development of mathematics as a purely formal system would not have continued to the extent that it has. What Lacan had in mind for the development of psychoanalysis was quite different to this. After more confusion about the nature of science, he finally arrives at the contradictory claim that psychoanalysis will derive its justification from its curative efficiency. As for that, there has been no word from Paris of any controlled (or even uncontrolled) observation of cure rates by Lacan and his school, so there is no reason to assume that he could do any better in this direction than other psychoanalysts. (It is interesting to note that in 1966, at any rate, Lacan was not claiming that his psychoanalysis was yet a science. Althusser and his English admirers, who have had no professional engagement with psychoanalysis, let alone with any real science, have not been so restrained in the claims they have made on his behalf.)

The nature of Lacan's attempts at 'formalization' of his psychoanalysis can be indicated by an example from *Subversion of the Subject and Dialectic of Desire* in *Écrits* (page 317). Here he takes the basic symbolic representation in Saussurean linguistics:

$$\frac{Signifier}{Signified} = \frac{S}{s} = statement$$

as an algebraic expression, which it is not, and puts 'signified' and 'statement' equal in the case of a proper noun, so obtaining $S = s^2$. Now according to his theory in this particular case the signifier corresponds to that which is not the Ego Ideal, and so by another ordinary algebraic manipulation Lacan obtains

$$signifier = \sqrt{-(Ego\ Ideal)}$$

Apart from the initial misuse of Saussure's expression for a linguistic statement as a division of signifier by signified, the use of algebraic operations by Lacan without first showing how they are defined for his own system inevitably leads him to the ridiculous nonsense of the final expression.

Another and more serious instance of Lacan's use of subjects of which he does not understand to bolster his ideas and hoodwink his audience occurs in one of a series of lectures that are included in *Four Fundamental Concepts of Psychoanalysis* (Hogarth Press, 1977). Here, in discussing his concept of 'alienation' on page 210 (in the original French on page 191 of *Le Seminaire - Livre XI*), Lacan appeals for support to symbolic logic, and in particular to its concept of the logical relation 'or'. He says that there are three kinds of 'or', all of which he insists on referring to as the Latin *vel*, and his examples of these three kinds are:

1. "I go either here or there – I make a choice between the two places." This is indeed the exclusive 'or' as recognized by formal logic, but it corresponds to the Latin *aut*, not the Latin *vel*.

2. "I go to one side or the other, I don't care which." As far as logic is concerned, this is not different to the first 'or', but just another example of the exclusive 'or', i.e. *aut*.

3. "Your money or your life." Lacan would have us believe that this is yet another kind of 'or' from the logical point of view, but in fact it is exactly the same as the other two, as the hearer is being offered an exclusive choice. What might happen after he has made his choice is irrelevant. It seems that at this point Lacan is ignorantly groping for the inclusive 'or' of logic, which alone corresponds to the Latin *vel*, and which can be exemplified by the statement "A native citizen of the United States is someone who is born of American parents, or born on American soil." This statement defines a category of people who fulfil both conditions as well as those who fulfil just one of them.

The confusion of Lacan's already quite incorrect statements is worse confounded in Stephen Heath's presentation of Lacan's position in *Screen* (Volume 18, No.4), by the substitution of 'exhaustive' for 'exclusive', so reversing the meaning, which is thus made even more incorrect. Lacan follows this point by a further appeal to the algebra of sets in which he says that the number of elements in the union of two sets is different to the number of elements resulting from their addition, quite failing to realize that the second operation does not exist in the form of ordinary arithmetical addition in the algebra of sets. The importance of all this wildly fallacious confusion is that it is supposed to provide the justification of a concept called the 'suture' introduced into attempts at film theory created by Lacan's followers. (See *Cahiers du Cinéma* Nos. 211 and 212, April and May 1969, and *Screen* Vol.18 No.4). According to the latest version, the 'suture' is supposed to inhere in the operation of practically every feature of film, including the soundtrack – image relationship, the effect of the edge of the frame, the occurrence of reverse- angles, and every cut in a film. As usual with French theory, no description of exactly how it does this in general is provided, and the way it is invoked arbitrarily in any specific instance irresistibly suggests the use of 'the Will of God' in low-grade mediaeval thinking. The absence of the 'suture' has been invoked to explain some cases of 'distancing effects', but there is no necessity for it in this case either, as distancing effects are already easily recognizable and explicable in their action by making comparison with films in which they do not occur, and hence in terms of their unexpectedness.

What we have here, as in some other instances of the activities of Lacan's disciples, is something exactly analogous to a man going round a picture gallery and drawing lines around the already visible outlines of the objects in the pictures, and then saying that this 'explains' the pictures. The need for a special new 'theory of the subject', which Lacanian psychoanalysis is supposed to supply, is not felt at all by truly scientific psychology, and it might be advisable to point out to likely readers of this chapter that that discipline has been making considerable concrete and useful progress in many directions in the last few decades; with the prediction of behaviour, the analysis of perception, in making connections with neurophysiology, and even in producing rapid cures of phobic neurotic states under controlled test conditions. Of course, the more scientific psychology advances, the more difficult it is for literary intellectuals to understand it, so I quite expect psychoanalysis to hold its ground for some time as the current form of 'literary psychology'. (Compare the psychology of humours, phrenology, etc. in past centuries.)

Cahiers du Cinéma and Young Mr. Lincoln

Lacanian psychoanalysis has provided the model for a new kind of interpretation of narrative films which has been propounded and demonstrated in *Cahiers du Cinéma* No.223 (1970), and translated in *Screen* Vol.13 No.3. In principle this simply consists of finding (or inventing – "...we shall not hesitate to force the text ...") 'gaps' or 'lacks' in a film, which are then interpreted like symptoms in psychoanalysis to give an indication of what the film, like a patient, is repressing. This ingenious inversion of older procedures of interpretation has attracted a lot of attention from those interested in creating interpretations of films without taking any regard for their possible validity. There is of course nothing wrong in itself in taking over a theoretical model from one discipline into another, but it is not usual to do this with one that does not work in its original application, as is the case with psychoanalysis.

The authors of the *Cahiers* article *John Ford's 'Young Mr. Lincoln'* claim that their work "... will not be a new interpretation, i.e. the translation of what is supposed to be already in the film into a critical system ...", but since they say a few paragraphs later that their aim is to carry out "... an active reading to reveal what is already there, but silent ...", and since they are undoubtedly working in terms of a special Freudian-Marxist system in doing this, we must disbelieve their initial claim. In any case, in their practice it is quite clear that what they are doing at least some of the time is interpreting negative (i.e. absent) features of the film. The writers of this article say that their principal aim is to show that the film is about "... the reformulation of the historical figure of Lincoln on the level of myth and the eternal ...", and that anything that conflicts with that end, such as sex and politics, is omitted from the film. I think anyone would agree with this interpretation when it is simply put to them in those words after they have viewed the film, and would do so without twenty pages of Marx and Freud, hardly any of which bears on this particular point in any case. The observation I have just made is supported by the fact that in a contemporary review of the film in 1939, Graham Greene wrote, "... it is intended to be legend, not history ...". I would expect any film engaged in a similar project and made around that period to proceed in a roughly similar way, though it is to be noted that John Ford was more inclined to leave sex out of his films than the average Hollywood director.

A major section of the *Cahiers* analysis of *Young Mr. Lincoln* is to do with the alleged political and economic determinations of the film's production, and here large amounts of totally erroneous information about American economic and social history are produced by the writers, as has often been pointed out, even in the pages of *Screen* by Ben Brewster (Vol. 14, No. 3).

Returning to *Cahiers'* psychoanalytical interpretation of the film, we find that the authors very quickly slip back into the usual kind of interpretation of features actually *present* in it, rather than absent, although they show no recognition that they are doing just what they said they were not going to do (note their treatment of the various occurrences of the Mother and the Law (book), of Carrie Sue's kissing Lincoln, and so on). They even descend to psychoanalysing the personality of the fictional character of Lincoln as he is presented in the film, twice describing the behaviour of this invented person as denoting his paranoia. But I shall return to the fundamental defects of the psychoanalytical approach when I deal with the general matter of interpretation.

3. THE INTERPRETATION OF FILMS

The question of what should count as a valid interpretation of a film or other work of art, and why it should, is one that most people do not seem to be willing to face. For brevity we can consider the alternative positions on this question as being stretched out along a spectrum from the most conservative or restrictive position to the most extreme or radical. At the restrictive extreme the possibility of true, or at any rate fairly certain, interpretation is denied altogether, and at the other extreme all interpretations, however generated, are regarded as equally valid. In between these two extremes are various positions where smaller or larger numbers of different systems of interpretation are considered to be valid. There is also a tendency for the amount of unjustified personal intuition used by the critic or interpreter to increase towards the more radical end of the spectrum.

The most restrictive position, which is the denial of the possibility of any valid interpretation at all, does not concern us, since anyone who held it, but still produced interpretations of films, could be fairly regarded as wasting everyone's time. The next most conservative position is that all interpretation should be controlled by, and compatible with, what we know about the way the film was produced, including the context of the other films of that time and place, and also what we know about the ideas and personality of its maker. By these standards, a religious interpretation of a film on a non-religious subject by an irreligious film-maker would be regarded as invalid, as would an interpretation that read significance into eye-line mismatches in a European film of the nineteen-twenties, since most films of that time and place contain some 'wrong directions' of all kinds. (This last error of interpretation has become increasingly common in recent years.) The contextual limitation on interpretation which I have just put forward is one that I myself hold to, and I put it into operation in a consideration of the films of Max Ophuls in a later chapter. Although I arrived at this position on interpretation independently, I have found that a very similar position had been earlier argued at length with respect to literature by E.D. Hirsch Jr. in his book *Validity in Interpretation* (Yale University Press, 1967). It is also an attitude that is in part implicit, perhaps in a not very conscious way, in some conventional film criticism. It seems to me that a well-known figure like Andrew Sarris is applying it in arriving at his excellent interpretations of the films of Josef von Sternberg (Museum of Modern Art, 1966), though elsewhere he sometimes lets his imagination and prejudices take complete control.

When a critic allows his private view of the world to determine his interpretations, as often happens, we are moving into a more extreme position, where systems of doubtful relevance and truth are used to create interpretations. One

variant of this position, which has been entertained by by Jonathan Rosenbaum and Bruce Kawin, is a conscious adoption of complete subjectivity in interpretation. Though in practice I don't think they have really followed this program through fully. When considering the application of more extended systems of ideas to interpretation, a factor that becomes important is the degree of certainty that can be attached to the assignment of meaning to any particular feature of a film. Possible concrete illustrations of this point are innumerable, but I shall return to psychoanalytic interpretation to provide an example.

Taking up again the specific instance of the *Cahiers du Cinéma* article on John Ford's *Young Mr. Lincoln*, we find that Lincoln's fixed stare in that film is always interpreted as 'castrating', whereas according to another psychoanalytic authority, quoted by Peter Wollen in his comments on the *Cahiers* article in the same number of *Screen* (Vol.13, No.3 1977), fixed stares are phallic, a symbol of rape. This situation, in which totally different interpretations of works of art are explicitly accepted by the devotees of psychoanalysis as equally valid, is quite common. In the reverse way, an interpretation that sees quite different features of the film as meaning the same thing can also be accepted as valid in psychoanalytical interpretation, as also happens in the article mentioned. In section 19, Lincoln is identified by the authors with the Law, but in an addendum to the article it is claimed that the mother represents the Law. Because of these various multiple connections between features of the film and the symbolic features that the psychoanalytic interpretation connects with them, it is impossible to trace back connections from the symbolic plane to that containing the features of the film with any certainty at all. What we have here is an aspect of the essential arbitrariness of psychoanalytical interpretation, or in mathematical terms, the lack of any definite functional relationship between the features of the film and the set of symbols to which they are supposed to relate. Seen in yet another way, the system of the features of the film and the psychoanalytic symbolic system do not have the same kind of relation to each other that two natural languages have, for in the case of natural languages one can always make a fairly accurate translation of a text from one to the other, and then back again. This point was made long ago by Ludwig Wittgenstein, and of course this sets psychoanalytic interpretation totally apart from the nature of explanation in the real sciences, and may well have something to do with the failure of psychoanalysis as therapy. It is well worth noting at this point that the concept of 'overdetermination' introduces an almost equal arbitrariness into Marxist 'explanations' of the existence of various features of cinema.

Not very surprisingly, these ambiguous and arbitrary features of psychoanalytic interpretation usually lead to muddled thinking in general, not to mention a high-handed attitude to evidence bearing on the point in question. A good example of this is provided by an article in *Film Quarterly* Vol.33, No.1, 1981, entitled 'The Lady Vanishes'. The central point of this article rests on a psychoanalytical interpretation of the alleged absence of female magicians from early trick films, but the author, although told that there were female magicians in Pathé trick films (for there are indeed quite a number of Pathé films made around 1908 featuring a female magician), did not bother to investigate this. Whether there were a lot of female magicians in early trick films, or only a few, or none at all, clearly did not worry the author of the article, for although the facts undercut her main thesis, she was obviously not really interested in films in themselves, but only in using them to provide bogus support for quite other aims. This kind of attitude has unfortunately become very common in recent years.

Faced with the kind of situation in which there are competing interpretations of a particular feature of a film, the response of anyone with any scientific inclinations or training is to use some extra system of real knowledge to determine the relative pertinence and validity of these different interpretations. This has also been part of the practice of art historians dealing with painting and the other fine arts during this century. The literary types who are so interested in psychoanalysis show no interest in doing this, presumably because they are only interested in interpretation for its own sake, as a form of self-expression, or in the pursuit of some extra-artistic concerns, rather than in creating relatively certain knowledge about films which can be built upon further. Because of the essential arbitrariness of psychoanalytic interpretations there is no possibility of basing any generalizations on them that have true explanatory or predictive powers with respect to the features of other films. As has proved to be the case in the past, psychoanalytic interpretations are shifting sands on which nothing solid can be built.

One justification sometimes advanced for the most extreme position on interpretation, which is that all interpretations are equally valid, is that some modern artists sometimes say that their work means whatever a member of their audience wants it to mean. But in fact it will be found that such artists nearly always reject interpretations that clash strongly with their beliefs when confronted with them. Andrei Tarkovsky is a case in point. Although he has sometimes said to enquirers that his films mean whatever they mean to the individual person watching them, when it was suggested that the mother in *Zerkalo* was an unloving mother, he instantly rejected this, as he did other interpretations which he didn't agree with.

A variety of the extreme position on interpretation, which has not so far tempted anyone interested in film, is indicated by the program advocated, but only feebly attempted, by Julia Kristeva with respect to literature. (See page 229 of *Essais de Sémiotique Poétique* (1971), edited by A.J. Greimas). This program involved using random operations on texts to generate new words from them; the new words so generated constituting the interpretation. Nevertheless, something approaching this degree of arbitrariness has been used by Raymond Bellour in a study of Hitchcock's *North by Northwest*, published as *le Blocage symbolique* in *Communications* Vol.23, 1975. I will consider the part of it dealing with the well-known crop-dusting sequence, starting from page 295 of the article.

Bellour claims that, amongst the numerous codes imbued with significance in this film, there is one that involves the directions of the arrivals and departures of the vehicles at the cross-roads where this sequence takes place. After illustrating the arrivals and departures with the following diagram:-

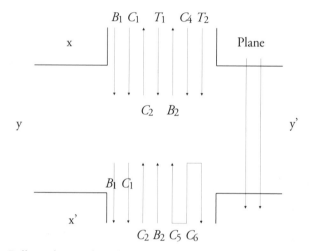

Bellour then makes a series of statements about the alleged operation of this code:

"The first bus appears from the direction x, and it disappears in the direction x'...

The first car repeats this movement of appearance and disappearance from x to x'. A gap is inscribed from the bus to the car in terms of the kind of vehicle ...

The second car operates a path exactly inverse to that of the first. The differentiation of the bus is reinforced by this symmetry in the measure where this second car constitutes a closed sub-ensemble with that which it immediately precedes. The first truck which follows it accentuates the opening of the system. It arrives from x like the bus and the first car from which it differs by its kind, but inversely to the preceding three vehicles it is not seen to disappear in the opposite direction, and so leaves an empty term in x in the equilibrium of the systems of which the sub-ensemble of the two cars proclaims the constraint. The appearance of the third car marks a radical opening of the system. It adds to the axis xx' the axis yy'...

The arrival of the second bus allows, like the arrival of the second car following the first, a relative closure of the system of which the third car underlines the differential expansion. It strictly inverts the effect of the third bus ..."

And so on. This might seem quite impressive at first glance, but an instant's thought should tell one that Bellour's procedure is meaningless. To demonstrate this, take the case that one creates a similar diagram of arrivals and departures of vehicles at a cross-roads by a totally random process of coin-tossing to determine what the direction should be, whether the arrival or departure is shown, and what kind of vehicle is involved. Although in this situation the diagram will be totally without any meaning, nevertheless Bellour's sort of interpretation can still be carried out. I shall show this for one example created by just the sort of random coin-tossing I have described, and which I illustrate below:

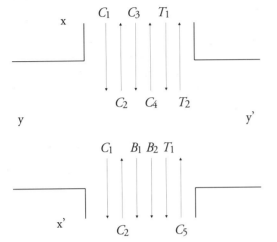

We can easily repeat Bellour's procedure to find a pretended significance in this diagram as follows:

"The first car appears from the direction *x*, and disappears in the direction *x'*...

The second car operates a path exactly inverse to that of the first, so constituting a closed sub-ensemble together with it.

The opening of this system is announced by the arrival of the third car without its departure being shown.

The departure of the bus which follows it underlines the differential expansion of the system which is further accentuated by the next two departures.

Two successive trucks departing in opposite directions now produce an opposaitional symmetry that signals the stabilization and relative closure of the system before the final departure of truck 2 produces a radical re-opening of the system, accentuating the total dissymmetry which compensates for an equal dissymmetry in the movements of the vehicles aligned with the *yy'* axis."

The fact that my interpretation, though based on a meaningless diagram, is indistinguishable in its nature from Bellour's interpretation demonstrates the pointlessness of his approach, and I could produce the same kind of interpretation for an infinite number of arrangements. To reinforce my point, I will similarly deal with another and even more extreme instance from the same source. When Bellour is interpreting the movements of the crop-dusting plane in the same scene from *North by Northwest*, he represents them by the diagram at the top of the next column

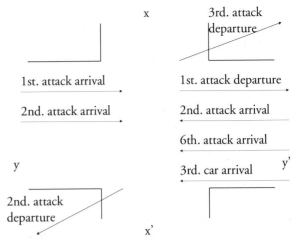

In this diagram, as before, only the arrivals and departures of the aeroplane that are actually shown in the film are represented by arrows. A careful comparison with the film itself shows that Bellour has created a bogus extra symmetry by displacing the centre of the attacks to the centre of the cross-roads, when in fact they are centred at a number of points in the bottom right quadrant formed by the cross-roads, and he has also represented the sixth attack as taking place along the *yy'* axis, when it is actually oblique to it. Having done this, Bellour then says:

"One can see: a) that the attacks 1, 2, 3 and 6 of the aeroplane are arranged symmetrically two by two in the directions *y* and *y'* with respect to their arrivals, but that: b) the departures progressively draw away from the rigorous symmetry of the first attack: either in marking a distortion of their paths in relation to the axis (departures 2 and 3), or in being different iated by the exigencies of the action (attack 6). c) that the car involved in the sub-ensemble of features connected with 'aeroplanes' doubly accentuates this disequilibrium, enhancing in one way the number of arrivals, and in another the prominence given to the direction *y'*."

Of this last point, Bellour also says:

"... this reprise accentuates the constitutive dissymmetry which, sliding into the heart of the repetition, allows this series of operations to be tied up."

I hope it is obvious that any random set of directions laid down at various points in a plane could just as well be 'assimilated' (as Bellour puts it) to a pair of perpendicular axes nearby. Consider the diagram below, which I constructed by drawing a pair of axes, and then dropping ten pins which fell onto the sheet in the marked positions.

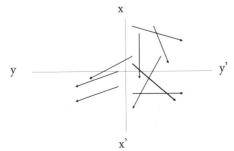

The random direction of those pins which happen to lie close to those of the axes have been 'assimilated' to them, and then the arrival and departure and ordinal designation have been assigned by a random coin-tossing operation to give the next diagram:-

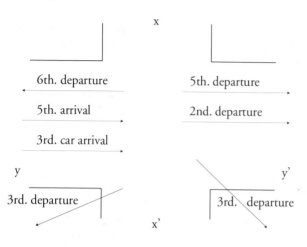

One can then construct an interpretation of this diagram of exactly the same kind as that produced by Bellour, as follows:

> "One can see: a) that the attacks 5 and 6 of the aeroplane are arranged symmetrically in the direction *y* and *y'* with respect to their arrival, and that: b) the departures progressively return to this same rigorous symmetry, producing a relative closure that is broken by the final departure, which in its turn: c) is compensated for by the arrival of the third car."

And again the result is indistinguishable from Bellour's kind of interpretation, even though deriving from an intrinsically meaningless set of features.

That Bellour should be unable to see the total arbitrariness of his method becomes less surprising when we look back to the way he introduced it on page 294 at the beginning of his article, before beginning his 'analysis':

> "The progression is double, at the same time profoundly linear and non-linear; on one side tying together the elements of the system step by step in a contiguity more or less immediate, from one series, from one alternation, from one rupture to another; on the other hand tying at a distance, at a greater or lesser distance, according to a play of echoes which produces simultaneously a perpetual contraction and expansion of the system."

With such a system that simultaneously uses the totally contradictory ideas of linearity and non-linearity, contiguity and non-contiguity, and expansion and contraction, absolutely anything can be fitted in, even if it be a series of totally random features.

Only occasional touches of this sort of procedure have appeared in the writings of the English admirers of French theorizing, for instance in Stephen Heath's *Film and System* in *Screen* Vol.16, Nos. 1 and 2, 1975, and the charitable assumption is that this denotes a better sense of what is reasonable than Raymond Bellour has. But equally unjustified over-interpretation of a more general kind has appeared from time to time in the last couple of decades in more conservative journals. The sort of thing I have in mind is the reading of major significance into such features as the directions of panning shots, or the actual length of particular shots, without regard for the plausibility of this. An early example of this sort of tendency was the almost legendary occasion when the writers of *Movie* asked Vincente Minnelli the meaning of a wobble of the image in his *The Four Horsemen of the Apocalypse*. Minnelli replied that the wobble was not in his film but in their projector. To be fair, the *Movie* writers were taking the right general approach in checking their interpretations with the film-maker, but they should have done it with some awareness of the techniques and aesthetic attitudes that he was likely to use.

It is worth noting that ordinary academic film criticism frequently suffers from some of the same kinds of illogicality as those in the examples I have been considering. Recently, many good examples of the basic flaws in the arguments used in interpretation have been given by David Bordwell in his *Making Meaning: Inference and Rhetoric in the Interpretation of Cinema* (Harvard University Press, 1989), but he does not also consider the frequent lack of simple correspondence with the facts to be found in academic criticism. When such faults are not present, what we usually get is a mixture of unthinking reactions produced by the critic's personal system of beliefs, mixed in with more reasonable interpretation that is controlled in an implicit or unconscious way by just the kind of checks for relevance that I have advocated at the beginning of this chapter. This latter component of criticism *can* produce observations of lasting interest about a film, so that not everything that is sweepingly dismissed by would-be theorists as 'impressionistic' criticism is worthless, though this is no reason to encourage its proliferation. Rather it is to be hoped that its practitioners might come to differentiate, both for themselves and for others, between the various kinds of approaches to film that they are employing unthinkingly.

4. FRENCH FILM THEORY INTO ENGLISH

The principal channel for the presentation and advocacy of French film theory in English translation has been the magazine *Screen*, one of the Marxist journals subsidized by the British Film Institute. From 1971 French theoretical writing of the kind I have already commented on has been translated in *Screen*, and more recently such ideas have been presented in rewritten form, and nearly always totally uncritically. Indeed, the claim has often been made in *Screen* that these French inventions represent new truths that render all other ideas about film worthless, and that they provide new standards of 'rigour' and exactness. Many would agree that the standard of previous discussions of cinema could be improved, and that moves in the direction of improvement are to be welcomed, but only if they produce new and constructive knowledge, and not just more empty words.

At first sight, those original articles by members of the *Screen* group which attempt to apply French ideas to actual films look quite impressive, for they mimic the appearance of scholarly articles in established disciplines, with very large numbers of footnotes and references, and often also elaborate analytical tabulations. But when one looks more closely at the references, one finds that they are not to well-established results, but at best to a source where a chain of dubious arguments rests on baseless assertions, and at worst to some bald assertion by an ignorant and badly-educated Frenchman. As for analytical tabulations, I will just mention one in an article by Stephen Heath on *Touch of Evil* in *Screen* Vol.16, Nos. 1. and 2. In this there is a large chart covering a number of pages which tabulates, amongst other things, the Scale of Shot for the shots in a section of that film. But the Scales of Shot given are written down incorrectly and inconsistently, and then *no use is made of this chart in the course of the article*. No doubt the model for this kind of pointless procedure is the list of Actions at the end of Roland Barthes' *S/Z*, of which that author too makes no use whatsoever.

The novel but unnecessary terminology which is used in these articles in *Screen* may have helped to conceal their inadequacies from their authors, and as an example of this I will mention two articles by different authors in Vol.17, No.4 and Vol.18, No.3, which deal with the first twelve shots in *Un Chien Andalou*. Both authors repeatedly describe the first four shots of this film, which comprise a repeated pair of reverse-angle cuts on action between a shot of a man sharpening a razor and a detail Insert of the sharpening action, as an 'alternating syntagm'. Now although Christian Metz's 'Grande Syntagmatique', which had previously been expounded at length in *Screen*, is quite unnecessary and productive of no extra precision, Metz has made it quite clear that by 'alternating syntagm' he meant what is ordinarily referred to

as cross-cutting between parallel actions in different places, and certainly not continuity cutting within an ordinary scene, which is what we have in these four shots. This misunderstanding of the basic 'theoretical' ideas being used leads the authors of these articles on to further confusions about the placing of the camera and the actors, and then this confusion is reinforced by a failure to recognize the eye-line mismatches still common in European films made in 1928.

Leaving aside further similar confusions, I will mention yet another kind of characteristic failing in the original articles written for *Screen*, and I will take as an example an article by Roger Silverstone in Vol. 17, No.2 called 'An Approach to the Structural Analysis of the Television Message'. This purports to apply to a contemporary television play the system of narrative analysis developed by Vladimir Propp for Russian fairy tales in his *Morphology of the Folk Tale* (University of Texas Press, 1968). In Propp's work various narrative functions describing parts of the stories are defined specifically to relate to the nature of events in Russian fairy tales, and in fact Propp's aim was to show that all Russian folk tales of a fantastic nature had a similar structure, with the narrative functions occurring in the same order, and hence that all Russian fairy tales derived from a common original tale. In his attempt to fit Propp's narrative functions onto a modern drama, Silverstone uses them sometimes with the literal meaning Propp attached to them, but sometimes he can only get them to fit the events in the television drama by widening their meaning to take in a figurative sense. For instance, Propp's function which relates to the giving of a magical object to the hero is used by Silverstone to apply to the wife giving breakfast to her husband, and so on. For the instances when even this illegitimate tactic will not work, Silverstone has no hesitation in inventing a series of new *ad hoc* functions for his analysis. Even so, he cannot get all of Propp's functions to occur, and in their correct order, but this does not stop him claiming that he has done a Propp-type analysis, and that it fits the television play well! But there is more to come. Silverstone has now added more material to his original article and it has all been published without alteration in book form as *The Message of Television* (Heinemann, 1981). However he has also included in an appendix an entirely different analysis of the teleplay using Propp's functions, which he claims is the same as his original analysis which is in the body of the book! The acclaim with which Silverstone's work has been greeted by other sociologists gives one some idea of the intellectual standards prevailing in sociology as well as in *Screen* magazine.

In the last several years there have been various other attempts to force Propp's functions onto film narratives, and they have all shown the same kind of faults as those in

Silverstone's work. However it is only *Screen* that has made repeated claims that the articles it publishes meet new standards of rigour. As a summation of the failings of the *Screen* approach to film theory, I will consider in more detail another article in that magazine which has been frequently referred to as though it contained profound truths about the nature of photographic reproduction, whereas in fact the case is quite the contrary.

Narrative Space

An article by Stephen Heath in *Screen* Vol. 17, No. 3 (1976), which attempts to draw a number of topics together under the heading of *Narrative Space* has since been cited in various articles as support for erroneous positions and ideas. It perpetuates some common misunderstandings about the nature of photographic reproduction, and buttresses what it says on this and other topics with a large number of factually incorrect statements, so a closer look at the matter is in order. To do this concisely it is necessary to go back to a consideration of photographic reproduction from first principles.

A real scene has light waves coming from it, and then arriving at any particular point in front of it, in a way that is in principle completely determined, and this is the case whether there is an eye or a camera at that point or not. The ideal of perfect photographic reproduction is to have light waves coming from a screen or other source to a point in front of it in exactly the same way as regards direction, wavelength, intensity, etc. as was the case for the corresponding point in front of the original scene. And this is again to be so whether there is an eye to look at the reproduced scene or not.

If this aim is perfectly achieved, an eye placed in the two corresponding positions before the real scene and before the reproduced scene in succession will of course not be able to distinguish which is the original scene, and which is the reproduction. The eye-brain combination has difficulty distinguishing cases where the absolute intensity of the rays in the two versions is different, but still in the same relative proportion one to another *within* each of the versions, but beyond that there is very little leeway for the brain to compensate for deviations from the ideal to give the illusion of perfect reproduction when it does not exist. If this were not the case there would be no possibility of deciding which was the more accurate of two differing reproductions of a scene, and this we can certainly do, and agree about as well. To take the crudest instance, we can easily agree about which of two photographs is more in focus, but the case extends to much more subtle details than that. The existence of visual illusions is irrelevant to the matter, since nearly all of them exist in the same way in a real scene and also in the best possible photographic reproductions of that scene. Nearly all the writers on visual perception, and also on perspective in reproduction, fail to realize this, including the ones Stephen Heath cites, and they are eventually led to the puzzled (and false) conclusion that we should not be able to recognize the similarity or otherwise of two scenes, whether reproduced or not. J.J.

Gibson's *Perception of the Visual World* (Houghton Mifflin, 1950) is a case in point. After mentioning the correct view of the matter that I have presented above, he fails to discuss it at all. Other discussions of perspective in reproduction confine their attention to the case of painting, though sometimes bringing in black and white photographic prints on paper, which is not much help as far as the general case is concerned.

At the present time one can in practice achieve various approximations to the ideal reproduction of visual reality. One approach is through central projection (in both the geometric and cinematic senses of the word) onto a hemispherical screen with a 'fish-eye' (180° field) lens used for both taking and projection. An even more nearly perfect reproduction for two-eyed humans can be made by using a stereoscopic pair of cameras and projectors in this situation. But these arrangements are not economically attractive, so we ordinarily have the usual reproduction of a restricted part of the visual field from a flat surface, so introducing the possibility of artistic composition of the image. (The possibility of image composition does not really exist with hemispherical projection, since in that case the edge of the image can not be seen properly when looking near the centre of it.)

In the arrangements so far described, movements of the eyeballs of the spectator are allowed, but if one wants to maintain the perfection of reproduction as well as possible, movements of the head are not. (Stephen Heath fails to distinguish between these two types of eye movement.) Perfect reproduction of *part* of the visual field in a manner that accomodates the head movements of the spectator can be accomplished with holography, and motion holography was achieved nearly two decades ago, but this is still being ignored in theoretical discussions of these matters. And holograms can be synthesized from ordinary photographs taken from a large number of different angles to a scene, so that the visible world *can* be considered as "... a sum total of possible photographs ...", and not the contrary, as Stephen Heath wrongly claims on p.78 of his article.

Short of having one of these two more nearly perfect, but at the moment highly inconvenient systems, we settle for the next best, which is, as already stated, the optical and geometrical projection of a scene onto a flat surface. The way the eye-brain combination works is quite irrelevant to all this, as there is no way it can change the physical information (the light waves, that is) impinging on the eye, and that is *all* that determines whether the brain has a chance to 'see' a perfect reproduction or not. Some sort of vague impression that the brain, eye, and external world are bound together into a kind of un-analysable whole seems to have become quite widespread amongst literary intellectuals in recent years. This is quite false. Only light waves (or photons if you like) go into the eye, and nothing goes back the other way, so that one can make a simple separation between what goes on in the external world, and what goes on in the eye-brain combination.

In Stephen Heath's attempt at an account of the significance of photographic reproduction, which is more a free fantasia round miscellaneous quotations than a logical argument, the principal idea put forward is that the form of photographic reproduction results solely from a 'code' invented in the Quattrocento (15th. century) for painting, as a result of a sudden new philosophical or ideological conception of space itself. This superficial and false idea is not original, but along the way of rehearsing it from pages 73 to 81 of his article, Heath produces a number of factually false statements, starting with the claim (page 73) that representation is a matter of discourse. As I have indicated, true representation is just a matter of optical correspondence, regardless of whether there is any observer to give the possibility of calling it 'discourse'. Next, from page 75 onwards, the idea that there was a "... perspective code of Quattrocento painting ..." appears. Now the specific characteristics of Quattrocento painting are actually due to the way a convention of composition interacts with the reproductive system then in use, through the lining up of the edges of solid objects with the perspective construction lines. As every art historian knows (Gisela M. Richter, *Perspective in Greek and Roman Art*, Phaidon, 1970), correct perspective renderings corresponding to the results of central projection had been achieved in classical antiquity, presumably in the pursuit of *mimesis*. These renderings do not have the *centralized compositional convention* of Quattrocento painting, but that does not prevent them from having correct perspective. If one insists on talking of codes, even though it is not necessary and the use of that word tells us nothing new, then one has to say that there are two codes involved in this matter – a perspective code, and a compositional code. The first is a simple mechanical code like Morse code (from a mathematical point of view even simpler than Morse code), and if it is altered very much it just vanishes, ceasing to be a code. The first signs of a revived interest in it can be seen before the Quattrocento, possibly due to concerns with the new popular religious teaching. As for the specific Quattrocento compositional 'code', interest in this convention departed remarkably suddenly around 1520, after which compositional interest in paintings shifted to complex figure arrangements in a shallow space, or alternatively to landscapes done freely without construction lines. In the first case there are sometimes bits of architecture dim in the backgrounds of the paintings, but the renderings of these are sufficiently inaccurate from a perspective point of view as not to count as perspective. If the reader wishes he can check the above statement against any sufficiently large sample of Renaissance paintings, such as Freedberg's *Italian Painting in the Sixteenth Century* in the Pelican History of Art series.

In film terms, the independence of centrally organized compositional conventions from the reproductive system is demonstrated by the existence of alternatives to their usual co-presence. In horror films, anamorphic images (in the general geometrical sense: i.e. distorted, without correct perspective reproduction), but *with* centralized composition, are sometimes used for expressive purposes, and in some avant-garde films one sometimes gets images that have no centralized

composition, but do have correct perspective, as in Hall and Sinden's *Edge* (1973). The rarest combination is images having neither correct perspective nor centralized composition, but some of the distorted shots in Abel Gance's *la Folie du Docteur Tube* (1915?) just about fill the bill.

In his failure to understand these facts, Stephen Heath has put himself in the position where he can uncritically quote statements like: "The public has come to believe that geometrical perspective, so long as it does not involve unfamiliar points of view, is 'true', just as a long time ago it was believed that the old geometry of Euclid was 'the truth'." I have already indicated that as far as getting the most accurate reproduction of visual reality onto a flat surface (and off it again) is concerned, geometrical perspective is the 'truest', and of course Euclidean geometry is still accurate as far as all practical purposes are concerned. It is only when dealing with cosmological matters that one has to take account of Riemannian geometry. In using a quotation like this, Stephen Heath is clearly confused about what constitutes useful knowledge, and he goes on to emphasize this by using as part of his argument quotations relating to film construction from authors who have not worked in fictional film-making, and hence whose ideas have no direct relation to film practice.

Then, on page 81 of his article, Heath makes an attempt to associate with the Renaissance the existence of pictures and their frames as entities independent from wall decoration and other applied uses. Apart from the fact that, contrary to his claim, paintings were made on freely movable rectangular panels of wood and terracotta with painted borders in classical antiquity, he is also flatly wrong in stating that "... the Quattrocento system cannot be realized without it (i.e. the frame) ...". In fact, perspective by central projection does not require that the projection plane have any limits; the semi-infinite volume of the visual world which exists on the other side of the infinite projection plane from the projection point can be projected onto that infinite projection plane in exactly the same geometrical way as for the projection of a limited volume of space onto a limited area of the projection plane, which incidentally can be of any shape.

After more pages stitched together from quotations of varying reliability, (e.g. the Lumières did not restrict themselves to audiences viewing the screen from one side, but the alternative used at the Paris Exposition of 1898 required the inconvenience of keeping the screen continuously wet), Stephen Heath arrives at a favourite statement that he has repeated in other places. This is: "The 180 degree line that the camera is forbidden to cross answers exactly to the 180 degree line of the screen behind which the spectator cannot and must not go ...". In fact it is quite easy to find examples of crossing the eye-line in scenes involving two people in Hollywood films; about once in every twenty films if one looks for it carefully. For example, inside a couple of weeks I have seen instances in *Pilgrimage* (John Ford, 1933), *Lady in a Jam* (La Cava, 1942), and *The Unsuspected* (Curtiz, 1947). Obviously these occurrences were not considered of any importance at the time, as retakes were usual to correct faults in those days. When one turns to European films of the nineteen-thirties it is quite easy to find orgies of eye-line crossing: as in Paul Czinner's *Escape Me Never* (1935), and Duvivier's *Un Carnet de Bal* (1937). From all this the only possible conclusion is that 'crossing the eye-line' is far less important than is usually supposed, and since the rule is far from *exactly* held, there is no way for it to correspond to the line of the screen, as Stephen Heath would have it.

This article on 'Narrative Space' ends with four pages of mixed rhetoric, description, and frame enlargements centering on a tiny peculiarity of one scene of Oshima's *Death by Hanging*, a peculiarity that has nothing to do with 'narrative space', but a lot to do with the difficulty of getting a cat to do what you want when shooting low-budget location film, but Heath is incapable of recognizing this last point.

Can we do better than this sort of thing?

5. PRACTICAL FILM THEORY

I take the aim of film studies to be arriving at, and then communicating, the maximum amount of useful knowledge about all sorts of films from the past to the present. I also believe that the best sort of knowledge is constructive, meaning that it has its basis in what we can be fairly sure about, and also that it can be used as a sound basis to build upon further. To handle this task practically, there must be methods of analysing and evaluating as objectively as possible the hundreds of thousands of films that have been made. Analysis is necessary, for nothing can be said accurately without it. Evaluation is necessary, because only some films can be considered, saved, and made available out of many. The maximum amount of objectivity is necessary, because that permits the maximum communication of knowledge. (In a world where total subjectivity and relativism reigns, no meaningful communication is possible.) This means that serious study of the cinema should strive towards, without being able to attain, the nature of the established sciences such as biology and physics, which are identical in England and Russia, America and China. Film studies are unable completely to become a real science because of the essentially innovatory, idiosyncratic, and complex nature of the art object. There are no eternal laws of aesthetics.

Principles like these, though not usually expressed, doubtless because they are obvious, have guided the fruitful development of musicology and art history during this century. An important aspect of this approach is that only as much theory as is necessary to deal with the matter in hand is used; there is no point in the pursuit of totally unnecessary and unobtainable rigour and generality. As P.B. Medawar observed, in the real sciences there are no prizes for tackling too difficult a problem and then failing to solve it. Though in the humanities it seems that if this is done with enough flashy rhetoric one can collect one an admiring crowd of ignorant disciples for a while, not to mention providing a comfortable living for oneself. The other main error of film critics has been too great an eagerness to say just what sort of film is good and what sort bad; by an unconscious desire to justify personal preferences. The two sides of film theory – the analytical and the evaluative – should be separated as much as possible, and for both the individual film should be central, not the director or the genre or anything else.

Analysis

Analysis of films can proceed in two directions, and these are far from equivalent. Most importantly, films can be analysed in terms of their construction and their relation to their makers: analysis in this direction is mostly ignored in theorizing about films. This is strange, because if one insists on describing a film as a coded message, that coded message must have been constructed by the films immediate makers, and the only way to get an accurate decoding must be to reverse the process of encoding. Actually, it should be noted that the film medium, in terms of its narrative function, is not a simple communication channel, but a complex object that is also a representational system, but neverless with aspects that function in other ways, such as communication.

Less importantly, films can be analysed in terms of the response of their spectators. Of course film-makers also form part of the audience, and they are the part that is capable of the fullest response and understanding. It is in relation to them that the film comes closest to being something like a language system.

The obvious factors that influence the creation of a film – previous films, the technical and other production constraints from inside the film industry and craft, and the more general influence of society and culture – all act through individual film-makers whose individual differences play a large part in producing the visible variety of films: a variety that will be underlined in the following chapters. Attempts at the type of large-scale 'cultural history' or 'culture critique' generalizations that ignore the relations of individual film-makers to their work and try to explain everything about films in terms of such tenuous and imprecise abstractions as 'bourgeois ideology' invariably founder on the sheer variety of films. The generalizations of cultural history, Marxist or otherwise, are always either banal or false, and indeed experience shows that one generation's cultural history, however diverting it was at the time, is the next generation's waste paper.

Most of the numerous features of a film are the way they are because of conscious decisions by the director, writer, cameraman, etc. (There is a possibility that this was slightly less true in some cases in early cinema, but it is fairly easy to tell the occasions when this happened, if one has seen enough examples of films from the period in question.) So in the first place the narratives of films should be looked at in the terms used to construct them. Besides the well-known vocabulary of 'scenes', 'sequences' and so on, these terms are mainly of dramatic origin, but there are other more specialized terms such as the 'switch'.

The conventions of editing and lighting are already supplied with descriptive terms, and where there are gaps they can be filled by the natural extension of existing expressions. For example the existing description 'core lighting' can be extended to cover another common type of lighting of figures by the term 'angled core lighting'. The other dimensions of the medium are similarly provided with their analytical concepts and terminology. More generalized forms of classification such as 'genre' and 'style' form themselves in the usual way on a secondary level, after this primary analysis has been carried out. The fact that this is fairly obvious and straightforward does not make it incorrect and unsatisfactory.

The film-maker's beliefs, aesthetic and otherwise, undoubtedly influence the product, and they certainly must be considered, as might also the connection of the film-maker's personality with what he does. For this latter purpose, scientific personality theory is sufficiently advanced to guide the investigation without recourse to baseless Freudian speculations.

Towards the Spectator

Unlike the relation of the finished film to its makers and production process, which is fixed and definite for all time once it is complete, the relation of the film to its audience not only varies between audiences of different filmic sophistication as already mentioned, but this relation also varies with time: the reaction of a contemporary audience to a silent film is often quite different to that of an audience in the nineteen-twenties. This fact alone renders this side of film analysis less important, but nevertheless it is well worth pursuing. Proceeding in this direction we are led to the once popular investigation of the sociological effects of films, then to what is essentially part of the psychology of perception, and finally to a consideration of how audiences understand films. As far as the psychology of perception of film is concerned, what is needed is the kind of research begun some time ago in painting and music into the response to the simplest elements of these arts, and then working up to more complex structures. Recently there has been quite a lot of interest in the branch of perceptual psychology called cognitive psychology, though so far this has mostly produced a great deal of theorizing, with little in the way of experimentally supported conclusions of any but the most banal kind. Nevertheless, we should keep our eyes open for more in the way of solid scientific results in this area. The evidence so far in the other arts shows that the response to combinations of artistic elements can be predicted from the response to the elements (colours, shapes, etc.) themselves taken individually, despite the unsupported speculations of Gestalt theorists that this would not be so. It is also undoubtedly the case in these other arts that the personality of the spectator affects his artistic preferences. (See D.E. Berlyne, *Aesthetics and Psychobiology*, Appleton-Century-Crofts, 1971). Would-be film theorists are *still* proceeding as though all the members of the film audience are identical.

Leaving aside the understanding that film-makers and those with equal knowledge have of film, the major part of film audiences probably understand film in a very simple way. In fact as an intensified and extended dramatic representation – i.e. like a stage play with knobs on. Although the idea awaits full experimental verification, my suggestion is that the mass audience does not register in any significant way any minor infractions of editing and other conventions as long as rough temporal continuity is preserved within a sequence. The way

a naïve audience comes to understand film representation quite quickly gives some idea that the understanding is as simple as I have suggested. On the other hand, most avant-garde film is quite meaningless to the mass audience, for in that case its appreciation depends on an understanding of its relationship with other films, other arts, the conventions, and other things. Avant-garde film is the most difficult area of all to handle, and most recent film theorizing has little to say about most of it.

The Nature of the Medium and Film Form

The first crude holographic films have already been made, and we can anticipate a complete, all-surrounding audio-visual representation of reality being possible at some time in the future. So the most useful basic way of regarding the medium (and this includes television) is as a more faithful or less faithful reproduction of audio-visual reality. One extreme, as technically possible at the moment, would be a series of 70 mm. colour stereoscopic films with multi-channel sound taken of an unstaged event, and projected so as to fill the complete area of possible vision, while the other extreme would be some kind of small-screen abstract film with synthetic sound, or no sound at all. All films can be considered to lie on a spectrum between these two extremes, with a greater or lesser degree of distortion (or transformation) of reality being introduced in various ways: by making cuts between shots rather than running the camera continuously, using zooms and camera movements within shots, shooting in black and white rather than colour, using various degrees of non-natural sound, filming acted events, and so obviously on. The amount of distortion of reality introduced in the separate dimensions of the medium (cutting, photography, sound, acting, the events represented, etc.) is not necessarily parallel between each of these dimensions and the general effect of the film itself, though there is not usually a great divergence.

These dimensions can even be considered in a semi-quantitative way in many cases; for instance the 'strength' of a cut or other shot transition can be defined in terms of the amount of discontinuity in space and time introduced into the action by the cut. Another possibility is a precise analysis of the number of shots having various shot lengths in a film, and also the numbers with various degrees of camera closeness and camera movement. It might be claimed that this is a rather arid approach, but considerations of how long a shot is to be, where the camera is to go, and so on, are some of the things with which the director of a film is principally concerned. (Note also that acting style has been included as a dimension of the medium as well.)

Film Style

Questions of style arise when we consider films in relation to other films. If analysis along the lines just mentioned has been carried out, then the distributions of these quantities (shot length, etc.) for a particular group of films, say by a particular director, when compared with those for other directors working at the same place and time, give a sure indication of the existence of a personal style; in fact this is what formal style is. (Analogous analyses have long ago been carried out for the style of literary and musical works.) To give a simple example, in the middle of the nineteen-thirties the cutting rate (or better, the Average Shot Length) in Mervyn Le Roy's films was near the norm for Hollywood films of that time (an Average Shot Length of 9 seconds), whereas in Michael Curtiz's films it was around 6 seconds, and in John Stahl's 14 seconds or longer. Using a measure like this, or indeed other more complex ones, it is also possible to compare the range of variation characteristic of American films with the different range holding for the contemporary French films, and so on. When this method of norms and differences is generalized to all the features of films it can help to avoid the frequent error of describing as unique what is in fact a common feature of a large class of films from a particular time or place or genre. For instance, Noël Burch has described the use of dissolves from a Long Shot to a closer shot in *Caligari* as "subverting the codes" (a pointless synonym for 'breaking the conventions'), whereas in fact this usage was fairly common in German and American films during World War 1, and indeed through into the 'twenties in Europe. The error of failing to take the context into account is very common in writing about older films, and I have already referred to another instance of it in a previous chapter.

It could be argued that often the individuality of a film-maker lies in the verbally expressible content of his films, and indeed it often does in part, but this individuality of content will mostly be found to be allied to formal individuality if the analysis is carried far enough.

The importance of formal style analysis is beginning to be realized, but it still has not got much further than remarking things like the fact that Howard Hawks keeps the camera at eye-level and doesn't move it if possible. But in fact there are other directors of his vintage who do this too. For instance Henry Hathaway. (Keeping the camera at eye-level makes for efficient shooting because the actors can be kept well-framed at all distances without tilting the camera up. If the camera were tilted up, the lighting set-up would sometimes have to be changed to keep the back-lights out of shot.) The real stylistic distinction is that further than this, Hawks keeps his Average Shot Length a little longer than normal, whereas Hathaway uses faster cutting.

Some attempts at style analysis have unfortunately been conducted in spurious terms that ignore conditions imposed on the director, and also the relation between the approach of a particular director and that generally prevailing at the period in question. For instance, the style of Douglas Sirk cannot be simply pinned down by talk about mirrors and flat shiny surfaces. Mirror shots are quite common in dramas made by ordinary Hollywood directors from the nineteen-thirties on-wards (it makes shooting a studio scene more interesting for the director), and insofar as Sirk's films have flat, glossy surfaces this is due to the art directors at Universal Studios and the deficiencies of CinemaScope lenses. (The squeeze ratio of CinemaScope lenses varied with object distance, so emphasiz-ing the existence of the picture plane.) Actually, Sirk's formal style is distinguished by a so-far unremarked excess of low-angle shots over the norm. To judge by an unprompted statement of Sirk's, this resulted from a seeking for expressivity on his part.

The formal spectrum covered by the cinema, that I de-scribed in the previous section, when translated into terms of style becomes a spectrum stretching from extreme naturalism to extreme expressivism.

If one looks back to statements made by Hollywood directors in past times, it is apparent that they mostly saw their task as one of expressing the material in the script – 'putting the story across' – in the most effective way, and a point at issue between them was just how much expressivism to use, and how much naturalism. The general desire was to affect the audience in the appropriate way, and this called for the application of unmentioned supplementary principles, un-mentioned because traditional in the drama and other arts, and so obvious to film-makers, such as internal consistency in all aspects of the film to maintain suspension of disbelief. This is closely related to Victor Perkins' principle of internal co-herence. Incidentally, many of the examples discussed in *Film as Film* are cases of the expression of the script content through formal devices. Indeed discussion of the detail in a film in these terms is not new, but it has nearly always taken place within a framework that unfortunately assigned aesthetic values to particular styles and contents.

Of course nearly all commercial films occupy a fairly small central region of the style and form spectra, but the extremes are increasingly taken up by films of the avant-garde. These are still denied satisfactory discussion, partly because the terms for this are lacking, partly for less creditable reasons.

At this stage questions of value, of aesthetics, are still excluded, but there are still lots of things that can be said about films, even in a more general way. For instance, we can say that Bergman preferred to film in black and white rather than colour at that period when he had a choice, because he wished to make films that were more expressivist than the norm. We can talk about how the degree of naturalism of the average entertainment film has changed over the years, and about many other interesting matters. And we can talk about films like Godard's which have different parts made in different styles.

In other words, the interaction between style and content is basically a second-order effect that can be dealt with once the first approximation in the analysis has been carried out, by treating style and content separately.

The Evaluation of Films

Now that form and style have been considered, aesthetic evaluation can be dealt with without creating confusion. My criteria for doing this are, in the order of the weight to be attached to them: firstly, the originality in all respects of the film; secondly, the influence it has on other films; and thirdly, the degree to which the film-maker has fulfilled his intentions in the finished film. The criterion of influence on other films should also be weighted according to the excellence, by these criteria, of the films that are influenced by the film in question. These criteria are the most objective possible, and are equally applicable to every type of film, which cannot be said of previously proposed criteria.

My first two criteria are completely realizable in principle, with the proviso that the iterative part of the second criterion, which requires that the influence on other films takes account of the quality of the films influenced, has to be calculated with a reducing factor applied on each repetition, in which case it can be cut off after a fixed number of cycles to give a sufficiently correct answer. The third and least important criterion does present some difficulties in application. Nevertheless it can be worked well enough for practical purposes, even when it has greater weight thrown upon it by the inapplicability of the second criterion when we are considering new films. The conscious intentions of the film-maker (or makers) can usually be found out or reconstructed with sufficient accuracy for this purpose by taking a little trouble. Although something has been done in this direction already by interviewing film-makers, a certain amount of misleading information is produced because interviewers do not know enough about the subjects on which they ask questions. A case in point is the many manifestly untrue things that are said about 'north light' in Charles Higham's *Hollywood Cameramen*. Such errors are partly produced by the asking of incorrect leading questions, to which Hollywood types have a tendency to reply with the answer expected of them, and partly by the boastful exaggeration endemic in Old Hollywood. In fact my principles provide the justification, which is otherwise lacking, for the interviewing of film-makers.

Although the criteria I have put forward here are the most objective possible, they do not quite provide a calculus which can be operated mechanically to crank out values. They need to be applied by people who have viewed large numbers of films with analytic understanding in the ways I have indicated, and indeed there have always been some people in this position. They have had significant things to say about films, even if unclear principles have sometimes led them astray.

The evaluation of films by aesthetic criteria to which their makers did not subscribe also seems fairly pointless, and tends to look foolish in the light of history; the most famous example being the attitude of Socialist critics to von Sternberg's films in the early 'thirties. As is also recognized now, Bazin's consideration of the films of Welles and Wyler in terms of concepts that were not those of their makers was also factually inaccurate and logically confused. More recently the evaluation of films purely in the light of moral educational concepts such as 'maturity' has risen and fallen, and now purely political values are being pushed to the fore again. There is no doubt that large numbers of film-makers do not subscribe to these values, and so the extremely limited usefulness of these ap-

proaches in film terms should be recognized.

The Auteur Theory Revisited

It does not seem to be fully appreciated that, in its original form, the 'Auteur Policy' as it developed in *Cahiers du Cinéma* was influenced by the way that film-makers see films; the people who were its leading proponents were just starting to direct films, or were thinking about doing so, and they were looking at films of the past, or what was then the present, for guidance about how to handle the camera, when to cut, and so on. The operation of this interest enabled them to see individuality and skill at work in films where it was invisible to the ordinary critic, but it also led them to slightly overvalue many of the American films of the nineteen-fifties.

The ghost of this semi-conscious use of film-makers' ways of seeing persisted in the form that Andrew Sarris gave to the Auteur Theory. Amongst the numerous subsidiary evaluative criteria that he introduced, mostly to demote the film-makers whose films were unsympathetic to him, was the criterion of craftsmanship. This is a relevant criterion, and it is included as a part of the third general principle that I have proposed, which is that the film succeeds in fulfilling its makers intentions.

Because of all this, my theory, when applied to the American sound cinema, produces evaluations rather similar to those of Sarris in the upper ranks of film-makers. But it moves Stroheim and Wilder up a step, and it moves Raoul Walsh down as being little more than an excellent craftsman, to mention only the more obvious adjustments. Since my approach works through individual films in the first place, important film-makers are just those who have produced important films. There is nothing in my theory that says that all films by a particular film-maker must be good, or even interesting, and in fact for most film-makers their most important work is concentrated towards the earlier parts of their careers. This is because the strength of will and body needed to control the film production process, necessary to a far greater degree than in the other arts, decreases with increasing age.

The principal reason that my theory of film evaluation produces rather similar results to the Sarris Auteur Theory is that 'originality' and 'expression of the maker's personality' amount to almost (but not quite) the same thing in practice, but a subsidiary reason is Sarris' personal sensitivity and the fact that he has seen and compared a very large number of films. Apart from the elements of confusion and illogicality that spoil Sarris' work, he himself admits that there are exceptions to his theory: films such as *Casablanca* that are better than their directors. There are *no* exceptions to the theory advanced here. The importance or excellence of *Das Cabinet des Dr. Caligari* is not because Robert Wiene was a great director, but because of its originality and influence.

In Conclusion

One of the merits of the theoretical framework for film

put forward here is that it has spaces to accommodate quantities of useful work, writing, and information that have been produced in the past, and are still being produced by a large number of people interested in films. For of course it is hardly likely that intelligent people who know a great deal about films could be totally mistaken in everything they say. Yet this seems to be the position of those who hold the ideas described in the first section of this book. And even further, they appear to believe that by reading a few approved books and articles, and seeing a small number of approved films, one is in a position to understand everything about cinema that matters. It is a conception of the cinema that would limit it to serving some extra-filmic concerns of the moment, and in its most extreme form wishes to dictate what sort of films should be made.

There is no royal road to knowledge about films, or about any other art for that matter.

By contrast, the theoretical framework that I propose for film studies puts the difficulties where they belong, in dealing with individual problems, and makes it possible to deal with those that are soluble one by one in a sound and useful way, as I hope the rest of this book demonstrates.

If film-makers did not make films, following as they do their own ideas about what they are doing, there would be nothing to support would-be film theorists who write about films. At a time when there are already a number of film-makers who are as well-educated, as clever, and who certainly know more about films than most theorists, a certain humility should be in order.

6. FILM THEORY WITH AN AMERICAN ACCENT

In the nineteen-seventies there was a massive expansion of film studies courses in American higher education, accompanied by all the usual institutional appendages, such as the award of higher degrees, and the appearance of academic societies with their annual conferences, and their journals for the publication of their members' papers. In some of these academic publications there is a display of exaggerated and pointless pedantry, to the extent of some articles having end-notes as long as the articles themselves. Indeed some American film studies academics can even be found childishly boasting that their work is better than anyone else's just because it is longer, and has more footnotes. In the 'seventies the works and persons of people like Christian Metz, Stephen Heath, and Raymond Bellour were received with awe by many American academics, and they provided a pernicious model for American film studies. For now there had to be native American academic film theory as well, and it had to contain striking new concepts and terminology, with little regard paid to its possible validity. So in the United States in the last several years there have been various attempts to produce new theories about all, or part of, the cinema, but mostly these are not worth taking seriously, being vulnerable to the same kinds of objections as the French-derived theories discussed in the previous chapters. The major exception to this generalization is one of the earliest contributions to American theorizing, which came from David Bordwell and Kristin Thompson, starting at the beginning of the nineteen- eighties. They called their theoretical approach 'Neo-formalism', which indicated that it was directly derived from the Russian Formalist aesthetics of the nineteen-twenties, as propounded by Boris Eikhenbaum, Victor Shklovsky, Yuri Tynjanov, and others. Their immediate inspiration came from a rash of English translation and comment concerned with the work of the Russian Formalists that was published in the nineteen-seventies in various places, including even *Screen* magazine. (The publication of my ideas on film analysis, which have a quite independently formalist aspect, from 1974 to 1977 in *Sight & Sound* and *Film Quarterly*, may also have had some influence on Bordwell and Thompson, since David Bordwell certainly read them at the time.) The one change that makes Bordwell and Thompson's version of the ideas of the Russian Formalists 'neo- ', is that they have replaced the speculative psychology of the nineteen-twenties, which the Russians used to attempt to analyse the relation of the work of art to the spectator, with more recent speculations about perceptual psychology.

The basic ideas of Neo-formalism are fairly simply stated, as can be seen in David Bordwell's *The Films of Carl-Theodor Dreyer* (University of California Press, 1981) and Kristin

Thompson's *Breaking the Glass Armour* (Princeton University Press, 1988).

"The fundamental assumption is that art is an affair of perception, and as such it presents the perceiver with problems of unity and disunity. The unity springs, of course, partly from patterns within the work, such as composition in a painting, sonata form in music, or narrative in cinema. Unity also emerges from the art-work's relation to the history of the medium. Thus conventions and the art-work's use of other works lead us to expect unity. Yet the Formalists also stressed the importance of disunity in aesthetic experience. The force of art arises from shocks and disturbances which it gives to our perception. Viktor Shklovsky called this *ostranenie*, 'estrangement', 'defamiliarization', 'making-strange'." (*Dreyer*, p.3)

"Disunity is also perceived in the art-work's relation to other works. The text defines its strangeness not by imitating tradition but by violating it – by breaking conventions, reordering tried elements, shattering our expectations. In all, Formalism's conception of art as a struggle between a stable unity and a dynamic estrangement has a usefulness that transcends any particular medium." (*Dreyer*, p.4).

"But if a series of artworks uses the same means over and over, the defamiliarizing capabilities of those means diminishes; the strangeness ebbs away over time. By that point, the defamiliarized has become familiar, and the artistic approach is largely automatized."

"These assumptions about defamiliarization and automatization allow neoformalism to eliminate a common feature of most aesthetic theories: the form-content split. Meaning is not the end result of an art-work, but one of its formal components. The artist builds a work out of, amongst other things, meanings." (*Glass Armour* p.11)

This last claim that Neo-formalism eliminates the form-content split is obviously self-contradictory, since its very wording attests that 'meaning' for a Neo-formalist is a separable element of the art-work, and indeed Bordwell and Thompson do treat all the parts of what is ordinarily considered content as something separable when they analyse particular films. This is particularly evident in their *Film Art: an Introduction (3rd. edition, 1990)*. All they are doing is to include meaning as a sub-section of 'form', which is purely a verbal trick, and contributes nothing extra to more traditional analytical methods such as my own, which already deal with the form-content interaction to produce the same sort of results, insofar as they are valid.

Indeed, a great deal of Bordwell and Thompson's theorizing is a matter of replacing existing terms and concepts that were already in wide use with new names, and then discussing these renamed concepts at length in an unnecessarily pedantic and tedious way. One example is 'background', which just corresponds to the concept of 'context' of a work of art, widely used long before, and another is 'device', which just means a significant element in an art-work. Yet others include the 'stairstep construction' of narrative, which is nothing but the series of '*stufe*' (steps) which form part of Gustav Freytag's theories about dramatic construction in his *Die Technik des Dramas* of 1876. And 'defamiliarization' is a direct result of the original features in an art-work, and so on.

Amongst other concepts taken over by Bordwell and Thompson from the Russian Formalists as part of their theory of narration, and in this case altered in meaning, are 'fabula' and 'syuzhet'. Like 'stairstep construction', the original Formalists had these from a long tradition of dramatic theory stretching back to Aristotle, which was already well-known to practical Russian playwrights like Chekhov. In the form Bordwell and Thompson use these notions to analyse narrative, they don't actually do anything extra either.

To Bordwell and Thompson 'syuzhet' means the narrative events as they are actually presented in a film, including gaps and possible irregular time schemes, while 'fabula' refers to the complete, continuous and chronological events in a world just like ours which the audience reconstructs in their minds in the course of understanding the incomplete scenes they are seeing shown on the movie screen before them. Although this distinction is unarguable, their choice and application of the name 'syuzhet' is particularly unfortunate, as it is the Russification of the French word '*sujet*' (i.e.'theme'). But when it comes to their application of these terms to the analysis of actual films, this distinction between fabula and syuzhet is hardly ever used, and most of the detail of the examples David Bordwell discusses in *Narration in the Fiction Film* deal with the interaction of syuzhet and style. This is exactly equivalent to that good old analysis of the interaction of content and form, which is so theoretically despised nowadays. And there is nothing wrong with that equivalence in my eyes, as it merely reverses the way most films are constructed, with a script being written first, and then a director filming it, and including what he considers suitably expressive or stylistic effects. The really novel and interesting interaction of what Bordwell and Thompson call fabula and syuzhet is sufficiently rare for examples of it to be discussed in an ad hoc way using existing terminology, without the need for special new general terms for this purpose. In their actual analyses, Bordwell and Thompson also make hardly any use of another of the Russian Formalist's basic concepts, the 'dominant', and in the little use

they do make of it, it could just as well be replaced by existing terminology again, with a little periphrasis.

The analysis of art-works in terms of the 'unity-disunity' between their elements has actually been a commonplace of literary criticism since the New Criticism of the interwar years. Since any feature of a film or other artwork can be taken to contribute to either its unification or the contrary, in practice this approach is subject to the same kind of abuse that I demonstrated in Bellour's analysis of *North by North-west* in a previous chapter. According to Bordwell and Thompson's own principles, this danger should be eliminated by taking the context of other art-works from the same place and time into account, and I would agree with this, provided that the context also includes the way the films were made, and what the film-makers thought they were doing at the time. But because they refuse to take these last two restrictions into account, and also because of their lack of full knowledge of this context, they often attribute aesthetic significance to features of films that really have no such significance. This is particularly the case in Bordwell's *Dreyer* book, where many features that he analyses formally in terms of 'unity-disunity' are the meaningless small-change of film style in a European backwater. The danger of such misinterpretation when a theory like this is in the hands of truly ignorant people is even greater.

It is usually considered that Russian formalist aesthetics was severely limited in dealing with the history of art, because it refused to deal with historical causation in the creation of particular works of art, and also in the development of artistic styles. Bordwell and Thompson have likewise rejected the consideration of the way the actual makers had put any particular film together when they are analysing its form, as can be seen in the most recent edition of their *Film Art: an Introduction*. However, in practice they are guilty of a fair amount of 'double-think' on this point. In particular, for their analyses they use the basic analytical terms that were invented by film-makers to describe what they were doing, and which are also part of the film-makers' own theories about what they are doing. So that when we look at Bordwell and Thompson's actual consideration of film historical matters, in their *The Classical Hollywood Cinema* (1985) and elsewhere, we find that it is carried out purely in terms of standard art-historical analysis, just as it was in other people's earlier work, such as my own on historical stylistics done in the nineteen-seventies. Indeed, some of the key methods and observations that Bordwell and Thompson use in the last-mentioned book are taken from my work. But strictly speaking, my approach to film analysis rejects the reading of any meaning into features of a film that was not put there intentionally , whereas theirs does not. Despite this, they now say that their Neo-formalism is necessary, not just for considering the interaction between the perceiver and the work of art, but also for the proper analysis of film history. Indeed, David Bordwell has recently, in the last chapter of his *Making Meaning* (Harvard, 1989), taken my theoretical framework for film analysis and interpretation that you have just seen outlined in the previous chapters of this book, and which he too had read in the first edition of 1983, and appropriated it as a new part of his Neo-formalism, calling it 'Historical poetics'. He does not mention where these ideas came from, but that seems to be acceptable practice for ambitious American academics. He presumably did this because of the growth of serious interest in film history in the last dozen years, but because Neo-formalism as formulated by Bordwell and Thompson is essentially audience-centered, and insists on giving all spectators equal status, to claim that it is sufficient and necessary for doing film history is either self-delusion or flim-flam.

There is only one component of Bordwell and Thompson's Neo-formalism that is truly unique amongst contemporary film theories. This is the part consisting of their psychological ideas about the perception of films. The fullest form of their treatment of film perception is in Chapter 3 of Bordwell's *Narration in the Fiction Film*, but close inspection of this shows that it is made up almost entirely of pure speculation about the psychological processes involved in perception, and the references given are also almost entirely to recent speculative theorising by other people, likewise unsupported by experimental results. A major notion in Bordwell and Thompson's ideas about film narration is that, in contradistinction to a view of it as some kind of communication process, it "...is better understood as the organization of a set of cues for the construction of a story. This presupposes a perceiver, but not any sender, of a message." (p.62) This is not the only contradiction of this kind within Bordwell's arguments in support of his notion of narration, as Seymour Chatman has pointed out, though it is the only one that is contained within the one sentence. Such illogicality, in which the act of organization has no subject, must result from Bordwell and Thompson's eagerness, like so many academics, to downplay the relation of the significance of the features of films to the way they were put together, and in particular to what film-makers thought they were doing when they made them. The attraction of this attitude is that it makes the critic or analyst more important than the artist and the art-work, and it also means that he and his students don't have to know very much about how films are made, let alone having any film-making experience and ability.

My view of the matter is that film is the most complex artistic medium there is, and consequently has a number of different aspects, so it escapes any simple reduction that depends on describing it as *only* mimetic, or *only* linguistic, or *only* a simple communication system. Narrative film *is* basically representational, but it does have a component of its organizational structure that is like the vestige of a language system. Rather like the grunts and waves of primitive hominids before real language developed. And film undoubtedly functions as a communication system in transmitting a story from scriptwriter to audience. The representational aspect of the film medium presents no special theoretical problem, because our perception of it works just like our perception of the real world, for all practical purposes. Our perception of the purely filmic part of film construction, which mostly relates to shot transitions, is undoubtedly quickly learned by children or adults in their first acquaintance with cinema or television. Once you have learned it, you don't have to think about it anymore, but it is available to simple introspection, in a way that the truly natural part of film perception, which proceeds at a much deeper mental level, is not. Bordwell has made much of the notion of 'the viewer's activity', but there are good indications that most of the film audience is reluctant to engage in any extra conscious or semi-conscious mental activity while viewing films. Apart from the resistance most people have to watching avant-garde cinema, there is also a strong resistance to watching silent films, which also call for a fair amount of semi-conscious mental activity to fully follow their narratives. The recent failure to detect the 'Kuleshov effect' reported by Prince and Hensley (*Cinema Journal* Vol.31, No.2, Winter 1992) also shows that ordinary viewers do not really do much of the extensive positing and testing of perceptual hypotheses attributed to them in David Bordwell's speculations about film perception in *Narration in the Fiction Film*.

Eventually we will discover how the actual mental mechanisms involved in perception of the real world work, and then we will know how the perception of the representational part of the film medium works as well. But this will be done by scientists, and not by 'theorists' sitting in armchairs in the humanities department of universities. As for how the small part of purely filmic perception works, this will likewise have to be found out with active experimental research. It truly embarrasses me to have to state something which should be so obvious, but the conceit and self-deception involved in most recent theorizing about film forces me to do it.

7. FILM STYLE AND TECHNOLOGY: 1895-1900

Before 1900 the volume of film production was small when compared with that of the next several years, and formal development of the medium was restricted and desultory. The few makers of fictional films active at this time were mostly occupied with the fairly close copying of one another's films by restaging them, though there were already a few signs of the elaboration and variation that later became so important in filmic evolution. On the other hand, this was obviously the time when the influences from pre-existing artistic media were most important.

Photography and Cinema

In the beginning, the cinema benefited from the flexible film developed in 1889 for the Kodak and other hand cameras that had been designed to use it. It seems that the same negative emulsion was used to coat Eastman motion picture film as was used on Kodak film for still photography; certainly it was treated in the same way as regards exposure. The restriction of the colour sensitivity of this orthochromatic film to blue and green light was less serious than is usually supposed, since at that time, much more so than now, the things in the world that were coloured bright red or orange were few and small, so that their reproduction in a heavy black tone had little significance. The 'speed' of this film in our contemporary sense was largely immaterial, since it was developed by inspection to the correct density under a red safelight, just as is now done in still photography when making positive paper prints. In fact the development of motion picture negative at that time had the advantage over the development of ordinary still photographic film and plates in that a test section of several inches from the beginning of each shot was always torn off and given a separate development first. This whole procedure continued to be standard till the end of the silent period.

What *is* important, as far as any possible visible effect in films is concerned, is the lens aperture that was used. This was about the same as that used for hand-camera photography at that time: i.e. an aperture of f11 to f16 for ordinary scenes under direct sunlight. Most fiction film-making was done out of doors at first, with the exception of some of the Edison company films made in their well-known 'Black Maria' studio. This was *not* modelled on the typical still photography studio of the time, but seems to have followed some idiosyncratic Edison idea about fixed scientific experimental conditions. It was rotated to follow the sun, and fitted with a clear glass ceiling, so that filming was always done under direct sunlight coming from high front to the actors and set. This model was imitated by some other small studios built for other companies in the next few years, but it was quickly realized that it was an impractical design once the new century began. The new standard was provided by the studio Georges Méliès had built in 1897. In May of that year Méliès had a studio with glass-roof and glass walls constructed after the model of large photographic studios of the time, and it was fitted with thin cotton cloths that could be stretched below the roof to diffuse the direct rays of the sun on sunny days. The soft overall light without real shadows that this arrangement pro-

A view of Georges Méliès' studio about 1900, showing the camera end. (The camera is in an alcove behind the small black curtain in the centre of the picture.) Movable square frames with thin cotton diffusers stretched on them are suspended just below the front part of the glass roof.

duced, and which also exists naturally on lightly overcast days, was to become the standard for film lighting for a decade, but for a few more years after 1897 no-one but Méliès had the facilities to produce it.

It is interesting that some of the well-established techniques of the still photography of this period were not taken over into film photography; among them the use of arc floodlights with diffusing screens in front of them, which was already a standard principal light source for still photography by 1894, and also the intentional production of 'soft focus' by lens manipulation, which was a standard technique in still photography by 1898. Reflecting screens were also being used to bounce light on to the shadow sides of figures in portrait still photography before the turn of the century. (It is most regrettable that no existing histories of still photography deal with the standard techniques and styles of still photography in this century, but on the contrary deal only with the exceptional work of the Steichens, Westons, and the like.)

Summing up on the question of the influence of the style of still photographic lighting on that of films, I can say that there was no intimate connection between the two, since film lighting was restricted to frontal sunlight, whether diffused or not, while studio still photography mostly used light from the side or side-front.

Before leaving the subject of motion picture film stock, it should be mentioned that initially, from 1895 onwards, both negative and positive film were supplied in rolls of an approximate length of 65 feet by Eastman, and 75 feet by the English company of Blair. The positive film was, as it still is, of much slower speed, finer grain, and higher contrast than the negative film. Unexposed rolls of negative could be cemented together in the darkroom to make longer rolls if this was absolutely necessary, though this rather troublesome procedure seems to have been mostly avoided in fictional film-making. For actuality filming this creation of rolls of the order of 1000 feet length out of the standard size rolls began as least as early as American Mutoscope and Biograph's filming of the Jefferies-Sharkey fight in November 1899.

Cameras

In the first several years of the cinema one of the two most important classes of cameras descended from the Edison Kinetograph. In its initial form the Kinetograph was contained in a very large and heavy casing, and was driven by a variable-speed electrical motor. For the purpose of producing films for the Edison Kinetoscope peep-show machine it was run at 46 frames per second, but from 1898 onwards it was also used to produce films for projection at the usual speed of approximately 16 frames per second. Its intermittent mechanism, which depended on a Maltese-cross gear to drive the sprocket wheel that transported the film through the exposure gate, was not reversible. This last drawback did not hold for the camera that R.W. Paul based on the Edison design in 1896, for Paul's camera had synchronized sprockets driving the film both above and below the film gate. Georges Méliès

based the first camera he had built for himself on this Paul design, and eventually, though not till 1898, took advantage of the facility it gave for controlled winding back to produce superimpositions in the camera. Although the Paul double Maltese-cross mechanism had the advantage of reversibility, it also had the disadvantage of poor registration, at least when compared to the Lumière mechanism. This is evident in the Robert Paul trick films that involve superimpositions.

The other major type of camera mechanism was represented by that of the Lumière camera of 1895. In this case the intermittent pull-down of the film was accomplished by a claw driven by two cams, one of which produced the vertical motion of the claw, and the other its insertion into the sprocket holes in the film before pull-down, and then its withdrawal afterwards. This mechanism could produce reversed film motion too, but all the remaining types of camera intermittents – the Demeny beater or 'dog' movement, the Mutoscope (later Biograph) camera of Dickson, the Prestwich epicycloidal sprocket wheel, and others – could not be reversed.

In general, the cameras of the first several years had no separate view-finding systems that could be used to check what was in frame during the time that the shot was being taken. The shot had to be framed and focussed beforehand by opening the back of the camera, and then inspecting the image in the gate through a hole of the same dimensions as the frame that was cut in the back pressure plate. When actually taking the shot it was largely guesswork as to exactly what was in frame and what was not, unless the limits of the frame were marked on the set.

Camera Supports and Camera Movements

The first movie cameras were fastened directly to the head of their tripod or other support with only the crudest kind of levelling devices provided, in the manner of the still-camera tripod heads of the period. Movie cameras were thus effectively fixed during the course of the shot, and hence the first camera movements were the result of mounting a camera on a moving vehicle. It is claimed that this was first done by Alexandre Promio, one of Lumière's travelling cameramen/exhibitors, when he put a camera in a gondola to film *le Grand Canal à Venise* in 1897, but certainly by 1898 there were a number of films shot from moving trains, and made by English film-makers as well as French. Although catalogued under the general heading of 'panoramas', those films shot straight forward from in front of a railway engine were usually specifically referred to as 'phantom rides'.

Also in 1897, R.W. Paul had the first real panning head made for a tripod, so that he could cover the passing processions of Queen Victoria's Diamond Jubilee in one uninterrupted shot. This device had the camera mounted on a vertical axis that could be rotated by a worm gear driven by turning a crank handle, and Paul put it on general sale the next year. Some European film-makers acquired this device in the next couple of years, but in general it was scarcely used before 1900.

Shots taken with a panning head were also referred to as 'panoramas' in the film catalogues of the first decade of the cinema, though the description of the film concerned almost invariably makes it clear which meaning was intended.

Lenses

Lenses having focal lengths from 50 mm. to 75 mm. seem already to have been considered standard before the turn of the century, and any lenses that were available with slightly shorter focal length seem not to have been used. On the other hand long lenses, already referred to as 'telephoto' lenses, were occasionally used in actuality filming, though I have not seen anything longer than about 100 to 150 mm. used in surviving films. Many film-makers apparently had a range of lenses for their cameras, even though there were no standardized mounts, and each owner had to have each lens individually fitted to match his camera. As a consequence, lenses were not made with a focussing scale on their barrels, and focussing on the film in the gate was unavoidable. Maximum lens apertures were mostly within the range f4.5 to f5.6, with some cameras such as the Lumière having lenses of even smaller maximum aperture. With the latter, filming was restricted to fairly bright days.

Projectors

Many of the earliest cameras could be quickly converted into projectors by opening their backs and putting a lamp-house and condenser lens behind them. Light sources were either arc-light, or lime-light produced by a high temperature oxy-hydrogen flame playing on a stick of lime, and a water cell was invariably placed between the condenser and the film to absorb heat radiation. Purpose-built projectors used the same sorts of intermittent mechanisms that have already been mentioned in connection with the cameras of the period. The problem of pulling film intermittently from a roll longer than

about 100 feet without the sudden jerks breaking it was solved in 1896 with the invention of the 'Latham loop'. This was a free loop of film between the continuously driven sprocket wheel now placed below the feed reel to pull film off it continuously; the small changes in the size of the free loop absorbing the effect of the intermittent intake into the gate below. This addition to the mechanism of projectors was already widely diffused by 1897, well before anyone had started to think about making longer individual films, which did not happen until 1899. The demand for such an improvement to projectors was caused by the desire to splice a number of short individual films together onto one reel for convenience in projection, as Hepworth's book *Animated Photography* (1897) makes clear.

Photographic Framing

The relationship of the framing in the first films which Louis Lumière made in 1895 – *l'Arrivée d'un train, le Gouter de Bébé* and *l'Arroseur arrosé* – to the kind of framing previously occurring in amateur and professional photography before the birth of the cinema has often been pointed out, and this is one of a limited number of instances in which I think received ideas are adequate. For the sake of completeness I must also mention the use of nearly axial movement towards the lens in the first of these films; a usage the force of which was recognized immediately, but not fully applied in fictional films until the new century. However, it does not seem to have been noticed that in Méliès' *l'Affaire Dreyfus* (1899) these features are reproduced in a staged narrative. In the scenes of the attack on the lawyer Labori and the fight in the courtroom at Rennes, the camera is placed at eye-level, and bystanders and observers of the action fill the space between the principal actors far in the background and the front of the scene in a way that was also commonly found in actuality footage of street scenes at the time. In the scene in the courtroom at

Fighting reporters exiting towards and past the camera in the scene of the courtroom at Rennes in l'Affaire Dreyfus *(Georges Méliès, 1899). This shot is lit by sunlight diffused by a thin cotton shade stretched over the top of the set.*

3. The first scene, "The Observatory", of Méliès' la Lune à un mètre *(1898).*

The second scene, "The Moon at One Metre", of Méliès' la Lune à un mètre. *This shot is joined onto the first one by a straight cut. Note the displacement of the furniture across the cut, and that, despite the similarity, the set is completely rebuilt.*

Rennes there are also exits past the camera in the way that became standard in 'chase' films after 1903. It is possible that these intimations of staging in depth and the use of a truly 'cinematographic' angle may have been forced on Méliès by the small initial dimensions of his studio, for though weaker forms of this kind of staging occur once or twice in Méliès' big films of the next two years, such as *Jeanne d'Arc* (1900), after he had extensions built onto the sides of his stage in 1902 they no longer occur. From that date onwards entrances into, and exits from, the shot in Méliès' films always take place from the sides; in fact from the equivalent of the wings of a theatrical stage.

Theatre and Cinema

Pre-existing theatrical forms have their only strong influence on the development of cinematic forms in the films of Georges Méliès and his imitators. As is well known, Méliès' earliest one shot trick films are in the manner of a straight recording of his earlier stage presentations in the Théâtre Robert-Houdin, but an important point in this connection arises with the transition to multi-shot films in 1898. There are other aspects of this matter which will be dealt with in later sections, but in 1898 Méliès made a film entitled *la Lune à un mètre* which was closely based on one of the miniature fantastic shows that he had previously staged in his theatre. *la Lune à un mètre* was made up of three scenes, representing first 'The Observatory', in which an aged astronomer looks at the moon through a telescope and then falls asleep; next 'The Moon at One Metre' in which the moon descends from the sky and swallows him up; and lastly 'Phoebe', in which he meets the goddess of the moon. The second scene and the beginning of the third were intended to be understood as the dream of the astronomer, who wakes up in the middle of the final scene when the goddess he is chasing vanishes by a stop-camera effect.

This was the first of a long line of films made over the next

couple of decades that used the device of a dream story turning back to reality at the crucial moment, but the most important thing about *la Lune à un mètre* was that this whole concept was not immediately apparent from the film itself. This was because there were only small changes made in the décor between one scene and the next, so that there was no way for the viewer to instantly notice the transition between what took place when the astronomer was awake and what took place when he was asleep. Since films in those years were nearly always shown with an accompanying commentary by the showman who projected them (just as in the earlier lantern-slide shows), this was not such a great handicap, but Méliès must have felt that the way he had treated the matter was not ideal, for in his next fantasy film, *Cendrillon* (1899), he joined all the scenes by dissolves, just as was the practice in most slide shows. In this and all subsequent long films made by Méliès during the next seven years, dissolves were used indiscriminately between every shot, even when the action was continuous from one shot to the next – that is, when there was no time lapse between shots. The dissolve was used in the same indiscriminate way in the slide shows that pre-existed the cinema, and hence in both cases the dissolve definitely did *not* signify a time lapse. The theatrical style of the scenes filmed for this and subsequent long films by Méliès extended to the films' large-scale construction, because they all ended with an apotheosis added to the strict narrative, and this feature was taken over into the Pathé films modelled on them in the next century.

Trick Effects

Although there is no question that Georges Méliès' trick films were the source for a wide diffusion of trick effects during the first decade of the cinema, his origination of all (or indeed any) of these trick effects is by no means certain. The apparent transformation of objects in the middle of a shot by stopping the camera, and adding or subtracting the objects in question

Inset scene within a vignette mask that has been placed by superimposition on the black background of the main scene of Santa Claus *(G.A. Smith, 1899). Both scenes have been shot under direct sunlight on an open stage.*

from the scene before starting the camera again, was first carried out in *The Execution of Mary, Queen of Scots* made by the Edison company in 1895, and this film probably reached Europe with the Kinetoscope machines well before Méliès started to make films in 1896. His first film using the stop-camera technique was *Escamotage d'une dame chez Robert-Houdin* (1896),

As for trick effects depending on superimposition, some time before July 1898 G.A. Smith in England made *The Corsican Brothers*. This film was described in the catalogue of the Warwick Trading Company, which took up the distribution of Smith's films in 1900, thus:-

"One of the twin brothers returns home from shooting in the Corsican mountains, and is visited by the ghost of the other twin. By extremely careful photography the ghost appears *quite transparent*. After indicating that he has been killed by a sword-thrust, and appealing for vengeance, he disappears. A 'vision' then appears showing the fatal duel in the snow. To the Corsican's amazement, the duel and death of his brother are vividly depicted in the vision, and finally, overcome by his feelings, he falls to the floor just as his mother enters the room."

The accompanying frame enlargements in the catalogue show frames including the two main effects. The ghost effect was simply done by draping the set in black velvet after the main action had been shot, and then re-exposing the negative with the actor playing the ghost going through the actions at the appropriate point, which was already a well-known technique in still photography, and referred to as 'spirit photography'. Likewise, the vision, which appeared within a circular vignette, was similarly superimposed over a black area in the backdrop to the scene, rather than over a part of the set with detail in it, so that nothing appeared through the image, which seemed quite solid. This idea too was already used in lantern slide shows and graphic illustrations to suggest visions, and also sometimes to suggest parallel action. Nevertheless, Smith applied for a provisional patent on these techniques as they applied to film, but this did not prevent other film-makers subsequently using these ideas when they felt inclined. Although at this date Georges Méliès had been making trick films for more than a year, his films seem to have used the 'stop camera and substitution of objects' technique exclusively, and his first films depending on superimposition on a dark ground, which were *la Caverne maudite* and *l'Homme de têtes* were made just after *The Corsican Brothers*.

The only surviving film of this kind made by Smith is *Santa Claus*, made later in 1898. Here the 'dream vision' of Santa Claus on the roof getting down the chimney, as the catalogue again describes it, appears to two small children asleep in bed on Christmas Eve. In this case, the circular inset vignette could also be taken as a depiction of parallel action, even though not described as such, since when it vanishes after Santa has disappeared down the chimney, he then appears out of the fireplace on the set, and fills the children's stockings with presents.

Méliès actually made very little use of total direct superimposition, but he greatly elaborated the use of superimposition on visible black background areas from *l'Homme de têtes* (1898) onwards, principally to produce dismemberment and displacement of parts of the human body. These devices all depend on winding back the film and making a second exposure in the camera, and make no demands on film technique beyond that.

G.A. Smith also made the first films with the trick effect of action running backwards in time. One motive for making reverse-order prints was supplied by the public interest in the custom that the Lumière cameramen/exhibitors had of winding their actuality films backwards through the projector after projecting them forwards in the normal way, and so reversing the course of the actions of the people and objects in the film. A favourite Lumière subject for this treatment from 1896 onwards was the actuality *les Bains de Diane à Milan*, which showed swimmers diving into the water. But as already remarked, some types of projector could not be run backwards, and hence the desire to have reverse sequence prints. In the first examples from G.A. Smith, the trick was done by repeating the action a second time, while filming it with an inverted camera, and then joining the tail of the second negative to that of the first. The first films made using this device were *Tipsy, Topsy, Turvy* and *The Awkward Sign Painter*. *The Awkward Sign Painter* showed a sign painter lettering a sign, and in the reverse printing of the same footage appended to the standard print, the painting on the sign vanished under the painter's brush. The earliest surviving example of this technique is Smith's *The House That Jack Built*, made before September 1900. Here, a small boy is shown knocking down a castle just constructed by a little girl out of children's building blocks. Then a title appears, saying 'Reversed', and the action is repeated in reverse, so that the castle re-erects itself under his blows.

Robert Paul made a contribution to trick effects with a somewhat similar technique in *Upside Down; or, The Human Flies* made some time before September 1899. This shows people in a room set jumping from the floor onto the ceiling, where they walk around upside down. This was done by making a trick cut on action as they all jump upwards to a second shot made with the backdrop showing the wall behind them and the furniture upside down, and shot with the camera inverted. This idea was copied, with variations, by the Pathé company and Georges Méliès in 1902 in *la Soubrette géniale* and *l'Homme-mouche* respectively.

Printing

At the very beginning, the printing of positive film from negative film was done by passing the developed negative through the gate of a projector or camera with its emulsion in contact with the emulsion of the unexposed positive film strip, while shining light through the negative image onto the positive. This was the standard form of contact printing, and exposure was regulated either by the distance of the light source from the printing-gate aperture, or by the speed with which the two films were cranked through. Purpose-built printers were produced from 1896 onwards on the pattern of various projector and camera film gates and movements, but it was realized almost immediately that the only type of mechanism that gave good registration between the positive and negative was that with an intermittent claw pull-down, as in the Lumière camera/projector.

Actuality Into Fiction

The starting point for the influence of actuality film and its exhibition on fictional film has to be, as far as present knowledge goes, the claim by Francis Doublier, one of Lu-

mière's travelling cameramen/exhibitors, that in 1896 he showed a series of actuality shots of soldiers, a battleship, the Palais de Justice, and a tall grey-haired man, as a film of the Dreyfus case. Such multi-shot assemblages, of which there were quite possibly others in the first few years, were no doubt helped in their public acceptance by the continuous spoken commentary that usually accompanied the projection of films. The next step was the reproduction of news events on film, or 'drama documentaries' as we would now call them. Here too Méliès was the man who got in first, with his series of single shot films on the Greek-Turkish War made in 1898, and then his similar series on the sinking of the American battleship Maine in Havana harbour during the Spanish-American War. These latter films were, as entered in the Star Films catalogue of 1898: No.143 *Collision and Shipwreck at Sea*; Nos.144-145 *The Blowing-up of the 'Maine' in Havana Harbour*; No.146 *A View of the Wreck of the 'Maine'*; and No.147 *Divers at Work on the Wreck of the 'Maine'*. No doubt these four films were often spliced together by their purchasers and exhibited as one film, but in any case during the next year Méliès made *l'Affaire Dreyfus* using the same form of single-shot scenes without continuous narrative connection between them, and this was sold only as a unit. Méliès did little with reconstructed actualities after this, though they had a brief and limited attraction for some other film-makers for a few years.

The Multi-shot Film and Film Continuity

The earliest film that we can be certain was made with more than one scene was R.W. Paul's *Come Along, Do!*, shot around April 1898. This film was undoubtedly made up of two scenes, each consisting of a single shot, and was filmed on constructed sets. So far it seems that only the first shot, which shows an old couple lunching outside an art gallery, and then following other people in through its doorway, survives. However, there also exist stills showing both the two scenes, and it is clear that the second scene was shot on a set representing the interior of the gallery, where the old man closely examines a nude statue, until removed by his wife. The probability is that these two shots were joined by a simple splice, since there is no sign of the beginning of a dissolve after the actors exit the frame in the first scene, but the exact nature of the transition still remains to be determined. This film was preceded by Méliès' *Sauvetage en rivière* from early in 1896, which was twice as long as the standard length, and sold in two separate parts, but we have no way of telling whether it was really in two different scenes, or the nature of any action continuity between the two parts. In any case, the available evidence still says that Paul's *Come Along, Do!* was the first film made up of more than one scene joined together, and sold as such.

About July 1898 Paul also produced a series of four films, each made up of one scene done in one shot of 80 feet length, under the general heading of *The Servant Difficulty*. These films were sold separately, but dealt with a series of incidents involving the same characters. But such things were exceptional in R.W. Paul's output, which both before and after

The set representing the railway carriage interior for G.A. Smith's The Kiss in the Tunnel *(1899). This scene is again shot on an open stage in direct sunlight.*

1900 was mostly actualities, or single shot knockabout comedies.

So in 1899 the development of the multi-shot fictional film was definitely on its way in France and England, but not in the United States, where the Edison company was still only making single shot knockabouts and inferior imitations of Méliès' single shot trick films. Méliès' *l'Affaire Dreyfus* and *Cendrillon* have already been mentioned, and in the latter, though it is more nearly a continuous narrative than the former, the causal narrative connections from one shot to the next are still to a considerable extent obscured by long processional entries and exits irrelevant to the main line of the story. And in *Cendrillon* there is no action continuity across the dissolves that separate the shots.

The next film after *Come Along, Do!* developing action continuity from shot to shot was G.A. Smith's *The Kiss in the Tunnel*, made before November 1899. The Smith film shows a set representing the interior of a railway carriage compartment, with blackness visible through the window, and a man kissing a woman. The Warwick Trading Company catalogue instructs that it should be joined into a film of a 'phantom ride' between the points at which the train enters and leaves a tunnel, an event which many 'phantom rides' included, and this is indeed the case with the surviving copy of this film. (G.A. Smith had made a 'phantom ride' film, which was the result of fixing a film camera on the front of a train, the year before, as had other film-makers, but it is difficult to tell which 'phantom ride' is which amongst the few that still remain out

The third and final shot of the surviving copy of G.A. Smith's The Kiss in the Tunnel *. This shot is part of a 'phantom ride' taken from the front of a train emerging from a tunnel.*

The first shot of the Bamforth company's The Kiss in the Tunnel *(1899).*

of the many that were made in the first decade of cinema.) In any case, the catalogue instruction as to the point at which the cut should be made shows that the concept of action continuity was understood by Smith. A few months later, the Bamforth company made an imitation of Smith's film with the same title, which developed the idea even further. Bamforth & Co. were a well-established firm making and selling lantern slides and postcards in Holmfirth, Yorkshire, before the owner, James Bamforth, took them into film-making. Their version of G.A. Smith's *The Kiss in the Tunnel* was made at the very end of 1899. This put their version of the scene inside the railway carriage between two specially shot scenes of a train going into a tunnel, and then coming out the other end. Since these shots in the Bamforth film were objective

shots, with the camera beside the track, rather than 'phantom ride' shots, they made the point of the continuity of the action quite clear, rather than forcing the viewer to work it out by logical deduction.

Finally, another film in the Warwick Trading Company catalogue dating from 1899, *Fire Call and Rescue by Fire Escapes*, should be mentioned, as the title and length of 175 feet show that it must have been made up of more than one shot – in fact at that length fairly certainly of at least two shots. Given subsequent developments, the obvious conjecture is that it was made by James Williamson.

Conclusion

As might be expected, with the limited and sporadic nature

The second shot of the Bamforth company's The Kiss in the Tunnel *(1899).*

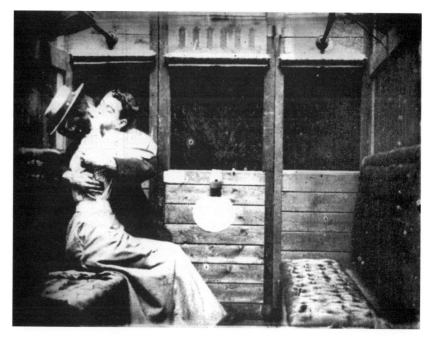

of film production by most of the film-makers except Méliès in the four years up to 1900, there is not much purely filmic evolution – in the sense that the distinctive features of particular films derive more from other films than from external sources. The copying of subjects that has already been mentioned as taking place – by Méliès of Lumière and Paul subjects, and by the Edison Co. of Méliès – was no more than simple plagiarism, and did not give rise to the variation, elaboration, and combination that was to be a powerful motor for the evolution of film form from 1900 onwards. Most of the features of films made before 1900 can be strongly connected with those of pre-filmic media, but with *The Kiss in the Tunnel* and its continuity cuts from real exterior to studio interior, the first purely filmic device had certainly arrived.

8. FILM STYLE AND TECHNOLOGY: 1900-1906

It seems to me that in the years 1900-1906, before the Nickelodeon boom and subsequent world-wide increase in film production, that the commercial pressures on the evolution and development of the forms of cinema were low. The only absolute demand from audiences was that the films be photographed (and printed) sharply in focus and with the correct exposure. Even after 1900 there were still substantial audiences somewhere for just about anything that moved on the screen. Despite the absence of any noticeable changes in the conditions of film exhibition, there was from the beginning of 1903 a sharp increase in the number of longer multiscene films being produced, though the total number of titles did not increase that much. There was, nevertheless, an extremely rapid evolution of film form, and I take this to be an instance of the way that many developments during the first decade of film history depended largely on the individual wills of the film-makers.

In my approach to these developments, the *descriptive* norms are provided by what most films come to be like, and all the surviving films are taken into consideration as far as possible, without respect to their artistic worth. More than 1000 fictional films still exist from the years 1900-1906, and I have viewed most of them, and mostly more than once. This is quite easy to do, because they are in general very short, many hundreds of them consisting of only one scene done in one shot. When they are seen quickly over a week or two the genetic interconnections between them spring to the eye. Indeed one way of looking at the rapid formal developments in these early years (and later years too) is by analogy with biological evolution. (Of course, the developments in film form, like all kinds of cultural evolution, are more like the Lamarckian than the Darwinian concept of evolution, though without exact correspondence even to the former.) This shows itself in the way that novel features which suddenly appear like mutations are sometimes rapidly taken up, forming a line of descent, while on other occasions original devices die out because they have some unsuitability of a technical or artistic nature. One obvious instance of this last effect is the use of dissolves to join all the shots of a film together, which had a fleeting vogue at the beginning of the century.

On the other hand, looking at the situation from the point of view of the film-maker, I find it useful to follow E.H. Gombrich in thinking in terms of artistic problems, and then the solution to these problems being created by using models derived from other films, or indeed other art-works in general. In this period one of the cruder problems was how to make longer films which would be readily understood by audiences, and apart from the obvious solution of filming well-known

stories of sufficient length, another rather simple-minded approach was to use repetitions of actions and events. Many examples of this can be found in the early 'chase' films and films about keyhole-peeping.

Studios

Initially, staged interior scenes were filmed in the open under direct sunlight, and even after 1906 one can see many films made by the minor companies shot under the same conditions. Amongst many surviving examples can be mentioned *The Missing Legacy* (Alf Collins, 1906), and *The Hundred-To-One Shot* (Vitagraph, 1906). However in 1899 Georges Méliès had begun to shoot his films with the direct sunlight falling on the set diffused and softened by thin cotton sheets suspended over the stage, as can be seen in *l'Affaire Dreyfus*, for instance. Other major companies then also took up the use of glass-roofed and glass-walled stages with the sunlight diffused either by thin cotton sheets stretched below the roof, or by the use of ripple glass covering the roof and walls, or both. At first only the European companies followed the Méliès model exactly, with glass walls as well as ceiling to their studios, and even they did not use cotton diffusers that could be pulled across under the roof to soften the direct sunlight until after 1902. With the continuing expansion of their production, Pathé opened an even larger studio in 1905, and in this they built remarkably extensive sets for some of their films. Then having built them these big sets, they showed them off with wide panning shots. The scenery lift in this big studio can be seen disguised as a mine lift-cage to make up part of the set in *Au pays noir*. Pathé also built a large-sized tank in their studio grounds in 1904, and this was used to stage scenes requiring action in water, as in *Un Drame dans les airs* (1905), in which the gondola of a balloon was filmed falling into the water in front of a painted back-drop representing the sea stretching to the horizon. This tank also sometimes had elaborate sets built around it; for instance one showing Venetian *palazzi* and canals in *Un Drame à Venise* (1907).

Photography and Lighting

The transition from filming under direct sunlight to filming under diffused sunlight took place at Pathé in 1902, and at Biograph and Edison at about the same time. The first company to use artificial light to any extent was probably Edison, after they built a new roof-top studio in New York in 1900. It seems to me that this studio was a confused compromise between their original 'Black Maria', which used direct sunlight through clear glass onto its small set, and the standard construction of a still photographer's studio of the

One of the staircase shots in Par le trou de la serrure *(Pathé, 1905) lit by a mixture of diffuse daylight and light from arc floodlights. (Note the sharp-edged shadow of the bannisters cast onto the wall by the arc floodlight out left.)*

time. Certainly there are clear signs of extra arc lighting from overhead on the Edison film *Why Jones Discharged His Clerks*, and what looks like mercury vapour lamp lighting on *The Mystic Swing* and *Uncle Josh in a Spooky Hotel*, all of which were made in 1900. As far as the second two films are concerned, it is possible that the soft lighting with rapid fall-off in intensity coming from the side may be from a small area of glass wall in the inadequate studio mentioned above, but the very poor quality of the prints available make this difficult to tell. The arc lighting units used were mostly based on the kind of arc lamps used for street lighting at the time, if they were hung overhead, or the on the kind of arc flood-lights on floor stands already used by still photographers. In the United States the mercury vapour lamps were usually

referred to by the name of their principal manufacturer, Cooper-Hewitt, which produced them for indoor lighting in large buildings. Mercury vapour lamps were large glass tubes about three feet long and three inches in diameter which produced monochromatic blue light from mercury vapour ionised by an electric current passing through it, on exactly the same principle as modern fluorescent tubes, though without the white phosphor coating which produces white light as well in these latter. Mercury vapour tubes were invariably used in groups of several tubes held side by side in large wooden racks, which gave lighting rather similar to that from a very large version of the 'soft light' or 'North light' used nowadays for film lighting.

By 1903 extra artificial lighting is certainly visible in a few

A studio interior scene from The Silver Wedding *(F.A. Dobson, 1906) lit almost entirely by the soft light from a rack of Cooper-Hewitt mercury vapour tubes high at the left side and just out of shot. Note the very rapid fall-off in brightness of the light away from the source.*

In this model shot from Un drame en mer *(Pathé, 1905), the beam from a lighthouse shining onto a sinking ship is simulated by a sharp edged black mask placed in front of the camera lens.*

films from all the three major film companies, such as *The Divorce* from Biograph, and *Lotion miraculeuse* from Pathé. By 1904, Biograph was using a completely enclosed studio entirely lit with many racks of Cooper-Hewitts suspended from the ceiling and on vertical floor stands; indeed so many that the effect was quite like the overall diffuse daylight illumination in the large glass studios Pathé and Méliès were using. At Pathé arc lights were frequently used to supplement the diffuse daylight through the studio roof and walls, as in scenes shot on the Pathé staircase from *Par le trou de la serrure* (1905) onwards.

When the French Gaumont company expanded production and built a large new glass studio in 1905, they also installed arc floodlights, just like Pathé, and likewise used them on floorstands to put extra fill lighting onto the figures from the front, at least some of the time. The first big Gaumont production, *la Vie du Christ*, made in 1906, used rather large and complex sets for the time, and on these there was a fair amount arc light used for fill on the figures, and also to get some light into the dark corners. The resulting patterns of lighting are sometimes quite striking, but it is not clear to me whether these were merely a matter of reproducing the look of the engravings on which the scenes of this film were based. Certainly, other Gaumont films of this time are nowhere near as interesting from the lighting point of view, though the compositions their cameramen produced when framing exterior scenes are usually quite elegant.

The use of arcs to create effect lighting really begins in

One of the deep sets, with action on many levels, in la Vie du Christ, *with extra light from arc floodlights above and on floor stands.*

Studio interior lit solely by the light from a small electric arc concealed in the lantern held by the actor in Falsely Accused *(Hepworth Co., 1905). The power cable taking the current to the arc is just visible dangling below it.*

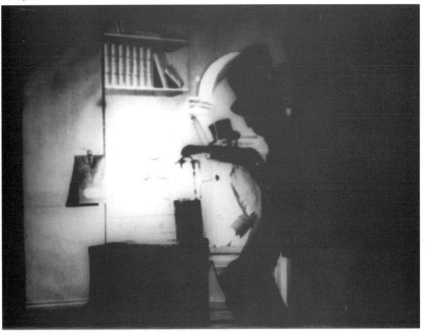

1905, with such films as Edwin S. Porter's *The Seven Ages*, in which the scene representing 'Old Age' has a fire effect done with an arc floodlight hidden in a fire-place before which an old couple sit, illuminated solely by its light. Another very early attempt at a lighting effect is the use of the sun reflected in a small mirror to produce a patch of bright light which is intended to simulate the light from a lantern in *After Dark: The Policeman and His Lantern*, a G.A. Smith film of 1902. An entirely different approach to the simulation of a beam of light occurs in a Pathé film of 1905, *Un drame en mer*, in which a scene lit by a beam from a lighthouse is revealed within the confines of a diagonal band delineated by a mask in front of the camera lens; this being supposed to represent the outline of the beam of light.

Returning to the eruption of effect lighting in 1905, another extremely interesting example is in *Falsely Accused*, from the Hepworth studio. In this film a man searching a totally dark room by lantern light is photographed doing just that, the sole illumination of the scene coming from a tiny electric arc concealed in his lantern! It was several years before this technique turned up in films again. There would seem to have been someone at Hepworth aware of the possibilities of available-light photography, because in the same year *Stolen Guy* includes a bonfire scene lit solely by the light from the bonfire.

Some moderately innovative camera work was also being

The studio set showing the scene in the gypsy's attic in Recued by Rover *(Lewin Fitzhamon, 1905). This is lit in part by arc floodlights simulating the light through the window and casting the multiple shadows just visible on the back wall.*

done at this time by G.W. Bitzer and F.A. Dobson at Biograph. 1906 saw the appearance of *The Paymaster* photographed on location by Bitzer, and featuring an available-light interior scene in a watermill, in which sunlight coming through the windows from the side produces a strong chiaroscuro effect. In the same year F.A. Dobson produced *The Silver Wedding* and *The Tunnel Workers* doubling as director and cameraman, as was quite common in this period, and in these films, more by the nature of the sets he had constructed than by the sources of light used, he accidentally created scenes in which foreground figures went into silhouette at some points; scenes of a type that were not extensively exploited till a decade later. There are similar effects, which likewise may be more accidental than intentional, in some Edison studio scenes as well, and in this case the lights are arcs suspended above the back area of the scene, with little light on the foreground figures. Examples from 1905 include *The Watermelon Patch* and the scene showing 'The Judge' in *The Seven Ages*. Partial uses of arc lighting also occur in the Hepworth company's *Rescued by Rover*, in which the scenes in the gypsy's attic are illuminated by a pair of arc floodlights simulating the light from the window at the side, though only as an addition to the general diffuse natural light, and in *The Firebug* (Biograph, 1905) arc floodlights are used on the emblematic shot of the firebug himself brandishing a lighted torch.

At least one cameraman with the Vitagraph company began working on effect lighting in 1906. In *Foul Play* there was a moderately successful attempt at simulating the light coming from a property lamp shown within the shot by using arc floodlights just outside the edge of the frame, and on the evidence of production stills this kind of work with lighting seems to have continued over the next couple of years at Vitagraph.

Coloured Films

In the 1900-1906 period all-over tinting and toning of prints was not generally used, but there are examples of what were to become the standard tints appearing in some films. The first and last shots of Williamson's *Fire!*, which show the exterior of the burning building, are tinted all-over red in the surviving print, the sky scenes in R.W. Paul's *The ? Motorist* (1906) are tinted blue, and there are also some examples of night-time scenes being tinted all-over blue. But a large number of films, almost entirely from Méliès and Pathé, were made available with their images hand-painted frame by frame in several colours. Such prints cost 3 or 4 times as much as the same film uncoloured, and the subjects treated were usually of the fantastic or exotic-historical kind. Even though the hand-applied colours did not exactly correspond to the various ostensibly coloured surfaces in the image, and also jiggled about from frame to frame, they added greatly to the appeal of these films both then and now, compensating to some extent for the way most of them were conducted entirely in Very Long Shot. In the case of Méliès' films the effect was particularly suitable given the broad and simplified style of

scene painting he used, and the combined effect of colour and flat scenery quite transforms a film like *le Royaume des fées* (1903), giving it the look of a series of popular 19th. century block-coloured wood-cuts which have been animated.

The Pathé Studio Camera

Although it did not come into wide use for several years, the Pathé studio camera first became available from 1903. Its design was closely based on that of the original Lumière camera, but it was rather larger, and it also had a few extra features. The main body of the Pathé camera was made of wood, and measured about 12 inches in height, 8 inches in width, and about 4 inches from front to back. Instead of having just a single small spool-box containing the unexposed negative mounted on the top of the camera as with the Lumière camera, there were two square wooden magazines, each capable of holding 400 feet of film, mounted one behind

Back view of a studio model Pathé camera on a simple panning head without tilting mechanism. The tachometer and crank handle are just visible on the back of the camera. This photo dates from around World War I, but the camera in it is essentially the same as the original models, plus an added supplementary viewfinder on the left side. Note the slate held by the assistant cameraman. (Photograph courtesy of Kevin Brownlow)

the other on top of the camera body. Again like the Lumière camera, the crank handle driving the mechanism projected from the back of the camera, rather than the side (as was to become usual with later cameras), and the claws pulling down the film were driven by the same double cam mounted on a single shaft as in the Lumière camera. However the Pathé camera also had a toothed sprocket-wheel mounted above the gate aperture which pulled the film out of the feed magazine before it passed through the gate, and also drove it up into the take-up magazine after it had been exposed, as was necessary for the transport of film from the larger rolls being used. A loop of film ('Latham loop') was formed between the feed side of this sprocket wheel and the top of the film gate to allow for the conversion of the continuous movement of the film off the feed roll into the intermittent movement of film through the film gate, and a second Latham loop performed the same function for the film leaving the gate and going up onto the take-up roll over the other side of the continuously rotating sprocket wheel. The drive for the take-up magazine was provided by a flexible band driven from a pulley wheel in the camera body which turned another pulley attached to the axle supporting the take-up roll of film. The Pathé camera also had a footage counter to measure the approximate amount of film that had been driven through it.

Critical focussing of the image on the film was obtained by removing the film from the gate, and then putting a rectangle of thin ground glass in the film aperture. The inverted image formed on the ground glass surface was inspected by a magnifying lens. This procedure could only be carried out between shots, as the back of the camera had to be opened to put the focussing glass in place. A supplementary viewfinder attached to the side of the camera had to be used for checking what was in frame while the shot was actually being taken. At some fairly early stage this became an optical arrangement inside a rectangular tube with its own lens and ground glass screen showing an inverted image.

The Williamson Camera

The standard Williamson camera, which first appeared in 1904, was a simple rectangular wooden box about 20 inches high by 20 inches long, and about 6 inches in width. The crank handle driving the mechanism was in what was to become the usual place on the right hand side of the body, and as with the Lumière camera, one complete turn of the handle exposed 8 frames of film. The camera was loaded from the left hand side, with the feed roll of unexposed film carried inside a rectangular wooden spool box that was placed in its turn inside the main camera box. The film was pulled out of the spool box (or magazine) by a sprocket wheel inside the main camera compartment, and fed down into the gate. The intermittent mechanism pulling successive frames of film down between exposures was a pair of claws which engaged in one sprocket hole on each side of the film, and their up and down motion was produced by their being on the end of a lever attached at its other end to a pivot on the edge of a

continuously rotating disc. There was also a central pivot rod on this lever that slid up and down in a slot attached to the camera body near the gate, and because of this the rotation of the end of the lever attached to the disc gave its claw end an oscillating movement that drove it into the sprocket holes in the film during the down stroke, and then lifted the claw away from the film on the up stroke whilst the film was stationary and the exposure being made. Owing to its simplicity this type of intermittent movement came to be used in many early cameras, and indeed it has persisted in use up to the present day, but the Williamson version included an extra subtlety in that the slot in which the central pivot of the claw lever arm slid was curved rather than straight. This produced the optimum path for the claw tip on the pull-down part of its stroke; a straight line parallel to the film plane.

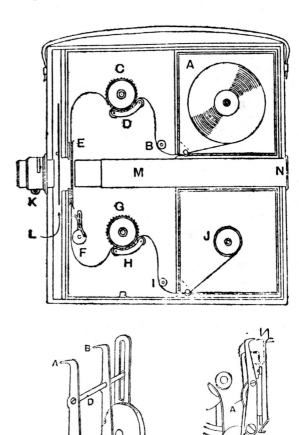

—Pin or Claw
Movement

—Williamson
Claw Movement

(Above) Standard interior layout of cameras of the English type, including the Williamson camera. A and J are feed and take-up magazines inside the camera body, MN the telescope for focussing on the image on the film in the gate, and F is the claw mechanism.
(Below) Close views of the standard English claw mechanism and the Williamson variant with curved path for the pivot at A.

After exposure the film was driven through another sprocket wheel, and then taken up into a second spool box of 400 feet capacity just like the feed box. The image in the film gate could be viewed and focussed only when the camera was stopped between shots, and this was done by replacing the film in the gate with a strip of special film which had the emulsion removed and the front surface roughened to matt translucency. The image on this focussing film was viewed through a telescope running from behind the film gate to the back of the camera, between the upper and lower spool boxes. Since at this period there were still no standardized lens mounts, even for cameras from the same maker, lenses had to be individually calibrated by their owners, but once this had been done it was possible to focus them by the distance scale their owner had engraved on them, without inspecting the image in the gate. Approximate framing during the course of the shot relied on a supplementary viewfinder fixed to the side of the camera. This lack of any precise means of determining the framing must have constituted some sort of pressure against the frequent use of panning shots, but it certainly did not prevent them being used at all, as some films of the period show. Like the Lumière and Pathé cameras, the Williamson camera and other similar English cameras ran just as well backwards as forwards, so permitting dissolves to be made in the camera if desired. Nevertheless, in English films of this period there is very little use of dissolves made in any manner.

Cameras modelled on the pattern of the Williamson and other similar early English cameras were widely made over the next decade by various companies in other countries of the industrialized world; for instance by Ernemann in Germany, and they were used by many film-makers for shooting fictional films, and used even more for shooting 'topicals' or for actuality filming.

The Biograph Camera

The American Mutoscope and Biograph company depended on a camera designed for them by W.K.L. Dickson, who left the Edison company after doing most of the work in creating the Edison camera and viewing apparatus. To completely avoid the Edison patents, the Biograph camera had a very peculiar mechanism for film transport. The film was pulled down through the usual gate where it was exposed by being squeezed between a pair of rubber covered rollers which rotated once for each exposure. Half way round each revolution the rollers lost their grip on the film because their rubber covering was cut away for half their circumference. Thus the film was stationary while the usual shutter opened in front of the gate aperture and the exposure was made. Unperforated film was used in the camera, and when the film strip came to rest for the exposure, a pair of circular punches cut through it to cut out two round holes on each side of the frame. Because of the nature of the rubber rollers, the amount that the film was pulled down for each exposure was rather irregular, and hence the spacing of the sprocket holes cut in it down the

length of the film likewise. This defect was compensated for by the special printer Biograph used to make positive prints. This was rather like ordinary printers, except that the moving claws that pulled the negative and positive through the printer aperture were spring loaded, so that they could go through the regularly spaced pre-cut perforations in the positive stock and slide on the negative underneath till the two sets of hole were brought into registration, when the claws went right through both sets, and dragged both positive and negative together to the point in the printer gate where the positive was exposed. This method worked quite well, and the vertical registration of Biograph films is quite good, though the sideways registration of the image with respect to the perforation in the positive is not so good, and a slight weave of the image from side to side is visible on close examination. Overall, the image steadiness of films shot with the Biograph camera is not that much better than the best from a new Pathé camera, or later from a Debrie.

Camera Movements

Panning shots rarely appear in dramatic films made before 1903, although they were well established in actuality filming by 1900. Those few that do are mostly in the nature of framing movements: i.e. pans of limited extent made to keep an actor who has unexpectedly moved towards the edge of the frame within its bounds. One such framing pan amongst a very small number in the production of the period occurs in *Caught in the Undertow* (Biograph, 1902), but in general shots on both exteriors and studio interiors were taken with a fixed camera.

The first sign of a quite different approach to camera movement occurs in an earlier Biograph film, *Love in the Suburbs* (1900). In this one-shot film, the camera pans (or panorams, as it would have been put at the time) with a woman being followed down a street by two men, until finally its motion discovers a policeman in their path. This use of an extensive pan to reveal the unexpected, either in the narrative incident or the background scenery, began to be really developed from 1904. In that year a new element in the plot is even more subtly revealed by a pan following the leading character in Biograph's *The Lost Child*, and Porter's *Stolen by Gypsies* (1904) and *Maniac Chase* (1905) use extensive pans that reveal more and more striking and unexpected backgrounds as they follow the action. Not surprisingly, all the examples of pans so far described, some of which cover more than 90 degrees, occur on real exteriors, but in 1905 the Pathé film-makers took up this use of panning shots and applied it to large-scale studio sets. In the context of the films of this period it is even more unexpected to see a slow pan which is following the action reveal a more and more extensive set filled with more and more actors, as happens in such films as *la Poule aux oeufs d'or* (1905) and *Au pays noir* (1905), and a number of others. For a few years this use of wide slow pans on studio sets was common in big Pathé productions, but not in those of any other company.

Tracking Shots

Unlike the extensive use of pans by Porter and the Pathé film-makers, which formed a small-scale evolutionary trend for some years, there were only a very few isolated instances of the use of tracking shots in the 1900-1906 period. Biograph produced a series of three single-shot films starting with *Hooligan in Jail* (1903), in all of which there was a slow track in from Long Shot at the start of the scene to a Close Up on the principal character's face. These films, the last of which was made at the beginning of 1904, seem to have had no progeny, and conclude the matter of tracking on static scenes for the next several years.

The use of tracking shots to show a view of a more or less static scene from the front of a moving vehicle was not generally taken over from 'phantom rides' to fictional films in this period, but there were nevertheless a very few isolated examples of the parallel tracking shot which shows one moving car taken from another preceding it or following it, starting with *The Runaway Match* (Alf Collins, 1903). The 1905 American remake of this film as *Marriage by Motor-Car* uses quite an elaborate series of these shots.

Trick Effects

It is my opinion that excessive attention has been devoted to early trick films, and particularly those of Georges Méliès, especially in view of the fact that they proved a dead-end as far as the development of the cinema is concerned. Nevertheless, such films still formed a substantial part of production in the early years of the century, though the decline in their commercial importance was already evident by 1906. This is not to say that they have no other interesting qualities; just that enough is enough. The basic techniques that Méliès and everyone else used had already been developed and established as standard before 1900, though there is one exception to this which will be noted below. There is no necessity for me to describe these well-known techniques, which can be summed up as: stopping the camera and adding or subtracting elements of the scene, superimpositions of various kinds made in the camera, including those made on a dark field within the background shot, and later on superimpositions on a white field made in the printer. Their occurrence and execution are always quite obvious, particularly since no cameras of the period had perfect registration of the image, and hence the two parts of a superimposition always move with respect to each other. There was no development in what Méliès did with these techniques either, with the possible exception of his science-fiction fantasies.

The transference of Méliès' techniques to scenes shot in real surroundings (rather than on a stage set) by English film-makers also has its place in the history books already, but since it largely happened after 1900 some discussion is in order. The earliest examples were made by the Hepworth company in that very year, and include *Explosion of a Motor-Car* and *How It Feels To Be Run Over*. The effects in the first were achieved in the standard way by stopping the camera,

substituting an imitation motor-car for the real one, then starting the camera again and exploding the imitation car, and so on. In the second film a motor-car drives straight at the camera, and when it is right up to it and out of focus there is a cut to a black frame decorated with stars and dashes and exclamation marks, and then a cut to the title 'Oh, Mother will be pleased'. The British motor-car trick films can be related to the extra-filmic tradition of British nonsense, and lead me to mention the climax of this sort of thing, which was *The Big Swallow*, made by Williamson in 1901. In this, a shot from what is meant to be a still photographer's Point of View shows a pedestrian approaching till his head fills the screen, at which point he opens his mouth to almost full screen size, then there is a cut to a shot of the photographer with his camera, all of which we had not seen in the previous shot, falling about in a black void, and then a final objective shot of the pedestrian in Long Shot walking towards the camera munching. An interesting technical point concerning this film is that the focus is adjusted to keep the image sharp as the actor approaches the camera. Such adjustment of focus during the course of a shot is extremely rare before World War I, though there are a few other early examples in this period, such as *Magic Bottles* (Pathé, 1905).

Hepworth also made *The Bathers* in 1900. This simply shows two bathers undressing and diving into the water, then the action apparently reverses in time, and runs its course backwards to the initial state. The reversed second half of the film was made using frame-by-frame reverse printing. The 1903 trade advertisements for films such as *The Robbery of the Mail Coach* and *Alice in Wonderland* give the fact that they have been shot with '...all natural scenery' as selling points, and from this and other indications, a comparison was clearly being made with Méliès' long films. Although this form of advertising suggests that audiences at the time may have preferred the British approach, it does not make it absolutely certain.

Optical Printing

Cecil Hepworth was one of the most technically able of all early film-makers, and he developed a way of making films with reversing action without having to stage the action that was to go into reverse twice, as had been the case before. The solution was to project the image from one frame of a negative in a projector onto positive film in the gate of a separate camera with the lens removed: the projector lens being pulled out till the image was of the same dimensions as the original frame. Then the film negative was moved forwards one frame, the positive moved one frame in the opposite direction, a second exposure was made, and so on. The arrangement I have described constitutes what is now called an optical printer, though on the rare occasions that one was used in the early decades it was referred to as a 'projection printer'. With this device Hepworth produced some rather complex treatments of reversed motion such as *The Frustrated Elopement* (1902), in which the actions reverse for short sections *within* the shot a number of times.

After this I have seen no *visual* evidence for the use of an optical printer for the next decade or so. On the rare occasions when one was reputed to have been used the result could have been achieved just as well by masking and the use of a contact printer in the standard way.

Camera Speeds

The camera speed used for filming had not stabilized in the early years of the century, for although all French films and some others from elsewhere had settled close to 16 frames per second, there were quite a number of English films which were shot nearer to 24 frames per second. On the other hand, a large number of Edison and Biograph films were cranked far slower, even as slowly as 10-12 frames per second. By 1906 there was beginning to be a closer approximation to 16 frames per second in all quarters.

Given these facts it is not surprising that intentional departures from a standard camera speed for expressive purposes were extremely rare, but I can report at least one interesting exception to this generalization. In *The Indian Chief and the Seidlitz Powder* made by the Hepworth company in August 1901, the beginning of the scene, which shows an American Indian drinking a large quantity of Seidlitz Powder, was filmed at about 16 frames per second, but when the Indian's stomach blows up like a balloon with gas the camera speed was increased to more than double this. The result was that the leaps he makes are in slow motion, which gives a balloon-like floating quality to his movements. It seems likely that cranking slowly ('under-cranking') to give accelerated motion had appeared before 1900 in R.W. Paul's *On a Runaway Motor Car through Piccadilly Circus* (1899), and there are certainly also one or two other examples of this technique prior to 1906.

Single Frame Filming and Animation

The most important development in trick effects during this period was the introduction of single-frame filming. It appears that the first stage in this development was the object animation carried out in Porter's *How Jones Lost His Roll* and *The Whole Dam Family and the Dam Dog* of 1905. In these two films cut-out letters are made to move about to form words by shifting them a small amount between each single frame exposure, so introducing at one stroke what was to be the standard filmic animation technique. For this purpose a camera with specially adapted gearing was needed, so that one turn of the crank handle exposed only one frame of film, rather than the eight frames per turn that was now standard. (Any attempt to produce the same result with an unmodified camera by turning the crank exactly one-eighth or one-quarter of a turn will inevitably produce some uneven exposure or 'flashing' of frames within any reasonable length of film put through.)

However it must be noted that it is possible to produce scrambled letters moving into place in other ways than that used by Porter in the films mentioned. The simplest of these is to lay the complete words out on a sheet and then shake it while filming the words with an inverted camera running backwards. When the resulting film is turned end for end and projected the letters will be seen to leap into place. This technique can be seen used in a French film of roughly this date, and it is quite likely that the advertising films which Georges Méliès claims to have made in 1898 with letters forming words also used this technique. Yet another possibility for moving objects about slowly is to use a series of shots about a foot or two long joined by short dissolves, as Méliès did in a film from 1904 which *does* survive, *le Roi du maquillage*. This shows what would nowadays be thought of as a 'Wolfman' type facial transformation with the gradual appearance of hair all over the face, and it is achieved by just such closely spaced and even dissolves between each stage of the addition of more hair.

The true single-frame animation technique was applied to a series of drawings by J. Stuart Blackton in 1906 to produce the first true filmed animated motion pictures in one section of *Humorous Phases of Funny Faces*, and it was only after this that single frame animation technique was used in European films. Claims that this happened earlier appear to be bogus.

Other Special Effects Techniques

The use of vignetted images inset within the frame, along the lines of G.A. Smith's *The Corsican Brothers* was further developed by Robert Paul in *The Countryman and the Cinematograph* (December 1901). This film shows an unsophisticated spectator at a film show of the period who takes what he sees on the screen for reality, and then tries to get into the action, demolishing the screen at the end of the film. The series of scenes on the cinema screen were shot as superimpositions by double exposing the original negative with a rectangular mask or matte in front of the lens to confine the screen image to the appropriate area. Edwin Porter made a copy of this film a month later, called *Uncle Josh at the Moving Picture Show*. His imitation even contains the same subjects shown in the film within a film in *The Countryman and the Cinematograph* – a dancer, a train, and a courting couple. Porter also introduced another variant on the use of mattes in *The Twentieth Century Tramp* (1902), in which the frame is split into two fields by a horizontal mask line, with the upper area showing a stationary airship shot on a studio set, and the lower part a panning shot across a city skyline to give the illusion of contrary motion of the airship through the sky. The upper half of the shot was masked off while the lower half was exposed, and vice-versa. This procedure would nowadays be referred to as using a matte and a counter-matte in succession. Porter repeated this trick in the better-known case of *Dream of a Rarebit Fiend*, and after several more years it came to be quite commonly used. Some other early attempts to handle similar stories involving flying, such as *Rescued in Mid-Air* (1906), used simple superimposition with white-coloured flying machines and people in an attempt to minimize print-

Cinema screen effect done by matting in a second exposure made on the original negative in Robert Paul's The Countryman and the Cinematograph *(1901). The cameraman did not succeed in giving the foreground scene and the background scene the same exposure, hence the darkness of the latter.*

through of the background scene.

Scene Dissection

The practice of dividing a scene up into a number of shots was pioneered by G.A. Smith in *Grandma's Reading Glass* (1900), in which the various objects a small boy is shown looking at with a magnifying glass in the establishing shot are cut into it as Big Close Ups of the objects seen from his Point of View (POV). As the Warwick Trading Company catalogue put it at the time: 'The conception is to produce on the screen the various objects as they appeared to Willy while looking through the glass in their enormously enlarged form.' In the Big Close Ups of the objects the actual magnifying glass is not used, but its field of view is simulated by photographing the object of interest inside a black circular mask fixed in front of the camera lens. In 1901 Smith repeated this device in *As Seen Through a Telescope*, which shows a man with a telescope spying on another man who is taking advantage of his helping a woman onto a bicycle to fondle her ankle. Into the Long Shot incorporating all this action is inserted the ostensible view through the telescope, which is represented by another Big Close Up showing the lady's foot inside a black circular mask. Unlike the previous film, there is only one cut-in POV Close Up rather than several, but in the development of *As Seen Through a Telescope* made later in the same year by the Pathé company, *Ce que je vois de mon sixième*, the man uses his telescope to spy through a number of different windows in succession, so combining the structures of both earlier Smith films. Also in 1901, G.A. Smith initiated the other major form of scene dissection with *The Little Doctor*. In this film, which now only exists in the essentially identical restaged version of 1903, *The Sick Kitten*, there is a cut straight in down the lens axis from a Medium Long Shot of a child administering a spoon of medicine to a kitten, to a Big Close Up Insert

The first shot of As Seen Through a Telescope, *showing a man using a telescope to watch another man helping a woman onto a bicycle.*

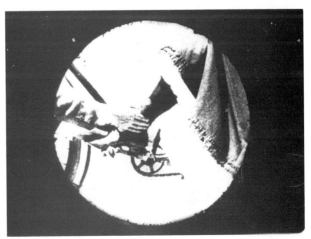

The second shot of As Seen Through a Telescope, *which is a Point of View shot simulating the view through a telescope with a circular vignette mask.*

The first shot of G.A. Smith's The Sick Kitten *(1903), which is an identical remake of* The Little Doctor *of 1901.*

The close shot of the kitten cut straight into the master shot of The Sick Kitten.

of the kitten with the spoon in its mouth, and then back to the Medium Long Shot again. As this is an objective shot of the kitten there is no masking as in the other films, and the matching of the position of the kitten across the two cuts is not perfect, as is hardly surprising given the nature of kittens, but it could be worse.

An interesting example of the evolution of filmic devices through copying and modification is given by Edwin S. Porter's *Gay Shoe Clerk* (1903), which combines, as so often with Porter, features from two or more previous films. This film, which shows a shoe salesman taking the opportunity to fondle a female customer's ankle in a Big Close Up Insert cut into the main scene, combines the general construction of *The Little Doctor* with the subject matter of *As Seen Through a Telescope*.

Another line of development of scene dissection using the POV shot goes through the Pathé film *Peeping Tom* (1902), which shows a man peeping through a series of keyholes, with what he sees shown inside a keyhole-shaped mask cut in at appropriate points. In *A Search for Evidence* (Biograph, 1903),

the series of keyhole peepings and associated POV shots lead a wife and detective to a confrontation with her unfaithful husband inside the last of the rooms spied on. In the previous films of this type, the person spying through the keyhole never entered the rooms, which were shown exclusively inside the POV keyhole vignettes or masks, but in *A Search for Evidence* the wife and detective open the door, and as they go through it there is a cut on action and change of camera direction through 90 degrees to show them actually going inside the room from an objective camera position also inside the room. Amongst these early peeping films there is one which does not have the Point of View shots shown inside a vignette. This is *la Fille de bain indiscrète* made at Pathé in 1902 quite early in the series. In this film, the bath maid in a hotel peeps at the occupants of the bathroom through the transom window above the door. The angles from which the inserted shots are taken do not really match her line of sight at all, and this is also the case for the only other Pathé example of the unvignetted POV shot from these years so far found. This is *Pauvre mère*, noted by Richard Abel in an article in *Screen* (Vol. 30,

The main shot of Peeping Tom *(Pathé, 1902), showing a hotel servant peeping through a series of keyholes.*

One of the series of Point of View shots with keyhole-shaped mask cut into the master scene of Peeping Tom *at the appropriate point.*

No. 3, Summer 1989). Here a little girl looks down out of an upstairs window at a passing military band, which is shown in a stock shot taken from pavement level with a panning camera. However, there is a British example of the use of the true Point of View shot in Alf Collins' *A Runaway Match* (1903), where the advertisement makes clear that these shots of the pursuing and pursued cars taken from each other in succession were meant to be the characters respective views. And they are from the correct angle, of course. The American remake of this film about three years later also includes repeated true POV shots. Comparing the large number of films with vignetted POV shots made in the first decade of the century with the handful of intermittent examples of the unvignetted POV shots and 'almost' POV shots, it would seem that most early filmmakers had some conceptual or aesthetic difficulty with a device that now seems so natural to us.

The Pathé Staircase

In the process of making longer films by the use of repetitions of the Point of View shot with keyhole mask, the Pathé company built a staircase set to give a home to all those doors with keyholes in them. Once having constructed this set, Pathé retained it, and used it whenever possible in their films subsequent to its first appearance in *Peeping Tom* (1903). After they had exhausted the keyhole idea, they just used this staircase set to give them an extra shot between a shot showing a character entering a house in an exterior scene, and then the inevitable shot of him entering a room interior set. This simple way of making a longer film was noticed by some American film-makers in the next few years, but it led them in quite different directions.

The Insert Shot

At this point it really becomes necessary to distinguish between the true Close Up and the Insert, which I define, following later nomenclature, as a close shot of some object or part of an actor's body *other than the face*. This distinction

seems to have been made by the end of this period, for there were studios such as Vitagraph, where from 1906 onwards the Insert as I have defined it was used, but not the true Close Up or Medium Close Shot of head and shoulders. The use of a close shot of a letter or other text at the point where it is written or read in a film obviously makes a vast difference to the possibilities of film narration, and early examples of textual Inserts that must be mentioned include the tombstone inscription in *Mary Jane's Mishap*, a cut to a Close Up of a notice on a gate in *Chien de garde* (Pathé, 1906), and an insert shot of a document in *Buy Your Own Cherries* (R.W. Paul, 1904). A very special use of the Insert Shot appears in G.A. Smith's *A View Through an Area Window* (1901). This shows the view through a basement window of feet going past on the pavement above, and through their movements the course of characteristic incidents can be deduced. I would guess that this idea was a transposition of a standard vaudeville routine done in the theatre with the front stage curtain raised a couple of feet, but I don't have the evidence yet. In any case, no continuation of the idea has been found later in this period, though there are developments of it after 1907. The more general use of inserts to show clearly details that were important to the story increased after 1903, as in *The Missing Legacy* (Alf Collins, 1906), and *Falsely Accused* (Hepworth, 1905), and many others, and from this point on we can consider the usage well established.

Cut in Close Shots

As with other devices, 1903 saw the real beginning of the *continuous* development of the use of closer shots cut into a scene, and the most remarkable instance occurs in that little-known master work, *Mary Jane's Mishap*, again from G.A. Smith. In the first scene of this film there is repeated three times a pair of cuts in, and then out again, from a Long Shot of Mary Jane lighting the fire to a Medium Close Shot of her. The matching of the actress's position across the cuts is not perfect, but careful examination shows that she is taking

The first scene in G.A. Smith's Mary Jane's Mishap *(1903).*

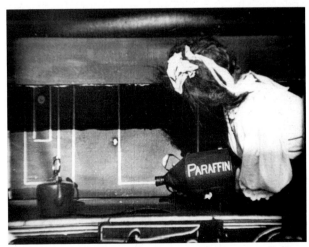

One of the series of Medium shots cut into the first scene of Mary Jane's Mishap *with static position matching.*

trouble to hold an exact position at the end of the first shot, which she also assumes within a couple of frames as the camera starts turning at the beginning of the closer shot joined to it, and so on for succeeding cuts. In other words, the idea of position matching across a cut within a scene had already been arrived at by G.A. Smith. Exactly the same observation can be made in some Pathé films of succeeding years; for instance *Ursus et son taureau lutteur* (1904), in which a Close Up is used to bridge a hitch in the execution of a stage act in which 'Ursus' wrestles a bull to the ground. He can be visibly seen taking direction as to how to strike the correct matching pose when the resumed Long Shot starts again.

It seems likely to me that the idea of position matching across a cut within a scene arose naturally from its use in those earlier trick films which involved transformations by substitution of one person or object for another after stopping the camera and then restarting it on exactly the same shot. Curiously enough, the first major exponent of this trick technique, Georges Méliès, never really took up the use of cuts to a closer shot within a scene, and a further oddity is that although trick substitutions in which a cut was made 'on action' when replacing one body with another were quite standard, the generalization of this to cutting on action to a closer shot, rather than to a held position, was never made in this period.

To give some further indication of the rapid spread of cutting in to a closer shot within a scene, I will just mention a few more titles out of many – most of these showing a cut in to Medium Shot from Long Shot – *The Strenuous Life* (Edison, 1904), *The Widow and the Only Man* (Biograph, 1904), *la Chaussette* (Pathé, 1905), *Rêve à la lune* (Pathé, 1905), etc., etc..

Shot Transitions

From *Cendrillon* (1899) onwards, Georges Méliès used dissolves rather than cuts from one shot to the next in his films,

and despite examples of what was to become the standard approach of using a straight cut for shot transitions being already available in the work of contemporary English film-makers, Edwin Porter and others took up the use of the dissolve as the standard form of shot transition. For instance, in *Life Rescue at Long Branch* made by the Edison Company in 1901, the transition from a Very Long Shot of a beach resuscitation to a slightly closer shot of the same was made with a dissolve, and in Porter's *The Life of an American Fireman* (1903), all the shots were joined with dissolves.

The adoption of the Méliès dissolve was not confined to the United States, for all the shots in the Pathé *Histoire d'un crime* are joined with dissolves, and in *Alice in Wonderland* (Hepworth, 1903) there are a number of transitions of this kind, including dissolves to a closer shot within a scene, and also dissolves when the actress walks out of one shot into the next. This is despite the fact that the position matching from one shot to the next in these cases in *Alice in Wonderland* was not too bad for the date when the film was made. In November 1901 Robert Paul made a great effort to outdo Méliès with his film *Scrooge; or, Marley's Ghost*. This was, as he described it in an advertisement in *The Era* (20 November 1901), 600 feet long, and in '...twelve tableaux, dissolving or otherwise.' Further, it had '...pithy letterpress titles on the film, which give the clue to each of the principal sections. These short introductions are imprinted on the film in a novel or pleasing manner, some of them appearing with a dissolving effect between the various scenes, others being disclosed by a rolling curtain, as if projected by a biunial lantern.' Most of this film survives, and it contains all the advertised features. The 'rolling curtain' effect is what we would call a soft-edged vertical wipe, and this is fairly well executed twice within the surviving material, around Scene II. As the advertisement implies, this kind of wipe effect was already commonly used on magic lanterns, but it was much more difficult to bring off on film,

A frame part of the way through the progress of a vertical wipe from a scene to the following intertitle in Robert Paul's Scrooge; or, Marley's Ghost *(1901). Part of the set from the previous scene remains visible at the bottom of the frame.*

and in fact close examination of the examples in *Scrooge; or, Marley's Ghost* show that in one case the blurred overlap between the out-going and in-coming scenes separates to leave a dark gap as the edge of the wipe moves up the screen. In the transitions to and from the later scenes in this film, Paul dropped the wipe effect, and used the simpler dissolve, and as far as I know, he never used the wipe again. The next occurrence of wipes, less perfectly done, is in G.A. Smith's *Mary Jane's Mishap* (1903). There are no more dissolves in the other surviving Paul films either, and virtually no other European examples of such use of the dissolve outside the films of Méliès. American examples pretty well vanish after 1903 as well.

Only Georges Méliès persisted in using dissolves between every shot after this date. (It must be emphasized Méliès was not using the dissolve to indicate a time lapse between shots in his films, since many of them occur between shots in which there is no time lapse possible between a character walking out of one shot into a spatially adjoining scene. Examples of this can be seen in *Barbe-Bleue* (1901) and *le Voyage dans la lune* (1902). In fact the use of the dissolve to indicate a time lapse did not begin to be established as a convention till the end of the nineteen-twenties.)

The use of fades was very rare in the early years of the century, but there are examples to be seen in one of the surviving prints of *Ali Baba et les quarante voleurs* (Pathé, 1902), where they begin and end each scene, and also similarly in Williamson's *The Old Chorister* (1904) and the Gaumont *la Vie du Christ* (1906). Those few fades that occur in *Alice in Wonderland* are probably unsuccessful attempts at making a dissolve in the camera by fading-out, then winding back and fading in on the next shot. The earliest cameras did not have footage counters, and a mis-counting of the number of backward turns with the crank handle could easily create a separate fade-out and fade-in rather than a dissolve. For this and other obvious reasons the use of dissolves made in the camera between every shot was not an efficient procedure of film

construction, and neither was making dissolves in the printer by the same process for every separate print of the film produced, so it is no great surprise that the usage disappeared after 1903.

The Cut as Shot Transition

And it was displaced by the English film-makers' use of simple cuts to join shots together, with action moving directly from one shot to the next. The earliest important example of this was a new version of *The Kiss in the Tunnel* made for the Bamforth company at the very end of 1899, which was a slightly varied imitation of G.A. Smith's film of the same title made a month or two previously. The Bamforth film actually shows the train going into the tunnel in Very Long Shot, rather than the view from a camera mounted on the front of it, then it shows the events in the interior of the carriage as before, and finally the train coming out of the tunnel, again seen in Very Long Shot.

The continuation of the development of action continuity through shots cut directly together occurs in a series of 1901 British films; Robert Paul's *The Waif and the Wizard*, and James Williamson's *Attack on a Chinese Mission Station, Stop Thief!*, and *Fire!*. The Robert Paul film is made up of two shots, with the principal characters walking out of frame at the end of the first shot, followed by a cut to a room somewhere else, into which they then enter. In other words, it uses the same continuity structure as Paul's earlier *Come Along, Do!*.

Attack on a Chinese Mission Station - Blue Jackets to the Rescue develops the dissection of a continuous action by breaking it down into a series of shots taken from different camera positions that had been begun in the G.A. Smith films. This film has often been discussed on the basis of the description and frame enlargements in the Williamson and Warwick Trading company catalogues, but now that a print of the film itself has finally re-appeared, its importance can be seen to be even greater. The full catalogue description of the action

Visitors are shown exiting top left up some stairs from the factory scene near the beginning of Méliès' le Voyage dans la lune (1902). The dissolve to the next scene, which can already be seen faintly superimposed, has just begun.

About 20 frames later the dissolve has just finished, and the visitors are emerging with time continuity up the top of the stairs onto the balcony on the roof avove the previous scene in le Voyage dans la lune.

appears in Low and Manvell's *History of the British Film: 1895-1906*, but the essence of what happens in and outside the grounds of a large house is as follows:- 1. Chinese Boxer rebels are attacking the outside wooden gates of a mission station. They break through, and rush into the grounds away from the camera. 2. In the grounds of the house a European family are taking their ease. When the Boxers rush past the camera towards them the missionary sends his family into the house, and he defends himself against the attackers, who finally kill him. His wife appears on a balcony and waves a handkerchief. 3. In a shot taken from the opposite angle, showing the open gate to the garden from the inside, we see a troop of marines, led by an officer on horseback, approaching the gate, which they rush through. Inside the gate, they pause, fire a series of volleys past the camera, then rush towards and past it. 4. This is the same camera set-up as shot 2., showing the garden and front of the house, with woman on balcony and besieging Boxers. The marines rush past the camera into the scene and engage the Boxers. There follows more varied action in this scene, but although the latter part of it is missing from the surviving print, it clearly contributes nothing further from the point of view of film construction.

What is most striking about the actual film is the smoothness of the cuts between movements passing from one shot into the next, and also the alternation of shots from opposite directions on continuous action. Because of these different directions of camera angle, the film has a greater feeling of flexibility in its dissection than the preceding films made by G.A. Smith. Some subsequent films by James Williamson keep this feeling, but they are not many, and none does it much better than *Attack on a Chinese Mission Station*.

Williamson's *Stop Thief!* takes action through more widely separated spaces, and is the source of subsequent developments in 'chase' films. It is made up of three shots. In the first shot the thief is chased out of the side of the frame, and then in the second shot set in a different place he runs in one side of the frame and is chased towards the camera and out of the other side of the frame, and then he runs into the third shot, where he is finally caught; all of these shots being joined by simple cuts. *Fire!* introduces this feature into a more complex construction. In this film an actor moves from a scene outside a burning building by exiting from the side of the frame and into a shot outside a fire station, then the fire cart moves out of this shot and next appears in the distant background of a shot of a street, advancing forward and out of frame past the camera. From this point the film moves back to the burning house, though not to the real exterior as before, but rather to a set showing a room inside the house. A fireman comes into the room from the top of a ladder outside the window, picks up a helpless occupant, and starts to lift him through the window. At this point there is a cut to the real exterior again, with the victim being lifted through the window and carried down the ladder. In the absolute sense the continuity of action across the cut from inside to outside is imperfect, as there is a second or so of movement across the window still missing, but

even to the modern eye, the cut *looks* smooth, in the same way that contemporary editing often elides small parts of movement invisibly. The film ends with more movement towards the camera and out of frame past it. The only other surviving films from 1901 that have continuous movement from shot to shot are French, namely the Pathé company's *Histoire d'un crime* and Méliès' *Barbe-bleue*, and these were made later than the first of the Williamson films. Also, in these two French examples the transitions from one shot into the next are covered with dissolves, as already remarked, rather than being straight cuts.

The consolidation of Williamson's methods of film construction was carried out by other British film-makers in 1903. The first of these was *Daring Daylight Burglary*, made by the Mottershaws at the Sheffield Photographic Company at the beginning of the year. This film starts with an onlooker leaving the high-angle first shot of a burglar breaking into the back of a house and running off into the next shot of a street elsewhere in which he alerts the police. Then there is another straight cut back to the original scene, and after a couple of shots a chase develops that is carried through several more shots, giving an overall structure to the film which adds that of *Stop Thief!* to the end of that of *Fire!*. *Daring Daylight Burglary* was one of the most commercially successful films made up to that date, and it was distributed in America by the Edison Company under the title *Daylight Robbery* several months before Edwin S. Porter made *The Great Train Robbery*. That Porter saw *Daring Daylight Burglary* is proved by the inclusion of the same trick effect, whereby a criminal throws a dummy purporting to be an actor off a height; a roof in the *Daring Daylight Burglary*, and the top of an engine tender in *The Great Train Robbery*.

The Emblematic Shot

Although *The Great Train Robbery* lacks the elaborated chase structure possessed by *Daring Daylight Burglary* and other English films such as *The Pickpocket - A Chase Through London* (Alf Collins) and *Desperate Poaching Affray* (William Haggar), which were made before it in 1903, it does possess original features of its own. The most important of these was the addition of what might be called an 'emblematic shot', which in this case shows a Medium Close Up of a cowboy bandit pointing a gun straight at the camera. This shot, which could be placed either at the beginning or the end of the film by the exhibitor, does not represent any action which occurs in the body of the film, but can be considered to indicate the general nature of the film. At any rate, when this device was copied subsequently in many other films, that was clearly the way that it was used. For instance, in *Raid on a Coiner's Den* (Alf Collins, 1904), the first shot shows a Close Up insert of three hands coming into the frame from different directions; one holding a pistol, another with clenched fist, and the third wearing a police uniform sleeve and holding a pair of handcuffs. These things suggest, without actually representing them, some of the principal features of the film. Similar instances occur in the famous *Rescued by Rover* (Hepworth, 1905), and various other films of these years, and the device continued to occur up to at least 1908, being used in some of Griffith's first films, amongst others, though by that time it was more likely to occur at the end of the film than at the beginning. In this position the emblematic shot shades into a kind of miniature apotheotic shot, and a connection is suggested with the extra shot showing a standard kind of theatrical apotheosis that always concluded the Méliès and Pathé multi-shot fantasy films at this period. Whatever the case, such initial or final shots in films like *Rescued by Rover* are quite distinct from the body of the film, even though the participants shown posed together are also present in the preceding or succeeding shot that is part of the action of the film proper. The emblematic shot seems to have first appeared in embryonic form in Porter's *Rube and Mandy at Coney Island*, copyrighted in August 1903, which is made up of a series of disconnected scenes at Coney Island, concluding with a close shot of Rube and Mandy eating hot dogs and grimacing at the camera.

The Chase Film

The style of overall construction stemming from *Fire!* that has been described above continued to be applied over and over again in the years after 1903, and applied to new versions of the subjects already treated without much variation. Though *Stolen by Gypsies* (Edwin Porter, 1905) has the chase in the middle rather than at the end.

But the genre of comedy chase films descending from *Stop Thief!* are invariably simpler in construction than the dramatic films incorporating chases, for they all just have a simple linear movement of the action through shots set in a succession of different locations, without cutbacks to an established scene. The most famous and influential of these comedy chase films was Biograph's *Personal* of 1904, and this was followed in the first place by total plagiarisms from Edison later in the same year – *How a French Nobleman Got a Wife Through the Personal Columns of the New York Herald*, and from Pathé in 1905 – *Dix femmes pour un mari*, and then by slight variations such as the Pathé *Chien de garde* of 1906.

Films using the chase construction all seem to be original film subjects, and they are nearly all without intertitles between shots. But there was also a category of films adapted from stage or literary works, or even actual events, in which a more complex narrative was handled within several minutes running time by using narrative or descriptive titles before all (or most of) the scenes. This form was of course established before 1900 in some of Méliès' longer films such as *l'Affaire Dreyfus*, and after 1904 it was sometimes combined with chase construction, as in the Pathé film *Au bagne* (1905). This film starts off with separate scenes depicting aspects of convict life, each preceded by an explanatory title, but when one convict escapes, a chase is carried through a succession of shots cut directly together. This sort of construction obviously leads on to the flexible form which became usual in subsequent years.

Before leaving the subject of overall film construction, it should be mentioned that more than half the fictional films surviving from before 1906 consist of just one scene done in one shot, and of course these have no relevance as far as film construction is concerned.

Directions

Georges Méliès seems to have realized fairly quickly the importance of 'correct' directions of entrances and exits for the smoothness of film continuity, even though he was using dissolves between every shot. Certainly by *le Voyage dans la lune* (1902) he was consistently using an exit frame right followed by an entrance frame left , and vice versa, when the characters moved out of one shot into another set in a different, but adjoining, location. This was not the case for most other film-makers at this period, though obviously anyone who stages the directions of entrances and exits purely at random, without having thought about the matter, is going to get them 'right' some of the time, just by chance. It must have been slightly easier for Méliès to come to grips with this problem, because he was working in the one single place, his studio stage, whereas most other people making multi-scene films were working in a number of different real locations in succession while making the one film, and these locations must have tended to suggest the way the action in each shot should be staged.

In multi-scene films shot on real locations the transition to the next shot was often cued by movement forwards out past the camera, as was already established in Williamson's *Fire!*, and in the next shot the actor or actors would be discovered already within the frame in a new location. For this type of transition it is almost immaterial on which side of the camera the exit (or entrance) is made. However, if the actors are discovered moving strongly in one direction not too far from the camera in the next shot, it gives smoother continuity (according to subsequent ideas), if they exit in the same direction.

In general in this period, as far as action continuity is concerned, one has either a series of shots with axial movement towards the camera from the far distance, or alternatively a series of shots with movement into the frame past the camera and moving away into the far distance, but the subtler combination of movement out of the frame past the camera followed by a shot in the opposite direction with movement into the frame past the camera, as in Williamson's *Attack on a Chinese Mission - Bluejackets to the Rescue* and Haggar's *Desperate Poaching Affray*, is extremely rare.

Cuts to Other Directions

The earliest cut to another direction within a scene occurs in *Ladies Skirts Nailed to a Fence* (Bamforth, 1900), in which the second shot is taken at 180 degrees to the first from the other side of the fence with time continuity. This was obviously done to make the action of the film clear. Interestingly, this cut is achieved by an ingenious cheat which depends on

The first shot of Ladies' Skirts Nailed to a Fence *(Bamforth, 1900)*

The second shot of Ladies' Skirts Nailed to a Fence*, with a reverse-angle simulated by moving the actors to the other side of the fence, without moving the camera.*

moving the actors to the other side of the same symmetrical fence, without moving the camera for the second shot. Following this, there is the case in *Attack on a Chinese Mission Station* already described, and then in the Pathé film, *Histoire d'un crime* (1901), the transition to the final shot is done by reversing the direction on the scene through the open gate to the execution yard painted on the backdrop with a dissolve to the exact opposite direction, with a match on the actors in static positions. Following this there are occasional films made through the next few years which show successive scenes with action through a door or window from opposite sides of the wall containing the opening, nearly all of them made on studio sets.

In 1903 Alf Collins made a group of films which use a cut to a different angle within a scene, all of them shot on real exteriors. The first of them may well have been the film currently only known by the descriptive title *The Interfering*

Lovers. This film begins by covering action on a park bench in Very Long Shot, and then cuts in closer to Long Shot with a simultaneous change of camera direction of 60 degrees, so covering slight discrepancies in actor position between the two shots and ensuring a smooth transition (as seen in subsequent terms). A cut of identical nature occurs in Collins' 1904 film, *The Child Stealers*, but before that Collins had also made cuts with angle changes in *The Pickpocket – A Chase Through London* (1903), and in *The Runaway Match* (1903). In the latter film the cuts are in fact reverse-angle cuts, from the pursuing car to the one pursued. These cuts within the scene are reproduced and elaborated in an American copy of this film made a year or two later, *Marriage by Motor-Car*. Collins also made a film in 1904, *The Electric Shock* (or *The Electric Bell*), which had a cut to the reverse direction from the other side of a wall to cover the action going through a doorway, and being him, he did it on location rather than on studio sets.

Marines come through the gate and towards and past the camera in the third shot of Williamson's Attack on a Chinese Mission Station *(1901).*

There is a cut to the next shot, taken in almost the opposite direction, and the marines enter it past the camera and go away forwards from it.

Despite the existence of these films, and also a few others which use cuts to the opposite angle on the other side of a wall during comedy chases, there was no general adoption of the use of cuts to a different angle during this period in any way comparable to the use of cuts straight in to a close shot.

Other Forms of Shot Transition

Mary Jane's Mishap, which has already been mentioned, includes a remarkable and quite unique pair of vertical wipes to effect the transition into, and out of, a closer shot of the inscription on her gravestone, and as well as this there are a few cases where fades were used intentionally in the years between 1900 and 1906. One fairly trivial instance is their use to begin and end each scene in *la Vie du Christ*, made by Victorin Jasset for Gaumont in 1906. In this case every scene is preceded by a narrative title put in between the fades. In *The Old Chorister* (1905), scenes are joined directly by fade-outs and fade- ins.

Another unique occurrence in these years is the use of a focus-pull transition in *Let Me Dream Again* (1900) by G.A. Smith. In the first shot of this two-shot film a man is seen kissing a beautiful woman in Medium Shot, then the lens focus is changed to reduce the image to an out-of-focus blur, followed by a cut to another shot similarly out of focus which then pulls into focus to show the same man in bed kissing his ugly wife, from whom he recoils in revulsion. When this film was remade by Pathé in 1902 as *Rêve et réalité*, the focus pulls were replaced by a simple dissolve. This gives just one instance of the superior technical skill of the English film-makers at this date.

Dreams, Memories, Visions, etc.

The filmic structure, and indeed the basic joke, of *Let Me Dream Again* came to be copied, elaborated, and extended over the next few years. The beginning of what was to be the standard form is already apparent in *Hooligan's Christmas Dream* (Biograph, 1903), in which the transition to the dream is made with a dissolve, but the transition back to the original scene and reality through an unexpected waking is made with a cut. The number of shot-scenes contained within such dreams gradually increased over the years; there are two shots within the dream in *le Cauchemar du caïd* (Pathé, 1905), and many more in *And the Villain Still Pursued Her* (Vitagraph, 1906). Although the dissolve into the dream, followed by the straight cut out of it, was mostly used at this time, there are a few films such as Robert Paul's *A Dancer's Dream* (1905) and Vitagraph's *A Midwinter Night's Dream* of 1906 which use a dissolve to get out of the dream as well.

The use of a small vignette scene representing the dream or vision, inset within part of the frame showing the main scene, continued to be used into the new century, and amongst the examples are Porter's *The Life of an American Fireman* and *Jack and the Beanstalk*. In these films, as in the earlier G.A. Smith films, the inset scene was produced photographically by masking and double-exposure, but in the Pathé film *Histoire d'un crime* the effect was produced by the stage device of having a series of small sets revealed behind a hole in the backdrop to the main set. On these inset sets the series of dream memories was played out, which is further confirmation that the Pathé film-makers had a lot to learn at the beginning of the century.

The representation of spirits, angels, and suchlike continued to be done by simple superimposition as before, and examples can be seen in *Uncle Tom's Cabin* (Porter, 1903), *The Old Chorister* (1904), *Drink and Repentance* (1905), and elsewhere.

Split Screen

Are You There? (Williamson, 1901) is again not completely intelligible from what is shown on the screen. It is the first attempt to deal with the problem of representing a telephone conversation on film, which it does by a split screen effect. This was created by building a split set, with a division down the centre of the frame separating the two telephones, which are understood to be in two quite different places. The edge of the wall near the camera now vertically divides the frame as a thick black strip, actually created by a strip of curtain material. What is said over the phone is vital to understanding the second scene of the film, which follows after a cut, but again this would have to be supplied by the showman's commentary when the film was projected. I have the feeling that there must have been at least one early film following on from *Are You There?* which treated a telephone conversation in the same way, but with the split screen effect done in the camera rather than by set construction. This is because there is a strange lapse of several years in the surviving films before this way of treating a telephone conversation reappears in 1907. The only other presentation of both sides of a telephone conversation before that date is in the American Mutoscope and Biograph company's *The Story the Biograph Told* (1904), in which the scenes at both ends of the line are totally superimposed on each other over the whole area of the frame. This makes it very difficult to decipher what is going on, and was obviously a bad idea.

Cross-cutting Between Parallel Actions

It should already be clear that the practice of cutting away to a scene set elsewhere for one shot became well established during these years, but the idea of doing so repeatedly was not. However the preliminary stages of this latter development can be detected in a few films such as *Rescued in Mid-Air* (Percy Stow, 1906), in which the shots alternate repeatedly between aerial events and those actions connected with them on the ground. But something much closer to fully developed cross-cutting is used in *The Hundred-To-One Shot* (Vitagraph, 1906). The sequence of shots in this film moves from a house interior with the family threatened with eviction, to a race-course where the son wins a bet that will pay off the debt, then to a shot of him racing towards home. This is followed by another shot of the house interior with the family in the process of being evicted, followed by an exterior shot of the son driving up to the house in his car, and finally another shot of the inside of the house into which the son enters and saves the day. There is still some way to go from this to true cross-cutting, but the Pathé film-makers got there a year later.

The Action Continuity Problem

But looking backwards at the period, the major problem turned out to be the action continuity problem. Of course a problem does not exist until it is more or less consciously recognized as such, and at first many film-makers did not recognize this one, because of the difference of the cinema from previous narrative media. Neither the stage nor lantern-slide sequences allowed the absolutely continuous visual representation of action moving from one space to another in the way that was possible in film, and indeed the nature of existing lantern-slide sequences could well have helped to delay recognition of the possibilities of film. For the fact is that most of these lantern-slide sequences showed what were essentially disconnected scenes, and they relied on their accompanying text, which was recited by the showman, to provide a continuous narrative thread. For instance, in one of the most famous sequences, *Bob, the Fireman*, the principal figure in successive slides is obviously a different fireman, but the text nevertheless always insists that he is 'Bob'. More than that, the series of scenes of the fire wagon leaving the fire station and racing to the fire (or fires) obviously take place at different times of the day or night. The same is true for nearly all other slide sequences I have seen – the slides each represent a dramatic moment that is explained and connected by the text in prose or poetry supplied with it. To put the matter another way, the lantern slides in a sequence are merely a set of illustrations to a verbal narrative.

This and other kinds of discontinuity are reflected in the first multi-shot films made by Edwin S. Porter and other American film-makers, of which the most often discussed is *The Life of an American Fireman* (1903). The first shot of this film shows a man wearing what might be a uniform coat dozing at an office desk while a circular inset scene showing a woman and a baby appears on a wall. When this inset scene disappears the man gets up and leaves the room. The next scene shows a Close Up insert of a hand ringing a fire alarm in a street, but there is no return to the first scene, and no way of recognizing whether the man in that scene takes part in subsequent events. The descriptive text supplied for the film in the Edison Company catalogue describes the man in the first scene as a fire chief thinking of his wife and child, and then of all the people who might be in danger from fire, but there is no way of telling this from the film alone, or indeed what is the connection between this scene and later ones in the film. Now although a commentary was pretty well essential for full audience appreciation of a lantern-slide sequence, it had already been demonstrated by 1903, principally by European film-makers, that it was possible to make longer films which were self-sufficient and could be understood by

audiences without commentary. One such example was James Williamson's *Fire!* of 1901, which unlike *The Life of an American Fireman* used the movement of recognizable characters from shot to shot, and action to action, to provide a continuous and comprehensible narrative.

Charles Musser has pointed out that there is another feature of *The Life of an American Fireman* which arises from the tendency to conceive of each shot as a detached unit on the model of lantern-slide sequences. This is the way that action that has been completed in one shot is repeated at the beginning of the next shot, firstly when the firemen leave their dormitory in succession down the pole (this sequence of actions being shown again from their place of arrival in the wagon room below), and secondly in a later pair of successive scenes showing events inside and outside the burning room, with the comings and goings through the window shown in full from both sides. I shall have more to say about this 'doorway problem' later, but at the moment it is only necessary to say that the only reasonable interpretation of these occurrences is that Porter did not recognize any continuity problem in such situations, whereas some other film-makers of the period did, and took steps to deal with it.

It must also be emphasized that the cases of repetition of the same action in successive shots that occurred in a small number of films in this period have no relation to the intentional use of a similar device twenty years later by Sergei Eisenstein, since in that case it resulted from a clearly conceptualized intention, whereas in the early years it was an accidental side effect of simpler ideas, or indeed of no ideas at all.

The Doorway Problem

Looking at Williamson's *Fire!* nowadays, one might think that since he had moved two people though a window on a cut from one shot to the next with a fair approximation to continuity of action, then the problem of how to do this in a film had been solved, particularly when we consider the handling of a somewhat similar situation in Méliès' *Barbe-bleue* made the same year. In this latter film, Bluebeard's last wife unlocks and enters the door to his secret room at frame right, and then there is a dissolve to a shot of the inside of this room with the wife coming through the door at frame left. In fact a perfect match. But although these two films were widely shown, just two examples were not enough when other film-makers had to deal with similar situations. In Porter's *The Life of an American Fireman* of 1903, two people exit in succession through the window of a burning room seen from inside, with their escapes being separated by a couple of seconds. In the next shot, joined on as in Méliès' film by a dissolve, both people are seen coming through the window from the outside in succession, which means that part of the action is repeated. Putting oneself back into that period, it is not so surprising that some film-makers had difficulty with getting several people in succession through a door from one shot to the next, since narratives in other media could not provide a guide. If just one person goes through a door it could be seen as a case of a positional match, which was fairly well established by 1903 in European films, and indeed there are no European examples of this kind of repeated action.

Amongst the several American films which show action repeated after a cut in this way are examples from both Edison and Biograph, e.g. *Next!*(Biograph, 1903), but rather strangely these coexisted with other films where the same situation was handled in what came to be the standard way. This happens in Biograph's *A Search for Evidence*, made later in 1903, in which the cut is made as the first of the two people entering a room opens the door. Yet *The Firebug*, made at the same studio in 1905, returns to the alternative of repeating the whole action, as a series of characters are shown getting through a window both from the inside and the outside.

The existence of two alternative forms for dealing with a feature of film construction has already been mentioned in connection with the two methods of joining shots together, the Méliès dissolve and the British cut, but in that case there was a clear practical and economic reason for preferring one of them. This was not the case with the doorway problem, though the logical generalization of the position match for cuts within one scene does support the result which we know became standard after 1906. Anything more to be said on this matter requires a careful consideration and comparison of *all* the films which were made in this period using *all* the ways of getting people through a door, etc. from one shot to another, which is not a very large task.

Smoothing it Out

A much simpler problem was the exact timing of the cuts between successive shots when the action moved from one into the other. When the whole idea of action continuity had just been invented, in Williamson's *Fire!*, and other similar films over the next couple of years, there will typically be a couple of feet of film after an actor has left the frame to move on to the next shot before the cut is actually made to the succeeding location, and then a foot or two more of the new shot before the actor moves into it. This seems particularly strange to modern eyes, when the movement from one shot to the next is not horizontal, but a vertical fall under gravity. However, by 1905 a number of film makers were doing something about this, and making the cut to the next shot just after the actor has left the frame. This sharpening up of the cutting around 1905 is particularly noticeable in Pathé films, but some of the British film makers were getting quite good at it too. The best-known film which shows the elimination of the delay on movement from one shot into the next is Hepworth's *Rescued by Rover*, but other examples from 1905 include Pathé's *Cache-toi dans la malle!*, and *Demenagement à la cloche à bois*, whereas Porter's *The Watermelon Patch* is notable for the sluggish cutting from one shot to the next in the earlier 'chase' part of the film, particularly when contrasted with other Pathé chase films from that year such as *Chien de garde*. In fact over the next couple of years, as their production increased greatly, Pathé became the definite world leaders in smoothness of continuity as well as in production values.

Intertitles

As the comments above on Robert Paul's *Scrooge; or, Marley's ghost* indicate, it was in 1901 that the usefulness of having explanatory titles preceding each scene came to be realized. It may have been Méliès who first used them, but since there were few multi-shot films before 1903, they were not used much till after that date. Also, towards the end of this period there are isolated instances of dialogue titles being cut in before a scene in place of the usual narrative title, but the films being produced at this time were still not long enough to contain a continuously developed complex story in which the usefulness of such a feature would be obvious. The earliest example I have noticed occurs in *Ali Baba et les quarantes voleurs* (Pathé, 1902), and here the dialogue title is the minimal but immortal speech, 'Sesame, ouvre-toi'. Later examples with a single line of dialogue quoted in them include *la Vie du Christ* (Jasset, 1906), and Porter's *The Ex-convict* of 1904. There is an English film of unknown name produced by the Urban company in 1906 which contains more than one dialogue title. It is catalogued as *'Father, Mother wants you'*, which is actually the first dialogue title it contains, well into the body of the film. But such films are indeed very uncommon during these years.

Acting

It is very difficult to make any generalizations about the acting in the films of this period, with one exception. This is that the acting in the numerous films of the life of Jesus Christ which were made from the beginning of the century was always extremely restrained, and sometimes naturalistic as well. Extremely naturalistic acting, though not common, can also be found in a number of other films, one of the earliest being Williamson's *The Soldier's Return* (1902). In this particular case the naturalness of the acting was advertised as such in the contemporary distribution catalogues, and so was clearly quite intentional. In fact, a tendency towards more naturalistic acting can be seen in all of Williamson's films. Other random examples of very restrained acting include Biograph's *The Course of True Love* (1905), and Porter's *The Kleptomaniac* (1905), but it is far from certain that such examples were intentional, for they may well have resulted from letting particular actors do it their own way without direction. On the other hand, most films had fairly broad, stylized acting from the principals at least, and sometimes wildly melodramatic acting, particularly at key moments in the drama. An obvious example of the latter is Porter's *The Great Train Robbery*, so that overall it is very difficult to see any consistent patterns emerging, either by studio or director, with the exception of the films of James Williamson.

The Broad View

It must be emphasized that the films made before 1906 which still exist are only a fraction of the production of that period, and so if a particular feature is found in several of them it is quite probable that it also appeared in many more that are now lost. For instance, if about 30 surviving films made at different times and places during these years have closer shots cut into the middle of a scene, as is indeed the case, then it is likely that there were more than 100 films made with this feature. On the other hand, if there is only a unique occurrence of a particular feature in surviving films, then it may well have been unique at the time. An obvious example of this is the three Biograph films previously mentioned which consist solely of a track in to a Close Up of a character. Now although there were three of them, they were all made within several days of each other to judge by the copyright dates, so it seems fairly safe to conclude that since there now exist no other films using a similar tracking shot before 1906, then there were probably no others made at all. And we can certainly conclude that this usage was not well established at this period. Keeping all these considerations in mind, we can say that the major trends in the development of film form that emerged during this period were the practice of cutting in to a closer shot of one kind or another during a scene, the use of masked Point of View shots likewise cut into a scene, and the mastery of the rather more complex matter of the movement of action from shot to shot in separate locations, as in 'chase' films. All of these developments really solidified between 1903 and 1906, and since the proliferation of examples shows that these specifically filmic techniques were consciously mastered, there does not seem to be much point in referring to films in general made during the next decade as constituting 'primitive cinema', any more than an art historian would call the work of Duccio and the Siennese school 'primitive painting'.

Other definite formal trends that emerged after 1904 were the use of panning shots to follow action, arc lighting both for effect and for general lighting, and transition to a dream sequence made with a dissolve. There is also the beginning of cross-cutting between parallel actions. These trends I have been describing, though also detectable in American films, were much more firmly established in French films during these years, and in particular those made by the Pathé company. This must have been due in part to the fact that the multi-scene film was established slightly earlier in Europe than in America, but an associated hindrance to American progress could have been that the film-makers of the two major American companies, Edison and American Mutoscope and Biograph, were simultaneously producing films for both cinema exhibition and for showing in the Kinetoscope and Mutoscope peep-show machines. Some multi-scene films were exhibited in these machines by putting each successive scene in one of the machines making up a row in the Kinetoscope or Mutoscope parlour, so that to see the whole film the viewer had to put a coin in each machine in turn. In this situation it was obviously preferable that the film exist as a series of discrete scenes, each prefaced by a title, and obviously without action passing continuously from one scene to the next. One typical example from 1903 is Biograph's *Kit Carson*, in which

the successive scenes, apart from being complete in themselves, do not have much obvious connection with each other. These two points about American film production may also have something to do with the existence of American films having repeated action on either side of a cut.

Lines of Influence

The films made in the years 1900-1906 provide a most striking demonstration of the influence of one film on another, and anyone inclined to doubt that it is possible to determine this kind of influence is advised to spend a week or two going through several hundred of them. Apart from the examples of formal influence which I have mentioned earlier, there are of course also the large number of reworkings of the same subject, such as the numerous films about the kidnapping of children. These may very well start with *The Kidnappers* (Biograph, 1903), and they certainly continue through *Weary Willie Kidnaps a Child* (Edison, 1904), which has a similar narrative structure to the earlier film, but uses exterior instead of interior locales. Then comes a combination of some elements from both these two films into a longer film made in England in 1904, *The Kidnapped Child*, and then a further elaboration in the well-known *Rescued by Rover* (1905), where the new element is the activities of Rover. Later in the same year there was *Stolen by Gypsies* (Edison), which adds a developed chase sequence as well as 'Porter pans', and then a number of other variations on the formula, both immediately and later. Sometimes it was a matter of simple copying, and sometimes of variation and elaboration, which might or might not throw up interesting new features.

A very interesting case in point is the Edison studio film *Dream of a Rarebit Fiend* (1906), which is quite closely modelled on the Pathé film *Rêve à la lune* (1905), both in its story and in its form. *Rêve à la lune* in its turn incorporates a couple of elements from Méliès' *Voyage à travers l'impossible* (1904), though in general it is not that close to the Méliès film, and also from Winsor McKay's comic strips *Dreams of a Rarebit Fiend*. The interesting differences between *Rêve à la lune* and the Edison film are that the former includes a detail insert of a key groping for a keyhole in the hands of the drunken protagonist which is omitted in the Porter film, while the latter replaces a simple shot of the drunk clinging to a rocking lamp-post with a similar shot which has superimposed on it two whip pans across a row of buildings inclined at opposite angles to the horizontal. This extremely striking shot is an isolated example of the representation of a subjective state by filmic means, and seems to have had no immediate successors. *Dream of a Rarebit Fiend* also lacks the perfect cutting on action that the Pathé film contains, and this is as typical of an Edison film as the lack of the Insert Close Up.

The Status of Edwin S. Porter

If we accept that all the Edison films of these years were made by Edwin S. Porter, where does the fact that many of these Edison films were closely modelled on various predecessors from other hands leave our estimate of his importance?

The answer is implied in the discussions of the various films concerned that I have given above. Because there were a few features that Porter introduced were either very original or highly influential, even when the film in which they were included was otherwise very closely based on previous films, there is no question but that Porter was one of the major figures of the period, but on the other hand, there were a number of other film-makers of whom the same could be said. But there is also no question that Porter did *not* originate any of the basic features of film construction – cutting within a scene and continuity of movement from shot to shot, or indeed film editing in general. Indeed not only did he *not* invent these things, but when others had developed them, he clearly had some difficulty handling them properly.

Film and the Other Entertainment Media

Much has been made of the influence of the theatre, the comic strip, and the slide show on the creation of purely filmic constructional devices, the earliest instance of this being A. Nicholas Vardac's *Stage to Screen* (1949). A more general treatment of the notion can be found in John Fell's *Film and the Narrative Tradition*, but the problem with this idea is that the devices which are alleged to be derived from other media were used in films before they appear in any noticeable way in the other media. For instance, cutting in to a close shot appeared in films before any example so far found in comic strips or slide shows. However, I think it is well worth looking in to this further, particularly with respect to lantern slide series, because something may yet turn up; for instance a source for the masked Point of View shot construction, apparently invented out of nothing in *Grandma's Reading Glass.*

Film Form and Society

It has been suggested by Noël Burch that various features of some of the films of the first decade present a vision of an alternative form of 'working class' cinema which was suppressed by the middle class, who then produced the form of cinema that developed over the next several years after 1906. I find it difficult to see the point of these speculations, since it seems to me that the general form of cinema was inevitably determined by the middle class from the beginning, and whatever its form, there could never be a purely working class cinema anywhere. In Europe, contrary to what Burch claims, all the first major film-makers were of middle class origins, from Méliès to G.A. Smith and James Williamson, and in America, even if some such as G.W. Bitzer were of more humble origins, by the beginning of the century, if not earlier, they were being paid such large wages that they had definitely entered the middle class. This is an aspect of the generalization that whoever has truly mastered the application of advanced technology — which the cinematic apparatus was at the beginning of the century — inevitably moves up in status and automatically reaps the rewards in *any* industrialized society. Beyond that, it should be noted that only under capitalism is technological innovation possible, as the record of the last seventy years shows. There has been zero technological innovation in socialist societies in that period, and they have been completely parasitic on the capitalist world for any technological advance at all. This is very evident in the sphere of film technology in particular.

It is true that the subject matter of films was biased towards material from vaudeville, melodrama, and music hall before 1903, particularly in America, but that is largely a reflection of the fact that a film only a couple of minutes long is not capable of containing anything more subtle. In any case it should be noted that a large part of the material used in vaudeville, melodrama, and music hall was already being produced by professional writers and composers who were no longer part of the working class in any real sense. The other major sources of the subject matter of the nascent cinema; slide shows, comic strips, and legitimate drama, were being produced by members of the middle class for an audience of mixed composition. Note also that slides for slide shows were being produced on an industrial scale before the cinema came into existence. Once films began to move on to longer running times after 1903 the basic elements of continuity cinema that I have described were truly established, and audiences of all classes voted with their pennies for coherent stories presented in what we now think of as a coherent manner.

9. FILM STYLE AND TECHNOLOGY: 1907-1913

Once there was a sufficient accumulation of story films several minutes long, it was possible to set up film exhibition in permanent venues. So in the year following the opening of the Nickelodeon in Pittsburgh in 1905, three thousand of these small, sub-200 seat cinemas opened in the United States, and a world-wide film production and consumption boom had begun. To meet the rapidly accelerating demand, production of fictional films started in Italy, Germany, and Denmark where there had been none before. After a year or two, yet more countries joined in, most importantly Sweden and Russia. Reports of the comments of exhibitors from 1907 onwards in the trade periodical *The Moving Picture World* show that audience response was heeded by the exhibitors and distributors, and presumably transmitted back, however imperfectly, to the producers, so constituting some kind of selection pressure on the evolution of the forms. But this pressure cannot have been strong, to judge by the large range of competence (as seen from the point of view of the subsequent evolution of mainstream cinema) that continued to exist in America up to the First World War. In other words, it was still not that difficult to satisfy the taste of the continuously expanding market. Or to put it yet another way, in the previous period the formal developments I have described took place purely through the independent will of the film-makers, and though this was still to a considerable extent the case after 1907, it was no longer completely so.

The word 'art' began to be increasingly associated with films in writing about them and reviewing them from 1909 onwards, and this no doubt encouraged some film-makers to seek originality in what they did. The major event in changing attitudes on this point was the obvious one: the release of the French Film d'Art company's first film, *l'Assassinat du Duc de Guise* in November 1908. This company was formed with a definite aesthetic programme, which was to make films written by established serious writers, acted by some of the best stage actors, and supported by music specially written by good composers. Although their films were to be released by Pathé, the latter company nevertheless immediately set up its own subsidiary, Societé Cinématographique des Artistes et Gens de Littérature (S.C.A.G.L.), with the same sort of programme. The fact that other companies took notice of all this is indicated by the full titles of some 1909 films. For instance, just after *l'Assassinat du Duc de Guise* opened in New York, Vitagraph made *The Judgement of Solomon* and *Oliver Twist*, and issued them with the extra descriptive subsidiary title 'A Vitagraph High Art Film', and in Italy there was Cines' *La campana*, also made in the latter part of 1909, which had the descriptive addition to the title, 'Artistic Pictures from Schiller's Poem'.

But it is clear from the reviews in *The Moving Picture World* and *The New York Dramatic Mirror* that their film reviewers were often slow and sometimes obtuse in understanding the technical developments which I will describe below, and indeed they continued to resist some of these developments long after they had become standard with many film-makers, so that what little these reviewers had to say on detailed technical points must have mostly been ignored.

(A collection of such reviews can be found in *Spellbound in Darkness* by George C. Pratt (New York Graphic Society, 1973). This book concentrates excessively on the reviews of D.W. Griffith's films by Frank Wood, and these are not exactly disinterested in what they have to say, since Wood was selling film stories to Biograph from quite early on in Griffith's career as a director. Wood only comments on stylistic developments after they occurred, and presumably only after they had been explained to him by the people at Biograph, and he seems to have known little about what happened before 1908, or at places other than Biograph later.)

Direct, unmediated competitiveness between American film-makers seems to have become important from about 1911 in producing intentionally conspicuous features in their films, and I will refer to some of these instances below, but here I will just let Vitagraph's *Over the Chafing Dish* (Larry Trimble, 1911), a story told entirely through Close Ups of hands and feet, stand for all of them.

So in the years from 1907 onwards the evolution of film form was still proceeding very quickly. Because films were still mostly only one or two reels long it is possible to see a large number of them in a short time, and so get a good idea of comparative developments in a way that is no longer possible when we reach the period when most films become several reels long. If one takes advantage of this situation and looks at most of the two or three thousand films still extant from between 1907 and 1913, one finds that the accepted picture of what happened in those years, based as it is on a few handfuls of films by D.W. Griffith and one or two others from elsewhere, is largely mistaken. The reader who has reached this point will not be too surprised to discover that the usual idea that Griffith invented most of the features of mainstream cinema is quite wrong; but more than that, he has not been given credit for all the things he *did* develop. However, it must be made clear that I am not challenging Griffith's position as the man who made the *best* films before 1913; to justify his standing in this respect one needs to take other things into consideration as well. A further complication to investigation of this whole matter is provided by the fact that nearly all of D.W. Griffith's 450 films made for Biograph up to 1913 survive, whereas only about three times that number still exist from all the other American film-makers working in the same period; a period when the total production was about ten times as much. The unrepresentative survival of films is particularly severe for the years 1907 and 1908 – from those years there seems to be only a few score films from American production companies other than Biograph in the world's archives. In particular, there are only about a dozen films from the Vitagraph company, which already had a larger output than Biograph, and maintained this position through the period under consideration. Nevertheless, partly by extrapolation from the films surviving from either side of this gap, one can reconstruct the outlines of what was happening.

Film Stock

Eastman Kodak continued to dominate the film stock market without making any change in the negative and positive emulsions which it offered in rolls of 200 feet length. Minor competition came from the Lumière company with a range of negative film from their Blue Label stock, with a speed of about half that of Eastman negative, to their Violet Label stock, which was comparable in speed to Eastman negative. In 1907 the Pathé company bought up the English company of Blair, and used their production for their own films, supplementing it from 1910 by collecting old unwanted prints from all over Europe which they stripped and recoated with new emulsion. The German Agfa company, which began producing film stock in 1913, had no appreciable sales outside the local market until after the First World War. There were a few other small companies making film stock in this period, but their production was small, and its quality inferior. In particular, the emulsion of the negatives they produced was a lot slower than Kodak negative, and much of it was only blue sensitive, rather than orthochromatic.

A large part of the 35 mm. film stock produced was still sold by the makers as unperforated strips, and then the sprocket holes were punched in it by the purchaser, using special punches bought for the purpose. These were made by different small engineering firms in the major film producing countries, usually those also making film cameras or projectors. Although the resulting perforations were meant to have some sort of fairly close correspondence with those used by Edison and Lumière, they still often differed one from another, and so there was a general lack of standardization in this area. This began to change from 1908, when the new Bell & Howell company of Chicago began to manufacture film perforators for general sale. Designed by Arthur Howell, these were so superior to the competition that they quickly came to be generally used in the United States. In particular, Eastman Kodak bought them to produce pre-perforated film stock for sale, and eventually the shape, dimensions, and spacing of the perforations for negative film produced by the Bell & Howell perforator became the world standard, which remains the case up to the present, as far as 35 mm. camera negative film is concerned.

Production Procedures

Karl Brown's memoirs, together with other sources, give a picture of the way filming procedures were becoming standardized by the end of this period. First the camera was set up in a position that covered the area in which the scene was to be played, and then the cameraman's assistant marked out on the ground or studio floor with chalk or tape lines the limits within which the actors could move while remaining within the frame. The cameraman's permanent assistant, if there was one at all, was limited to menial tasks like this, including carrying the camera, and also to keeping a primitive continuity record. Anything connected directly with the camera, including loading the magazines, was done by the cameraman himself. At Biograph in 1913 the continuity record contained no more than the length of the take, the lens aperture setting, and which side of the frame the various actors concerned made their entrances and exits. The shot filmed was identified by a number giving its order in the sequence of shooting; this number being written in chalk on a school slate held in front of the camera either at the beginning, or more usually the end, of the shot. The end of the whole footage including the shots made under the same lighting conditions was marked on the film by either opening the back of the camera and tearing the edge of the film through to a sprocket hole, or if the camera was equipped with a built-in punch, by actuating this to punch a hole in the middle of the film. Then a fixed length of film a few feet long was exposed to provide material for test development, and the end of this was marked in the same way. This mark enabled the company's darkroom technician, who was now a specialist who had taken over this job from the cameraman, to separate the test strip by touch, and then give it a separate test development before processing the shot itself.

Laboratory Procedures

Both negative and positive film continued to be developed in batches, at most in 200 foot lengths, by either the rack or drum method. However in some French companies the continuous developing machines which had first been introduced by Gaumont in 1907 were being used. These ran a continuous length of film through vertical tubes containing the various chemicals. As far as negative development was concerned, the aim was to produce a series of negatives for all the shots that could be printed with the same intensity of the light source in the film printer. Negatives were in general developed to a much greater density than is now usual in still and motion picture photography. One good reason for this was that rush prints were not usually made from the developed negative for selecting takes and editing the film: the original negative itself was projected and handled, and the inevitable scratches resulting showed up much less on the final print when it was made from a dark negative.

Printing continued to be done on the kind of intermittent printers already described until 1911, when the Bell & Howell continuous printer was introduced. In this machine the nega-

A scene in the 1907 Vitagraph film Liquid Electricity; or, The Inventor's Galvanic Fluid. *The set is lit by diffuse sunlight through the studio roof, shaded off a bit towards the back. On the right is a Cooper-Hewitt rack on a floor stand, and hanging in on the left, above the actor's head, is an unlit arc floodlight of the street-lighting type. The actor is manipulating the light from another bare carbon arc mechanism on the bench, of the kind ordinarily enclosed in a projector lamp-house. Notice that the light from the mercury vapour tubes makes very little impression against the brightness of the daylight, whereas the arc does.*

tive and positive were held in contact while wrapped on the sprockets half way round the diameter of a continuously rotating drum. Light was shone from an incandescent bulb through an aperture of appropriate size onto the films, and its intensity was regulated by a manually set aperture.

For the production of the distribution prints the shots still had to be handled separately because they were now mostly tinted different colours, and so the individual shots and titles were all cemented together for every individual print by teams of female workers. The necessity of this system removed any demand for the machine processing of positive prints in the way that we have it today, and in fact machine processing was not adopted in the United States for a decade, as far as feature films were concerned.

Film Lighting

As already described, the major production companies were already equipped with what was to be the basic studio lighting equipment for the next decade – arc floodlights of one kind or another, and racks of mercury vapour tubes. The new, smaller production companies that sprang up in America with the coming of the film boom did not acquire and use such equipment with any rapidity, but often made do with diffused sunlight on open-air stages, or on simple glass-roofed stages. This was particularly the case in California, where artificial light seems rarely to have been used before World War I. In shooting interiors back East the general tendency at first was just to supplement the daylight with Cooper-Hewitt banks or arc floodlights when there was not enough of it, but with some of the large companies new tendencies depending on the increased use of arc lights gradually developed. The same tendency is apparent in European films of the period, though there were some national differences there. For instance, the introduction of the visible use of artificial light

seems to have been slightly slower in Italy than in the U.S., and some of the Italian companies, particularly Cines, tended to shoot their interiors with the diffuse daylight coming through the glass studio walls from the side, rather than the front, as was more usual in American films. And the Scandinavian companies tended to use arc floodlights more or less exclusively, without any use of banks of mercury vapour tubes.

On the evidence of surviving films and also the film clips deposited in the Library of Congress for copyright, the Vitagraph company led the way in the USA. (A discussion of these Vitagraph clips, together with reproductions of some of them, can be seen in Ben Brewster's article 'Frammenti Vitagraph alla Library of congress' in *Vitagraph Co. of America*, edited by Paolo Cherchi Usai, published by Edizioni Studio Tesi in 1987.) Although the first real Vitagraph studio was very like the earlier studios built by Méliès and Pathé, with roof and walls made of diffusing glass, they were more inclined to use overhead arc lights, rather than arcs on floor stands, to supplement daylight. These overhead arcs were of the standard kind used for street lighting, which had the arc enclosed inside a hanging glass bell cover, and they shone their light equally in all downwards directions. The major American manufacturer of such lights was Aristo, and this became the generic term for such lights for a while. They were mostly used hung in on a movable light temporary beam of wood where and when needed, which was basically when the daylight through the studio ceilings and walls was weak and needed boosting. They were also used mounted on floor stands, either singly, or in groups on the one stand at Vitagraph. They were fitted with improvised metal reflector sheets half way around them to ensure that the light went only towards the set, and to keep it from shining back into the camera lens. For dates before 1912 these lights usually did not make a great difference to the general look of the lighting, and there is no discernible

A.E. Smith filming The Bargain Fiend *in the Vitagraph studio in 1907. The street lighting type arcs with their improvised shades hanging from the roof beams are not lit. Note that the set-up has the camera at an angle to the walls of the simple L-shaped set.*

pattern as to which kind of scenes they were used on in general. For instance, these overhead arcs contribute a large part of the light to a number of varied scenes – a low dive, some factory interiors – in *The Mill Girl* (1907), though always without any attempt to simulate the effect of actual light in the real situations. The standard lighting method at Edison was very similar, and this general approach, which had most of the supplementary light coming from rows of overhead flood-lights, came to be the model for newer American companies as they stepped up their production. By 1910 arc lighting in this manner is noticeable in films from all the New York and Chicago studios, though not in the films made by the units from these companies already working in the West and South of the United States.

A scene in a drinking den in Vitagraph's 1907 film, The Mill Girl *. It is mostly lit by two or three arc floodlights hanging in a row overhead the actors at the table, as can be seen from the shadows on the figures and the walls. There is only a small contribution from the diffuse daylight through the studio roof.*

The filming of a studio interior scene from Vor Tids Dame *(E. Schnedler-Sørensen, 1912) at the Nordisk studio in Copenhagen. The cameraman is Axel Graatkjaer, and three European-style arc floodlights on floor stands are in use, one left, two on the right.*

Around 1912 a new kind of arc floodlight made it appearance, adapted from the type used in photo- engraving. This had the arcs in a metal box with the front open, and was mounted on a floor stand. In America the principal maker of these was M.J. Wohl and Co. At Vitagraph these were mostly used for special effects at first, though at Pathé and Gaumont in France similar lights were already being used by 1906 to sometimes produce a significant part of the lighting on an ordinary set. This is most noticeable in Gaumont films from 1908 onwards, where the contribution of arc lighting to the illumination of the picture became greater than at any other studio, and the more so the smaller the set that was being lit. The lights used were mostly the kind on floor stands just mentioned, and they were arranged in a rough line in front of the set on either side of the camera. There were also some street lighting arcs hung overhead, but these had much less of an effect on the look of the lighting. The standard Gaumont arrangement of lights produced a fairly crude kind of overall lighting of the scene, with the actors casting multiple shadows onto the set. This arrangement produced a certain amount of separation of the figures from the background, since by the time the light reached the back walls of the set its intensity had fallen off a little, and so the walls are slightly darker than the actors when they were several feet in front of them. But on a small set crowded with actors, as in the 1908 'Concierge'

comedies, it is all a bit of a visual mess.

In contrast, the look of the lighting is quite different in Pathé films of the same period, for these often show no obvious effect from additional lighting. Nevertheless, there is usually some faint frontal light from distant arcs on floor stands putting fill light into the actors faces in Pathé films, and sometimes these lights are a bit closer, as in the examples mentioned and illustrated in the previous chapter. When this happens, the figure modelling is better than in Gaumont films, and the general effect visually cleaner. The Pathé look is more like, but not identical to, that of the standard American studio lighting.

Lighting Effects

Returning to novel lighting effects at Vitagraph, *Foul Play* (1906) has the effect of light from a table lamp within the shot simulated rather well by an arc floodlight just out of shot on the same side of the frame. This seems to have been an innovative idea in movie-making, and the Vitagraph cameramen returned to it from time to time, though not very frequently, and it spread to films made elsewhere after a few years. Not quite so novel was the use of a small arc light placed inside a domestic light, such as a table lamp, which formed part of the decor of the set. In *After Midnight* (1908), the dominant lighting of a night interior scene is provided by a small arc light concealed in a hanging lamp over a table, and throwing light onto the actors. In this and other similar lighting set-ups in *Cupid's Realm* and *For He's a Jolly Good Fellow*, which were also made early in 1908, there is always a much weaker general diffuse light over the scene, but this in no way detracts from the strikingly natural effect. Also, in *After Midnight* one of the actors carries a hand lamp round the darkened set, lighting it up with the small arc concealed inside it, in a subtler repeat of a similar usage in *Falsely Accused*, the Hepworth film of 1905. Exactly who was responsible for introducing such lighting effects is not known, but it is possible that it was Smith and Blackton themselves, since they habitually operated the camera on the films they personally directed, at least up to 1908. The orgy of lighting effects tried out at Vitagraph in early 1908 also includes a studio scene in *'True Hearts are More Than Coronets'*, in which people stand at an open door lit from a constructed exterior set beyond it by horizontal artificial light simulating the sunset. Vitagraph films also used the standard effect of light from a fireplace, done by hiding an arc light inside it, after the model of Porter's *The Seven Ages* (1905), but none of the early Vitagraph examples has the expressive force of the device as it was used in D.W. Griffith's *The Drunkard's Reformation* (1909). However, Vitagraph may well have been the first to give a flicker to the arc light to better simulate the effect of flames, as they did in *Washington Under the American Flag* (1909).

Lighting at Biograph

The standard lighting used at Biograph continued, as it had at the end of the previous period, to be done entirely with Cooper-Hewitt mercury vapour tube racks in their completely enclosed studio. These were on floor stands and hung from the ceiling. The light from the average rack of Cooper-Hewitts was much less than that from one arc floodlight, perhaps a quater as much at a couple of yards distance from the unit, and this meant that quite a lot of them had to be used in a completely dark studio like that at Biograph. The standard set there had two walls in 'L' shape, i.e. a back wall and a side wall coming towards the front, and the Cooper-Hewitts were lined up on the other side and overhead shining down, with usually another couple of racks standing on either side of the camera at the front. Given the number of Cooper-Hewtitts used, and their width, there was not a great deal of space between each unit, and they came close to being a wall of light. Or rather, two walls and a ceiling of light. This arrangement basically still mimicked the natural lighting in a large old-style still photographer's studio which had a glass ceiling and a glass wall at one side, though the diffuse light straight on to the actors from the frontal racks had no equivalent in still photography. Since the Biograph company persisted with this standard lighting arrangement through to 1912, there came to be a subtle difference in the look of the lighting at Biograph from that used at other studios, where the supplementary lighting was mostly from arc floodlights. When it was necessary to have a set with three walls to hold another door required by D.W. Griffith's

peculiar use of action moving from room to room, only a short third wall coming out from the flats at the back was built. In this case some of the side Cooper-Hewitts could not be used, and the back of the set was appreciably underlit compared to the standard arrangement. The Biograph lighting arrangement obviously placed certain constraints on the stagings, of a sort which did not hold in other companies' studios, and may have helped to produce the markedly frontal arrangements of the actors that D.W. Griffith habitually used.

It was well into 1909, after having made a hundred films without showing the slightest interest in the use of artificial lighting for special lighting effects, that D.W. Griffith and his cameramen first tried their hand in this area. When they finally did so, although only using well-established techniques, it must be said that Griffith's placement of lighting effects within his narratives was singularly forceful. The first film in which this happened was *The Drunkard's Reformation*, in which the final scene showing the reformed drunkard reunited with his family before the hearth is lit by an arc floodlight hidden in the fireplace to simulate the light of a real fire, in exactly the same manner as Porter's *The Seven Ages* (1905). The strength of this application by Griffith lies in its contrast with the initial shot of the film, which shows the effects of unreformed drunkenness on family life, using the same camera set- up in the same room. But in this case the scene was lit with the standard general diffuse lighting of the period, with no fire effect. Similar and more elaborated examples occur in Griffith's films over the next year or so; for instance in *The Cricket on the Hearth* (1909), in which the general lighting of the set by Cooper-Hewitts is reduced during the scene so that the fire effect shows more strongly. In *Edgar Allen Poe* and *The Slave*, also from 1909, a window light effect with an actor standing or sitting by the window frame and lit by broad diffuse light coming through it appears for the first time in a Griffith film, though this too had been used elsewhere earlier. This kind of shot of a person inside a room lit by the soft light coming through a window later became a great favourite with American and European filmmakers, but it hardly ever recurs in subsequent films by D.W. Griffith.

Another aspect of the expressive use of lighting effects is the isolation of important actors in a scene. In Vitagraph's *The Life Drama of Napoleon Bonaparte and the Empress Josephine*, Napoleon and Josephine are singled out by rather stronger lighting in their area of the scene during the proceedings of their divorce. This film was released on 6 April 1909, on which very day Griffith's *A Baby's Shoe* was being shot, which is the first of his films to contain a similar use of lighting to isolate the principal in a scene. Admittedly the Griffith film develops the idea further, in that the localized area lighting is more strongly distinguished from the general lighting, and also it is produced by lowering the lighting on the surrounding set during the course of the scene. *Napoleon Bonaparte and the Empress Josephine* also uses an incomplete fade-out on the scene of Napoleon's leave-taking from Josephine, four months

The scene of Napoleon abandoning his
Empress Josephine in Vitagraph's Napoleon
Bonaparte and the Empress Josephine
(1909). Here the arrangement of the set
actors, and light source produces brighter
lighting on the principals.

before the first use by Griffith of the fade-out in his *Fools
of Fate*.

Griffith's *Pippa Passes*, which was made later in 1909 than
the films I have so far mentioned, contains a rather more
complex lighting set-up. In this film the effect of dawn light
appearing and shining through Pippa's window into her room
was achieved by opening shutters in front of two separate
lights; one to produce the light coming through the window,
and the other to put a patch of light on her bed. As well as this
the room was weakly illuminated throughout the whole
length of the scene by a few Cooper-Hewitts placed at the
front. The light levels had to be regulated by shutters, because
arc lights and Cooper-Hewitts cannot be dimmed satisfactorily by reducing the current through them, as incandescent
lights can. After a certain amount of dimming, arcs and
mercury tubes are likely to go out suddenly and unexpectedly.
The lighting of this particular scene in *Pippa Passes* was
certainly done by Arthur Marvin, but the authorship of other
complex lighting effects in Biograph films made in 1909 and
1910 is not clear at this point. Certainly after Arthur Marvin's
death early in 1911 the subsequent films lit by G.W. Bitzer
alone contain very little in the way of effects done with
artificial light. These early uses of lighting effects in Griffith
films were not always completely successful; for instance in
The Necklace (1909), there is an attempt to reproduce the
lighting of *The Cricket on the Hearth*, but the cameraman,
whether he be Marvin or Bitzer, does not get the relative light
levels from the various sources correct.

But all this was fairly exceptional, and even in 1910, the
use of effects with artificial light which are clearly intended for
the creation of mood is quite rare. In Vitagraph's *The Mystery
of Temple Court* (1910) there is a scene with lower key lighting
for a murder, but in their *Auld Lang Syne* more than a year
later, two carefully arranged low-key scenes showing two

different dark cottage rooms, each lit only by the light from a
fire and from a small window, and which are much better
handled than anything Billy Bitzer ever did, seem to be done
without expressive intent, and must be taken as purely decorative or naturalistic. However, by 1911 there begin to be
European examples of well-applied effect lighting for mood
from major companies such as Pathé, Nordisk, and then
Gaumont. Films to be mentioned include *le Courrier de Lyon*,
in which a robbery scene takes place in a room only dimly lit
by the light through the window, and a series of lonely low
key rooms similarly lit by window light in the Feuillade series
'la Vie telle quelle l'est', such as that in *la Tare*, with the
heroine ending in the depths of despair. Some slightly different examples of sinister mood effects from 1911 Danish films
are described below.

Location Lighting

All the work just discussed was done on studio sets, but
another area in which there was a slight development over
these years was in using available light in interior scenes filmed
in real locations. Although there had been a few extremely rare
and isolated examples of interior scenes shot on location
without extra lighting added, it was not until 1910 that a small
tradition of using the technique developed. Exactly who
started it is not certain, but the earliest example from this year
that I have seen is in D.W. Griffith's *Ramona*, where a scene
in a chapel is shot using available light. The only other Griffith
film using the idea during that year, and maybe for ever after,
is *A Child's Stratagem*, released in December. In this film a
scene is shot in a tram also with available light. Other examples
occur in *The Telephone*, made at Vitagraph in the middle of
the year, in which one scene takes place in a large New York
telephone exchange, without any extra artificial light being
added, and interiors in a real police station in *Clancy*, made

Location lighting with arc floodlights in a real bank vault in Coronets and Hearts *(Vitagraph, 1912)*

late in the year. In 1910 there are also shots taken inside a railway carriage on the move in *le Malheur qui n'a pas lieu* made by Lux, a minor French company, and the German *Heimgefunden; oder, Von Stufe zu Stufe - die Leibesbeichte eines Probiersmamsell*, where a café interior was also shot as found. I suspect there were other such cases in the many French and Vitagraph films from that year now lost. From this point onwards the technique, though infrequently used, can be considered to be standard.

The Vitagraph cameramen seem to have had the edge when it came to putting film lights into real locations which were too dark for filming with the available light, and a prime instance of this is in *Coronets and Hearts* (1912), though this is not the only example from Vitagraph. In this film there are

three scenes shot in a real bank, two of which are down in the bank vault, and in these the action is entirely lit by sets of arc floodlights specially brought in. I have seen nothing like this anywhere else in about one and a half thousand films made between 1906 and 1914.

The other major development in the use of artificial lighting that began in 1909, though not in Biograph films, was the first attempt at the expressive use of shadows. Vitagraph's *Oliver Twist* made in that year has a scene in Fagin's den in which an arc floodlight placed low on the floor out of shot to one side casts Fagin's shadow up on the wall when he gets near it. Although this effect does not show up too well against the general frontal diffuse lighting of the shot, it is quite clearly intentional, since the arc light was not switched

A studio interior scene from Oliver Twist *(Vitagraph, 1909) lit mostly by diffused daylight, but with an arc floodlight just out of shot low left casting Fagin's shadow up onto the wall over the foot of the stairs.*

A studio interior scene from Ved Faengslets Port *(August Blom, 1911), with lamplight simulated by an arc floodlight just out of shot left. The figure in the background (also lit by an arc floodlight) is actually out of shot, but is seen reflected in a mirror within the shot.*

on during the first occurrence of this set-up earlier in the film. A similar and slightly more obvious use of this device occurs in *Den sorte Drøm* (Urban Gad, 1911), in which a set of arcs was placed low down on the floor at the front so that at the emotional climax of the scene the actors could cast looming shadows on the back wall by moving forwards towards the lights. This usage, which was little seen before the nineteen-twenties, undoubtedly derives from the theatre of Max Reinhardt, in which it was first used in his 1906 production of Ibsen's *Ghosts*. No doubt the Vitagraph example also derives from an unknown American theatrical source. But the standard use of lighting features like these could not be developed to their full extent until it became the practice to eliminate the contribution of daylight through the studio roof, and film

interior scenes entirely by artificial light, which was not to happen for another several years.

Scandinavian Lighting

Another of the aspects of Scandinavian lighting in which they were sometimes slightly ahead of American practice was in the simulation of lamp light. In 1911, in films such as *Ved Faengslets Port*, the cameraman Axel Graatkjaer was achieving a more convincing rendering of lamp light than the earlier American attempts, by more precise control of the placement and relative intensities of the lights, though the basic set-up was no different, with a floodlight just outside the frame. A couple of years later it had become quite usual to put small arcs inside oil lamps to produce a practical light source casting

A studio scene lit in low-key by the cameraman Specht in the Gaumont company's Roman d'un mousse *(Léonce Perret, 1913). The light comes in part from a small arc in the standard lamp behind the actors, but also from an arc floodlight in front of the camera.*

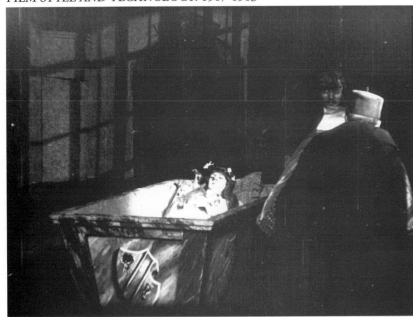

A macabre scene in Bedraget i Døden
(Dr. Gar-El-Hama I), *made at Nordisk in
1911. The low-key lighting effect here has
been obtained by control of daylight with
blinds or screens.*

a photographically effective light in such films as *Ingeborg Holm* (Victor Sjöström, 1913) and *Det Hemmelighedsfulde X* (Benjamin Christensen, 1913), and *Roman d'un mousse* (Léonce Perret, 1913). A variant of this lamp light effect has the arc light source above the top of the frame casting light straight down onto a small area of the scene beneath, without there being any ostensible source of light within the shot. Here the earliest example I know of is in a Nordisk film, *Den hvide Slavehandels sidste Offer* (1911). Like many other Danish innovations, one can see this being diffused into German films a few years later in *Der Student von Prag* (Stellan Rye, 1913). Another Danish interest was in light changes within the duration of the shot ostensibly caused by the actors switching the room lights on and off. This technique had first appeared in American films earlier than 1909, and was done with a stop-camera effect and an almost invisible cut in the shot while the lighting change was being made. But again the best Danish cameramen were able to produce a more convincing result by 1911, and the incessant use of this effect came to be a feature of Benjamin Christensen's films.

Yet another of the Danish interests in lighting was in doing low-key effects with controlled daylight, as in *Bedraget i Døden (Dr. Gar-El-Hama I)* made by Edouard Schnedler-Sørensen in 1911. In this film a small patch of direct sunlight illuminates the point of interest in a macabre interior scene of a coffin in a crypt being opened, while the surrounding set in the shot is heavily shaded off from the light so as to be dark and murky. Similar effects continue intermittently through the succeeding years in *Den flyvende Cirkus* (Alfred Lind, 1912), and other films. This particular sort of lighting seems to have been unknown in other countries at this time, and together with the lighting from a low angle already mentioned, and also other features of Danish camerawork, forms

a major influence on what is usually called German 'Expressionist' cinema.

(The word 'Expressionist' has been so abused by being attached to so many disparate things that I propose to use instead the term 'expressivist' to describe such lighting effects, and also other related filmic devices.)

Silhouette and Contre-jour Effects

The exact way silhouette effects came to be intentionally used in an integrated way in film stories is still not clear, but at the moment, 1909 seems to be a crucial year. The Italian Aquila company made a film with the a figure in semi-silhouette against window lighting in *Floriana de Lys* early in the year, and D.W. Griffith produced some much more striking examples shortly after. His *In Old Kentucky* has a skyline silhouette showing a sentry at his post, and there are semi-silhouette figures in *Lines of White on a Sullen Sea*, though in both cases they are used purely pictorially, without strong expressive connotations. The only example after this date of this feature in Griffith's Biograph films that I am aware of is a shot of figures silhouetted against the sunset in *The Yaqui Cur* (1913). Italian film-makers developed the contre-jour technique further in the Cines *Patrizia e schiava*, from near the end of the 1909, which includes a number of striking *contre-jour* shots of boats on the sea. Cave mouth contre-jour shots are found in *Il Cid* (Cines, 1910), and at the end of the Milano company's version of *L'Inferno* (1911). This last example is finely judged as an expressive effect, given its correspondence to the last four lines of the poem. But by this date a number of other film-makers had taken up the idea, principally in Europe, mostly using it for pictorial purposes, though with a gradual move over to more expressive ends. Films to be mentioned in this connection include *Ekspedi-*

The final shot of the Milano company's version of L'Inferno *(1911), with Dante and Virgil silhouetted against the light at a cave mouth as they emerge from Hell.*

tricen (August Blom, 1911), and *Dødspringet til Hest fra Cirkuskuplen* (Schnedler-Sørensen, 1912), in both of which the silhouette effects were again achieved by shooting figures in an unlighted room against the fully daylit exterior seen through a large window. An even more forceful use of silhouettes brings us back to America in 1912, with an Indian burial shot in skyline silhouette in Francis Ford's *The Indian Massacre.*

By 1913 the technique was becoming fairly standard, though still infrequently used. Many examples can be found from Italy (*L'antro funesto, Jone* and *La lampada dell nonna*), but the idea had even got as far as Russia (*Sumerki zhenskoi dushi*). Léonce Perret's *Roman d'un mousse* (1913) makes a special feature of silhouette shots, and the influence of this was

carried over into one of the films inspired by it, Benjamin Christensen's *Det Hemmelighedsfulde X* (1914), in which silhouette effects done both with daylight and artificial light, as well as with all sorts of extreme chiaroscuro of other kinds, are used throughout its entire length. Here these effects are definitely used to contribute to the atmosphere implied by the title.

Shadow Play

The only example of shadows being used expressively in this period that I know about are in Luigi Maggi's *Satana* of 1912. In this the scene of the scourging of Christ has the main action taking place off-screen, but the actions can be seen by the shadows they cast within the picture frame.

One of the silhouette shots in Léonce Perret's Roman d'un mousse *(1913).*

A scene filmed 'contre-jour' (against the light) in the Cines company film Patrizia e schiava *of 1909. The sand on the beach is scattering light back onto the back of the foreground figure, so that detail can be seen in his clothes, and the exposure has been calculated to allow for this. The other alternative would have been to expose for more detail in the sea, and let him go to a silhouette.*

The Influence from Still Photography

Backlighting on exteriors and interiors had appeared in still photography before it ever did in motion pictures. Martin Bray has located examples from the turn of the century in the work of Constant Puyo, a well-known French member of the 'Pictorialist' movement in artistic still photography. Back-lighting seems to have been his speciality, and he created numerous examples done both outdoors and in the studio. He habitually shot exterior scenes in the country with a clothed or unclothed model in the middle of them lit by the sun from behind, and exposing for the front of the figure, without any extra fill light. In studio photographs he shot close shots in the same general way, but here the backlight was usually an arc floodlight either above the model or behind her, as in one of his best known photographs, *Effet de lumière*. As well as that, in these studio photographs there is some extra fill light put onto the face from the front in one way or another. Very few of the other well-known photographers of the time used this technique, but there are some photographs by Clarence H. White, a prominent member of the American 'Photo-secession' group, which also use backlighting from the sun on exteriors. However, these are a arranged in such a way that the backlighting from the sun produces less of a rim-lighting effect, and is does not particularly draw attention to itself. From a little later, Bray has found examples of fully developed 'three-point lighting', with a backlight, plus a keylight and a fill-light from the front; for instance in a studio picture by Eva Watson, *Head of a Young Girl*, published in the January 1905 number of Stieglitz's *Camera Work*. Nevertheless, these were not common techniques in still photography, and it was several years before they began appearing in cinematography.

Backlighting with Reflector Fill

The introduction of backlighting with extra fill-lighting shone onto the front of the figures from the camera side represents another small mystery. As is well-known, credit has been claimed for this idea on behalf of D.W. Griffith by Billy Bitzer, but there are much less well-known counter-claims on behalf J.S. Blackton by his daughter Marion and by Norma Talmadge. Although most of the Vitagraph films are now lost, *Washington Under the British Flag*, which was made in the middle of 1909, and released on June 27, does have exterior scenes lit by the sun overhead, but slightly behind the actors. There is also a certain amount of light bouncing back and up into their faces from something, but it is possible that this is a natural accident, rather than specially arranged. The point is that it is possible to produce an effect that looks rather like reflector fill-lighting under certain special location and atmospheric conditions by 'splitting' the exposure. This means setting the aperture to half-way between the correct exposure for shooting with the sunlight and the correct exposure for shooting against the sunlight. Under hard sunlight from the back of the scene this usually results in over-exposed backgrounds and slightly under-exposed faces, but under diffuse or hazy sunlight the result can be quite good. Anyway, the effect in *Washington Under the British Flag* is much the same as when the technique became standard in outdoor filming in American films a year or so later, when such scenes were usually taken with the sun somewhat lower down from the zenith. The first D.W. Griffith film in which there is any possible backlighting is *The Message*, which was shot after the Vitagraph film and released a month later. This is the first of a small group of films which he made at Greenwich, Connecticut, around the beginning of June 1909, and there may also be similar weak backlighting in the others, which include *The Cardinal's Conspiracy* and *Sweet and Twenty*, but it has not been possible to confirm this, as the only prints available at the moment are 16 mm. copies from the paper prints de-

One of the scenes from Washington Under the British Flag *(Vitagraph, 1909) which is backlit by the sun. There is also light being reflected back up onto the figures from some very light coloured surface in front of the actors and below the bottom of the frame.*

posited for copyright in the Library of Congress, and the quality of these is rather poor when compared to good 35 mm. duplicates from an original. (It is worth remarking in passing that one can miss details of the lighting even when viewing good 35 mm. prints on a viewing machine; often only high intensity projection can reveal such finest details as whether reflectors or artificial light were used in location exterior lighting.) But if this was indeed intentional backlighting in these films, the mystery is why the technique was not used in the other Griffith films made on other locations around the same time, or in the fifty films he made afterwards through the rest of 1909. The query as to the exact method, if any, used in this group of Griffith films from 1909 arises because there were contemporary reports of arc lights being used on location exteriors in British film-making, although I have seen no visual evidence of this. But in American films there is a surviving Vitagraph film from 1909 which has arc lighting on an exterior scene. This is *Betty's Choice*, in which a garden scene shot under dullish daylight has the light on the figures boosted and sharpened by the light from an arc floodlight just out of shot.

In any case, after the mysterious hiatus, the use of backlighting on exteriors came back to stay in Griffith's films with *The Threads of Destiny*, one of the first he made on the Biograph company's first trip to California in 1910. There is no question but that the process was now one of reflecting sunlight coming from behind the figures of the actors back towards their faces with a sheet of matt white reflecting material. The credit for applying this device to film has been given to Billy Bitzer, but Arthur Marvin was also on camera during this trip, and in any case the technique of reflector fill-light had been standard in studio portrait photography for about a decade.

The use of reflector fill-lighting on exteriors spread to other American cameramen over the next few years, and by 1914 it

was applied quite generally on location filming whenever it was possible and appropriate. This was not the case in Europe, in part because the light there is less suitable, with relatively few days of bright direct sunlight each year. Even late in the 'twenties one sees major European films all of whose exteriors are shot with direct frontal sunlight.

Figure Lighting

Backlighting of the actors combined with fill-light from the front is the start of figure lighting as a technique independent of the general lighting of the scene, and from the beginning it was used to make the actors look more attractive regardless of other considerations bearing directly on the particular narrative. Right at the end of 1910 Bitzer and Griffith made the obvious application of the technique to a studio interior scene in the same way that they had been doing it for a year on exteriors. The film was *Fate's Turning*, but thereafter it was used only infrequently by them in the occasional single scene in a film. For instance, the well-known shot of Mae Marsh in the hall of her parents' house in *Birth of a Nation* is the only occurrence of this technique in interiors in the whole of that film. Other studios did not take up this technique for interior photography at all within the period we are considering.

However, a variant of this approach did begin to appear amongst the interior shots lit in the established simple frontal style in some of the films from other major companies in 1912 and 1913. This was what one might call 'three-quarters back lighting', and was applied from arc floodlights and sometimes Cooper-Hewitt banks on floor stands (i.e. at about eye-level), and placed rather behind the actors and off-screen at one side. This arrangement produced marked figure modelling as well as separation from the background, as one can see from the illustration.

The exact evolution of figure lighting over these few years

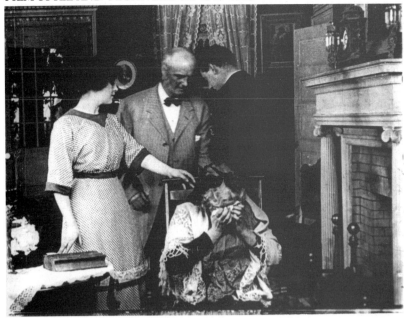

A studio interior scene from A Brother's Devotion *(Vitagraph, 1910), showing the Vitagraph angle and staging up to the 'nine-foot line'. the lighting is partly from general diffuse lighting, and partly from a group of arc floodlights on floor stands out of shot to the left. Note rapid fall-off in light level towards the back of the set producing a degree of separation of the figures from the background.*

is not yet completely clear to me, but the example illustrated, and others like it from 1913, may have alternatively evolved through the gradual movement of lighting units from the quarter front position to a side position, as in the illustration from Vitagraph's *A Brother's Devotion* (1910). This scene is largely lit by groups of arc floodlights ranged out of shot at the left, and this arrangement already produces quite good figure modelling. Because of the rapid fall-off in intensity towards the back of the set inherent in floodlighting, it also gives fairly good separation of the figures from the background, and that to a greater degree than the standard overall frontal lighting of the period. By 1912 much stronger lighting from directly at the sides, and producing nearly all the illumination on the scene, can be seen in a number of films,

particularly those from the Rex company, where the light was applied in this manner from *both* sides. Examples can also be found in the films from other companies made in 1913, but like all advanced work with artificial lighting in this period, these were confined to films produced in the New York area, and only a limited number of those at that. After this development of side lighting it may be that the move to three-quarters back lighting seemed the next obvious move, and was made as such.

As this work on figure lighting developed at other studios, Bitzer and Griffith *did* have one or two tries at it, as in *Friends* made in July 1912. In this film, as in a few others from this time, Bitzer did use arc lights to get some light into the back corners of a set with a staircase built in. (Sets with a proper

The combination of 'three-quarters back' lighting coming from the left behind the characters in the foreground, plus the more usual lighting from sets of arc floodlights from the right and left front. A studio interior scene in Vitagraph's Coronets and Hearts *(1912).*

This scene from D.W. Griffith's Friends
*(1912) is lit with the Cooper-Hewitt
arrangement usual at their New York studio
- lights left, above, and front.*

staircase built into them are extremely rare in Biograph films, probably because the small size of their New York studio made this difficult.) But more importantly, *Friends* has some Medium Close Ups of Mary Pickford cut into a couple of the scenes, and when these were taken the lighting was adjusted from that in the general shot of the scene, which was the usual Biograph Cooper-Hewitt arrangement. An arc floodlight was brought in from side-front to the actress, and with the exposure adjusted for the now higher light level, the background to the shot became very dark. This is the earliest obvious example of this kind of lighting readjustment (or 'cheating', as it came to be called), that I have noticed.

Around 1912 there was a definite move in all the major film-making countries towards having the majority of the lighting in studio scenes provided by artificial light, rather than by the diffuse daylight through the studio roof and walls, which was the usual case before. However, this is more visible in the films of some companies than of others, and of course Gaumont had already arrived at this position on their own several years before. The other important exception was Biograph, but in that case the Cooper Hewitt lighting in their New York studio almost perfectly mimicked the diffuse daylight in other company's studios, so from a visual point of view it was not an exception at all. This change over to a greater contribution from artificial light was accompanied by greater diversity in exactly how the light was applied to different parts of the scene.

As far as standard studio lighting was concerned, Vitagraph

*For the Medium Close Up cut into
the previous scene shown above, the camera
has been moved almost straight in, and an
arc floodlight has been added high left front.
This light is doing most of the lighting of the
face, and the exposure has been adjusted to
take account of this. Thus the background
has got relatively darker. The mismatch in
the position of the actress across the cut is
quite typical of Griffith's practice.*

Low-key lighting in Conscience *(Vitagraph, 1912). The scene is solely lit by groups of arc floodlights in the side alcoves out right and also out left in the back alcove. There is also a single weak arc light out left to light the man sitting in the chair.*

was the most advanced company, and a good example of the best practice there in 1912 is provided by the film *Conscience*. A key scene in this film is the first genuine example of low-key lighting (i.e. most of the frame is very dark) that I have seen done solely with artificial lighting. In other scenes in this film the dominant lighting is from small groups of arc lights on either side of the camera at about 45 degrees to the lens axis. When an actor is closer to one set of lights than the other, that set of lights acts as the key (principal) light, and the other set as fill light, and vice-versa. This approach gives a fairly natural fall-off in light intensity towards the walls of the set, and much improved modelling of the features. It also gives fairly good separation of the figures from the background, though not as good as that with overhead back-lighting with its bright rim effect. The same approach was also sometimes applied by

Vitagraph cameramen to location interiors, these being totally lit with arc floodlights for the first time ever, as in scenes in a real bank vault in *Coronets and Hearts* (1912).

Parallel developments in lighting to those I have described can also be observed a year or so later in the films of the major French companies, particularly Gaumont. There arc lighting was regularly used to touch up the modelling of parts of a large scene in the previous period, and can be seen continued in various films from *The White Slave* (1909) to *Good for Evil* (1913). Italian practice, which at the beginning of the period entirely followed French models, and in the middle of it shows influences from Vitagraph and Nordisk as far as contemporary subjects are concerned, finally developed an element of individuality in some aspects of film lighting. One example of this is the use of lighting applied from a low angle in Guazzoni's

Another studio interior scene in Conscience *lit almost entirely by arc floodlights out side left and side front right. Their reflection can just be seen in the milk bottle sitting on the table. Note how the light intensity from this arrangement falls off rapidly towards the back wall of the set.*

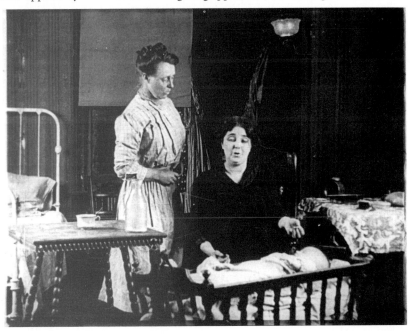

Nero plays while Rome burns in Quo Vadis? *(Enrico Guazzoni, 1912). The shot is lit solely by an arc floodlight well below the camera angle shining upwards.*

Quo Vadis? (1912). This usage was then carried further in *Cabiria*, where the effect was similarly naturalistically motivated by a large-scale fire out of shot. In another scene in *Cabiria* the source of this low-angle lighting was actually in the shot, and the aim was apparently to suggest a weird atmosphere. Semi-silhouette effects also occasionally appear in Italian films. Finally, the most massive use of arc lights up to this date took place on some of the giant sets of *Cabiria*.

Advanced and Retarded Styles

The photographic features which have been discussed in the previous few pages were not, at the date of the particular films mentioned, typical of most films made in that year. However they did come into use a few years later in the majority of films made in their place of origin, and for this reason I find it useful to describe them as advanced stylistic features. In this context this expression is purely descriptive, and does not imply a value judgement. On the other hand, particularly in this early period, there were always a minority group of films that were still using the forms of the majority of films of an earlier period, and such forms and features I will describe as retarded. Obviously, what constitutes advanced and retarded features keeps changing with the time and place of production of the film under consideration, as the norms applying to the majority of films change. An example of a retarded photographic feature is given by those films made in 1908 or later in the U.S.A. which have their interior scenes still shot solely under direct, undiffused sunlight. This feature was still so common in European films in 1908 that it does not constitute a retarded feature in that context, though it does by 1913. The concepts of advanced and retarded features also have application to other dimensions or aspects of style such as the amount of cutting within scenes, and so on.

Tinting and Toning

During the years 1907 to 1913 the conventions of tinting can be observed stabilizing, and the position was being reached where most films were coloured in one way or another. In 1907 the use of blue tinting for night exteriors actually shot in full daylight, as they all were, was fairly standard, as was the use of red tinting for interiors being consumed by fire, and both can be seen in Vitagraph's *The Mill Girl.* By 1913 the other standard colour was orange or amber (yellow-brown) for candle-lit or lamp-lit scenes. Green tinting was sometimes used for weird or gruesome scenes, and light pink for early morning, but daylight exteriors and modern interiors understood from the context to be lit by daylight or incandescent light were usually left untinted.

The use of toning – the alteration of only the black silver part of the image by chemical treatment – was less common because of the greater cost of the chemicals involved, and films such as *The Great Train Hold-Up* (Pathé, 1910), which has the exteriors toned green and the interiors toned sepia, are rare. The toning is quite effective in this particular instance because grass and forest trees form most of the backgrounds in the exteriors. Where such tonings exist in the original copies they are virtually never reproduced in modern duplicate prints made from them.

Pathé Stencil-Tinting

A process for mechanically colouring different parts of the image in different colours was developed by the Pathé company from 1905, and reached its perfected form in 1908. This process largely replaced the hand-painting of copies of their films which had been a speciality of the company before 1908, and the new stencil-tinting continued to be used by them on some films up until the nineteen-thirties. In the years we are concerned with its use seems to have been restricted to trick films and exotic and historical subjects, both fictional and documentary. Pathé also re-released some of their popular films made earlier than 1908 in stencil-tinted form, which has created a certain amount of confusion. The technique involved taking one positive print for each colour that was to appear in the film being stencil-tinted, and then cutting out the areas in every frame that were to be coloured that particular colour, so forming a stencil, (or rather a series of stencils), for every frame down the length of the film. The stencil film for one colour was then run through a machine sandwiched against an uncoloured print, while rotating brushes applied dye of the appropriate colour to the film through the stencil. The other colours were applied through their own lengths of stencil film in successive applications on successive machines. Although the labour involved in cutting the stencils was considerable, the efficiency of the subsequent stages made the process worth-while in view of Pathé's large sales world-wide. At first the cutting of the stencils was done directly with a scalpel, but in 1907 an improvement was introduced, in which the frame being worked on was projected onto a screen, where the operator traced the outline of the area to be cut out with a pointer linked by a reducing pantograph arrangement to an electrically driven vibrating needle which actually cut out the small required area on the film frame itself. The process must also have helped the appeal of the 'Film d'Art' series after 1908, for these films were otherwise somewhat retarded in style.

The colours in surviving copies of Pathé stencil-tinted films made using the improved method after 1907 are rather pale when compared with those of hand-painted films, and it seems probable that they were so originally, and that this was a characteristic of the process. The registration of the colours is quite good from frame to frame, even on the garments of moving figures, so that the general effect is as if one of the carefully hand- tinted photographs or post-cards so common at the beginning of the century had come to life.

The Kinemacolor Process

The only genuine colour process to become a commercial reality before Technicolor was the Kinemacolor process, which was developed by G.A. Smith from an earlier unsuccessful attempt by Edward R. Turner at a three-colour additive process. This in its turn was a direct application of the Clerk Maxwell system of three-colour still photography which was in use at the turn of the century.

To reproduce approximately the full range of colours in natural scenes, analysis and synthesis in terms of three correctly chosen spectral colours is necessary, but until the nineteen-thirties only markedly imperfect two-colour systems had to suffice in films. In the Kinemacolor process in its final form the film was shot with an ordinary Moy-Bastie camera slightly modified by having an extra co-axial disc with two gelatine filter segments mounted behind the ordinary shutter. This was geared to revolve at half the shutter speed so that for the first

exposure the red filter was interposed in front of the film frame while the shutter was open, while for the next exposure the green filter was in front of the frame, and then the cycle continued to repeat for successive pairs of frames. Various filter combinations were used for different types of scene and light conditions, the most usual being a red and cyan (blue-green) pair, which indeed in principle should give the most satisfactory combination for a two-colour system. The red frames gave a record in a black and white silver image of the intensities of the red light from various areas of the scene, and the alternating green frames gave a record of the complementary intensities of green (or blue-green) light from the appropriate parts of the scene. The negative used was ordinary orthochromatic film specially sensitized by the Kinemacolor company to produce a panchromatic emulsion which would respond to red light as well as to blue and green. The exposed film was developed and printed in exactly the standard way, and the result was a positive with a succession of black and white silver images, of which the odd-numbered ones had light areas corresponding to the most intense sources of red light in the picture, and the even ones had their lightest areas corresponding to the most intense sources of blue-green light. White areas in the original scene produced an equally light area in both records.

The Kinemacolor film was projected with a projector of one of the standard designs, but having the same modification of an extra filter disc coaxial to the shutter as in the Kinemacolor camera. Both taking and projection speeds were 32 frames per second, and the shortened exposure time resulting, plus the extra light absorption by the camera filters, meant that films could only be satisfactorily shot under bright sunlight. This ruled out scenes made under the best studio lighting conditions of the period. The limited number of fictional films made by the Kinemacolor company were also unsatisfactory in other respects, and this was responsible for the final demise of the process, for in the absence of competing colour processes the other faults of Kinemacolor were less noticeable at the time. These faults included the inability to reproduce certain colours, particularly blue and yellow, and also the colour fringes produced by objects in fast motion. Since the red image was taken and projected 1/32nd. of a second after the corresponding cyan image, a fast moving object had time to change its position in the frame, and hence be seen as two separate red and green objects. This 'motion fringing' was the downfall of many later attempts at colour cinematography, particularly those using an additive system of colour combination. As well as this, all additive systems, including Kinemacolor, which by their nature reproduce white light by adding together red, green, and blue (or red and cyan) light from separate image records, give less brightness on the screen than either ordinary black and white film, or the subtractive colour processes which were ultimately successful. However, the most irritating characteristic of the process, at any rate to my eyes, is the heavy flicker noticeable on scenes which included a large amount of white, or near-white, in the

The Debrie Parvo seen from the front with the door to the compartment holding the 400 foot feed magazine open, and also the front containing the shutter and lens lifted up to show the film path through the gate.

Seen from the front with the front section closed. Note the supplementary viewfinder attached to the right of the body. this consists of a small square diverging lens at the front of the camera, and a set of peepsight holes at the back to allow for different degrees of parallax correction.

picture area, as a result of the alternation of bright red and green frames on the actual film. (The eye does not actually distinguish the separate red and green frames of course, but the impression of white synthesised by the brain seems to flicker violently.)

Kinemacolor was exhibited successfully from 1908 to 1915 in the larger cities of the major film distribution areas, most of the films shown being documentary subjects. A two hour film of the Delhi Durbar of 1911 was particularly successful.

Cameras

A new camera of major importance, the Debrie Parvo, made its appearance in 1908, though it was not extensively used till after 1914. This was largely because it was much more expensive than the existing cameras. The Debrie Parvo was the smallest professional-quality camera available, being entirely enclosed within a rectangular wooden casing measuring 6 inches by 8 inches by 10 inches. Unlike other cameras of the time, this wooden casing was no more than an enclosing shell, and the gears, film gate, etc. were mounted on, and contained within, a metal chassis. The film was fed from one pre-loaded 400 foot spool box inserted into one side of the camera,

through the gate and into another spool box inserted into the other side of the camera coaxially with the first. The gearing and claw movement were between the two boxes. The Parvo had a 'one turn – one frame' animation crank-handle position, and a shutter with adjustable opening, as was now the case for all professionally-used cameras, and the usual eyepiece at the back of the camera for framing and focussing the image on the back of the film before shooting. Its supplementary view-finder for use while actually taking a shot was a simple rectangular negative lens fastened to the side of the camera at the front in which, when the eye was placed behind a peep-sight at the back, a tiny reduced erect image of the scene in shot could be seen. This arrangement left something to be desired as a means of checking what was in frame during the course of the shot. The Debrie Parvo design was copied by the German Ernemann company in 1909 for one of the models in their range of cameras, presumably under some sort of license from Debrie.

An alternative arrangement for viewfinding during shooting came to be added to the Pathé Studio camera during these years; a supplementary viewfinder that formed a real, inverted image on a ground-glass screen at the back of a tube fastened to the side of the camera. This image had the advantage that it was larger and could be viewed by the eye from various directions. The inversion of the image, though no great encouragement to making panning shots, was not so great a disadvantage as it might seem nowadays, since all cameramen at this time had been still photographers, and were quite used to working with inverted images on the ground-glass backs of the still cameras of the period.

The Bell & Howell Camera

By 1910 the Bell & Howell company of Chicago were well established as the major maker of film perforating machinery in the United States, with a very superior product, and in that year they produced their first film camera. This was built on the English pattern inside a rectangular wooden box, with the magazines for the film also inside. It had one unusual feature, which was that the lens was mounted on a plate which could be slid up and down vertically on the front of the main camera casing. This acted in a limited way like the usual rising front

The Bell & Howell studio camera on its panning and tilting head. The camera has been slid over to the right of the head into the fine focussing position, with the taking lens rotated to the left side of the turret. The focussing eyepiece is immediately in front of the crank handle. The gears producing the tilting movement of the head can be seen on the circular base.

on a plate camera for still photography, and enabled the converging verticals in the image to be corrected when taking a shot centred above or below the horizontal. A few models were sold to the local film companies in Chicago, Selig and Essanay, but these companies did not adopt it as their standard camera. After considering their experience with this model, and also what cameramen seemed to consider desirable in an ideal camera, Bell & Howell designed the 2709 model, which was first made available in 1912.

This camera was unusual in being constructed entirely of metal, with the body machined from cast aluminium, and it was approximately 15 inches tall including the magazines on top, 15 inches long, and 7 inches wide. Its total weight was about 27 lb. The gears ran in ball-bearings at the crucial points, and the variable opening of the shutter could be changed while the camera was running, so making fades in the camera possible at any lens aperture. The film movement was quite different to any that had been before; a 'shuttle gate' lifted up the film away from the front of the gate onto the claws, which then moved it forward, after which the shuttle gate pulled it down off the claws onto the fixed register pins protruding from the back of the gate aperture plate. This was in fact the first camera to have register pins holding the film completely steady and in a precise position with respect to the evenly spaced perforations in the film, and it was alone in this for a long time. (Although the Biograph camera had punches cutting the perforations as the exposure was made, and so holding the film steady, its pull-down mechanism using rubber pinch rollers did not give perfectly even spacing of those perforations.) Another important feature that was built into the Bell & Howell was an accurate frame counter which facilitated the making of accurate dissolves and other special effects. In fact all the features of this camera so far mentioned contributed to making it outstandingly suited to filming special effects of every kind. The lenses were mounted on a rotatable turret with space for four lenses, which was fixed on the front plate of the camera. Focussing was accomplished by rotating the turret through 180 degrees so that the lens which was to be used in taking the shot was in front of the ground-glass screen on the other side of the camera, where the image on it could be viewed through an eyepiece to the side of the camera. Before this was done the camera was slid sideways on the special baseplate on which it was mounted so that the lens was restored to the position in space that it would occupy when the shot was actually photographed – the two displacements by rotating the camera turret and moving the body cancelling to eliminate the parallax that would otherwise occur. The camera also had a supplementary viewfinder system for use when the shot was actually being taken. Although the Bell & Howell camera was first made available in 1912, very few cameramen acquired them before 1914, despite their many advantages. This must have been because of its very high price, in the region of $2000.

Camera Movements

Although the unsatisfactory viewfinding arrangements on the cameras in regular use must have provided some pressure against the free use of panning shots in this period, but they did not prevent skilful cameramen from occasionally making them. Although the majority of films were shot with a totally static camera, the place the occasional panning shot is most likely to turn up is in the exteriors of American Westerns, where the uncertainty as to the precise movements of the actors in action sequences demanded the ability to adjust the framing during the shot. Danish films also include occasional framing tilts and pans, and even fully developed pans, even on interior scenes, from *Røverens Brud* (Viggo Larsen, 1907) onwards. Taking production for this period as a whole, camera movements are more likely to occur than they were in the previous several years, even if they are still not common, and in this respect D.W. Griffith's films conform to the general pattern, with about one in ten containing a camera movement of some kind to keep the action in frame. However, a few of them are exceptional, in that it can be seen that pans supplied by the cameraman at the end of the shot have been cut off in the editing, as in *The Drive for Life* (1909) and *The Massacre* (1912), presumably in the pursuit of an increased cutting rate to speed the action.

An example of the kind of conscious virtuoso effect which I mentioned at the beginning of this chapter as beginning to be introduced into films in these years is provided by the complex series of pans and tilts within the length of one continuous shot following a group of horsemen on a zigzag path down a hillside in Allan Dwan's *The Fear*. The extensive pans over the landscape (not following action), which begin and end Griffith's *The Country Doctor* (1909), are completely exceptional in his work, and I have not seen anything else of this nature from this period, except the 270 degree pan round the deck of a liner in the middle of *Captured by Bedouins* (Sidney Olcott, 1912). American film-makers had a strong prejudice against wasting valuable screen time on atmosphere, when it could be used to accommodate more central story material.

Tracking shots of any kind were still extremely rare, and it was only in 1912 that we can see the beginning of a real tradition in their use. I think that film-makers in the silent period, and to some extent later, made a distinction between those tracking shots that followed people around in some way, whether with the camera on a special carriage moving beside or in front of walking actors, or on a powered vehicle moving along with another powered vehicle containing the action, and on the other hand those tracking shots which moved the camera relative to a fixed scene. Some film-makers have undoubtedly gone on record as condemning the latter variety as drawing attention to the technique of filming, and their relative rarity in the silent period suggests that this feeling was general. Nevertheless, there are rare examples of the use of tracking relative to a quasi-static scene in this period, and a number of them come from the Hepworth (or Hepwix, as it

was now known) company in Britain. In the earliest of these surviving, *An Old Soldier* (1910), the camera tracks very slowly in and out over a small distance almost imperceptibly during some very long scenes. There seems to be some sort of relation between these moves and the dramatic course of the action, so presumably they are intended to have the kind of intensifying function that became standard much later. There are other Hepworth examples from 1910 and through to 1912, and these include *Church and State* and *The Deception*, though in these the tracks in and out are even smaller.

Also in 1912, in the United States, we have the very impressive instance in *The Passer-by* (Oscar Apfel, 1912), in which the camera tracks slowly in from a Long Shot of a man addressing a table of diners to a Medium Close Shot of him, which then dissolves into a flashback of the story he is narrating, and at its conclusion the process is reversed. I think there may well have been other examples of this sort of thing at the time, for the handling is quite assured in this film. The next case of a tracking shot used on a more or less static scene that comes to mind is towards the end of *Traffic in Souls* (1913), where the camera tracks sideways in front of a row of prison cells containing some of the villains of the piece. In the Hepworth company *At the Foot of the Scaffold* (1913), the camera tracks sideways from one room into another past the wall dividing them, to follow an actor who goes through the door joining the two rooms. Despite all these earlier examples, there is no question but that the really influential use of tracking shots on quasi-static scenes occurred in *Cabiria*, made in Italy by Giovanni Pastrone in 1913, but not seen elsewhere till the next year. This film contains a number of slow diagonal tracks into spectacular scenes from Very Long Shot to something only a bit closer, and so great was this film's fame that the tracking shot on a quasi-static scene was referred to in America for some years afterwards as the 'Cabiria movement'.

The more common kind of tracking shot, with the camera moving alongside or in front of a moving vehicle, has a sparse but continuous existence carrying through from the previous period and the elopement chase films. Hepworth again contributed examples in *John Gilpin's Ride* (1908), but some of the most striking examples after 1908 occur in D.W. Griffith's films. In his *The Drive for a Life*, a car-mounted camera tracks in front of another car containing an amorous couple, and the shot continues while a cab containing the man's abandoned mistress drives up behind and observes the couple until their car drives out of shot, leaving the mistress's chagrin to register before the end. It is in the detailed way a piece of staging is invented and worked out here, as in a hundred other differently unique cases, that the achievement of D.W. Griffith lies, and not in his having been the first to use the parallel tracking shot, or anything else for that matter. But it is from 1912 that the use of the parallel tracking shot really increases in films from all the major film producing countries, usually following action on cars or trains. Examples include Griffith again in *The Girl and Her Trust* using a car-mounted camera to film a train running alongside, Schnedler-Sørensen in Denmark filming a trolley ahead from a train following it, and so on.

Camera Speeds

The impression of 'rush and turmoil' in Griffith's films that troubled some critics, but not anyone else that we know about, may have been due in part to the curious fact that many of them are shot slower than 16 frames per second throughout. In this period most other American and European cameramen had settled down to this steady cranking speed (though perhaps just slightly faster at Vitagraph and some of the European companies), but many of Griffith's films made in 1913 are shot at around 14 frames per second, or even a little lower. The result of this would be that if the projectionists ran them at the same speed as other films, the actors would have moved about appreciably faster than was natural. Kevin Brownlow has suggested to me that Griffith used the slower speed so as to get a longer film into the length of the single reel to which the Biograph management limited him, and since these 1913 Griffith films are all very full reels, being very close to 1000 ft., this seems quite plausible.

Slightly later, in 1914, Griffith went on record as expecting projectionists to give him expressive variations in *their* cranking speed to go with the nature of particular scenes in his films made in that year, but since many reminiscences tell us that what projectionists did was not predictable by the film-makers, I think that the chances were that a film that was shot slower than 16 frames a second stood more chance of being projected too fast than one shot at 16 frames a second, and the chances of getting expressive variations throughout the length of a film were very poor.

Expressive variations in cranking speed of a crude kind that were made by cameramen, not projectionists, had already begun in this period, as the undercranking of chases and slapstick scenes was already being used in comedies. Severe undercranking down to several frames per second was also being used to make a particular joke in comic scenes about people moving much faster under the effect of some peculiar stimulus, as in *Liquid Electricity* (Vitagraph, 1907).

Special Effects

Various special effects techniques that had earlier only been used in little 'trick' films came to be used in substantial dramatic films in these years. One instance of this is provided by that variety of composite photography in which the upper part of the frame is masked off in the camera while a scene occupying the lower part is filmed, and then a second exposure is made on the same length of film, with the inverse masking of the lower part of the frame with a counter-matte. There are a number of examples of this in obscure films of the period, but the most spectacular examples are in some of the big Italian films such as *L'Inferno* and *Cabiria*. In these films a scene in a real landscape is extended by painted or model sets in the upper part of the frame. Although it was possible with care to get apparently seamless images, as in the first film

mentioned, usually there was a fuzzy black line between the two parts of the combined image, representing inaccurate relative positioning of the matte and counter-matte on the successive exposures. Another problem was caused by relative motion of the two parts of the image; that is, a jiggle due to poor registration of the frames of the film in the camera gate. This is inevitably worse in cameras without registration pins, as was the case for all makes at this date, particularly when they have seen a lot of use. However, it was possible to reduce this fault considerably by careful choice of the camera used.

This was done in the Pathé trick films which continued to be made on the Méliès model throughout the years 1907-1912, presumably by picking out those brand new Pathé cameras with the best registration as they came off the production line. Although these Pathé trick films mostly used techniques pioneered by Georges Méliès, they brought greater precision to their execution as far as trick position matching and cutting went, as well as in image registration. They were also shot closer in and used more attractive performers than Méliès did, so beating him on his home ground. A number of these Pathé films make use of miniature human figures interacting with a full-sized one on the pattern of a Robert Paul film of 1901, *Lilliputians in a London Restaurant*, though they surpass their model in precision, as can be seen in *les Pantins de Miss Hold* (1908).

The basic technique of making objects move by single frame animation had been well established by Edwin S. Porter and J. Stuart Blackton in earlier years, but when Segundo de Chomon and other Pathé film-makers finally came to understand the method in late 1907 they applied it to making transformations in clay sculpture and silhouettes as well as for moving solid objects about. In *Sculpture moderne* (1908) figures of birds, people, etc. made in modelling clay gradually metamorphose into one another, apparently without human intervention, by the use of small changes made to them between the exposures of a succession of single frames.

There is a Pathé film of unknown original title in the Moscow archive which dates from around 1908, and which is an anthology of just about everything that the trick film unit of the company could do at that date. Its basic framework is a standard live-action 'haunted inn' story, but it includes sequences of simple stop-camera tricks, frame by frame object animation, live action silhouette projections, and also the novelty of objects animated as silhouettes, in what we now think of as the Lotte Reiniger manner. This was pretty well a clean sweep of the animation field (though they missed out computer animation), and as icing on the cake the film also contains numerous cuts in to a closer shot during the live action sections. To be perfectly honest, all this adds up to a rather messy film overall, and even with these new techniques the trick film staggered to its commercial doom over the next few years.

Glass Matte Painting

Although strictly speaking the technique of glass matte

painting was invented in 1910, it was not really used in fictional films till after 1913, so I will deal with it in the next chapter.

Camera Lenses

By 1912 Zeiss lenses of 35 mm. and 40 mm. focal length were available, but it is very doubtful that they were used to any great extent. Certainly I have seen no definite visible effect of the use of any lens as wide as 35 mm., but I cannot be absolutely sure, since the stagings of that time did not have things up close to the camera during a scene, and in any case the tiny amount of perspective distortion produced by a 35 mm. lens when compared to the reproduction with a 50 mm. lens is very hard to recognize. Some cameramen at the time referred to a 40 mm. lens as a wide-angle lens, which it certainly is not in the sense of producing perspective distortion, since that focal length gives correct perspective with an image of the silent film size. It also seems that some people regarded a 3 inch lens as a standard lens during this period, but this seems to be a reflection of newsreel and 'topical' film-making attitudes rather than being the best professional practice in fictional film-making. The 35 mm. lens I first mentioned had a maximum aperture of f4.5, but the maximum aperture of 2 inch lenses was around f3.5 at this time; the principal manufacturers being Voigtländer, Busch, Dallmeyer, and Taylor-Hobson besides Zeiss. The only appreciably faster lens was a Dallmeyer 3-inch lens with an aperture of f1.9, but though this may have been used in actuality filming, there is no reason to suppose that it was ever used for fiction films, particularly since it would have given poor definition at its maximum aperture. In fact even the standard lenses of the time had noticeably inferior definition at maximum aperture, as can be seen in the famous scene in Griffith's *Pippa Passes* (1909) in which the dawn light comes into Pippa's room. This was filmed with just sufficient light to get an exposure, and hence at maximum aperture, and the effect on the image definition is quite noticeable. Long lenses of several inches focal length continued to be readily available, but they were still not used except for wild-life filming.

Shot Transitions

Although all the special forms of transition from one shot to another – fade, dissolve, wipe, and iris – had appeared as isolated instances in earlier years, it was only in this period that we can see the beginnings of their general use by film-makers. Fades continued to be fairly rare until 1912, mainly occurring to represent transitions into or out of dreams, as in the Pathé film *Rêves d'agent* (1908). But in 1909 the Vitagraph film *Life Drama of Napoleon Bonaparte and the Empress Josephine*, released on 6/4/09, has a fade-out which does not go to complete blackness after Napoleon says farewell to his Empress Josephine. It could be claimed that this use of the fade-out has an emotional function as well as indicating a time lapse, since there are other time lapses in this film which are just bridged in the usual way with an intertitle. When D.W.

Griffith first took up the fade a few months later in *Fools of Fate* the fade-out was used to end an exterior scene which was supposed to be taking place at the end of the day, and it seems possible that here the fade was intended to represent sunset taking place. Certainly the next scene starts after an intertitle indicating that it is now the next day. In *Lines of White on a Sullen Sea* there is a fade-out used to indicate a time lapse, but over the next year or so there are only two or three fade-outs in Griffith's films, and they are either at the end of the film or at the end of a sequence. In the latter case they represent the beginning of the convention that a fade-out represents a time lapse between shots. By 1912 this usage was beginning to become common in American films, often with the fade-out followed by a fade-in, rather than the straight cut to the next shot as had been the case earlier, e.g. *The One She Loved* (D.W. Griffith, 1912) and *The Flaming Arrow* (Bison 101, 1913). However it must be noted that in 1913 there were a number of films which also use the same transition of a fade-out followed by a fade-in to indicate a flashback of the kind I have described in a previous section. Although some European film-makers had been involved very early in the development of the flashback, and indeed used fades for this in the two films of *L'Inferno*, they were a bit slow on the whole to take up the fade, and it is only in 1913 that we get an a fair number of films using fades for time lapses, or to go to a mental image represented in a single shot. The one exception to this generalization was the British Hepworth company, which around 1912 seems to have adopted a policy of taking all, or nearly all, the shots in their films with a fade-in at the beginning and a fade-out at the end. Often these fades were trimmed off in the editing, sometimes only partially, but whichever was the case, the idea didn't help the speed of the narrative in Hepworth films. In the American production there are a few films which contain fade-out – fade-ins used both to indicate a transition to a flashback, and for time lapses as well, as for instance in *The Tiger* (Fred Thomson, 1913). Clearly the context determined the meaning of the types of transition used, then as later. It is also quite possible that some of these fades are really failed attempts at dissolves made in the camera, as had happened in earlier times, for cameras were still not fitted with accurate footage counters.

Dissolves were still used sometimes for indicating the transition into a dream during this period, but mostly they were used for indicating entry or exit into or out of a flashback, and hardly ever for indicating a time lapse. Just about the only other thing that I have found a dissolve used for during these years is as an alternative to the cut in going to a parallel action, and this only in two European films. These are the Hepworth company's *A Woman's Treachery* made in 1910, and in the well-known *l'Enfant de Paris*, made in 1913 by Léonce Perret. Given that there are a few other European films made after 1913 that use the same device for initiating a sequence of parallel action, I think there may well have been other examples of this before 1913 in films now lost. Besides all the preceding, there are a few curious uses of the dissolve in

Vitagraph films. In their famous *Haunted House* of 1907, a dissolve is used to bridge the transition from the exterior of the house, shown in a model shot, to the interior, which is a studio set, and in *The Battle Hymn of the Republic* (1911), dissolves join each image illustrating the poem. This latter usage could obviously be considered to be a hangover from the lantern slide show conventions, but at the same time it might be thought to look forward to the montage sequence, which was not very far away in the future.

The use of the iris-in and iris-out also begins during 1913, but the priority for this between D.W. Griffith and the Thomas Ince company remains uncertain, for both made a few films in that year that include irising, for example *Just Gold* (Griffith), and *In the Nick of Time* (K.B.-Broncho).

Both irising and fading require adaptations to the camera lens; the former the addition of an extra-large variable iris diaphragm a few inches in front of the lens, and the latter some sort of internal adaptation permitting a complete closure of the internal aperture control diaphragm if a fade to complete blackness was to be achieved in all circumstances. Under studio conditions, when the aperture being used was about f5.6, it *was* possible to achieve a reasonably complete fade-out by reducing the ordinary lens aperture to the minimum possible value, which was around f32 to f45, but on exteriors, when working as was usual at about f11, this approach would not give complete blackness at the end of the fade. In fact the unsatisfactory results of attempting an aperture fade on exteriors can sometimes be seen in the films made when fades first became popular.

The addition of an extra-large variable iris diaphragm in front of the lens was certainly more convenient than the internal adaptation of lenses, since one design could be fitted to any camera, regardless of the particular lens being used. This may well explain why irising rather than fading became so popular for a few years after 1914. Before that date neither irising nor fading were used in European films in the way I have described above.

The only way in which it was possible and convenient to make fades, other than in the camera at the time of shooting (for production volumes now forbade making fades in the printer for each separate print), was by a chemical bleaching process on the developed negative. The beginning and/or end of the shot was lowered slowly in to the bleaching solution, and when the point where the fade was to start was reached, the negative was immediately slowly pulled out again. The result was that the silver image was completely removed at the very end of the shot, and the negative was quite transparent there, while at intermediate points the negative image was lightened to various degrees. When prints were made from this negative they had various degrees of darkening along the way to total blackness at their ends. Chemical fades can be detected in some films from 1913, because the process, which continued to be used in cheap little film laboratories into the 'thirties (as in Renoir's *Toni*), was slightly uneven in its effect over the area of individual frames, and this enables it to be

recognized. For this reason it was not used if it could be avoided, but it was certainly much commoner in the 'teens of the century than later. The final fairly obvious point to be made is that for dissolves to be made in the camera, which was the only efficient way at this period, the camera must be capable of being cranked backwards. The Biograph camera was not, so there are no dissolves in Biograph films.

High and Low Angles

In the previous period we find the occasional rare use of a just slightly depressed or elevated lens angle, but these were always in shots taken at a considerable distance from the actors, and arose out of the nature of the specific location that was being used. Such was the case for instance in *Daring Daylight Burglary* (1903) and *The Pickpocket – A Chase through London* (1903), which were described in the previous chapter. This sort of thing occasionally appears in this period too, usually in the form of a slightly low angle shot of a window which features in the film story. The opposite kind of high angle shot made more or less necessary by the surroundings of the scene, or alternatively done to show clearly what is going on, is also used on rare occasions, as in a high angle shot of horses in the 1907 Pathé *Voyous de l'ouest* and the shot of Brutus' funeral pyre in the Vitagraph *Julius Caesar* (1908). This sort of thing was not to be found on studio interior scenes of course, as it would have produced obviously converging verticals in the set, which everyone was intent on avoiding. However, extreme high and low angles now began to appear on rare occasions on location exteriors. Such shots fall under the concept of the 'cinematographic angle', which I owe to Jean Mitry. This denotes those types of compositions and framings which did not and could not occur in the still photography of this period and earlier. Marked departures from a horizontal lens axis often produce images which can be rendered comprehensible and acceptable in films because the activities in them are already understood from the previous movements of the narrative and the actors in it, which would not be the case in a still photograph. It appears from the examples he quotes that Mitry believes that such composition only began to appear in films around 1914, but in fact numerous films show that it was some years before this that such features had begun to appear occasionally. Extreme high- and low-angle shots first appeared to my knowledge in the Vitagraph film *Back to Nature* (1910), which shows a lifeboat floating beside an ocean liner in a shot taken downwards from the ship's deck, and then the opposite angle of the watchers at the ships rail taken from the lifeboat. This pair of steep high and low angles could be taken to be a pair of Point of View shots, since the people in both places are watching each other, but there is also another high angle shot in this film taken from the bridge of the liner of the action on the deck, which is certainly a purely objective shot, since there is no kind of shot showing anyone on the bridge on either side of it. There are a small number of other American films from the next few years that include a true high or low angle shot, virtually

Low angle shot of people on the deck of a steamer in
Vitagraph's Back to Nature *(1910).*

*The reverse of the previous shot: a high angle Point of View
shot of a lifeboat below. The lightning and rain effect have
been painted onto the negative of the film.*

always as a part of a Point of View construction, such as the
Vitagraph *Cardinal Wolsey* (1912). High and low angle shots
are very rare in European cinema, with the exception of some
Danish films, beginning with *De fire Djaevle*, which was made
by Alfred Lind, Robert Dinesen, and Carl Rosenbaum in
1911. Since this film dealt with the lives and passions of circus
trapeze artists, the use of high- and low-angle shots would arise
fairly naturally in the filming of their act, but it is clear that
the use of extreme angles was consciously pushed much
further the next year in Schnedler-Sørensen's *Dødspringet til
Hest fra Cirkuskuplen* and *Den Staerkeste*.

(These extreme angle shots, together with the strong
chiaroscuro lighting effects which I have already described,
plus some favourite Danish subjects such as the 'fiendish
master criminal' thriller, all had a strong influence on what is
often unfortunately referred to as 'German Expressionist cinema'. This happened because up to 1916 the Danish film

industry, together with the Pathé company, dominated the
whole Northern European market – Germany, Russia, and
Scandinavia. The Pathé films did not include the stylistic
features I have just mentioned.)

D.W. Griffith's films are not stylistically advanced at all in
this respect, and it is only in 1912 that the few well known
high angle Extreme Long Shots on Western landscapes appear
in some of his films. By this time some other American
producers were beginning to follow the Vitagraph lead in the
use of extreme angles, and in 1913 this feature is beginning to
appear in European films from countries other than Denmark. In 1913 even a film from distant Russia could now
include a true objective high angle shot of a courtyard.
(Bauer's *Sumerki zhenskoi dushi.*)

But as films came to be shot from closer in to the actors,
even slightly low- or high-angles come to be visually significant. In Vitagraph films again we have a low angle shot of a

High angle shot in De Fire Djaevle *(Lind, Dinesen, &
Rosenbaum, 1911).*

The corresponding low-angle shot in De Fire Djaevle.
*Neither of this pair of shots is readly understood as a Point of
View shot.*

A low angle shot of one of the principals in Ralph Ince's Strength of Men *(1913).*

couple taken from fairly close on an exterior scene in *Poet and Peasant* made by William V. Ranous in 1912, and the next year a pair of Medium Shot low angles of the two principal men in Ralph Ince's *Strength of Men*. In fact, the *Moving Picture World* review of this film is the first mention I have been able to find of 'camera angles' in connection with films. *Strength of Men* also includes some extreme high-angle shots as well.

The Vitagraph Angle and the 'American Foreground'

Besides their influence on the polishing up of action continuity across cuts, the Pathé films of 1905-1908 also had subtler influences on American films. One of these was in the matter of the height cameras were used at in shooting ordinary scenes. Ben Brewster has noted that for some years before

1907 many scenes in Pathé films were shot with the camera at waist height, whereas most other films were usually shot with the camera at shoulder level, which was more convenient for the operator. In both cases, the lens axis was kept horizontal when shooting on studio sets, so that the vertical lines in the sets stayed parallel to the sides of the film frame and did not slant, as 'correct' still photographic technique had long required. With most still cameras it was possible to use the camera at any height with horizontal lens axis and still get the required height of a scene into frame, while also preserving parallel vertical lines in the picture. This was because they usually had a 'rising front', with the lens mounted on a board that could be slid up and down vertically with respect to the photographic plate, so producing the framing that would result from a tilt, but removing the optical effect a tilt gener-

The standard height used for filming at Pathé after about 1908, with the camera at hip level. The film is Max - artiste cinématographique *The Pathé studio camera has had a tubular lens hood added to it.*

A shot from the final sequence of l'Assassinat du Duc de Guise *(Calmettes & le Bargy, 1908), showing the Duc de Guise about to walk from one antechamber of the royal palace into the next behind.*

The immediately following shot in l'Assassinat du Duc de Guise, *cutting to the opposite angle from inside the room that the Duc de Guise is about to enter. The camera is set about waist level.*

ated in a rigid box camera. At the beginning of the century there had been one or two British movie cameras that had the lens mounted on a sliding board which could be moved up and down on the front of the camera, so producing the exact equivalent of a rising front still camera, and as previously noted, the first wooden box Bell & Howell camera had this feature as well. However, it is clear that this was considered an unnecessary complication in movie cameras, and the simpler solution of shooting everything with the lens horizontal, when there were conspicuous rectangular features in the background, was the one adopted.

When the actors are distant from the camera, as was mostly the case for films made before 1908, the camera height makes no visible difference to the look of the image. But if the camera is close enough for the actors to fill most of height of the frame, and if they are also disposed in depth within the scene, the waist level camera position gives a very distinctive look to the image, with the actors in the foreground markedly overtopping the actors in the background. The film that demonstrates this development in the most obvious way is the famous *l'Assassinat du Duc de Guise*, made by Calmettes & Le Bargy at the end of 1908 for the Film d'Art company, because it has the camera slightly closer to the actors than in most previous films, so that they fill most of the height of the frame, and also because there is a certain amount of staging in depth in it as well. In *l'Assassinat du Duc de Guise* there is a definite sensation of looking up at the actors, as though from the stalls of a theatre. It certainly struck some American critics at the time, as they described the appearance of the actors in it as like 'heroic figures'. As already remarked, the Vitagraph company signalled that they had taken note of *l'Assassinat du Duc de Guise* by giving two of their films made just after *l'Assassinat du Duc de Guise* had appeared in New York, namely *The Judgement of Solomon* and *Oliver Twist*, the extra descriptive subsidiary title 'A Vitagraph High Art Film'. *l'Assassinat du Duc de Guise* also introduced into films another stylistic

component which was gradually taken over as part of the characteristic Vitagraph 'look' from 1909 onwards. This involves allowing the actors in the foreground of a group to turn their backs to the camera if it is appropriate to the action of the scene, as with a group of people in a real scene caught unawares. Whereas in the vast majority of French and American films it was, and continued to be, the practice to keep the central foreground clear of actors, and also to allow any actors in the foreground to angle themselves at least side-on to the camera. The extreme case in the way actors were placed within the shot in films made up to 1914 was to allow them to play directly to the camera lens, and this can frequently be seen in European dramas, though much less so in American films. (In comedies address to the camera has always been permitted.) Amongst American film-makers, D.W. Griffith was notable for the way he persisted with a frontal organization of his stagings right through into the 'twenties, even when everyone else had followed the Vitagraph example.

Shooting Closer

In 1907 and 1908 the most common way to shoot a scene was in Long Shot, with the actors shown at full length with a fair amount of space around them. However, already by 1907, some American films, particularly those from Vitagraph, have the camera closer, with many scenes staged so that the actors occupy nearly the full height of the frame (Full Shot). e.g *Francesca da Rimini* and *The Mill Girl*. This is also true of many Pathé films made at the same time.

In 1909 there was still very little cutting in to a closer shot in the middle of a scene, and most shots in most films were taken at LS or FS. However, there were the first signs of a movement towards shooting the ordinary master scenes in American films from even closer, so that the feet of the actors were cut off by the bottom of the frame. This seems to have developed as a competitive thing between the Vitagraph and Biograph companies, with a number of scenes in a minority

One of the earliest occurrences of the
'nine-foot line' and the Vitagraph angle,
with the camera at waist level, can be seen
in this studio shot from Romance of an
Umbrella (1909). The lighting is solely
overhead daylight, slightly diffused, and
with no artificial fill from the front.

of Vitagraph films being shot with the actors working up to
what the company called the 'nine foot line' towards the end
of the year. This was a line, or in the case of studio scenes, a
plank, laid down nine feet in front of the camera lens, and at
right angles to the lens axis, and it represented the closest the
actors were allowed to come forwards towards the camera.
With the usual studio lens aperture setting of f5.6 to f8 a
standard 50 mm. lens would give sharp focus from nine feet
to about 50 feet if the focus was set at 15 feet. There are some
Vitagraph films made in 1909 that begin to show the effects
of this practice, such as *Romance of an Umbrella*, but the
stagings in them do not take the actors quite as far forward as
the nine foot line, though sometimes they do get to within 11
feet of the camera. At this distance the bottom of the film

frame cuts the actors off at the thighs, and the top of the frame
is about a foot above their heads. (The exact height included
within the frame for the silent aperture when a standard 50
mm. lens is used is 3 foot 9 inches at 10 feet, since of course
the actors would not stand right on the nine-foot line, particularly when it was a plank of wood, and in the case of the
usual European forward limit of 4 metres the height within
the frame would be 5 foot 2 inches at that distance.) At the
same time, a small number of Biograph films have some scenes
in them shot with actors cut off at the ankles, which corresponds to them acting up to a line at 12 feet from the camera.
In 1910 the nine foot line became fairly common in Vitagraph
films, and as the year wore on this closeness began to be
adopted in Biograph films too.

Staging of the action right up to the
nine-foot line in the Vitagraph film Daisies
(1910). This shot also shows the characteristic
Vitagraph willingness to let the actors have
their backs to the camera, if this happens
naturally. At this point in the scene, the woman
in the background is rather unhappy, as you
might guess.

Emblematic Shots and Cameo Introductions

In Europe in 1910 such closeness of camera was still unknown on master shots. These were still being taken at Full Shot at the closest, though there were of course the rare closer shots cut into the middle of a scene. The other important exception to this generalization was the continuation of the tradition of the use of a close emblematic shot to begin or end a film. As in the previous period these can be recognized by the fact that they are not a continuous extension of the narrative, and generally are posed, with little or no movement. For example, the last shot of D.W. Griffith's *The Curtain Pole* shows the protagonist filmed in Medium Shot against a blank black background biting a chunk out of the pole in question, with no relation to the action in the previous shot. The introductory emblematic shot also continued into this period, and a gradual change of its style took place. Vitagraph's *Shakespeare's Tragedy, King Lear* begins with a posed shot in a special set of the principal characters in the play, with their names lettered underneath them on the set. Another striking example was *Luigi XI, re di Francia* (Ambrosio, 1909), which starts with a posed Medium Shot of Louis XI in front of a background of hanged men. There are other examples of this sort of thing amongst surviving films, and over the next few years it modulated into the much more familiar introduction of the main characters in a series of cameos. These were moderately close shots of the principal characters in the film shown in front of a black curtain, and perhaps also enclosed within a black vignette mask. Sometimes the actor playing the character would be identified by a title at the bottom of the frame as well. Examples can be seen in *Zigomar, peau d'anguille* (1913) and other films from most countries. However, such things only occurred in a minority of movies.

Getting Closer Still

It must be understood that in the analysis of closeness of filming, I am basically concerned with studio scenes, for there was a general tendency to keep the camera further back on location scenes at this period and later, presumably because it had cost the production company a certain amount of extra money to ship their actors and technicians to perform in front of these novel backgrounds. The other caution that must be observed in analysing camera closeness is that the frame in nearly all 16 mm. prints of silent films is cropped at top and bottom and one side, because they have been printed down from 35 mm. as though they were sound films. The result is that a 16 mm. print usually gives the impression that the camera was quite a bit closer than it actually was when the film was shot.

As Vitagraph adopted the 'nine foot line' there were occasional mistakes made, because it required careful adjustment of the focus under studio conditions to have the depth of field just cover from 9 feet to the farthest part of the set, about 30 feet away. For instance, although the action is staged up to the nine foot line in *Victims of Fate*, made at the beginning of 1910, the foreground is out of focus in one set-up.

In 1911 and 1912 the trend towards using more and more shots taken up to the nine foot line continued at Vitagraph, and at Biograph Griffith did likewise. By 1912, Griffith had perhaps drawn a little ahead in the number of scenes in his films staged right up to the nine foot line, but the effect of this on the look of his films was quite different. This was because the camera height in his films now tended to be mostly up around the head or shoulder level, and also because his stagings still had the acting strongly organized towards the front. The exact balance in this closeness of shot competition at this time is hard to determine, because both companies made some films which made little use of the features I am discussing, and in 1912 Griffith in particular was still quite capable of making films such as *Billy's Stratagem* and *Man's Genesis*, which were nearly entirely conducted in Long Shot and Full Shot.

Over the next few years more and more of the Vitagraph films show stagings that make use of this 'nine foot line' set-up, but it is not until 1913 that one finds some shots in them that have the actors standing right on the nine foot line, at which distance they are cut off at the hips.

American film producing companies besides Biograph followed the trend towards shooting closer in, but more slowly, in fact a year or more behind. Edison and Essanay were closest behind the leaders, then Kalem, followed by the rest. But no other company made as much use of actors positioned with their backs to the camera. The use of actor groupings with some natural back turning did begin to appear in a few Edison and Essanay films in 1911, and more so in 1912, but elsewhere there was virtually none of it. Tom Gunning has noted that there are some examples of actors turning their backs to the camera in Griffith films, but in my opinion they are very few indeed compared to the Vitagraph practice. Gunning has also postulated a difference in the expressive application of the practice in the two company's films. He considers that in Vitagraph films the back turning occurs at dramatically unstressed moments, whereas in the Griffith films it is applied only at the most dramatically effective moments, such as when a character has been made particularly unhappy. I agree that there might be some tendency in this direction, but nevertheless, the back-turning technique is also used in Vitagraph films in an expressive way, for instance in *Daisies*, when one of the girls has just received bad news in a letter.

Despite the fact that this kind of natural staging with some of the actors having their backs to the camera had first appeared in a French film, French and other European film-makers proved unable to develop the idea, and they also kept their limit on actor closeness at 4 metres, though they did respond to the closer camera placement in Vitagraph and other American films over the next couple of years after 1909 by sometimes moving the actors right up to the 4 metre line. When French films finally began to use a true Medium Shot or nine foot camera closeness in a few rare shots cut into the course of a more distant shot about 1913, they referred to this as the '*plan américain*', and in the United States the distinction was now being made by the terms 'French foreground' for the 4 metre line and 'American foreground' for the effect of the full use of the nine foot line.

By 1912 the Vitagraph angle was being used for most of the scenes in Vitagraph films, and then some Vitagraph films began to include scenes that slightly departed from the company's standard camera set-up by being shot with the camera even lower than waist level, as in *The Spirit of Christmas* and others.

Although the Vitagraph company was easily the most important American company in the European market, the 'Vitagraph angle' was not taken up in its pure form by any European film-makers. In France in 1913 even the most advanced among them were still confining themselves to the rare cut in to Medium Shot (the 'nine foot line', but without the low camera position) in the course of a scene, which would otherwise be shot from further back, at the four metre line at least. The same is true of the Danish cinema, but in Sweden in 1913 the limited staging in depth which was used in the Vitagraph films – from Medium Shot to Long Shot – was extended by Mauritz Stiller and Victor Sjöström to action moving back from Medium Shot into Very Long Shot in some exterior scenes, and even in some interiors. A good example of this is provided by Sjöström's *Ingeborg Holm*.

(*Ingeborg Holm* is also interesting because, although it is stylistically retarded for its date, in that it contains no cuts within its scenes apart from a couple of letter Inserts, it nevertheless shows how such formal qualities can be largely irrelevant to the total aesthetic value of a work. For this film has a dramatic depth and power, resulting almost entirely from the handling of narrative and acting, that is superior to anything that Griffith or anyone else had put together by 1913.)

In Italy too there was some copying of the subject matter and techniques of the Vitagraph films, but again no wholesale adoption of the Vitagraph angle.

Before leaving this subject I should mention that the dominant position of the Vitagraph company in Europe was supported by the fact that from 1909 onwards they were the only American company that actually printed copies of their films there as well as in the U.S.A. This was done in their factory outside Paris, using a second negative which had been shot simultaneously with the negative for the American distribution prints in a second camera set up beside the main camera on the studio stage. There was even a period of a couple of years around 1911 when Vitagraph used a special double camera to produce the two negatives, but this did not last.

By 1913 shooting in closer was becoming a craze, and even Keystone comedies tried using Close Ups and Medium Shots to cover slapstick action, as in *His Chum the Baron*. This was of course foolish, for it meant that much of the slapstick movements were taking place outside the edge of the frame, and the whole point of the genre was being lost. The Keystone film-makers grasped this point almost immediately, and re-turned to using mostly Long Shot by 1914, but this brief episode is indicative of the extent to which closer filming became competitive before 1914.

The Insert Shot

From the very beginning of this period it was completely standard practice with all the major film producers in America and Europe to cut Insert Shots of letters and other objects into a scene otherwise conducted in continuous Long Shot, whenever it was really necessary and appropriate. For instance, Vitagraph's *Francesca da Rimini* (1907) contains both these kinds of Insert Shot. There are also a number of examples of a highly specialised form of the use of the Insert Shot, in which the entire film story is carried in close shots showing only part of the actors, to be found in this period. This idea appeared very early, with G.A. Smith's *A View Through an Area Window* (1901), which shows a series of casual incidents, done in just one shot showing the feet of the people involved. I have seen no sign of this technique reappearing until the Ambrosio company made *La storia di Lulu* in 1909, though Vitagraph's *The Story the Boots Told* of 1908 *does* use some close-ups of feet doing this and that as part of a moralising story, but most of its narrative is carried on in ordinary shots showing the characters fully. *La storia di Lulu* on the other hand tells a story in several scenes by using nothing but insert shots of the feet of the actors. Unfortunately the narrative organization of this film is rather confused. Later on the American Vitagraph company returned to the idea, with variations, in *Over the Chafing Dish* (1911) and *Extremities* (1913), which in their turn may have had something to do with Ambrosio having another more extended try at the same idea in *L'amore pedestre* of 1914.

Scene Dissection in General

From 1907 to 1909 cuts within a scene, other than cuts to Insert Shots, continued to be rare, with the exception of the numerous trick films which continued to be made at Pathé in 1907 and 1908. These films, which mostly consist of just one scene, regularly use at least one pair of cuts straight down the lens axis from Long Shot to a closer shot, usually with quite good position matching of the actors across them. (I must emphasize that I am not talking about 'invisible' trick cuts here, which these films also contain in abundance.) Sometimes these Pathé trick films contain quite a number of these cuts in and out, and the closer shots can be anything from Medium Long Shot to Medium Close Shot, as in *En avant la musique* (1907) and *Sculpture moderne* (1908). Those two films, and many others like them, were all imported into New York and the rest of America, and anyone attending several cinema programmes at the time that D.W. Griffith started directing would have had great difficulty in *not* seeing at least one of them. Despite the fact that this kind of cut to a closer shot had occasionally been used in Biograph and Edison films before 1906, both companies, along with Vitagraph seem to have almost abandoned the practice in 1907 and 1908, and

A scene in The Physician of the Castle *made by Pathé early in 1908.*

This Medium Close Up is cut into it, and both the background and lighting have been adjusted, with the phone table moved, and arc fill light added.

the Vitagraph and Edison film-makers did not return to it for some years. In French films from 1908, on the other hand, there are a few non-trick films like *The Physician of the Castle* which also have a close shot cut into a scene. The best that D.W. Griffith managed in 1908 after he started directing was a cut from Very Long Shot to Medium Long Shot once in *The Ingrate*. However, in 1909 Griffith did indeed make a couple of films that cut into and out of a Medium Shot in the middle of a scene, but in this case their function was to show an important detail, just as in an Insert Shot that only includes the object, and not the person using it. In the case of *The Medicine Bottle* this is the mistaken choice of bottle made by a child. On the other hand, in the Pathé films that Max Linder made from 1908 onwards, such as *The Would-be Juggler* (1908) and *A Young Lady-Killer* (1909), the function of the Medium Shot cut into the middle of the scene seems to be to get the maximum out of his facial expression. In 1909 there are more of these, and the usage had spread to a few Italian films, not all of them comedies. In all of the instances so far mentioned, the camera is moved straight in down the lens axis, and the matching of position of the actor across the cuts is nearly always poor. On the odd occasion when the position matching is better, my feeling is that it is more a matter of good luck than good judgement.

The situation did not change much in 1910, with only a couple of Biograph films using a cut in to a closer shot in one scene, and also at least two Vitagraph films doing likewise, while there is rather more of this sort of thing amongst French and Italian films. In 1911, out of 124 American films that I have analysed, only 16 use cuts in to a closer shot in the middle of a scene, while amongst 130 European films there are no less than 28 using the technique. These are mostly French and Italian films, but there are also three Danish films involved as well. Before being too impressed by these figures, it is worth remembering that by 1911 American films, and particularly Vitagraph and Biograph films, had their master shots taken closer in on the average than European films. And even more

importantly, 1911 was the year when some of the Griffith examples of the technique, as in *The Battle* and *The Lonedale Operator*, were used at a point in the narrative which would have a considerable emotional impact. Although Griffith may have been the first to realise the dramatic effectiveness of going in to a close shot at the right moment, he was not alone in 1911. The director of the Edison company's *The Switchman's Tower* cuts in to a Medium Close Up of the switchman at the moment that he realises that a train is headed for disaster.

In 1912 the idea really caught on in the United States, and film-makers at most of the companies joined in, with 40 films using the technique out of 216 seen, which is now about the same as the proportion in European films of that year. This remained pretty much the same in 1913, though there were now a few examples of cuts all the way in to a true Close Up in American films, and also some examples of a change of angle on cutting in, but this was not true of European films. As well as that, the matching of actor positions across the cuts was getting much better in American films, and even to some extent in European films. However, in all this, we are still talking about the use of cuts in to a closer shot in only one or two scenes in a film. The above facts explain why Italian film-makers in 1915 were dismissive of the recommendations in a pamphlet Charles Pathé had published in Italy, called *Manuale per uso dei direttori di scena italiani*, as part of his plans to take advantage of Italian production facilities. It was written by Louis Gasnier, the chief director at the Pathé studios in New York, and amongst other things, recommended the greater use of the *primo piano* by Italian directors. The reason for the Italian rejection of this advice, with the claim that they knew all about using the *primo piano*, was that though in 1915 Gasnier was meaning what *we* understand by a Close Up, which had by then come to be frequently used in American films, the Italians understood it as what they had been occasionally doing since 1910, which was cutting a somewhat closer shot into the occasional scene. But these closer shots in Italian films were only what we would call Medium Shots, showing the body from the hips up, and were taken at a distance of nine feet, because that was as close as they took anything, except inserts.

It is also possible to break down a scene into more than one shot by changing the camera angle across the cut, as had already happened in a few films in the previous period. This kind of cut continued to be quite rare until 1913, unless the camera was forced away from the standard move straight down the axis by the physical nature of the set or location. An early example of a cut within a scene with a large change of angle is given by *Røverens Brud* (Viggo Larsen, 1907), in which there is a cut from a Very Long Shot of a group in an exterior scene to another Very Long Shot from the opposite angle. (This scene is described, with illustrations, by Marguerite Engberg in *Iris*, Vol. 2, No.1, 1984). It is naturally much easier to do this sort of thing on real exteriors than in studio shots, where special pre-planning and set-building are called for if opposite angles are to be used within a scene. Nevertheless this point has been taken account of in a pair of reverse angles in *Romance of an Umbrella* (Vitagraph, 1909), in which the shots are taken from *behind* each of the two characters interacting, and the set reconstructed to make this possible.

Reverse Scenes and Reverse-Angles

To cover the development of reverse angle cutting properly, I have to return to the crucial case of *l'Assassinat du Duc de Guise* yet again. For this film contains yet another novel feature that proved to be much more significant for American than for European film-making. This is in the final pair of shots in the sequence showing the Duke's progress through various antechambers in the Royal palace to a waiting room crowded with conspirators. In the first of these two shots the Duke is seen walking away from the camera up to an open doorway through which can be seen the final room and some of the conspirators in it, and then there is a cut to a continuation of the action as he walks through the doorway, which is

shot from the opposite direction, so that the conspirators are now in the foreground and the doorway and the room the Duke is leaving is in the background. To obtain these two shots, both sets had to be specially constructed with movable back walls to enable the camera to get far enough back to cover the figures seen full length in the foreground of each shot. This is something no film-makers had thought worth the bother of doing before this date. Although shots taken from opposite directions to a scene had been put together well before this date, as far as I know this very infrequent practice had always involved at least one of the scenes being shot outdoors on location, which eliminates the set rebuilding problem. Starting with Williamson's *Fire!* there had always been occasional films which show action on a set with a window in the back wall, with a backdrop behind it, followed by a shot on location of a window seen from the other side, with more or less matching action, or the opposite arrangement. After *l'Assassinat du Duc de Guise* had appeared in New York, D.W. Griffith used a variant of reverse-angle construction like that used in *The Runaway Match* and its imitators in an interior scene in *The Drunkard's Reformation* of 1909. In this case the cuts are between Long Shots of The Drunkard (and the rest of the audience), and Long Shots of the play they are watching. The shots of the audience are taken from a slightly high angle so that the rows of seats in the auditorium fill the frame, and no extra set construction was necessary. It is really only this sub-category of reverse angle cuts which are also Point of View cuts that Griffith was ever easy with, and further than that, he only used them when he was showing characters in the kind of theatrical situation where their use is practically essential. As the years went by the use of reverse-angle cutting became a standard technique in American films, but by the early 'twenties it was clear that Griffith was unable or unwilling to use them freely, and this contributed to the 'old-fashioned' look of his films. Or as I would put it, his films became stylistically retarded in this respect. To be absolutely accurate

A studio set representing two different offices in two separate buildings separated by a street in Vitagraph's The Romance of an Umbrella *(1909).*

The opposite angle to the preceding shot taken from inside the office which was formerly in the background. The man seen in the previous shot has just walked out of frame in the background before the cut to this angle occurs.

about this matter, there *are* one or two instances also of Griffith using reverse-angle cuts in a chase when the hunter and hunted are in sight of each other, though still in Long Shot or Very Long Shot. However in most scenes involving a pursuit Griffith shot the hunter and hunted from the *same* direction, as did most other film-makers at this time.

To return yet again to *l'Assassinat du Duc de Guise*, the sort of set-up where a scene is shown from two opposed directions in succession immediately caught on in a small way. Vitagraph used the idea from time to time, as in *Romance of an Umbrella* (1909) and *Uncle Tom's Cabin* (1910), and so did other people, including Viggo Larsen again, in his *Revolutions-bryllup* of 1909. In all of these cases except *Romance of an Umbrella*, the use of the reverse scene was quite gratuitous, and added nothing to the exposition of the narrative from any point of view. By late 1910 the reverse scene had begun to move outdoors, in the Yankee company's *The Monogrammed Cigarette*. However, in all these cases, the camera is well back from the actors, who are in Medium Long Shot at the closest, at about 12 feet distance. By 1912 the device was commonly referred to as a 'reverse scene' in the United States.

At this point it is important to distinguish carefully between the several fairly distinct classes of reverse-angle shots. The earliest example, as in *Røverens Brud*, in which the camera is far back from the actors in the shots from opposite directions of the same scene, is the least common in modern times. The next major class is of a pair of shots from behind the backs of the two characters who are interacting, and slightly to the side of the line joining their eyes (the 'eye-line'), as in *Romance of an Umbrella*. This form was rarely used in the decade following its first appearance, though there are some other examples in Vitagraph films such as *Uncle Tom's Cabin* (1910), and it is still not the most common form of reverse-angle construction. I shall refer to it hereafter as 'behind the shoulder reverse-angles'. The major class of angle – reverse-angle cuts, from this period forever onwards, was what can be described as 'in front of the shoulder' reverse-angles. In these, each of the pair of characters interacting appears alone in a reasonably close shot directed approximately frontally at them, and the presence of the other person whom they are looking at has to be inferred from previous information. This sort of reverse-angle cutting, first appears in *The Loafer* (Essanay, 1912), a Western made by Arthur Mackley at the end of 1911, in which there are repeated cuts between Medium Shots of two men talking, both taken from the front with the camera just off their eye-line so that they do not look into the lens. It seems quite possible to me that this variety of the reverse-angle had begun evolving earlier than the example that I have just mentioned, since its handling in *The Loafer* is already quite assured.

The further development of the 'in front of the shoulder' reverse-angle over the next year or so is entangled with the beginning of the free use of unvignetted Point of View shots, and seems to have taken place on exterior scenes, and mostly in California. This is not very surprising, since studio shooting on the fairly small sets usual in America at the time presented obstacles to the free use of reverse angle cutting. Many sets were constructed with only two walls in 'L' shape, which made shooting the opposite angle almost impossible, and for those sets with three walls, shooting would have to stop while a wall was removed, because of the small size of the sets. (Remember that even a Medium Shot, from the waist up, requires that the camera be nine feet back from the actor). So we find that there are quite a number of films made late in 1912 on exteriors that have either simple reverse angle cuts, or reverse angles which are also part of watcher-POV pairs of shots. Arthur Mackley later made *The Shotgun Ranchman* for Essanay towards the end of 1912, and this contains many reverse angles. On the New York side, there are a couple of Thanhouser films from late 1912 that have reverse angle cuts, *Treasure Trove* and *In a Garden*, and both also contain also POV reverse angles as well as plain reverses. At Vitagraph's California unit, the director Rollin S. Sturgeon had picked up the idea, and used reverses in *The Craven*, *Out of the Shadows*, and *Una of the*

A dialogue exchange conducted in Medium Shot in The Loafer *(Essanay, 1911). The actor is back-lit by the sun, with fill light reflected up into his face from a matt white board.*

The reverse-angle to the previous shot in The Loafer. *This is also lit with sunlight from one side and reflector fill from the other. These two shots are repeated in this scene.*

A scene in Ralph Ince's His Last Fight *Vitagraph, 1913), shot on location.*

The opposite angle, showing the watcher whose Point of View the previous shot was.

Sierras. From here the idea seems to have got over to the main Vitagraph studios in New York, and was taken up most enthusiastically by Ralph Ince, though films from other directors contain the occasional reverse angle cut by 1913.

His Last Fight, which Ralph Ince made in the middle of 1913, is quite remarkable in that of the 75 shots that make up its single reel, 25 form part of reverse-angle pairs. It seems that it was a number of years before any other director used such a high proportion of reverse-angle cuts in a film. Some of the reverse-angle cuts in *His Last Fight* are between a shot of a watcher and a shot representing her Point of View (POV), and this category is also rarely represented in this period, though it occurred as early as the 'objective' form of reverse-angle construction which I have been describing.

(Since Ralph Ince plays an important part in the story of the development of 'continuity cinema' or 'classical cinema', I must make it clear that his career was not at all associated with that of his better-known elder brother, Thomas Ince. Ralph

Ince began as an actor at Vitagraph before he moved over to directing for that company in 1912, and he never worked with his brother, or for his brother's various companies.)

In European films made in 1912 and 1913 one finds a few extremely rare instances of reverse-angle cutting, but only under the same severely limited conditions as in Griffith's films. Basically that means in scenes involving a theatre and audience, such as Nordisk's *Desdemona* and *Et Drama paa Havet* of 1911 and 1912. However, most scenes involving a theatre audience's reactions in European films were still shot with a small angle change from the front-on view of the stage to a shot of the watchers in a box near the stage, or even through the back of a box looking towards the stage, with the occupants turning a bit towards the camera so that the faces are readable.

Point Of View Shots

True Point of View (POV) shots are shots representing

One of the shots continuing this scene in His Last Fight, *in which the Point of View shot is taken from closer in.*

And in the matching reverse angle, the watcher is also shot from closer as the excitement mounts.

what a person shown in a film sees, cut in at the moment when the person is looking, and taken in the direction in which they are looking. There are two categories of such shots: those in which the view is shown in a full-frame shot, and those in which the view is surrounded by a black vignette mask, representing the view through a telescope, or binoculars, or a keyhole. This latter sort appeared very early, and in considerable numbers, as has already been described in the previous chapter, but the former variety only began to appear in any quantity after 1908, so clearly showing that they had an entirely different conceptual status for film-makers of the time. This is another case of something that seems to us to be an obvious generalization of a technical device failing to be made by early film-makers. Nevertheless, there are one or two cases of what are *almost* unvignetted POV shots from before 1908. I have mentioned the 1905 *Pauvre mere*, and then there is *Løvejagten* (1907) from Nordisk, in which shots of hunters looking for their prey are alternated with shots of wild animals taken in zoo enclosures from a high angle which completely fails to match the direction in which the hunters are looking. It is noticeable that all the vignetted POV shots used in films from the very beginning are fairly correct in the directions they are taken from, unlike these gropings for what seems to us an obvious extension of the idea.

In 1908 Pathé produced another example, *The Shrimper*, in which the matching of angle of the scene viewed to that of the watcher's look is rather better than before, and then later in the year D.W. Griffith developed a special case of the true POV shot which proved very influential. This was when showing an audience watching a play or other show. The first film in which he did this was *A Wreath in Time*, made at the beginning of December 1908. In this film there are shots which show part of a theatre audience in a stage box reacting to a play, shot from the side, alternating with shots of the stage taken head on, and the direction of these stage shots matches the direction in which the watchers are looking fairly well. Several weeks later Griffith made a much more powerful film, *A Drunkard's Reformation*, in which the audience is shot from head-on in Full Shot, as are the actors on the stage, so that the shots are reverse angles as well as POV shots. Strangely enough, after this film, Griffith very rarely used the Point of View shot, and when he did, seemed unable to use it in its general form outside theatre scenes. It was only in 1913, when a number of other film-makers were adopting a correctly realised POV structure in general situations, that Griffith managed a few films in which he too got it right, namely *The Massacre*, *Olaf, an Atom*, and *The Telephone Girl and the Lady*. Then he seems to have abandoned any further attempt to come properly to grips with the POV shot, and I believe there are none at all in *Birth of a Nation*, other than in the theatre assassination scene.

Amongst the film-makers who really developed the standard Point of View shot after 1909, the people at Vitagraph played a particularly important part. In their *C.Q.D.; or, Saved by Wireless* (1909), there is a series of three shots taken

forwards from the bow of an unseen ship sailing into New York harbour, followed directly by a Long Shot of sailors on the deck of the actual ship looking out to one side of the frame and pointing, which implies, not entirely convincingly, that the previous shots were their Point of View. This kind of 'revealed' POV structure, in which the shot of the looker does not precede the POV shot, but only comes after it, was extremely rare in the beginning, and has remained so to this day, for obvious reasons. The only example I have picked up from several hundred films made over the next few years is in *Sallie's Sure Shot*, made at Selig in 1913.

The more conventional presentation of the Point of View shot, as the unvignetted view seen by one of the characters we have seen looking at something in the previous shot, occurs in *Back to Nature* in 1910, in which we see a Long Shot of people looking down over the rail of a ship taken from below, followed by a shot of the lifeboat they are looking at taken from their position. However, the Vitagraph film-makers continued to be a little uneasy with the device, as a true POV shot is introduced by an explanatory intertitle, 'What they saw in the house across the court' in Larry Trimble's *Jean and the Waif*, made at the end of 1910. But a few months later, Trimble made *Jean Rescues*, which has POV shots introduced at an appropriate point without explanation. After this, unvignetted POV shots began to appear fairly frequently in Vitagraph films; in fact in five more titles released in 1911 among 31 prints viewed, as compared with only three films from the same year among the 93 prints from other American companies that I have so far seen. These latter are *The Corporation and the Ranch Girl* from Essanay, *The Little Soldier of '64* (Kalem), and Edison's *The Switchman's Tower*, which is still using a 'What he saw' intertitle to explain the nature of the following POV shot.

The really big surge of interest in the POV shot happened in the latter part of 1912, and in 1912 and 1913 taken together, Vitagraph films continued to lead the way. There are 28 examples among 92 Vitagraph films from those two years, whereas amongst 295 films from other American companies there were only 45 which included anything like POV shots, and more than half of these were shot from angles which clearly did not actually correspond to the angle of the watcher's sight, whereas only 4 of the Vitagraph sample did. In other words, although film-makers outside Vitagraph were becoming interested in using the POV structure, they were having considerable difficulty mastering it. It is noticeable that Allan Dwan at American Film Manufacturing was one of those who could not get it quite right, and at Essanay, the same is true of a couple of attempts in G.W. Anderson's films, whereas the Essanays directed by other directors get the POV directions correct. Given the importance of integrating the faked wild animal action into many of the Selig company's films, it is perhaps not surprising that their directors, despite their generally low level of competence, were managing to get some POV shot structures correct by 1913.

The way that POV shots could be used for the maximum

dramatic impact is best illustrated from Vitagraph films. Such films are still not very frequent, but William V. Ranous' *Poet and Peasant* (1912) is one striking example. Here the story is about a country hunchback who secretly loves a beautiful peasant girl, and the shots in question are cut in from his POV when he sees the girl with a visitor from the city with whom she has fallen in love. In this film the shots of the watcher are as usual taken from the side or back, as also occurs in *Jean Rescues* (1911), and *Cardinal Wolsey* (1912). But we are now at the point where the emerging use of the Point of View shot as a standard constructional device blended with the new reverse angle idea, so that the shots of watcher and their Point of View could also form a angle – reverse angle pair of shots taken from closer in. A very polished example of the combination of the two techniques occurs in *Out of the Shadows*, made by Rollin S. Sturgeon late in 1912. In this film the watcher is shown from the front looking out past the camera in a series of shots which cut in closer to her as she becomes more disturbed by what she is watching unobserved. This use of cutting to a closer shot to increase the intensity of emotional expression in a scene, rather than just to show something more clearly, dates back to about 1904, and though early examples are extremely rare, one finds a good example in *The Physician of the Castle* (1908). After this, D.W. Griffith was the person who used the device of relating the scale of the shot to the emotional intensity most effectively, though not till after 1910. However, because of his inability to handle the general form of reverse-angle cutting outside a theatrical audience situation, he was not able to develop the idea further, as was done by other film-makers in films such as *Out of the Shadows*.

There are just a few European examples of the device, but in most of these, the directions are again wrong. The continuing European resistance to using any form of scene dissection in this period is sufficiently indicated by the number of scenes in European films which were staged with a watcher lurking behind a bit of scenery in the background, while what he is watching is in the foreground of the same shot, just as it would have been staged in the theatre, rather than by using a POV shot.

Position Matching on Cuts

As already remarked, the Pathé trick films made before 1908 have fair to perfect matching of the actor's position across a cut to or from a closer shot within a scene, but as such cuts became more common in the work of other film-makers, principally in America, the position matching across their cuts was often poor. This was definitely the case in that small minority of D.W. Griffith's films that include cuts within scenes. This would seem to be due to the way he shot scenes, for according to Karl Brown (*Adventures with D.W. Griffith*), it was his practice to vary the action in each shot in every take he made of it. Thus there would have been no way of remembering the exact movements made in any individual take if it were decided to film a closer shot to insert into the master

scene. Griffith's interest would seem to have been less in continuity, and more in the dramatic effects he could achieve, in particular by eliciting performances from his actors, as is also indicated by their tendency to play to the front (i.e. towards The Master).

However, there are some Griffith films that have good cuts on action within a scene, even quite early, such as *After Many Years* (1908), where a cut from a very distant shot to a Full Shot is done in the middle of the action of the castaway leaping for joy. And of course there is *The Squaw's Love* (1911), where multiple cameras were used to shoot the scene. Before 1911 there are a few signs of film-makers elsewhere working on the perfecting of cuts on action, as in Vitagraph's *The Telephone* (1910), where the possibility of a smooth cut is definitely not due to the use of multiple cameras. In *The Telephone* the cut in question is from a location exterior shot of a woman falling away from an open window, to the same action seen from inside filmed on a studio set, the cut being perfect to the frame, and the actress's movements identical. The handling of the cutting of movements out of one shot into the next elsewhere in this film confirm that the example of cutting on action mentioned was no accident. Still, progress was slow, and as far as D.W. Griffith was concerned, it is still quite easy to find films from 1912 like *Friends*, where there are substantial mismatches on cuts in and out from a close shot.

As far as directional continuity (having the directions of the actors' movements match as they walked out of one shot into the next) is concerned, there is a noticeable improvement in American films towards 1913, due to the institution of simple procedures to keep a check on this particular kind of continuity during shooting. For instance, although Griffith's control of directional continuity was never good, even in the 'twenties, there was a definite improvement in this respect in his films during the period we are considering, presumably due to the introduction of these procedures of recording continuity. In 1911 a film of his like *The Lonedale Operator* still has a number of 'wrong' directions of movement from location to location, but by 1913 this was much less noticeable in his films. European directors were in general worse at handling continuity, and in some Danish films of 1911 and 1912 one can still see what we would now call hard 'jump cuts', in which a character who has been left in shot in one scene is discovered in shot in the next scene in a quite different location, without there being any explanatory intertitle. However some of the best European directors such as Victorin Jasset and Benjamin Christensen were definitely making progress in this respect by 1913.

Cutting Rates

The increasing use of the practice of breaking a scene down into a number of shots, along with the spread of the practice of cross-cutting between parallel actions, meant that the number of shots in a film increased throughout the years 1907-1913. To give some idea of this process in action, Vitagraph's *Francesca da Rimini* contains 14 shots and 8 intertitles, while their *Napoleon - Man of Destiny* of 1909 contains 27 shots and 11 intertitles. These films are fairly typical of the general mass of production in this respect, but in that same year of 1909 D.W. Griffith's *Drive for a Life* had 42 shots and 5 intertitles. I do not have many figures for 1910, but of these, Vitagraph's *The Telephone* has the fastest cutting, with 35 shots in only 440 feet. In 1911, still considering one-reel films with the usual length of about 900 feet, we find that *The Loafer* contains 39 shots including intertitles, and is rather typical at that, while Griffith's *The Voice of the Child* has 90 shots in the same length. Other American examples from 1911 for comparison are *The Colonel's Daughter* (Rex) with 29 shots in 937 ft., *The Lost Freight Car* from Kalem with 39 in 713 ft., and *A Cowboy for Love* from Bison with only 19 in 923 ft. For comparison, some European examples from 1911 are *Angelo tutelare* from Cines, with 25 shots in 735 ft. and *La morte civile* from FAI with 27 in 803 ft. An entirely typical Danish example from 1911, *Ekspeditricen*, has only 70 shots in four fairly full reels. A Max Linder film from Pathé in 1911, *Voisin-voisine*, has 22 shots in 581 feet, more nearly approaching the American speed, but this is exceptional. French dramas from all companies have far fewer shots in them, as indicated by the Gaumont film *Panther's Prey* made in 1913, which has only 81 shots in 1737 feet. In 1912 *Conscience* (Vitagraph) contains 49 shots, and by 1913 a film typical of the better end of production, the Thanhouser Company's *Just a Shabby Doll*, includes 60 shots in a little less than a reel. But in the same year D.W. Griffith's *The Coming of Angelo* has 116 shots. Looking at these figures, and also considering hundreds of other films from these years in this respect, the unavoidable conclusion is that D.W. Griffith alone led the way towards faster cutting, and other film-makers very definitely tagged along behind him. This is in sharp distinction to the development of closer camera positioning in American films through these years, which was to a large extent competitive all the way.

The increase in cutting rate was noticed at the time, as one can see from an article in *The Moving Picture World* (August 10, 1912), which has been republished in George Pratt's *Spellbound in Darkness*. This article quotes more figures for the number of shots and intertitles of the kind I have given above, but in this case for films made in 1912. The author of the article is however rather confused between true scenes, and the shots they might or might not be divided into, and he tends to think of all shots as separate dramatic entities, like the scenes of a play. Because of this, he considers the shots to be much too short in some films, particularly those from Biograph. Not for the first time a critic in *The Moving Picture World* failed to understand a stylistic development that was already well established and successful with the general public, as the magazine finally acknowledged a year later.

As far as D.W. Griffith was concerned in all this, it must be reiterated that cuts *within* scenes made relatively little contribution to the number of shots in his films, for even in 1912 some of his films have no cuts within scenes at all, e.g. *The Three Sisters*. Besides the contribution of cross-cutting to

the large number of shots in his films, there was also his technique of playing a scene across a number of adjoining locations, with cuts at each move from one to the next. In a number of films, such as *The Battle* (1911), he reaches the point where a scene which would be played in one location and one shot in any other director's film of this date is spread across three adjoining locations and four cuts.

Another Pathé Example

In 1907 Pathé films were still the dominating presence in the American market, and the film-makers of the two major American companies derived some major stylistic features from their example. The Vitagraph film-makers took note of the way the Pathé film-makers had been using extra shots of the comings and goings of their actors on the Pathé staircase to increase the length of many of their films. As Albert E. Smith, one of the directors and founders of the Vitagraph company put it in his autobiography, *Two Reels and a Crank* (1952), 'No one complained about this until it became evident that Pathé was using its goings and comings over and over again. The stories varied, but sandwiched in would be the same goings and comings. This aroused a two-horned complaint: the audiences were getting tired of the same goings and comings, often having little relation to the story, and secondly the buyers weren't going to pay fifteen cents a foot for this surplusage. They said the story was better without the goings and comings, and so they began to scissor them out of the picture, paying Pathé only for what was left.'

Now although this anecdote is rather exaggerated in its details, there is no doubt that many Vitagraph films lack transitional scenes showing the movement of the actors from place to place, and some even omit the less important dramatic scenes in their stories, which are merely reported in the narrative titles bridging the shots. Although the Pathé example had a largely negative effect on Vitagraph practice, this does not mean that the flow of movement from scene to scene is not well handled in Vitagraph films on the occasions when it was judged appropriate. It is just that there is less of it than in most of the other American companies' films.

The Space Beside

At Biograph, D.W. Griffith drew exactly the opposite lesson from the Pathé example, and developed further the practice of transferring part of the action of a scene into adjoining hallways and rooms even when this was not strictly necessary, although in his case what the actors were doing was certainly always relevant to the development of the story. Ben Brewster has suggested to me that the first Griffith film that shows a sign of this manner of staging action is *An Awful Moment*, and I am certain that it is embryonically visible in *The Broken Locket* and *A Wreath in Time*, which were also made at the very end of 1908. From this point onwards the amount of movement from room to room slowly increases in Griffith's films, until by 1911 it has become obsessive. What this practice gave Griffith was the same amount of action split

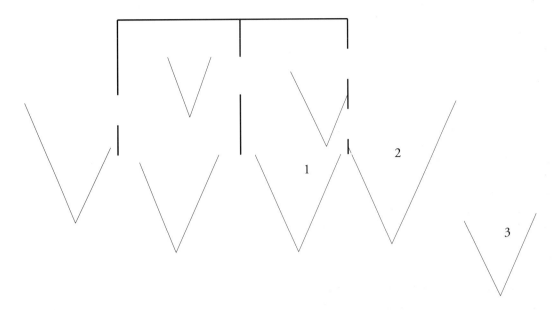

The camera set-ups used for the scenes in and around the house in D.W. Griffith's The Battle *(1911). In the first shots of the film, the two principals play a continuous scene through camera set-ups at 1, 2, and 3, and then continue back again. At later points in the film, action moves in the same way back and forth sideways through the other areas indicated.*

up into a greater number of shots, and this greater number of shots within the same length of film was undoubtedly the major feature of the dynamics of his films. The other way that Griffith used what we might call 'the space beside' was to provide an extra delaying stage in the advance of the villains on his helpless heroines in his suspense films – the next room had one more door they had to break down while the rescuers got closer in a cross-cut scene of parallel action. By 1910 he had also expanded the method to include in the same way action spread backwards and forwards across what were effectively adjoining spaces in exterior scenes. There are innumerable examples of this, but mention of cross-cutting to parallel action brings us to the other major feature of his style that Griffith derived from Pathé films.

Cross-Cutting to Parallel Action

As noted in the previous chapter, embryonic cross-cutting showed signs of emerging before 1907, and further examples of its development occurred before its alleged invention by D.W. Griffith in the latter part of 1908. The Vitagraph film, *The Mill Girl*, which was released in September 1907 has a scene with two chains of action going on inside and outside a house shown in a series of shots which alternate between the inside and outside three times, though really these actions are directly connected, since the person inside the house is reacting to what is going on outside after the first inside-outside alternation. Likewise in *le Thé chez le concierge* (Gaumont 1907), the many repeated cuts between the inside and the outside of the building are directly connected by the ringing of the bell inside to the actions of those ringing it outside.

However, in the Pathé film, *le Cheval emballé*, made late in 1907, and released at the beginning of 1908 in America, the actions shown inside and outside a house are truly independent. In this film there are repeated cuts back and forth between four pairs of shots showing a delivery man's horse demolishing a grain merchant's stock outside the house, and his driver dawdling on his calls to various flats inside (more Pathé 'goings and comings'). And in *Je vais chercher le pain* made about the same time, a similar piece of cross-cutting with a mild suspense element is set up. But far more striking is *The Physician of the Castle*. This was released in New York on 28 March 1908 under the title *A Narrow Escape*, and had its story, and even the staging of one of the scenes, reproduced in Griffith's film *The Lonely Villa*, which he made in May 1909. The basic plot of *The Physician of the Castle* is that two criminals lure a doctor away from his home to a local chateau with a false telegram, then break into his house, where his wife and child remain, killing a maid in the process. The doctor's wife barricades herself behind a series of doors with her son, and rings her husband at the chateau. The two strands of action have already been shown in alternate scenes at this point, and then we get a pair of Medium Close Shots of the doctor's wife and the doctor taking on the telephone, using this method of representing a phone conversation for the first time ever, as far as I am aware. There is then a cut back from the MCU of the doctor to a Long Shot of the scene. After this the doctor is driven in his car back to his house in a series of four shots, followed by a shot back inside his house of the criminals breaking though the second barricade. The rescuers then burst into this scene to save the day. The use of a cutaway to the other end of a telephone conversation can also be seen used in the 1907 Pathé version of *l'Affaire Dreyfus*, along with the other alternative way of treating a telephone conversation, which was to use a split screen effect to keep both speakers on the screen at the same time. Both methods slowly became standard methods of treating a telephone conversation over the next few years.

Even at Biograph there was a weak example of cross-cutting between parallel actions before Griffith started to direct for them. *Her First Adventure* made in May 1908 by Wallace McCutcheon, when Griffith was already acting there, has repeated cuts from the kidnapped child and her captors to shots of those pursuing them further back down the streets they are travelling through.

There does not seem to be much doubt that Griffith saw *le Cheval emballé*, for his film *The Curtain Pole*, which was made later in 1908, has some of its action quite closely based on the Pathé film, but it also has to be said that his first use of cross-cutting in *The Fatal Hour*, made in July of 1908, has a much stronger suspense story served by this construction than those in the surviving Pathé examples. And it has to be admitted that whoever made the Pathé films did not recognize the potentialities of this technique, and that from this point onwards Griffith certainly developed the device much further, gradually increasing the number of alternations between the two, and later three, sets of parallel scenes, and also their speed. He used a cross-cutting structure in approximately a quarter of his Biograph films made in 1908 and 1909, but this usage was only slowly taken up by other American film-makers. Examples from other production companies, such as Vitagraph's *The Telephone* of 1910, are extremely rare until 1913, when cross-cutting began to appear in films from the Thomas Ince company and some others.

Just why this was so is not completely clear to me, but certainly film stories have to be specially constructed to be suitable for cross-cutting between parallel actions, particularly in one-reel films. Griffith was in a position to do this, since he worked with what were described at the time (1912) as 'on the flap-of-an-envelope stories'. So although he did not invent the technique of cross-cutting, he did consciously develop it into a powerful method of film construction. It is also important to note that Griffith described cross-cutting indiscriminately as the 'switch-back' or 'cut-back' or 'flash-back' technique, and that by the last of these terms he did *not* mean what we now understand by 'flash-back'. The true 'flash-back' also developed in this period, but not at all under Griffith's hands.

What Griffith Really Did

There are some aspects of Griffith's work which have been satisfactorily described and emphasized in the past, and the most obvious of these are the large-scale constructional symmetries in some of his films. The best place to read about these effects is in Tom Gunning's book *D. W. Griffith and the Origin of the American Narrative Film* (University of Illinois

Press, 1991), though some films such as *The Country Doctor* (1908) have been analysed before, by Robert M. Henderson, Vlada Petric, and others. The peak of Griffith's efforts at a complex large-scale narrative structure in the Biograph period was *A Corner in Wheat*, and you can read about the significances of the form of this film in Gunning's book.

Richard Schickel has pointed out in his *D.W. Griffith* (Pavilion, 1984), that one of Griffith's most important methods was the invention of striking bits of expressive business for the actors to do. The examples of this are almost innumerable, but a good one that recently caught my attention is the enraged and jealous husband in *The Voice of a Child* (1911) walking around his office chomping on a cigar and puffing clouds of smoke out of it through clenched teeth.

One aspect of this last technique which has not been properly brought out before this is that because of the various methods of narrative dissection which he *did* develop, i.e. cross-cutting between parallel action and the use of the 'space beside', by 1909 Griffith was moving towards the point where most shots in his films contained no more than one action which was significant for the plot. In fact at this date there already begin to be shots in his films which contain nothing that advances the story, but just show someone moving quickly through them on the way to the next scene. However, when this was the case, Griffith always tried to get the actor to make a movement of some noticeable kind. This is frequently no more than a brief halt to look back towards their pursuers, or a gesture towards where they are leading their companion, as in *What the Daisy Said*, or perhaps a pause for a self-satisfied chuckle towards the camera by the seducer, as in *The Voice of a Child*, and so on, and on, and on.

Another feature of D.W. Griffith's direction that becomes noticeable from about 1910 onwards is that he arranges the action so that one of the principals is left alone, and clearly thinking about their predicament. There then ensues a passage of silent acting, though without formal mime gestures, directed towards the front. The earliest example I have particularly noted, though it is probably not the first, occurs in *The Light That Came*, when the heroine, who has been badly scarred in an accident, sits in front of a mirror looking at herself. It has already been established, basically by means of narrative titles, that she fears that the blind man with whom she has fallen in love will reject her if his sight is restored by an operation, which could be financed with her savings. The whole plot of the film has clearly contrived to produce this situation, and so to give an opportunity for this piece of solo acting. As the examples multiply over the following years, they become rather more blatant, particularly since the acting in the big scene becomes more obviously directed towards the front. The recipient of this acting opportunity is usually, though not always, one of the inexperienced young girls Griffith now started to engage as actresses.

Also from about 1910, there was a move towards shooting Griffith's films with a camera at head height, and together with the other features of staging which I have already described; the frontal organization in groupings and the use of side by side spaces, the faster cutting, and so on, the effect hardens into idiosyncrasy.

Most of the more obvious particular aspects of D.W. Griffith's style were inevitably adopted by the other directors at Biograph from 1910 onwards, so that Frank Powell, Mack Sennett, and later Tony O'Sullivan and Dell Henderson made films that used a fair amount of cross-cutting, the 'space beside', and general frontal organization. Their films look much more like Griffith films than they look like anything from other companies made at the same time. However, these other directors created at Biograph were much less talented than Griffith at inventing dramatically expressive gestures for their actors, or indeed even non-dramatically expressive gestures. Even Biograph actors who did not direct films under Griffith, but left and became directors elsewhere, such as James Kirkwood, took up the more obvious features of Griffith's style. In particular, the rapid and immense success of Mack Sennett's films at Keystone from 1912 meant that the major features of the Griffith style were generally adopted in America as *the* way to make slapstick comedy for quite a number of years.

Flash-Back Construction

There are two principal classes of flashbacks: those that show scenes in the past that someone is remembering in their own mind, and those that show past scenes that are being narrated by someone to an audience within the framing scene. This distinction may not have been clear to early film-makers, but since it is objectively quite definite, it is worth making here just to be on the safe side. The earliest known example of a narrated flashback occurs in the Cines film *La fiabe della nonne*, made in the middle of 1908. This begins with a Long Shot of the grandmother of the title telling a story to a group of children, and then there is a dissolve, without any explana-

tion, to the fantastic story she is telling them, which continues through a number of scenes, these being joined by straight cuts and intertitles. These intertitles do not seem to be the grandmother's actual words, but just the briefest of continuity explanations. The flashback is finally left through another dissolve back to the scene of the grandmother telling the story.

The other form of flash-back construction would seem to have developed out of the way dreams were represented in films of the previous period. Dream scenes were already being done in multi-shot form before 1907, and when they showed past events all that was required for them to become true flashbacks in the modern sense of the term was that the person shown having them should be awake rather than asleep. The first film that I know of in which this happens is Vitagraph's *Napoleon - Man of Destiny* made in 1909. Here, Napoleon is shown sitting in his palace in 1815 after the battle of Waterloo, awake and remembering his past life, scenes of which are cut directly into the framing scene after a superimposed title has appeared naming the event to come. The film ends with a *flash-forward* to what is, in the context of the film story, the future scene of his imprisonment on St. Helena. The only example of flashback construction from 1910 that I have so far come across is in the Swedish film, *Fänrik Ståls Sägner*. This is based on a narrative poem by the nineteenth century Finnish poet, J.L. Runeberg, and the story is presented as a flashback inside a scene which shows an actor representing the poet reading it. I think it highly likely that there was further development of true flashback construction during 1910, and one reason for this belief is that the scriptwriter George Rockhill Craw, writing in *The Moving Picture World* (Vol.8, no. 3, 21 January 1911, p. 178), suggests that it should have been used to improve on the script construction of Vitagraph's *Three Cherry Pips*. (Of course he does not use the actual word 'flashback', but 'vision', which had now extended in meaning to include what we call 'flashbacks', as well as describing the

Napoleon in the late Empress Josephine's bedroom in Napoleon – Man of Destiny *(Vitagraph, 1910), with the superimposed title which has just appeared to announce the transition to the last of the flashback scenes in this film.*

imaginary or dream visions already used in films.). In 1911 flashback construction got under way properly in Italy, with at least three films. In the Italian Milano company's *L'Inferno*, the story of Paolo and Francesca, and also other stories told by the inhabitants of Hell, are introduced and narrated by dialogue titles cut into them, and with the beginning and ending of the flashbacks marked by fade-outs and fade-ins. The same method is used to present the same stories in the competing version of *L'Inferno*, made almost simultaneously by the Helios company. The flashback made its next appearance in a surviving film in Luigi Maggi's *Nozze d'oro*, from later in the same year. In this film an old couple on their golden wedding anniversary tell their children that they will describe how they met, and immediately after the intertitle conveying this information there is a straight cut to a series of scenes continuously depicting those past events, which form the body of the film. At the end of the film the framing scene is returned to by means of a fade-out and a fade-in. In *The Passer-by*, made by Oscar Apfel for Edison in 1912, the flashback was presented in what was to become one of the classic forms; the camera tracks into Close Up on a character who has started to narrate a series of past events through dialogue titles to a gathering of people, and then there is a dissolve on his features which leads directly to the first shot of the flashback. this is done without any *descriptive* intertitle separating the present scene and the remembered scenes, and explaining that the scenes to come happened in the past. Doing flashbacks like this obviously depended on the use of a camera which could be wound back for dissolves, and this method was also facilitated by the recent introduction of dialogue titles cut into preceding scenes to make a preparation for the flashback.

Examples of true flashback construction like those just described can be found in a few films from most countries in 1912 and 1913, even from Russia (*Bratya Razboinki*) and

Australia (*The Sick Stockrider*), and for a few years the device stood beside the gradual adoption of cross-cutting as a way of introducing complexity into film construction. One of the more notable examples of 1913 was *Just a Shabby Doll* (Thanhouser Co.), in which one of a series of flashbacks includes another flashback inside itself. This is done as another scene inset within part of the frame which shows the main shot of the flashback. A number of flashbacks in films in this year are just single shot scenes with the transition made by a fade-out and a fade-in. When the flashback started to become really popular in 1912, Griffith tried it out just once in *Man's Genesis*, where a character in the framing scene narrates the main story of the film, which is set in pre-historic times. However, his unease with this form of construction is demonstrated by the fact that when he remade the same story a year later as *In Prehistoric Days*, the past story is represented as a dream.

The Space Behind

There was another peculiar and distinct form of staging that was developed in some French films of this period, as has been pointed out to me by Ben Brewster. His own account of this phenomenon can now be read in his article 'Deep Staging in French Films 1900-1914', which is included in *Early Cinema: space - frame - narrative* (ed. T. Elsaesser, BFI Publishing, 1990). What was involved was a combination of certain special features of the set design with the staging of action within it. In the form in which it arose in interior scenes, the room sets were built with a large door at the back through which could be seen another full-sized room. Part of the action of the scene, though usually not the most important part, would be played in this back space, being visible through the door from the unchanging camera position. This usage, which may have had a theatrical origin, is first visible in embryonic form in *l'Assassinat du Duc de Guise* (1908), and

Staging in depth and the use of the 'space behind' in Ekspeditricen *(August Blom, 1911). This shot is lit solely by daylight.*

its development can be traced through other films of the 'Film d'Art' genre such as *le Siege de Calais* (1911). This latter film includes a variant form of the technique carried out on exteriors, in which a large gateway with more open set behind it took the place of the doorway to the room behind.

In the next few years this sort of staging spread to contemporary subjects such as *Roman d'un mousse* (Léonce Perret, 1913), and inevitably it also spread to the other European countries most influenced by French cinema, which were Denmark, Sweden, and Italy. Amongst a number of Danish examples could be mentioned *Ekspeditricen* (August Blom, 1911), and it could still be seen as late as 1918, as in *Mater Dolorosa* by Abel Gance.

This form of staging was rarer in American films during this period, for they had quickly reached the point of development where any adjoining room, whether beside or behind the one where the main scene took place, would be entered by the camera with a cut if the action moved there. Nevertheless, there are a certain number of American examples of this, particularly towards 1913. The Vitagraph company was the most fond of this type of set design, though even in their films it was a minor feature. They sometimes used a weak form of this staging by making a reverse angle cut that finally entered the room behind after the scene had been going on for some time. For instance, in *Uncle Tom's Cabin* (1910), Eliza can be seen in the background behind the big half-open doors of the back room eavesdropping on a conversation, but after this shot has gone on for a while in the European manner, there

Staging in depth in Léonce Perret's Roman d'un mousse *(1913). This studio interior is largely lit with arc floodlights. most of them out right in the foreground room, but there is also one out left lighting the boy in the chair. The light in the rear room is coming from a group of floodlights out left.*

A Vitagraph studio set for The Inherited Taint *(1911), with a space behind constructed to accomodate background action.*

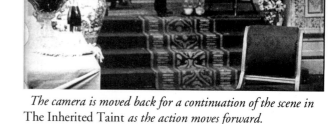

The camera is moved back for a continuation of the scene in The Inherited Taint *as the action moves forward.*

is then a cut to the reverse-angle on the scene from behind Eliza, looking into the other room which is now in the background. In these rare American examples the sets were never constructed on the large scale common in the European use of the form.

When Vitagraph used this kind of set with the space behind without it being part of a reverse scene construction, it was usually for scenes at grand parties, of which they were quite fond. (Not very surprisingly, given J.S. Blackton's taste for social climbing in his private life.) However, in such cases, the room visible behind was only used to contain extras dancing, or the like, and not to contain part of the main action. (This could really be considered to be an indoor variant of the Red Indians or fisher folk going about their colourful business behind the main action in the shot, which D.W. Griffith introduced into his outdoor subjects from 1909 onwards.) A particularly fine early Vitagraph example is in *The Inherited Taint* (1911), in which the camera steps back during the course of the scene as the actors move forwards, so revealing more and more depth in the set. During the war the simpler form of this sort of set design and staging for big party scenes spread to other American companies.

From a general point of view one could consider the European use of the space behind to be an attempt to get more variation in the image during the course of the shot (and of the film) to make up for that variety which was otherwise provided in American films by the greater use of cutting.

Set Design

The use of the space behind just described obviously depends on the space being created beforehand by the set builders, and indeed designed by a set designer. Of course there had to be such people from the moment films began to be produced on an industrial scale by the Pathé company, and the biggest American companies, Vitagraph and Edison, not to mention the Italian companies, had them as well in this period. At Biograph, the studio sets were so nondescript that

it is possible that they did not have a real set designer, and the same applies to the lesser American companies. In most films of this period, it was still usual to shoot the scenes with the camera flat on to the set, but there are numerous European films on historical subjects from 1909 onwards where the master shot on a scene is taken at an angle to the set. The same applies to some Vitagraph films of the same kind, such as *Richelieu* (1909). All this bespeaks the use of a set designer. Although such films still involved a fair amount of cheating, with pillars and other three-dimensional objects painted onto flat surfaces, the craftsmanship of this was mostly so good that even the modern viewer is not particularly aware of it. The finish on contemporary sets got better during this period, and more importantly, as the camera got closer in, and the genuine solidity of the furniture occupied more and more of the foreground, middle ground, and back ground, the sense of naturalism increased a great deal, getting close to what we consider normal in a film. About 1912 a strange concept emerged in the set design for some American films. This involved painting the walls of the set a very dark uniform colour, which came out on film as a very dark grey, near to black. Although most visible in many Vitagraph films, the treatment can also be seen in films from Biograph and other companies. I can only conjecture that it was intended to produce extra visual separation of the figures from the background. A minor interesting idea from Pathé was the building of a set representing the interior of a house on two levels, with more than one room on each floor being simultaneously visible to the camera. This kind of multi-storey cross-sectional set, like the view of the back of a doll's house, was used in at least two 1909 films, *Why Jones Couldn't Sleep*, and *Uncle Richard*, and there may well have been more. In the two examples cited, after a scene has started in what seems to be a perfectly ordinary set, a pan or tilt continuously follows a character through the wall or up through the floor to the next floor. This set design concept has kept reappearing in films every several years ever since.

Other Types of Staging

Throughout the years 1907-1913 most films, including those of D.W. Griffith, but largely excluding Vitagraph films, had the grouping of the actors oriented towards the camera and the putative audience after the manner used on the legitimate stage. The degree to which this is noticeable varies, and sometimes in American films it could extend as far as the leading players looking straight at the camera, though this was rare. Even in comedy, American films use acting addressed straight to the camera less than European films, where it was still very common in 1913. To put it another way, by 1913 blatant and continuous direction of the acting towards the camera can be regarded as a retarded feature in American dramatic films.

Although he did not use staging in depth in the strict sense, which calls for dramatic connection between actors in the foreground and others well in the background, Griffith did develop a weaker related form of staging. In this approach extras were placed in the background in Very Long Shot engaged in activities that provided an atmospheric background to the main action. This is most noticeable in his films on Indian and fishing community subjects, beginning with *Comata, the Sioux* and *Lines of White on a Sullen Sea*, both made late in 1909. Actually this procedure can be seen as a substitute for the filming of acted scenes in the foreground of a real situation which had real people going about their ordinary business without taking too much notice of the camera, as other film-makers continued to try to achieve on suitable occasions. Griffith himself had tried this approach earlier, as in *Romance of a Jewess* (1908), which has scenes shot in the Jewish quarter of New York, but in later years he turned to completely staging the background action, quite possibly from preference. But in the period under consideration, other film-makers only followed his lead in this to a limited extent.

This leads me to consider the way scenes of mass action were staged at this time. At first theatrical tradition continued to provide the model, as it had in earlier years, but by 1910 other influences had begun to appear, particularly in Italy. In that country the effect of the graphic art of the recent past can be seen in *L'Inferno* (Giuseppe di Liguoro, 1911) and *La caduta di Troia* (Giovanni Pastrone, 1910), and others. The compositions of *L'Inferno* are largely modelled on Gustave Doré's engravings for *La divina commedia*, and in *La caduta di Troia* the influence is from the Alma-Tadema type of salon painting. However, mixed in with the more derivative approaches to large-scale staging, the emergence of a more purely filmic approach can also be seen in some films. Sometimes this is just a matter of the conjunction of the topography of the location and the relatively unorganized enthusiasm of the extras, and sometimes it is the result of camera placement, as in some scenes in *La caduta di Troia*. As is well-known, the Italians pushed the staging of large-scale scenes much further in the next few years, and both the Salon Painting strain in staging and the purely filmic approach developed side by side in such films as *Jone* (Vidali, 1913) and *Quo Vadis?* (Enrico Guazzoni, 1913). The kind of composition that is sometimes used to combine principal figures with massed extras in D.W. Griffith's films from 1913 onwards is anticipated in *La sposa del Nilo* (Cines, 1911), though this may not be a matter of influence, but rather of directors with similar backgrounds producing a similar solution to the same filmic problem.

Film Acting

Although the patternless diversity of acting styles current in the previous period still continued to exist in 1907, the next several years saw the emergence of greater consistency in this dimension, and also substantial modifications of the general approach. Some of the last of the pure melodrama poses can

An example of the influence of late 19th. Century Salon painting in the manner of Alma-Tadema on the design and composition of film images in Italian cinema. A shot from Jone, *directed by Giovanni Enrico Vidali for the Pasquali company in 1913.*

A staging in La sposa del Nilo *(Cines, 1911),*
similar to some of those later used by D.W.
Griffith in his spectacle films.

be seen in Vitagraph's *The Mill Girl* of 1907, but already a
good deal of the acting of the principals in this film is no longer
directed towards the audience. Broader acting from the principals surrounded by naturalistic playing from the supporting
actors was quite common, though decreasingly, in American
films throughout this period. The classical mime style, which
uses fully extended gestures of the arm with flowing movements and a smooth line to them in the ballet manner was
usually used for subjects having a high-class literary derivation,
as in Vitagraph's *Francesca da Rimini* (1907). Interestingly,
the acting in the French 'film d'art' was much more restrained,
for the creators of this genre explicitly sought a new acting
style appropriate to film with emphasis placed on still moments, and they avoided the classical mime style quite intentionally, as can be seen in *l'Assassinat du Duc de Guise*.

An example of acting from the naturalistic extreme of the
spectrum that already existed in American cinema is given by
Biograph's *Her First Adventure* made early in 1908. In this
umpteenth entry in the 'baby kidnapping by gypsies' genre,
all the acting is so naturalistic that it is questionable whether
it should be called acting at all, or just behaving. Such an
acting style may well have been less effective with audiences
than broad mime, particularly since this film was shot so far
back from the actors. Certainly the acting in D.W. Griffith's
first films made a few months later is much broader than in
Her First Adventure, though the very first of his films, *The
Adventures of Dolly*, is essentially a remake of the same film,
which Griffith presumably seen, as he was already working as an actor for Biograph when it was made.

It is difficult to generalize about the acting in Griffith's
films made in 1908 and 1909, since although much more
restrained acting appears in some of his films from *The Stolen
Jewels* (September, 1908) onwards, there is no consistency in
this. There continue to be many of his films, such as *Tragic*

Love (December, 1908) that use very broad acting, and so it
continues through the years. It may be that these differences
are due to the varying actors used in all these films, with less
than complete control over their performances being exercised
by the director, but to determine this for certain involves a
major piece of research. However, it may also be that since
Griffith had been brought up on melodramatic acting, he did
not worry very much about its presence. It is noticeable that
Florence Lawrence and Harry Salter give nice light comedy
performances in the first half of *A Calamitous Elopement*
(1908); performances of a kind that never reappear in Griffith's films, and it is also noticeable that the films of his first
year all have adult female leads, presumably inherited as part
of Biograph's stock company. The transition to the well-
known skittering nymphets comes after this.

It is only at the beginning of 1910 that a fair proportion
of the acting in Griffith's films becomes markedly restrained,
but even then it does not reach the degree of naturalism
evident in some of Vitagraph's films such as *The Telephone*
(1910) and *The Law and the Man* (1910). It would seem from
Romance of an Umbrella (1909) that Vitagraph had been
ahead of Griffith all the time in this particular. This high
degree of naturalism was consolidated by the Vitagraph actors
over the next few years, and the best of them managed to
project with great intensity, despite the constraints of doing
very little physically. Their achievement in this direction was
explicitly recognized and admired in Europe, as can be seen
from Victorin Jasset's comments on the Vitagraph films in
1913. Whether it was as highly valued in the United States is
open to question, and it is quite possible that the broader
acting style that was the norm in American films, including
those of D.W. Griffith, was more effective with the audience
there.

(Following the general principles I am using, I do not hold

that naturalistic acting is intrinsically superior to stylized acting. Indeed I believe that there is much to be said for a very individual style that falls some way short of naturalism, such as that Asta Nielsen developed in this period. Her movements and poses, which owe a lot to the stage dancing (though not ballet) of this period, combined with an occasional well-placed 'thinks' look towards the camera, formed a powerful instrument of expression in films made by Urban Gad from *Afgrunden* (1910) onwards.)

The generalizations that I have been making about acting in American films must be understood to be taken against a background of certain differences in the way that various racial types were presented at this time – American Indians were presented with broader acting than white men, and Mediterranean types were acted in an even broader way. Again, the acting in historical subjects was everywhere broader than in contemporary stories, and this difference was also observed in European films.

Narrative Construction

The vast increase in film production after 1906 inevitably brought specialist writers into film-making as part of the increasing sub-division of labour in the interests of increased output, and these people both in themselves, and also as a response to that demand, introduced a greater variety in the types of story used in films. The use of more complex stories derived from literary and stage works of the recent past also contributed to developments in film construction. The general American tendency was to simplify the plots borrowed from novels and plays so that they could be dealt with in one reel and with the minimum of titling and the maximum of straightforward narrative continuity, but there were exceptions to this. As I have already said, the Vitagraph tradition was to incorporate the information that was difficult to film and lacking in strong dramatic interest into narrative titles before each scene, rather than simplifying the story, and this was also mostly the custom in European films of the more seriously intended kind.

Narrative titles in American films also had another indirect function, which was to eliminate what we would now call 'jump cuts' between scenes. For the most efficient use of the 1000 feet of film per reel that was all that was available for standard films, it was very frequently necessary to start the next scene with some of the actors from the previous scene already in shot, even though the new scene was taking place later and in some other place. By 1908 it seems that there was already a strong feeling in the American industry that this 'jump' in narrative time was disruptive, and so one frequently finds narrative titles between scenes in American films supplying information that is completely redundant. Sometimes European film-makers used narrative titles in this way, but they were much more inclined to do without any title between scenes, unless more information was absolutely necessary. Hence many European films of the period have jump cuts between scenes. This is particularly noticeable in Danish films,

and to a lesser extent in Italian films. European comedies of the cruder kind were particularly likely to include this sort of jump cutting.

As far as the move away from cramming the story from a whole novel, opera, or full-length play into a one-reel film is concerned, it is possible that D.W. Griffith was a major influence. Before he came onto the scene, there were many films that had stories nicely adapted to being narrated within the limits of the form, but equally, there were many that were not. At first, the Griffith Biograph films frequently used stories that were not well adapted to being clearly presented in one reel, but this changed after several months. In any case, by the middle of 1909, Griffith was starting to make some films that had much less story content than any previous films which were one full reel in length. The earliest Griffith film that I have noticed which has sharply reduced content is *The Message*, made in May 1909, and released 21 June 1909, and the second is the much better known *The Country Doctor*, which was made a few days later. In *The Message*, a good deal of the time is taken up with the characters interacting in a not particularly dramatic way while they wander round the farm location. Nevertheless, the detail of their behaviour is well worked out, and there is always a fair amount of visual interest in the scenes, and none of this actively interferes with the simple triangle story, but rather makes it seem more real. In *The Country Doctor*, the action is no more than various people, including the doctor, hurrying backwards and forwards between the doctor's house, where his child is sick, and a neighbouring cottage, where another child is also sick. From this point on, there are many Griffith films where he seems to be consciously demonstrating how the audience's attention can be gripped with the slimmest story possible. Of course, before this date he had made suspense thrillers like *A Drive For Life* (22/04/09) which had very slight plots, but that sort of Griffith film always had lots of action events in it, even if the basic story was very simple.

Other film-makers also began working in this way at least some of the time. For instance, although Vitagraph films usually had more plot in them than Biograph films, they could produce a film like *Jean Rescues* (1911), which had as little plot as any Griffith film. However, such Vitagraph films are usually confined to the Light Romance genre. By 1912 and 1913, there are beginning to be many films from many American companies, particularly Selig, that rely on applying novel decoration to the story rather than supplying any twists of the drama itself to sustain interest. (In the case of Selig films, the decoration was the wild animals the company owned.)

Dialogue Titles

In 1907 and 1908, as in previous years, the use of intertitles containing lines of dialogue was extremely rare, and it was definitely not standard procedure. But this began to change towards the end of 1908. *An Auto Heroine; or, The Race for the Vitagraph Cup and How It Was Won*, released 17 October 1908, contains a couple of dialogue titles, and the same firm's

Julius Caesar, released on 1 December 1908, includes three lines of dialogue from Shakespeare's play quoted in intertitles, finishing with 'This was the noblest Roman of them all'. Since there were a number of other Vitagraph films from 1908 based on classic stories which are now lost, it is quite likely that some of these also contained other famous lines of dialogue in their intertitles. In any case, starting from 1909, a small number of American films, and even one or two European ones, came to include a few dialogue titles, or 'spoken' titles as they were called. Film-makers slowly progressed from putting these dialogue titles before the scene in which they were spoken, to cutting them into the middle of the shot at the point at which they were understood to be actually spoken by the characters. This transition began in 1912. The logical reason for making this change was that since the scene almost always contained more than one person talking, it could be difficult for the audience to instantly recognise who was supposed to be speaking the words that had appeared before the scene started. Once underway, the trend was aided by the move towards the increasing use of cuts within scenes in American films. In 1913 the proportion of American films using dialogue titles at all was 63 out of my total sample of 171 for that year, and only about half of these dialogue titles were cut in at the point when they were spoken. Hardly any of the films where this happened were D.W. Griffith films, and indeed many of his 1913 films still contain no dialogue titles at all. Although a few European film-makers picked up the trend towards using dialogue titles, they did not pick up on the move towards cutting them into the scene at the point at which they were actually spoken until a few years later.

The introduction of dialogue titles was far from being a trivial matter, for they entirely transformed the nature of film narrative. Not only does a dialogue title take less time to read than the narrative title it replaces, but when it is cut into the point at which it is spoken, it interrupts the flow of the narrative far less. When dialogue titles came to be always cut into a scene just after a character starts speaking, and then left with a cut to the character just before they finish speaking, then one has something that was nearly the same as a sound film, or indeed much closer to an audio-visual recording of a stage play, if one likes to look at it that way. On the other hand, with nothing but narrative titles before each scene, one has something tending more in the direction of an illustrated book. Indeed, a case could be made that as the film stood at the beginning of this period, though not at the end, it was more nearly a unique aesthetic medium than it came to be some decades later, at any rate as far as mainstream cinema was concerned.

Illustrated Titles

Although they were fairly typical of American companies in the way they handled intertitles, Vitagraph did toy with a novel idea in their presentation in 1910 and 1911. In 1910, perhaps in response to the new striving after 'art' in film-making which had just begun, they made a few films which had special illustrated borders round the intertitles. The most striking example from 1910 was *Daisies*, in which the whole plot turned on that flower, and which was present in most of the film scenes in various forms. Here the intertitles had a border of daisies, instead of having the standard 'picture frame' style decorative border. A few weeks before this the company presented *Hako's Sacrifice*, a Japanese subject, in which the intertitles had a border made of bamboo rods, though the bamboo played no part in the story. Another surviving example of illustrated borders on titles is *Auld Robin Grey* from a couple of months later, and it is quite likely that there were a some more similar Vitagraph films from this period.

In 1911, the Vitagraph film-makers made a small extra step forward, in *Consuming Passion; or, St. Valentine's Day in*

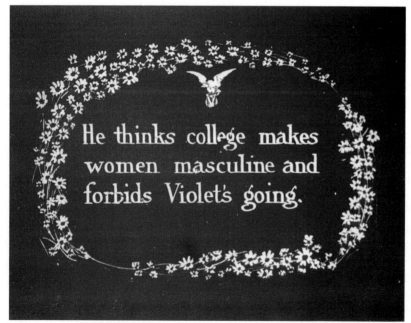

A decorated border used for the intertitles in Vitagraph's Daisies *(1910).*

Extra small drawings placed around the standard Vitagraph titles to illustrate the events in the story in Consuming Passion; or, St. Valentine's Day in Greenaway Land *(1911).*

Greenaway Land, which told a story of school infant love and gingerbread hearts, acted in slightly stylized settings reminiscent of the paintings by the famous illustrator of children's books. The costumes of the children followed the Kate Greenaway style closely, too. In this case, although the borders of the intertitles were the same throughout the film, they included drawings of toys and other things which changed in accordance with the course of the narrative. This was a remarkable anticipation of the vogue for illustrated intertitles which only started properly in American films in 1916, and lasted into the early 'twenties, but there are no other early examples of this feature among the surviving Vitagraph films. The most likely explanation for this was that by 1911 the larger part of Vitagraph's film sales were overseas, and the difficulty of reconstituting these illustrated intertitles on the title cards for every foreign language, which had to be remade at their Paris factory, was not considered worthwhile. This last point probably also explains why the idea was only taken up generally in American films in 1916, when it was clear that most of the foreign market was cut off by the Great War, and also why the practice died out again after the war.

The Multi-Reel film

As is well-known, the transition to the production of films more than one reel long was a gradual process involving a number of well-separated stages. Almost from the beginning of film history there were films of the life of Christ that ran longer than one reel, but it is only in the 1907-1913 period that a substantial number of multi-reel films on other subjects began to appear. The earliest American examples, such as Vitagraph's *Life of Moses* (1909), were released as separate parts of one reel each in successive weeks, though exhibitors naturally turned to showing these parts together as a continuous film more or less straightaway. The general way such films were structured was to have the dramatic action shaped

to give a natural 'act' break at the end of each reel, and this continued to be usual in multi-reel films for some time, and indeed was recommended in script writing manuals around 1913. However, not all long American films show this structure, as can be seen in the now well-known *Traffic in Souls* (1913). Here the incident- packed plot speeds over the reel changes without being particularly shaped to their occurrence.

Subjective Effects

It is not until the next period that subjective camera effects really start to develop properly, but there are some striking forerunners from 1912 and 1913. The first of these is in Victorin Jasset's *Zigomar contre Nick Carter.* This film contains a sequence in a opium den, and the drugged vision of one of the clients is represented as a series of superimpositions overlaid onto the main scene, and these eventually build up into a set of multiple images within the one frame. There is a development of this idea the next year in the Itala company's *Tigris.* This is mostly a rather clumsy imitation of the earlier 'Zigomar' criminal master-mind thrillers by Jasset, but a drug vision in it takes the device closer to the later standard form of the montage sequence. As the effect of the drug takes hold, this is represented by tilting the frame sideways, then superimposing a series of disjointed images fading and dissolving in and out on a patterned background. Apart from these very special cases involving chains of superimpositions, in many films there are of course quite a lot of ordinary visions shown within one shot as *single* inset scenes, or as *single* superimposed scenes, or both, just as there had been before 1907.

'Symbolism' and the Insert Shot

As a result of the increasing artistic ambitions of filmmakers during this period, poems and other 'literary' subjects began to be transposed directly into films. Griffith's filming of Browning's *Pippa Passes* is well-known, but the same impulse can be seen at work elsewhere, as in the Italian Cines company's film *La campana* (1909), based on Schiller's poem *Die Glocke*. These films are no more than live illustrated versions of the verses of the poems, which precede the various scenes in them. Griffith was capable of moving on from this to an adaptation of the poetic refrain to visual form in an original film subject *The Way of the World*, made a year later, which although it featured repeated Insert Shots of bells again, was more than a simple illustration of a poem. However it took some years for Griffith to develop the Insert Shot further as a force in its own right, as a way of drawing attention to narrative objects with significant connotations. In his other 1910 films the Insert Shots were still just used to show things clearly, as had been a long established usage. When one of his films such as *Simple Charity* centred on the role of an object, in this case a girl's dress, it was not singled out by being given its own exclusive Insert anywhere in the course of the film. When one gets the rare Insert shot in his films, it is only there to make an object or action visually clear when that is impossible in the more distant shot in which the scene is being conducted. Not very numerous examples include the poisoning of the candy in *Drive for a Life* (1909), and the adjustable wrench pretending to be a gun in *The Lonedale Operator* (1911).

Later in 1910 Griffith made a couple of films that make explicit claims to 'symbolism' in their titles, namely *The Two Paths - A Symbolism* and *A Modern Prodigal - A Story in Symbolism*, but despite their titles, neither contain any special new filmic usages in this area. However, by 1912 there were the first signs of the special use of the Insert which was to prove so important from that date onwards. Early in the year the Italian Ambrosio company released *La mala pianta*, directed by Mario Caserini. This film, which involves a case of poisoning, begins with an Insert shot of a snake slithering over the 'Evil Plant' of the title. Another of the still very rare examples is in Griffith's *The Massacre*, which was made at the end of 1912. This includes an Insert Shot of a candle at a sick man's bedside guttering out to indicate his death. Yet another is in the Ambrosio company version of *Gli ultimi giorni di Pompei* (1913). This film includes a scene, preceded by the title 'The thorns of jealousy', in which a rejected woman overhears the man she loves with another woman, and this is followed by a fade to a shot of a pair of doves, which then dissolves into a shot of a bird of prey. Unfortunately this is about the only point of interest in this film, which is otherwise much cruder than the contemporary Pasquali version of the book, *Jone*, directed by Enrico Vidali. The inspiration for the use of the symbolic effects in *Gli ultimi giorni di Pompei* may have been the original novel by Bulwer Lytton on which it is based. The heading of the chapter which includes the original of the scene just described is 'The Fowler Snares Again the Bird that Has Just Escaped, and Sets His Nets For a New Victim', and other chapters in the book also have metaphorical titles, like 'A Wasp Ventures into the Spider's Web' and other similar ones.

10. DRAMATIC CONSTRUCTION FROM STAGE TO FILM

Theories about how the film screenplay should be structured began to be articulated at least as early as 1908, when film production and exhibition had standardized into programmes of single reel films. All of these theories were variants and adaptations of the basic ideas that had developed in the nineteenth century about writing stage plays. These ideas about play construction were in their turn a development of the original Aristotelian conception of what drama should be, and were well known to, and thoroughly internalized by, most writers of plays. Theories about play construction current at the end of the nineteenth century became even more important for American film scriptwriting once the long feature film became established in the United States, so I will quote a summary of the main points from the most practical and complete of these treatises on how to write a play. This was *The Art of Playwriting*, by Alfred Hennequin, published by Houghton Mifflin & Co. in 1890. The author, despite having the same name, was *not* the well-known French playwright from slightly earlier in the century. However, this American Hennequin *was* an acquaintance of George Bronson Howard, who was considered to be the first American playwright of real worth, and it seems that Hennequin's ideas about constructing plays agreed with those of Bronson Howard, not to mention those of others who followed him.

Hennequin on Playwriting

Extracts from p. 85 - 91 of Chapter XV - *"What Constitutes a Story?"*

'Every story that has any value for dramatic purposes may be reduced to the following formula:-

A (standing for one or more characters) is trying to achieve some purpose. A is opposed by B (representing one or more characters), who tries to carry out his design. After a series of incidents, in which first one and then the other seems to have the upper hand, A finally succeeds in frustrating the designs of B, and either accomplishes the end sought, or is killed.

Characters.
(1) The characters must be suited to the story – the story to the characters.

(2) The characters must be clearly distinguished one from another.

(3) The characters must be self-consistent.

(4) The characters must be selected and arranged that each one may act as a foil to another.

Completeness
A story is complete when it is told so that the listener does not need to ask what happened before it began, nor care to ask what happened after it concluded.

Unity
Unity in the sensible view is, that all the incidents of the story must be made to cluster about a single central animating idea. One purpose must be seen to run throughout the whole series of incidents, they must be so woven together that, at the end of the story, it will be evident that one could not have taken place without the other. This constitutes the *unity of action.*

Motived Incidents
The incident must be *motived.* This means that the cause of every incident must be apparent in some incident that has preceded it, and serves as a motive for it. Every event must be seen to grow naturally out of what has gone before, and to lead naturally to what has comes after. An incident which is introduced arbitrarily, simply for effect, is called *clap-trap.*

Next I quote extracts from pages 92 to 96 of Chapter XVI *"What constitutes a play – means of creating interest"*

1. *Interest and Pleasure*
The story must interest and please. This is the fundamental law of modern drama. It is not forbidden the dramatist to point a moral, or discuss a social problem; but these are side issues, extra-dramatic effects, which he must undertake at his own risk.

2. *Novelty*
An important requirement of a dramatic story is that it be fresh and original. .... Still it must not be forgotten that an old story, told in a new way, possesses all the charm of a new one. A certain interest also attaches to well-known events in history that compensates for their lack of novelty.

3. *Variety and Contrast*
Monotony is the bugbear of the dramatist. In order to escape it he must exercise all the inventive power of which he is possessed to vary the character of the incidents as they follow one another. Pathos must be followed by humour, wit by eloquence, "talky" passages by quick-succeeding scenes of incident, soliloquies by the rapid give-and-take of dialogue. The entire act should be a rapidly shifting kaleidoscope, presenting new features at every turn.

Variety not only destroys monotony, but it secures the powerful effect of contrast. A bit of humour is twice as effective if it follows an instant of pathos or even of commonplace.

4. *Suspense*

Suspense is the nervous system of the drama. In some form or another, it must exist throughout the entire progress of the story. At various points of the play, generally at the close of each act, it may be partially relieved, but it must always be done in such a way as to give rise to new suspense, or to leave one or two particulars still unsettled. etc.

5. *Surprise*

Nevertheless, surprise is one of the most potent of stage effects. .... Surprises are most valuable in light comedies, which sometimes consist of little more than a succession of startling incidents. In more serious plays, too sudden surprises give the story an unpleasantly abrupt and "jerky" character. The surprise, in such cases, must be in a manner prepared for; the audience must be made to have a dim foreboding of the impending disaster, while its exact nature is to be left a matter of surmise.

5. *Climax*

A regular increase of force and interest culminating in a strong situation is called a *climax*. A dramatic story should be full of climaxes from beginning to end. Every act should have several lesser ones scattered through it, and should invariably end with one of greater importance. Toward the end of the play should occur the great climax in the technical sense of the word, i.e. the point at which the interest of the play reaches its highest stage.

7. *Humour and Pathos*

Except in the lighter sort of comedy the two elements of humour and pathos are always introduced into the modern drama. No one any longer thinks of writing pure tragedy for the stage, and, on the other hand, the most saleable comedies are those which have a few touches in them of genuine pathos.'

And next, extracts from pages 109 to 116 of Chapter XVIII – *Growth*

'2. *Conflict and Plot*

Every dramatic story is founded on the conception of a character striving to accomplish some purpose in which he is thwarted by another character. This brings about a *conflict*, or clash of interest which becomes more serious and more complicated as the play proceeds, and forms the *intrigue* or plot.

(conflicts of virtuous and the wicked are to be found in all serious plays.) (In comedy, the clash or conflict usually comes about through misunderstandings – but these can also cause pathetic or tragic events.)

8. *Episodes*

However interesting an episode may be of itself, however

humorous or pathetic, it should be ruthlessly cast aside unless it in some way helps on the principal current of the story.

9. *Series of Climaxes*

If the story grows continually in interest, the introduction of various characters with their conflicting aims, will lead to a series of situations and climaxes, which themselves will be arranged in a climax.'

At this point Hennequin introduces a rising saw-tooth diagram, with a sudden fall after the grand climax, illustrating the dramatic progress of Bulwer's *Lady of Lyons*.

This is an elaboration of the kind of diagram that appeared in Gustav Freytag's *Die Technik des Dramas*, of 1876. Hennequin also says that the Grand climax should occur in the latter half of the play, and comments that multiple climaxes are now fashionable. He considers them inartistic, even though the "gallery" likes them. But they will be in demand, so make the later ones of multiple climaxes stronger.

Incidentally, Hennequin, and the writers he was discussing, including Bronson Howard, deMille Senior, and Belasco, were *not* talking about and writing melodrama, but what they considered *good* plays, which they all distinguished from the American melodrama of the time. They considered their work was realistic, and they all frequently included an intentional moral message in it.

Methods of Plot Generation

Chapter XXIII of Hennequin's *Art of Playwriting* gives a demonstration of how to create a play plot from a basic situation by logical steps. The example of a situation that he gives is "A young woman and an elderly woman in love with the same man", then, by expanding it by introducing another main character, and adding complications by making two of the characters related, and thinking of situations leading to the revelation of the character's feelings, and so on, he eventually constructs a plot he reveals to be that of Scribe's *Duel en amour*.

Although Hennequin does not say so, this technique for generating a plot is a generalization from the methods used by Bronson Howard, at least in one particular case, which the latter described in a lecture to the Harvard University Drama Club, published in the Boston *Herald* of 27 March, 1876.

A later manual on constructing plays that became popular with would-be scriptwriters was W.T. Price's *Analysis of Play Construction* (1908). Price identified the same basic constituents of a correctly constructed play as Hennequin and his other predecessors, but he suggested a different method for creating the plot. This involved a series of rational and causal steps starting from the beginning of the plot, rather than working outwards from the basic central situation, as with Hennequin. Price's term for the situation at the beginning of the plot was the "formula", and it included a *critical condition*, an *excitant*, and a *result*.

An example of a critical condition is:- "Anne Cavendish, who loves and is loved by Arthur Renwick, has ambition which has been inflamed by the artful encouragement of George Sylvester. She must choose between love and ambition. What shall be the result of her choice?" Here the excitant or disturbing factor is George Sylvester, and then the result of Anne Cavendish's choice gives rise to a new situation or formula, which is worked out in the same way, and so on.

I believe that a recent computer programme written to generate film plots uses this latter method.

Dramatic Ideas on the Screen

When there began to be extended theorizing about film script construction from 1910 onwards, these ideas from playwriting were taken over largely unaltered, with the fairly inevitable simplification that the one reel film was considered to be only capable of accommodating one climax, and also left no room for sub-plots or contrasting episodes. However, at first there was a certain amount of confusion about the basic nature of film dramaturgy amongst theorists, because there was in general no dialogue in films made before 1909. Hence the notions invented to deal with this lack, some of them derived from pre-existing ideas about the art of theatrical mime, confused the matter. Other irrelevant ideas about using short story writing as a model for film script writing also surfaced at first, but these were already being questioned by 1910, and by 1913 it was generally recognized that short story writing technique had little to contribute to film scriptwriting. This was because by 1910 even the ordinary commercial short story writing of the day had come to rely more on "colour" and fine writing than dramatic construction.

In the American one reel film the requirement that the character or mood of succeeding incidents be varied was usually not met, though it *is* actually possible for really skilled film-makers to do this with a certain amount of effort. Some of D.W. Griffith's Biograph films do contain one or two lighter incidents, verging on comedy, amongst the more dramatic scenes that make up the bulk of his films, and he and other people also made some comedies that involved suspenseful scenes amongst the more usual fooling.

Then, once films became several reels long, and having their dialogue rendered in intertitles, it became fairly easy in principle for them to accommodate all the desirable dramatic features indicated by Hennequin, though this did not happen instantaneously. Early gropings to more fully satisfy the "Variety and Contrast" criterion include the unnecessary part of a scene at a party in *The Avenging Conscience* in which Mae Marsh does her "silly flapper" routine, and the suicide scene

in Cecil B. DeMille's comedy *What's-His-Name*, both from 1914. On the other hand, another 1914 film adaptation of a successful stage play of the period, *The Spoilers*, does not manage to use variation of mood to any great extent.

The advent of the long film brought more and better people from the American theatre into the movies, together with recently successful stage plays, so it was inevitable that *all* the standard features of play construction would be eventually accommodated in motion pictures. Actually, most good nineteenth century plays were just waiting for the long film. Close examination of stage works all the way from Boucicault's *The Colleen Bawn* to Ibsen's *The Wild Duck* shows that their continuous scenes are actually broken up into sub-scenes involving different groups of people, with the playwright having to use various forced pretexts to get some characters off stage, and others onto it, for the next section of the scene and the further advancement of the plot. Hence it would be more natural for these sub-scenes to take place at other times and locations, as permitted on film, but not by the practicalities of the stage.

The full assumption of theatrical methods of dramatic construction by American motion pictures took place at the same time that the final features of continuity cinema were being generally polished and diffused, during the First World War. The perfection of standard film dramatic construction particularly involved people like Mary Pickford, who had starred in Belasco plays in New York, and who worked to incorporate features from such plays into her films when she became an independent producer. Sometimes she did this against the resistance of her collaborators, for instance Maurice Tourneur, who was very unhappy with the comedy scenes that Pickford insisted on having in *Poor Little Rich Girl* (1917). 1917 was really a crucial year for some of the new leaders of the American film industry, because, besides Pickford finally getting these things right from *Rebecca of Sunnybrook Farm* onwards, Chaplin began to introduce pathetic scenes into his comedies, and Douglas Fairbanks moved beyond his stodgy early works like *His Picture in the Papers* to better shaped constructions.

By the end of the war it was generally recognized that the model for the dramatic construction of ordinary commercial films should be theatrical, as can be seen in Howard T. Dimick's *Modern Photoplay Writing* of 1922, and other subsequent manuals on the subject. However, writing "how to do it" books about film script-writing died out in the late 'twenties, because American film studios stopped buying film scripts, and turned to having them developed by their own employees. After this, the techniques I have described were passed on inside the Hollywood studios for many decades by word of mouth and by example, but were forgotten in the outside world. This has meant that it has recently become possible for someone like Robert McKee to become very successful selling advice on film script-writing that is little more than the nineteenth century Hennequin recipe.

11. FILM STYLE AND TECHNOLOGY: 1914-1919

During the years of the First World War there was not a great deal of development in film technology, but stylistic development continued rapidly in the United States of America. It is often said that the way the war cut off the European film producers from many of their markets was responsible for the post-war dominance of the American film industry, but in fact the American industry was moving into a commanding position even before the war started at the end of 1914. This can be seen from the figures for the numbers of films shown in Germany in 1912, and those put on sale in France from 1911 to 1914, as quoted in Georges Sadoul's *Histoire Générale du Cinéma* (Tome III, 'Le Cinéma devient un Art', Premier Volume, p.10). In 1912 as many American films as French films were shown in Germany, and in Berlin in particular far more, while in France the French industry's

share of the home market fell steadily from 1911 to 1914, with the share taken by American films rising steadily to take the leading position in 1914. Eye-witness accounts of the American takeover of the market in Paris can be read in Richard Abel's *French Cinema: The First Wave 1915-1929* (Princeton, 1984). Italian films held third place in both the French and German markets throughout, followed by Danish films, and then the rest. The rapid expansion of the American industry pre-war must have been aided by the size of its home market, but when one compares a sample of American and French films made in 1913, one can see that what the European cinema-goers were already voting for in the fairly free competition for their money was:- more shots per reel, more shots in each scene, more close shots, and more naturalistic acting. In other words, a semblance of the more interesting parts of

The studio of the American Film Manufacturing Company in 1916. Sunlight diffused by thin cotton sheets suspended just above the sets still forms a large part of the lighting, but the figure modelling is sharpened by arc floodlights on floor stands shining in from the left, with a reflector being held to the right of the camera to bounce sunlight as fill on to the actors. A row of arc floodlights ('scoops') suspended on a beam across the top of the walls of the set are not switched on.

reality improved and accelerated by leaving out the dull bits, and serving the exciting bits right up to the audience. The years 1914 to 1919 in the American cinema were concerned with the further development of these formal features, and also with the appearance of the newer features of 'continuity cinema'.

The most obvious characteristic of the period, which was the establishment of films several reels long as the major part of production, had little influence on most aspects of the formal developments taking place, though it did contribute to the increasing profitability and expansion of the American film industry. The many new directors entering the profession, mostly drawn from the ranks of the actors, were important in establishing the new developments, since they were not hidebound by the earlier formal practices, and in fact the decade from 1914 onwards was the period when film directors had their greatest power in the American cinema. This is indicated by the slogan of the Triangle Distributing Corporation: "The greatest pictures by the greatest movie-makers", and by the fact that many directors who had made a name for themselves were able to set up personal production companies towards the end of the war.

Film Stock

In 1916 the standard Eastman Kodak camera negative was improved to give what became known inside the company as Cine Negative Film Type E. A year later this was replaced by Type F, but this had no major visual effect, for it had the same speed as the previous Kodak negatives, and like them had an orthochromatic emulsion. It seems likely that there was some improvement in its granularity and definition, however. Some years later this standard Kodak movie negative came to be called Negative Film Par Speed (Type 1201). There were no other developments in this area during the years 1914-1919.

Lighting Equipment

As is well-known, these years saw the introduction of spotlights for the lighting of studio interiors in America, but the details of the process are not simple. The lighting units themselves were standard theatrical-type spotlights, with the carbons producing the arc contained in an oblong box of black sheet steel, and the light from the source being concentrated into a beam by a large glass lens several inches in diameter set in the front of the casing. By later standards they were rather inefficient, since only a small fraction of the light from the arc made its way through the lens, and most was scattered around inside the walls of the housing. These spotlights could be focussed by moving the arc inside the housing with respect to the lens, and from 1915 they were used in a range of sizes, from those drawing 60 amperes of electricity to those drawing 120 amperes. The principal American manufacturer of such lights for theatrical purposes was Kliegl Brothers, and they, and later others, supplied them for film purposes as well.

Theatrical spotlights had been used as props within the scene in a number of films with a backstage story from at least as early as 1911 (*A Stage Romance*), but in these cases they were just standing round in the background unlit. The earliest possible instance of an arc spot effect being used as part of the lighting scheme is in *At the Foot of the Stairs*, where the principal scene is lit in low-key for suspense purposes. This Universal film was released in July 1914, well before Wyckoff and DeMille had done anything with arc spots. But it is very difficult to make out exactly which type of arc light is doing the lighting unless the instance is in a very low-key situation, so I may have missed something earlier amongst the films I have seen.

The use of arc spotlights was very limited at first, and most American films continued to use no backlighting on interior scenes for the next few years. In this matter, as in others to do

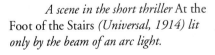

A scene in the short thriller At the Foot of the Stairs *(Universal, 1914) lit only by the beam of an arc light.*

A studio interior shot in Between Men *(Reginald Barker, 1915), with the actors backlit by the slightly diffused light from the sun behind them, and with the general diffuse daylight from the front supplemented by an arc floodlight just to the left of the camera.*

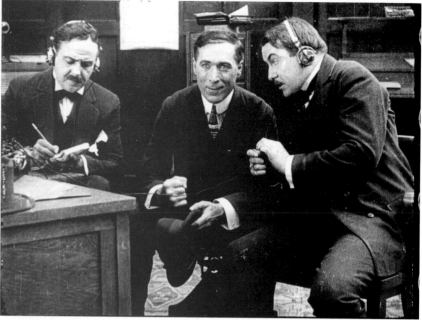

with film lighting, there was something of a split between films shot in the East Coast studios and those shot in California. In the years 1914-1916 films from the East, though more completely lit by artificial light than the Californian ones, stayed with either frontal light, or side, or three-quarters back light done with arc floodlights in the way that had begun to develop before 1914, while the films from the West Coast had more of a tendency to use full backlight on interiors. This backlighting of the actors was still sometimes done with sunlight in 1915, as in the illustration from *Between Men*, which was made in the Thomas Ince studios in that year. This kind of backlighting was done by constructing the set so that the sun was *behind* the actors, with its light diffused by the usual overhead cotton screens, rather than in front of the actors, as

had previously been the case. The frontal light came from Cooper-Hewitts and arc floodlights as usual.

On New York films at this date three-quarter backlight from arc floods on floor stands was sometimes used on close shots, and rather more often than in the previous period. Indeed by 1916 the usage was just starting to spread to some European films, as in some close shots in *Signorina ciclone*, as was the idea of using diffuse sunlight through the studio roof to give a weak backlight.

By 1917 backlighting with an arc spotlight from overhead was appearing in more American features such as *Forbidden Paths*, and for the first time cameramen tried using *two* slightly separated arc spotlights from high behind so that they hit the side of the head from glancing angles on either side, producing

An interior scen in Their One Love *(Thanhouser, 1915), lit by general diffuse light, plus light from an arc spotlight of the theatrical type hitting the back of the head of the more distant actress.*

(Right) A Close Up from Daddy-Long
-Legs *(1919) lit by Charles Rosher with
two backlight spots coming in from an angle
a little to each side of the head, plus key and
fill lights of almost equal brightness to the
left and right of the camera at the front.
There is no softening of the image by the use
of a diffusing filter in front of the lens.*

*(Below) A large arc spotlight of the type
based on the military searchlight introduced
in 1918, and referred to as a 'Sunlight' arc.
the beam is focussed by a parabolic mirror
behind the arc. The carbons between which
the arc is struck are just visible in the centre
of the housing behind a protective screen
stretched across the front opening.*

a bright rim round the whole of the upper side of the figure. This began to appear in a limited number of close shots in some Famous Players-Lasky films in 1917, for example *Rebecca of Sunnybrook Farm* and *A Mormon Maid*, lit by Walter Stradling and Charles Rosher respectively, and it seems the idea spread slowly from there. Walter Stradling took it with him to the other Mary Pickford films he lit afterwards, such as *Stella Maris* (1918), and Rosher also began to use the idea consistently. By that year a *single* backlight was being used in some, but not all, interior scenes in other quality American features; e.g. *A Modern Musketeer* (Allan Dwan, 1918) and *The Gun Woman* (Frank Borzage, 1918). Walter Stradling had also begun to use arc spotlights for key and fill lighting on the front of figures as early as 1915, in *Mr. Grex of Monte Carlo* (1915), and frequently followed the practice thereafter. However, most cameramen continued to use floodlights for the key and fill in figure lighting, but there were exceptions in this, as can be seen in *The Ghost of Rosie Taylor* (1918), which is also lit using spots for much of the key and fill on the figures.

In 1918 another major technological development in lighting equipment occurred with the introduction of a new type of arc spotlight, which was based on the military searchlight. This formed the spot beam with a large parabolic mirror a couple of feet in diameter, *behind* the arc, and it had no lens in front of the arc. This type of spotlight was much more efficient, and could throw a fairly broad beam over a large area from a distance, although this beam was less precisely controllable than that from the earlier type of spotlight. Over the next few years such reflector spotlights, referred to as 'Sunlight arcs', came to be principally used for lighting large-scale night exteriors, but it would seem that in some of the daylight exterior scenes of *Daddy Long-Legs* (1919), the cameraman Charles Rosher used them for long-range fill light on the figures on daylight exteriors, rather than using the usual

An exterior scene in Daddy Long-Legs *lit by high sunlight from the left back with fill light from big arc reflector spotlights out of shot at the right front. Note also the soft-edged vignette mask around the edge of the shot.*

reflected sunlight. He also tried using the 'Sunlight arc' as a floodlight on at least one interior scene in the film.

Yet another important technical development in lighting during these years was the introduction of diffusing screens which were fixed in front of arc floodlights. These screens, which were made of ripple glass or spun glass sheets, were fixed to the front of the arc housing, completely enclosing the carbon arc inside it, rather than letting the arc shine unimpeded through the square opening as before. These diffusing screens completely changed the quality of the light coming from arc floodlights, making it more diffuse, so that it now cast softer-edged shadows instead of the hard-edged shadows that had been so characteristic of arc floodlighting. This was particularly significant in figure lighting, as the shadows cast by the protuberances of the human face upon itself were also softened, and if the key floodlight was fairly close to the actor's face, the result was an approach to the sort of 'soft lighting' coming from a north-facing window that had long been considered attractive in portrait photography. (It must be made clear that this sort of softening of arc floodlights was only *tending* in the direction of modern 'soft lighting', as the diffusing screen over the arc opening was only about 15 inches across, which is far smaller than true softlight sources.)

The origin of this use of diffusion on arc floodlights, which came in fairly suddenly in the work of the better cameramen about 1916, is not clear. *Fanchon the Cricket* (1915) is the earliest film that I have noticed with the light from arc floodlights softened. Since arcs had been used for filming for over a decade in many studios, and since the use of diffused arc light in still photography goes back years before that to the beginning of the century, it is a little difficult to see its sudden appearance as late as 1917 as due to the influence of still photography, though that is not completely impossible. Another possibility is that it arose accidentally as a side effect of

the attempt to cure the 'Klieg eye' condition that began to afflict film actors a couple of years before, when the use of arc floodlights first started to become the main source of light on the East coast, rather than just a supplementary addition. 'Klieg eyes' was an inflammation of the eyes resulting from their irritation by the fine dust in the studio atmosphere coming from the burnt carbons of the arcs, perhaps supplemented by the large amount of ultra-violet light given off by the arc flame. (Arc lights were generically referred to as Klieg lights at this time, after the Kliegl company, the principal American manufacturer of arc lights for theatrical use. In Germany arc floodlights were called 'Jupiter lights' for similar reasons.) Certainly the cause and cure of 'Klieg eyes' was a subject of considerable discussion in 1916-1917, and even if this was not the reason for putting glass diffusion screens on the front of arc lights, their enclosure in this way certainly stopped the arc dust getting out into the atmosphere, and also absorbed the ultra-violet radiation, as ordinary glass is opaque to it. On the other hand, the fact that some 1917-1918 films use arc floodlights both with and without diffusion in various scenes might suggest that the use of diffused arcs was a purely aesthetic decision, as a response to the dropping of the general frontal diffuse light which had previously concealed to some extent the harshness of the light from open arcs. This point can probably be decided by further research.

Although by this period most of the studios were using electricity from their own direct current (D.C.) generators to power their arc lighting, one can occasionally see one of the cheaper films that has scenes lit by alternating current (A.C.) arcs. The visible result is a periodic fluctuation of the light level several times a second due to the stroboscopic effect between the frequency of the A.C. fluctuations and that of the opening and closing of the camera shutter. This is quite a different matter from the occasional flicker of unsteady burning or near extinction to which arc lights have always been prone, as a result of irregularities in the automatic feeding mechanism advancing the carbons as they burn away in the arc. Although the carbon feed mechanisms were improved over the decades, all older cinemagoers will have sometimes experienced the dimming and extinction of an unattended arc-source film projector resulting from the same cause.

Mention of both shortcomings of arc light sources, the first eventually eliminated by the use of D.C., and the second still with us, can often be found in the reminiscences of people who were in films in that period, and both can be seen in its films, as retakes were not usual in the early silent period if an arc floodlight lighting a minor part of the background happened to go out in the middle of a take. This attitude began to change in the nineteen-twenties.

Throughout the years 1914-1919 the general large-area lighting of sets continued to be supplied by racks of Cooper-Hewitt mercury vapour tubes, and in some of the smaller companies by arrays of street- lighting type arcs hung overhead.

The General Development of Lighting Style

The first generalization to be made about the development of American film lighting during these years is a fairly well-known one – it speaks of a transition from films being lit with the help of the general diffuse light through the glass studio roofs, to films being shot entirely under artificial light in blacked-out studios by 1919. Although the latter situation is fairly true, as already indicated there were a number of films shot in East Coast studios even before 1914 which had scenes lit entirely by artificial light, and this separation between the lighting practices on the two sides of the United States persisted to some extent till around 1918. This is best made clear with some examples. To speak of Californian film-making first, the interiors of *Birth of a Nation* (1915) were lit entirely by daylight controlled in one way or another, and a sketch of

G.W. Bitzer's lighting procedures can be read in Karl Brown's *Adventures with D.W. Griffith*. There are one or two pieces of backlighting on interiors in this film done by letting in a patch of direct sunlight through a gap in the overhead cotton screens, and the 'spotlight' effect on Lincoln's assassin was created with sunlight reflected from a mirror. An even better example of what could be done solely with controlled daylight is given by the lighting of Raoul Walsh's *Regeneration* (1915), for which Georges Benoit created remarkably precisely controlled gradations and localizations of sunlight across some of the interior scenes. He also used sunlight for backlight in many of the interiors, with the key light coming from reflectors put in front, in the same manner as was now standard for exterior scenes.

Even by 1915 the more common approach, both on the East Coast and on the West Coast, was to add some arc lighting to sharpen up the general diffuse lighting of the set; in the New York studios the diffuse light came mainly from Cooper-Hewitts, and in California from diffuse daylight. One of the most elegant demonstrations of this earlier (and about to be superseded) style is given by the lighting of *David Harum* (Allan Dwan, 1915). Although the photography of this film has been recently credited to Harold Rosson, it seems probable to me that he was only assistant cameraman on this film, as he was only twenty years old at the time, and his next claimed solo credit was four years later.

The less common, but more advanced, style to be observed in 1915, which consisted in lighting a fair number of scenes principally or entirely with arc lights, seems to have been confined to some of the New York and New Jersey studios. A good example of this is given by the remarkable short film *His Phantom Sweetheart*, which was made by Ralph Ince for Vitagraph. In this film the majority of the interior scenes are lit solely with arc floodlights; by necessity in the case of those shot inside a real theatre auditorium and its foyer. As can be seen from the illustrations, the theatre interior is lit with two

A scene in His Phantom Sweetheart *(Ralph Ince, 1915) shot on location in a real theatre and lit by a group of arc floodlights out left. The focus is set slightly forward so that the image of the actress in the background is a little soft.*

The reverse-angle to the previous shot from His Phantom Sweetheart. *In this case the actors in the background are in focus.*

The next shot in the series of alternating reverse-angles in the theatre scene of His Phantom Sweetheart. *In this Medium Close Up lit with a single arc floodlight the actress is still kept slightly out of focus.*

A low-key interior shot in His Phantom Sweetheart *lit solely by a small arc concealed under the shade of the table lamp.*

groups of arcs, one on each side of the camera, and both coming in at roughly 45 degrees to the lens axis, on the pattern established at Vitagraph some years before. What is new in this film is the scale and complexity of the scenes. *His Phantom Sweetheart* also contains a climactic scene lit with genuinely low-key lighting done with arcs to contribute to a succession of moods – sensuality, suspense, and terror. The rather similar, and much better-known example in Cecil B. DeMille's *The Cheat* (1915) is no more thoroughgoing and extended in its use of low-key arc lighting.

By 1916 there were many films coming out of the East Coast studios that had most of their studio interior scenes lit solely with arc floodlights. One example is *Silks and Satins* (J. Searle Dawley), which had the lights disposed so as to give a stronger key light from one of the side-front directions, and

weaker fill light from the other, and also sometimes three-quarter back lighting through a real or implied door or window opening in the set. (Due to the way that the light intensity from an arc floodlight falls off rapidly with distance, it was not possible to use one to do backlighting from directly behind and above in Long Shots. This was only possible with spotlights.) In *Silks and Satins* no diffusing screens were used on the lights to soften them. Relatively unsubtle arc flood-lighting like this, or worse, can still be seen in some films made in 1918, particularly in California, e.g. *A Modern Musketeer.*

By 1917, as already remarked, the floodlights were being diffused a good deal of the time on some films, and one of the better examples of this was *The On-The-Square Girl.* (Although the cameraman and director of this film are named on the titles as Morris E. Hair and Frederick J. Ireland, Kevin

A studio interior shot in Silks and Satins *(J. Searle Dawley, 1916) lit by three arc floodlights through the doorway ay left. As can be seen from the sharp-edged shadows, there are no diffusing screens in front of the openings of the reflectors of the floodlights.*

A studio interior scene in The
On-The-Square Girl *(1917), lit by an arc
floodlight with a diffusing screen in front of it,
so producing slightly soft-edged shadows.*

Brownlow has suggested to me that these are pseudonyms for Arthur Miller and George Fitzmaurice. Given the high quality of the lighting and direction of this film, and that it comes from George Fitzmaurice's company Astra, and also that it was listed in a trade source at the time as a George Fitzmaurice production, this seems quite likely.) A fully accredited example of what the change to diffusion on arc lights looked like is given by *Till I Come Back To You* (Cecil B. DeMille, 1918), which was lit by Alvin Wyckoff and Charles Rosher. In this film there was still some contribution from the old-fashioned general overall light as well as the well-managed directional components from diffused arc lights on the closer shots.

Figure Lighting

From these years onwards it became the practice in America to treat the lighting of the closer shots of the actors separately from the general lighting of the set as it was visible in Long Shot, and indeed to make changes in the positions of the lights when shooting the closer shots which were to be cut into the main scene. (Naturally there has to be some sort of very rough correspondence between the look of the lighting in more distant and in closer shots, but nevertheless quite substantial changes are not noticed by the audience, now as well as then.) Although the essentials had already been independently developed in a crude way, it was around 1917 that a few of the best cameramen such as Walter Stradling and Charles Rosher polished up what were to be the standard patterns of figure lighting, presumably drawing on still photographic practice.

The most basic pattern of figure lighting is to have a key (or brightest) light directed at the figure from the front on one side of the lens axis, a weaker fill light from the other side of the lens axis, and a backlight shining forwards onto the back

of the actor. What would be considered the ideal angles along which to direct these lights depended in the first place on the exact direction in which the actor was facing with respect to the camera, and in the second place on the shape of the actor's face. Besides the skill required in selecting the angles for the lights, there was also the matter of arranging the relative levels of brightness of the key and fill lights. It was here that there began to be a marked improvement over the practice of a few years before, for earlier it had been quite common to have the lights from either side of the camera of equal, or nearly equal, brightness. This produced two shadows from the nose, one falling on either side of the face.

Charles Rosher's progress in this respect can be illustrated by the difference between his work on *The Sowers* (1916) and *The Secret Game* (1917). In the former the lighting on the figure is rather flat, since the key and fill lights are of almost equal brightness, but in the latter the relative intensities and positions of the lights are very well judged. The key light was still being placed only slightly above actor eye-level in most films in 1917, but by 1919 some cameramen were beginning to place the key light rather higher when appropriate, as did George Barnes in *Dangerous Hours*.

As already mentioned, a modification to the initial use of a single backlight now began to appear, with a few cameramen using two backlights, one directed from each side at the back of the figures. This can be seen intermittently in such films as *Fighting Odds* photographed by René Guissart in 1917, and *Stella Maris* and *The Whispering Chorus*, photographed in 1918 by Walter Stradling and Alvin Wyckoff respectively. This use of double backlights could be combined with either a single key light and no fill from the front to give an alternative form of three-point lighting to the basic form described above, or with both key and fill from the front to give four-point lighting, which was less common initially.

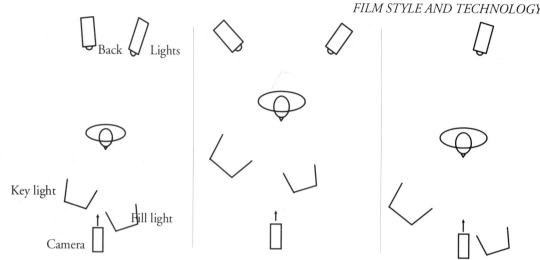

Left *Early use of close double backlights.*   **Centre** *Double backlights spread apart.*   **Right** *Single backlight with key and fill*

Later the use of two backlights and a weaker light straight on from the front came to be the standard way of treating a 'profile two-shot' (two actors facing each other), but this did not happen at first.

It is at present impossible to tell who were the principal forces behind the developments I have outlined above, in part owing to the lack of cameraman credits before 1917, which was the year in which it became usual to name the cameraman on the better class of production. We also do not know what were the aesthetic assumptions behind the adoption of the standard techniques, though it might be possible to find out more about this with extensive research.

Interior Lighting in Europe

In 1914 the best European lighting of interiors was being done in a rather similar way to that in America, with general diffuse lighting through the studio roof being sharpened up a little with arc floodlights in many scenes, but also with the rare

occasional scene done mostly with arc floodlights when a special lower key effect was wanted. Over the war years in Scandinavia there was a tendency, just as there was in America, to move towards heavier use of arcs, but the Scandinavian studios were never blacked out permanently at this time, and even in the early 'twenties many scenes were still being lit in part with diffuse daylight, as can be seen in the films of Dreyer, Stiller, and Sjöström.

The most accomplished Danish cameraman during this period was Johan Ankerstjerne, and his work on Benjamin Christensen's *Haevnens Nat* (1916) shows the way that a few European cameramen were also developing the kind of three-point lighting that has already been described in American films. But Ankerstjerne only did this on closer shots, where the light applied from the three-quarters back position could come from an arc floodlight. There was no introduction of backlighting from directly behind with spotlights in Europe, nor any use of spotlights at all for that matter, until well after

Well-placed figure lighting by Johan Ankerstjerne in Hævnens Nat *(1916). Side-back lighting from the left, and side lighting from the right, both produced by diffuse sources.*

One of many low-key scenes in Verdens Undergang *(August Blom, 1915). A simulation of light from a hand-held lamp.*

the end of the war. Ankerstjerne also did some notable low-key work – such things as a hand-held lamp casting looming shadows in a flight down subterranean passageways – in *Verdens Undergang* (1915), which was yet another of the speculative and apocalyptic epics like *Civilization* which were produced during the early stages of World War I. *Homunculus* (1916), a German contribution to this genre, shows the retarded state of lighting in that country, in that its low-key effects were done solely by the control of daylight with blinds and the way the set was constructed, in the manner of the Danish films of some years before.

By 1918 the Germans had fallen badly behind in lighting, as is obvious even in a Lubitsch film such as *Die Augen der Mumie Ma*, in which the interiors were still done with general overhead diffuse light, with only a little sharpening here and there with arc floodlights. And even this was not well done. Things began to improve a little in 1919, particularly in the best productions of that year (Lubitsch again), but in most films the way light was applied to the figures was still rather crude by American standards.

The flowering of Swedish cinema during the war also involved some notable camerawork by Julius Jaenzon and others, and not surprisingly the styles used owed quite a lot to earlier Danish and French examples. The most common approach in Sweden to lighting the general shot of a scene was to bring the light in from one major direction, either from the side or from above at the front of the set. The source of side light was usually a large opening such as an actual (or implied) door or window letting in the diffuse daylight coming through the glass wall of the studio. The result was not an even flood of light over the whole extent of the set, but moderately localized light in one area tailing off into the further corners. Sometimes foreground features of the set or actors were left relatively dark. A good example of this is given by the lighting

of Mauritz Stiller's *Balletprimadonnan* (1915). An alternative form of this localized lighting with natural light which was very popular with the cameramen at Svenska Biografteatern was to allow direct sunlight to fall frontally from high above onto a central area of the foreground of the set where most of the action took place, with more general diffuse lighting working its way into the farther parts of the set to light them more dimly. This second method of using mostly natural light gave somewhat the same effect of separation of lighter figures from darker background that had earlier been achieved by American cameramen using artificial light sources. When using both these methods of lighting the placement of the actors at the various stages of the evolution of the scene becomes quite important if their faces are to be clearly visible, and not heavily shadowed when they move into some parts of the set. It also precludes the use of a lot of cutting around to different angles within the scene. As the Swedish directors only used a limited amount of cutting within scenes at this point in history, they experienced no difficulties because of this. Nor did the major exponent of a somewhat similar approach in America.

Maurice Tourneur and Cinematography

There were some American film-makers who used lighting styles other than those already described, and the most important of these was Maurice Tourneur. His cameramen used the most precise and subtle form of lighting from a single direction, and had probably evolved it from the rather more primitive French forms current before 1914. Although Tourneur used more cuts within a scene than the Swedish directors, he overcame the problems in staging associated with the single direction lighting style by having a certain amount of localized fill light on the actors when they were in some positions, and also by unobtrusive relighting for the closer shots.

The most obvious visual feature of Tourneur's films, which was the creation of foreground silhouette effects, fitted in well with the handling of the main light source as described above, but this particular feature does not appear continuously in every scene in his films. On the contrary, during the years 1914 to 1916 many of the scenes in his films are lit in the more conventional manner usual at that time in American films. In fact, some of Tourneur's most striking images were obtained purely through the compositional arrangements in shots which were lit in a high key, i.e. with moderately even illumination over the whole frame.

Although hardly any of their films from this period have survived, it seems probable that the other emigré French directors at the Fort Lee studios – Perret, Capellani, and Chautard – worked in similar, though less exalted, versions of this 'pictorialist' style. (The sense of the description 'pictorialist' is that the compositional style is closely based on that used in the painting of past periods – say the Salon painting of the end of the nineteenth century – as opposed to the relatively nondescript compositions of the already existing film tradition, where the connection with fine art is at second or third hand.) The principal continuers of this tradition in America during the 'twenties were Rex Ingram and Josef von Sternberg, though in the case of the latter it evolved into a style with quite new qualities. Traces of the Tourneur influence can occasionally be seen elsewhere, for instance in von Stroheim's *Foolish Wives*, and also in the films of Clarence Brown, Tourneur's former assistant.

The Italian Picture

One aspect of the decline of the Italian cinema during the First World War was the pursuit of pictorialism, particularly in exterior scenes, regardless of its relevance to the narrative. In short, the story stopped while the leading characters stood around in a beautiful landscape picture. This can be readily seen in the Eleanora Duse vehicle, *Cenere* (1916), but it touched even the best Italian films of the period, such as *Assunta Spina* (1915).

The Photography of Night Exterior Scenes

In 1914 exterior scenes purporting to be taking place at night were still exclusively shot under full daylight, and the impression of night was conveyed by the standard blue tinting, usually with the help of a previous descriptive title. But in 1915 the first night scenes actually shot at night with the help of artificial light appeared in a few American films. Notable early examples include a street scene in Cecil B. DeMille's *Kindling* which was lit by Alvin Wyckoff solely with a few strategically placed arc floodlights, and a night battle scene done the same way in a short Thanhouser Company production, *Their One Love*. G.W. Bitzer's cruder solution to the same problem in *Birth of a Nation* was to use pyrotechnic flares to light the scene of the farewell ball before the battle. By 1916 the use of arc floodlights on moderate scale night exteriors was becoming more common in the better American films, and by 1918 even an ordinary Western such as Henry King's *Six Feet Four* has a large-scale night street scene lit in this way. But very distant landscape scenes still had to be given normal daytime photography, and then integrated with closer shots which had been photographed 'night for night' with artificial light by applying the same overall blue tinting to the whole sequence. Some cameramen and directors show the first signs of trying to improve on this method however, and there are a few very rare cases where distant night scenes have been photographed in the half-light of dusk (*Female of the Species*, 1916), or where the upper part of the scene has been darkened by putting a partial filter over it in front of the lens, as in *Less Than the Dust* (1916). In such cases the cameramen avoided getting any appreciable amount of sky into the shot, but in general such an approach was neither possible nor striven for.

A battle scene shot at night, and lit solely by arc floodlights in Their One Love *(Thanhouser, 1915).*

The shadow of the villain slides into frame before he does in Maria Rosa *(Cecil B. DeMille, 1915).*

In Europe the idea of lighting night exteriors with arc lights was also just beginning to appear, as in Bauer's *Zhizn za zhizn* (1916) and Sjöström's *Berg-Ejvind och hans Hustru* (1917). Elsewhere I have seen no sign of this technique before the 'twenties, but it must be emphasized that I am discussing location or 'back-lot' exterior scenes, and not sets representing exteriors constructed inside a studio, such as those in Lubitsch's *Die Puppe* (1919), or the subsequent *Das Cabinet des Dr. Caligari* (1920).

Shadowplay and Other Lighting Effects

It was not until this period that the use of cast shadows for expressive purposes began its true development, though occurrences still remain fairly rare. Cecil B. DeMille began using the shadows of objects outside the frame cast into the frame area as early as 1915. The well-known example here was the shadow of the prison bars falling on the husband in *The Cheat*, but the first instance of this in DeMille films was earlier in 1915 in *The Girl of the Golden West*, where a rope casually dangling on the set casts the threatening shadow of a hangman's noose at an appropriate moment. Variants of the idea also occur in *Maria Rosa*, where the villain casts his shadow on the wall before he enters the scene, and it had spread to other countries by 1916, e.g. Protazanov's *Pikovaya Dama* and Abel Gance's *Barberousse*, where the shadow of the clutching hand of a criminal slides onto the white pillow of the sleeping heroine. After a scattering of other similar examples we find a natural part of the set creating the shadow of a cross on the

The shadow of a threatening hand slides over a sleeping woman's face in Barberousse *(Abel Gance, 1916).*

heroine at a suitable moment in *Until they Get Me*, by which time such devices were available to any really enterprising director. Looming shadows had begun to spread to other directors by 1917, e.g. *The Whip* by Maurice Tourneur, and *Kidnapped*. And DeMille's *The Whispering Chorus* of 1918 uses looming shadows cast on the walls from lights placed low in a scene in which the hero begins to stray into wrong-doing. There was no apparent light source in this scene motivating these upcast shadows as there had been in the earlier Italian examples of low placed lights that I have mentioned, and this is also the case in Sidney and Chester Franklin's *Going Straight* (1917), in which a low placed light shining up into a face in Close Up was used in a nightmare sequence without any apparent or reasonable source, purely to convey a sinister atmosphere as the hero's fears and worries were played out.

Cameras

It was during these years that the Bell & Howell camera, described in a previous chapter, began to displace the Pathé studio camera as the major tool for American cameramen. Another new camera, the Akeley, was first produced in 1917, but since it was a few years before it had any significant use, I will defer a description of it till the next chapter.

Angle Shots

In this period shots taken from really high- or low-angles continued to be rare, and mostly they were used in a situation where they could be understood as representing the Point of View of one of the characters in the scene in question. However, there are examples of extreme high-angle shots which are objective, and definitely not POV shots, in films from most countries, from America to Russia. When they do occur, the allowance is one per film. Ignoring distant shots from the ground towards a first floor window, or something similar,

real low-angle shots are even rarer. By far the most striking instance in this class is a low-angle Close Up in Abel Gance's *Barberousse*. This is of the titular protagonist, at the point where he declares that he is 'the King of the Forest', and this must be intended to be expressive.

Camera Movements

During the years 1914-1919, just as in previous years, there was little change in the way the vast majority of shots were taken with fixed framing, particularly in interior scenes. Very rarely one finds panning shots being used to follow actors across a set, as in some Reginald Barker films such as *Typhoon* (1914) and *Between Men* (1915), but there was some increase in the use of framing movements – i.e. small pans and tilts to keep the actors well-framed – as some directors started to take even more of their shots closer to the actors. (When shooting close in it *is* possible to avoid the use of framing movements if the movements of the actors are carefully controlled, but if the cameraman had the ability to turn the panning or tilting crank while also cranking the film drive, it was easier on the actors to let the camera conform to them.) Early examples of this slight trend towards the greater use of framing movements can be seen in *David Harum* (Allan Dwan, 1915) and *The Right Girl* (Ralph Ince, 1915), but by 1919 it is much easier to find examples amongst the increasing numbers of films that were now being shot from closer to the actors; e.g. *Jubilo* (Clarence Badger, 1919). As before, exterior action scenes were the likeliest place to find camera movements.

Tracking Shots

Parallel tracking shots, in which the camera moves at a fixed distance from actors moving on a parallel course, continued to occur on rare occasions such as car and train chases, but tracking towards and away from groups of actors who were

A Cloe up shot from a very low angle in Abel Gance's Barberousse *(1916). The character in the shot has just boasted that he is 'The King of the Forest'.*

not moving a great deal (which I call 'tracking on a quasi-static scene') had a world-wide vogue in the wake of the Italian film *Cabiria* (1914). Such tracking shots were referred to at the time as '*Cabiria* movements', for it seems that no-one had taken much notice of the earlier tracking shots on quasi-static scenes in American and English films, except perhaps Giovanni Pastrone, the director of *Cabiria*. At the time Pastrone stated that his intention was to create a 'three-dimensional' effect in the photography to show off the vast solid sets of his film, and for this reason his tracking shots were made moving inwards on a diagonal to his sets. These tracks are also of a fairly limited extent, slow, and do not end too close to the actors. In 1915 and 1916 every bright young director had to have one or two '*Cabiria* movements' in one of his films, but they used them slightly differently to Pastrone.

To pick just a few examples of this fashion from well-known directors, I will mention *David Harum* (Allan Dwan, 1915), *Ditya bolshogo goroda* (Yevgeni Bauer, 1914), *Evangelimandens Liv* (Holger Madsen, 1915), and *The Vagabond* (Chaplin, 1916), all of which move in much closer to the actors rather faster than the originals in *Cabiria*, and also have trajectories fairly straight in or out from the scene. And all of these tracking shots incorporate a certain amount of panning as well, which those in *Cabiria* did not. The example in *The Vagabond* is the most elegant application: a track out from a close shot of a painting reveals the people standing around looking at it. Everyone seems to have been satisfied with at most two tracking shots on quasi-static scenes in their films, with one well-known exception. This was *The Second-in-Command* (William J. Bowman, 1915), which though of no great interest otherwise, contains about two dozen tracking shots. These go closer in to the actors than those in any of the other films, even as close as a Big Close Up at one point, and one of them is of greater complexity than any in other films as well. The tracking shot in question follows a couple round a dance floor amongst other couples, panning the while to keep them in frame, and the general effect is exactly the same as it would be twenty years later in any tracking shot following a dancing couple. *The Parson's Horse Race* (Edison, 1915) has a track back from the final group of characters at the end of the film, and can be seen as a development of D.W. Griffith's idea for the conclusion of *A Girl and Her Trust* (1912).

By 1917 the tracking shot craze in America was declining as fast as it had arisen, and by 1918 and 1919 tracking shots on quasi-static scenes had again become rare, the only examples I have come across being in *The Blue Bird* (Tourneur, 1918), and *Stella Maris* (Marshall Neilan, 1918), though there probably some more amongst the large number of lost films. The example in *Stella Maris* is a further development of a usage that was to become popular much, much later: as the hero and heroine embrace in the final shot of the film the camera pulls back from them, and there is a slow fade-out. There are also still a few examples in European films, such as *Herr Arnes Pengar* (Stiller, 1919), *Jacques Landauze*, and *Malombra*.

Camera Movement and Expression

Cases where a camera movement could reasonably be considered to produce meanings through its conjunction with the action in the filmed scene are hard to find in this period, apart from the marginal case in *Stella Maris* mentioned above. The only other instance that springs to mind is in von Stroheim's *Blind Husbands*, in which what was to be a characteristic effect in his films first occurs: a Point of View shot tilting up from the feet to the face of a potential prey as the villain sized her up.

Depth of Field and Other Photographic Variables Influencing the Film Image

Depth of field (often erroneously called depth of focus) is one of the central factors controlling the appearance of the film image, and it is really necessary to get a clear understanding of the way it is related to other variable factors if one is to appreciate the interconnections between the visual qualities of films and film technology. The four central quantities whose variations are strictly connected one with another are *Depth of Field, Lens Aperture, Focal Length of Lens*, and *Lens Focus*.

Depth of field is the range of distance in front of the camera lens inside which objects produce sharp images of themselves *as seen on the cinema screen* when the film is finally projected. The boundaries of this range of sharp focus are approximate, as objects just outside it appear only slightly unsharp, or may even perhaps appear in focus to the casual glance at the cinema screen. The range of sharp focus as it appears on the ground-glass screen of any camera view-finding system is not necessarily the same as that on the cinema screen, though usually close to it.

Lens Aperture is the size of the variable opening in the diaphragm built into the middle of the lens. Its size is measured in 'f-numbers' or 'stops', and these f-numbers are inversely related to the actual diameter of the lens diaphragm opening. the basic series of f-numbers runs f1, f1.4, f2, f2.8, f4, f5.6, f8, f11, f16, f22, f32, f45, f64, though other numbers may appear on actual lenses. Each of these f-numbers is said to differ from the next by 'one stop', and each change of a stop proceeding from left to right along the series halves the amount of light passing through the lens to the film, and conversely in the other direction the amount of light passing is double for each change of a stop. The smallest aperture on a film camera lens is now usually f22 or f32, but in the early days it could be f45, and the largest or maximum aperture was usually between f2 or f4.5. Determining the correct exposure means determining the amount of light that has fallen on the scene and is then reflected from it into the lens, and then determining the lens aperture that will permit just the right proportion of this light to fall onto the film to give the right amount of activation of the silver halides contained in it. It is colloquially said by cameramen that when there is twice as much light on the scene, then the light has 'increased by one stop', and that a photographic film that needs only half as much light as another is 'faster by one stop'. Likewise, a film that needs four times as much light as another is 'two stops slower', and so on.

Focal Length of a Lens is the distance behind its 'optical centre' of the plane in which an image of an infinitely distant object is formed. The 'angle of view' of a camera lens is inversely proportional to its focal length for the same size of film frame, so short focal length lenses have a wide angle of view, and are colloquially referred to as wide-angle lenses, and long focal length lenses have a narrow angle of view. This brings me to the awkward question of what constitutes a standard lens. the opinions of film cameramen on this point have changed during this century, and as already remarked, some cameramen before 1914 considered a 3 inch (75 mm.) lens to be standard, though most considered a 2 inch (50 mm.) lens to be standard, which was exclusively the case in the 'twenties. Later on, there was some move towards considering even shorter focal lengths as standard, as I shall detail later. There has been another approach to this problem through experimental investigation of which *camera* lens focal length gives audiences the best impression of correct perspective in projected images of real scenes, and this work suggest that in this sense a standard lens has a focal length of around 35 mm. to 40 mm., with the uncertainty corresponding to a real experimental variation.

Lens Focus is of course the distance at which lens focus is set so that objects at that distance will produce the very sharpest images on the film and on the screen.

Now the value of any one of these four quantities is determined by the values of the other three, but it is usual to consider the effect of the depth of field of holding any two of the other three fixed, and varying the third. The results of this are nowadays set down in depth of field tables, but these were not used in the period we are considering, and cameramen relied on experience to determine what would be in focus or not. Given that the other two factors are kept constant, the depth of field increases with (1) reduction of lens aperture, (2) decrease of focal length of the lens, (3) increase in distance at which the lens focus is set (up to a certain distance called the hyperfocal distance).

As has already been indicated, the aperture cannot be freely chosen in any particular case, for it depends in its turn on the light level on the scene to be photographed, and also on the sensitivity to light (the 'speed') of the particular type of film in the camera. And on this point there was no real choice till the end of the silent period.

Lens Apertures Used In 1914-1919

Towards 1919, for the first time since the use of diffused sunlight was established for the filming of studio interior scenes, there began to be signs of a change in the lens aperture used, and hence in the depth of field. In a few films such as *Stella Maris* (1918) and *Jubilo* (1919), there is quite clearly a visible reduction in the depth of field when the actors are in Medium Shot, when compared with the situation at that closeness previously. I estimate that in these cases, and one or two similar ones that I have seen, the depth of field corresponds to an aperture of about f4 with a 50 mm. lens. Although these examples presaged the trend of the next few years, they were not typical in 1919, but restricted to the work of a limited number of leading film-makers. This phenomenon may have had something to do with the move towards shooting in totally blacked-out studios which was taking place around this time, for although in general the background of diffused daylight that was lost in this move was replaced with

An exterior scene in Clarence Badger's Jubilo *(1919), backlit by the sun, but with some extra fill from the front on the foreground figures. There is quite a shallow depth of field here, and the man several feet behind the people in the front is already a little out of focus. This corresponds to a camera aperture of about f4. Note also the irregular soft dark border around the frame, done with layers of black net in the matte box in front of the lens.*

greater use of Cooper-Hewitts and diffused arcs, it seems likely that this replacement was not complete, and hence the overall light level dropped slightly. However the majority of the studios were probably still working at an aperture of about f5.6 most of the time, just as before the war. Certainly the now minor and declining studios of Vitagraph and Edison were, according to an article in *The Transactions of the Society of Motion Picture Engineers* (No.8, 1919). However this is a suitable point to warn against taking such reports of particular cases as applying in general, for it is clear from the detailed description in this article of the kind of lighting set-ups being used at Vitagraph and Edison in 1919 that the cameramen there had not advanced from the standard procedures of several years before. Whereas in the major studios there had been the considerable changes in lighting style that I have described earlier. Similarly, a reminiscence by a cameraman that he once took an exterior shot at f45 around this time does not mean that this was standard practice. It wasn't.

Lenses

There was no change in the variety of camera lenses available during the years 1914-1919, but the first signs of the use of long focal-length lenses appeared in entertainment films. There are isolated shots in a crowd scene in *Civilization* (1916) and the battle on the pyramid in *The Woman God Forgot* (1917) which are taken with lenses of focal length in the region of 4 to 6 inches, both scenes clearly having been shot with multiple cameras. This kind of usage remained very rare for decades, even in similar mass-action scenes, as most film-makers preferred either to arrange the scene so that they could get one of the cameras in closer with a standard lens, or alternatively to restage parts of the action for a separate shot.

Another harbinger was Hendrik Sartov's use of a long lens for shooting Close Ups in *Broken Blossoms* (1919), though when this practice became common in the next decade most cameramen were satisfied with something like a 4 inch focal length, rather than the 6 inches plus used by Sartov.

The Use of the Iris Mask

The use of the iris mask came to a peak during the years 1914-1919, both as a way of beginning and ending a scene, and also to create a static mask or circular vignette around some shots. Whether or not Griffith and Bitzer originated irising and the use of the iris vignette, it seems highly probable that the well-deserved prestige of D.W. Griffith and the success of *Birth of a Nation* were responsible for the popularization of this device. By 1914 Griffith had settled on the standard procedure of beginning every shot with an iris-out (i.e. opening the iris diaphragm in front of the lens), and concluding it in the reverse way, though some of these irisings were removed later in the editing process. Nevertheless, in Griffith's films a sufficiently large number of shots, even within scenes and sequences, remain with the irising still present to create a very discontinuous impression. Very few film-makers in America went as far as Griffith in this direction,

and those few who did soon abandoned the extreme of the practice, but Griffith himself persisted with it into the 'twenties. This may be because Billy Bitzer kept using a Pathé camera, which did not have a fading shutter, throughout this period, whereas other cameramen were switching to the Bell & Howell as soon as they could afford it.

The films made at the Ince studios contain relatively few iris-ins and -outs, and those few are confined to the beginning and end of sequences. At the Ince studios, as elsewhere, fades also continued to be used for the purpose of beginning and ending sequences, without any consistent relation to the temporal connection between the sequences they separated. By 1918 the use of the iris to begin and end sequences was starting to decrease in the United States, though in Europe it was just starting to become fashionable. At that date it is quite easy to find American films such as *Stella Maris* in which only fades are used.

A variant of the simple iris opening out from the centre of the frame appears at the beginning of 1915 *The Girl of the Golden West* and *Birth of a Nation*. In this procedure the opening and closing centre of the iris started from whichever point in the frame contained the subject of principal interest in the scene, and it had an effect somewhat analogous to a modern zoom shot. There are very few other examples until 1917, when the device became slightly fashionable. However, the effect was always used very sparingly, and in most films that have ordinary irising it does not even appear. To produce 'directional' irising of this kind required a special sliding mount for the iris diaphragm that enabled it to be centred in front of the appropriate point in the frame.

Yet other variants of the simple iris appeared at this time, and in these the mask opening or closing in front of the lens had shapes other than circular. One of the more frequent of these shapes could be called the opening slit; a vertical central split appears in the totally black frame, and widens till the whole frame is clear, revealing the scene that is about to start (*The Cossack Whip*, 1916). Eventually the diagonally opening slit appeared as well. Another form was the single mask that pulled up from the bottom like a theatre curtain, or down from the top, or back from one side, and yet another was the diamond-shaped opening iris, as in *Poor Little Peppina* and *Alsace* (1916), rather than the usual circle. Again, all of these variant forms were very infrequently used, and when they did occur in American films it was usually in the introductory stages. Before leaving the subject of irising, I should also mention that by 1918 the edges of ordinary circular irises were becoming very fuzzy in American films, sometimes to the point where it is difficult to distinguish an iris-out from a fade. This is a reflection of the move that was beginning towards photography at larger apertures, and hence reduced depth of field, which put the iris mask in front of the lens further out of focus than it had been some years previously. The edge of the iris mask in European films stayed rather sharper and more distinct into the 'twenties, because the trend to filming at larger apertures had not yet developed there.

The Return of the Wipe

The true wipe – i.e. a boundary line of some shape moving across the frame and erasing the image as it passes over it to leave a new image behind it – which seems to have dropped out of use after being invented by Robert Paul at the beginning of the century, now made its return around 1917. *The Angel Factory* (1917) includes several wipes as transitions to and from scenes representing a character's thoughts. These wipes have a curved edge rather than the original straight edge of those used by Paul and Smith, and they proceed from side to side rather than up and down. A wipe of the same kind gets half-way across the screen to reveal a mental image before stopping in *Old Wives For New*, and there is an instance similar to that in *The Angel Factory* in *Twin Pawns* (1919), so there were probably at least a few other films that used wipes at the time. There were also various approximations to the wipe as a form of transition between sequences, as in *The Ghost of Rosie Taylor* (1918), where an iris-out is overlapped with an iris-in, and there were quite probably other examples of these kinds of procedures in the vast numbers of films which are now lost, so the simultaneous iris-in and iris-out from opposite corners of the frame that is used a couple of times in *Das Cabinet des Dr. Caligari* (1920) is not as unprecedented as has been suggested.

'Soft Focus' and Lens Diffusion

The earliest use of a form of 'soft focus' of which I know occurs in *His Phantom Sweetheart* (1915), and in this case it is done by putting the lens very slightly out of focus. That the effect is intentional is shown by the fact that it occurs twice in successive shots; first as a mysteriously seductive woman is introduced in Medium Shot behind foreground actors who are sharply in focus while she is slightly out of focus, and then in a Medium Close Shot of her alone which is again slightly

out of focus. A more fully developed example of this technique occurs a few months later in Mary Pickford's *Fanchon the Cricket*, in which there is repeated series of Medium Close Shots of Mary Pickford in an exterior scene with her face well out of focus, and with strong backlighting as well. The only other example of soft focus that I have come across from before 1918 is in *Ablaze on the Rails*, No.96 in the 'Hazards of Helen' series of films. This film, which was made in 1916, opens with a close shot of the actress playing the heroine of the film in a glamorous gown introducing herself in the working clothes of the films. The central area of the frame covering her face is softened by some means, presumably the use of a special lens on the camera, and then this softening vanishes on a dissolve to the next shot, which has an identical set-up. Although I know of no other examples of this technique from the next couple of years, this does not mean that they did not once exist, and indeed there has been a claim made for the use of 'soft focus' in another film made in 1916, but which is now lost. What one *does* find in the next few years is the use of extremely out-of-focus circular vignette masks, which are so out of focus that the blurred edge of the mask extends its effect to the centre of the frame, slightly reducing the definition of the image there. Then in 1918 there was a completely new development in D.W. Griffith's *Broken Blossoms*. In this film all the Close Ups of Lillian Gish are heavily diffused by the use of layers of fine black cotton mesh placed in front of the lens, and also by the intrinsically poor definition of the special long focal length lens used by Hendrik Sartov to photograph these shots. Heavy lens diffusion was also used on all the other shots carrying forward the romantic and sentimental parts of the story, though whether these were done by Sartov or Bitzer is not known. Heavy lens diffusion was also used in a similar way in France by Marcel L'Herbier in his film *Rose-France*. This could well have been a case of direct influence, since that

A Close Up in Fanchon the Cricket *(1915), with the focus sharp on the frame of leaves in the foreground, but with the actress behind appreciably out of focus. She is backlit by the sun, and there is strong reflector fill from the front as well.*

Elaborately shaped vignette mask used for a shot in a children's battle scene in The Little Patriot *(1917).*

film was first shown at the very end of 1919. After that date lens diffusion occasionally appears in a more limited way in the works of the so-called 'French avant-garde', but not elsewhere in Europe for a few more years.

Masking of Other Kinds

Masks of shapes other than circular also began to appear in American films during the years 1914-1918: first such simple shapes as the 'cinemascope'-shaped narrow rectangle formed by a black band masking the top and bottom of the frame in *Intolerance*, then moving on to more complicated shapes such as a mask with a cruciform cut-out in *Stella Maris* (1918). *The Girl Without a Soul* (Wm. Bertram, 1917) also has shaped vignettes, while *A Little Patriot* (Pathé, 1917) has

elaborately shaped vignettes used on a scene of a children's mock battle, and also a white vignette to concentrate attention on a detail. In 1918 Maurice Elvey in Britain took up the idea, and, along with a number of other new tricks, introduced it into his *Nelson; The Story of England's Immortal Naval Hero*. This has a couple of scenes framed in a heart-shaped mask, as does his subsequent *The Rocks of Valpré* (1919). The most elegant variants occur in some films Ernst Lubitsch made in 1919 and later. In *Die Austernprinzessin* a triple layer of horizontal rectangles with rounded ends enclose sets of dancing feet at the frenzied peak of a foxtrot, and in *Die Puppe* a dozen gossiping mouths are each enclosed in individual small circular vignettes arranged in a matrix. Unlike most of the vignettes used in American films, the vignettes used by Lu-

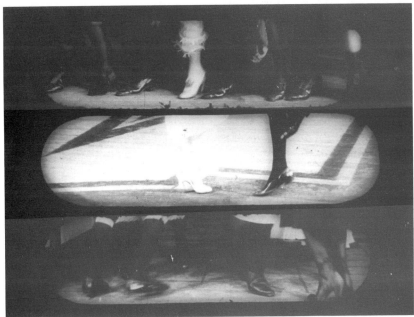

A hard-edged vignette mask of complicated shape enclosing three sets of fox-trotting feet in Lubitsch's Die Austernprinzessin *(1919).*

bitsch were 'hard' or sharp-edged, as was necessary for clarity in his particular application. In France again, unusually shaped masks play a large part in *Rose-France* (1919), and later continue to appear in a small way in subsequent films.

For the sake of completeness I should also mention another celebrated use of hard masks in these years, and this was the characteristic arch-shaped mask used by Maurice Tourneur in his films to denote fantasy or hallucination. As far as I can remember he used it consistently for this purpose, and not merely for decoration. Certainly in *Poor Little Rich Girl* the arch-shaped mask is used solely on the shots of the heroine's hallucinations.

Anamorphosis

The use of anamorphic (distorted shape) images first appears in these years with Abel Gance's *la Folie du Docteur Tube*. In this film the effect of a drug administered to a group of people was suggested by shooting the scenes reflected in a distorting mirror of the fair- ground type. Although this film still exists, it was not shown at the time of production, which Gance claims was 1915. It would be nice to have some independent confirmation of this date. There may well have been other uses of anamorphosis during the war years, but in any case the next use I know of was in *Till the Clouds Roll By* (Victor Fleming, 1919). Here it was used to depict the nightmare effects of indigestion in a comic manner. In fact, like so many film effects that distort the representation of reality, anamorphosis was first used exclusively in comic contexts.

Other Subjective Effects

In fact, it was during this period that camera effects intended to convey the subjective feelings of characters in the film really began to be established. These could now be done as Point of View shots, as in Sidney Drew's *The Story of the Glove* (1915), where a wobbly hand-held shot of a door and its keyhole represents the POV of a drunken man. In *Poor Little Rich Girl* a rocking camera shot is intended to convey delirium, and by 1918 the idea had got to Russia, in *Baryshnya i khuligan*, where the Hooligan's infatuation with the Lady is conveyed, in a less than ideal way, by his Point of View of her splitting into a multiple superimposed image.

'Poetic Cinema' and Symbolism

Symbolic effects taken over from conventional literary and artistic tradition continued to make some appearances in films during these years, and it is possible that there were yet more examples among the vast number of films from the war years that are now lost. In D.W. Griffith's *The Avenging Conscience* (1914), the title 'The birth of the evil thought' precedes a series of three shots of the protagonist looking at a spider, and ants eating an insect, though at a later point in the film when he prepares to kill someone these shots are cut straight in without explanation. The inspiration for this may well have come from the widely distributed Italian film *Gli ultimi giorni di Pompei*, which I mentioned in this connection in the previous chapter.

Possibly as a result of Griffith's influence, 1915 was a big year for 'symbolism', allegories, and parables in the American cinema. Films following this route invariably included female figures in light, skimpy draperies, and indeed sometimes wearing nothing at all, doing 'expressive' dances or striking plastic poses in sylvan settings. Titles include Lois Weber's *Hypocrites*, Vitagraph's *Youth*, someone else's *Purity*, and so on. All of it was thumpingly obvious, and usually done at considerable length, as in *The Primrose Path*, which starts with a large painting illustrating the concept, which dissolves into a replica of the same scene with actors posed, and then they come to life. This is amplified by closer detailed live action representations of stations on 'The Primrose Path' before the film proper gets under way.

Giovanni Pastrone's *Il fuoco* (1916) represents an advance to some extent, in that the symbolic effects, though admittedly fairly obvious, were not explained as they occurred. *Il fuoco* was an entry in the already established 'vampire' genre, of which the best-known example is Frank Powell's *A Fool There Was* (1915), but in fact these tales of a man enticed and destroyed by an evilly seductive woman had been developing in European cinema for years before that. The central figures of *Il fuoco* are introduced as 'He - The Unknown Painter' and 'She - The Famous Poetess', and the three stages of the affair are introduced by illustrated titles showing The Lightning Flash, The Flame, and The Ashes. Throughout the early stages of the film her dress and poses are arranged so as to suggest a bird of prey, and at a key moment a shot of one is cut in without explanation. An interesting German example from a few years later is Robert Reinert's *Opium* (1919), which has some notable innovations in the use of Insert shots to help convey the sensation of the drug reveries. These are travelling landscape shots taken from a boat going down a river, and they are intentionally shot out of focus, or underexposed, or cut into the film upside down. The last of these devices in particular seems to me very striking, and also quite successful in conveying a feeling of disorientation.

Symbolist art and literature from the turn of the century also had a more general effect on a small number of films made in Italy and Russia. The supine acceptance of death resulting from passion and forbidden longings was a major feature of this art, and states of delirium dwelt on at length were important as well. Although such features were mostly in what I would call the content of these films, there was an interaction of this content with their formal features, so I will mention some of them. The first Russian examples were all made by Yevgeni Bauer for Khanzhonkov during the First World War, and include *Grezy*, *Schastye vechnoi nochi*, and *Posle smerti*, all from 1915. These to some extent live up to the promise of the 'decadent' aesthetic suggested by their titles; *Daydreams, Happiness of Eternal Night*, and *After Death*. *Schastye vechnoi nochi* includes a visually very striking vision of a medusa- like monster superimposed on a night-time snow scene, and *Posle smerti* has a somewhat subtler dream vision of a dead girl, picked out by extra arc lighting, walking through a wind-blown cornfield in the dusk. Later examples from the rival Ermoliev company such as Protazanov's *Pikovaya dama* and *Satana likuyushchi* lacked the true Symbolist feel. In Italy, another country somewhat isolated filmically by the war, the same kind of realization of the *fin de siecle* decadent symbolist aesthetic can be found, mostly in films associated with the *diva* phenomenon. I have already mentioned *Il fuoco*, but there were others afterwards developing the theme further, such as *Malombra*, and the most complete example, which also has decor to match, is Charles Kraus' *Il gatto nero*. This last is one of the few films of this kind to use atmospheric insert shots to heighten the mood. Films from other countries did not show this tendency to any significant extent, either because Symbolism had never had much of a grip on their major arts, or in the case of France and Germany, because newer artistic movements had made Symbolism thoroughly old-fashioned.

The first film explicitly intended by its maker to be a visual analogue of poetry, Marcel L'Herbier's *Rose-France* (1919), continues further along these same paths.

Art Direction and Design

The general style of design for film interiors remained a tidied-up naturalism, and it is during this period that it became established that room sets in American films be built about 50% bigger than they would be in actuality. The other generally notable characteristic of interior sets in American films is that the walls are always of a rather dark tone. It is largely this convention, which lasted till the end of the nineteen-twenties, that gives the films of these years their 'old-fashioned' look. As is well-known, it was during the war years that greater attention came to be paid to art direction, and as well as care being given to visual co-ordination in films with contemporary subjects, the first efforts at stylized design were made in a few films. Most of these have often been discussed and illustrated, but a brief survey should mention *The Female*

of the Species (1916), in which the art director Robert Brunton did not go much beyond what might have been the very latest ideas of refinement in actual interior decoration. Though the abstract designs round the intertitles in this film are a little more advanced. The same concern for putting into a film the latest kind of 'modern' elegance that a wealthy contemporary with the most advanced taste might hypothetically use in his home can be glimpsed in some of the sets in Benjamin Christensen's *Haevnens Nat* (1916) and Ernst Lubitsch's *Schuhpalast Pinkus* (1916).

In *Fighting Odds* (1918) Hugo Ballin went beyond this to a real degree of stylization; the furniture is sparse to a point well beyond the simplifications of the stylized naturalism in ordinary films, and such solid features of the decor as fireplaces are simplified to the barest possible geometrical shapes, and integrated into the walls by being covered with the same coating of uniform dark grey paint. This rather peculiar approach was not copied in other films of the period.

The films made in Russia during the war by Yevgeni Bauer are quite interesting from a design point of view, and some of them closely reproduce what was the most advanced work there in the interior design of real houses, mostly that being done by Fedor Shekhtel'. Most of this does not appear particularly forward-looking today, with one exception. In *Yuri Nagorni* (1916) the sets are done by Bauer himself in a slightly simplified, rectilinear way that resembles the mature style of Shekhtel', as in his Yaroslavl' Railway Station interior of 1902, and his 1903 project for the new Moscow Arts Theatre, and the furniture in *Yuri Nagorni* is clearly influenced by the work of Ivan Fomin from the same period. This is perhaps not so surprising, as advanced stylized set designs had appeared in the Russian theatre before the war, and Bauer had been a set designer in the theatre before he turned to film-making. Also, Ian Christie tells me that Bauer knew Shekhtel' quite well. It is also worth mentioning that some of the exterior scenes of

An set with décor in the style of the most advanced Russian interior design of the pre-World War I period in Yevgeni Bauer's Yuri Nagorni *(1916).*

Bauer's films have a definite flavour of the paintings of Konstantin Somov done in the early years of the century, with their peculiarly Russian blend of Symbolism, Art Nouveau and Impressionism.

The film *Thais* (1916) made by the Italian Futurist Bragaglia is usually mentioned as the first instance of the use of fully stylized decor, and this does seem to be correct, though it only applies to one set used in the last few scenes. The greater part of *Thais* seems to be a very conventional and inept entry in the 'diva' genre that gripped the Italian cinema at the time – those films in which a female star anguished for love in the midst of rich and glamorous suitors and surroundings, struck Art Nouveau poses, and then died desperately. (It is *just* possible that *Thais* was intended as parody, but if that was the case it is still inept.) However, the decor of the final fatal room is highly stylized, with the walls covered with sets of alternating black and white rectangles and triangles nesting inside each other, but, contrary to some suggestions, the geometrical regularity of these designs sets them apart from true Expressionist art.

Maurice Tourneur's *The Blue Bird* and *Prunella*, both made in 1918, were rather more in the mainstream of cinema. In the first of these films some of the sets were partially done as simplified and stylized scenery painted on backdrops behind the action area. The style used for this was rather like some of the most advanced commercial art of the time, but certainly not in any of the manners used in the most advanced easel painting such as Cubism or Expressionism, or one of the abstract styles. Other parts of the design of *The Blue Bird* went straight back to nineteenth century Salon painting. In *Prunella* the stylization of houses, trees, etc. in the decor into simplified flat patterns was carried much further, with much more consistency. *Prunella* was also unusual in that these stylized sets were part of the framing action, which was set in a fantasy world, whereas the central section of the story was set in the real world, and had realistic sets, so reversing the usual large-scale construction of such films. Both films were designed by Ben Carré.

Then in 1919 Ernst Lubitsch moved in the same direction with the decor of *Die Puppe*, though in this case the very definite 'Toy Town' stylization of the sets was justified by the framing presentation of the narrative as representing the doings of dolls from a toy-box. Lubitsch's *Die Austernprinzessin* made earlier in 1919, and likewise designed by Ernst Stern, also used slightly stylized sets, but this did not go much further than the enlargement and geometricalization of the kind of decorative features to be found on the walls of real houses, etc.. Incidentally, all this happened before *Das Cabinet des Dr. Caligari* was made at the very end of 1919. (Its premiere was on February 20, 1920.) The use of stylized decor in *Die Puppe* may well have suggested a similar approach in *Caligari*, though Ernst Stern's work had nothing to do with the characteristic forms of Expressionist painting. The choice of a truly Expressionist style for the design of *Caligari* was presumably due to the impact of the stagings of Expressionist plays in the Berlin theatre that year. For instance, Toller's *Die Wandlung*, which was premiered on September 30, 1919 had decors by Robert Neppach in a genuine Expressionist style.

Glass Shots and Glass Matte Shots

Although the earliest examples date from the previous period, extensive use of glass shots did not occur till after 1914, in part because of the poor registration of cameras prior to the introduction of the Bell & Howell. Norman O. Dawn made the first glass shots in 1907 by painting additions to the scene being photographed – which were roofs for roofless buildings – on a sheet of glass fixed several feet in front of the camera. The progress of the painting had to be continually checked by examining the image focussed on the film to ensure that additions to the image exactly obscured the unwanted parts

One of the many sets with "Toy Town" stylization in Ernst Lubitsch's Die Puppe *(1919).*

A glass matte shot in Daddy Long-Legs *(1919) combining a real exterior scene in the bottom right corner of the frame with a painting occupying the rest of the frame.*

of the scene, and also exactly matched the other parts of the scene in tone and shadow disposition. In this initial form of the technique the camera and glass had to be shielded from direct sunlight by canvas to prevent reflections in the glass, and the painting had to be specially illuminated, either by reflected sunlight or by artificial light. There were many obvious disadvantages to this process, not least the time required to make the painting, so in 1911 Dawn introduced a modified form of the process called the glass matte shot.

In glass matte painting a sheet of glass is set up in front of the camera as before, but it is not specially shielded or lit. A matte or mask of opaque black paint is applied to the glass so as to obscure the unwanted areas of the scene in front, and this can be done rather quickly, checking the image on the film the while to see that just the unwanted parts of the scene are covered. Next the scene is filmed with the action taking place in the areas still visible through the parts of the glass which are not blacked out, and further lengths of test footage are exposed in the same way. Back at the studios one of the test sections, but not the main negative, is developed, and then threaded in the gate of a camera which is set up in front of an art board on an easel. Light is shone through the back of one frame of the test film to project an image of the test film onto the white art board. Then the artist is free to slowly build up painted additions to the scene, checking all the while for matching, and he finally blacks out the parts of the board where the filmed parts of the scene fall. The resulting painting is then filmed as a second exposure on the undeveloped negative after a series of test exposures and developments have been made using the other undeveloped test sections. In this way a correctly combined scene can be obtained on one negative after it has been developed.

The successful application of this technique can be seen in *Civilization* (1917), and the result of trying to make matte combinations in a camera with poor registration can be seen in *Birth of a Nation*, in the 'burning of Atlanta' scene.

Titling

During the war years the trend towards carrying most of the narrative through dialogue titles used in combination with the action solidified into standard practice in the American cinema, though all films still continued to use a small proportion of narrative titles. However, as with other aspects of film form, there were a few directors who clung to older practices to a greater or lesser extent, and here D.W. Griffith was one of the extreme cases. He continued to use large numbers of narrative titles into the 'twenties when such a practice was quite obsolete. In Europe, as usual, these developments lagged some years behind American practice, with most directors using few dialogue titles even in 1919.

It must not be understood from what I have just said that *all* the lines of dialogue which were visibly spoken by the actors came to be given in intertitles; what is at issue is the proportion of dialogue to narrative titles. All films continued to leave some visibly spoken lines of dialogue untitled, and as early as 1915 there were films such as *David Harum* and *The Cheat* which mainly used dialogue titles, but still left a large number of spoken lines untitled. In these films and many subsequent ones quite active co-operation from the audience was needed to deduce what might be being said. (I am not talking about lip-reading here, but about purely intellectual deduction, given what had happened in the film up to the point in question.) In *The Cheat* one of the many untitled lines quite clearly contained a proposition which would have been unacceptable to the various censorship boards of the time, though not because it was obscene in the strict sense. From this point onwards the pleasure of guessing what was being said came to be an occasional and intentional feature supplied to audiences by the brighter film-makers. One of the masters of this device was Ernst Lubitsch, though he did not use it in all of his silent films. His earliest really distinctive use of untitled dialogue occurs near the beginning of *Carmen* (1918).

Art Titles

Even in the early years the development of most formal and stylistic features of film was gradual, with one or two isolated instances appearing first, and then over the next few years an increasing frequency of examples. But the use of 'art titles', which were title cards with illustrations on them, occurred rather suddenly, without preparation, in 1915. At least two Lasky films of that year, *The Girl of the Golden West* and *Mr. Grex of Monte Carlo* have illustrated titles, as does Maurice Tourneur's *Trilby*. Then in 1916 quite a large number of American films use the device. Usually the art work, which sometimes covered the whole frame area with the text superimposed, was an illustration of, or comment upon, the intertitle, but sometimes it was just a neutral decorative background or border. The style of the illustrations and decorations was almost always that used in middle-brow book and magazine illustration of the period, but the abstract backgrounds to the titles in *The Female of the Species* (1916) were in the manner of the embryonic Art Deco style, which was the very latest thing at that date. Art titles never caught on in Europe to any great extent.

A unique way to treat dialogue titles also turned up in this period, but it was not generally adopted for technical reasons. In *Dolly's Scoop* (J. De Grasse, 1916), the lines of dialogue at the climax of the film are superimposed directly over the image of the person speaking them, rather like the sub-titling used in modern films. However, in this case the lines of dialogue were superimposed across the *top* of the frame rather than the bottom. Obviously this would create problems with the production of foreign versions of a silent film, not to mention the extra difficulty of carrying out the superimposition in the camera at exactly the point at which the lines were spoken, so it is no surprise that there were no more examples of this technique.

A clever variation on the illustrated title idea which obviously had no future was the use of live action vignetted into decorative cut outs around the title in the title card in *Twin Pawns* (1919).

Acting

During the years 1914 to 1919 the range of acting styles used in American films narrowed, basically by the elimination of the last traces of the more exaggerated kind of miming. Acting towards the camera had been fairly well eliminated in American dramatic films by 1914, but this was not altogether the case in European films, and it is still easy to find examples of this in 1919. In the previous period Asta Nielsen had established the occasional look into the camera lens as an element of personal acting style, and in Russia the famous Mozukhin pushed this further, with the aid of the more

frequent close shots that were now appearing even in the films of that distant country. The other aspect of European film acting, which had already begun to appear years before this period, was its slowness. There were theories about this sort of acting when it appeared on the stage, and these apparently were still in vogue in Russia where it had its most extreme manifestations in the films of Yevgeni Bauer. It was just possible to do work in this style that still seems striking, as does Aleksandra Rebikova in *Yuri Nagorni*, but frequently it just seems like very protracted ham acting to the modern sensibility, as in the case of Emma Bauer's acting in the same film.

The most naturalistic extreme of American acting after 1914 occurs in some of Maurice Tourneur's films – some of the performances in *A Girl's Folly* come close to being not acting at all – and it is difficult to think of anything going further in this direction until recent decades. By 1919 American acting style had developed to a point that left the acting in D.W. Griffith's films at the more emphatic end of the spectrum. What had earlier been outstanding invention of acting detail in the context of the general production of the time was now beginning to show its contrivance – the hand of the puppet-master was becoming visible. In any extended piece of acting by the young actors in *Birth of a Nation* one can clearly see that they make the moves and expressions registering one thought or emotion, then there is a brief pause before they register the next thought and emotion, and so on. This is presumably the result of Griffith talking them through the scene, and although the general and detailed dramatic construction of his films was still sufficiently strong to override this flaw, this was not to be the case in the next decade, when exaggeration in acting was a thing of the past. After 1919 dramatic acting became so standardized in American films that there are no more general trends to be discussed, though the fine detail and differences in individual performances can be profitably considered in other contexts.

The Rise of Continuity Cinema

The years 1914-1919 in America also saw the consolidation of the forms of what was to become the dominant mode of commercial cinema – that mode which I shall call for sharpness and brevity 'continuity cinema'. During this period there were other styles that were still important, and these can be considered to lie along a spectrum between the best examples of 'continuity cinema' at one extreme, and at the other extreme the 'discontinuity cinema' of D.W. Griffith.

There are a number of factors involved in the strong and apparent visual discontinuities between successive shots in Griffith's films, and the use of cross-cutting between parallel actions is only the most obvious of these. Cuts within the duration of a scene are still relatively infrequent in his films, and when they do occur they are frequently from Long Shot or Medium Long Shot (which were the shots he most used) to a Big Close Up of an insert detail which only occupied a small part of the frame in the previous shot. This in itself introduces a fairly strong visual discontinuity across the cut, but as well as that, the cut-in shot might often have a circular vignette mask if it were a Close Up of a person, so reinforcing the effect. And sometimes the now-standard Griffith iris-out and iris-in might also be left on the inserted shot, even though it had action continuity with the shots on either side of it. As well as all this there was Griffith's habit of moving the action into another shot in an adjoining space, and then back again if it was at all possible, which produced a marked change in background which also made its small contribution to the discontinuity between shots. This discontinuity between shots in Griffith's films can be demonstrated in a particularly striking way by taking a reel from towards the end of *Birth of a Nation* or *Intolerance* and showing it out of context alongside any other climactic reel from a film made by anybody else at that time or later.

Because of the custom of attributing all technical developments to D.W. Griffith, the first masters of continuity cinema are largely unsung, and sometimes even unknown, but it is possible to mention films that show particular continuity techniques making some of their early appearances. One of these techniques involves the exact way the movement of actors from a shot in one location to another in a neighbouring location is handled. At best this kind of transition had previously been dealt with by having the directions of travel of the actor in the two shots correspond on the screen, though there were still some directors in 1914 who could not manage that much. But in a film such as *The Bank Burglar's Fate* (Jack Adolfi, 1914), one can see shot transitions in which a cut is made from an actor just leaving the frame, to a shot of him well inside the frame in an adjoining location, which have the positions and directions so well chosen that to the casual eye his movement appears quite continuous, and the real space and time ellipsis between the shots is concealed. So thorough-going is the demonstration of barely noticeable shot transitions (in my terminology, 'soft' cuts) in this film that I am tempted to take it as a consciously virtuoso performance by the director. Strangely, this film, so exceptionally advanced for 1914 in this respect, and also in other respects, entirely lacks dialogue titles, as the story is entirely supported by narrative titles. Anomalies between the sophistication of the handling of the different dimensions of the medium are not uncommon during this period; for instance crude acting sometimes occurs in films with good scene dissection, but this is the most singular example of this kind I have noted. Other good examples of this technique for eliminating several yards of waste space and a few seconds of waste time can be seen in Ralph Ince's films, particularly *The Right Girl* (1915), and by 1919 it was widely diffused in American films, but not in those made in Europe.

Exactly the same approach came to be applied to breaking interior scenes down into a number of shots – a character could leave one shot and be picked up immediately several feet away on the other side of the room in the next shot, again with apparent continuity. This became important as more and more of the shots in a scene came to be taken from close in during the war years in America, but for the technique to work really well, it was necessary that there also be a substantial angle change between the two shots. This is because if both shots were taken directly from the front, the omission of several feet of the actor's path across the room would be more apparent from the obvious sudden background change. All this connects with the rise of the use of cutting to different angles within a scene during the years 1914-1919, and in particular to the development of reverse-angle cutting.

Reverse-Angle Cutting

It was only in 1915 that cutting to *different* angles within a scene became well-established as a technique for dissecting a scene into shots. As already described, this approach had appeared a few times in earlier years, but in general cuts to or from a closer shot within a scene were still being made more or less down the lens axis as established in the Long Shot of the scene in question. There were a few instances in which the disposition of objects within the filmed scene were such as to prevent the camera being moved absolutely straight forward to take the closer shot, but the deviations were never so great as to have the camera shooting in the opposite direction. This applies to D.W. Griffith as well as nearly everyone else, but I must make one more exception to this generalization, and this is in connection with scenes taking place in a theatre. In such cases cuts with a change of direction of approximately 180 degrees between shots of the audience, and of the show they were looking at, were used even in Europe before 1914.

The leading figure in the full development of reverse-angle cutting was Ralph Ince, who has already been mentioned in this connection in the previous chapter. Films that he made at Vitagraph in 1915 such as *The Right Girl* and *His Phantom Sweetheart* show him putting the final polish on the technique of using a large number of reverse-angle cuts in interior, as well as exterior, scenes. Other directors were also just starting to take up this style in 1915, for instance Reginald Barker in *Bad Buck of Santa Ynez*, but none matched Ralph Ince's command. It must be emphasized again that this development has nothing to do with Thomas Ince, for the films he most closely supervised, such as *Civilization* (1916), lack the features I am discussing, and indeed it is quite possible that Thomas Ince was responsible for the other positively retarded features of *Civilization*. As for Griffith, in *Birth of a Nation* there are just eight cuts to reverse-angle shots in the scene in Ford's Theatre, while elsewhere throughout the two-and-a-half hour length of this film there are only four more true reverse-angle cuts. (I define a reverse-angle cut as one in which the camera direction is changed by more than 90 degrees, which corresponds closely to the way film-makers use the term.) None of these cuts occur at any of the major climaxes in *Birth of a Nation* where they would be most effective, such as the pursuit of Flora Cameron and her leap from the cliff, whereas there are more than a dozen such cuts within the ten minute length of Ralph Ince's *His Phantom Sweetheart*.

WARNING Since *Birth of a Nation* is such a frequently seen film I must point out that to the uninstructed glance there might appear to be more reverse-angles in it than I have stated, but careful consideration of the relative positions of the actors will show that in what might at first appear to be possible instances of reverse-angle cuts the camera is in fact shooting from almost exactly the same direction in the adjoining shots; i.e. from the 'front'.

Nevertheless, the Griffith style of film-making was still followed in its full idiosyncrasy, with extensive use of side by side spaces and a definite 'front' for the camera, in most slapstick comedy, and this was because of the success and influence of the Keystone company, which was already rigidly using this style before 1914. Directors of dramatic films such as James Kirkwood, Lloyd Ingraham, and W. Christy Cabanne, who had all previously worked for Griffith, also followed his style fairly closely, though by 1916 Ingraham could sometimes manage to use the occasional reverse-angle cut when the two shots concerned also formed a watcher-POV pair. In fact the Griffith style, with only a slight weakening of his relentless frontality of scene dissection, was the standard for films made by his Fine Arts section of the Triangle company, and was followed by all who worked there. D.W. Griffith's prestige ensured that many American film-makers elsewhere were very slow to adopt true reverse-angle cutting during this period, and on into the years after the First World War.

By 1916 there are a number of films in which there are around 15 true reverse-angle cuts per hundred shot transitions – which I shall refer to as 15% reverse-angles – and two such are *The Deserter* (Scott Sidney) and *Going Straight*. By the end of the war such films form an appreciable but minor part of production: e.g. *The Gun Woman* (F. Borzage, 1918) with 18% reverse-angles, and *Jubilo* (Clarence Badger, 1919) with 16%, and by that date most directors of quality films were making more use of reverse-angle cutting than D.W. Griffith did, though they tended to restrict the device to one or two major climaxes in their films. Anyone who did not move with this trend when it became dominant in the next decade was in danger of having their films look old-fashioned, and such was the fate of D.W. Griffith himself. Other qualities in a film could surmount this handicap, but not if it was combined with yet other retarded stylistic features, and old-fashioned subject matter as well. All this hardly concerned European cinema, where those few reverse-angle cuts used were mostly between a watcher and what he sees from his Point of View, both being filmed in a fairly distant shot. However, after the end of the war some of the brighter young directors such as Lubitsch started using a few reverse-angle cuts, mostly in association with Point of View cutting.

Cutting On Action

A major feature of 'continuity cinema' was the establishment of cutting on action as a standard way of smoothing the transitions between cuts within a scene. This meant making the cut to or from a closer shot, not when the actor concerned was more or less stationary, as had usually been the case, but when he was in the middle of a definite movement, and as well as that, making sure that the movement across the cut had reached exactly the same point, to the very frame, in the shots on each side of the point where the cut was made. As in other aspects of the development of continuity cinema, a leading figure was Ralph Ince, and his 1915 films contain a number of demonstrations, for the first time, of how to do this in a number of standard situations. *His Phantom Sweetheart*, *The Right Girl*, and *The Juggernaut* use perfect cuts on action in such places as the middle of the movement of a person sitting down in a chair, or when they were making some other sort of broad body movement, and increasing numbers of other American film-makers took this up over the next few years.

Editing Equipment

Those film-makers concerned with the development of continuity cutting seem to have felt the need for some mechanical assistance with the editing task under these new stylistic conditions, for around 1916 the first editing viewers appeared in the United States. Initially these machines were no more than a projector film-gate through which the film was pulled by the usual intermittently moving sprocket wheel, which was driven by the Maltese Cross gear mechanism which was now becoming standard in projectors. The gear train was driven in its turn by a small crank-handle at the side of the device, and the frames passing through the aperture were viewed through a magnifying lens supported a few inches in front of the film by a tube attached to the front of the gate. The whole device was only several inches high and was mounted on a little stand which could be put on the top of an editing bench. As the film was cranked through, it had to be fed into the bottom of the gate from a small roll held in the hand, and illumination of the frame of film in the gate was from behind in some sort of *ad hoc* manner. There were no loops of film formed in the machine to smooth out the intermittent motion through the gate, so the editor had to keep unrolling the film from the feed roll so that there was no tension between it and the machine. This was not too difficult to do for small rolls of film. No doubt this machine was only used to deal with the most tricky points of action-matching across a cut when the figures were small in the frame, since it is actually quite possible to do good continuity cutting 'in the hand' most of the time, with no aid other than a simple magnifying glass, as had been done before, and as still continued to be done.

The Use of the Insert Shot

As already described, the use of Insert Shots – Close Ups of objects other than faces – was established very early, but apart from the special case of Inserts of a letter that was being read by one of the characters, they were infrequently used in American films of the previous period, and hardly at all in European films. It was also before 1914 that D.W. Griffith had begun to bend the use of the Insert towards truly dramatically expressive ends, but he had not done this often, and it is really only with his *The Avenging Conscience* of 1914 that a new phase in the use of the Insert Shot starts. As well as the symbolic inserts I have already mentioned, *The Avenging Conscience* also made extensive use of large numbers of Big Close Up shots of clutching hands and tapping feet as a means of emphasizing those parts of the body as indicators of psychological tension. Griffith never went so far in this direction again, but his use of the Insert made its real impression on other American film-makers during the years 1914-1919.

Cecil B. DeMille was a leading figure in the further development of the use of the Insert, and by 1918 he had reached the point of including about 9 Inserts in every 100 shots in *The Whispering Chorus*. He also pushed the insert into areas of visual sensuality inaccessible to D.W. Griffith, with such images as a Close Up of a silver-plated revolver nestling in a pile of silken ribbons in a drawer in *Old Wives for New* (1918).

The impact that the increased use of the Insert Shot had at the time is difficult to recapture now, for at that date there had never before been accurate images of relatively small objects presented with such definition and enlargement in any medium, be it painting, photography, or whatever. Things like pistols when shown in Big Close Up could be several times the size of a real pistol when held at arms length, and for instance in *Her Code of Honour* (John Stahl, 1918), the scratches on the metal and the movement of the internal parts as the trigger is squeezed can be quite clearly seen in an Insert Shot of an automatic. Since the evolution of the use of the Insert had been quite gradual in the United States, there was no comment upon it there, but in France a number of young aesthetes felt its full force in 1917, when the American films that had been withheld by the war during the previous three years were suddenly released to the public. Louis Delluc and others then explicitly formulated the *idea* of the Point of View shot and the Insert in their critical articles, and this had a significant influence on the development of the so-called 'French avant-garde' of the early nineteen-twenties. (Detailed information on this subject can be found in *French Film Theory and Criticism* by Richard Abel (Princeton University Press, 1988). When Louis Delluc and others of like mind came to make films after the war, the fact that they had conceived of these sorts of shots as a separate idea tended to promote their use in a more isolated and discontinuous way than in their original source. Combining this with the influence of Griffith's cross-cutting in its most extreme form in *Intolerance* helped to promote a European avant-garde cinema of discontinuity which was some distance apart from the mainstream of continuity cinema that had already formed in the United States.

The Atmospheric Insert

Like many other devices that were more fully developed in Europe during the next decade, what could be called the 'atmospheric Insert Shot' made its first appearance in American films during the years before 1919. This kind of shot is one of a scene which neither contains any of the characters in the story, nor is a Point of View shot seen by one of them. It first appears to my knowledge in Maurice Tourneur's *The Pride of the Clan* (1917), in which there is a series of shots of waves beating on a rocky shore which are shown when the locale of the story, which is about the harsh lives of fisher folk, is being introduced. Simpler and cruder examples from the same year occurs in William S. Hart's *The Narrow Trail*, in which a single shot of the mouth of San Francisco Bay taken against the light – the Golden Gate – is preceded by a narrative title explaining its symbolic function in the story. This film also contains a shot of wild hills and valleys cut in as one character comments that the country far from the city is so clean and pure. By 1918 we can find a shot of the sky being used to reflect the mood of one of the characters without specific explanation in *The Gun Woman* (Frank Borzage), but it must be emphasized that these examples are very rare, and did not either then, or within the next several years, constitute regular practice in the American cinema. The Tourneur example just mentioned also could stand as part of the beginning of the 'montage sequence', which probably had its true origin in American films during this period. Another case that has crossed my attention is in *The Woman in 47*, which includes a chain of shots joined by fades discovering the heroine in the middle of typical New York scenes, as she discovers the city for the first time. Maurice Elvey's *Nelson - England's Immortal Naval Hero* (1919) has a symbolic sequence dissolving from a picture of Kaiser Wilhelm II to a peacock, to a battleship, which is probably more startling now than then, given our awareness of Eisenstein's subsequent films.

The atmospheric Insert began its notable career in European art cinema in Marcel L'Herbier's *Rose-France*. Here amongst the intentionally 'poetic' uses of vignettes and filters and literary intertitles, a shot of the empty path once trod by the lovers is used to evoke the past.

The Flash-Back

The fashionable interest in the flash-back continued into this period, and it could now be entered with very little preparation, as in *Between Men* (Reginald Barker, 1915). In this film the hero reads a letter which refers to a past incident in his life – we see the letter in an Insert Shot – then after a cut back to him sitting thinking, there is a dissolve which goes straight into a representation of the past scenes referred to in the letter, without any explanatory titles occurring at any point. During these years the usual way of entering and leaving a flash-back was through a dissolve, and this was in fact the principal use at this time for this device.

(The subsidiary use for a dissolve was to bridge a suspected mis-match in actor position on a transition from a Long Shot to a Close Up, and although the technique of American directors and actors was already sufficiently good to render this unnecessary most of the time, there are enough occurrences of this usage in 1915 and 1916 for it to be described as standard.)

On the other hand the dissolve was *still* not being used to denote a time-lapse, though there are one or two films in 1914 where it does happen to correspond to a time-lapse as well as to other things. In that year the enthusiasm for the new possibilities of the medium led to considerable complexity being crammed into one reel of film, as in *The Family Record* (Selig, 1914), in which an aged man and woman separated for most of their life have his flashback and then hers shown in succession within the framing story. In fact fully developed flashbacks occur in more Selig films during this period than in those from any other company contained in my sample. The Vitagraph company's *The Man That Might Have Been* (William Humphrey, 1914), is even more complex, with a series of reveries and flash-backs that contrast the protagonist's real passage through life with what might have been, if his son had not died. In this film dissolves are used both to enter and leave the flash-backs, and also the wish-dreams, and also for a time-lapse inside a reverie at one point. But fades are also used for these purposes in this and other films of the period, and flashback transitions are also done with irising in other films, and even straight cuts in Bauer's *Grezy* and *Posle smerti*, so that all that one can say on the basis of these examples is that the understanding of a particular transitional device depended totally on the context. To reinforce this point, I will mention what seems to have been a unique occurrence of a novel way of getting into a flashback during this period. In *The On-The-Square Girl* (F. J. Ireland, 1917), a flashback is shown as a succession of scenes inset into the centre of a letter which one of the characters is reading. Since this is a fairly standard sort of film, it would seem that this device was expected to be as understandable to an audience then, on its first occurrence, as it is now. This kind of lack of regularity in the significance of

style features, which was to become even more marked with the emergence of the avant-garde in the 'twenties, is one of the main reasons for the failure of attempts to create a science of film considered as a language system. This is not to say that aspects of film cannot be studied by scientific methods, or that there are no regularities in the forms of films at all, but just that these regularities are insufficient, and also change too fast, to be considered as a language system.

The fashion for flash-backs at the beginning of this period was such that one gets some instances where the use of flash-back construction was completely pointless, but on the other hand there are instances where an extensive series of flash-back scenes serves a contrasting function essential to the plot, as in *Silks and Satins*. During the war the use of flashbacks occurred in films from all the major European film-making countries as well, from Italy (*Tigre reale*) to Denmark (*Evangeliemandens Liv*) to Russia (*Grezy* and *Posle smerti*), where it arrived in 1915. As the years moved on a sudden decline in the use of long flash-back sequences set in around 1917, but on the other hand the use of a transition to and from a brief single shot memory scene remained quite common in American films. However, I have come across one more final example of complex flash-back construction in American films in the case of W.S. Van Dyke's *The Lady of the Dugout* (1918). This film has a story that happened long before narrated by one character in the framing scene, and initially accompanied by his narrating dialogue in intertitles, though after a while this stops, and the intertitles then convey the dialogue occurring within the flashback. Inside this main flashback there develops cross-cutting to another story, happening at the same time, and at first apparently unconnected with it, though the connection eventually appears. Next, inside this first flashback, the Lady of the title narrates another story, presented in flashback form, but with cut aways inside it back to events occurring in the time frame in which she is

The beginning of the flash-back scene in The On-The-Square Girl *done as a series of shots inset into the middle of a letter recalling the past events in question.*

doing her narrating. Actually, all this is fairly easy to follow while watching the film, in part because what happens in all these strings of action is relatively simple.

Cross-Cutting Between Parallel Actions

After 1914 cross-cutting between parallel actions came to be used whenever appropriate in American films, though this was not the case in European films. It should be noted that a good deal of the American use of cross-cutting was not the rapid alternation between parallel chains of action developed by D.W. Griffith, but a limited number of alternations to make it possible to leave out uninteresting bits of action with no real plot function. In Europe, some of the most enterprising directors did use cross-cutting sometimes, but they never attained the speed of many American examples, and their lack of ease with it is indicated by the fact that some of them felt it necessary to make the initial transition to the first shot of the alternate strand of action with a fade, as in Benjamin Christensen's *Haevnens Nat* (1916) and the Cines company's *Il sogno patriottico di Cinessino*. And in 1918 the quite experienced Russian director Protazanov still found it necessary to cover important simultaneous action inside and outside Father Sergius' cell in the film of the same name by having the wall of the set split apart to show these actions at the same time, rather than by cutting between them.

In the United States some directors became so enraptured with the idea of cross-cutting that they sometimes used it when it was not really necessary, and contributed nothing to the film; in other words, when nothing of any significance was shown happening in the alternate action, and no acceleration of the main action was accomplished either. One example of this is contained in the Selig company film, *The Lost Messenger* (1916). On the other hand, cross-cutting was used to get new effects of contrast, such as the cross-cut sequence in Cecil B. DeMille's *The Whispering Chorus*, in which a supposedly dead husband is having a liaison with a Chinese prostitute in an opium den, while his unknowing wife is being remarried in church. Or the sequence in *The Female of the Species* (Raymond B. West, 1918), in which a man is crawling into a woman's sleeping-berth on a train while in the cross-cut scene another train is speeding towards them in the opposite direction on the same track. The crash comes as they embrace.

Of course all this was simple compared to The Master's *Intolerance*, in which four parallel stories are intercut throughout the whole length of the film, though in this case the stories are more similar than contrasting in their nature. The use of cross-cutting within these parallel stories as well as between them produced a complexity that was beyond the comprehension of the average audience of the time, and effectively though unintentionally turned *Intolerance* into the first avant-garde film masterpiece. (Only loosely speaking, since *Intolerance* was intended to be commercially successful, whereas real avant-garde films are not.) The influence of *Intolerance* produced a few other films that combined a num-

ber of similar stories having similar themes, such as Maurice Tourneur's *Woman* (1918), but the box-office failure of *Intolerance* ensured that these later films had simpler structures. The true line of descent from *Intolerance* curves away from the mainstream through Abel Gance's *la Roue* (1921), and some of Eisenstein's films, to the real avant-garde.

Scene Dissection

Another new fashion of 1915 was the practice of beginning scenes with a close shot of some detail in them, and only then tracking or cutting back to show the whole scene, rather than following the usual practice of starting with a general shot, and only then cutting in closer. The first example I have come across is in the Thanhouser company's *The Center of the Web*, released at the very end of 1914, though this may not be where the idea started. This film begins with an insert shot, and then the camera tracks back to reveal the whole scene. Other instances of this new idea can be seen in *David Harum* (Allan Dwan) and *Elsa's Brother* (Van Dyke Brooke), released in 1915. A couple of years later, the Franklin brothers' *Going Straight* includes a scene which starts with a series of Close Ups of actors interacting with each other, before where they are doing this is revealed. Although not common, once it had been established, this new variant in the way of dissecting scenes never completely vanished after this initial burst of enthusiasm, but has been returned to from time to time ever since by imaginative directors.

The possibility of breaking a scene down into shots in markedly different ways that now existed in the American cinema was intimately connected with a number of developments, one of which has already been mentioned, namely the use of reverse-angle shots. Also involved was the general tendency to cut scenes up into more and more shots, and along with this the tendency to use a greater proportion of close shots. All these developments are obviously interconnected to some extent, but perhaps surprisingly they could also be relatively independent. And the films in which each of these different tendencies was most prominent may also be found a little surprising. For instance, by 1918 there were more shots per hour in a Kay-Bee Triangle film such as *The Hired Man* (Victor Schertzinger) than in Griffith's *Broken Blossoms*, while *Jubilo* (Clarence Badger, 1919) and *Until They Get Me* (Frank Borzage, 1917) are shot from much closer in throughout their length than contemporary films by the best-known names of the period. And Badger and Borzage used far more reverse-angle cuts than Cecil B. DeMille, while in his turn the latter used more Medium Long Shots than D.W. Griffith, who tended to avoid this range of camera closeness by 1918.

When I add that other films by other directors were now using various other combinations of these variables of film style, the response might well be to ask for a better, briefer, and clearer way of handling and describing all these matters than the imprecise words I have used up to this point. I shall now begin to provide this new approach in the following chapter.

12. STATISTICAL STYLE ANALYSIS OF MOTION PICTURES - PART 1

Since my work is basically concerned with establishing differences and similarities between films in the way they are put together, I have felt the need for a more precise method of analysis than the simple verbal descriptions that I have used in writing the previous chapters. Up to the present, everyone has been satisfied with statements like "...Fritz Lang, like Jean Renoir, puts the emphasis on Long Shots in his films...", and "*Muriel* contains twice as many shots as the average film", or even vaguer statements than these to describe a director's style. When concrete statements like the above *are* made in this area, they often turn out to be flatly wrong, as indeed are those I have just quoted. In fact *Muriel* contains a fairly average number of shots, and Renoir worked mostly with a camera distance of around Medium Shot, as did Lang a good deal of the time.

When I first started thinking about the problem of more accurate stylistic description back in the 'sixties, I took my inspiration from the use of statistical style analysis which had begun long before in literature and music. (For a survey of some of that work see *The Computer and Music*, edited by H.B. Lincoln, Cornell, 1970, and *Statistics and Style*, edited by Dolezel and Bailey, Elsevier, 1969.) However, I have recently discovered that I was not the first person with such thoughts about the style analysis of movies, for Herbert Birett had already published some suggestions along these lines in *Kinematographie I* (1962). (For Birett's other publications see issue No.2 of *Diskurs Film* (Munich, 1988)). Indeed, it appears that there were other researchers before him who put forward ideas about measuring cutting rates, not to mention the brief investigation by the Reverend Dr. Stockton in 1912 which has already been referred to in Chapter 9. In Birett's studies he has, like all previous investigators, worked with shot lengths, and has not investigated all the other major stylistic variables with which I am also concerned.

One filmic variable about which conscious decisions have to be made when a film is being shot is Scale (or Closeness) of Shot, and even before 1919 distinctions were already being drawn by American film-makers between the categories of "Bust" or Close Up, American Foreground, French Foreground, Long Shot, and Distance Shot. Although there was already a small amount of disagreement about precisely what shot scale corresponded to each of these descriptive terms, it is sufficient for the purposes of analysis to define carefully what one means by each category, and then stick to it. I will in fact use categories of Scale of Shot more like those used in the nineteen-forties and later, as follows: Big Close Up (BCU) shows head only, Close Up (CU) shows head and shoulders, Medium Close Up (MCU) includes body from the waist up, Medium Shot (MS) includes from just below the hip to above the head of upright actors, Medium Long Shot (MLS) shows the body from the knee upwards, Long Shot (LS) shows at least the full height of the body, and Very Long Shot (VLS) shows the actor small in the frame. It must be appreciated that the closer categories of shot are understood to allow only a fairly small amount of space above the actor's head, so that the kind of situation where just the head and shoulders of a distant actor are sticking up into the bottom of the frame with vast amounts of space above him would *not* be classed as a Close Up. Although all the analyses in this book are done with the above categories, it might be preferable for future work to subdivide the category of Long Shot into Full Shot, which just shows the full height of the actor, and Long Shot showing the actor so distant that the frame height is two or three times the actor height, and still reserving Very Long Shot for those shots in which the actors are very small in the frame.

Since there is very little camera movement in the films made in the period we are dealing with at the moment, and since the actors also tend to stay mostly at the same distance from the camera in them, it is not difficult to assign the shots to the appropriate category. However, if a shot does include extensive actor movement towards, or away from, the camera, it is always possible to carry out an averaging process for actor closeness within the length of the shot to any desired degree of accuracy, if one takes enough time and care over it. Also it should be noted that since we are considering films with 200 or more shots in them, there is a tendency for occasional errors in the assignments of shots to their correct category to cancel out.

To carry out an analysis of a film in this way, it is necessary to run it on some sort of viewing machine, so that it can be stopped and run backwards while difficult decisions are made as to the appropriate Scale of Shot. With practice it is possible to deal with most films in not much more than their actual running time. Although in the first place the total number of Close Ups, etc. in a film are recorded, for the purpose of the comparison between one particular film and other films which will include different numbers of shots in total, it is preferable to multiply the number of shots in each category by 500 divided by the total number of shots in the film, so that one then has the number of each type of shot per 500 shots. This "standardization" or "normalization" not only enables one to easily compare one film with another, but also gives a direct measure of the relative probability of a director choosing any particular closeness of shot.

First Results

When we look at the histograms (bar charts) for the number of shots in each category of Scale of Shot for some

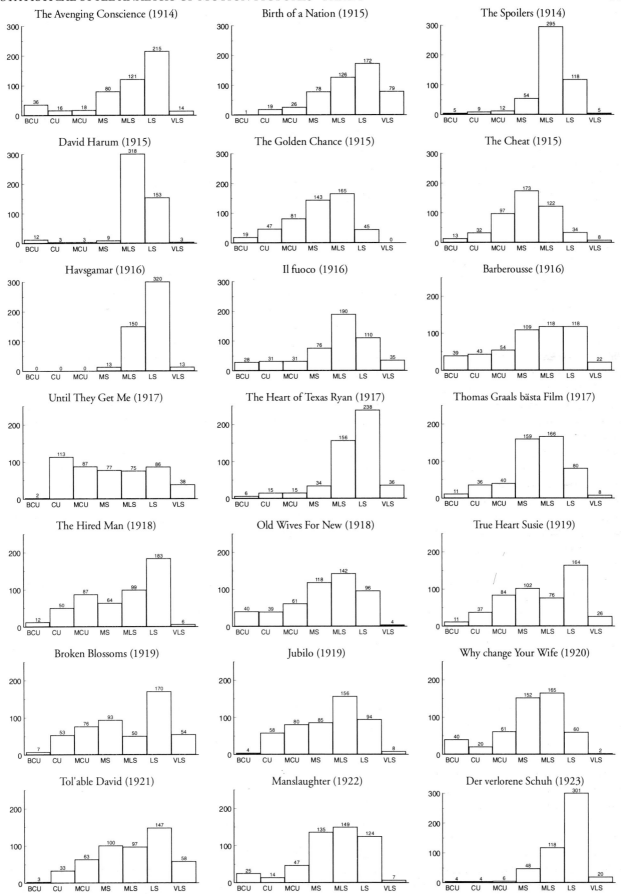

Number of Shots with the Given Scale of Shot per 500 Shots for the Films Named

American films released in 1914 and 1915, we can readily see a marked difference between them. In *The Avenging Conscience* and *Birth of a Nation* Long Shot is the most frequently used closeness of shot, while in *The Spoilers*, *David Harum* and *The Golden Chance* Medium Long Shot is much the most common. In the first two of these latter films, nearly all the shots fall into the Medium Long Shot and Long Shot categories. This was no more than the application to feature length films of the standard closeness of camera in most American films made around 1913, as has already been described. The Cecil B. DeMille films, *The Cheat* and *The Golden Chance*, have something of the same emphasis on Medium Long Shot, but they are starting to increase the proportion of closer shots. They are also shot with the camera up near head height, as had become the practice in 1915, rather than at the earlier low position, which can still be seen in *The Spoilers*. The figures for *The Cheat* illustrate one of the minor problems with the practical application of my ideas about statistical style analysis, since I had to use a 16 mm. print rather than a 35 mm. print, as I have been able to do for virtually all my other analyses. 16 mm. prints of silent films nearly always crop off part of the frame, and so make it appear that they were shot slightly closer in to the actors throughout than was really the case. Making allowance for this would give a distribution of the numbers of shots for each closeness of shot much closer to that for *The Golden Chance*. You will notice that the other three DeMille films from some years later still have the same sort of general profile of the scale of shot distribution as *The Golden Chance*, with the same sort of slope up to Medium Long Shot, but a little more emphasis on the closer shots.

It should be mentioned that I include in the category Big Close Up all shots in which the camera is as close to whatever is being filmed as it would be to give a shot of the human head alone filling the full height of the frame. Thus for most silent films this category is entirely, or almost entirely, made up of Insert shots of objects, except towards the very end of the 'twenties. I *could* separate out the two sorts of Big Close Up, since I have them recorded, but I judge that this would produce an unwanted complication in my presentations here.

Over the next few years after 1915, there was of course a trend towards closer shooting, particularly in the American cinema, and other examples I have selected from amongst a larger number in my sample indicate this, just as do the DeMille films. In Frank Borzage's *Until They Get Me* (1917), the closer shots definitely form the majority, but there were some other directors who were slow to follow the trend. Such directors as E.A. Martin, who directed *The Heart of Texas Ryan*, quickly vanished from sight. *Havsgamar* and *Il fuoco* illustrate typical European scale of shot distributions of the time, but there were one or two more advanced European directors who were following the American trend more closely, as shown by Mauritz Stiller's *Thomas Graals bästa Film* and Abel Gance's *Barberousse* from 1917, though they never completely caught up. I have more distributions which

support this statement, though to really prove it a large sample of analyses of Scale of Shot for this period is needed. Meanwhile, I hope you will accept my assertion, which is backed by a perception sharpened by carrying out a large number of analyses for later decades, that this is indeed so.

Notice as well that D.W. Griffith was also following the trend, though definitely not leading it, as can be seen from his two 1919 films, *True Heart Susie* and *Broken Blossoms*. Notice also the similarity of these two distributions, and in particular the curious avoidance of Medium Long Shot. I believe that this is a characteristic of many of Griffith's feature films, but in any case, this peculiar profile of the Scale of Shot distribution can be found in a number of other American films of the nineteen-twenties, as can be seen in the accompanying histograms for *Stella Dallas* (Henry King, 1925), *Sun-Up* (Edmund Goulding, 1925), *The Eagle* (Clarence Brown, 1925), and *The Son of the Sheik* (George Fitzmaurice, 1926). Despite the persistence of this single aspect of Griffith's style in the work of some directors, the other important idiosyncrasies of his scene dissection that I have previously mentioned were not copied by these directors. The above films by Goulding, King, Brown, and Fitzmaurice all show much greater use of reverse angle cutting, better position and movement matching across cuts, and far less irising and vignetting within scenes than there is in Griffith's films of the nineteen-twenties.

As new directors came into the industry in the nineteen-twenties, they tended to push the move towards closer shooting even further, as is shown in the distributions illustrated for *Docks of New York* (J. von Sternberg, 1928), and *It* (Clarence Badger, 1927), and some other established directors swung with them, as can be seen from Brown's *The Eagle* and *Flesh and the Devil*. One of the main alternatives for camera placement continued to be defined by a profile with the strongest emphasis on Medium Shot, and examples of this are shown here from the 1925 Clarence Brown films *Smouldering Fires* and *The Goose Woman*, as well as *Sun Up* and Victor Fleming's *Mantrap* (1926). The European films illustrated show yet other ways of shooting, with the camera still further back. The one exception to this last generalization that I have come across is E.A. Dupont's *Varieté* of 1925, which much impressed the American film industry, though only partly for this reason.

The other major point that begins to emerge from consideration of these Scale of Shot distributions is that films made by the same director often have profiles that closely resemble each other, as is the case for the DeMille, Lang, and Sternberg films here. This observation receives much more support from the extensive results which I will present later for films of the sound period.

Average Shot Length

In the previous chapters I have already commented on increases in the cutting rate in terms of the number of shots per reel of film, or in terms of the number in one hour's running time. Although other people have used these ideas in

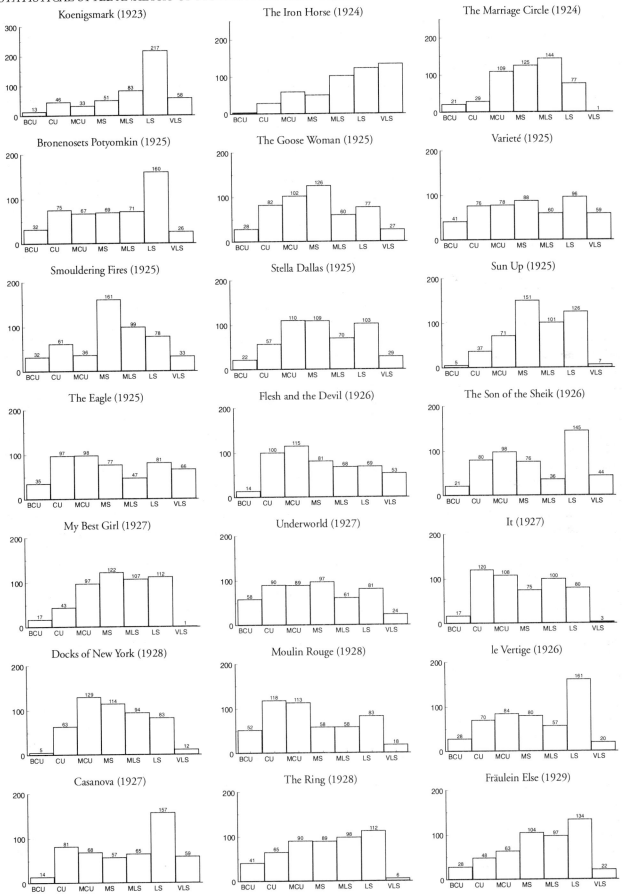

Number of Shots with the Given Scale of Shot per 500 Shots for the Films Named

a rough kind of way before me for making some kinds of limited comparisons between films, neither of these quantities is a very convenient or accurate measure of the general tendency for any particular film-maker to break a scene down into a smaller or larger number of shots. Instead I shall introduce the rather obvious concept of Average Shot Length (ASL), which is the length of a film divided by the number of shots in it, and which can be expressed as an actual physical length of film, or as a time duration. Such a measure provides strict comparability between films of different length. Because of the variations in taking and projection speeds that existed for silent films, and which will be further discussed in the next chapter, the use of feet of film as a measure of Average Shot Length (ASL) for silent films does not give a true impression of relative cutting rates when comparing films made at widely different times and places, so I express all Average Shot Lengths in seconds. This decision introduces the complementary problem that the correct running speed for a silent film must be estimated before the ASL in seconds can be finally determined, but this can always be accomplished within an accuracy of a few percent with a variable speed projector, and that is quite sufficient for most reasonable purposes.

So we find that in 1914 D.W. Griffith's *The Avenging Conscience* has an Average Shot Length of 7.7 seconds, and there were other American film-makers who were cutting just about as fast, as the ASL's for *The Italian* (7.5 sec.) and *A Florida Enchantment* (8 sec.) indicate. However, most directors were still using less shots in their films, as is suggested by the figures for *The Spoilers* (13.5 sec.), *The Wishing Ring* (11.5 sec.), and *The Three Musketeers* (11.2 sec.).

A wide range of values was still to be found in 1915, such as; *The Cheat* (De Mille) - 13.5 seconds, *Birth of a Nation* (Griffith) - 7.1 seconds, *The Coward* (Barker) - 11 seconds, *David Harum* (Dwan) - 20 seconds, *Madame Butterfly* (Olcott) - 16 seconds, and *Playing Dead* (Sidney Drew) - 9 seconds.

But by 1918, because of the rapid formal evolution that continued through the war years in the United States, we find that values for the Average Shot Length had decreased substantially, as the following figures show: *The Hired Man* (Schertzinger) - 5.5 seconds, *The Gun Woman* (Borzage) - 4.7 seconds, *A Modern Musketeer* (Dwan) - 4 seconds, *Stella Maris* (Neilan) - 7.5 seconds, *Old Wives for New* (DeMille) - 8.2 seconds, and *Till I Come Back To You* (DeMille) - 8 seconds.

To reinforce the point I shall add a few figures for 1919, as follows: *Broken Blossoms* (Griffith) - 7.5 seconds, *True Heart Susie* (Griffith) - 6 seconds, *When the Clouds Roll By* (Fleming) - 5 seconds, and *Jubilo* (Badger) - 5.5 seconds.

These figures give just one indication that stylistic development in the American cinema was just beginning to slow down and stabilize at the end of the war, and as well as that, if we note that the ASL for Cecil B. DeMille's *Don't Change Your Husband* (1919) is 8.5 seconds, and then compare it with the other values quoted for his films, we can also see the way that Average Shot Length comes to be characteristic for a

director once his individual style is fully formed. I will have more to say about this in later chapters.

In European cinema, I have found no films with an ASL shorter than 11 seconds before 1917, by which date a few clever and perceptive directors had finally begun to understand the new American methods of film construction. In Sweden, Victor Sjöström had all the devices of continuity cinema working properly in *Tösen fra Stormyrtorpet* (1918), with an ASL of 6 seconds. (His other films of this time, in which he acted as well as directed, unlike the one just mentioned, are slightly more retarded stylistically.) Mauritz Stiller also went some of the way down the same path in *Thomas Graals bästa Film* (ASL=9 sec.), but this was not typical for the Nordic region, as figures for films made by Georg af Klerker and others show. In Germany, Ernst Lubitsch seems to have been the first to get a grip on American methods, as is indicated by the ASL for *Wenn Vier dasselbe tun* (1917) of 8.5 seconds, while his *Die Puppe* of 1919 has an ASL of 5.5. seconds, not to mention the fact that he was already using a lot of reverse-angle shots by this date. His *Carmen* of 1918 has 14% of such cuts, and *Die Puppe* includes 19% reverse-angle cuts.

These changes and differences in cutting rates for a larger sample of feature films of the period can best be summarized by using another set of graphs on the next page which show the various numbers of films with Average Shot Lengths which fall within each of the ranges of one second width from zero to 26 seconds for the periods 1912-1917 and 1918-1923. That is, there were 20 films with ASLs of 5.0 seconds or greater, but less than 6.0 seconds, in my sample of 68 American feature films from the 1918-1923 period, and 17 films with ASLs of 6.0 seconds and greater, but less than 7.0 seconds, and so on. The speed-up in cutting rate is reflected by the fact that there are no American films in the sample with ASLs longer than 10 seconds in the 1918-23 period, and hence the mean value of the Average Shot Length for this period is 6.5 seconds, whereas for the previous six year 1912-1917, the mean value of the ASL for American features was 9.6 seconds. On the other hand, for European features, the 1912-1917 mean value of the ASL was 15 seconds, which only decreased to 8.6 seconds for the next 6 year period. And this difference of 2 seconds in the mean ASL's between America and Europe remained into the late 'twenties as well, and was quite obvious to people in the American film industry at the time. Two seconds may not seem much on the page, but it is a long time on the screen. Imagine all the shots in a film you know well having two seconds added to their duration, and you will get the idea.

Reverse-Angles

Another of the other major stylistic variables is the extent to which reverse-angle cutting is used. I define a reverse-angle cut as being a cut within a scene which changes camera direction by more than 90 degrees in the horizontal plane, since this accords well with film industry usage, not to men-

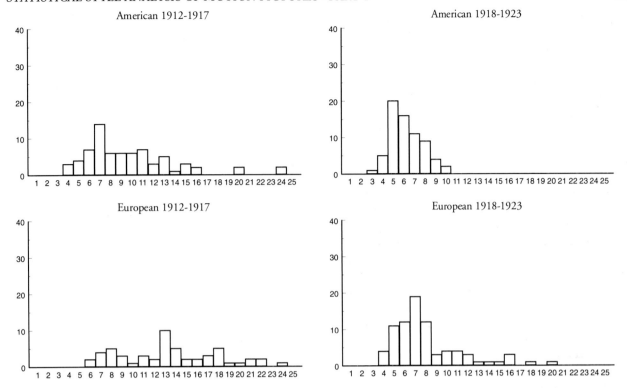

Numbers of Films with stated Average Shot Length for samples of American and European Films as indicated.

tion the common meaning of the words "reverse" and "angle". The proportion of reverse-angle cuts to the total number of shot transitions (including fades and dissolves) in the film is the appropriate measure for comparative purposes. This percentage of reverse-angle cuts often distinguishes between films by different directors which are otherwise rather similar with respect to the major stylistic variables already defined; for instance Henry King's films are rather similar to those of D.W. Griffith with respect to their Scale of Shot distributions, and even their Average Shot Lengths, but King used around 20% reverse-angle cuts, and Griffith hardly any.

During these early years, when American directors were only just discovering the usefulness of reverse-angle cutting, there was a tendency to make most of such cuts between a watcher and his Point of View, but this changed towards the end of the 'twenties, and in general in the sound-film period

most reverse-angle cuts are between two positions both of which are off the eye-line. It must also be remembered that in any period not all the cuts between a watcher and his POV are reverse-angle cuts – sometimes the watcher is shot from the side or the back – and of course not all reverse-angle cuts are between a watcher and his POV. Nevertheless, the amount of cutting between a watcher and his Point of View (or vice-versa) is also a variable that can distinguish between the films of different directors, and there is something to be said for recording this quantity for that purpose, as I suggested when I first made proposals for the statistical style analysis of films in 1968.

In Chapter 16 I will take up the question of what constitutes reasonable accuracy in the statistical style analysis of films, and also introduce further extensions of the technique, to the point where it begins to engage with expressive devices.

13. FILM STYLE AND TECHNOLOGY: 1920-1926

In the nineteen-twenties the general trend in the world film industry was, with certain exceptions, one of expansion, and in the United States in particular, profit ratios continued to be very high. This was because American films penetrated into all markets, but foreign films were not widely shown in the United States. The great commercial success of American movies no doubt encouraged a certain conservatism in their forms, though finally they proved susceptible to stylistic developments that took place in Germany in the first half of this decade. The so-called French Avant-Garde cinema of the early 'twenties was as inventive as some of the German films, but the poor production values and poor technical finish of its films tended to keep them out of other markets. The few Russian films which were seen by a limited audience in America after 1925, though applauded, had very little visible effect on American film styles.

The German and French advanced cinemas of the early 'twenties in their turn owed quite a lot to American films of the previous decade, in fact more than is now realized. A thorough investigation of this matter, as of others, is hampered by the relatively small numbers of films surviving from the early nineteen-twenties when compared with later years, and also by the fact that those which are usually seen are rather unrepresentative of the general production of the time, whether it be in America, France, or Germany. This matters because in the early 'twenties there was still a far greater range of styles in use in any country than was to be the case from the late 'twenties onwards, when the range in competence amongst film-makers came to be greater than the stylistic range. It can hardly be said too strongly that the Russian film industry between 1919 and 1925 was very small and feeble, and most of the films seen in Russia at that time were American or German. As far as can be told at the moment, the few Russian fictional films produced before 1924 were made in a rather retarded style, resembling the American films made a decade before. The influential Russian films were made *after* 1925, while the most influential German films were made *before* 1926.

The wildly mistaken idea that the German cinema of the 'twenties was distinguished from that of other countries by the practice of shooting film exteriors entirely on studio sets, rather than using actual locations, rests as usual on the consideration of a couple of handfuls of famous films, most of which were made by one company, Ufa. In fact Ufa produced less than 10% of German films throughout the 'twenties; a period over which the total German production amounted to about 2000 films. The French production for the decade was less than half that, fluctuating around 70 films per year, while the total American production of fiction films of four reels or

longer was nearly 7000 films.

These figures bring me back again to the problem of film availability when trying to make an accurate assessment of the main developments in film style during this period. My experience leads me to believe that with a sample of about 100 films from each year, one does not miss much in the way of general trends. A sample approaching that size has been available over the last decade for films made in the late 'twenties, but this has not been the case for the early part of the nineteen-twenties, and it is quite possible that more discoveries about developments in those years are yet to be made.

Film Stock

There were few major developments in the types of motion picture negative and positive stocks available up to 1925; each manufacturer continued to produce a single standard orthochromatic negative stock, and a single positive print stock as before. However, Eastman Kodak added a new 'Super-Speed Cine Film' to its range from about 1922. This was available to special order, and had to be used almost immediately it was manufactured, as the effect of the special sensitizing treatment applied to it wore off quickly. Also, the Eastman panchromatic negative, which had previously only been available to special order, was made a standard stock item from 1923. Kodak made efforts to encourage the use of this panchromatic negative by the industry, even financing a short feature, *The Headless Horseman* (1922), which was shot entirely with panchromatic negative to demonstrate its capabilities, particularly in 'day for night' filming. But because the price of panchromatic negative remained higher than that of the usual orthochromatic stock, no other films were entirely shot with it before 1926. There were, however, a few films in which some of the exteriors were shot on panchromatic negative, starting with *The Last of the Mohicans* (Maurice Tourneur, 1920), but this created problems of changes in the tones of the costumes between scenes shot on the two different stocks, as described by James Wong Howe in *Hollywood Cameramen*. Since it was still standard practice to tint all night scenes blue, there was no great need for a convincing 'day for night' technique of photographing exteriors as we know it from later years.

The other major advantage of panchromatic negative in exterior photography is in the rendering of blue sky with scattered clouds, but the importance of this should not be exaggerated either. In the first place, it is not generally understood that orthochromatic negative will *just* distinguish between sky and clouds if it is correctly exposed, since its emulsion has a small amount of yellow sensitivity, and this is particularly the case at sunset, or when there are heavy clouds all over the sky, and in the second place it had become customary to put clouds into the sky when necessary by glass matte painting or with a matted-in photograph, as can be seen in the desert shots in *The Thief of Baghdad* (1924) and elsewhere. Nevertheless, panchromatic stock was occasionally used to bring out cloud formations, but usually only on shots in which human figures were distant or absent.

In 1920 Eastman Kodak made its ordinary camera negative stock available in an optional alternative form with a resin coating on the back of the cellulose nitrate base. This was called 'X-back' stock, and its purpose was to prevent the build-up of charges of static electricity on the film as it ran through the camera, particularly in very cold weather. If these static charges formed, they could cause minute sparks to discharge onto the film surface as the film strip pulled off the feed roll. These sparks produced very fine black branching lines on the negative which thoroughly spoiled the look of the picture, and these static marks were a cause of great concern to the early cameramen. Although X- back stock may have reduced the incidence of static marks, it certainly did not eliminate them completely, for they can still occur on rare occasions with modern film stocks, which also have a special backing on the film. X-back stock was only used on the East Coast in the depths of winter, and it also had the slight disadvantage that it was almost opaque to transmitted light, so the older type of focussing arrangement in cameras that depended on viewing the image formed on the film from its back side could not be readily used with it.

The Prizma Process

Early attempts by William van Doren Kelly at creating a successful two-colour process for colour cinematography were fairly closely based on the Kinemacolor additive process, but in 1919 a further modification to the Prizma system produced a subtractive process that was used in a number of short films over the next couple of years. In this form the Prizma process used the same kind of camera as the Kinemacolor process, taking alternate frames on black and white panchromatic film through a rotating filter with red and green sectors, but after this stage the method was quite different. The red record frames and then the green record frames were separately printed onto two black and white positive films by using an optical printer that skipped alternate frames, and then these two films were separately dye-toned so that the black silver images in each were turned to red or green as the case might be. These two prints were then cemented back to back down their whole length to give a single print which could be projected in ordinary projectors at ordinary speed. Since the red and green records were taken successively in the same way as for Kinemacolor, there was some colour fringing round fast moving objects, but this was slightly reduced as the two records were projected simultaneously rather than successively. There was only one feature film made in the Prizma process, and this was *The Glorious Adventure* (1922), which

was shot in England by James Stuart Blackton of the Vitagraph company. Surviving material suggests that the process was biased in the red direction compared to other later two-colour subtractive processes, and this meant the general effect was one of browns and reds in the image, with the greens underplayed. The Prizma prints cost about six times as much per foot as ordinary black and white prints, and this may have been the reason the process was dropped after 1922.

Technicolor Cinematography

Like the Kinemacolor process before it, the Technicolor system of colour cinematography was initially a two-colour additive process incapable of reproducing the full range of natural colours. But after Kalmus and Comstock's first unsuccessful trials in 1916 with this additive process, they developed a new two-colour subtractive process with which *The Toll of the Sea* was made in 1922. A new camera was produced for this process which was quite different to the earlier model. This new camera used a different form of beam-splitting prism to produce the red and green images on the film, with a shorter path in glass for the rays between the back of the lens and the film gate. The new prism was made up of two separate prisms in the shape of equal right-angle triangles which were cemented together along their longer right-angled faces with a semi-reflecting filter layer between them. The light coming out of the back of the camera lens entered the prism through the hypotenuse side of the first prism, and after passing across it was split into two beams by the semi-reflecting filter layer. A red beam was reflected back into the first prism inside which it was reflected once again by the front surface down through the prism and out of its base onto the film to form the red image. Simultaneously the other beam of green light passed into the second prism and then across it to the back hypotenuse surface where it was reflected internally down through

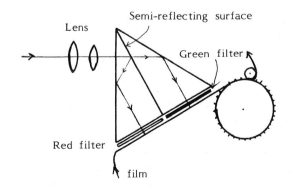

The beam-splitting prism arrangement used in Technicolor cameras during the 'twenties.

the base to form the green image on a frame of film adjoining that for the red image. The red and green images were inverted both laterally and vertically with respect to each other, and the other difference from the earlier camera was that the corresponding red and green frames were adjacent on the film negative rather than separated by two other frames. The film movement was novel in the new Technicolor camera as well, being based on a modification of the Bell & Howell shuttle gate mechanism. Most unusually, the film was pulled *up* through the gate which was set below the oblique bottom of the double prism block, rather than moved downwards as in all other cameras. Exact registration of the image for every exposure was accomplished by the part of the shuttle-gate mechanism which lifted and dropped the film off and onto fixed registration pins, but the intermittent advance of the film was produced by a large sprocket wheel above the gate which rotated intermittently by means of a Maltese Cross movement, rather than by the claws of the standard Bell & Howell mechanism. Although the light path in the prism block was now only about two inches, it was still not possible to use wide-angle lenses on the new Technicolor camera.

After development the negative was printed in an optical printer that moved the film down two frames at a time, while only moving the positive forward one frame for each exposure. The result was a positive that had all the red image frames printed on it, and then the process was repeated to extract the green record frames onto another strip of positive film. These two red and green record positive films were developed by a special process which hardened the gelatine of the emulsion in proportion to the amount of silver produced in each area of the individual images; i.e. in proportion to the intensity of the red colour or the green colour of the image, as the case might be. The result was a relief image for each frame in which the remaining gelatine of the emulsion was thicker where the red or green colour had been brighter. Then the red relief positive was treated with orange-red dye, and where it was thickest most dye was absorbed, and vice-versa. The green relief was similarly dyed with blue-green dye. This treatment of the red and green positives just described had also produced the usual black silver photographic images in the coloured gelatine reliefs, and though in principal it was possible to remove this by dissolving it out, this seems not to have been done. The red and green positives were next cemented together back to back with the corresponding red and green images in alignment, and the resulting film could be run in ordinary projectors when the pressure on the gate was slackened off a little to allow the double thickness of film through.

Contemporary reports speak of the subdued colours obtained with this process, and prints reconstructed from the surviving material of *The Black Pirate* (1924) do indeed show a very limited range in both hue and intensity of colour. This may be due in part to the fading of the dyes, but as the film now exists the two primary colours appear to be a pale salmon pink and a steel blue, and some of the time only one of these colours is present. In fact the process looks more like a one-and-a-half colour process than a two-colour process! Because the process also retained the black silver image, though in a weaker form than in ordinary black and white film, there is also some resemblance to the Pathé stencil-tinting process, which was still being worked in the 'twenties in France. A caution is necessary about the reconstructed prints of *Toll of the Sea* recently produced in the United States. These, which were made from the original negative by a quite different process to that originally used, give the impression that the process produced far brighter colours and far higher definition than was actually the case. These prints also reveal that the exposure of many of the original shots in 1922 was substantially incorrect, which is not terribly surprising given that the effective speed of the system was very different to anything that the cameraman was used to, and that it was being shot without an exposure meter.

The filming operation in this Technicolor system still suffered from some of the drawbacks of the earlier Kinemacolor. Because of the division of the light from the lens into two beams, and the interposition of filters into those two beams, not to mention the light losses in traversing all the length of glass in the prism system, the film effectively lost two stops or more in speed when compared with ordinary black and white photography. This meant using a very great deal of light in shooting studio interiors, and something approaching maximum aperture on exteriors. Also, because of the length of the path through the prism system, which was more than two inches, special lenses with large back focal distance had to be designed for the cameras. But the real drawback to the process was that the original negative had to be passed twice through the optical printer for every show print that was made, and this was a slow job compared to standard black and white printing in a continuous contact printer. This meant that there was little scope for lowering print costs as the process was expanded commercially. Another minor drawback was that the double-sided cemented prints wore out faster than ordinary black and white prints, and they were also liable to 'cupping', which meant that they became concave in cross-section after a while, and hence could not be properly focussed in the projector.

Laboratory Procedures

No great changes took place in laboratory procedures in the early part of the decade; negative continued to be batch developed in 200 or 400 foot lengths, and so mostly was positive, but there was a slow movement towards more machine (i.e. continuous) development of positive as the years passed, starting in newsreel production. 80 to 90% of prints were tinted, with the colours continuing much as before – blue for night, gold for day, orange for flamelight, red for conflagrations, magenta for romantic scenes, and sometimes green for ghastly happenings. As before, the tinting was applied by running the film through dye baths after printing and developing the positive, and then the different coloured shots were spliced together to make the final print. However in the

A scene from The Wanters *(John Stahl, 1923) being filmed on location. The cameraman Ernest Palmer is using a Bell & Howell studio model camera with matte box attached in front of the lens. At the front of the matte box is the mechanical arrangement for producing irises. The lights in the background are another form of the usual mercury vapour tube racks, and in the foreground arc floodlights can partially be seen. The one at the left sitting on the floor detached from its usual stand has a diffusing screen covering its opening. (Photograph courtesy of Kevin Brownlow.)*

'twenties there began to be some use of print stock with a pre-tinted base which now became available from Eastman Kodak or imported from Pathé in France. Toning was still very rarely used, except for the occasional climactic scene in major productions, and these were usually emotional sunset scenes which were blue toned and pink tinted, though other combinations were possible in other situations.

Lighting Equipment and Techniques

Although most American studio filming was being done on totally blacked-out stages at the beginning of the decade, this was not the case in Europe, as can be seen in the many films in which it is obvious that on the sets of large-scale interiors a good deal of the light is old-fashioned diffuse sunlight coming through the studio roof. F.W. Murnau's early films could be mentioned amongst many others in this connection. As the decade wore on it was inevitably the larger

companies in Europe which first moved over to filming entirely under artificial light.

The only major new piece of lighting equipment that came into general use during these years was the kind of arc spotlight in which the beam was focussed by a large parabolic mirror behind the arc, often referred to as a 'Sunlight arc'. They were widely used in the early 'twenties in Hollywood, almost entirely for the lighting of exterior sets and scenes, but it was only around 1922 that a large company such as UFA came to use them in Europe.

The principal use for these reflector arc spotlights was to light large sets 'night for night', i.e. to bring the light on a night-time exterior scene actually shot at night up to photographic level. This approach was already well developed at the major studios in 1920, as can be seen in *The Virgin of Stamboul* made at Universal, in which these large spotlights are used singly from various places outside the frame to light selected

Night exterior scene in The Virgin of Stamboul *(Tod Browning, 1920) shot on the studio backlot and lit 'night for night' with the new big reflector arc spotlights.*

areas of the streets just as it is done to this day. In the next couple of years one can see the same technique being used in better-known films such as *Foolish Wives* (1922) and *The Hunchback of Notre-Dame* (1923). In this application the reflector spotlights were used with their focus adjusted so as to give a spread or 'flood' beam, but in a related usage, the lighting of night-time trench warfare scenes, the arc spotlights were used with a tighter spot beam just skimming the ground from side-back to give a really low-key effect. The prototypical instance here seems to have been *The Four Horsemen of the Apocalypse* (1921), lit by John Seitz. He retained the same sort of lighting for the closer shots in the night trench scenes in this film, just adding a very little weak fill-light from the front, so that in all respects these scenes look exactly like such scenes

have looked ever since in movies.

Studio Lighting

The standard equipment for studio lighting continued to be Cooper-Hewitts, arc floodlights of one kind or another, and the older theatrical type of arc spotlights, but a few studios did not use Cooper-Hewitts, replacing them with extra banks of arc floodlights. The Cooper-Hewitts were used as they had been before, suspended from above the set or on floor stands to provide general overall background light on scenes lit to a middle- or high-key level, but they did not define the real modelling of the figures. Some cameramen also used a small pair of Cooper-Hewitt tubes rather than a diffused arc flood-light to give fill-light on closer shots. It was now universal

Night exterior scene of trench warfare in The Four Horsemen of the Apocalypse *(Rex Ingram, 1921) lit with reflector arc spotlights from left and right back.*

A Medium shot in The Thief of Baghdad *(1924) lit by Ernest Palmer with two backlights. The right one is fairly fine to the head, while the left one is coming in from 3/4 back at about 45° to the head. There is also a key light coming from the front just to the right of the camera. There may, or may not be, some weak fill from the front.*

practice in America to put diffusing screens over the front of arc floodlights when using them for figure lighting, and often these diffusers were heavy enough in their effect to produce a considerable softening of the shadows they cast.

As the years went on from 1920 to 1926 the rather varied approaches that still existed in American lighting practice converged towards uniformity. One of the general features which emerged in this transformation was the greater use of what might be called four-point lighting. I have already described how the use of two backlights had first appeared just before 1919, spreading from the lighting of close shots to the lighting of Long Shots as well in a small number of films, and this technique, in combination with use of two more lights as

key and fill from the front, spread to more and more camer-amen as the years passed. By 1925 some cameramen were using this arrangement fairly relentlessly on interiors, but others alternated it with other arrangements as appropriate, including the earlier three-point lighting using one backlight plus key and fill. Yet others stuck more or less exclusively to the earlier single backlight with key and fill from the front. Exactly which of these methods was used, and more import-antly, what the usual angles of the lights were with respect to the camera lens axis represented a stylistic distinction between cameramen. For instance, in the middle 'twenties John Arnold habitually used a single backlight, not too strong, and coming in at only a very small angle to the line between the lens and

Studio interior scene photographed by Henry Cronjager for Tol'able David *(Henry King, 1921), with backlight from an arc spotlight, and excessively flat lighting from arcs to the front.*

A Close Up in The Four Horsemen of the Apocalypse *which has been photographed with John Seitz's usual core lighting of this period, with two sources straight out each side. Exceptionally for this film, it also has heavy lens diffusion.*

the actor, while the key and fill lights from the front were fairly well separated. And so on. Another new and fairly general trend was the placing of the key-light a bit above the actor's eye-level, whereas previously it had usually been at or below eye-level.

As an example of one of the major lighting styles from the previous decade that was relegated to cheaper films and comedies as the years passed, I will quote Henry Cronjager's work on *Tol'able David* (1921). In this film the backlighting on interiors is done with a single spot directly behind and above the actors, and both the key- and fill-lights are almost equal in intensity, and applied to the actors too frontally, so that there is a flatness, a lack of modelling, over the parts of the face facing the camera. For this date this was not *bad* lighting, just not particularly distinguished. In *Tol'able David* what photographic distinction there is lies elsewhere, in the composition and camera placement on exteriors.

A very individual approach to lighting in the early 'twenties that was later lost in the tide of the general trend is to be found in the work of Charles Rosher. In 1919 he explicitly formulated the idea of creating very sharp images with very simple lighting applied from carefully chosen directions. This style can be seen most clearly in the more distant shots in *Daddy Long-Legs*, but he was still working in much the same way in *Rosita* (1923). After that date he gradually succumbed to the general movement that was already underway in the opposite direction; towards larger apertures and heavy lens diffusion. However the struggle between these two opposed styles of photography in Rosher's work meant that he had some difficulty in adjusting to the use of lens diffusion, as the less-than-perfect control of the gradation between differing amounts of diffusion on successive shots in *My Best Girl* (1927) shows.

Still another idiosyncratic approach to lighting that was much less at odds with the general trend was that of John Seitz,

working for the director Rex Ingram. The basic technique used by Seitz in lighting *The Four Horsemen of the Apocalypse* (1921) was what has now come to be known as 'core lighting' in still photography. This involves using *two* equally bright key-lights placed to either side of, and very slightly behind, the figure being lit. This kind of lighting leaves a dark vertical band of shadow down the centre of the figure – the 'core'. This kind of lighting set-up is nowadays included under the more general expression 'double cross back lighting'. For the more distant interior shots in *The Four Horsemen of the Apocalypse*, Seitz used groups of lights out of shot on either side, rather than single lights, though the effect was the same. He also had a little weak fill-light on the figures from the front, particularly on closer shots, but this was not strong enough to wipe out the dark core. Two years later, when he came to light *Scaramouche* for Rex Ingram, Seitz was starting to use a more varied approach, but some of the time he returned to a modified form of his original 'core' technique. Instead of having the two side lights at head height as he had placed them before, he moved them up and a little further backwards, so that they were now almost two backlights, and thus close to the way other cameramen were starting to use backlights. But what little fill-light Seitz used was far weaker than the frontal light used by other cameramen, so there was still a dark 'core' down the centre of his figures. Seitz also adopted very heavy lens diffusion for the Close Ups in *Scaramouche*, whereas he had mostly used the older soft circular vignette mask in *The Four Horsemen*. Though he did try lens diffusion at one or two emotional moments in *The Four Horsemen*.

In Europe these new American lighting techniques were picked up rather slowly in the nineteen-twenties, so that although there are some shots in European films with a single backlight from the beginning of the decade, this only happened sometimes when the actors were right in the middle of

Location exterior Medium Close Up in He Who Gets Slapped *(Victor Sjöström, 1924) lit with arclights right and left of the camera providing key and fill light of almost equal intensity, and the sun providing the backlight.*

the set and it was easy to get a back spot onto them. After a few years the use of double backlighting likewise makes the occasional appearance in the occasional European film, but it never became as common as it was in American films.

Cameras

The Akeley camera, designed with the special problems of wild-life filming in mind by a cameraman of that name, was first produced in 1919. It was very different in appearance from all other cameras, since its body was in the form of a squat cylinder of height 7 inches and a diameter of 15 inches standing on one curved edge. This drum could be rotated about a pivot supporting it from one side at the centre to give the tilting movement, by pushing on a panning and tilting

tiller fixed to the back, or on the handle on top. The panning pivot was also an integral part of the camera, and the casing which included both pivots also included flywheels that were driven by gears from the movements applied to the camera body by the panning and tilting tiller. The flywheel system smoothed out any unevenness in the panning and tilting pressures applied by the cameraman, as this kind of unevenness was particularly harmful when trying to follow unrehearsed action with a long lens. The whole camera weighed 22 lb.

On the front of the camera a pair of identical lenses were mounted side by side, one being the taking lens, and the other the viewfinding lens, and they were coupled together so that focussing the image through the viewfinding lens simulta-

The Akeley camera with the adjustable viewing system eyepiece angled upwards. The viewing lens is on the left of the taking lens on the removable lens board fixed to the front of the camera body. (Camera from Kevin Brownlow collection.)

A view of the other side of the Akeley camera, in which can be seen the way the camera body is supported from a pillar containing the flywheels and gears producing the 'gyroscopic' smoothing of the movement on panning and tilting. The cameraman actually controls the pans and tilts with the handle on top, and just in front of this handle is the knob which controls the lens focus remotely.

neously focussed the taking lens. These paired lenses were supplied in a range of focal lengths on standard quickly changeable mounts, and the image seen in the viewfinder was erect rather than inverted as with most previous cameras. The viewfinder tube, which ran up the side of the camera, was jointed in the middle so that the eye-piece could be set at a convenient height for any position of the camera. The film was loaded into 200 foot magazines which included the drive sprockets for film transport, and these pre-threaded magazines were then inserted into the camera body. This arrangement simplified loading in the heat of the action, for all that was necessary was to open the camera door, take out the used magazine, and then slip in the new one, sliding the pre-formed loop of film coming out of it under the usual kind of claw in the film gate. The whole camera, including pan and tilt mechanism, weighed 41 labs., and it entirely suited not only wild-life cameramen, but also second unit cameramen in ordinary commercial film-making who were shooting unrehearsed and unrepeatable action in war films and the like. Many Akeley cameras were used for this purpose up until the early sound period, though they did not entirely monopolize this application.

The most distinguished user of the Akeley camera was Robert Flaherty, and all his silent films from *Nanook of the North* (1922) onwards were shot with one. He did not make a great deal of visible use of its unique properties in *Nanook*, for there are only a couple of long-lens shots in that film, and also only a couple of shots with the smooth simultaneous pan and tilt movements that were possible with the Akeley camera, but not with ordinary geared heads. But in *Moana* (1926) there are a number of extensive sinuous camera movements involving simultaneous panning and tilting. As far as I know, no- one else made such use of the special properties of the Akeley, though one can occasionally see action followed with a long lens in Westerns such as *Tumbleweeds* (1925), and this was presumably shot with an Akeley camera. In 1926 the

Akeley pan and tilt head with its smoothing flywheel (or 'gyroscopic') mechanism was marketed separately without the actual camera body, so that it could be used for the same purpose with other cameras.

The Mitchell Camera

The basic design of the Mitchell camera was due to John E. Leonard, and not to the man whose name it bears. In some respects it was a logical progression from the Bell & Howell, which remained the major production camera in America for the rest of the silent period. Rather than moving the whole camera sideways on the tripod head to put the viewing lens in the position normally occupied by the taking lens for focussing, as was done with the Bell & Howell, only that part of the body behind the front plate, which carried the lenses on a turret, was slid over for this purpose. This obviated all the moving of the matte box backwards and forwards over the lens that was necessary to get a Bell & Howell across and back when focussing, and as well as that, in the viewing position the Mitchell through-the-lens viewfinding system showed the whole frame area clearly, which the Bell & Howell did not. When it was first made available in 1921, the Mitchell camera did not have the register pins it was later provided with in 1928, but the basic design was pretty much as it remained in later versions. The body, machined from cast aluminium, was slightly larger and heavier than that of the Bell & Howell, and like that camera it had a variable shutter which could be closed while the camera was running, so permitting perfect fades and dissolves to be made at any lens aperture. It also had detachable 400 foot magazines, and a lens turret with places for four lenses. Immediately in front of the film aperture adjustable mattes were built into the front plate behind the lens turret, and these could be screwed across the frame from either side, so blanking off part of the frame horizontally or vertically. This made split-field trick effects very easy to carry out. The claw movement was actuated by two cams working simultaneously to provide the combined in-out and up-down movement required, in a very general kind of way like the working of the old Pathé mechanism, though the disposition of the actual cam system was quite different. A third cam system clamped down the back pressure plate on the film while it was stationary in the gate during the actual exposure. Although this idea may have been suggested by the Bell & Howell mechanism, the way that it worked meant that the Mitchell in its first version could not achieve an image registration equal to that of the Bell & Howell.

Other Cameras

The Studio model of the Pathé camera was still extensively used in Europe in the early 'twenties, and even in America some impoverished or conservative cameramen continued to use it. In total numbers the Debrie Parvo was the most used camera in the world, if we take all kinds of film-making into account, but it was only in Russia after 1924 that it was regularly used as a studio camera on feature films. At the beginning of the decade a new model of the Parvo became available that had an automatic dissolve facility, and this made a fade mechanically over a fixed number of frames. A Debrie Parvo cost $1500 in America, while a Pathé Studio model cost $552. A Bell & Howell camera now cost $3500, and a Mitchell camera even more.

In 1921 Debrie also introduced a new high speed camera of quite different design to the Parvo. In general configuration this new camera looked like a larger and cruder version of the much later 35 mm. Arriflex camera, with the film fed in line through the gate from an internal 200 foot magazine which had the feed and take-up compartments lined up slantwise above the film movement and gate. The viewfinding arrangements were extremely simple, with none of the subtle mechanisms that were used in the American cameras. In its initial form the High Speed Debrie was hand-cranked with a top speed of about 200 frames per second. The great slowing down of motion that could be produced with this camera was immediately applied in *The Ropin' Fool*, which enclosed a long demonstration of Will Rogers' lariat twirling in extreme slow motion within a brief story. Subsequent to this date the occasional very slow motion shot turned up on rare occasions in comedy films such as *Feel My Pulse* (La Cava, 1928), just as less marked slow motion had already been used in comedies before 1920.

For the sake of completeness another camera that has had a long life, though almost entirely in the documentary field, should be mentioned here. This was the English Newman-Sinclair camera which was first put on sale in 1922. It was clockwork driven, with two springs which when fully wound would take through a full 200 foot magazine without rewinding them, and it had a very individual 'clapper gate' registration system. In this system the register pins were fixed as in the Bell & Howell, but the film was lifted off them, moved forward one frame, and then dropped onto them for the next exposure by a quite different mechanism. The entire camera

was inside a simple sheet aluminium box, and the single lens was simply mounted on the front. Through-the-lens viewing was possible by sliding a 45 degree prism in behind the film in the gate from the side. The film was pre-loaded into a 200 foot magazine which included the sprocket drive, and this in its turn was placed inside the camera body in the same way as in the Akeley camera described above. The advantage of the spring drive system was that it left the cameraman *both* hands free while filming, so that he could simultaneously change the focus and pan, or take other combinations of action, which was not the case with the usual hand-cranked cameras.

The Mobile Camera

At the very beginning of the nineteen-twenties the first phase of camera mobility in 1915 and 1916 seemed to be almost forgotten. From time to time one can see a small framing movement used in some films, particularly in America, but in general shot after shot stays quite fixed. In American and German films the only kind of tracking movement to be found, and that only extremely rarely, is the parallel tracking shot, in which the camera accompanies actors walking along at a fixed distance from it. But in 1923 there was a new explosion of camera mobility in France and Germany, and this time the effects were much more far-reaching. In France there were a number of films made in 1923 by the most advanced film-makers which included one or two tracking shots moving with respect to a quasi-static scene, and amongst these I will mention *Au secours* (Abel Gance), *l'Auberge rouge* (Jean Epstein) and *l'Inondation* (Louis Delluc), but at the moment it seems that the really influential line of development comes from the German cinema, and Lupu Pick's *Sylvester*. In this film there were many tracking shots moving through the atmospheric scenes, the *umwelt*, surrounding the main action, and a special dolly was built to carry a set of three cameras to take these shots as it moved through the set which showed a city street. *Sylvester* was intended to be the second part of a trilogy of films that started with *Scherben* (Lupu Pick, 1921), but as it turned out, the third part of the trilogy, *Der letzte Mann* (1924), was not directed by Pick but by Murnau. Nevertheless, this film carried on the use of tracking shots, many of which are parallel tracking shots, but a few of which are done on more or less static scenes. And it was *Der letzte Mann* that really caught the attention of other film-makers, and led to a very widespread interest in using the mobile camera again.

In America this new fashion for camera movement took a year to really get going, but there are a few films such as von Stroheim's *The Merry Widow* made in 1925 which use one or two tracking shots with panning movements in which the camera moves with respect to a quasi-static scene. Although the examples in 1926 become more numerous, those films which do use tracking shots still make do with only a handful, and they are still a very small minority amongst the total production. The same kind of observation could be made about the French and German cinema in 1925 and 1926.

Taking and Projection Speeds

The question of taking and projection speeds in the 'twenties is rather complex, but nevertheless a number of generalizations can safely be made by relying on discussions of the subject which took place at the time, in combination with making trials at different projection speeds of a number of films of the period. As far as making trial projections is concerned, it is not sufficient to project just part of the film, as the taking speed sometimes varies throughout the length of a silent film, and in the second place it is only possible to tell whether the people in the film are moving at just exactly the natural speed with certain kinds of human movement. The best kind of movement for showing whether the speed is natural is steady walking over a fair distance within the shot, and also steady running. Ordinary interior scenes, in which the actors move from one position to another with only a few steps, and make no fast movements of any kind, are not very good for this purpose.

In American films it is evident that on the average the taking speed had already increased beyond 16 frames per second before 1919, in fact to something like 18 frames per second. In a report on the subject in *The Transactions of the Society of Motion Picture Engineers* the situation was described as one in which projectionists had increased projection speed, and as a consequence cameramen had increased their taking speed. From this point onwards the excuse given by projectionists for this increase in projection speed was that the increased speed reduced flicker, which is certainly true, but it has always been considered that the real motive was to get more complete programmes into a day's screening, and hence sell more tickets. This seems a very plausible explanation to me. In any case, in 1923 a survey of the viewing theatres in the studios showed that they were projecting rushes and finished prints at speeds between 18 and 20 frames per second, and this tallies fairly well with the projection speeds at which films from around that year show correct speed of movement for the actors in them. In 1924 it was decided to attempt to standardize projection speed at 80 feet per minute (approximately 21 frames per second), presumably on the basis that this was the speed used in most cinemas, and this again squares well with the visible characteristics of surviving films. Despite the concrete evidence to the contrary, the American Society of Cinematographers claimed in 1925 that its members were still cranking at 16 frames per second! Apparently cameramen reserved all their attention for the scene being filmed, and never looked at the tachometer (speed indicator) with which all the major makes of camera were now fitted. The attempt to standardize projection speed did not succeed, and it continued to increase, so that when a survey was made of first-run cinemas in 1926 with a view to fixing the sound film speed, it was found that the projection speed had become 24 frames per second on the average. However in this year it is clear from the prints of films themselves that the taking speed was a couple of frames per second less than this – about 21 to 22 frames per second in fact.

In Europe there was also an increase in taking speeds through the 'twenties, which was inevitable given that American films were widely shown everywhere, but European taking speeds lagged behind those used for American films of the same date. French films only reached taking speeds of around 21 frames per second in 1929, but German films were closer behind the American speed increase, say about 20 frames per second in 1926. As might be expected, Russian films increased very little in speed during the 'twenties, not getting above 18 frames per second before 1925.

This whole story is further complicated by the fact that not only did individual cameramen's cranking speeds differ with respect to the averages I have been describing, but in some films whole sections were cranked at different speeds, presumably as a result of being shot by different cameramen. A very interesting case in point is *Ella Cinders* (1926), of which the first half is shot at around 18 frames per second, and the second half at around 22 frames per second. Further than this, since this particular film is about film-making, it includes a scene showing a film being shot by two cameramen side by side, as was still the practice, and the two cameramen are visibly cranking at quite different speeds. A European example that can be quoted is *Nosferatu* (1922), in which some scenes are shot at 18 frames per second and some at 20 frames per second. In *Nosferatu* there is also of course the scene of the phantom carriage which is very undercranked for expressive purposes, but this aesthetic use of different camera speeds within a film is yet another matter superimposed on the quite independent general effects I have been describing so far.

The moral of this story is that silent films can only be properly shown with a projector with continuously variable speed, and since they were habitually shown when they were new at a slightly higher speed than their taking speed, it can be considered legitimate to do this today, *but only to a slight extent*. Showing films from before 1920 at sound speed should be out, for instance.

Expressive Variations in Taking Speed

The example of undercranking, and hence of accelerated motion on the screen, which has just been mentioned in *Nosferatu* might be conjectured to have been intended to convey the feeling or idea of supernatural velocity, but it certainly does not achieve this now, and it is questionable if it ever did so. Film technique had already advanced to the point, at any rate in America, where it was realized that the most audience-effective way to lead into such unnaturalistic distortions was through the use of reverse-angles and Point of View shots, but if one has seen Murnau's other films from the beginning of the 'twenties it will be realized that even in German terms his control of the medium was imperfect. By 1924 this was no longer the case, and he himself repudiated his early films, though as far as *Nosferatu* is concerned, the instance under discussion is the only major blemish on it.

The common uses of undercranking continued to be in comedies, and also to produce accelerated motion in races

An objective low-angle shot from Vanina oder die Galgenhochzeit *(Arthur von Gerlach, 1922)*

against time in dramas, where something approaching double speed was used for this purpose in some films right up to the end of the silent period. On the other hand, overcranking to produce a slight slowing of movement was less common, but it was sometimes used in love scenes, and also to make some actions such as mounting a horse more graceful. An example of a rather rare type of related use of overcranking to provide a lyrical feeling is given by some of the shots which show the eponymous heroine of *The Merry Widow* (1925) waltzing in the big ball scene at the centre of the movie.

Angle Shots

In the 'twenties the use of high- and low-angle shots continued to be rare in American films, but in the German and French cinema there was a move from using them as distant POV shots, which was the only way they had been consistently used before, to shooting them without such motivation, and from closer in as well. Stages in this development can be traced from the use of a few objective low-angle shots in *Vanina* (Arthur von Gerlach, 1922) and *Die Strasse* (Karl Grune, 1923), to the shooting of the whole of the Ivan the Terrible episode in *Das Wachsfigurenkabinett* (Paul Leni, 1924) with the camera near floor level and fairly close in to the actors. From this point onwards the technique was a standard option in German practice, but it was not used with great frequency. There was some tendency to associate low-angle shots with the creation of an imposing impression in the figures so treated, despite the fact that they were never presented as the Point of View of a character in the film. A parallel development of extreme angle shots was taking place in the French cinema, though here there was more emphasis on high-angle shots taken from close in than on low-angle shots. Examples of such non-POV high-angle shots taken from close in can be seen in *l'Auberge rouge* (Jean Ep-

stein, 1923) and *la Souriante Madame Beudet* (Germaine Dulac, 1923), and a general shot of a scene taken straight down from directly overhead in L'Herbier's *L'inhumaine* (1924). Despite the admiration of many American film-makers for *Der letzte Mann* (1924) and *Varieté* (1925), both of which continue the use in German films of a small scattering of extreme angle shots, there was considerable and vocal resistance to this usage in America after those films appeared there, and the only examples of low angle shots taken from ground level and fairly close to the actors that I have come across before 1926 are in David Smith's *Captain Blood* (1925). It was not till the very end of the 'twenties that rather more low-angles shot from close in make their appearance in American films. By then the German example had been reinforced by some Russian films which had amplified the use of extreme angles.

The first Russian film in which this happened was Sergei Eisenstein's *Stachka* (1924), and this presumably owed its low-angles to the large number of German films imported into Russia in 1923 and 1924. However Eisenstein and other later Russian film-makers pushed the use of low- and high-angles to much greater extremes, particularly in using them on Close Ups, and their smooth integration into a moderately conventional narrative in *Bronenosets Potyomkin* (1925) had the greatest impact in other countries.

Dutch Tilts

The use of shots taken with the camera body tilted sideways to the horizontal made their first appearance in this period. Such an arrangement of the camera means of course that all true verticals and horizontals within the scene are tilted that same amount with respect to the edges of the frame. This kind of shot eventually came to be called a 'Dutch tilt' after it arrived in American cinema some time later. So far the earliest

An objective low-angle shot in l'Affiche
(Jean Epstein, 1925).

examples I have seen are in French films from 1925 and 1926, *Poil de carotte* and *le Vertige*, made by Julien Duvivier and Marcel L'Herbier respectively, but there may be others that I have missed. In both cases they are probably intended to be expressive of the feelings of characters in the films. In *Poil de carotte* the Dutch tilt is one shot in a montage sequence depicting the atmosphere of a fairground, and in *le Vertige* it is used to suggest the vertigo of the title from which the protagonist suffers at one point.

Lenses

Much wider-angle lenses than had been available before became available fairly early in the nineteen-twenties. These had focal lengths in the region of 25 to 30 mm., but I have so far not been able to discover the precise technical details. A new generation of standard lenses also appeared in the 'twenties, and here the leading manufacturer was undoubtedly the British firm of Taylor, Taylor, and Hobson. They introduced an f2 lens of 50 mm. (2 inches) focal length in 1920. Bausch and Lomb produced a standard lens with a maximum aperture of f2.7 in 1922, and Zeiss produced new Tachars of maximum aperture f1.8 and f2.3 in 1925, though the latter seems to have been the one preferred by film cameramen. The longer lenses of focal lengths 75 and 100 mm. now extensively used for shooting Close Ups continued to be of smaller maximum aperture, about f3.5. As already mentioned, the smallest maximum aperture of a set of lenses being used by a cameraman tends to have a regulating effect on the aperture chosen for all

A tilted low-angle shot with looming shadows cast on the wall and ceiling in Die Strasse *(Karl Grune, 1923).*

Selective soft focus in L'Herbier's Eldorado *(1921), with a special diffusing filter in front of the lens that only softens the image of the central figure.*

the photography in the studio scenes, once the move has been made to shooting at the lowest possible light levels. This move towards shooting at maximum lens aperture was now well underway, *before* the general use of panchromatic film.

Lens Diffusion

It was only in 1923 that lens diffusion started to become really fashionable in the United States, and this was remarked on at the time. Although there had been a few films using lens diffusion in the years following *Broken Blossoms*, amongst which can be mentioned (nay, has to be mentioned) *Sex* (1920), most cameramen had rather surprisingly been content to stay with the soft iris mask already described when they wanted to add 'beauty' to the image. During this initial period in the development of lens diffusion it was usually carried out by putting sheets of coarse gauze in front of the lens, close enough to be out of focus, and sometimes this was supplemented by using a special lens constructed to give poor definition even when it was nominally in focus. Vaseline-smeared glass plates and specially made glass diffusing filters were yet to come.

In 1923 lens diffusion was only applied to Close Ups, and not to more distant shots, and this produced an abrupt transition from the sharp image of the general scene into which the diffused Close Up was cut. At the time this must have been seen as unsatisfactory, for by the next year some cameramen were starting to use intermediate amounts of diffusion (i.e. smaller numbers of sheets of gauze) on the shots immediately on either side of the Close Ups which had been shot with heavy diffusion. By 1925 this modified approach was becoming more common, though far from universal, and an alternative solution, that of using heavy diffusion on *all* the shots, whether near or far, had also appeared, as in *Zander the Great* photographed by George Barnes. This alternative never

became common.

In France, Marcel L'Herbier moved on from his use of simple lens diffusion in *Rose-France* to invent a new variety in *Eldorado* (1921). In this film the heroine is first seen in Long Shot sitting in the middle of a row of performers in the cabaret of the title, and though everyone else in the shot is in sharp focus, her face is blurred by a spot of localized diffusion covering it alone. In the next shot from another angle that includes her, the spot of diffusion remains over her face, but as she starts to perform it disappears, or rather she moves from behind it, and it only returns when she has finished performing. From subsequent developments in the narrative it would seem that this device was meant to indicate her mental abstraction from her surroundings, but like other such devices used by advanced French film-makers of the 'twenties, its appearances in this film are far from consistent, so we cannot be certain of this. This use of lens diffusion in a selected area of the frame was used in some of Jean Epstein's films up to *l'Affiche* (1925), but after that it seems to have been dropped in favour of the conventional use of lens diffusion over the whole frame area. Despite these examples from the 'avant-garde', the use of lens diffusion was in general taken up more slowly in Europe after 1924 than it was in America.

Another rare variation in the use of 'soft focus' occurs in René Clair's *le Mystère du Moulin Rouge* (1924), in which it was used exclusively to denote night-time in scenes actually shot under full daylight. This curious usage crops up elsewhere on rare occasions, and so accounts for the heavy diffusion applied in the 'night' scenes of Carl Dreyer's *Vampyr* (1932).

Lens diffusion works best when the lens is set at maximum aperture, which by 1925 was at least f3.5, and the increasing use of lens diffusion in American films no doubt helped to encourage the further reduction in the depth of field which is quite visible in many films made in 1925 and 1926.

A scene staged in depth in Scaramouche *(Rex Ingram, 1923), and lit by John Seitz in the modified 'core' style he used in this film. There is no true deep focus in this scene as the foreground actors are about 20 feet from the camera, and the focus softens beyond the furthest small doorway in the background. all this is consistent with the use of large aperture photography in the region of f2.8 – f4 and the use of a 40 mm. lens.*

Depth of Field

As in other dimensions of the medium, there was a considerable range of variation in the handling of depth of field in American films made in the earlier part of the 'twenties. Because previous commentators have only considered a handful of films from this period, not going much beyond the famous comics, von Stroheim, and Griffith, they have concluded that there was no reduction in the depth of field from that usual before 1914: i.e. a depth of field corresponding to a lens aperture of f5.6 on interiors. As I have already noted, this was indeed true for some films in 1920, but in many others the trend towards filming at increased aperture which had just begun before that date continued to gain ground. *Scaramouche*, which has already been discussed, is a case in

point. The interiors in this film are shot at apertures in the region of f2.8 to f4, and even a few of the exteriors are shot in this way too. The staging in depth that is used in some scenes in this film does not conflict with this, as the foreground figures and objects are not placed closer than 20 feet from the lens, with the focus extending from them to about 60 feet back, and this is quite possible with a 40 mm. lens set at f2.8.

The increasing use of lens diffusion may have encouraged the trend towards larger aperture filming in another way, as it is simpler to fix the lighting level for all the shots at the level used for the Close Ups shot at maximum aperture with gauzing, rather than reduce the lighting level specially for them alone. Another factor in this development was the use of long focal length lenses – anything up to 6 inches – for

An exterior shot in Love *(Edmund Goulding, 1928), in which the background is softened by a large sheet of fine net behind the actress.*

Another angle showing the other participant in the same scene in Love, *in which there is no screen behind him, and the true depth of field of the lens in this situation is revealed.*

shooting Close Ups, which threw the background well out of focus, even when no diffusion was used. This introduced another source of visual discrepancy between the diffused Close Ups and the distant shots of the scene, unless the aperture was increased on them to throw their backgrounds a bit out of focus as well. One rather bizarre response to this last part of the problem was to leave the aperture and depth of field alone on the Long Shots, but to soften the sharpness of the background by placing a giant gauze screen *behind* the actors, and right across the full field of the picture. Examples of this are known from 1922 to 1927, but they do not seem to be very common.

A very minor trend in filming Close Ups in interior scenes was to put a completely black background in behind the actor just for these shots. The most glaring examples of this are in D.W. Griffith's films such as *America* (1924), where it accentuates even more the discontinuous features of his film construction, but occasional examples can be found in the work of other film-makers in the 'twenties. In the previous period, Griffith had also originated the occasional use of 'choker' Close Ups, which show only the front of the face, leaving the neck at least partly out of shot, and these came to be used by other American film-makers on rare occasions in the 'twenties. By the late 'twenties it was possible for an American and other film-makers to go even closer at a peak moment, into a shot showing only the eyes, as in *The Blood Ship* (1927).

Erich von Stroheim's obsessive pursuit of realism in his films led him against the tide in photographic matters, and accidentally produced greater depth of field in many of the images in his films. Stroheim wished to have his cameramen shoot scenes inside rooms, with at the same time a view of the action in the streets outside visible through doors and windows. This requires that the light levels inside the room sets be almost as high as that of the direct sunlight outside, and this in its turn meant that an aperture of about f8 or f11 had to be used for correct exposure. With the usual 40mm. or 50 mm. lens as used on *Foolish Wives* (1922), this does not give 'deep focus' in the modern sense, which means sharp focus all the way from Close Up to Long Shot, and in any case von Stroheim did not exploit all the depth of field he did have available in this film. But in the photography of *Greed* (1925), where similar considerations applied, many shots were taken with a truly wide-angle lens of about 30 mm. focal length inside small rooms, and this *did* give the depth of field associated with true 'deep focus'. But here again the stagings were not particularly arranged to take advantage of this, and only occasionally do the actors accidentally pass through positions that show this great depth of field. Von Stroheim's later films were lit more conventionally, as were those he made before 1920.

There was another peculiarity in the lighting of the two von Stroheim films I have just mentioned, and this was that the interiors were shot in room sets (or actual rooms) which had real ceilings in place, though these ceilings were not visible within the shots. This meant that backlighting from above

and behind could not be used, and the sets had to be lit with arc floodlights on floor stands. This gives many of the scenes a quite distinctive look, particularly when the reflections of the lights can be seen in the varnished wood of doors and furniture, which was something that was avoided in ordinary films.

In America, von Stroheim was alone in this accidental achievement of 'deep focus', but in Germany a similar situation arose in *Varieté* (1925), in the filming of location scenes in the theatre manager's office. There was a slightly greater tendency to use wide-angle lenses on studio sets in Germany than in the United States, and this is quite visible as early as 1923 in *Die Strasse* and *Das Wachsfigurenkabinett*. In these cases there was no increased light level to match exteriors as in the Stroheim films and *Varieté*, as they were shot entirely in the studio, and so were later UFA films such as *Am Rande der Welt* (Karl Grune, 1927) which also has scenes shot with wide-angle lenses. The case of *Der Schatz* (G.W. Pabst, 1923) is yet again different. In this film it is obvious that a conscious effort was made to obtain and use greater depth of field, and it is also clear that all the set-ups had been pre-designed before the film was shot; i.e. the camera positions were not freely chosen by the director during shooting. A number of the sets in *Der Schatz* have heavy low ceilings visible in shot, and this was also the case for some UFA films of the same kind.

Vignetting

The use of soft-edged vignette masks, particularly on closer shots, continued into the early 'twenties, but this practice was still not completely general. The form of the mask was still often that of a circular iris diaphragm in front of the lens, well out of focus so that its edge was completely blurred and indistinct. On Close Ups it continued to serve in some films as an alternative to the use of gauze diffusion over the whole frame, but now those cameramen using it in this way led into its use by putting a wider circular vignette, which just entered the corners of the frame, on the adjoining shots. The use of the hard-edged circular vignette had pretty well entirely vanished in America, where a new kind of soft mask now made its appearance, and quickly came to be quite widely used. This was a sort of black semi-transparent edging that projected just a little way into the frame to which it made a faint small irregular border of rectangular shape. This kind of mask is so unobtrusive that one hardly notices its presence, and it was produced by layers of coarse black gauze with rectangular holes cut in their centres positioned in front of the lens in a matte box. This matte box was now a standard accessory fixed in front of the camera lens, and it usually incorporated the vignetting iris diaphragm into itself at the lens end.

In Germany Lubitsch continued and elaborated his experiments with unusually-shaped hard-edged decorative masks in *Sumurun* (1920) and *Die Bergkatze* (1921). The latter film is packed with masks in all sorts of complex and symmetrical shapes such as a double ogive, and these shapes have been carefully chosen to harmonize with the decorative stylizations

One of the many differently shaped vignette masks in Die Bergkatze *(Ernst Lubitsch, 1921).*

of the sets. However, after this film Lubitsch completely abandoned this approach, and nothing like it has been seen since.

A quite different kind of complex but irregular masking was developed a few years later in Murnau's films, but this involved the use of black semi-transparent gauze masks rather than the solidly opaque masks Lubitsch used. These semi-transparent irregularly shaped masks first appear in *Der letzte Mann* (1924), and for a good deal of the film they do not reach much further into the frame than the American edging masks which may have been their model. However on some of the shots they do cover a fair amount of the frame area, and only leave an irregular central opening in which the actors do their stuff. These masks are not very noticeable, particularly on poor prints of this film, because they integrate with the other dark areas inside the frame, and in particular with the smudgy dark patches painted onto the walls of the sets, which were a characteristic feature of the design of many German films in the 'twenties. In *Der letzte Mann* the central area of the frame in the closer shots is usually illuminated with a spotlight which casts a soft-edged patch of light, and this again blends with the very soft edge of the mask. However in the moving camera shots in *Der letzte Mann* the masks can be clearly seen, as the moving backgrounds show through them. There are still quite a number of shots in this film which do not have the masks I have described, but in *Tartüff* (1926) nearly every shot has them. It may be because these masks show up on moving camera shots, and also when actors walk behind them when they walk out of shot, that Murnau almost entirely abandoned

Irregularly shaped soft-edged and semi-transparent mask covering most of the frame in Murnau's Faust *(1926).*

White bordered vignette masking used in
L'Herbier's Eldorado *(1921).*

camera movement in *Tartüff,* and also arranged his scene dissection so that the actors did not walk out of the edge of the frame at all. The result is that the actors are literally trapped inside the clear central area of the frame, and personally I find the effect extremely oppressive.

For whatever reason, Murnau relaxed this total use of the broad-edged soft black mask in his next film, *Faust* (1926). The masks in this film, which are not used on every shot, though of the same soft-edged black semi-transparent kind, are much more varied in shape, and many of them have at least one side open. On the other hand, there are a few of the masks in *Faust* that encroach much further into the frame area than ever before, leaving only a small part of the frame clear for the action. The example illustrated from the duel scene would be a high-key shot lit brightly all over by direct sunlight but for the mask, which effectively turns it into a low-key shot, and helps give the impression that the whole scene was taking place at night. After this final well-balanced use of this technique Murnau dropped it, and it has never been seen again .

In France, the use of simpler regular decorative shapes in mattes or masks with fairly hard edges after the earlier American manner was continued into the early 'twenties by L'Herbier in *l'Homme du large* (1920) and *Eldorado* (1921). In the former film there does not seem to have been much reason for the particular shapes chosen, but in *Eldorado* a shape such as that illustrated – an oblong white mask – could be related to an implied comparison between the decadent character shown within it, and the similarly framed Aubrey Beardsley drawing he has on his wall. This use of decoratively-shaped masks disappeared in France too in later years.

Special Forms of Shot Transitions

In the early 'twenties the use of the dissolve continued to be rather limited. The dissolve continued to be the principal way of getting into and out of flashbacks, but flashback construction became much less popular. The dissolve also continued to be used for smoothing out a suspected mismatch in the transition to (and from) a closer shot of an actor, but the necessity for this was now rare in American films, and less frequent too in European films. The dissolve now also began to be used to string together the first montage sequences with tightly packed sequences of shots, and in some of these it does happen to correspond to a time lapse between the shots joined by it, as in the brief excerpts from a series of variety acts in *Varieté* (1925). In other montage sequences made earlier and later, the dissolves joining the shots do not always correspond to time lapses, but I would still suggest that the later use of the dissolve as denoting a time-lapse arose by generalization from those montage sequences in which it does, since it is only at the very end of the 'twenties that the dissolve between ordinary scenes begins to denote a time lapse with some certainty.

In these years a time lapse between ordinary scenes was still mostly indicated with a title card or a fade-out and fade-in, but the iris-out and iris-in still appear sometimes, and even occasionally an overlapping iris-out and iris-in. As might be expected, even more elaborate combinations appeared in some of the films of the French avant-garde, utilising various forms of moving masks in front of the lens. The opening-slit iris was overlapped with fades and ordinary irises to make some of the transitions in L'Herbier's *l'Homme du large* (1920), and devices of equal visual complexity were also used in his *Eldorado* (1921). However most of the shot transitions in these films were more conventional, as was the case for the work of other film-makers using such effects. There seems to be no specific reason for which particular form of shot transition was used at which particular point in these French avant-garde films.

Wipes

Eldorado also includes a number of true wipes: i.e. transitions in which a straight line moves across the frame removing one shot as it goes, and leaving another shot revealed behind its line of travel. In *Eldorado* the control of the moving boundary between the two shots was very imperfect, and the effect was very roughly done when compared with the wipes from later times with which we are familiar. The same imperfections can be seen in the wipes in Eisenstein's *Stachka* (1924), in which the disappearing and appearing shots are separated by a broad black bar which changes in width as the wipe progresses. These faults arose from the difficulty in making the transition directly in the camera, as had to be done before the introduction of special duplicating films a couple of years later. To make a wipe in the camera a mask has to be slid across in front of the lens from one side to the other at the end of the first shot, and then the film has to be wound back past the beginning of the wipe before starting the second shot. At the start of the second shot the mask has to be slid sideways from the other side *at exactly the same speed, and starting from exactly the same frame* to open up the second shot. Now although this procedure resembles that for making a dissolve in the camera, as was always done at that time too, it happens that small errors in the speeds and starting points of the fades that make up a dissolve are not visible at all in the finished effect, in the way that they very definitely are in wipes. It *was* possible to make a perfect wipe at this date by taking enough time and trouble, and also being prepared to go back and try again if it did not come out properly the first time, as a perfect wipe in Victor Sjöström's *He Who Gets Slapped* (1924) shows, but most Hollywood film-makers apparently did not think it was worthwhile. Another original way of making an expanding circle wipe, in which the second scene appears inside a circle which enlarges to fill the frame, appears in *Das Haus am Meer* (1923). This was achieved by punching out a series of circles of increasing size in successive frames with punches of

increasing diameter at the end of one scene on the negative, and repeating the operation at the beginning of the next scene, but in this case keeping the circular punch-outs, and cutting off the remnants of the frames. These punch-outs were then cemented into the holes of the same size in the frames at the end of first scene, and then sticking the next shot from the first full frame onwards after the circle has reached full frame diameter. It works in a rough kind of way.

Anamorphosis

In the early 'twenties distorted images (i.e. anamorphic in the original and literal sense of having the 'wrong shape') had quite a run of popularity in European films with artistic pretensions, where they were used to suggest subjective states in a character in the film concerned. Having said that, it must be admitted that there is a certain ambiguity of intention in one of the earliest examples in *Von Morgens bis Mitternacht* (1920). In this film the six-day bicycle race that the protagonist watches at one point in his adventures is shot with a lens that stretches the image out sideways. It is not clear whether this is intended as a subjective effect representing the way the protagonist sees the race, or whether it represents the feelings of the cyclists taking part, or whether it is simply an attempt to match the visual stylization of the rest of the film, in which all the decor and costumes are painted with distorted black and white patterns in an extension of the *Caligari* manner. I incline to the last view myself, but there is no way of deciding the question on the internal evidence in the film itself. In an American instance from 1925 in *The Lady*, directed by Frank Borzage, the use is comic, and is certainly intended to suggest subjective drugged vision.

When anamorphosis became popular with the French avant-garde in the next year or two, there was the usual tendency for it to be inconsistently applied as an expressive

Anamorphic effect in the court scene of Crainquebille *(Jacques Feyder, 1922)*

effect when it was used more than once in a film, as is the case in *la Souriante Madame Beudet* (Germaine Dulac, 1922). In this film the neurotic depression and anxieties of the woman of the title are established by conventional means, and then this impression of her state is reinforced by a horizontal stretching of the image in a number of shots, some of which are from her POV, and others objective Close Ups of her. To accentuate the effect in some of these shots the squeeze ratio of the anamorphosis is varied slightly during the course of the shot, so that the image expands and contracts a little in one direction. Germaine Dulac used this effect again in *la Coquille et le Clergyman* in 1928. Even a director like Jacques Feyder who was closer to the mainstream tried out anamorphosis in 1923 in *Crainquebille*, in this case using a diagonal stretching of the image strictly in POV shots to indicate the old man's boredom and confusion when in the dock in court. After this date it again becomes extremely rare in conventional films.

In all the cases I have described, it seems probable that the anamorphic effect was created by putting a simple cylindrical lens in front of an ordinary camera lens, with the cylindrical axis of this supplementary lens in the appropriate direction for the distortion required. As well as producing the required distortion, this procedure also severely degraded the definition of the image. However, it is also easy to get a simple anamorphic effect with a cylindrical mirror reflecting the scene back into the lens, and this alternative may have been used in these films.

German Expressionist Cinema

From an art historical point of view, which is the only way to approach the matter with a useful and productive degree of accuracy, Expressionism was an artistic movement that began in Germany before the First World War, reached its peak around the end of that war, went into sharp decline in 1922, and had fairly well vanished by 1924. It was in fact one of the most sharply defined artistic movements that there has ever been, and its products in the various arts all have quite definite characteristics. Expressionist paintings, which were always figurative, used distorted, irregular, and jagged shapes in unnatural, vivid colours to depict their subjects. Expressionist literature used brief, telegraphic fragments of sentences, and Expressionist drama added to that literary style simple, elementary, and violent plots with anonymous protagonists, and also a special form of acting. As is usually the way in general artistic developments, Expressionist painting appeared first, several years before the First World War, followed by Expressionist literature just before the war started, and then finally Expressionist plays were written during the war, and staged from 1917 onwards. In 1919 these Expressionist plays were just starting to be staged in settings derived from the style of Expressionist painting before *Das Cabinet des Dr. Caligari* was made, and Expressionist cinema entered the scene. What was really singular about this event was that never before or since has an advanced artistic movement entered the commercial cinema so quickly. Another peculiarity of *Caligari* that has

confused the issue is that it contains a supernormal element in its story, which has led some people to describe every German film that contains supernatural elements as Expressionist. In fact Expressionist art was completely free of supernatural elements, whereas there had long been a tradition of the fantastic in German art and also in the German cinema. Most of the German films involving the supernatural and the fantastic were the work of Paul Wegener and Henrik Galeen, working together or separately from *Der Student von Prag* (1913) and *Der Golem* (1914) onwards. Hans Janowitz's story for *Caligari* was one of the limited number of outside contributions to this cinema tradition, and the *Caligari* story owes absolutely nothing to Expressionist drama and literature, though it does contain a component derived from the international genre of 'master criminal' movies.

The films which had strong connections with Expressionist art in one way or another were *Das Cabinet des Dr. Caligari* (Robert Wiene, 1920), *Genuine* (R. Wiene, 1920), *Von Morgens bis Mitternacht* (Karl-Heinz Martin, 1920), *Torgus* (Hans Kobe, 1921), *Raskolnikov* (R. Wiene, 1923), and *Das Wachsfigurenkabinett* (Paul Leni, 1924). Even within this small group of genuinely Expressionist films one can see a weakening of the style by 1923, so that in *Raskolnikov* the costumes, furnishings, and even a few of the sets are realistic, and in *Das Wachsfigurenkabinett* only the 'Jack the Ripper' episode is substantially Expressionist. If I include these, perhaps I should also include *Metropolis* (1926), as that has a plot heavily indebted to the first half of Georg Kaiser's *Gas* trilogy of Expressionist plays, and some Expressionist acting as well, not to mention mass stagings derived from the work of the theatrical producer Georg Jessner. All the first six films I have named have their visual design strongly based on Expressionist art, they all contain Expressionist acting, and *Von Morgens bis Mitternacht* is a filming of another genuine Expressionist play by Georg Kaiser. But apart from that, none of these films has any of the other characteristics of Expressionist drama and literature. One might ask if there were films that were heavily indebted to Expressionist drama, without having any Expressionist visual elements, and the answer must be that there were indeed a few films which had a simple plot with un-named principal characters, and a small number more which had somewhat Expressionist acting from one of the principals, but I don't see that that makes them Expressionist any more than one raisin turns a suet dumpling into a Christmas pudding.

Expressionist Acting

There was an explicit theory of Expressionist acting, according to which broad and slow gestures gave the audience time to think about the emotions being felt by the characters in the play, and also amplified those emotions as they were communicated. This conception was probably erroneous at the time, and is certainly so today. Owing to the elementary nature of Expressionist plots, the emotions that the characters are likely to be feeling are only too simple and obvious, and can even be guessed in advance of the moment. At first glance

Expressionist acting in films seems no more than bad old-style melodramatic acting done very slowly, but there were a small group of top actors such as Conrad Veidt and Werner Krauss and a few others, all of whom had appeared in Expressionist plays at the end of the war, who could come up with an original twist in their characterizations. Amongst the major themes on which variations were played were the use of hands clawed this way and that, and shoulders pushed in various directions. Incidentally, since there was still a tendency at the beginning of the 'twenties for most European film acting to be rather broad and slow, it can be a little difficult to tell where Expressionist acting leaves off, and ordinary film acting begins. However by 1926 the last vestiges of Expressionist acting were diluted enough to be ignored in a general survey.

Expressivist Features

The small group of genuinely Expressionist films had little influence on later films, for it was mostly the other famous German films of the early 'twenties which used the looming shadows and extreme camera angles which are usually thought of as 'Expressionist'. For instance, *Die Strasse* (1923) and *Schatten*, which respectively feature extreme angles and looming shadows, both have perfectly conventional sets, and the acting in the first of these films is quite normal for the place and time it was made. As I have already made clear, extreme angles had already appeared in Danish and American films before 1920, and they continued to appear in films which had no connections with the genuinely Expressionist films. For this reason I prefer to use the term 'expressivist' for the non-naturalistic distortions which existed in film before and after German Expressionism. This usage also leads to greater precision in analysis, so it is naturally to be favoured for art historical purposes rather than the catch-all vagueness of 'expressionism', which encourages laziness, ignorance, and journalistic imprecision in dealing with the cinema of the nineteen-twenties and later. In previous chapters I have described many kinds of expressive effects such as low-key lighting, superimpositions, montage sequences, etc. occurring in American, French, and Danish and Russian films from before 1920, and these continued to occur in films from other countries into the early 'twenties before any influence from *Caligari*, or indeed from other Expressionist art could have occurred. An obvious American example now known to many people is Charles Giblyn's *The Dark Mirror* of 1920, which has a delirious narrative of confused identities played out mostly at night in dark rooms and streets.

Optical Printing

In the 'twenties there was a revival of the use of optical printing, and this may have been connected in some way with the introduction of reduction printing for the making of copies of existing 35 mm. films in the new amateur sub-standard gauges of 16 mm. and 9.5mm., when these were introduced in 1923. A number of optical printers had to be made specially for this purpose, and it was suggested at the time that they could be used for enlarging or reducing parts of the image from one 35 mm. film to another 35 mm. film. In any case, specialized optical printing (or projection printing, as it was still called) services were provided by independent operators from about 1924. The leading figures in this field at the time were Irving Knechtal and Max Fleischer, and they had of course built their own optical printers, presumably in the way it continued to be done, by adapting Bell & Howell cameras to serve as both projector and special camera, with a lens system in between, and the whole lot mounted on a lathe bed with screw controls for traversing the main component units in any direction separately.

Not much use seems to have been made of these facilities until the late 'twenties, which is not surprising, since optical printing inevitably involves the making of an intermediate positive film from the original negative or negatives, and then a new combined negative with the final optical effect on it. This produced, as mentioned before, a noticeable deterioration in image quality, since ordinary positive and negative film had to be used for these stages. A good example of the result of this deterioration in image quality resulting from the use of ordinary negative as an intermediate duplicating stock can be seen in a trick shot in *Der müde Tod* (Fritz Lang, 1921), though this was probably not done on an optical printer. In the scene in which the magician produces a miniature army for the Chinese Emperor, the high-angle shot showing the tiny figures of the army in the foreground with the Imperial court in the background was made by combining two separate negatives of the two groups, with the area the miniature army occupies blanked out on one negative by a fixed matte or mask, and vice versa on the other. The 'positive' stock that these two negatives were printed onto to make a combined positive was actually ordinary camera negative, which was used yet again to make a new negative from which the final distribution prints were made. As a result this particular shot can be seen to be much grainier and also less contrasty than the surrounding shots if a good 35 mm. print of this film is inspected, and this would have been even more obvious on the original prints shown at the time.

The earliest optical enlargement of part of the frame, or 'blow-up', that I have seen occurs in *Womanhandled* (Gregory La Cava, 1925), where a letter important to the plot, which is not very visible in the Long Shot in which the scene is conducted, is revealed more clearly by enlarging part of the frames containing it to full frame size, and then cutting this new footage back into the existing shot. Because of the enlargement of the original negative, as well as the effects of the use of unsatisfactory duplicating stocks already mentioned, the image quality of this insert is very poor indeed. Even after the introduction of special intermediate print stocks with improved qualities in 1926, such a use of optical printing remained very rare, since for ordinary studio scenes it was almost always quicker and cheaper to restage the scene and shoot a Close Up insert of the unclear detail, possibly with a stand-in for the actor involved. As far as using optical printing

A combination shot made with fixed mattes in Der Müde Tod *(Fritz Lang, 1921). Unusually for this period, the combination has been made by double printing using camera negative to make the intermediate positive and then the combined internegative, rather than by using double exposure in the camera.*

for reversing action and producing 'freeze frames' is concerned, the important film seems to have been *Hollywood* (James Cruze, 1923), but a much better-known example where the effects of these techniques are central to the plot is René Clair's *Paris qui dort* (1924). These devices, though continuing to appear intermittently in lighter films, were never used in serious dramas till after World War II, when Frank Capra took up the idea for fantasy purposes in *It's a Wonderful Life* (1946), in a way rather similar to *Paris qui dort*.

Travelling Mattes

The first true travelling matte process also dates from the beginning of the nineteen-twenties. I have already described methods for combining into one shot scenes of action which take place within separate areas of the frame, but there had been no way of combining a moving actor with a shot of a moving background scene immediately behind him that had been taken separately. In principle the Williams process was supposed to change this situation. As described by its originator much later, the process consisted of shooting the foreground action on a stage in front of a white backing which was brightly illuminated, and then from the negative of this scene a positive print was made of such high contrast that the moving figure became a black silhouette surrounded by clear film. This positive 'travelling matte' was then put in a printer sandwiched between the negative of the background scene which had been separately shot, and the print stock on which the final combined image was to appear, and the printing exposure was made. On the final positive, which was not developed at this stage, there was no exposure recorded in the silhouette area, but around that there was the latent image of the background scene, which could contain movement of its own. Then a second pass was made through the printer with the original negative of the foreground moving figure, and

provided the first frames of each film had been correctly aligned, the image printed of the moving figure would exactly fill the empty spaces in the frame when the combined positive was developed.

However, there are a number of good reasons for believing that this was not how the Williams process was carried out in the majority of cases. It has been said by people actually working in the 'twenties that what was actually done by the operators of the Williams process was to rotoscope (project frame by frame) the negative of the foreground action onto a series of large sheets of paper on which counter-silhouettes were painted by hand around the changing outlines of the moving figures on every frame, and then to refilm these hand-painted mattes frame by frame onto positive film stock which was given high contrast development. From this point on the printing process continued as first described. Clearly the process was very slow and expensive in this form, and so it was rarely used, and then only on larger budget films. The earliest example of the Williams process that I have been able to find is in Cecil B. DeMille's *Manslaughter* (1922), where it was used to put a moving background behind a close shot of the heroine driving her car. In this case the quality of the combination is fairly good, although there is a thin black line just visible round the foreground action. (A 'minus' in the jargon of the trade.) In another early example that I have been able to examine closely in a good 35 mm. print, the shot of clowns surrounding a giant spinning globe in *He Who Gets Slapped* (1924), the irregularities in the hand-painted mattes are clearly visible, though they cannot be made out in the usual poor 16 mm. prints.

It seems that after this there were some attempts to work the Williams process in the original form described, for instance in *The Fire Brigade* (1925) and *The Torrent* (1926), but the result was that the photographically produced mattes were

A travelling matte shot in Cecil B. DeMillle's Manslaughter *(1922). A dark matte line (or 'minus') can just be made out behind the white veil blowing out from the woman's hat.*

not dense enough to hold back the part of the background image where the figures were to be placed, and as a result the background 'prints through' the figures in these films. A further drawback to the Williams process in both forms before the introduction of intermediate duplicating stocks was that unless the double printing process was carried out separately for every print made of the film, there was marked deterioration of the image quality, of the kind I have previously mentioned in connection with *Der müde Tod.*

Film Splicers

Despite the introduction of the Bell & Howell semi-automatic splicer for joining both positive and negative film (particularly the former), there was no standardization of the width of splices used, though much narrower splices, down to 1/32nd. of an inch, were now usual. The Bell & Howell splicer, which is still being used for the same purpose today, was a free-standing machine on a pedestal, with the film cutting and clamping actions operated by foot pressure on pedals, though the scraping of the film and the spreading of the cement still had to be done by hand. Nevertheless it was a considerable improvement over the simpler type of splicing clamp, which continued to be used for editing the work copy (cutting copy) of the film.

Editing Equipment

In 1924 an improved version of the first editing viewers of several years before was produced under the name of the Moviola. This was essentially the same as the earlier machines, but the mechanism was now driven by a small variable-speed electric motor controlled by a foot pedal, and the illumination was now provided by a built-in light bulb. The previous machine had no shutter, but the Moviola was provided with a shutter behind the film gate which swung into place and

started revolving when the speed of film transport exceeded several frames per second. The machine was now usually mounted on the top of its own small table rather than standing free on the editing bench or elsewhere. It was in fact just the same as the basic picture head on the Hollywood Moviola of today. (Since the original Moviola has given the generic name to all other subsequent types of film viewing machines, it and its sound version will henceforward be referred to as the Hollywood Moviola, as is done in the industry when the distinction has to be made.) It soon became the practice to have a Moviola handy on the set in Hollywood when difficult points had to be decided about matching a shot which was about to be taken to existing shots.

Matters of Continuity

Although most of the standard methods of securing smooth continuity of action through the cuts between shots, and also for giving a correct sense of direction in the movements and placements of actors were well understood in the United States at the beginning of the 'twenties, this was not generally the case in Europe. In particular, when it came to the matter of eye-line matching in reverse-angle cutting between shots, the chances were that the average European director would get this 'wrong' nearly half of the time, since he was not aware of the existence of any convention in the matter. This can be illustrated in Fritz Lang's *Der müde Tod* (1921), for instance, in the introductory scenes in the inn. Other examples can easily be found up to 1926 and beyond, in French and Russian films as well as German films, e.g. *la Glace à trois faces* (Jean Epstein, 1926) and *Oblomok Imperii* (F. Ermler, 1929). Naturally this minor failing in craftsmanship (and the fact that nearly all those concerned stopped doing it later on when they found out about it shows that it was a matter of craftsmanship) was most common in the works of the avant-garde or 'art cinema'. But whatever the films concerned, if their proper context is taken into consideration there is no way that any profound meaning can be read into failures of eye-line matching, as some have tried to do in recent years. Even in American films there are plenty of lapses in the correctness of eye-line matching in the 'twenties, and that includes the films of directors like Frank Borzage who were some of the first to use reverse-angle cutting extensively. (For example *The Circle* (1925) and *Seventh Heaven* (1927)). My feeling is that although the rule against crossing the eye-line may perhaps have been formulated by the beginning of the decade, there was no general attempt to observe and enforce before the last years of the 'twenties.

Scene Dissection

The basic Griffith style of scene dissection, with cuts in to a closer shot made from the frontal direction, without any substantial angle change, continued to be practised by many film-makers into the early nineteen-twenties, both in America, and particularly in Europe. In the United States people who made dramas tended to be more subtle than Griffith about the way they did this, which was by arranging the actors in a group in the wide shot in such a way that their faces were angled at about 45 to the lens axis. Thus, when there followed a series of cuts to close shots of individuals taken straight from the established 'front', there was created the *illusion* of them facing each other in a reverse-angle arrangement.

Another feature of Griffith's style in the use of Close Ups was also copied by other film-makers in the 'twenties, particularly in Europe. This was his practice of having the actors look straight into the lens in such shots. Other American film-makers only did this very rarely, and then at a few peak moments in the drama, but it was much more common in films from continental Europe.

Reverse-Angle Cutting

In America in the early 'twenties more and more directors came to use a substantial proportion of reverse-angle cuts when they were breaking scenes down into shots. Even at the beginning of the 'twenties a point had been reached where 20 to 25 percent of the shot transitions in many American films were from a shot to its reverse-angle. This was particularly true for those who began directing in the late 'teens when the usage was already starting to be consolidated. But on the other hand many older directors such as Cecil B. DeMille were not particularly inclined to use reverse-angle shots. In between these two extremes there were directors who restricted their use of reverse-angle cutting to just a few main climaxes in their films. (Slapstick comedy is excluded from this consideration, as even in its more elevated reaches reverse-angle cutting continued to be relatively rare right through to the end of the silent period.) In Germany most directors used reverse-angle cutting relatively little, or in some cases not at all, and only Ernst Lubitsch had truly mastered American methods of scene

dissection. Even famous names such as Murnau were working in a retarded style at the beginning of the 'twenties; shooting from far back with slow cutting and without reverse-angles. The position was somewhat the same in France, and because of these features – sometimes referred to disparagingly as the 'Old Country style' – European films, with the exception of those of Ernst Lubitsch, were unsaleable in the United States until 1925.

The Eye-Line Match

As the extensive use of reverse-angle cutting consolidated in the United States, film-makers must have gradually become aware of a new problem of directional continuity. It was not consciously formulated before 1919, but it must have been increasingly considered within the next several years in the United States. The point is this. When a great many shots within a scene come to be made from many different angles and closenesses to the actors, should the camera be put anywhere, or should some positions be preferred?

A little thought shows that a better sense of the relative positions of the actors and the set under these conditions is preserved if the camera is kept roughly in a position to the 'front' side of the actors, even though its *direction* varies through nearly 180 degrees for different shots. (Please note that this is quite different to the Griffith practice in which the camera was kept in the 'front' and only *one* lens direction was used.) One can nowadays visualise this approach (in a very rough way) as being like covering the scene in one continuous shot while quickly panning the camera from actor to actor and also making fast zooms in and out as appropriate, and then removing the zoom and pan parts of the footage in the editing, to leave the scene broken down into the remaining fixed shots cut together. The whole can then be seen as rather like what a spectator before the actual scene would see, standing to one side of it, and casting his glance from this point to that point within it. For various reasons which it is not appropriate to go into here, rather more license in camera (or spectator) position is desirable, and of course this license was already being used before 1919. But to prevent what the film-makers themselves experienced as disorientation, a simple rule came to be devised that covers not only this problem, but also a related one having to do with the positions of objects on the screen in successive shots. This rule was that the camera should be kept on the same side of the line joining two actors who are interacting when its position is changed between successive shots of them. This notional line later came to be called the 'eye-line', or sometimes just 'the line', and the rule involved is now referred to as an 'eye-line match', or 'not crossing the eye-line'. When more than two people are involved in a scene, the line keeps changing according to which of them are interacting at any point in the scene, and this means that it is possible, without breaking the rule, to make a complete circuit of camera positions around a group over a sufficiently large number of cuts, though this is hardly ever done.

Much has been made of this rule recently by would-be film

theorists, but in fact it seems that infractions of it are of no great importance to audiences, since they are certainly not noticed by even habitual, but non-professional, film viewers, and it can even be difficult for an expert to be certain whether the rule has been rigidly observed in a film on the basis of a single screening. For instance, although I think there are no eye-line crossings amongst the substantial number of reverse-angle cuts in *Jubilo*, a film from 1919, I would not stake my life on it without seeing the film again, preferably on an editing machine. As final empirical evidence on people's failure to notice eye-line mis-matches, I note that many trials with groups of students in a school for film-makers have shown that most of them, even when alerted, do not notice eye-line crossings in Hollywood sound films.

My main reason for doubting that the eye-line rule had been formulated in the 1914-19 period is that nearly all the films made in these years that include an appreciable number of reverse-angle cuts have at least some of them 'crossing the eyeline'. It is not surprising that a certain number of reverse-angle cuts should be correct even before the rule was consciously expressed, since the usual physical arrangements of set and actors in the shooting of interior scenes tends to make unintended observance of the rule probable, but not certain. On the other hand, those many directors who still only used reverse- angle cutting in one or two climaxes of their films certainly had not realized the principle, for many of their eye-line matches are 'wrong'. There are various other subsidiary facts supporting the idea that the rule about not crossing the eye-line was not generally taught in Hollywood till the late

'twenties, but I will just mention one of them. This is that Maurice Elvey, one of the important British directors of the previous period, came to Hollywood and made five films there in 1924 and 1925. Before he came, his films were nearly totally innocent of reverse angles, but after he resumed directing in England in 1926, his films included a fair proportion of them. But the eyelines for these cuts were very frequently wrong. They had taught him about reverse angles in Hollywood, but that teaching did not include not crossing the eyeline.

Flashbacks and Cross-cutting

As already remarked, there had been a reaction against the use of the long multi-shot flashback sequence, and this form of film construction continued to be quite rare through the 'twenties. On the other hand, cross-cutting between parallel actions continued to be used when appropriate, without pushing the idea to quite the D.W. Griffith extreme. I can't resist mentioning a particular example of cross-cutting for expressive purposes that continues the tradition established in the previous period. This is in Louis Mercanton's *l'Appel du sang* (1920), where a love scene inside a room at night is cross-cut with a fireworks display that is taking place not too far away outside.

Cutting Rates in Silent Films of the 'Twenties

To give an impression of the sorts of cutting rates to be observed in particular silent films of the nineteen-twenties I will quote a fairly random collection of Average Shot Lengths selected from the figures I have obtained from more than 200

Twin Pawns	1920	Leonce Perret	6.5 sec.
The Virgin of Stamboul	1920	Tod Browning	4.5 sec.
The Four Horsemen of the Apocalypse	1921	Rex Ingram	7.0 sec.
Tol'able David	1921	Henry King	6.0 sec.
The Old Swimmin' Hole	1921	J. de Grasse	6.0 sec.
Foolish Wives	1922	E. von Stroheim	6.0 sec.
A Woman of Paris	1923	C. Chaplin	5.5 sec.
Smouldering Fires	1924	Clarence Brown	7.0 sec.
Ben-Hur	1924	Fred Niblo	4.0 sec.
Forbidden Paradise	1924	E. Lubitsch	5.5 sec.
The Merry Widow	1925	E. von Stroheim	5.0 sec.
Stella Dallas	1925	Henry King	5.5 sec.
The Phantom of the Opera	1925	Rupert Julian	5.5 sec.
The Magician	1926	Rex Ingram	7.5 sec.
Don Juan	1926	Alan Crosland	3.5 sec.
The Winning of Barbara Worth	1926	Henry King	5.0 sec.
Skinner's Dress Suit	1926	W. Seiter	8.0 sec.
Mantrap	1926	V. Fleming	4.5 sec.
Son of the Sheik	1926	G. Fitzmaurice	4.5 sec.
The Unknown	1927	Tod Browning	5.5 sec.
The Dress Parade	1927	Donald Crisp	5.5 sec.
The Cradle Snatchers	1927	Howard Hawks	4.5 sec.
White Shadows in the South Seas	1928	W.S. Van Dyke	6.0 sec.
Laugh, Clown, Laugh	1928	H. Brenon	6.5 sec.
The Crowd	1928	King Vidor	5.0 sec.
A Girl in Every Port	1928	Howard Hawks	5.0 sec.

Sumurun	1920	E. Lubitsch	6.0 sec.
Von Morgens bis Mitternacht	1920	K-H. Martin	12.0 sec.
Scherben	1921	Lupu Pick	16.0 sec.
Schloss Vogelod	1921	F.W. Murnau	9.5 sec.
Die Bergkatze	1921	E. Lubitsch	6.5 sec.
Vanina	1921	L. von Gerlach	11.0 sec.
Danton	1921	D. Buchowetzki	6.5 sec.
Dr. Mabuse der Spieler	1922	Fritz Lang	7.5 sec.
Eine versunkene Welt	1922	A. Korda	7.0 sec.
Das alte Gesetz	1923	E.A. Dupont	6.0 sec.
Die Strasse	1923	Karl Grune	13.0 sec.
Der letzte Mann	1924	F.W. Murnau	10.0 sec.
Orlacs Hande	1924	R. Wiene	11.0 sec.
Variete	1925	E.A. Dupont	6.0 sec.
Die Bruder Schellenberg	1925	Karl Grune	7.0 sec.
Tartuff	1926	F.W. Murnau	6.5 sec.
Der Geiger von Florenz	1926	P. Czinner	10.0 sec.
Die Villa im Tiergarten	1926	Franz Osten	6.0 sec.
Die Unehelichen	1926	G. Lamprecht	7.0 sec.
Die letzte Droschke von Berlin	1926	Carl Boese	6.0 sec.
Metropolis	1926	Fritz Lang	7.0 sec.
Die Hose	1927	H. Behrendt	5.0 sec.
Adieu Mascotte	1929	W. Thiele	6.0 sec.
l'Homme du large	1920	M. L'Herbier	7.0 sec.
Eldorado	1921	M. L'Herbier	5.0 sec.
l'Atlantide	1921	J. Feyder	8.0 sec.
la Souriante Madame Beudet	1922	G. Dulac	5.0 sec.
Visages d'Enfants	1925	J. Feyder	5.5 sec.
Gribiche	1925	J. Feyder	5.5 sec.
Poil de Carotte	1925	J. Duvivier	5.0 sec.
la Glace a trois Faces	1927	Jean Epstein	5.5 sec.
les Deux Timides	1928	Rene Clair	6.0 sec.
les Nouveaux Messieurs	1929	J. Feyder	6.0 sec.
Neobytchainye prikhoutennaia Mistera Vesta v strane bolchevikov	1924	L. Kuleshov	6.0 sec.
Aelita	1924	Y. Protazanov	7.0 sec.
Bronenosets Potyomkin	1925	S. Eisenstein	3.0 sec.
Po zakonu	1926	L. Kuleshov	6.5 sec.
Devushka s korobkoi	1927	Boris Barnet	4.0 sec.
Dom na trubnoi	1928	Boris Barnet	4.0 sec.
Novyi Vavilon	1929	Kozintsev/Trauberg	5.0 sec.

films of the period. These values correspond to projection speeds estimated to give natural movement to the characters in the films.

As can be seen, the slowest cutting in the American films listed for the period 1920-1925 is an ASL of 7.5 seconds, whereas there are 8 German films with slower cutting, and in fact with ASL's of up to 18 seconds. It is also noteworthy that the slowest cutting in American films is in the works of the leading American 'pictorialist' of the period, Rex Ingram, with ASL's of 7 seconds for *The Four Horsemen of the Apocalypse*,

Scaramouche, and *Mare Nostrum*, and 7.5 seconds for *The Magician*. Clarence Brown also had tendencies in the same direction. The slower cutting in European films still tended to be reinforced by the slow pace of their narratives and acting, but even if narrative and acting had been faster, silent films such as *Scherben* which have many shots longer than 30 seconds would still not seem fast.

A rather more conclusive demonstration of these points is given by comparing the Average Shot Length distributions for much larger samples of American and European silent films

American 1918-1923

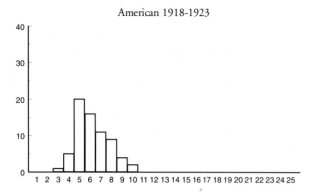

European 1918-1923

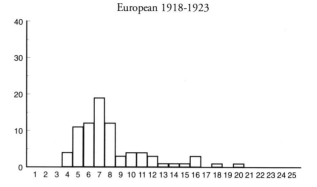

American Silent 1924-1929

European Silent 1924-1929

for the six year periods 1918-1923 and 1924-1929. As you can see, for samples of about 70 films from 1918-1923, there are no American films with ASLs longer than 10 seconds, whereas there are about a dozen European ones, and the modal values of the ASLs in the two cases are respectively 5 seconds and 7 seconds. When we move on to the ASL distributions for 1924-1929, which are based on well over 100 films in both cases, the American sample shows only a very small speeding up, while for the European distribution the modal (most popular) value has decreased to 6 seconds from the 7 seconds of the previous period. The mean values of the two distributions are now 4.8 seconds and 6.6 seconds respectively, and the European cutting rates are still about 2 seconds slower on the average, just as they were in the previous period of 1918-1923.

These results reflect a conscious attempt in the latter part of the nineteen-twenties by European film-makers to follow the earlier developments in American film style. This process was referred to as 'Americanization' from 1925 in the German cinema, and something similar was apparently going on in French and British cinema from around this date. This 'Americanization' also included closer camera placement and some changes in photography as well, not to mention the elimination of the last traces of Expressionist acting in Germany. In America itself, the distributions indicate that there continued to be some speeding up in the cutting rate in silent films from the early to the late 'twenties, for although the most poular ASL continued to be about 5 seconds, there were a much greater proportion of the film in 1924-1929 with ASLs of 4 and 5 seconds.

The shapes of the distributions of numbers of films with a

given ASL are in general assymetrical, like most of those just illustrated, but you can see that the distribution for American silent films of the 1924-1929 period is very nearly symmetrical, and bears a strong resemblance to the Normal (or Gaussian) distribution. This distribution is one that describes many natural phenomena, such as the heights of people in a population, or the distribution of errors in measuring a length accurately. Analogy with the second case just mentioned suggests that the approximation to the Normal distribution for American films of the late 'twenties may be due to film-makers unconsciously aiming at a standard cutting rate, and failing to hit it due to a variety of disturbing factors. The ASL's of American films in the late 'thirties are again approximately Normally distributed, but elsewhere this is not so.

The Atmospheric Insert

Prior to the nineteen-twenties there had been no real tradition of using a general shot of a scene which did *not* contain any of the characters in the story to give a feeling of mood or atmosphere to the narrative at an appropriate point. Isolated instances of this had occurred, but it is only in France and Germany after 1920 that the use of the inserted atmospheric shot became a definite principle of construction. In Marcel L'Herbier's *l'Homme du large* (1920) there are a small number of shots of scudding clouds and tumultuous seas cut into scenes at points at which they could be taken to indicate the feelings of the principal characters, even though those characters are not present at the place where the Insert Shot was taken. As with most of the expressive uses of Insert Shots in the cinema, the audience's understanding of this device depended on conventions or clichés established far earlier in the other arts, and particularly in nineteenth-century literature. A more developed example of the use of atmospheric inserts is provided by the shots of the docks of Marseilles which are cut more or less at random into the narrative of *Fièvre* (Louis Delluc, 1921), which otherwise takes place entirely inside a bar frequented by sailors. In this case these atmospheric inserts are not specifically expressive, since they do not appear to relate to the specific emotions which might be felt by any of the characters at the point where they are cut in, but rather they provide a kind of generalized 'port' atmosphere.

(Delluc explicitly proposed the idea of illustrating psychological states with shots of objects, etc. in one of his theoretical articles in *Cinea* (9 December 1921 p.14), and indeed similar ideas had been advanced by other French writers earlier than this, including the future film-maker Marcel L'Herbier in his *Hermès et le silence* of 1918.)

In parallel with these developments in France, but perhaps unconnected, a similar use of atmospheric inserts began to appear in German films from 1921 onwards: in *Scherben* with shots of the railway line and the outside of the house, in *Vanina* with cuts back to an empty ballroom when the action has moved elsewhere, in *Dr. Mabuse der Spieler* with the empty stock exchange likewise, some shots of the eponymous street in *Die Strasse* (1923), and then after that *Sylvester*. Descriptions of the extensive tracking shots in this film which showed the *umwelt*, or world surrounding the action, but not connected with it, can be found in Lotte Eisner's *The Haunted Screen*.

Made almost simultaneously with *Sylvester* at the end of 1923, Louis Delluc's last film, *l'Inondation*, also used tracking shots showing the village market and river which eventually floods as background atmosphere, in much the same way as *Sylvester*, though in the case of *l'Inondation* these scenes event-

ually come to have a connection with the action of the plot. It may be that this use of atmospheric tracking shots in both films had a common inspiration, but if so it is still obscure. The use of shots independent of the narrative to create atmosphere (or *Stimmung*, as the German film-makers put it at the time), never went beyond the extreme reached in *Sylvester* in mainstream cinema, but in the Art Cinema or avant-garde of the late 'twenties the mode was pushed much further. In a sense the 'cross-section of a city' films from *Berlin - die Symphonie der Grosstadt* (1927) onwards are nothing but *Stimmung*.

The Documentary Montage Sequence

A development closely related to all this, and which is indeed not completely distinguishable from it, was the appearance of what could be called the 'documentary montage sequence'. This was a series of fairly connected shots showing the actual events and unstaged action going on in some particular place that the characters in the film happen to be in, without it making any great emotional or expressive contribution to the narrative. The first example here was the Holy Week procession included in *Eldorado* (1921), and this was followed by the series of shots of the street market that begins *Crainquebille* (Jacques Feyder, 1923), and then by the shots of popular Sunday recreation on the outskirts of Paris near the beginning of *l'Affiche* (Jean Epstein, 1925), and so on. The last mentioned instance also has expressive connotations, and is one of those cases that escape any simple classification, and so have to be described in detail to indicate their true nature. Both Feyder and Epstein continued to use documentary sequences in their films throughout the 'twenties, and in many of these such as *la Glace à trois faces* (Epstein, 1926), the effect is startlingly like similar usages that appeared in the 'Nouvelle Vague' films of the nineteen-sixties.

Multiple superimposition in the montage sequence showing the attractions of the big city in Die Strasse *(Karl Grune, 1923).*

The 'Classical' Montage Sequence

The early evolution of the 'classical' montage sequence, which is a sequence of short shots joined by dissolves or other optical effects that are so close together that one transition starts shortly after the one before ends, is another topic that is still not completely elucidated. I have already mentioned examples of atmospheric montage sequences in French films before 1923, but in these the shots are of appreciable length, with the transitions between them, be they cuts, dissolves, or fades, well separated from one another, and the same can be said for the first German example I have seen. In 1922 Murnau's *Phantom* contains what seems to be the first attempt at what later became the standard method of suggesting a subjective feeling of dizziness, or vertigo, or loss of consciousness in a character in a film. In this film there were a series of moderately long shots joined by dissolves, each shot rotating about the central point of the screen. (The rotation of these shots was achieved in various ways; partly by building special small sets which were actually rotated in front of the camera, and partly by putting a special rotating prism in front of the lens to produce the effect in a purely optical manner.)

Die Strasse (Karl Grune, 1923) contains one of the very first fully realized montage sequences in the classical form, in which the dissolves take place absolutely continuously, so that there is always a changing sequence of superimposed images present on the screen. In this film the series of images are intended to represent the alluring attractions and excitements of the Big City street as seen by a timid bank clerk who is looking out of his window at it. In some parts this sequence is further complicated by splitting the frame into multiple images side by side. A similarly-used montage sequence in Murnau's *Sunrise* is also very similar in form and content, though more precise in execution, and far more elegant visually. Also in 1923, Robert Wiene's *Raskolnikov* has a fairly fully developed example of a montage sequence in the what was to be the classical style.

The German film most admired in Hollywood, *Varieté* (1925), also has its montage sequence, which is a series of shots showing short details of the acts on the bill of the variety program, and this is again used to convey atmosphere. In these few years development had been rapid, and by 1926 even ordinary German films had to have a montage sequence, as in *Die Villa im Tiergarten*, where the montage sequence suggesting a loss of consciousness has attained its canonical form. A series of dissolving images is surrounded by a nebulous swirling vortex matted in towards the outer edge of the frame.

Again there had been a parallel development of the classical montage sequence in France, though in this case I have a strong feeling that the German example had priority. Instances can be mentioned in *Coeur fidèle* (Jean Epstein, 1923), and later films. But even in 1926 in America there were only a limited number of directors just starting to use full montage sequences in films such as *What Price Glory?* (Raoul Walsh), *So This is Paris* (Ernst Lubitsch), and *Mantrap* (Victor Fleming). The last of these is an early example of a montage

sequence indicating a spatial transition, being made up of a series of panning and tracking shots of scenery which dissolve one into the next smoothly along a passage from the wilderness to the city.

The Things Take Over

The atmospheric Insert Shot is only one variety of the general class of Insert Shots, which is made up of shots of objects and also shots of the body apart from the face. The use of the general class of Inserts shows a marked increase in the films of all countries throughout the decade, so that by 1925 we find that both *Varieté* and *Smouldering Fires* (Clarence Brown) include about 45 inserts of all kinds; i.e. about 10% of their shots are Inserts. Although this tendency had its roots in American practice before 1920, it then developed quite independently through the early 'twenties in both Europe and America. The highest form of the use of the Insert was when the object shown alone in the close shot could be made to perform a double function in the narrative, though the occasions when a director could manage this were very rare. An example of this is given by Tod Browning's *Outside the Law* (1921). In this film the protagonist strays into criminality, and while he is hiding from the police he befriends a little boy for whom he improvises a kite. Later his criminal predicament suggests even worse crimes, and now the sticks of the child's kite, which has been lost and dangles broken from above the window outside, cast a crucifix-like shadow on the floor of the criminal's hiding place. This naturally recalls him to the paths of righteousness. Both the kite in its original form, and also its shadow, are repeatedly shown in Insert Close Ups at various points throughout these scenes. This may sound corny, but it is quite a trick to work effects like this into a film in an unforced way, which is what Tod Browning certainly does.

Already in 1924 the real avant-garde had produced a film composed almost entirely of Inserts (*le Ballet mécanique* by Fernand Léger and Dudley Murphy), and in the later 'twenties the use of a large proportion of Inserts became the norm in the new international Art Cinema in films such as Dmitri Kirsanoff's *Brumes d'automne* (1928), not to mention the advanced Russian cinema of Eisenstein and others. When some critics around 1930 were writing about the 'art of the silent cinema' and lamenting its loss, it was basically the extensive use of Inserts and montage sequences that they were talking about. I find it difficult to be sorrowful about the matter, since it seems to me that by 1929 these usages were becoming an established style which was starting to be used unimaginatively and unthinkingly by lesser talents. Sometimes even the better directors used these and other devices to hammer home dramatic points that were already quite obvious, as in Clarence Brown's *Flesh and the Devil* (1926), not to mention large numbers of lesser known European films with artistic pretensions.

The Hard Cut

Under the influence of *Intolerance*, which reached France

towards the end of the war, Abel Gance made his first experiments with fast cutting in the battle scenes of *J'accuse* (1919). Whereas in Griffith's films the hardest cuts (i.e. those creating the greatest physical discontinuity between shots) are mostly between parallel actions, and have been created largely in the pursuit of heightened suspense, in Gance's style this was changed to a linear progression through very disparate shots, without a true parallel line of action. There were already signs of a development like this in American cinema, where I have come across a humorous short film from 1920, *The Perils of Paul*, which depicts a wild drive in a car by intercutting shots of the car and POV shots from inside it with big Inserts of the speedometer and of a foot on an accelerator. This is the kind of thing that was developed further by Gance in *la Roue* (1922), in the scene of the train proceeding towards a crash. Many of the shots intercut with general shots of the moving train are of static parts of it such as pressure gauges, etc., and this produces a different effect to that in Griffith's films, where there is nearly always some movement in the shots. As well as that, the cutting in some parts of *la Roue* is even faster than anything in Griffith's films, with some of the shots only one frame in length. Although Gance did not completely carry through his original intention of creating simple regular metrical patterns with the lengths of shots, an element of mechanical rhythm, oblivious to what is represented in successive shots, remains in the film. This is most marked in the final climactic sequence which intercuts shots of the peasants' round-dance with shots of the dying engineer. The sequences in *la Roue* that I have mentioned represent a definite move in the direction of cutting together static, and at the same time very disparate, shots that later became important in Eisenstein's films, and also in fully avant-garde films like *le Ballet mécanique*.

The Interaction of Form and Dramatic Content

By the beginning of the 'twenties, the construction of American features through the filmic variables like Scale of Shot, cutting rate, angles chosen, and so on, had been largely brought into line with the standard form of dramatic construction which was now fully taken over from the theatre into the cinema. In particular, the alternation of different types of scene in the way described in Chapter 10 was accompanied in films by variations in the local cutting rate according to the type of scene concerned. This can be illustrated by the example of John Ford's *The Iron Horse* (1924), a film which is fairly easily available for study in Britain and the United States in a 16 mm. print produced by Killiam Shows. This print does have some short sections in which scenes of very fast action are 'stretched' by step-printing so that they do not appear ridiculously fast at sound speed, but these are sufficiently few and sufficiently short not to upset my demonstration. It is also important to realize that the Average Shot Lengths are here calculated for a projection speed of 20 frames per second, which is close to the speed at which the film was shot, and *not* for the sound projection speed of 24 frames per second.

The overall ASL for *The Iron Horse* is about 6.5 seconds, and the local ASL's for particular scenes fluctuate about this rate, according to their nature. The general pattern of these variations, which is fairly standard for ordinary American films from the First World War onwards, is that action scenes are cut faster than the norm, and sad or comic scenes slower than normal. In the case of *The Iron Horse*, the first few scenes, which are basically concerned with introducing the characters, do not depart very far from the overall norm, but after the young protagonist's father has been killed by Indians, the two scenes in which he buries and mourns him slow down considerably, to an ASL of 15 seconds. Then a scene in the corridors of Congress, which mostly contains exposition of the situation 20 years later in the story, returns to something like the norm, with an ASL of 8.5 seconds. This is followed by a scene which trades in the suspense as to whether Lincoln will sign the bill opening up the West, and this has a smaller than average ASL of 5 seconds. The next scene is neutral in mood, showing general 'documentary' views of the building of the transcontinental railroad out from the West Coast, and this proceeds at a pace slightly slower than the norm, with an ASL of 9 seconds. This is succeeded by another such scene, but since this includes more intense action and a dramatic mishap, it is cut much faster, with an ASL of 5 seconds. Next is action on the Eastern end of the railroad which is again somewhat similar overall to the previous scene, though longer, and starting slowly, then building up to the faster climax of an Indian attack in the middle before slowing down again. The ASL of this scene overall is 5.9 seconds. Yet another scene at the eastern end of the railroad building follows, but this time it starts slowly, with a comic section in the middle, followed by faster action at the end. Overall the ASL equals 5.1 seconds. The next section is pure action, representing a buffalo hunt, which is cut even faster, with an ASL of 4.6 seconds. This is followed by a short factual and non-dramatic scene of winter tracklaying which is made up of a couple of long takes, both about 24 seconds long. After a time lapse, another long action scene follows, with an ASL of 4 seconds, followed by another sad burial scene, which is slow cut, like the earlier one, at 12.5 seconds. After a long sequence of scenes to do with the building of the Eastern end of the railroad, which have an overall ASL of 5.6 seconds, there follows a long pair of basically comic scenes in the portable saloon which follows the construction gangs. These scenes have a slower cutting rate than average, as is usual with comedy scenes, with an ASL of 8.3 seconds. There follows a seduction scene, which slows down even further, to 11.2 seconds, and so it goes on.

As hinted in the above simplified summary, by the early 'twenties American films had also adopted the variation of type of dramatic action *within* scenes, as well as from scene to scene. Even within a continuous scene, dramatic sections are followed by comic sections, which are followed by action sections, and then pathetic sections, and the cutting rate varies in the same standardized ways to go with these different sections within the scene, and so indeed do other formal features like Scale of Shot. More detailed illustration of this point tends to be tedious in a book, but further examples of these standard constructional procedures are illustrated in a later chapter dealing with the films of Max Ophuls.

14. FILM STYLE AND TECHNOLOGY: 1926-1929

Because of the overlap between the production of the first sound films and the last silent films in the United States during the years 1926-1929, and also because only silent films were made in Europe during these years, my consideration of the period is rather difficult to organize. There has always been an unfortunate tendency not to make any distinction between the nature of silent films from the early 'twenties and those from the late 'twenties, and on the other hand to fail to notice the close formal similarities between the last silent films and sound films from the beginning of the nineteen-thirties, and I can only advise close attention to the points which bear on this, as I have been unable to think of a better way to cover these developments than to continue the pattern of the previous chapters.

To recapitulate the well-known outline of the industry's transition to sound cinema production in the United States: only a handful of sound films were made in 1927, in 1928 a minor part of the production was sound films, but in 1929 the majority of the films produced by the major studios were part-talkies at least. By April of 1929 about 2500 sound projectors had been installed in American cinemas, mainly in the first-run theatres in the larger cities. By the end of 1929 all the major studios had stopped making silent films, though they did convert many of their talkies to silent films by replacing the sound-track with intertitles for the benefit of unconverted cinemas.

In Europe on the other hand no sound films were made till the end of 1929, so film- makers there were free to develop certain stylistic features of the last silent films to an extreme that was impossible in the United States. This was particularly the case in France. In that country the development of stylistic extremes in an 'Art Cinema' was also encouraged by the fact that there were no large, highly organized production companies in the latter part of the decade, and each film was a separate enterprise for those concerned. If it failed, they could just walk away, and get the money for the next one from someone else, because that was what was done anyway. This approach was only possible to a limited extent in Germany, and hardly at all in America. In Russia centralized artistic control was imposed from 1928, but before that the production situation was sufficiently confused for those determined enough to make films pretty much how they liked. After 1929 only the slavish following of the party line in matters of content could give Dovshenko, Dziga Vertov, and others some freedom in formal matters for a few more years.

Film Stock

The new contestants in the film stock market were the E.I. Dupont de Nemours company in the United States, and Gevaert in Belgium, both of which began making motion picture negative and positive during this period, but without making any great impression, since their products were not as good as those of Eastman Kodak.

In 1926 the reduction of the price of Eastman Kodak's panchromatic negative stock to that of their standard orthochromatic negative precipitated the swing to the general use of panchromatic negative over the next few years. Almost instantaneous conversion in the studios should have been possible in principle, but no doubt the usual conservatism of most cameramen helped to prevent this. It was claimed at the time by cameramen that the new panchromatic negative was more contrasty than orthochromatic negative, but this claim is almost impossible to substantiate now, given the extreme difficulty there is in seeing a reasonable number of original prints of films shot on both stocks. It is certainly not obvious on duplicate prints of such early all-panchromatic films as *The Son of the Sheik* (1926), but on the other hand it may have something to do with the rather unusual look of the figure lighting in *The Winning of Barbara Worth* (1926), another early entry on panchromatic film. In this film it can be seen that the skin tones are reproduced as a mid-grey rather than the usual very light grey, yet even so the highlights on the protruding cheek bones, etc. are completely burnt out to an undifferentiated white. This is indeed an extremely contrasty effect, but it could have been achieved by special development or the like. This particular look to the photography of faces had been used to some extent over the previous several years in still photography, but it had never been a dominant style there, and I have never seen it used in another film. In any case, by the time that the majority of films were being shot on panchromatic stock in 1928, Kodak had replaced the original panchromatic emulsion with a new one which was certainly not more contrasty than ordinary orthochromatic stock, even though it was still approximately the same speed as both the original orthochromatic and panchromatic stocks. Agfa, Gevaert, and Pathé also made similar panchromatic films stocks available in parallel with Eastman Kodak.

Eastman also introduced a Superspeed Negative in 1926, as did Agfa in Germany and Pathé in France, and these would seem to have been about twice as fast as ordinary negative: i.e. about 40 A.S.A. in present-day terms. These fast stocks were in general little used for feature film-making, except to get the occasional large-scale night exterior, but the fast Agfa stock was essential for obtaining some of the interiors shot with available light in *Berlin - die Symphonie der Grosstadt* (Ruttman,1927). The graininess of some of these shots suggests that special forced development was given to the negative as well. Also in 1926, the firm of Dupont de Nemours started

Medium Long shot in The Winning of Barbara Worth *(1926) shot on panchromatic film with distinctive contrasty effect of dark skin tone and burnt-out highlights on the face of the seated character. Note also the heavy lens diffusion often used in this period.*

marketing its own film stocks in the United States, though without dislodging Eastman Kodak from its position of dominance.

The other major development in film stocks in the late 'twenties was the introduction of the first duplicating positive and duplicating negative stocks by Eastman Kodak in 1926. By making a print of an original negative on duplicating positive stock, and then printing this onto duplicating negative stock, it was now possible for the first time to create a duplicate negative that had almost as good definition and as low contrast as the original negative, and so capable of being used in its place either to make duplicate prints, or optical effects in the printer without much loss of quality. These duplicating stocks were undoubtedly created in response to the demand for a more convenient way of producing a second negative for foreign distribution than using two cameras side by side, and also for a more efficient way of making the increasingly popular optical effects such as dissolves, etc. Despite the availability of these duplicating stocks, it would be a mistake to think that everyone in Hollywood stopped making their dissolves in the camera; as usual the change took a few years, but the possibility of making dissolves between any pair of shots at the editing stage, using the optical printer, was immediately useful for putting together the newly popular montage sequences. By 1928 a film such as *Lonesome* (Paul Fejös) could include a vast number of dissolves, almost turning it into a single feature-length montage sequence, thanks to these intermediate film stocks and optical printing. In Europe such facilities seem not to have been available till the end of the decade, and certainly the 'Art Films' that also made great use of dissolves between shots had to have them made in the camera as before, e.g. *Menilmontant* (1926), *Un Chien Andalou* (1928), etc. etc.

Technicolor Dye Imbibition Printing

In 1928 Technicolor finally introduced the unique method of printing that continued for the rest of the life of their process. The initial stage of printing continued to be the same, with two hardened gelatine relief positives being produced for the red and green images, but now these were not used to make up the final print, but instead a single pair of them were used as matrices to absorb dye, and then deposit it on the final print somewhat in the manner of lithographic printing. To be precise, the gelatine relief absorbed more dye in the thicker parts of each frame corresponding to the areas where the colour to be printed was brightest in the original scene, but instead of leaving the dye there as before, it was transferred to a blank gelatine emulsion on another strip of 35 mm. film pressed against it. The crucial dye transfer or imbibition operation was carried out on a very large machine that essentially consisted of a thin endless stainless steel belt running between two large pulley wheels about 50 metres apart. This belt was 35 mm. wide, and had small stainless steel pins set down each edge with dimensions and positions exactly corresponding to the perforations in 35 mm. positive film. The blank print stock was settled onto the pins at the beginning of the top length of the belt after it had passed over the first pulley, then the dye-soaked matrix (gelatine relief) was pressed down onto the pins on top of the blank film, and it stayed there as it and the film passed down the whole length of the belt through a series of drying chambers. As the films reached the other end of the belt they were stripped off it, and the relief matrix was led back as a continuous loop to receive a new charge of dye and endlessly repeat the process.

At this stage in the history of Technicolor the blank film was actually coated with emulsion on both sides, and after one of the two colours had been printed onto one side in the manner described, it was further dried, and then passed on to another identical dye transfer machine, and the other colour was printed onto the other side in the same way. The printing matrix was the length of one whole reel of film, and after 50 to 100 prints had been made, the two matrices were removed from the transfer machines, and those matrices corresponding to the next reel to be printed were put on, and the process repeated. If a larger number of prints than this were needed, new gelatine relief matrices had to be made again by optical printing from the original negatives, as the printing process wore out the perforations, and the further use of the original matrices would lose the perfect registration of the two colours on the print.

The two primary dye colours now used were cyan (blue-green) and an orange-red, and these two colours permitted fairly good reproduction of the skin tones of people of most races, and also good blacks and whites. But yellows in the original scene were reproduced as pink, and pure blues and pure greens were both reproduced as not very different shades of blue-green. Pure reds were reproduced as the orange-red primary. A special fast emulsion had to be used on the camera negative for the Technicolor process, and as a result the image was very grainy when compared with that for black and white film, and the definition was much poorer. It should also be noted that the cyan dye was much more inclined to fade with time than the red primary dye, so that many surviving prints are reduced to orange-red fuzzy images, with the blue-green colours nearly (or entirely) lost.

One of the first demonstrations of the capabilities of the new Technicolor printing process was Victor Schertzinger's *Redskin* (1928), and this film was also unusual in that the section of the film dealing with the youthful education of the American Indian of the title in an Eastern college was shot in black and white, so creating the first strong example of the use of expressive contrast between sections of a film through the use of both colour and black and white film.

The Use of Colour Film Against Black and White Film

The series of films that have intermittently followed *Redskin* over the decades in using the contrast between colour and black and white film to distinguish between sections set in different 'worlds' shows the way that expressive conventions (or codes) fail to solidify even in the case of one of the simplest formal distinctions. In *Redskin* the colour/no colour distinction is presumably intended to suggest that the wild country of the Indian reservation is superior or preferable to the equally real world of civilization, whereas in *The Wizard of Oz* (1939) a fantasy world is shown in colour, and the real world, which is explicitly stated in the film to be superior, is in monochrome. The next film to use this distinction, *The Secret Garden* of 1942, reverts to something like the *Redskin* usage – the secret garden, which is quite real, is in colour, but then one comes to *A Matter of Life and Death* (1946), in which the real world is in colour, and the fantasy world is in black and white. Later films continue to show this failure to establish

any fixed convention of meaning with respect to this distinction, and eventually we reach films where the occurrence of black and white and colour sections is totally arbitrary with respect to their narratives, but not with respect to their production circumstances. For example *Un Homme et une Femme* (1966) and *If* (1968).

Tinting

It was not possible to tint sound films in the way silent films were still being tinted in 1927, because the tinting dyes covered the sound track area as well as the picture area, and so the transmission of light through the sound track changed from section to section as the tinting dyes changed. Special tinting dyes that did not interfere with sound reproduction in this way were developed after a few years, but the tinting of films never became standard practice again, though there were isolated examples of tinting in the'thirties. The increasing number of films using colour processes of one sort or another no doubt helped to make tinting less attractive as well.

Film Laboratory Procedures

By 1928 the continuous development of positive film in machines, rather than the old style of batch development, had been in use in some Hollywood studios for a year or two. Then in that year Universal Studios instituted machine development of camera negative as well, and the other major studios followed suit quickly. This change was encouraged by the necessity for very precisely controlled and reproducible conditions of development for sound track negative, which implied machine development, and so the same might as well be done for picture negative. The use of machine development in its turn meant that exposure conditions for film had to be standardized for the whole production of the studio, although this did not lead to the use of exposure meters as might have been expected. Photoelectric light level meters already existed for illumination engineering, as did purpose-built photographic exposure meters of the comparison type, but Hollywood cameramen were so experienced, and lighting was so standardized, that their determinations of exposure were already sufficiently precise to satisfy even the requirements of machine development. On the rare occasions when cameramen might be in some doubt as to the correct exposure, they could still expose a test section and have it developed immediately.

Lighting Equipment

With the swing to the use of panchromatic negative from 1926 onwards came the swing to using incandescent tungsten lighting, and in the first place this happened *before* sound films needed incandescent lights ('inkies') for silence. For instance, incandescent lights were used on the silent films *The First Auto* and *The Rose of Monterey* at Warners and First National in 1927. Although in general incandescent (tungsten) lights give less light when used in the same lighting unit as that in which an arc light has been used, they have the advantage that they do not require the constant trimming by hand that arcs do, and they are far less likely to go out in the middle of a shot. This means that less manpower is needed to tend them, and hence greater efficiency. At the time, scientists employed by Eastman Kodak and the incandescent light manufacturers made much of the idea that the greater sensitivity to red light of panchromatic emulsion matched the greater amount of red light from tungsten sources, but this was not strictly speaking effective, as there is already a fair proportion of red light in the arc flame. In fact panchromatic film is slightly faster with arc light of the same intensity than with tungsten light, and at least half the light on the sets at the time was coming from arc lights. However cameramen may have believed this propaganda, which had been put out in technical journals for years before 1926. And it *is* true that incandescent lamps are more efficient for panchromatic film than the mercury vapour lamps (Cooper-Hewitts) that were still being used to provide the general background light on the sets.

In any case, panchromatic film came in together with the partial use of incandescent lights, with some arcs being retained at first. Then almost immediately, as the production of sound films began, the remaining arcs had to be abandoned as well, as they emitted a hum that was picked up by the microphones. In the first stage of the transition, the Cooper-Hewitt banks were replaced by closely packed rows of incandescent floodlights having large tungsten filament globes in hemispherical metal reflectors. These were used in exactly the same way as the Cooper-Hewitts – either suspended at an angle above the set, or on floor stands. In the second stage of the transition, that necessitated by sound filming, the previous arc floodlights and spotlights were replaced by incandescent floodlights put into the same housings. There was however some tendency to replace the old trough-shaped reflectors carrying arcs, which had been used for flood lighting from floor stands, with new hemispherical reflectors containing incandescent globes, and to use these for figure lighting. Because the incandescent globes were in general less powerful than the arc units used in the same housings, there was also a tendency to use the reflector type of spotlight in the open drum housing rather than the enclosed theatrical type of spotlight with lens when doing figure lighting. However, both types of spotlight continued to exist side by side. From 1926 onwards, 10 Kilowatt, 5 Kilowatt, and 2 Kilowatt incandescent globes were used in the various types of lighting unit.

As far as interior shooting was concerned, the change over to tungsten lighting made no appreciable difference to the style of film lighting; a silent film such as *Don Juan* (Alan Crosland, 1926), which was shot on orthochromatic negative with the older type of lighting, looks much the same in this respect as an early 'thirties Warner Brothers film. According to information supplied to Kevin Brownlow by its cameraman, Byron Haskin, *Don Juan* was shot at f3.5 with a Bell & Howell camera, mostly hand-cranked, though with some extended takes shot under motor power. A range of lenses from 25 mm. to 100 mm. were used, though as far as I can

see the 25 mm. was used rarely and inconspicuously. The lighting units used for figure lighting, which were described by Haskin as standard, were arc floodlights ('broads') for key-lighting, small two-tube Cooper-Hewitts for fill-light, and arc spotlights for backlighting. Arc spotlights were also used for general set lighting along with the large Cooper-Hewitt racks. Production photographs for other films made at this date and earlier confirm that this was indeed standard lighting before the advent of panchromatic film.

By 1927 there are some signs of further reduction in depth of field in the photography of American silent films. For instance, most of the interior shots in *My Best Girl* (Sam Taylor, 1927), which was photographed by Charles Rosher, have hardly any depth of field at all. To be more precise, even in Medium Shot the depth of field is about 1 to 2 feet, which corresponds to an aperture of between f2 and f2.8. The photography of the exteriors of this film show an almost equal reduction in depth of field, and such a reduction in depth of field on exteriors can also be seen in some other silent films of the period, such as *Winners of the Wilderness* (W.S. Van Dyke, 1927). With the general switch to panchromatic film, and then the further transition to sound filming a couple of years later, the light level on the sets of all films dropped to the level that was already being used in some films such as *My Best Girl*, and apertures of about f2.5 became standard. Although this increase in the aperture by one stop in the photography of films in general reduced their already reduced depth of field still further, there were also other factors affecting this variable, as I will describe below.

The general trend in film lighting during the late 'twenties was the way the methods introduced in the early 'twenties by the most advanced cameramen spread downwards to the lesser cameramen. In other words, it was a period of standardization of the basic lighting style in Hollywood films.

Exterior Lighting

From the middle of the nineteen-twenties onwards there was a major new development in the lighting of exteriors. This involved the use of large incandescent reflector- type spotlights for figure lighting; not only for the key- light, but also for the backlight and/or fill-light. In some cases the direct sunlight was even shielded off the actors with a large shade, so that the total result was an approximation to the way figures were being lit in studio interiors. Examples of this approach from 1926 include *Rose of the Golden West* and *Mantrap*. Although in succeeding years this was to become the usual way of lighting figures on exteriors, at this stage most exterior scenes continued to be lit with direct sunlight plus sunlight bounced off reflectors, as had been done before. The use of spotlighting for exterior scenes required mobile electric generators to be taken out on location, which had sometimes been done even in the early 'twenties, but the trouble and expense of this was now regarded as worthwhile. In Europe no such subtleties developed in exterior lighting during the late 'twenties, so though it was now quite common there to use back-

Close Up in an exterior location scene in
Mantrap *(1926) completely lit by artificial*
light. Spotlights provide both the key and
fill-light from left and right of the camera,
and also the two backlights.

lighting from the sun on the figures, plus reflector fill on their front, it was still possible for a quality film such as *Die Liebe der Jeanne Ney* (G.W. Pabst, 1927) to have its exteriors lit solely with frontal sunlight.

Cameras

The Bell & Howell Eyemo and the De Vry camera were the principal totally new cameras introduced in this period, and both became available in 1926. They were small cameras that took 100 foot rolls of 35 mm. film on daylight loading spools and they were really intended for amateur use. Both were driven by clockwork mechanisms powered by hand-wound spring motors. The Bell & Howell Eyemo, which was the superior design, weighed 7 lbs., cost $600, and initially had a mount for a single lens only. Taylor-Hobson lenses from 40 mm. upwards were available for this camera, and from 1929 it was supplied with a lens turret holding three lenses. It had no means of framing the image through the lens, so a supplementary finder attached to the side of the camera had to be used for this. However critical focussing could be accomplished in the same way as with the large Bell & Howell Studio camera, by rotating the taking lens to the other side of the turret, where the central part of the image only could be examined with an eyepiece behind a ground glass screen. Unlike the larger camera, the Eyemo did not have registration pins in the film transport system, but only a simple reciprocating double claw pull-down.

The De Vry camera had rather similar specifications, though without any critical focussing system, and it was slightly heavier at 8.5 lbs. Both cameras could be hand-held quite easily, though neither was the ideal shape for this. The Eyemo was immediately put to work to get the occasional unobtrusive hand-held shot, as in *The Passionate Quest* (J. Stuart Blackton, 1926), *Quality Street* (Sidney Franklin,

1927), and *King of Kings* (Cecil B. DeMille, 1927). Thereafter the Eyemo was similarly used on the rare isolated occasion in feature films up to the end of World War 2, and both the Eyemo and the De Vry were also extensively used as combat cameras to get documentary footage in that conflict.

The major studio cameras continued to be the large Bell & Howell and the Mitchell, and in 1927 the latter was fitted with the double register pins and curved extension to the bottom of the gate that it has to this day. The change in the angle of action of the claw system so that it now worked within the new curved extension to the bottom of the gate was necessary to make space for the new register pins that were to fix the film accurately into place during exposure. With this modification the Mitchell could now offer the facility of completely accurate registration that had previously been restricted to the Bell & Howell amongst studio cameras.

In Europe in 1927 the through-the-lens viewfinding system of the Debrie was altered so that instead of viewing the image on the film through its back, the whole gate holding the film was displaced by turning a handle to slide a ground glass screen into its place. Amongst other advantages, this meant that the single frame of film that happened to be stopped in the gate was not fogged by critical checking of the image, and also that opaque coated-back negative could be used in the camera.

The first American synchronized sound films were shot using Bell & Howells and Mitchells indiscriminately in sound-proof booths with glass fronts, but when sound-proof coverings ('blimps') began to be applied directly round the camera body itself from 1929, only the Mitchell camera could be used, as its rack-over through-the-lens viewfinding system was far easier to use under these conditions, and also because its mechanism ran more quietly than that of the Bell & Howell. The particular measures that were taken to reduce the running noise of the Mitchell camera included the replace-

The film movement used with no real change in Mitchell cameras from 1927, through the NC and BNC models, and also in early Panavision cameras. The film path is outlined in white, and vanishes into the gate at the left of the picture. The claw mechanism is at the bottom left corner, with the register pin system immediately above it, going horizontally into the middle of the gate. (Photo by Michael Anderson)

ment of ball bearings by sleeve bearings, and also the replacement of some of the steel gears in the drive mechanism by fibre gears. The Bell & Howell was not modified in this way, so from 1930 it became obsolete as a standard production camera.

Camera Supports

The new increase in camera mobility that occurred in the latter half of the nineteen-twenties called forth changes in camera supports to facilitate it. Apart from the tendency to use more tracking shots, there was also a return to the greater use of the small pans and tilts to keep actors well-placed in the frame as they moved about, of the kind that had first developed at the beginning of World War I in the United States. The small geared head which was still universally used was just able to cope with simple combined tracking and panning at moderate speeds when following moving actors, particularly when the panning gear was disengaged, but anything beyond that required the use of the new friction heads. Such makes as the 'True Ball', which appeared in 1926, were similar to modern friction heads, with the camera movement about vertical and horizontal pivots controlled by hand pressure on a pan bar or tiller attached to the camera support plate, with the speed of these movements being regulated by adjustable friction in the pivots. When the first blimped cameras began to be used in 1929 they were always mounted on larger and heavier versions of these friction heads, which had in addition internal springs to partially counterbalance the greater weight of the blimped camera when it was tilted forward or back. These large spring-loaded friction heads continued in use up till the end of the nineteen-thirties.

The improvised camera dollys of earlier years continued to be adequate as far as tracking movements were concerned,

though they were supplemented on occasion by such things as fork-lift trucks with the camera tripod mounted on a platform on the forks. This improvised device made possible limited camera rises and falls combined with a tracking movement of the kind that can be seen in Harold Lloyd's *For Heaven's Sake* (1926). (Harold Lloyd was the only one of the great film clowns whose films showed an interest in the latest stylistic developments of their day, not only in camera movement, but also in other things such as lighting.) An even more remarkable and elegant use of camera movement occurs in his *The Kid Brother* of 1927, in which the camera rises straight up for about 20 feet to keep Harold in frame as he climbs a pine tree, finally giving an over-the-shoulder-shot of his distant view of the object of his affections. Although presumably achieved with some improvised arrangement, this equivalent to a crane shot indicates the kind of interests that led to the construction of the first true camera crane in 1929. The stylistic interests of Harold Lloyd fitted well with his comedy, which was mostly set far more definitely in the real world than that of the other film clowns.

Camera Cranes

As is well known, the first real camera crane was built under the direction of Paul Fejös for the Universal Studios production of *Broadway* in 1929. It had a camera platform big enough to accommodate two cameras on tripods suspended below the end of a 25 foot arm, and this counterweighted arm pivoted on a column mounted on a large wheeled chassis which could be moved under the power of electric motors. This crane was used extensively and very noticeably on *Broadway* to carry out long takes that traversed the many levels of the vast night club set during the musical numbers, but not for the dialogue scenes.

Camera Movement in General

Although it was not uncommon to find 10 or more tracking shots, not to mention large amounts of panning, during the length of some of the last American silent films such as *The Red Dance* (Raoul Walsh, 1928), in Europe this trend went a little further, particularly in France. In part this was because there were none of the constraints of early sound filming there until 1930, and in part because stylistic developments have always been pushed to greater lengths in the 'Art Cinema' section of film production. So one gets some films like Marcel L'Herbier's *l'Argent* (1928) in which most of the shots involve camera movement of one kind or another, often of a very conspicuous nature. It seems likely to me that the obviousness of a lot of the camera movement in this film and others such as Jean Renoir's *Tire au flanc* (1928) was due to lack of technical skill. This deduction follows from the fact that as *l'Argent* goes along the camera movement, though remaining just as extensive, becomes less conspicuous because it is fitted in better with the movements of the characters, presumably as a result of the practice that the director and operators acquired in the earlier part of the film. There have been a number of examples before and since of European film-makers learning their craft in front of the paying public. Something of the same lack of complete control can sometimes be seen in American films using a lot of camera movement at this date, but it does not go so far. When extensive camera movement is used close in to the actors, with panning and tilting as well as tracking, such films now look quite modern in appearance. Examples that spring to mind in 1929 silent films include Jacques Feyder's *The Kiss* and Wilhelm Dieterle's *Ludwig der zweite – König der Bayern*.

Although tracking shots with sync. sound appear in a number of American films made in 1929, for instance besides *Broadway* one could name *The Saturday Night Kid* and *The Virginian*, not to mention the well-publicized instance of *Applause*, still it must be realized that these are all instances of *parallel* tracking shots, in which the camera moves on a straight path with the actors, and without any large panning movements. This is because in nearly all of these instances the camera and operator were inside a glass-fronted camera booth on wheels, and the dimensions of the window to this sound-proof booth (or 'bungalow' or 'ice-box') prevented very large panning or tilting movements. However there *were* some films made in 1928 and 1929 that do show free panning and tilting on tracking shots: films such as *The Singing Fool* (1928), *Hearts in Dixie* (1929), and *Chinatown Nights* (1929). But in these cases the shots in question were taken with an unsynchronized camera, and the sound laid under the shots in the editing.

Of course there were also a number of sound films made in 1928 and 1929 that were shot from fixed camera positions, though not without pans and tilts to keep the actors in frame, but then this was the case for quite a large proportion of American silent films in the late 'twenties also. The noticeable difference was that in the sound films the shots went on far longer while a lot of lines were spoken by static actors. The 'all talking, all singing, all dancing' revue films that were made in 1929 and 1930 were a special case which were indeed filmed almost entirely in Long Shot with a totally fixed camera. But if one makes a rough addition of all the cases, one finds that in fact there was remarkably little discontinuity in the use of camera movement across the transition to sound in Hollywood; what discontinuity there was mostly existed in other dimensions of the medium. The use of the mobile camera in their early sound films by such second and third rank talents as Eddie Sutherland (*The Saturday Night Kid*) and Paul Sloane (*Hearts in Dixie*) attests to the vigour with which a burgeoning fashion could be pursued in the face of technical obstacles.

Lenses

Lenses of focal length even shorter than 25 mm. were tentatively tried out in the late 'twenties in various countries, though they all had rather poor optical performance. In France a 14 mm. lens called a 'brachyscope' was used by Abel Gance on *Napoléon* to cover a very wide angle indeed in a tight corner, but it suffered from severe distortion and very poor definition round the edges. The next year it was used in a rather more rational way by L'Herbier in *l'Argent* to suggest a subjective effect of shock in a Close Up. In America Clarence Brown also used a very wide-angle lens – about 20 mm. I would judge – in a similar way in a scene showing a young man in an alcoholic stupor in *A Woman of Affairs* (1928), though in this case the shot was a Full Shot. This latter film also includes an interesting use of a 25 mm. lens to get a semi-'deep focus' effect. A pair of handcuffs are held up in the foreground by a detective at Close Up distance, and sharp focus is carried from them back to the man who is about to be arrested standing in Medium Long Shot in the background. This amount of depth of field under these circumstances is quite compatible with the shot being filmed at an aperture of about f2.8.

Another film which makes even more extensive use of wide-angle lens filming than any of those so far mentioned is Grémillon's *Gardiens de phare* (1929), where something like a 25 mm. lens is used extensively on both exteriors and interiors. On the interiors many of these shots are also high or low angles, and taken together with the large amount of white in the sets this makes the film look rather like something made twenty years later.

The first experimental models of what was to be called the 'zoom' lens appeared in this period. These had a number of shortcomings, in particular that their maximum aperture was only about f11, which made them difficult to use for studio work, or even for exterior shooting under poor light. As well as that, their focus had to be adjusted at the same time as the focal length was changed with the 'zoom' control. Although these experimental zoom lenses were not taken up for general film-making, there are a number of American films from 1926 onwards which contain one or two zoom shots, nearly all made at Paramount studios, such as *The Grand Duchess and the Waiter*. The exception is *After Midnight* (1926) made at MGM, but since the director, Monta Bell, had Paramount connections, the same lens may have been used. Most of these examples don't do anything special with the zoom effect, but in *It* (Clarence Badger, 1927), there is a striking zoom out from a sign on the top of a department store, followed by a tilt down and zoom in on the front entrance.

Lens Diffusion

By 1926 the use of lens diffusion had become so common that Kodak was selling ready-made sets of diffusion filters producing various amounts of diffusion. However some cameramen were not satisfied with such simple means, and started using a glass plate smeared with vaseline in front of the lens. In the example illustrated from *Love* (1926), which was photographed by William Daniels, the streaky softening of the image round the edge was created (I think), by leaving a clear area in the centre of the frame and stroking the vaseline outwards radially towards the edges. This is a relatively re-strained example from the period; other cameramen went much further. Charles Rosher had a special lens – the Rosher Kino Portrait – designed for him, and this produced a rather similar effect of progressive softening of the image towards the edges, and can be seen used in *Tempest* (1928). On the whole however, by 1929 there were signs that the extremes of lens diffusion were being abandoned in both sound and silent films. This was connected with the increasing use of camera movement, which also caused the last traces of vignetting to be dropped. As well as that, there was a school of thought in the studios around 1929 and 1930 which considered that lens diffusion should be dropped entirely in sound films, as the 'realism' added by synchronous sound filming supposedly demanded that everything in the image be sharply visible, just as it was all now sharply audible. This idea had only a limited and passing influence.

Vignette Masks

As more and more panning and tracking shots came to be used in the last silent films, and more panning and framing movements in sound films, the use of soft black semi-transparent vignette masks round the edges of the frame rapidly vanished. This was because, as I have already mentioned in connection with Murnau's use of masking, the way that moving objects showed through the masks drew attention to their presence. However there were still a number of films being shot with a mostly static camera, and in these one still finds some use of soft circular vignette masks just coming into the corners of the frame, as in *The Crowd* (1928).

The Dunning Process

It seems probable that the Dunning process was the first really successful travelling matte process in which the masking effect was generated purely photographically, in contrast to the Williams process where the patented process did not work properly in its photographic form. Although the Dunning process was only fully described and patented in 1928, there were reports of a two-negative travelling matte process in which the foreground action was shot in front of a blue backing being operated in 1926, and this may well have been an early form of the Dunning process. My uncertainty about this point really results from the obsessive secrecy about the technical side of all sorts of special processes, including colour, that existed in those days.

In any case, in the Dunning process as described, the background scene that had to be combined into one shot with the foreground action was shot first in the ordinary way, and then from the resulting negative a special positive print called the 'Dunning plate' had to be produced. The exact details of the preparation of this positive were never revealed, but it was described as consisting of red positive images of the back-

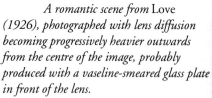

A romantic scene from Love *(1926), photographed with lens diffusion becoming progressively heavier outwards from the centre of the image, probably produced with a vaseline-smeared glass plate in front of the lens.*

ground scene made by dye-toning an ordinary positive, which simultaneously contained negative images of the same scene in black and white. The actors whose actions were to be combined with the background scene then performed in front of a blue backing sheet illuminated with white light, while being filmed with a camera loaded with a double layer of film passing through it. This double layer of film was made up of the Dunning plate in front of the unexposed panchromatic negative on which the final combined image was to be produced, the two films forming a sandwich or 'bipack'. The stated effect of doing all this was that the blue light from the backing sheet printed a negative image of the background from the red positive, which was opaque to the blue light in the appropriate places, but no image from the background was produced where the actors blocked the blue light from the lens. On the other hand the actors, being illuminated with white light (which contains a component of red light) would reflect this red light from their costumes and faces, and it would pass through the red image sections of the Dunning plate without being affected by them. In the area of the image occupied by the actors only a very weak image of the background scene would be produced by the blue light component of the white light reflected from the actors. This very weak image must have been balanced out by the effect of the black and white negative image component of the Dunning plate, though on the face of it, it would seem to have been more logical to have illuminated the actors with red light separately from the white light illumination of the background.

Whatever the process used to produce them, travelling matte shots made in the late 'twenties continued to show either black lines round the actors ('minuses'), as in *My Best Girl*, or alternatively some print-through of the background scene.

Microphones

In the first days of sound, complex scenes were recorded with multiple microphones scattered about the set in fixed positions, most of them being suspended over the actors by a network of ropes, but with some also hidden behind props, as colourful anecdote has it. The electrical signals from these microphones were mixed and passed to the disc or film recorder. Nearly all the microphones used for film sound recording for the first several years were of the capacitor ('condenser') type, and worked on the same principles as modern capacitor microphones. However they were far larger, and had to have an amplifier unit weighing several pounds right next to the diaphragm unit which actually responded to the sound waves and produced the initial electrical signal. Also they were all omni-directional; that is, they responded equally to sounds coming from every direction. For this reason they had to be as close to the actors as possible, to reduce the level of any small background sounds relative to the actor's voices, but even so, incidental sounds such as bacon frying and feet crunching on gravel came through rather louder than was usual several years later, when such noises were either post-

synchronized as sound effects, or entirely eliminated in the way the scene was staged.

The first generation of microphones had a frequency response from 50 Hertz to 7 kiloHertz (50 to 7000 cycles per second), but although this was a restricted range by recent standards, it was about as much as could pass through later links in the sound reproducing chain and be put out into the cinema auditorium. The microphone response also had a hump around 4 to 5 kiloHertz, and the extra emphasis this gave to frequencies in this range may have had an adverse effect on certain kinds of voices, and thus helped to end some actors' careers.

It seems that experiments were very quickly made in moving microphones about above the actors to keep them close when the actors moved, at first by manipulating the sets of ropes suspending them, and then in 1929 with the first crude improvised microphone booms.

Sound Film Systems

Restricting my attention as usual to the technology that was commercially applied to actual films, and ignoring all the experimental attempts which can be studied elsewhere, I can say that the position as regards sound systems being used in the American studios in May 1928, when sound films started to be produced in appreciable numbers, was that M.G.M., Paramount, United Artists, Warner Brothers, and Universal had adopted the Western Electric system, R.K.O. had adopted the R.C.A. Photophone system, and Fox the Movietone system. All these systems offered the alternative in the cinemas of projection from a sound-on-film track or from discs, and all were compatible in the two modes. Other than this, the Movietone system was essentially similar to the Western Electric system except for the light valve used in the sound recording camera, and the only difference these two had from the R.C.A. Photophone system was in the nature of the sound track on the film itself.

Sound on Disc Recording

Initially in 1927 in *The Jazz Singer*, *Lights of New York*, et al, recording and reproduction of film sound was done solely from discs. The electrical signals coming from the microphones on the set were recorded onto wax discs in the same way as for the making of gramophone records at that period, but although the discs for film recording ran at 78 revolutions per minute, they were 16 inches in diameter and the grooves were cut from the centre outwards, and so they ran for 10 minutes on their single side. The disc cutting machines were locked in synchronism with the cameras since both were driven by synchronous motors powered by the same alternating current source. Up to 1928 it was customary to shoot a scene, or part of a scene, with several cameras running simultaneously for its whole length, which was made as long as was reasonably possible. The usual arrangement was to have the cameras arranged in an arc around one side of the scene, with two of them covering it in Long Shot from different directions, and two or three more with long lenses covering each of the principal actors in Medium Shot or Close Up. A number of identical wax discs of the sound were cut simultaneously so that one could be preserved for making the master from which to press the shellac discs for distribution with the finished film, and the others could be used for immediate playback to check the sound quality and the actor's vocal performances.

The use of multiple camera booths in 1928, 1929, and also to some extent in 1930 forced the use of longer focal length lenses than had been usual before to get some of the shots. For instance, in the years mentioned, a Medium Shot would quite probably be taken with a 75 mm. lens rather than the usual 50 mm. lens, and consequently the depth of field was even further reduced, becoming so shallow that everything but the actor was conspicuously out of focus. With the appearance of blimped cameras it was once more possible to get the camera, fitted with any lens, closer to the actors again, and so this extreme shallowness of depth of field disappeared.

Sound-On-Film Recording

The only essential difference between sound-on-film recording and disc recording was the replacement of the disc cutting machine by a sound recording camera. In the sound camera the sound track was recorded photographically down a length of negative of the usual dimensions, just inside the sprocket holes on one side, in the position it was to occupy on the final print. The emulsion coated onto sound film negative was of a special fine-grain high contrast type, and it was given special high contrast development. The sound recording camera was similar in layout to the ordinary American studio cameras used for filming the picture, with a detachable 1000 foot magazine on top, and the film driven through toothed sprockets just like those in the Mitchell and Bell & Howell cameras. But instead of being pulled through a film gate by an intermittent claw mechanism, the sound negative was guided by a set of rollers to wrap around the circumference of a smooth drum, which was attached by a shaft through a high quality bearing to a small flywheel driven freely by the friction of the film round the drum. This last device was absolutely essential to the satisfactory functioning of the sound camera, as the inertia of the freely running flywheel in its turn smoothed out the irregularities in the motion of the film, which were due to the engagement and disengagement of the sprocket drive teeth with the sprocket holes in the film 96 times per second. This film transport smoothing mechanism was patented by the German Tri-ergon company, and all other creators of sound systems had to buy a license from them to design a satisfactory sound camera.

It was at a point on this smoothing drum that a thin transverse slit of light as wide as the sound track was focussed to produce the image on the sound track as the film moved past it. This beam of light came from a light source called the 'light valve' or 'galvanometer', and it was varied or modulated in different ways depending on the system being used. In the

R.C.A. Photophone system the width of the beam was varied by the varying electrical signal, and so produced the black sound-track band of oscillating width characteristic of the R.C.A. system. In the other two systems the width of the beam of light through the slit was constant, and its brightness was varied, so giving rise to the full width pattern of transverse stripes made up of varying grey tones that can still be seen in modern Western Electric recordings. After the sound track negative was exposed and developed, a positive print was made of it for editing purposes.

Sound Editing

At first the editing of sound films was a matter of selecting the required parts of several simultaneous takes from each of the cameras that had been running for the whole length of the scene, and then relocating them in sequence to make up the edited picture track. This final edited picture track had to be exactly the same length as the individual camera takes, because that was how long the single sound recording corresponding to them was unalterably, as sections could not be cut out of the disc recording. The tool developed to keep the multiple picture tracks in synchronism during the editing process was the synchronizer, and this is still used in its original form, but for the different purpose of negative cutting (U.S. 'conforming'). It is now referred to as a mute or silent synchronizer, to distinguish it from the modified form with added sound heads now used for sound track editing. The original synchronizer was just a series of large sprocket wheels, each exactly one foot (16 frames) in circumference, rigidly attached one behind the other on a common axle. The synchronous picture tracks were fed from a series of spools on a winding arm at one end of the editing bench, over the appropriate sprocket wheel while held against it by rollers, and then to a series of take-up spools, one for each picture track, on another winding arm at the other end of the editing bench. By cutting out and transferring equal length sections from one picture track to another before the film passed through the synchronizer, it was possible to build up the desired series of shots on the front track, just as is now done when editing multiple *sound* tracks. Since in those days two frames were lost from the film every time a section was cut out and rejoined, considerable care was needed to avoid a mistake that would lose synchronism.

Although in principle this method gave the flexibility to make as many cuts as desired from one camera angle to another within a scene shot with multiple cameras, in practice the difficulties mentioned were a strong disincentive to the use of fast cutting in the first sound films. In fact it can be observed that the mean Average Shot Length for American films roughly doubled with the coming of sound, as can be seen by checking the figures for this variable I have quoted elsewhere. The change can also be sharply observed within any of the early sound films that have large sections shot 'wild' (i.e. without sound) and then post-synchronized. For instance in *The Singing Fool* (1928), the sections shot wild have an Average Shot Length of less than 4 seconds, as was quite common for the last American silent films, but the sections shot with full synchronous sound have an A.S.L. of 10 seconds. This latter figure is again quite typical for early sound films, though many are a lot slower than that.

The method of editing synchronous sound films that I have outlined above began to change in 1929, in part because some of the more accomplished directors began to shoot sound with a single camera, running it for only the length of the shot that they knew they required in the final film – they were 'cutting in the camera'. Then they simply assembled these individual shots in the correct order together with their equal lengths of sound track to give the finished separate picture and sound tracks. Something like this process produced such films as von Sternberg's *Thunderbolt* (1929), but this was only possible when the studio concerned had decided to abandon the issue of their films with sound-on-disc recording. This began to happen in 1929, though Warner Brothers continued to make their films available in an alternative sound-on-disc version for a couple more years.

Post-Synchronization

The addition of music and effects (i.e. noises) to a film shot silent had been practised from the very beginning of the sound cinema with the sound track added to *Don Juan* (1926), although in that case the synchronization was not very exact. By 1928 it was quite common to add music and effects to sections of a sound film that had been shot silent, and this was done, as it still is, by projecting the section of the film in question, and recording the musicians and effects-makers performing to match the action in the film on a recorder synchronized with the projector. The mixing of sounds from different recorded sources into a combined new recording was tried out from almost the beginning of sound movies. In 1927 disc recordings of sound effects and music were mixed and re-recorded onto disc for the last reel of *In Old San Francisco*, and after that there were sometimes more elaborate mixes of this kind used for sections of sound films. However, this was a quite tricky process, and was avoided as much as possible.

Synchronization to Playback

In 1929 the inverse process was used in the filming of the musical *Sunny*. In this case the musicians and performers recorded a disc or sound track of the musical numbers first, and then mimed the appropriate lip movements etc. to the sounds played back from the sound track, while they were filmed with cameras locked in synchronism with the playback machine. However not all musicals were made in this way after this first appearance of the 'sync. to playback' technique; for a year or so many continued to be made with the musical items shot live and recorded directly in synchronism.

Some Things That Were Done With Sound

For the first couple of years of sound cinema quite a number of Hollywood directors made experiments with the novel formal effects that the new dimension made possible.

These were such things as the way the title and credits for *The Terror* (Roy del Ruth, 1928) were spoken by the shadow of a masked man, and the way a final 'Well folks, that's all there is.' was spoken directly to the audience in *Caught in the Fog* (Howard Bretherton, 1928). *The Bellamy Trial* (Monta Bell, 1929) starts with a documentary sequence, and then goes straight into the narrative without any credits, and so on. Other examples of such devices are described in Alexander Walker's *The Shattered Silents* (Elm Tree Books, 1979), but the most interesting film of the period from this point of view was Cecil B. DeMille's *Dynamite* (1929), which seems almost to be searching for a whole new form for the medium. It contains scenes which are carried through with dialogue from off-screen, a semi-improvised scene, and another in which three layers of diverse sound are continuously superimposed. This last happens in a scene of a wedding taking place in the condemned cell of a prison, with the dialogue of the wedding service combined with a sentimental song sung by a prisoner in another cell, and the sounds of the construction of the scaffold outside. Unfortunately such directorial exuberance quickly died out in the next decade.

Cinema Projection

For the sound-on-disc method of sound film projection the modifications required to the existing models of projectors were fairly simple. The direct current electric motor driving them had to be replaced by an alternating current synchronous motor running on mains electricity, and a special disc turntable had to be added to the back of them driven by a shaft and gearing from the film transport mechanism. Once the needle of the gramophone had been placed on an index mark in the run-in groove of the disc, and the film had been threaded with a special mark on the leader placed exactly in the gate of the projector, the projector could then be started safe in the knowledge that synchronism would be rigidly maintained through the length of the reel, *provided the film did not break*. A film break was unlikely with a print in good condition, but if one should happen there was no way to regain synchronism for the rest of the reel, once the film had been re-threaded in the projector and restarted from the point of the break. Another minor disadvantage of disc sound was the surface noise inherently associated with reproduction from shellac discs. Sound-on-film suffered from none of these disadvantages, and as a further bonus it made possible the return to the projection of 2000 foot reels, as had been standard with silent films for the whole decade.

The modification to projector design for sound-on-film reproduction was also fairly simple. It involved an extension to the film path beneath the projector gate and before the final drive sprocket, along which path it passed around a drum roller attached to a free flywheel similar to that already described in the sound camera. In the projector another thin transverse beam of light was focussed onto a point on this smoothing drum that was exactly twenty and a half frames ahead of the frame in the film gate. This beam of light passed through the sound track in varying amounts depending on the varying density (or varying clear area) of the sound track, and fell on a photoelectric cell on the other side where it excited a current that varied correspondingly. This current was amplified in the usual way and drove the loudspeakers beside the cinema screen. Ways were shortly discovered to make the cinema screen transparent to sound while still reflecting the light of the picture, and then the loudspeakers were placed behind the screen. The same 'sound head' on the projector served equally well for both the variable area sound track system and the variable density ones. Also sound-on-disc and sound-on-film could easily be combined in one dual-purpose projector.

Scene Dissection

The general trends in scene dissection in silent films of the late 'twenties have already been indicated in the previous chapter. To recapitulate, these were that in the American cinema there was only a small increase in the speed of cutting through the decade, though there was fairly certainly a slight tendency by many directors to shoot even closer in as the decade wore on. The Scale of Shot distributions illustrated in

Chapter 12, together with others I have not illustrated, support this subjective impression. Likewise, there was some increase in the use of reverse-angle cutting in American films through the 'twenties, with an overall increase of a few percent in the amount used from the first half of the decade into the second. I think this was not so much a matter of individual directors increasing their use of reverse-angle cutting slightly, as of many directors like Lloyd Ingraham or Herbert Blaché who stayed with the older Griffith style being removed from their chairs. These generalizations only apply to silent films, for at first there was a sharp reduction in the amount of reverse-angle cutting in the early sound films. Here are some figures for the use of reverse-angles in silent films of the 'twenties, drawn from a collection that includes another couple of hundred. Incidentally, all the indications are that there are no strongly preferred values for the amount of reverse-angle cutting used in any period, unlike the case for Average Shot Lengths, where the distributions are always strongly peaked.

In European cinema during these years, the conscious process of 'Americanization' lead to progressive changes in the treatment of the stylistic variables which has also been men-

Fool's Gold	1920	Trimble, Larry	10%
The New York Idea	1920	Blache, Herbert	7%
Why Change Your Wife?	1920	De Mille, Cecil B.	19%
The Affairs of Anatole	1921	De Mille, Cecil B.	23%
Tol'able David	1921	King, Henry	24%
Without Limit	1921	Baker, George D.	12%
The Girl in the Taxi	1922	Ingraham, Lloyd	9%
Hungry Hearts	1922	Hopper, E. Mason	19%
The Lure of Gold	1922	Hart, Neal	18%
The Marriage Circle	1924	Lubitsch, Ernst	28%
The Iron Horse	1924	Ford, John	8%
Lady Windermere's Fan	1925	Lubitsch, Ernst	23%
Smouldering Fires	1925	Brown, Clarence	24%
The Goose Woman	1925	Brown, Clarence	28%
Stella Dallas	1925	King, Henry	17%
Sun-Up	1925	Goulding, Edmund	9%
Mantrap	1926	Fleming, Victor	22%
The Son of the Sheik	1926	Fitzmaurice, George	15%
The Winning of Barbara Worth	1926	King, Henry	17%
The Blood Ship	1927	Seitz, George B.	15%
My Best Girl	1927	Taylor, Sam	33%
The Toilers	1928	Barker, Reginald	7%
Die Spinnen(Part 2)	1920	Lang, Fritz	9%
Das Haus am Meer	1923	Kaufman, Fritz	7%
Zur Chronik von Grieshuus	1925	Gerlach, Arthur von	14%
Varieté	1925	Dupont, E.A.	19%
Venus im Frack	1927	Land, Robert	14%
Angst	1928	Steinhoff, Hans	16%
Samson und Delila	1922	Korda, Alexander	11%
Das unbekannte Morgen	1923	Korda, Alexander	15%

The Wonderful Story	1923	Cutts, Graham	15%
The Rat	1925	Cutts, Graham	25%
The Pleasure Garden	1925	Hitchcock, Alfred	14%
The Third Round	1925	Morgan, Sidney	5%
The Lodger	1927	Hitchcock, Alfred	13%
Downhill	1927	Hitchcock, Alfred	25%
Moulin Rouge	1928	Dupont, E.A.	27%
The Ring	1928	Hitchcock, Alfred	24%
The Farmer's Wife	1928	Hitchcock, Alfred	42%
Champagne	1928	Hitchcock, Alfred	30%
The Manxman	1928	Hitchcock, Alfred	31%
Alley Cat	1929	Steinhoff, Hans	10%
l'Arlésienne	1922	Antoine, André	7%
Coeur fidele	1923	Epstein, Jean	14%
Koenigsmark	1923	Perret, Leonce	12%
Violettes impériales	1924	Roussell, Henri	10%
l'Inondation	1924	Delluc, Louis	3%
la Belle Nivernaise	1924	Epstein, Jean	18%
Pierrot/Pierette	1924	Feuillade, Louis	16%
Nêne	1924	Baroncelli, Jacques de	12%
le Miracle des loups	1924	Bernard, Raymond	15%
Pêcheur d'Islande	1924	Baroncelli, Jacques de	12%
Jim la Houlette	1926	Lion, Roger	19%
le Vertige	1926	L'Herbier, Marcel	28%
Michel Strogoff	1926	Tourjansky, Victor	15%
Casanova	1927	Volkoff, Alexandre	21%
Verdun, visions d'histoire	1928	Poirier, Léon	8%
Maldone	1928	Gremillon, Jean	17%
le Tourbillon de Paris	1928	Duvivier, Julien	19%

tioned in the previous chapter. There the way cutting rates increased in European films in the latter part of the 'twenties was demonstrated, and the selection of figures above for the use of reverse angle cutting in European films in the 'twenties gives an indication how this stylistic variable also changed. In particular, you can see how Alfred Hitchcock became very enthusiastic about the device after a couple of years, though his colleague Graham Cutts picked it up first. In fact, Hitchcock had sets with four walls, rather than the usual three, built for *The Farmers Wife*, and it was this that made the very high percentage of reverse angle cuts in that film easier to achieve.

Acting

There were no conspicuous developments in the acting in American silent films during the nineteen-twenties, since a style of only slightly stylized naturalism consistent with the general approach of American cinema had been arrived at in the previous decade. After a little uncertainty from some directors and actors during 1928 and 1929, when there was a some excessive elocution, the style of sound film acting quickly settled into the same approach. In France, and particularly in Germany, the conscious 'Americanization' in other dimensions of the medium was accompanied by a move towards greater naturalism in acting in the latter part of the decade. In this, as in other things, there was a tendency for the better directors to get there first. However there were occasional outcroppings of the earlier melodramatic style, even in the works of such major directors as Fritz Lang and Abel Gance (in *Napoléon*). The latter case may be due to a certain megalomaniac isolation from current events, as indeed may the former, assisted by the fact that Lang had made no films on realistic contemporary subjects through the 'twenties. Also in Germany those leading actors schooled in Expressionist stage acting may have been a little more difficult to shift from the individualistic elaborations of pose and gesture they had developed. Nevertheless the isolated cases of broad acting that occurred in German films of the late 'twenties are always quite well integrated with the nature of the films in question, which could not be said of the acting in Abel Gance's films.

Russian Film Acting

It was only in Russian films that there were any really new developments in acting during the nineteen-twenties. Unlike other features of the new Soviet cinema after 1924, this did not owe very much directly to film developments in the West, but rather stemmed from slightly earlier developments in advanced Soviet stage work. More detail on this point is available elsewhere, so I will just briefly mention Meyerhold's theories of 'Biomechanics' in acting, and the dramatic work of the theatre director Foregger. These lead in their turn to the stage work of the FEKS group (Kozintsev, Trauberg, Yutkevitch, et. al.), and the pre-film-making studies of the Kuleshov group. Sergei Eisenstein in his stage work also had connections with Meyerhold, the FEKS group, and Foregger. Besides having a derivation from popular spectacles and shows, and also from more theoretical conceptions, the novel acting styles evolved by all these Russian groups also owed something to American slapstick comedy of the higher and lower kinds.

The influence from American slapstick comedy shows in some of the films, particularly in the case of the Kuleshov group, which included the future directors Boris Barnet, Sergei Komarov, and V.I. Pudovkin. In the first film directed by Kuleshov with this group, *Neobytchainye prikhoutennaia Mistera Vesta v strane bolchevikov* (1924), the group's acting style can be seen in as extreme a form as it ever reached. The most thorough exponent of the new style was Kuleshov's partner, the actress Olga Khoklova, and she invented the most bizarre poses to express character and psychological states. The novelties of the style lay more in the poses than in the movements joining them, and in subsequent films by Kuleshov this acting style was rapidly diluted in the performances of the actors other than Khoklova. A trace of Khoklova's style also appears in Galina Grauvhenko's performance in Komarov's *Kukla s millionami* (1928).

Despite the word 'eccentrism' heading their program, the acting in the films of the FEKS group was not as idiosyncratic as that in Kuleshov's films, and by the time they made *Shinel* (Kozintsev and Trauberg, 1926) and *S.V.D.* (Kozintsev and

Trauberg, 1927), any special acting style was largely confined to the performances of their leading actor, Sergei Gerassimov. Actually Gerassimov's work in these films looks rather similar to the sort of thing done by some of the best German Expressionist actors in earlier German films, just as the visual aspect of these FEKS films strongly resembles earlier German films.

The influence of Meyerhold's 'Biomechanics' combined with that of the circus and similar popular comedy can occasionally be seen in Eisenstein's silent films in the acrobatic poses struck on ladders and similar constructions from *Stachka* (1924) onwards. A particularly striking moment in this vein is the grotesque series of positions that the mechanic delivering the new tractor in *Staroye i novoye* (1929) gets into all over it when it breaks down.

By the end of the 'twenties Soviet acting had begun to develop a few special clichés of its own, the most tiresome of which is the proletarian glare from under the eyebrows with head slightly lowered – and of course directed at the class enemy. It can be studied at great length in Pudovkin's films from *Mat* (1926) onwards, not to mention others. This trick lasted into the sound period, but the other styles did not, with the sole isolated exception of the acting in Kuleshov's *Velikii uteshitel* (1933).

Another major innovation in acting in Russian films during this period was the use of non-actors – ordinary people untrained in acting – in prominent roles in some of the better known films, not to mention in crowd scenes. And in one or two cases, such as Eisenstein's *Staroye i novoye*, even in the leading role. When one also notes that such non-actors performed without make-up, and in their ordinary clothes, it is not surprising that there was some tendency in the West in this period to think of the films concerned as documentaries rather than fiction films. Even despite the move towards greater naturalism in some German films from 1925 onwards,

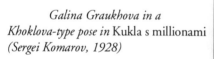
Galina Graukhova in a Khoklova-type pose in Kukla s millionami *(Sergei Komarov, 1928)*

nothing so extreme in this respect had been produced in Western Europe at this date.

The limitations of non-actors fitted in well with the tendency of Eisenstein's style towards the use of relatively static images, and in any case he had evolved a theory of 'typage' which required the use of actors whose basic appearance crystallized the essence of the characters they were playing, and their roles in the drama. This theory was really only an extension of the well-established Hollywood practice of type-casting, and in this it resembled other Soviet theories about other aspects of the cinema. Nevertheless the fact that it *was* an extension in theory and practice had significant results in a few films. The majority of Russian films of this period did not use non-actors, and for obvious reasons the practice did not survive the introduction of sound.

The Kuleshov Effect

Kuleshov formulated the idea in the early 'twenties that different feelings would be attributed to an actor according to the nature of whatever object he was shown looking at, by means of a cut from an expressionless Close Up of his face to a Point of View shot of the object in question. It has been questioned whether this idea was ever put to the test by Kuleshov and his associates, but be that as it may, the source of the idea was his close analysis of the new American films that became available in Russia during the First World War, just as he became involved in film-making. As previously noted, most of these films had developed the use of a large proportion of POV shots, to an extent that was unknown in Europe at the time. There were no American theories about the use of this device, as it had evolved gradually without conscious thought over the previous decade. Much the same could be said of another of Kuleshov's ideas, which had to do with the possibility of creating an apparently continuous but actually synthetic space, by cutting together a series of shots taken at different times and places and joining them with action continuity. This latter idea was even less remarkable, since it had been used in practice even in European films since near the beginning of the century, but here, as with the 'Kuleshov effect' proper, the fact that it had been explicitly formulated led to novel extensions in film-making practice, but not by Kuleshov or his group. For the curious thing is that Kuleshov's own films make absolutely no use of the 'Kuleshov effect' that goes any way beyond standard practice in Western films. However, it may well be that his ideas influenced Sergei Eisenstein in his practical investigations of the novel effects that might be obtained by the juxtaposition of wildly disparate shots, and subsequently his theories about this practice. Incidentally, there is now evidence that the hypothetical 'Kuleshov effect' does not exist. The details of a recent experiment on this point by Stephen Prince and Robert E. Hensley can be read in *Cinema Journal* (Vol. 31, No. 2, Winter 1992). This does not surprise me very much, since I have long believed that the emotional effect that movies have on audiences depends in the first place on the nature of what is represented

in the individual shots, and that the limited range of purely filmic devices, such as POV shots, only act as intensifiers of this shot content to a limited extent.

About Eisenstein

Sergei Eisenstein's first film, *Stachka* (1924), lacks most of the distinctive features that his style was to develop over the next few years, but it does contain a number of devices adopted from the earlier advanced cinema of the West, such as expressive superimpositions and elaborate irises and wipes, which were to be dropped from his later films. The extensive use of high and low-angles is already present, as is the emphasis on mass movement, but Eisenstein's special way of putting shots together is not yet really apparent. If one looks closely, one can see scattered throughout the film individual instances of the kind of discontinuity between shots that he was later to exploit extensively, but in this film they only occur in the way that Inserts of details that are not closely connected with the surrounding shots are cut into an otherwise normally constructed scene. One example of this is the repeated Insert of thrown tools hitting the floor, which is cut into the scene of the workmen leaving the factory at the beginning of the strike, without there being any shot of the workmen actually throwing the tools. In *Stachka* there is also a fair amount of lack of continuity from scene to scene which has had to be bridged by awkwardly placed explanatory titles, but this must be due to inexperience, haste, and lack of resources.

In his next film, *Bronenosets Potyomkin* (1925), Eisenstein developed much further the repetition of shots within a sequence to produce visual rhythms, but this is sufficiently well-known to excuse me discussing it. I will just remark that what Eisenstein was doing from this point onwards seems to be a conscious development from the effects of discontinuity and resulting contrasts between shots that had tentatively appeared in *Stachka*, reinforced by the examples of highly discontinuous cutting he had observed in D.W. Griffith's films and Abel Gance's *la Roue*. His theories about his particular approach to film construction which were written down in 1929 can be read in English in *Film Form* (Harcourt, Brace and Company, 1949). In 1929 Eisenstein called his basic concept the 'montage of conflicts', and this related to various kinds of strong contrasts between the features of two adjoining shots on either side of a cut, and also to strong visual contrasts within a single shot. In the case of the 'conflict' between shots, even when this was not directly related to the purely visual qualities of the two shots, as was the case for his category of 'intellectual conflict' between shots, the result was still to produce a strong visual contrast between them most of the time.

With Eisenstein's next film, *Oktyabr* (1928), the full exploitation of the 'montage of conflicts' produced a film that was almost entirely moved forwards by the way a series of nearly static but highly disparate shots succeeded one another. The success of this technique depended to a considerable extent on the use of a very short Average Shot Length, down to 3 seconds in the case of *Oktyabr*. Though this was shorter than that of the fastest cut American films, which did not go below 3.5 seconds, the *narrative* pace in this and other Soviet films of the late 'twenties was much slower than that in American films. Of course in American films most of the cuts were continuity cuts rather than Eisenstein's strong 'discontinuity' cuts. The effect was heightened in his films by the use of sections where the cutting speeded up to give strings of shots each only several frames long, but this was counter-balanced by other sections where all the shots were very long. Since in these latter sections the shots also tend to be static, some people find the effect rather wearing. In the films he made through into the nineteen-thirties Eisenstein stayed with this style, ignoring the contemporary fashion for the moving camera that had developed in the West.

The use of sections of very fast cutting became a fashion in the Russian cinema of the end of the 'twenties, but most of the other novice directors who took it up applied it without Eisenstein's talent, and it adds nothing whatever to their films, as can be seen in Ilya Trauberg's *Goluboi ekspress* (1930). On the other hand, there were directors such as Fyodor Otsep and Yakov Protazanov working in Russia in the late 'twenties who ignored all this, and made perfectly conventional movies, though their work lacked the final polish of Western films in most dimensions of the medium.

In fact the major factor necessary to the success of Eisenstein's use of almost static shots was the graphic quality of Eisentein's individual images. These had the same kind of characteristic outline shapes that he produced in his drawings, both those made for film purposes, and those made independently of this. That Eisenstein's silent films work in the way I have indicated is conclusively demonstrated by the reconstructed version of *Bezhin Lug* (1935) produced in 1967 by Sergei Yutkevitch. After Eisenstein's death all that existed of this film, which had been banned on completion, were short clips several frames long from every shot of it, and these

were extended as still frames by step-printing, and then edited together in script order with a music track. I judge the result to be very nearly as effective as Eisenstein's original films.

Modern Art and Image Composition

The ferment in advanced art in the nineteen-twenties had very little visible effect on the static composition of film images, apart from the truly avant-garde cinema made by established artists like Fernand Léger and Man Ray. The handful of German Expressionist films in which the shots were completely pre-designed by the art director have already been mentioned, but apart from this there is little else that is not a matter of set design, as in the Martian scenes of Protazanov's *Aelita* (1924). The main exception to this generalization again involves the Russian films of the late 'twenties. Apart from those of Eisenstein, even films by secondary figures like Boris Barnet occasionally contain an image produced purely by camera placement, rather than by pre-designing, which would not have been created but for the influence of the visual art of the early nineteen-twenties in Russia. An obvious example of this is the still that is always used to illustrate Abram Room's *Prividenyie, kotoroye ne vozvrash-chayetsya* (*The Ghost That Never Returns*, 1930). Such direct influence of advanced painting on film composition was not to reappear till the nineteen-sixties.

There is however another individual case of the influence of advanced art on image composition in mainstream films of the 'twenties, and this is in the films of Fritz Lang. As early as 1919 one can occasionally see in Lang's films the use of strongly marked crossing diagonal lines in the composition that derive from the geometrical abstract painting that had begun to appear at the end of the war. Major figures in this development in abstract art included Lazlo Moholy-Nagy, and in fact when Moholy-Nagy turned to the photography of real scenes about 1924 he used the same sort of compositions that Lang was sometimes already using in his films.

15. FILM STYLE AND TECHNOLOGY IN THE THIRTIES

There were no major changes in the industrial organization of American film production during the nineteen-thirties. The sharp fall in public attendance at the cinemas during 1932 and 1933 produced severe financial problems for the major companies, and although they all recovered as the decade wore on, this experience may have contributed to the marked decline in innovation in stylistic details after the first few years of the 'thirties. Within the film companies the already existing trend towards a closer control of the details of the film-making process through a hierarchical structure of production supervisors or producers steadily continued. I will have a little more to say about that later. The general situation in the other major Western film-producing countries was similar during the 'thirties, but not in quite such a marked way. American films continued to dominate foreign markets, either in specially made foreign language versions for the first couple of years, or later in subtitled and dubbed form until the very end of the decade, when they were excluded from some countries by political action.

Film Stock and Processing

At the beginning of the nineteen-thirties the most commonly used negative stock continued to be the Eastman Kodak panchromatic negative of the type introduced in 1928, but similar negative materials were available from Agfa, Dupont, and Pathé. All these were slow emulsions that were still used as though they had a speed of around 20 ASA in present-day terms. The Russian film industry was still using orthochromatic negative in 1930, but a year or two later they finally began to use panchromatic film. The faster Agfa negative which was already available, and the new Eastman Supersensitive Negative which became available in 1931, were not in general use in Hollywood except for filming the odd largish-scale night exterior, but Jacques Feyder's *Daybreak* (1931) was one film that was entirely shot on Supersensitive negative. As one might expect, the images in this film have slightly less contrast and rather more graininess than those in films shot on standard negative, and this point must have been what prevented the greater use of Supersensitive stock. Eastman Supersensitive Negative was the first camera stock to have an anti-halation backing applied to the cellulose nitrate base on the opposite side from the emulsion. This opaque grey

backing prevented extra-bright beams of light being reflected back into the emulsion after they had passed through it once, which would produce a halo of scattered light around very bright parts of the image, such as street lamps in a night exterior. The anti-halation backing on Eastman Supersensitive was dissolved off during the developing process so that it did not interfere with the printing process, and eventually, over the next several years, all camera negative came to be manufactured with anti-halation backing. In the early 'thirties photography on interiors continued to be at maximum aperture, which was between f2 and f2.5, depending on the make of lenses in use.

New improved duplicating negative and positive stocks were made available by Kodak in 1930 and 1933 respectively, and these were directly connected with the developments in optical printing that will be discussed below. The duplicating negative and positive stocks were improved yet again in 1936, but I have seen definite signs that the French and German industries did not benefit from these or similar improvements. Throughout the 'thirties the dissolves, etc., in French and German films look much more grainy and contrasty than those in Hollywood films, so presumably they were made using inferior local duplicating stocks. The same applies to the negatives used to shoot background scenes for back projection or travelling mattes in European films, which are noticeably grainy and of poorer definition than American examples. In 1933 Eastman Kodak had introduced a special Eastman Background Negative in the United States for these purposes, in response to the rise of background projection, but apparently European film-makers had to go on using ordinary negative to shoot the film used for background projection. (Film shots used for background projection are called background plates). Eastman Background Negative had very fine grain, and this made it possible to obtain shots whose graininess would not be evident on the new giant background projection (B.P.) screens. This was a case where the demand very definitely produced the technical development, but in fact the causal chain can be traced back even further to the exigencies of sound recording at this time.

In 1934 Agfa-Ansco introduced their 32 ASA Superpan negative to the American market, and the next year Kodak riposted with Super X which had a speed of approximately 40

ASA. These new stocks had better definition than their predecessors, but the decisive innovations occurred in 1938, when Eastman Kodak introduced Plus X and Super XX with speeds equivalent to 80 ASA and 160 ASA respectively, and Agfa introduced Supreme and Ultrapan (64 ASA and 120 ASA). Of these negative materials, Plus X immediately proved the most popular, for it gave definition comparable to the earlier slow stock for the first time, and in fact the vast majority of Hollywood films were shot with it for many years afterwards. But in most cases in the late 'thirties the extra two stops of speed that Plus X gave were not used to stop down by that amount from the usual maximum lens aperture, and so secure increased depth of field. On the contrary, the major effect of the switch to Plus X was that light levels on the sets were reduced: in 1937 typical values were 250 to 400 foot-candles for black and white film, and 800 to 1000 foot-candles for Technicolor, while in 1940 typical values were 75 to 150 foot-candles for black and white and 150 to 400 foot-candles for Technicolor. These lower light levels reduced the heat on the set, and made working conditions more comfortable, particularly for the actors.

But at some of the major studios not all of the speed advantage of the new stocks was absorbed in this way. A common approach was to slightly over-expose them rather than use them with the light level intended by the maker for a given aperture. This over-exposure was then compensated for by giving the negative reduced development, and this finally resulted in a flatter (less contrasty) print, so that there were more middle greys in the image, and fewer true blacks and whites. M.G.M. and R.K.O. were the studios which went furthest in this direction, and all in all this practice was responsible for the distinctively pearly grey look of many late 'thirties films when compared with those of the early 'thirties. But there was one studio which used part of the extra speed in quite a different way. At Twentieth Century-Fox the extra

speed of Plus X *was* partly used to film at slightly reduced aperture. About the end of 1938 a rigid policy was instituted there to film everything at f3.5 on interior sets. The reason for this policy is so far unknown to me, but its result was that from that date onwards Twentieth Century-Fox films have a slightly greater depth of field, and also a slightly greater image sharpness than those from other studios, at any rate until the latter began to change their photographic practices several years later. A minor unfortunate side effect of this use of reduced aperture was that it made it difficult to integrate background projection invisibly into a studio scene, as the B.P. screen tended to be sharply in focus in the more distant shots, whereas this had not been the case previously with the larger lens aperture. This can be seen in *Frontier Marshall* (1939), and other films.

The major long-range effect of this studio rule at Twentieth Century-Fox may have been through Gregg Toland's experiences when he went there to photograph *The Grapes of Wrath* at the end of 1939. More will be said on this matter in the next chapter, but briefly I note that in one or two shots in this film there is a noticeably large depth of field, though advantage is not really taken of this in staging the action. In the shots concerned, the depth of field corresponds to the use of a moderately wide-angle lens of about 28 mm. focal length shooting at the standard Fox studio aperture of f3.5, but they are the kind of shots in which a wide-angle lens would have been used by any cameraman to photograph a large studio set filling most of the sound stage. I can only think the unsought for result must have taken Gregg Toland's fancy, for before this there was no sign of extra depth of field in his work, and after it he alone went on to strive for even greater depth in *Citizen Kane*. Other cameramen who had similar experiences at Twentieth Century-Fox clearly did not think further about the matter, just as those who had inadvertently produced the same results for the same reasons in the odd shot in the

A wide-angle lens shot taken by Gregg Toland on a studio set in The Grapes of Wrath *(1939), in which the depth of field extends from just in front of the foreground figure to more than sixty feet away.*

A set with solid ceiling representing the interior of a roadside lunchroom in The Grapes of Wrath, *which has been lit solely from the front with two lights on floor stands.*

'twenties had not. Incidentally, *The Grapes of Wrath* has a scene in a roadside lunch-room which is shot on a set with a low and visible ceiling, and this set is lit solely by floodlights on floor stands, though there is no noticeable use of a wide-angle lens.

In the late 'thirties manufacturers finally began to give speed ratings to their film stocks using the Weston system, for by this date the use of exposure meters was becoming quite common when shooting exteriors, though not when shooting interiors in black and white. The Technicolor Corporation insisted on foot-candle meters being used to determine the light levels when exposing Technicolor both on exteriors and in studio interiors, and the increasing familiarity of leading cameramen with Technicolor filming, as well as the difficulty of coping with the new and changing range of black and white stocks helped to promote the use of exposure meters of one kind or another.

(The Weston photoelectric reflected-light meter had been available from the beginning of the 'thirties, as had the General Electric incident-light foot-candle meter, and also the Bell & Howell spot photometer. This last instrument measured the absolute brightness of a small area of the scene by comparison with a standard source, and was very similar to the still-available S.E.I. photometer.)

Two-Colour Technicolor and Other Two-Colour Systems

In the early 'thirties there was a large increase in the number of films that were shot wholly or in part with the two-colour Technicolor process. This continued to be carried out in the form established in 1928 using a special Technicolor camera with a beam-splitting prism producing the red and green images simultaneously on two frames of a single strip of panchromatic negative. The gelatine relief matrices were made as before, and the dye transfer or imbibition process also

carried out as earlier, but around 1930 a change was made to printing on blank film with the emulsion on one side only, rather than the film with emulsion on both sides that had been used before. There seems to have been a fair amount of improvement in the system over this period, mostly as regards definition – *Mystery of the Wax Museum* (1933) has quite sharp images when compared to say *King of Jazz* and other early Technicolor films. Graininess and contrast were also somewhat reduced, though still remaining higher than with black and white film. (Of course when considering prints of the early 'thirties it is important to take into account their history of being copied; original prints are more or less unobtainable.) The speed of the negative stock used in shooting Technicolor was now effectively half that of ordinary black and white negative, taking into account the light losses in the beam-splitting prism and the filters in the Technicolor camera. The slow film speed called for about twice as much light as ordinarily used for black and white filming, and then this requirement was doubled again, because the fastest lens available for the Technicolor camera had a maximum aperture of f3.2.

All the other two-colour processes employed commercially in the early 'thirties: Multicolor, Magnacolor, Harriscolor, etc., etc., were in fact essentially the Prizmacolor process of the late 'twenties, whatever they were named. This process continued to be carried out by exposing bipack negative in an ordinary camera (Mitchell or Bell & Howell) modified to take the double thickness of film in the gate, and with a double magazine formed by mounting a second magazine on top of the existing one. The two films fed emulsion to emulsion through the gate, the front film being orthochromatic to record the blue-green component of the image, and the back one being panchromatic with a red-orange filter layer on its surface so that it recorded only the red-orange component of the image. Printing was done from the two negatives in succession onto the two sides of 'duplitized' print stock specially made for this purpose by Kodak and Dupont. This special stock had an emulsion layer on both sides of the cellulose nitrate base, with one emulsion containing a yellow dye to prevent the second image printing through to it, this yellow dye being dissolved out later. When the duplitized print stock had been developed in the usual way, the silver images in the two emulsions were separately toned by floating the film on the surface of two toning baths, one containing an iron salt to give a blue-green tone, and the other uranium salts for an orange-red tone.

Although this process used ordinary cameras with the full range of lenses, it had its own peculiar drawbacks. The main one of these was that it was impossible to get the two images on either side of the film perfectly in focus at the same time on projection, and the film was also liable to the 'cupping' and wear experienced with the Technicolor film on double-sided stock.

Three-Colour Technicolor

In 1934 the new Technicolor three-colour process was used for the first time in live-action filming to make the short film *La Cucaracha*, and the following year saw the first feature

film in three-colour Technicolor, *Becky Sharp*. The three-colour system was made possible by the introduction of the new special Technicolor three-strip camera, which had a 45 degree split-cube prism behind the lens to produce two images, one of the green part of the spectrum on a panchromatic film directly behind the prism block, and another deviated by 90 degrees onto a bipack of two films with their emulsions in contact in another gate, to record the blue image and the red image respectively. In this second gate carrying the bipack, the light passed through the transparent base of the first film before forming an image in the blue-sensitive emulsion and then through a red filter layer coated onto its surface before forming the red image in the panchromatic emulsion on the second film facing the first. The definition in this image was the least good, since the light had passed through so many layers of material to get there, and this accounts for a tendency to blurriness in the green of foliage shown in filmed scenes. The green colour was principally formed by the cyan (blue-green) dye in the final print, and this was controlled by the inverse densities in the red negative record.

The Technicolor camera was to a certain extent modelled on the Mitchell camera, and was not all that much larger, except that the magazine was three times as wide to accom-

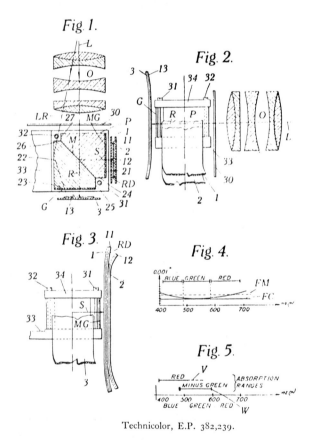

Technicolor, E.P. 382,239.

(**Left**) The Technicolor three-strip camera. (**Right**) The patent application drawing showing the construction of the beam-splitting prism of the three-strip camera. In the plan view of the prism top left 'M' indicates the semi-reflecting coating between the diagonal split surfaces, 'G' indicates a green filter on the back surface of the prism block, and 'MG' indicates a minus-green filter letting all wave lengths but green through to the bipacked films in the other gate, which have a red filter 'RD' coated on the one surface between them.

modate the three rolls of negative side by side. The bipack of two negatives face to face that went through the gate at 90 degrees to the lens axis was formed and separated by rollers on either side of the gate, and the pull-down mechanism in both gates was the Mitchell type, with the same register pin system, etc. Unlike the Mitchell camera there was no rack-over arrangement for rapid through-the-lens viewing of the image, and focussing was usually done by using the scale on the lens, though there was a kind of through-the-lens system involving moving one of the film gates to one side. The larger reliance on the supplementary viewfinder this caused may have produced a tendency towards less precisely composed images in Technicolor when compared with the best black and white photography of the 'thirties and 'forties. It took at least three minutes to change magazines and rethread the film with the Technicolor camera, whereas this could be done in under a minute with the Mitchell camera, so it was the usual practice to have a second Technicolor camera on the set ready threaded so that there would be no halt in production. Such was not the ordinary practice in black and white filming.

Because of the prism block between the back element of the lens and the film gates, ordinary lenses could not be used in the Technicolor camera, and so a special set had to be designed and made by Taylor-Hobson Ltd. The widest angle lens of this set was a 35 mm. f2 lens, and the focal lengths went upwards through a 50 mm. f1.7 lens to one of 140 mm. focal length. In other words there were no wide-angle or very long focal length lenses for Technicolor filming. However at the end of the 'thirties a true wide-angle lens of about 25 mm. focal length was made for the Technicolor camera, and it can be seen used in a few shots in *Gone With The Wind* (1939). These shots are readily recognizable because as well as the usual steep perspective due to the wide-angle reproduction, there is a lot of barrel distortion and some reduced definition in the image. The people concerned must have been well aware of this, and so this lens was only used when a very broad scene had to be encompassed from a limited camera distance.

The Technicolor lens apertures were not calibrated in f-stops, but in a series of special numbers that were related to fixed levels of key-light that had always to be measured on the set with a photo-electric foot-candle meter. In fact, photography in the studio seems to have been carried out at, or near, maximum aperture. In the initial period of the three-colour system the key-light level was set at 800-1000 foot-candles, but in 1939 a new negative stock was introduced and used on *Gone With The Wind*, and this was 2 to 4 times faster than the previous stock, and was considered to have a speed equal to Super X black and white negative, i.e. 40 ASA. The key-light level was now around 250 foot-candles. There was a change in the colour sensitivity of the new negative stocks now used, and the colour filters cemented to back of the beam splitting prism block in the Technicolor camera were no longer necessary, and were removed.

From the beginning, the response of the whole Technicolor three colour system was arranged to give correct colour balance under sunlight, or in the studio under arc lights fitted with 'light straw' coloured filters. Flood lights were used rather more for Technicolor filming than they were in this period for black and white filming, which made for flatter lighting on the whole, but this fitted in well with the usual desire of the producers and of Technicolor to show as much colour as possible in each image. Nevertheless, compared to later years there were a fair number of films made up to the beginning of the 'forties such as *The Garden of Allah* (Richard Boleslawski, 1936), *A Star Is Born* (William Wellman, 1937), and *The Return of Frank James* (Fritz Lang, 1940), in which a strong-minded director, or cameraman with a good visual sense, managed to use quite a lot of heavy chiaroscuro, including the use of foreground figures in black silhouette. Even *Gone With The Wind* shows tendencies in this direction, though in that case the production designer, William Cameron Menzies, was certainly responsible. Also striking was the very 'modern' simplicity of the lighting of *The Trail of the Lonesome Pine* (1936), done by W. Howard Greene, but apparently this approach was not very popular at the time.

Printing of three-colour Technicolor was a straightforward extension of the imbibition process already used for two-colour Technicolor; each of the three negatives was used to produce a gelatine relief positive matrix, and these matrices applied the three dyes, which were now Yellow, Cyan, and Magenta, to the blank in succession on three pin-belt machines. But now the blank stock carried a weak fourth 'key' image of black silver created in it beforehand photographically by printing from one of the three separate camera negatives, and the purpose of this was to get good solid blacks in the appropriate places. The green negative was usually used to produce the key image, but there were exceptions to this, and in particular for *Becky Sharp* the blue record negative was used. The purpose of this key silver image in the printing blank was to add extra black to the densest areas of the positive image.

Despite this departure from the theoretically optimum procedures of colour reproduction, the Technicolor process was capable of remarkably accurate reproduction of colours on natural exterior scenes by 1936, and this is the true test of a colour process. Initially the system was extremely contrasty, roughly comparable in this respect to present-day broadcast-quality colour video, with the unfilled shadows solid black, and very bright areas such as white clouds tending to 'burn out' (i.e. become undifferentiated transparent areas without detail on the positive print). However with the advent of the new camera negatives in 1939 this contrastiness was somewhat reduced. As far as faithfulness of colour reproduction is concerned, it must be noted that for a couple of years from about 1937 to 1939, original Technicolor prints were apparently made with a bias in the direction of orange, and such prints do not provide a true idea of the fidelity that the system was capable of at that time.

(FURTHER WARNING: A number of early Technicolor films such as *Becky Sharp* and *A Star Is Born* were later reissued in two-colour Cinecolor prints, and these have very little relation at all to the colour, definition, and contrast of the original prints.)

(LATEST WARNING: In the last several years new prints of a number of Technicolor films of the 'thirties and 'forties have been made either from the original camera negatives, or from an original positive print using modern colour stocks, and the colours of these do not correspond exactly to those of the originals either, though being fairly close in general. For instance, in the modern *Becky Sharp* prints the reds and yellows are more intense, and the blacks are not so black. The image definition of this class of modern reprints is often *better* than that of the original prints.)

Returning to the original Technicolor three-strip process, the printing of the relief positive matrices was carried out in an optical printer as before, and this printer had a facility for making fades and dissolves directly and automatically, without going through an interpositive and internegative as was necessary in black and white. It seems that this printer also could make a restricted range of simple wipes in the same way, but these were not used as often as they were in black and white films of this period.

Because the light level on a background projection screen has to match the light level of the scene being filmed in front of it, the high light levels required for Technicolor before 1939 prevented the use of big B.P. screens, with the upper limit being about ten feet. After 1939 the problem was minimized by the faster stock then available, and also by the development of a triple background projector at Paramount. This had the images from three projectors perfectly superimposed on the B.P. screen to give three times the usual screen brightness. The restrictions on background projection before 1939 may have contributed to the large amount of location shooting in the Technicolor films of the late 'thirties when compared with black and white films of the period, and also when compared with the Technicolor films of the 'forties.

Although the basic Technicolor camera, which weighed 77 lb., was not much bigger and heavier than a Mitchell NC, the blimp for the Technicolor camera was a lot bigger and heavier than the usual blimps for Mitchell cameras, with its basic dimensions being about 2 feet by 3 feet by 3 feet. It might be speculated that this bulk and weight militated against using the large number of camera set-ups that were required by directors working at the short end of the Hollywood Average Shot Length range, but the sample of films available is not large enough to confirm this. Certainly Wellman's *A Star Is Born* (1937) has an ASL of 9.5 seconds compared with his habitual 5 to 6 seconds, and Henry Hathaway, who also worked in that range on his black and white films, went to slightly slower cutting on *The Trail of the Lonesome Pine* with an ASL of 7 seconds. It is doubtful if there was any such effect on directors working near the mean Average Shot Length for the period, for John Ford's *Drums Along the Mohawk* has an ASL of 9.5 seconds, which is close to his usual figure of around 9 seconds.

Gasparcolour

Gasparcolour was purely a three colour printing process involving the variable destruction of dye colours in two emulsion layers on one side of the print stock, and in a third emulsion layer on the other. It could only be used for printing animated films as there was no satisfactory three-colour camera included in the system. On the surviving evidence it was capable of producing quite saturated colours, but I have some doubts about the colour fidelity of the system which are impossible to confirm, since animated films give no reference point in their entirely artificial colouring. The present-day Cibachrome process for making reversal colour paper prints in still photography is descended from the Gasparcolour process.

Dufay Colour

Dufay Colour was the only successful three-colour additive process that there has ever been in the cinema, but it only had a limited commercial application to one feature film and a number of short subjects made after 1938, mostly in England. In its initial form in 1934 it was a reversal process, in which a panchromatic emulsion was exposed through a filter layer made up of patches of red, green, and blue dye arranged in a *reseau* (a grid or regular mosaic) with spacing of 20 elements to the millimetre. After reversal development in the normal way for black and white emulsion, the film became a positive which could be projected. Although the 16 mm. form of this version of Dufay Colour had some success in the European amateur market, the 35 mm. form was only used for two short sequences in *Radio Parade of 1935* (Arthur Woods, 1934). At this stage of the development of the process the results left a lot to be desired when compared with Technicolor. All colours lacked saturation, and the blues and yellows were not strongly present or accurate. The reds had the dull red-orange quality that was usual with the older two-colour processes, and indeed the look of the image could be described as a two-and-a-half colour process. As well as this, the outline of the *reseau* was visible to most of the audience on the screen. In white areas of the scene a kind of 'boiling' effect was also visible owing to the presence of the minute discrete patches of red, green, and blue moving about in position from frame to frame. After further development, particularly of the optics of the printing process to partially suppress the image of the *reseau*, a negative-positive version of the process was made available in 1938. It was at this point that the commercial cinema use of Dufay Colour really began, but the process did not survive the war. From the existing material it seems that the negative-positive Dufay Colour process still had inferior definition and reduced saturation of hues when compared to Technicolor. Like all additive processes it produced a lower level of brightness in the screen image than the usual subtractive colour processes, but the importance of this should not be exaggerated, since the screen brightness was still perfectly satisfactory under good 35 mm. arc projection.

Agfacolor and Kodachrome

These two subtractive reversal colour processes, both using integral tripack film with three emulsion layers, were only initially available in 16 mm.; Kodachrome from 1935, and Agfacolor from 1936, and so they had no application to commercial film-making. However in 1939 Agfa produced a negative-positive material in 35 mm. film, and this was used for feature film production in the nineteen-forties.

Coloured Films

There was a slight revival of tinting and toning during the later 'thirties under the pressure of the increasing number of Technicolor films being produced. In Hollywood this was mostly a matter of using a simple restrained sepia tone applied throughout the entire length of a black and white print, but in France Max Ophuls made distinctive use of blue tinting to accentuate the romance of a moonlight scene in *Werther* (1938), and of pink and blue tinting to distinguish amongst the various levels of flashbacks he used in *la Tendre ennemie* (1936).

Lighting

By the beginning of 1930 electrical circuits to silence the hum of arc lights had been devised and produced, but in most studios in that year their use was extremely limited, and most of the lighting for sync. sound shots was done, as in previous years, with tungsten light sources. However Fox had returned to the principal use of arc sources, and the slightly sharper shadows and modelling to be observed in their films from that year, when compared with those from other studios, was the result.

In 1931 all studios had returned to the free use of arcs when convenient, but 80% of the lights used continued to be various types of tungsten light. This was no doubt to realize the worth of the investment already made in these incandescent lighting units, but also in part because cameramen appreciated the unique qualities of lighting that could be obtained with some of these units. In particular the 'rifle light', which had a large tungsten bulb of 1 kiloWatt in a hemispherical metal reflector with a fluted surface, gave a much softer light than any arc floodlight.

In general, the light from tungsten-source lighting units was slightly softer than the equivalent unit with an arc source, and when used for figure lighting they produced attractive soft-edged shadows on the face. Some cameramen took more advantage of these possibilities than others, but Victor Milner can stand as an example of those who most exploited the softness of tungsten light. In such films as *Ladies Man* (1931) and *The Man I Killed* (1932), where the key lighting was done with the hemispherical reflector tungsten floodlights on floor stands even in Long Shot, the cast shadows on the walls, as well as the modelling shadows on the faces, are as soft as can be achieved, short of using the type of 'soft light' unit which only became available in recent decades.

To sum up, the basic types of lighting units used in this period, to a greater or lesser extent, were first of all floodlights, either with tungsten bulbs of about 1 kW. in hemispherical reflectors of various types, or alternatively with arc or tungsten sources in trough-shaped matt-surfaced reflectors ('broads' and 'scoops'); all of which provided a fairly even flat coverage over an angle of about 90 degrees. Alternatively there were spotlights with either arc or tungsten bulb sources, and these could be either the searchlight type with a large parabolic mirror and open front, or the theatrical type where the source was totally enclosed and the light concentration and focussing was achieved by a spherical lens of several inches diameter at the front. Both types could be focussed to give a beam spread over a range from several degrees to about 40 degrees.

A Medium Shot from The Man I Killed *(1932), lit by Victor Milner with a large hemispherical tungsten floodlight on a floor stand high left. The light has a diffusing filter on it, and the result is the very soft shadows seen on the walls. There is also a spotlight from high right behind the actors backlighting them.*

Stylistic Peculiarities in Lighting

In general it is difficult to recognize individual styles in film lighting, much less to describe them accurately in those particular cases where they do exist. To take a concrete example, I can see little obvious connection between the strong chiaroscuro appearance of the lighting in *The Murders in the Rue Morgue* and the rather pedestrian mid-key look of *Back Street*, both photographed by Karl Freund for Universal in 1932. However, when Freund's work is juxtaposed with that of William Daniels on *Camille* (1937), a difference is recognizable. The point where Freund took over the lighting of this film from Daniels is fairly obvious, because Freund used far less lens diffusion in his photography, perhaps none at all on most of the shots, and also because on the average he used slightly simpler lighting set-ups, with less lights used to light the same sort of scene. Although the use of less lights and less diffusion is a general European characteristic, this distinction is not absolute, as can be seen if we look at another film on which two different cameramen worked. The point at which Rudolph Maté took over the lighting of *Come and Get It* (Hawks/Wyler, 1936) from Gregg Toland is also quite obvious, for in the last several minutes of the film, after the party scene, it can be clearly observed that in the closer shots the modelling shadows on the figures are much better handled, with a softness of edge that Toland could never achieve. And the European Maté used slightly more lens diffusion than the American Toland, and he used it more subtly. But despite being able to recognize the difference in some cases between the work of two cameramen when presented with their lighting side by side, I would never claim to be able to guess the name of the cameraman who had lit a film I did not know, if I was shown it 'blind'. And I don't believe anyone else can, though I can't prove this assertion.

James Wong Howe was perhaps the cameraman who tried the most individual things in the early 'thirties. For instance, on *Transatlantic* (William K. Howard, 1931) he did much of the photography with a 25 mm. lens, specifically to secure increased depth of field. But the result was far from being 'deep focus' in the modern, post-*Citizen Kane* sense, which means sharpness of focus from Big Close Up to Long Shot, since the range achieved by Wong Howe was only from 5 feet to 30 feet, which is from Medium Shot to Long Shot with a 25 mm. lens. These figures mean that the aperture used was approximately f4, and the light levels to secure this were little more than twice those usual at this time. The strange thing about the photography of this film is that having secured this increased depth of field, Wong Howe threw away most of the effect of it, by using heavy lens diffusion on nearly all the shots. Incidentally, it should be noted that the 'Waterhouse stops' that cameramen from this period often mention using are really irrelevant in themselves to deep-field photography; the fact that the design of wide-angle lenses at this period necessitated the use of a series of multiply-perforated slides, rather than the usual built-in iris diaphragm to change the aperture, made no difference to the image or the depth of field obtain-

able with a particular focal length at a particular aperture.

Wong Howe has said that he was nick-named 'Low-key' Howe at this period, and although the reason for this is not particularly evident in *Transatlantic*, there are some subsequent films where it *is* justified. In *After Tomorrow* (1932), many of the daytime room interiors are lit in a way that approximates the effect of filming in a real room lit only by the light through the windows, without supplementary light. The result is that the room goes very dark away from the windows, and many framings in these scenes are truly low-key. In everybody else's lighting of such scenes in the 'thirties far more fill lighting would be used on such sets, and the result would be at most 'mid-key' lighting. In *The Power and the Glory* (1933), again directed by William K. Howard, Wong Howe extended this approach slightly in the scenes in the tycoon's office, where he managed to duplicate even more exactly the fall of diffuse North light from large windows to one side of a room. There is no backlight or light from any other angle, as there would have been if any other cameraman had lit this scene in the standard way, and the effect is very close to reality. Ignoring a few instances involving close shots of people in other films, this is the only instance I have noted before recent years of anything that could reasonably be called 'North lighting' on a studio set.

It would appear that Wong Howe was not further encouraged in such individual efforts, as he did not do anything very unconventional again till the 'fifties; indeed the later 'thirties were a period of conformism in all respects in films made everywhere. Directors who had a taste for experiment like William K. Howard were not encouraged either.

Lighting in the Late 'Thirties

The really important development in lighting practice in the latter part of the 'thirties was the introduction of a new range of spotlights with Fresnel lenses, which came into use in the United States within a couple of years from 1934. For the first time it was possible to have large diameter lenses (up to 3 feet) close in front of a powerful light source, either arc or tungsten, as well as having a parabolic mirror behind the source. In this way the efficiency of the light and its controllability were vastly increased, and this type of lighting unit has remained standard from that time to the present. The range of units available extended all the way from those with 500 watt tungsten light sources up to the biggest arc spotlights, and all had a beam spread that could be varied from 8 to 48 degrees. The beam from these Fresnel-lens spots had a soft edge spreading over an angle of a few degrees through which the light intensity fell off very rapidly from almost maximum intensity to almost nothing. With these new lights there was now a trend to do more of the main and key lighting with spotlights than before in Hollywood movies, and though there was no sharp break with previous lighting practice, some Hollywood cameramen such as Tony Gaudio dignified the use of the new Fresnel spots with the name 'precision lighting'. (Journal of the Society of Motion Picture Engineers, Vol. 29,

A location exterior scene in Quai des brumes *(1938) shot on a slightly overcast day with heavy lens diffusion. The lighting is produced by weak sunlight from behind, and the face of the actor at the right is lit by the beam from a small spotlight.*

no. 2, p.157).

But the new Fresnel spots were slow to arrive in Europe, and there, even in the late 'thirties, the main lighting of shots continued to be done much more with floodlights. Since there was a tendency for European sets to be smaller, this was not such a drawback as it might appear, and in fact the greater use of floodlights often (but not always) made the lighting of European sets slightly more naturalistic in the strict sense of the term. Apart from the lack of these new Fresnel spots, there seem to have been few, or perhaps none at all, of the very large arc spotlights ('brutes') of the older kind available in Europe, and this shows up in the lighting of location exteriors. In films such as *Quai des brumes* (1938), one can see that the fill light on the figures is being applied from a small spot fairly close to

them, and hence covering a rather small area, rather than the large area that would be evenly covered by a very large arc spotlight in the case of such a scene in America.

Aside from these technological considerations, there are other occasional peculiarities of the lighting of German and French films in the nineteen-thirties. In German films there was a tendency, which did not exist at all in American films, to let the relative simplicity of the lighting sometimes put the face of a character into shadow, even though he or she had significant lines of dialogue to speak. This can happen in an ordinary conversational scene without any expressive connotations being intended, as in the one illustrated from *La Habanera* (Detlef Sierck, 1937). It must not be thought that this is a standard feature of German lighting, for there are

A shot of a conversation in La Habanera *(1937), in which the simple lighting from behind and from the right side leaves the face of the participant in the centre in shadow.*

Villainy in Quai des brumes *photographed in a high key on a light coloured set.*

many films in which the effect does not occur at all: it is just a small tendency. Likewise the contrary feature that can be found in some French films of the late 'thirties. Some French dramas that have definite sinister, twisted, or downbeat elements in them are nevertheless lit in a fairly high key more or less throughout, as far as the interiors are concerned. *Quai des Brumes* again provides an example, but the effect can be found in other lesser films such as *Macao – L'enfer de jeu* (Jean Delannoy, 1939). In part this high-key effect seems to be a result of a certain tendency to favour very light-coloured sets, but it is certainly abetted by the lighting. Faced by such a set in anything but a comedy or a musical, an American cameraman would surely throw a few more shadows on it than Eugen Schüfftan does.

But all in all, any distinctive look that some French and German films of the period have is due far more to set and costume design than to features of their photography and scene dissection. Throughout the later nineteen-thirties, just as in Hollywood, European photography continued to be at, or near, maximum aperture, and the faster film stocks were not used to achieve smaller apertures and hence greater depth of field. For the last time, there is *no* 'deep focus' in Jean Renoir's films, just extensive use of staging in depth, sometimes beyond the limits of sharp focus. And occasionally he uses a surreptitious focus-pull to sharpen the background slightly when the main interest in the shot moves there, and vice-versa.

With the beginning of three-colour Technicolor in 1934,

A scene in La Habanera *in which, in a way quite common in German films of the late 'thirties, the general dark effect is produced by the dark tones of the costumes and the sets as much as by the lighting.*

there was a need for more powerful floodlights, and Mole-Richardson introduced a new 'broad' or, as they called it, a Side Arc type 29. This had a rather better arc feed mechanism, and passed more current, but it was still basically the same as previous models. There was also a new Scoop of similar design, for hanging overhead. The most successful model was introduced in 1939, and known as the Duarc. Still containing a pair of arcs within the one housing, the arc feed mechanism was vastly improved, so that it could run for hours without needing to be trimmed or restarted by hand. The reflecting surface inside was chromium plated, and there was a built in diffusing filter over the front opening, made of pebbled and sand-blasted pyrex glass. This unit became a standard film light for decades, used whenever a really powerful floodlight was wanted, either on floor stands, or hung at an angle overhead.

Cameras

In 1930 Warners were the only studio still using the 'ice-box' type of sound-proof booth containing both camera and operator for sound filming, but in 1931 they joined all the other studios in using Mitchell NC cameras in hand-made blimps of their own various designs. So although Warners had fitted some of their booths with wheels, as had other studios during 1929, there was still during 1930 a limitation on the use of panning simultaneously with tracking at Warners, a limitation that no longer held elsewhere.

(Cameras inside sound-proof booths were limited by the size of the booth window to pans of about 30 degrees on either side of the forward direction, whereas both blimped and unblimped cameras can be pointed in any direction while the dolly they are mounted on is being tracked along.)

The first Mitchell BNC cameras were produced in 1934, but at first none of the studios except the minor Goldwyn company bought them. The BNC was developed from the Mitchell NC by adding a closely fitting soundproof cover integral to the existing base-plate and front plate over which the main body slid when being 'racked over' for focussing. This shell allowed just enough space for this 2 inch sideways movement of the body and magazine, and no more. The rotating lens turret on the front plate of the NC was eliminated, and replaced by a fixed mount for a single lens. Otherwise there was no essential change in the basic design of the camera, but the dimensions and weight (135 lb.) were appreciably less than those of an NC camera in a blimp. Although not totally silent, the sound level from the camera was not detectable at normal microphone distances. Gregg Toland used the Goldwyn BNCs for years with no visible effect on the style of his camerawork, while everyone else continued to use Mitchell NC cameras in hand-built blimps, though towards the end of the 'thirties automatic parallax correction was applied to the supplementary viewfinders mounted on the outside of the blimps. The studios resisted buying the BNC model because it was only several years since they had paid out for the NC model, and the BNC offered no great improve-ment, while being quite expensive. In fact when Warners finally led the way towards general re-equipment with Mitchell BNCs in the Hollywood studios by buying 10 of them in 1938, the price was $10,000 each.

In 1935 another silent camera was designed for Twentieth Century-Fox, and in 1939 several were produced for the exclusive use of that studio, but further production was prevented by the demands made by World War 2 on the precision-engineering firms concerned. This Fox camera was an entirely new design. It had no extra sound-proof casing, just some sound-absorbing material on the inside of the main casing, and also smoothly running mechanical parts. Its cylindrical body could be rotated 60 degrees about its longitudinal axis to bring a ground-glass screen into the film position behind the taking lens for accurate focussing and framing. The magazine was of the usual belt-driven American style, with two separate 1000 foot circular film compartments mounted on top of the camera, and the whole machine weighed 85 lbs.

Both the Fox camera and the Mitchell BNC were slightly easier to get into extreme positions and slightly easier to use in general, but this really had no significance as far as studio filming was concerned. What was important was that in sync. sound filming lenses of wider angle than 25 mm. could now be used, which was not the case with blimped cameras.

European Cameras

Through the nineteen-thirties and 'forties there was only one significant sound camera of European origin. This was made by Debrie in France, and was closely based on their much earlier Parvo design. All that was done was to enlarge the dimensions of the body in all directions, so that the coaxial magazine chambers let into either side of the body would now take 1000 foot rolls of film in the circular cassettes, rather than only 400 foot rolls. The viewfinding arrangements were the same as those in the last silent models of the Debrie, with the film gate displaced to put a ground glass screen in its place, this being viewed through an eyepiece in the back of the camera. The camera was easily silenced by putting a simple rectangular box round its rectangular body, and the lens was also enclosed behind a glass cover at the front of the camera. The dimensions of the whole blimped camera were about 20 inches wide by 20 inches high, by 25 inches long, which were smaller than those of a blimped Mitchell NC, but the Debrie still lacked pilot-pin registration, as is quite obvious in the special effects of a number of European films. The Debrie sound camera was used all over continental Europe, including Russia, either as built in France, or as built in licensed or unlicensed copies in the other countries.

British Cameras and Technology

In Britain the cameras and technology used were mostly American, and the penetration of equipment from the Continent was small, mostly limited to a small number of sound Debrie cameras, until well after World War 2. For this reason I will have little more to say about British film technology until some indigenous innovations began to appear there in the nineteen-fifties.

Camera Supports and Camera Movement

Most of the major studios had acquired large camera cranes in imitation of Universal, and small cranes with a rise and fall of several feet appeared at Paramount in 1933, and at other studios shortly after. The tradition established by *Broadway*, and followed throughout the 'thirties, was that large craning movements were confined to musical numbers of one kind or another, and not used in ordinary dramatic scenes. Occasionally a director would use a crane movement on a spectacular scene in a non-musical context, as in *The Scarlet Empress* (1934) or *The Adventures of Robin Hood* (1938), or sometimes to follow actors up and down staircases, but even this was quite rare.

Ordinary tracking shots were done with small steerable dollies developed from the improvised dollies carrying a blimped camera on a heavy duty tripod common at the beginning of the sound period. These new dollies were on the general pattern of a low-slung platform about 3 feet wide and 5 feet long with wheels having solid rubber tyres, and with the rear pair of wheels steerable. The support column for the camera was now an integral part of the construction of the dolly, and could be raised and lowered a few feet mechanically, but not during the course of the shot. The pan and tilt heads used under the blimped cameras were mostly of the heavy spring-loaded friction type controlled with a pan bar, just like the still existing Mitchell and Vinten models. However in 1930 Mole-Richardson had produced a large cradle geared head very like the present-day type of geared head, though without the the gear change on present-day heads that makes high speed pans and tilts possible. For some reason this type of geared head was little used till the end of the decade.

With this equipment, the way was open to a complete continuation of the extensive use of the mobile camera that had characterized the work of many directors at the end of the previous decade. Although obvious names like Pabst and Milestone spring to mind, this fashion was very widespread, and was eagerly joined by newcomers like George Cukor and John Cromwell, as the latter commented in interview at the National Film Theatre in 1974. However, many abandoned the extremes of this fashion after a few years with the rise of faster cutting, as I shall describe later.

The prototype of a small, extremely manoeuverable dolly was used on Milestone's *The Front Page* in 1931, and this dolly was put into series production in 1932 as the Bell & Howell 'Rotambulator'. It had a camera mounting with built-in geared head that could rise and fall beside a central supporting column, and this column was fixed in turn to a circular base about 4 feet in diameter. There were three small wheels around the circumference of the base, two at the front having fixed direction, and one at the back that was steerable. This arrangement permitted very tight turns to be executed, and the Rotambulator's manoeuverability (but not its stability)

approached that of present-day crab dollies. The effect of its use can be seen in the Press Room scenes of *The Front Page*.

The Hollywood extreme of the 'long take with mobile camera' style of the early 'thirties can be represented by John Stahl's *Back Street* (1932), which with an Average Shot Length of 23 seconds inevitably includes quite a number of takes which are minutes long. (Remember that the approximately Lognormal distribution of shot lengths under these circumstances enables one to know roughly how many shots there will be of given length once the ASL is known.)

None of the dollies or cranes that became available in this period permitted lens heights much below 3 feet, and setting up ultra-low camera angles continued to require special time-consuming measures. Nevertheless such extreme low angles continue to make their appearance in a few films such as *Doorway to Hell* (Archie Mayo, 1930) and others, the inspiration presumably coming from various European films such as *Bronenosets Potyomkin* which had arrived in America right at the end of the 'twenties. Unmotivated high-angle shots were rather more frequent, though still not common in non-musical films. A good place to study the use of these and other expressivist devices at one Hollywood extreme of the expressivist–naturalist spectrum is *The Bat Whispers* (Roland West, 1931).

Whip or Zip Pans

A whip (or zip) pan is one which is so fast that the image becomes an abstract blur of horizontal streaks of black, white, and grey. Whip pans first began to appear in very isolated instances after 1926, perhaps accidentally once the fashion for extensive camera movement had started. They were taken over as an intentional structural device to join the items in newsreels together after 1930. From there they made their way back into fictional films, where they had a brief vogue around 1932. Examples occur in Mamoulian's *Song of Songs*, and most interestingly in William K. Howard's *The Trial of Vivienne Ware*, in which all the scenes are joined together with whip pans rather than dissolves.

Dutch Tilts

Dutch tilts (or 'off-angles') are shots in which the camera is set up with the sides of the frame skew to the vertical, and they had first appeared in German, and then in Russian films in the previous decade. They were mostly to be found in montage sequences in mainstream movies, and this continued to be the case in the 'thirties. However in this decade they sometimes escaped from inside montage sequences in the strict sense, and could on very rare occasions be found in scenes of a disturbing nature, or those involving violent action. A few of these rare instances can be seen in *The Painted Veil* (R. Boleslawski, 1934), *The Adventures of Robin Hood* (Curtiz and Keighley, 1938), and some of Robert Florey's films made at the end of the decade. Dutch tilts were not much more common in European films, but in 1937 two French films show them being used at much greater length than anywhere else. Raymond Bernard's *Marthe Richard – au service de la France* has all the more treacherous of the espionage scenes shot with dutch tilts, and Duvivier's *Un Carnet de bal* contains a long scene done entirely with the camera set skew to the vertical, while at the same time the camera is *panned* extensively about that vertical axis. Although the scene in question involves a drug-addicted abortionist, none of these tilted shots are POV shots, they are all objective shots.

Lenses

During the 'thirties lenses with focal lengths from 24 mm. upwards continued to be available, and the usual maximum aperture for standard lenses was around f2.3, with one very popular set being the Taylor-Hobson series with maximum aperture of around f2. Lenses from Zeiss and Astro with maximum apertures of f0.85 and f0.95 respectively became available in 1933, but these would certainly have had visibly inferior performance, and it is highly unlikely that they were used for anything but newsreel work.

Once into the 'thirties, sets were being designed on the assumption that the Long Shots would be taken with a 40 mm. lens, and this focal length is close to that which more recent research has shown gives the impression of correct perspective when a natural scene is reproduced by projection. For closer shots a 50 mm. lens was once more the usual choice, and of course for true Close Ups something like 75 mm. or 100 mm..

In 1932 the Taylor-Hobson 'Varo' variable focal length lens became available, and since this was an improvement over earlier experimental zoom lenses in that only the focal length control had to be adjusted while zooming, it had occasional limited use for a few years. The focal length of this lens could be continuously varied between 40 mm. and 120 mm., and it had a maximum aperture of f5.6. Apart from the rather small maximum aperture, which still precluded its use under the standard studio interior lighting set-ups of the time, the other drawback to this lens was that the focus was fixed at the hyperfocal distance, and closer objects had to be focussed by putting supplementary lenses in front of the front element. So focus-pulling in the middle of a shot was impossible. More than that, when the aperture setting was altered, the lens casing, which was a large and heavy oblong metal box about a half the size of the body of a Mitchell camera, had to be opened and the cam system controlling the internal moving elements changed. Shortly after the introduction of the Taylor-Hobson zoom lens another similar lens with a zoom range from 40 to 160 mm., but a maximum aperture of only f8, was announced by Durholz in the United States, but this did not make much impression. Zoom shots made with the Varo lens can be seen in the street scene opening of *Love Me Tonight* (Mamoulian, 1932), and also in the stag-hunting scene. It was also used in a number of other films at this time on exterior scenes, but after that these lenses seem to have passed into the care of the special effects departments of the studios, where they were occasionally used to get shots in montage sequences.

One such example is in *Private Worlds* (LaCava, 1935). I have heard that there was a zoom lens produced in Germany in the middle 'thirties, though I have been unable to get details of it. It may have been the Astro Transfocator, which was a supplementary zoom attachment put in front of an ordinary 50 mm. lens. There are certainly a few zoom shots in German documentaries of the late 'thirties, though I have seen none in fiction films from that country. There are also a number of zoom shots in the Italian film *Scipione l'africano* (1937), but again I do not know the details.

No new lenses of any significance were introduced in the second half of the decade, but attempts were made to get greater effective depth of field by Hal Mohr through the use of a swinging lens mount in the films *The Green Pastures* and *Bullets or Ballots* in 1936. The arrangement consisted of an ordinary lens set in a special mount that enabled it to be pivoted around a vertical axis through its optical centre. The idea was that the zone of sharp focus in front of the lens would be inclined to the camera axis when the lens was inclined to the forward direction, and objects on one side of the frame would be in focus forward of the previous closest position of sharp focus, while objects on the other side of the frame would come into focus at a greater distance than previously. This

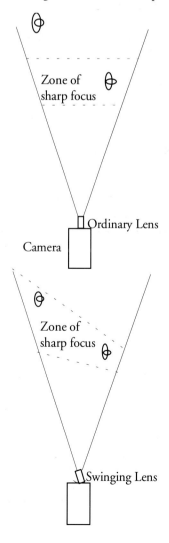

A shot in Bullets or Ballots *(1936) photographed by Hal Mohr using a swinging lens mount on the camera. The zone of sharp focus extends from the telephone right of frame diagonally backwards, passing behind the actor in the centre foreground, who is well out of focus, to cover the actors in the left background.*

kind of staggered depth of field is not greatly in evidence in *The Green Pastures*, but it was effective in a number of places in *Bullets or Ballots*. One of these is illustrated, and the shot also shows the drawback of the technique. The telephone at the right of the frame is in focus, as are the actors far in the background at the left, but the actor in the foreground centre using the phone is out of focus, because in the centre of the frame the region of sharp focus has to be behind him, in the middle distance.

This problem would not have arisen if the alternative method of getting different regions of focus on the two sides of the frame had been used. This involves the use of a split-field dioptre – a supplementary lens cut down the centre – which is placed in front of an ordinary camera lens covering the part of the field where the focus has to be brought forward. Then to deal with this particular case the split lens would cover the actor and the telephone, but not the background action, and all would be sharp. So the use of the swinging lens mount was a pointlessly elaborate technique for securing a result which could otherwise be obtained more simply, and in fact nothing more was heard of it after these two films. The real significance of this attempt is that it shows an interest in a kind of approximation to 'deep focus', prior to Gregg Toland inventing the real thing in the 'forties.

Wide Film Processes

In 1929 there arose a sudden interest in the use of film wider than the standard 35 mm. at some of the major studios.

Another similar set-up in Bullets or Ballots, *this time photographed with a conventional lens. Notice that in this case the image definition within the area of sharp focus is much superior.*

This may have been a development from ideas of producing larger images on the screen in the previous few years, which had included the first demonstration of Henri Chrétien's anamorphic process, and also some American use of wide angle lenses on cinema projectors to produce a bigger screen image from ordinary films. In any case, in 1929 Lorenzo del Riccio devised a process using 56 mm. film which he called Magnifilm. The only feature shot with this was *We're in the Navy Now* for Paramount. Fox developed a process called Fox Grandeur using film 70 mm. wide, which was used to film *Happy Days* in 1929 and *The Big Trail* in 1930. The special cameras for this process, like all the others, were based on the Mitchell mechanism. Other entries were George K. Spoor and P. John Berggren's Natural Vision, a 63 mm. process which was used on *Danger Lights* (1930) for RKO, and a Warner Bros. 65 mm. system used for *Kismet* (1930) and *The Lash* (1931). The Fox Grandeur 70 mm. process was also used on MGM's *Billy the Kid* (1930), but in this case the 35 mm. prints for ordinary distribution were obtained by optical printing from the centre of the wide image.

Finally, when the whole idea was in the process of being abandoned, the Spoor and Berggren Natural Vision 63 mm. system was used by Roland West for *The Bat Whispers* in 1931. All of these systems had image aspect ratios of around 1:2; i.e. the image was about twice as wide as it was high, and despite the fact that a few of them had film widths the same as present-day wide film with its 65 mm. negative and 70 mm. positive, none were exactly compatible with it. This was because the frame and sprocket hole positions were different, not to mention the size and placing of the sound track. All of the films mentioned except *Billy the Kid* were shot simultaneously with ordinary 35 mm. cameras standing beside the wide film cameras, and these 35 mm. versions were the ones generally shown when the films were originally released. Only a few show-case theatres were equipped for wide film projection at the time, and the whole idea was not a success at all.

Recently, prints of some of these films have been unearthed, and modern 'Scope or 70 mm. copies have been made from them by optical printing from the originals. The wide film version of *The Bat Whispers* adds nothing to the version shot on ordinary 35 mm., because the sides of its image are fuzzed out with layers of increasingly heavy black gauzing put in front of the sides of the frame when the film was originally shot. There seems to be a loss of focus of the picture out towards the sides as well, so that the only effective part of the image is restricted to an aspect ratio similar to that of the ordinary Academy aperture, and all the significant action takes place in this area. However, in the case of *The Big Trail*, it seems to me that the wide film version is superior to the ordinary 35 mm. version. This is not because the compositions are specially well adapted to the wide film ratio most of the time, though the final shoot-out round a giant fallen tree is striking from this point of view, but because the outer edges of the wide frame include extra background action in many scenes, and this adds considerably to the liveliness of the film.

Background Projection

From 1930 the earlier travelling-matte systems – the Williams and Dunning processes – used for combining live-action foreground scenes with moving backgrounds were largely abandoned, and replaced with background projection. In background projection a previously filmed background scene is projected in the studio onto a large translucent screen from behind, while the actors are filmed in front of it to give the combined image directly on the film in the camera. The very first background projection screens were made of ground glass, and they were limited in height to several feet. They were also inclined to show a 'hot-spot': that is, the part of the image near their centre photographed brighter than the parts round the edges. Attempts to use other materials to make large screens had other drawbacks, as can be seen in *The Dawn Patrol* (1930). Here very large screens, presumably made of some thin white cloth, were used in the final scenes showing the bombing of the German factory. The image of the distant parts of the bombed factory back-projected onto the screen are partially obscured with an all-over wash of white, either from the screen material itself, or from flare in the optical system of the projector. The result is a glaringly unconvincing mis-match between the background and the actors on the parts of the set built in front of the screen. Earlier in the film, close shots of pilots in aeroplanes made in front of smaller background projection screens are more satisfactory because the effect is less marked, and also because one expects aerial haze to wash out the background in the real situation being mimicked in these shots.

Because of these flaws, background projection was limited to showing things like the passing street through the back windows of cars, where small screen size does not matter, until the introduction of a new cellulose screen material and redesign of the optics of background projectors in 1932 made satisfactory projection possible on screens as big as 17 feet by 23 feet. However these improvements did not reach continental Europe for a decade or more, so background projection continued to be rarely used there, and when it was, the defects of small screen size and dim edges are very evident.

The new possibilities of background projection in America after 1932 can be studied with advantage in *King Kong* (1933), in which all the combinations of animated models with live action were achieved by background projection, often with the new large screens, though it would appear that the new fine-grain background negative was not available when the film was shot. It must be emphasized however that in this film some of the combinations of action in *different* parts of the frame were achieved with the older fixed-matte procedures. Also in one or two shots the silhouettes of birds flying past are made by simple superimposition, and in two or three very brief shots the Dunning process *was* used where its defects would not be too conspicuous.

Travelling Mattes

There were other rare occasions when the Williams and

Dunning processes had to be used, and one or two instances of this should be mentioned for anyone wishing to make a comparison. One case is when tiny human figures had to be combined with giant human figures within one shot, as in Tod Browning's *The Devil Doll* (1936). Here one can see the thin dark line (the 'minus') surrounding the foreground figures which often results from imperfect travelling matte systems, while in George Stevens' *Swing Time* of the same year, one can see 'print through' – the appearance of the background through the foreground figure, which is the other common fault – in the 'Bojangles' sequence.

In Europe travelling matte shots were often used in preference to the local alternative of inferior background projection, but both processes tended to suffer from another European deficiency, the lack of cameras with pin registration for shooting the background plates. The result was that European process shots almost invariably had jiggling backgrounds, sometimes quite badly. In Russia background projection seems to have been completely unavailable, so combination shots were done solely with very inferior travelling matte systems. The background print-through in the process shots in *Vesyolye rebyata* (Grigori Alexandrov, 1934) and *U Samovo sinyevo morya* (Boris Barnet, 1936) is so bad that the shots in question are little more than simple superimpositions.

Background Projection and Location Filming

As a result of the unavailability of good background projection during the early 'thirties, many films continued to include sync. sound location dialogue sequences, some of them quite lengthy, whereas after 1933 such scenes are very rare. Naturally the point about shooting what purport to be exterior dialogue scenes in front of a B.P. screen is that it gives total control over the environment – lighting, and weather, and background noise, and hence more efficient production. The reduction in background noise was particularly important given the kind of microphones available in the 'thirties.

Optical Printing

As mentioned previously, duplicating negative and positive film with fine grain and low contrastiness became available at the beginning of the 'thirties, and this permitted combinations of shots to be made and copied with little deterioration in quality, which had not been the case before. Series-built optical printers were made and sold by such firms as DePue from 1930, and with these the studios set up their own optical printing departments. Immediately such effects as front titles printed over live action started to appear, followed by the frequent use of the wipe as a shot transition from 1932. The first wipes in this new wave of fashion were straight-line replacement wipes with hard edges, but other shapes were flirted with, and the edge of the wipe line rapidly became slightly blurred. In the late 'thirties the edges of wipes became even softer, and they still continued to be used mostly to indicate a short time lapse, particularly in sequences of fast moving action. There was a definite tendency for wipes to be more common in Warner Brothers films than in those from other studios. The ready availability of optical printers also encouraged the proliferation of montage sequences with a faster flow of shots than had been usual at the end of the 'twenties, so that the usual montage sequence was now a continuous flow of changing superimpositions. In Europe optical printers came into use in 1934-1935, but the montage sequence never became as widely used as in the United States, possibly because the studios tended to contract out their film processing, and did not maintain their own optical effects departments, and hence the use of montage sequences was relatively more expensive.

Busby Berkeley and Brain Function

Before Busby Berkeley began producing his characteristic kaleidoscopic patterns with female bodies arranged to make images with several-fold rotational symmetry about the centre of the screen, similar overhead shots had already appeared a few times in such film revues and musicals as *The Hollywood Revue* (1929). But these isolated precursors have little impact when compared with Berkeley's vastly elaborated patterns in such films as *Footlight Parade* (1933), in which large numbers of dancers produce wave-like pulsations moving to and from the centre of the pattern by co-ordinated movements of parts of their bodies. Nowadays there is an obvious connection with the design of some of the abstract avant-garde films produced on the West Coast in the 'sixties like James Whitney's *Lapis*, which likewise works with patterns streaming and pulsing radially from the centre of the screen, but the connection is not just one of surface appearance. Behind the powerful, indeed physiological, visual effect of both sorts of films lies one of the so-far limited instances when the effectiveness of kinetic-visual stimulation in film can be related with some degree of certainty to the organization of nerve-cells in the brain.

The connection runs through the experimental investigation of the patterns in hallucinatory illusions observed under certain drugs, and also in other abnormal brain conditions such as migraine headaches. It is found that there are a very limited number of basic forms of these patterns in such illusions, and the two that concern us here are those illusions that appear like proceeding down a tunnel whose surface may be regularly patterned, and those that seem like a streaming of light radially away from a central point. Taking into account other results from neurophysiology dealing with the direct stimulation of the visual cortex, it appears that the patterns observed are the result of particular fixed patterns of connection of the nerve cells in the part of the brain handling visual information. (The details of this can be read in *Hallucinations: Behavior, Experience, and Theory*, edited by Siegel and West, John Wiley, 1975.) The implication of the above observations is that because of these particular patterns of neural organization, the brain shows particular sensitivity when presented with these visual patterns in actuality, as happens in the films under discussion and also in other films including shots tracking down tunnels taken with a wide-angle lens, when the same kind of weak physiological effect can be experienced. It seems possible that some other elements of film that work in this direct way in terms of neurophysiology will eventually be uncovered, but I expect that most recurring stylistic forms will turn out to be culturally conditioned.

Frame Size and Projector Apertures

In 1930 sound films were being photographed at all studios using what can be called for convenience the 'early sound aperture'. This was created from the full silent aperture (0.735 inch by 0.980 inch) by masking off the sound track area. This left an almost square frame area of Aspect Ratio 1:1.15, which corresponded to a *projector* aperture of approximately 0.687 inch by 0.825 inch. Films photographed with this aperture have only a thin line between the frames, and if the images have also been composed with respect to this aperture, it is quite likely that the heads of the actors will be cut off if the film is projected with the later standard Academy aperture. However this 'early sound aperture' is quite close to the present CinemaScope projector aperture, so the CinemaScope mask can be used in the gate of a projector to show early sound films if no specially cut mask is available.

In 1930 it was proposed that the sound film aperture should be 0.620 in. by 0.835 in., and in fact the Fox studios were already composing for this aperture, but most of the others were not. As cinema projectionists were already starting to mask off the picture to something like these dimensions the other studios came around to the same practice, and in 1932 the 'Academy aperture' of 0.631 in. by 0.868 in. for cameras, and 0.600 in. by 0.825 in. for projectors, was proposed by the Academy of Motion Picture Arts and Sciences. In fact most films made in 1931 can be satisfactorily projected with the 'Academy aperture', which has an Aspect Ratio of 1:1.33, but the only satisfactory way of deciding which projector mask to use when showing sound films made up to 1931 is to examine a section of the film to see where the heads of the actors come to, or even to make a trial projection. Of course this question is irrelevant if a 16 mm. copy is under consideration.

Technical Standards and the Film Industry Organizations

The way in which the sound aperture established by the Fox company was later adopted as the industry standard is absolutely typical of the creation of technical standards in the film industry, and for that matter in other highly technical industries in this century. The almost invariable sequence of events is that one company choses a standard for its own use, and then, either because the company concerned was first in the field, or because it establishes economic superiority, or because the standard is obviously a sensible and practical one, the other companies adopt it as well. Only after this has happened is the standard ratified by an industry body, such as the Society of Motion Picture Engineers or the Academy of

Motion Picture Arts and Sciences in the case of the film industry.

A brief consideration of the history of the major technical standards for motion pictures is all that is necessary to justify this assertion. The 35 mm. width of the film and silent frame size was due to the Edison company, the first to take satisfactory motion pictures and sell them. The initial standard of 16 frames per second for taking and projection, and the two turns per second of the crank handle, were established by the Lumière company because the first was more economic of film stock, and the second was associated with a more practical camera, which was eventually licensed for sale by Pathé. The pitch and dimensions of the perforations in 35 mm. film negative followed the standard set by the Bell & Howell perforating machine, which was much superior to competing machines, and the pitch and dimensions of positive perforations was set by Eastman Kodak, by far the largest manufacture of film stock. The failure of the industry bodies such as the Society of Motion Picture Engineers to standardise projection speeds as they increased throughout the early 'twenties has already been described, and there were a number of similar later failures in their attempts to establish a technical standard before it had been adopted in practice.

Following this, the sound speed of 24 frames per second was established for practical reasons by Warner Bros., the first company to succeed commercially with sound movies, and then adopted by everyone else, and next there was the business of the sound aperture that I have just described. Important later standards include the CinemaScope frame, squeeze ratio, and special perforations, again introduced by Twentieth Century-Fox, and then adopted by the rest of the film companies, and so it has gone on.

The only really important function of the Society of Motion Picture Engineers was as a forum for the dissemination and discussion of highly technical information, particularly from the 'thirties onwards. However, even in this area the activities of the film industry organizations were often irrelevant. For instance, the technician's branch of the Academy of Motion Picture Arts and Sciences, together with the American Society of Cinematographers arranged a series of 'Mazda tests' at the beginning of 1928, which were intended to demonstrate how to use tungsten lighting to film cameramen. But this was *after* many film cameramen had already found out how to use tungsten lighting and panchromatic stock for themselves, and were already in the process of disseminating this knowledge to their immediate associates. Altogether, technical developments would have followed the same course that they actually did, though perhaps very slightly slower in some cases, if the Society of Motion Picture Engineers, the Academy of Motion Picture Arts and Sciences, and the American Society of Cinematographers had not existed. The generalizations I have made at the beginning of this section about the mechanisms of technical change is confirmed by developments more recently in other highly technical industries in the electronics sector.

Sound Recording

1930 saw the final triumph of sound-on-film recording, and sound-on-disc was phased out. The microphones used for recording continued to be the capacitor type (or 'condenser' type as they were then called), and two principal models competed for favour. Both had quite a smooth response up to 2000 Hertz, then there was a rise to a resonance peak at 3000 Hertz, and after that the response fell away to zero by about 7000 Hertz. One model was made by Western Electric, and this had a small diaphragm unit swivelling below a tubular amplifier unit which was about 3 inches in diameter and one foot tall, while in the other model from RCA the amplifier and diaphragm unit were enclosed in one large spherical container several inches in diameter. Both models were suspended from microphone booms, essentially similar to present studio booms, which could be extended while in use, and the boom included a 'favouring' device at its end to change the direction the microphone diaphragm was pointing. The column supporting the swinging boom could be mounted on a tripod stand or a small pneumatic-wheeled carriage similar to present units. Mole-Richardson introduced a series-manufactured boom in 1930.

If several microphones were being used to record sound for a shot, their signals were mixed directly before being recorded photographically onto the sound negative in the sound camera. A wax disc recording continued to be made simultaneously for instant playback to check the actors' vocal performances, but in the middle 'thirties an acetate disc came to be used instead. The mixing of a set of film sound tracks subsequent to their initial recording to give a final combined re-recording was avoided if at all possible during the first years of the decade, as the extra recording stage onto sound film produced a just perceptible loss in quality. This meant that, although the post-synchronizing of voices to a film scene which had been shot silent could be carried out from 1929, it was mostly not used in the early 'thirties, and location scenes involving dialogue were always shot with direct sound. The point being made here is that it is mostly too difficult to get both the voices *and* the effects in the right place in one pass when post-synchronizing, and if they are recorded separately you are right back with the re-recording losses mentioned previously.

For location recording 'wind-gags' were already in use to prevent wind noise in the microphones, and in some situations ultra-directional microphones were created by putting ordinary microphones at the focus of large parabolic metal reflectors of up to 6 feet in diameter. In this way fairly good recordings could be made with the microphone 15 feet or more from the actors. Since all the microphones in use were omni-directional (that is, they responded to sounds equally whatever direction they came from), background noise pick-up could be a serious problem with location recording, and this was one of the pressures encouraging the change to the shooting of exterior dialogue scenes in the studio, as soon as good background projection made this possible.

Dynamic (or 'moving coil') microphones, and also ribbon microphones, had been available from 1931, but they were little used for film purposes, as their performance had serious shortcomings in one way or another. But in 1938 Western Electric produced a new moving-coil microphone, the model 630A, which was small and light in weight (14 oz.), and with a fairly flat response up to 10 kHz. Similar microphones became available from other companies, and they started to displace condenser microphones immediately in Hollywood. Although the response of the Western Electric 630A (colloquially called the 'ball and biscuit') was substantially omni-directional, it was commonly used with the sound direction at glancing incidence to the diaphragm, and at 90 degrees to its main axis, as the treble response was slightly higher in this position. Western Electric also introduced an improved smaller condenser microphone in 1938, and this had a very flat response up to about 9kHz., so dynamic microphones did not take over completely despite their size and weight advantages.

Around this time there were improvements in the design of ribbon microphones, particularly the RCA models, but despite their broad flat frequency response they were not particularly suitable for film recording under most conditions, because of their high sensitivity to mechanical vibrations, such as those produced by boom-swinging and favouring. Nevertheless they were sometimes used on film sets when such movements could be avoided, as they were the only type of microphones with sharply directional pick-up. And the better ribbon microphones made their contribution to better music recording in the late nineteen-thirties.

Improvements in Sound Recording Systems

In 1930 there had been three operational American systems of sound-on-film recording: the RCA variable area system, and the Western Electric and Movietone variable density systems. In Europe there was only one really satisfactory system, which was the Tobis variable density system similar to the Western Electric. The Western Electric system used a light-valve (variable aperture slit) controlled by the signal, and modulating the amount of light falling on the sound track area to expose it, and the RCA system used a galvanometer (an oscillating mirror system) likewise controlled by the signal in its deflection, so changing the width of the illuminated slit exposing the sound-track area. The Movietone system used a fixed light-slit and a variable intensity light (the 'Aeolight') which was modulated in brightness by the signal. During the early 'thirties the Aeolight system was not able to match the technical improvements made in the other systems, and it went out of use.

Throughout the 'thirties there were more or less continuous improvements in the two surviving types of sound-on-film recording system through attention to various aspects of their functioning, such as exposure and development control of the sound track negative, amplifier circuit improvements, mechanical refinements of the sound cameras and printers, and so on. But the really audible advance in the quality of recording began in 1931, and it was largely due to techniques for the suppression of noise in the sound track which were introduced almost simultaneously in the RCA and Western Electric systems. By 1933 it was possible to mix a separately recorded music track with the synchronous dialogue track recording *after* the editing stage without noticeable loss of sound quality from the extra sound film recording stage, and from this point on 'background music' came to be used more and more extensively. (Up to 1932 there was, roughly speaking, either dialogue or music on the sound track, but hardly ever both together, unless they had been recorded simultaneously.)

However, right from the beginning of the decade it was clear to the smartest technical people concerned that the RCA system was superior in principle, and by 1935 this was certainly the case in practice as well. Apart from what can be seen from careful reading of the technical discussions in the Journal of the Society of Motion Picture Engineers, the inferiority of the Western Electric process is indicated by examination of original prints of the period. For instance, on the track of *Front Page* (1931), the Western Electric track shows a 'blooped' sound cut corresponding to virtually every picture cut in the film, indicating that the original sound negative has been cut, assembled, and printed from directly, rather than being re-recorded to get a join-free track, as was the case for prints with RCA sound from this period. This necessity for avoiding making a second generation recording if possible continued to be indicated in this way for Western Electric sound prints for some years, although the sound track joins are no longer as frequent. Even at the end of the decade, it was considered necessary to change from the Western Electric track usual on a Selznick film print to an RCA track for the last reel of *Rebecca* (1940), to produce clear reproduction of a loud combination of music, sound effects, and voices.

In 1934 the U.S. Supreme Court rejected the Tri-Ergon company's claims for the exclusive patent on the sound smoothing drum at the sound head of recorders and reproducers, and the feeling in the business was that this would lead to more investment, and hence technical development by the American companies.

Reading the technical reports, the brilliance of the research work at the RCA laboratories at Schenectady is quite striking, and amongst many other things they produced a way of adapting RCA recorders to make superior variable density (Western Electric) type sound tracks. RCA also set the standard for recording sound on 16 mm. film with the design of a superior projector for this gauge. This is yet another example of companies rather than the industry bodies setting the technical standards.

Despite the evident superiority of the RCA system after 1935, most of the studios were reluctant to adopt it for release prints, though they all licensed it for possible internal use in the earlier stages of production. The reasons given were that prints with RCA soundtracks were more susceptible to deterioration through wear, and that they did not sound so good on inferior theatre sound systems. The first reason had dubious validity, and the second was probably the true one. (Older people may remember how the best new records often sounded unpleasant on old equipment during the 'hi-fi' revolution of the 'fifties.) The important point here is probably that absolute quality in sound did not matter that much to film producers in those days, or they would have shown more interest in getting exhibitors to improve their theatre sound systems.

The major improvement in sound recording in the late 'thirties was the introduction of 'push-pull' double sound tracks in both systems in 1935. This technique, which required a limited modification to the photocell system in sound reproducers to get the full benefit from it, was mostly used in the studio recording and mixing and re-recording stages, which could now go through more than one generation of sound track, and so almost any manipulation of the sound track that was desired could be accomplished. The only place that this made a real impression was in music recording, such as the use of the Western Electric version of push-pull tracks on M.G.M.'s *The Great Ziegfeld* (1935). Multiple-channel music recording and re-recording were used on the score for *One Hundred Men and a Girl* (1938), and other subsequent films where music quality was important.

European Sounds

As was now becoming usual in film technology, Western European developments in film sound recording followed one to two years behind those in the United States, and Eastern Europe was one or two years behind that. Sometimes, by means of the intricacies of patent procedures, local equivalents of the major American sound systems found a place, and soon the RCA and Western Electric systems were licensed in Europe as well, for those who were prepared to pay for the best. The major difficulties with making synchronized sound films were the necessity for sound-proofed studios and silent cameras. Because these were not always available at the beginning of the sound period in Europe, many films were completely post-synchronized, and this sometimes led to interesting formal features. The inevitable tendency in these cases was to reduce the amount of dialogue as much as possible, and to use background music alone to cover as much as possible of the action. So such films tended to be more like silent films, and one aspect of this was that they tended to have large numbers of Insert shots in them, just as late 'twenties silent films usually did. And these Inserts were very frequently used in the metaphorical way so common in late silent films. A readily accessible example of this is Hitchcock's *Blackmail*, but other excellent examples, with even less dialogue, can still be found in Eastern Europe in the early 'thirties, such as Machaty's *Ze soboty na nedeli* (1931) and *Extase* (1933). In Soviet films of the early 'thirties, which were inevitably totally post-synchronized as well, the quality of the matching of sound to image was very poor, and a lot of the time the makers did not even bother to try to dub sounds for all the prominent visible sources, as in Protazanov's *Tommi* (1931). The actual quality of Russian sound recording was also poor, and can be exemplified by *Aleksandr Nevskii* (1938), which was recorded using a Russian imitation of the RCA system. Here the noise reduction bands on the sound track actually cut into the peaks of the modulation in many places, which inevitably causes terrible distortion in the sound.

Editing

The basic tool for sound editing had already been introduced at the beginning of sound film-making, and this was the multiple synchronizer that has already been described. Originally its purpose had been to keep the several simultaneous picture tracks obtained from multiple-camera filming in synchronism with each other during editing, and hence finally with the sound track disc, but by 1930 both multiple camera filming and sound-on-disc were being abandoned. The synchronizer was then used just to manipulate the series of pairs of picture track and sound-on-film track, and to keep them in synchronism during editing. This simple procedure gave no way of hearing the words on the soundtrack, and so was not much help in editing scenes broken down into a large number of shots. But in 1930 the sound Moviola became available, and from 1931 the Average Shot Lengths in Hollywood films started to drop. The sound Moviola was a simple adaptation of the silent Moviola, with a continuously turning sprocket drive pulling the soundtrack film under a photoelectric sound head identical to that in a sound projector, the whole unit being mounted beside the standard Moviola picture head, and driven from it in synchronism by a rigid shaft drive. Basically the machine was the same as the present-day 'Hollywood' Moviola, except that the picture was viewed through a magnifying lens, and not back-projected onto a tiny screen. The soundtrack could be moved slowly by hand under the sound head, and the exact position of any part of a sound identified.

The other development that facilitated the fast cutting (in both senses) of sync. sound shots occurred in 1932, with the introduction of 'rubber numbering' or 'code numbering' for sound and picture tracks. 'Rubber numbers' are numbers stamped in ink down the outer edge of the picture and soundtrack for each shot, and they increase serially for each foot of the film that passes. The numbers coincide on the soundtrack and picture track at the points where the corresponding image and its sound lie. After rubber numbering has been carried out it is possible to shuffle about sections of picture and soundtrack longer than one foot in the editing process with perfect freedom, secure in the knowledge that synchronism can be regained when necessary by using the numbers.

As a result of the freedom provided by these developments, the Average Shot Length in the films of this period started to decrease in a way that can be exemplified by the work of William Wellman, for *The Public Enemy* (1931) has an ASL of 9 seconds, while *Wild Boys of the Road* (1933) has an ASL of 6.5 seconds, and Wellman stayed remarkably close to the latter figure for the rest of his career. Particular advantage of the possibility of speeding up the cutting rate was taken at the Warner Bros. studio, and this effect can also be seen in Michael Curtiz's films. But the pressure was not absolute, as can be seen from the work of Mervyn Le Roy, who stayed with a slower speed, in *Tugboat Annie* (1933) and later films, of about 9 seconds, combined with some use of camera movement. (It is obviously difficult, though not impossible, to use camera movement in a large number of shots when the ASL gets down around 6 seconds.) The other extreme of cutting speed, which was much more common in 1930 than 1933, can be represented by John Stahl's *Only Yesterday* (1933), which has an ASL of 14 seconds.

It was only in the middle of the nineteen-thirties that the technological developments in editing which I have described had their full effect. For a sample of 146 American sound films made during the years 1928 to 1933 inclusive, the mean Average Shot Length is 10.8 seconds, while for a fairly random selection of 184 American films made in the years 1934-1939 the mean of their ASLs has decreased to 9.0 seconds. This change is demonstated graphically by the accompanying histograms for the distributions of Average Shot Lengths in the two cases. Although this is still not a large enough number of results to make a really accurate year by year estimate of the changes in the mean figure, it appears that a minimum was achieved around 1937. This means that although there was a wide spread in the characteristic Average Shot Length used from director to director, most directors were taking some advantage of the ease of making a larger number of cuts within a scene in the middle 'thirties. But by 1939 a new tendency

American Sound 1928-1933

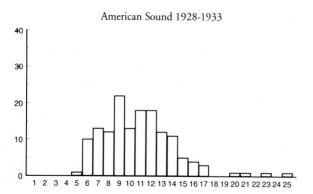

American Sound 1934-1939

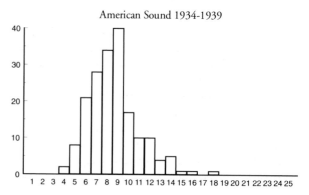

towards a move in the opposite direction was just beginning to appear: a tendency towards the use of long takes that only became fully developed in the 'forties.

To give some examples, George Cukor moved from ASLs such as 17 seconds for *Dinner at Eight* (1933) to an ASL of 10 seconds in 1935 for *Sylvia Scarlett*, and then back to long takes for *Holiday* (1938) with an ASL of 14 seconds and *The Women* (1939) with an ASL of 13 seconds, and similarly for subsequent films. Obviously this sort of movement with the trend was common (e.g. Wyler, Hawks) or the trend would not exist, but there were also a certain number of directors who stayed with what they were doing at the fast-cutting end of the spectrum. For example, Curtiz had already arrived at an ASL of around 7 seconds in the early 'thirties, and he continued right through the later 'thirties and early 'forties in the same way, with such films as *The Charge of the Light Brigade* (1936) with an ASL of 7.5 sec. and *Dodge City* (1939) with an ASL of 6 sec..

On the other hand, it was possible for just one or two directors to go against the tide without affecting the general trend, as John Stahl quite remarkably did. From an ASL of 13 seconds in *Imitation of Life* in 1934 he went on to use even longer takes in *Magnificent Obsession* (1935), which has many shots minutes long, and an ASL of 26 seconds. Even more distinctively, Stahl staged most of these long takes in 'profile two-shot', and he did not use much staging in depth as European directors who used long takes tended to do to a greater or lesser extent. Though none of these others went to such lengths as Stahl did. However by 1939 Stahl had retreated from this extreme position, with *When Tomorrow Comes* having an ASL of 14 seconds, and by the 'forties he was working near the norm for those years.

It might be thought that the Average Shot Lengths are related to the genre of the films concerned, and are not specific to the directors, but this is only true to an extremely limited extent. The most important case so far discovered after checking more than 2500 films is that of the musical, where if one includes the musical numbers in the count there is a definite tendency for a director to use longer takes than he would otherwise. This conclusion is of course dependent on the assumption that the way the musical numbers were shot was controlled by the named director, which was probably not always the case. And it is quite possible to make musicals which are fast cut throughout, as has been demonstrated in the last two decades. Another rare instance of the genre of the film dominating the way it was shot is given by the Tarzan films. Here the necessity of faking all the animal stuff ensured that the ASL was always close to 4 seconds from the 'thirties through to the 'fifties, regardless of who directed the films. Regular Tarzan directors such as Richard Thorpe never used such fast cutting in their later non-Tarzan films.

Another possibility that might occur to the reader is that the practices of individual film editors, and indeed of studio editing departments, might have some influence on the Average Shot Length of particular films. In the 'thirties it was claimed by technicians that the cutting was fast at Warner Brothers, and slow at M.G.M., and on the basis of the figures collected so far there seems to be some truth in this, though for the later 'thirties only. However, if we remember that the Tarzan films just mentioned were made at M.G.M., and also note that although there were no contract directors who went in for long takes at Warner Brothers, there were sometimes visitors such as Howard Hawks and William Wyler who made films tending in that direction, then we can see that the distinction was not absolute, but once more merely a tendency. Howard Hawks' *Ceiling Zero* of 1936 made at Warners has an ASL of 12 seconds, and Wyler's *The Letter* (1939) has an ASL of 18 seconds, despite their being edited by regular Warners editors, William Holmes and George Amy respectively. These editors did not impose on these two films the kind of cutting rates they used in their regular work for Michael Curtiz and others. In fact at this period Curtiz's films have an ASL of 6 to 7 seconds consistently, and Mervyn Le Roy's an ASL of 9 seconds, even though they were not all cut by the same editors, and indeed some Warners editors worked on films by both directors. Of the other Warners directors, Enright and Keighley worked with ASLs of 5 to 6 seconds, and Mayo and Goulding with 9 to 10 seconds. This last value was as high as Warner contract directors went in the 'thirties, but when the long take trend really got under way later in the next decade some of the Warner Brothers directors both new and old moved with it to some extent.

On the other hand one finds consistency of **Average Shot Length** from comedies to dramas to action subjects in the work of directors such as Hawks and Wyler and others, wherever they happened to be working.

European Scene Dissection

The adoption of American methods of scene dissection that had taken place in the European cinema in the late 'twenties was preserved after the transition to sound, but there were still some general difference in this respect between the films from the two areas. Again, this can be readily seen from the accompanying histogram showing the distributions of numbers of sound films with different ASLs made in Europe in general from 1928 to 1933 inclusive, and comparing them with that for American films of the same period. It is important to point out that the sample includes a certain number of films in which most of the scenes were shot wild, and then post-synchronized, usually in an approximate sort of way. In these cases the directors usually took advantage of this to use silent-style fast cutting a good deal, and it is these films which are represented by figures down to 2 seconds in the bottom end of the range. These were films like *Dezertir* (2.3 sec.) and *Niemandsland* (4.5 sec.).

There was not much speeding up of the cutting rate in the latter part of the decade on the continent of Europe, unlike the case in America, as can be seen by comparing the illustrated distributions. The mean ASL for the 1934-39 period for films made on the continent of Europe (i.e. excluding British films)

American Sound 1928-1933

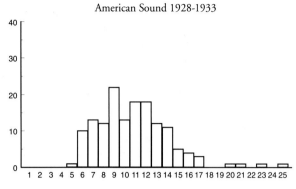

American Sound 1934-1939

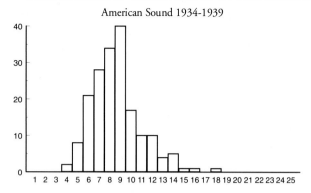

European Sound 1928-1933

Continental Sound 1934-1939

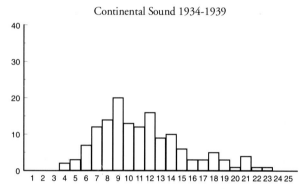

French 1934-1939

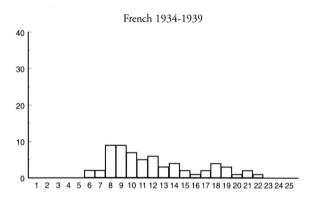

British 1934-1939

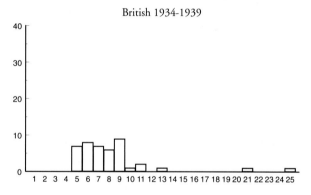

is 12 seconds for a 122 film sample, and in particular, for 64 French films made in this period there are only 4 with ASLs of 6 and 7 seconds. The mean value for this collection of French films was 13 seconds. The German situation was fairly similar, with slightly more emphasis on fast cutting, mostly due to the activities of Luis Trencker. The ASLs in his films were consistently very close to 5.5 seconds. Similar situations seem to have held in the other European countries in the late 'thirties.

On the other hand, the British sample gives a mean value for the Average Shot Length over the 1933 to 1939 period of 8 seconds, which is noticeably less than the value for American films of the same period. It seems that for later periods this tendency to cut English films slightly faster than American films has persisted, and it might be speculated that the source of this tradition was the influence of the famous Russian films of the late 'twenties that were regularly shown by The Film Society in London. The directors and editors of ordinary English feature films attended these screenings as well as the members of the British documentary movement, and there was nothing comparable to it in Hollywood.

On the Continent reverse-angle cutting was now used fairly freely, but the amounts used were several percent below typical American values, with most commonly around 20-25% of the shot transitions being reverse-angle cuts.

The Shock Cut

The 'shock cut', which is a cut to a different scene accompanied by a sharp discontinuity in the accompanying sound – say from near silence to loud music – seems to have been invented by Alfred Hitchcock. In his *Blackmail* of 1929 there is a scene in which the guilty murderess is surprised by noticing the slumped body of a dead-beat in a doorway. A woman's scream on the soundtrack then instantly accompanies a cut to the body of her murder victim elsewhere, and the next shot reveals that the scream has been emitted by another woman discovering the body. Hitchcock worked a variant on this transition in *The Thirty-Nine Steps* (1935), in which the shock cut was from a woman about to scream on discovering a body, to a shot of a steam train accompanied by a loud whistle on the soundtrack at the cut. In both these cases the cuts can be understood as being cuts to parallel action, with the second scene taking place at the same time as the first, but in the 'forties, following on from the example of *Citizen Kane* (1941), there are also a few examples of shock cuts that are also jump cuts, in which the transition is to a scene taking place not only elsewhere, but also much later. Although extremely rare, and always restricted to one example per film, shock cuts are more likely to be found in British films than anywhere else in the years prior to the nineteen-fifties. I have never seen one in an American film of the 'thirties.

The Life and Times of the Jump Cut - Part 1.

The origin of the jump cut as an intentional special form of transition used in sound films is obscure. It is quite possible that it worked its way out of early musicals, where it was less conspicuous because supported by a continuous music track, into ordinary dramatic films. For instance, in *Hallelujah* (1929), as the hero makes his way home from prison, he is shown in a series of shots singing and playing a song on the banjo while sitting on top of a train, and then on the back of a wagon, and then walking, with music continuity across a series of jump cuts that move him from one mode of transportation to the next. This is the weakest or softest form of the jump cut, in which the transition is not only from one place and time to a different and later place and time, but there is also continuity on the sound track. The most noticeable or hardest form of the jump cut, in which there is a transition with a straight cut to a later time in the same location, was unknown in this period. In the case of jump cuts in ordinary non-musical scenes, which are only found in European films in the 'thirties and the 'forties, the transition was always prepared and softened with dialogue in the scene being left. For example, in *la Crise est fini* made by Robert Siodmak in 1934, a scene ends with one actor saying to other actors gathered around him something along the lines of: 'There's a piano in the shop round the corner, let's have a look at it tomorrow.', and then there is a cut to a shot of the same group looking at the piano in the shop the next day. Other directors besides Siodmak who were inclined to use the jump cut included Max Ophuls in his mid-thirties films such as *Komedie om Geld* (1935), Alessandro Blasetti in *Vecchia guardia* (1935) and *La corona di ferro* (1941), and many German directors such as Karl Ritter in *Capriccio* (1938) etc. As with shock cuts, the standard quota of jump cuts was one or two per film, and no more.

Communist Cut-Ups

The fashion in Russian films made at the end of the 'twenties for including sections of very fast cutting indeed at climaxes, with shots a few frames long being cyclically repeated, lasted into the beginning of the nineteen-thirties, and into some of the early Russian sound films. This device can be seen

in Pudovkin's *Dezertir* (1933), for instance, where it is also combined with the kind of disjunctive use of sound recommended by Pudovkin and Eisenstein in their theoretical writings of some years before. This was something Eisenstein himself never tried, and after this film nobody else did in dramatic films either. *Dezertir* also shows that Pudovkin had no idea about how to get someone out of a shot on one side of a room into a shot on the other side when shooting sound, and like his other sound films confirms that he had always been a small talent doing his honest best to compete with the big talents of the Russian cinema.

The Dialogue Cutting Point

At the beginning of the 'thirties editors were starting to realize the importance of what might be called the 'dialogue cutting point' for making soft (i.e. smooth, unnoticeable) cuts when cutting from one speaker to another in a scene. In general the least noticeable cut from a speaker in one shot, to his listener who is about to reply in the next shot, will be made while the last syllable of the last word from the first speaker is still being spoken. Actually, most editors cut at the very end of the last syllable, which is almost equally acceptable, but virtually none cut in the middle of the pause between the two speeches, or just at the beginning of the reply. Of course deviations from this point can be made for reasons of emphasis and expression in general, most notably by cutting to a listener's reaction in the middle of a speech, but even there you will find that the cut in the picture usually falls on the last syllable of a sentence. Curiously enough, this principle is not to be found in most books on editing technique, so presumably it is passed on to apprentice assistants at the editor's knee, but in any case it should be immediately obvious to any would-be editor from watching a couple of films.

Some uncertainty about this point is still visible in some films from the first years of the decade, for instance Frank Capra's *Platinum Blonde* (1931), but by 1933 the principle seems to have been fairly well established in the editing of American films. The only later instances of bad dialogue cutting that I have particularly noticed are in the dialogue scenes of Astaire-Rogers musicals made by Mark Sandrich at R.K.O..

Narrative Construction

The early 'thirties was a period when some of the brightest spirits were still very active in trying out new devices for narrative construction in the mainstream sound cinema, and most of the instances are well known. Nevertheless for completeness sake I should mention such features that depend on the use of a soundtrack as the internal monologue in Hitchcock's *Murder* (1930), the visual illustrations supplied to speeches which continue on the sound track only in Fritz Lang's *M* (1931), and the subjective camera sequence opening Mamoulian's *Dr. Jekyll and Mr. Hyde* (1932). The narration of *The Power and the Glory* (William K. Howard, 1933) through a series of flashbacks in non-chronological order is also fairly well-known now, though the most daring feature for a dramatic film in *The Power and the Glory* is the flashback in which the narrator's voice quotes the remembered dialogue used on that occasion, and his words are made to coincide with the lip movements of the figures in the past apparently speaking them. The cinema audience is once more directly addressed by the principal character at the end of the film *Lucky Boy* (Alan Crosland, 1930), but then the camera pulls back to reveal that what had seemed an ordinary film up to that point was in fact taking place on a theatre stage in front of an audience. There are also a number of asides to the audience in Lubitsch's *The Smiling Lieutenant* (1931) and *Love Me Tonight* (1932), though we must remember that such liberties with the conventions have always been taken in comedies, and now this liberty was extended to musicals. The Czechoslovak cinema pushed slightly away from the norms with Vladislav Vancura's *Pred maturitou* (1932) and *Na slunecni strane* (1933). The former is notable for its narrative construction in terms of scenes written as autonomous blocks, without the standard causal lead from events at the end of one scene to those at the beginning of the next scene. Thus the relevance of most scenes only becomes apparent later in the film. This method could be seen as an anticipation of Jean-Luc Godard's methods in the nineteen-sixties. This feature is less important in *Na sluneci strane*, which puts more emphasis on apparently non-functional camera movement and extreme high angles on scenes. It seems that this film also had a good deal of theorising behind the costuming and performances of the actors, but the effectiveness of this for the unprepared spectator is doubtful.

The later nineteen-thirties were the cinema's most restricted and restrictive period, and although as already indicated the characteristics of films continued to occupy a large range in most of the major formal dimensions of the medium, there was very little indeed going on at the innovative extremes. Even documentary films, which had to a certain extent taken the place of the now non-existent avant-garde, were rather timid in the main, and one cannot point to much more in them than the rhythmic sound-and-poetry tracks of Cavalcanti's *Coal Face* (1935) and its successors, and the peculiarities of Dziga Vertov's *Tri pesni o Leninye* (1934). In feature films Dovshenko's *Aerograd* (1935), with its interjected choral songs illustrated on the picture track springs to mind, but otherwise one is left with very little else except the innovative games played with the medium in some of Sacha Guitry's films such as *Roman d'un tricheur* (1936).

Overall one can characterize the trend in the early 'thirties in mainstream cinema as an attempt to return to the main features of the last silent films, 1928 vintage, as soon as the various technological constraints on putting a film together were relieved. Having reached this point about 1937, new technological developments began to have some effect on film photography, and at the end of the decade a new trend towards longer takes was just starting to emerge independently of any technological pressures, a trend that was to flourish in the nineteen-forties.

16. STATISTICAL STYLE ANALYSIS OF MOTION PICTURES - PART 2.

If we want to establish the existence of an individual style in the work of a director, it is necessary to compare not only a sufficient number of his films with each other, but also, and this has always been forgotten until I pointed it out, to compare his films with films of similar genre made by other directors in the same period. This latter procedure is necessary so as to avoid describing as characteristic of a film-maker's work those features which are in fact shared with the work of other film-makers. For every period an even more absolute norm is needed as well, to give a standard of comparison that reflects the general technical and other pressures acting on the work of all film-makers at that time and place. And ideally *that* requires the analysis of a large number of films, both good and bad, chosen completely at random. Choosing one or two films to try to establish the stylistic norm for a period is close to useless. In parenthesis, I might add that this comparative approach should be applied to the discussion of the singularities of content in a director's work, as well as those of form. If this were done it would eliminate a lot of the wild over-interpretation of films that still continues to be produced.

The two and a half thousand values of Average Shot Length that I have so far collected go some way towards meeting these requirements, but though my collection contains a certain number of rather poor films, the many truly bad films that have been made are under-represented. About half as many films have been checked for percentages of reverse-angles, but so far I have not collected much more than two hundred and fifty Scale of Shot distributions. Nevertheless, I think that even that number allows many interesting and important conclusions to be drawn with a fair degree of certainty.

If you examine the further collection of Scale of Shot distributions for a number of sound films that are printed

here, you can see that some groups of them have a strong family resemblance – they are more like each other than they are like any of the other films. This applies particularly to the films made by Jean Renoir – *la Chienne* (1931), *Boudu sauvé des eaux* (1932), *Toni* (1934), *Une Partie de campagne* (1936), and *la Règle du jeu* (1939), and also to the many Ophuls films dealt with in the appendix. The group of von Sternberg films whose Scale of Shot distributions are illustrated in Chapter 12 and also here, and which span the transition to sound are even more alike with respect to this stylistic dimension, and give an indication of the degree of stylistic continuity there can be across the change from silent cinema to sound.

However, there does tend to be a change in Scale of Shot distribution for most directors between the early sound period, say up to 1932, and the later part of the 'thirties, as the technical pressures against close shooting are removed. The way that the work of directors can change over their working life, with their output breaking down into periods in which they shoot films in slightly different ways, is illustrated by a groups of Fritz Lang and Alfred Hitchcock films. In the case of Lang, there is a clear transition from his European films, with their emphasis going increasingly up to Long Shot, and his American films, which move over to much more emphasis on closer shots, and in particular the middle range of shot closeness. When such changes happen more or less simultaneously in the style of a number of directors, they give rise to the large scale stylistic trends which this book is mostly concerned with discovering and analysing. One such trend is hinted at by the Scale of Shot distributions for *It* (Clarence Badger, 1927), *Flesh and the Devil* (Clarence Brown, 1926), and a number of other silent films not illustrated. In these films the bulk of the shots are from Medium Shot or closer,

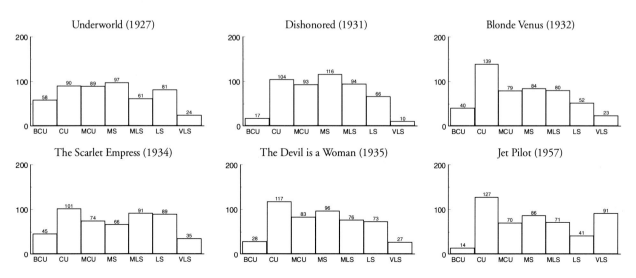

Number of Shots with Given Scale of Shot per 500 Shots in the Named Films

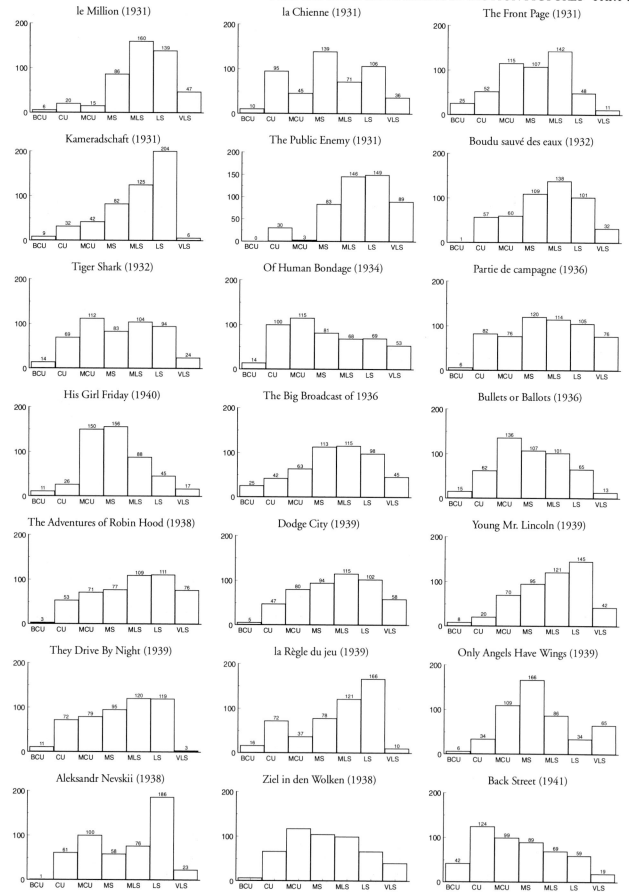

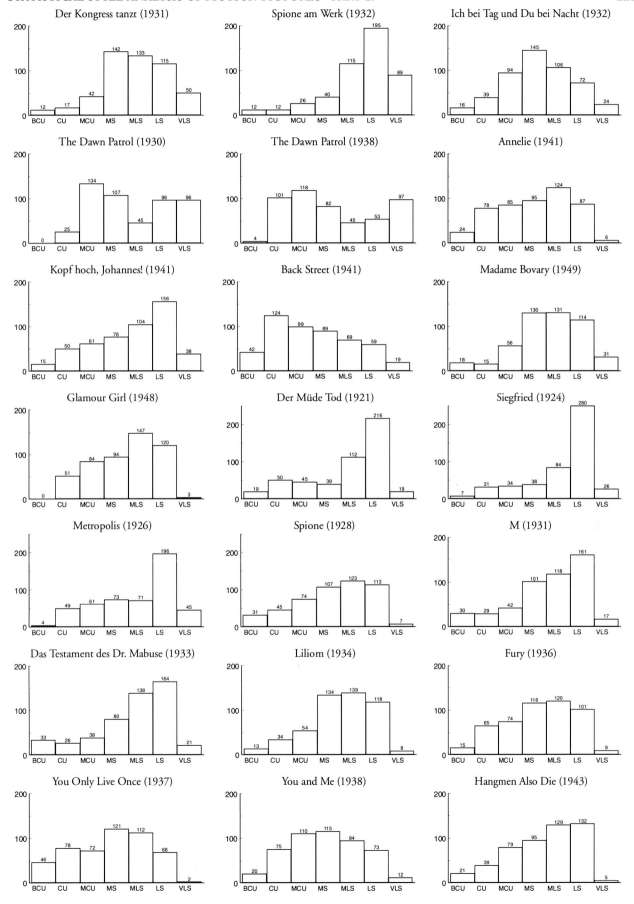

The Ministry of Fear (1945)

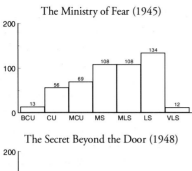

The Woman in the Window (1945)

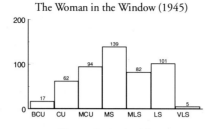

Cloak and Dagger (1946)

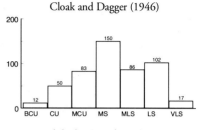

The Secret Beyond the Door (1948)

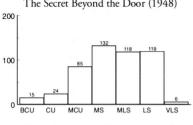

Human Desire (1954)

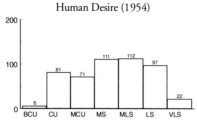

While the City Sleeps (1956)

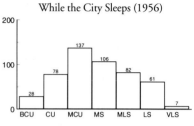

Beyond a Reasonable Doubt (1956)

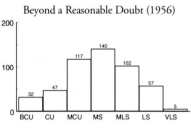

Der Tiger von Eschnapur (1958)

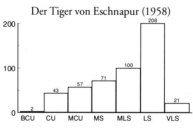

Die tausend Augen des Dr. Mabuse (1960)

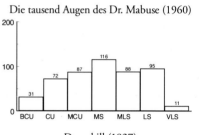

The Pleasure Garden (1925)

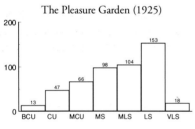

The Rat (1925)

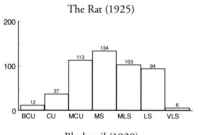

Downhill (1927)

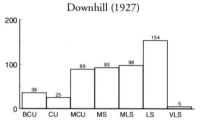

The Lodger (1927)

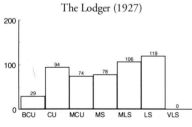

Blackmail (1929)

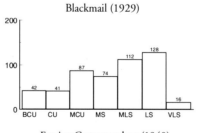

The Man Who Knew Too Much (1935)

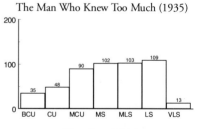

The Lady Vanishes (1939)

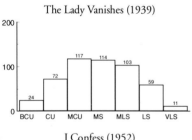

Foreign Correspondent (1940)

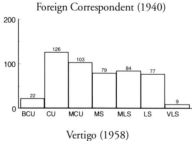

Notorious (1947)

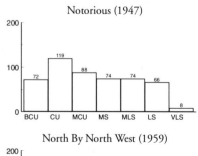

I Confess (1952)

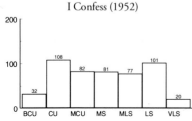

Vertigo (1958)

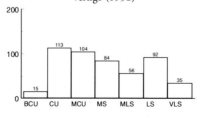

North By North West (1959)

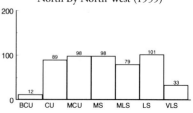

with the strongest emphasis on the Close Up, and an increasing number of American directors were coming to shoot their films in this way at the end of the 'twenties.

Another of the interesting points that emerges is the persistence of the weakened form of the early Medium Shot style, particularly in a number of European films. This was about as close in as European film-makers shot films; anything like the insistent close filming of *Of Human Bondage* (John Cromwell, 1934), *The Dawn Patrol* (Edward Goulding, 1938) and *Back Street* (Robert Stevenson, 1941) was unknown on the Continent. Another curiosity is the persistence of the D.W. Griffith type of Scale of Shot distribution in John Ford's *Young Mr. Lincoln* (1938).

The sharp-eyed reader will have noticed that a few films by *different* directors also have a close resemblance to each other with respect to Scale of Shot, but in these infrequent cases one always finds that the films are fairly sharply distinguished by other stylistic parameters. For instance, the Scale of Shot distributions for *The Public Enemy* (William Wellman, 1931), and *le Million* (René Clair, 1931) are very similar indeed, but we find that the former uses vastly more camera movement when we look at the tabulations of camera movement given below.

Camera Movement

The fashion for the use of extensive camera movement that arose in the late 'twenties and continued across into the sound period suggests the possibility of making stylistic distinctions in terms of the number of shots with different camera movements, since not all directors subscribed equally to this fashion. So the number of shots with panning, tilting, and tracking movements per 500 shots were found for a number of films, taking the movements as they occurred both separately and in their combined forms as well. A category containing shots involving the use of a camera crane was also used. It should be noted that where small pans and tilts were made merely to keep the actors nicely framed, which was an automatic action by camera operators from the end of the 'twenties onwards, then the shots were classed as static, as were those in which the camera was fixed relative to the actors while the background behind them moved: e.g. an actor filmed in a car. Incidentally, real camera movements are only made when authorized by the director, and further than that they are nearly always called for by him rather than anybody else, so I hope that one day we will see the end to the practice of film reviewers referring to such and such a cameraman's '..fluid and intricate camera movements..' In any case, once a director has decided on a tracking shot, the execution of it is usually supervised by the camera operator rather than the lighting cameraman (i.e. Director of Photography), at any rate in England and America.

Camera movements do not seem, on the evidence available so far, to be so characteristic of a director's work as Scale of Shot, but there is still a fair amount of resemblance between

	Pan	Tilt	Pan with Tilt	Track	Track with Pan	Crane
T. Graals bästa Film	1	0	0	0	0	0
The Hired Man	4	7	0	10	0	0
Erotikon	0	0	0	0	0	0
Hallelujah	3	0	0	3	3	0
The Public Enemy	36	3	3	36	18	0
Kameradschaft	61	25	12	76	51	0
le Million	16	4	2	2	0	2
la Chienne	45	9	3	44	17	0
Boudu sauvé des eaux	30	1	0	7	7	0
Toni	45	8	8	23	25	0
Partie de campagne	58	12	0	23	21	0
Sylvia Scarlett	22	4	0	15	11	0
His Girl Friday	82	0	0	20	9	0
The Big Sleep	77	3	1	36	64	0
The Front Page	0	0	6	39	65	0

Number of Camera Movements of the Specified Kind per 500 Shots for the Films Named

Renoir's films in this respect; however the large number of tracking shots in *la Chienne* must be noted, and the small number (for Renoir) in *Boudu*. This is undoubtedly intentional, and must relate to Renoir's statement with regard to the style of his films that he did different things in each of them; a statement that is somewhat surprising at first sight.

His Girl Friday has been included in the analyses because chance presented the opportunity of comparing it with *The Front Page* (Lewis Milestone, 1931), and so checking an assertion made by Andrew Sarris about the two films. He wrote on page 59 of *The Primal Screen* (Simon and Schuster, 1973) about *His Girl Friday*: '...Hawksian fluidity of camera movement and invisibility of editing was actually faster than Lewis Milestone's classical montage in *The Front Page*'. Now, *The Front Page* when analysed has a far greater number of tracks of both kinds than the Hawks film; objectively it has far greater fluidity of camera movement. The Average Shot Length of both movies is the same, but the Milestone film achieves this by having a larger number of very short shots, and also a larger number of very long shots, and this is certainly a very idiosyncratic feature, and hence not 'classical' as I shall show below. As far as Scale of Shot distributions are concerned, the difference between the two films, though real, is not very large, and in any case it is by no means clear what 'classical' might mean in this context. The cutting in *The Front Page* is standard continuity cutting, just as it is in *His Girl Friday*, but I do admit that there is a further idiosyncrasy in Milestone's film, which it shares with others he made around this date, and that is the inclusion of strings of fast cut Close Ups at two or three points in the film. However these only make up a minor part of the total length. *His Girl Friday* is not free of patches of fast cutting either, and the sequence of violent action after the escape of Earl Williams is shot and edited in a very similar way in both films.

Actually the effect of greater speed in *His Girl Friday* is largely due to the fact that the actors in that film move around a great deal, and indulge in a lot of 'business' as they deliver their lines, and also because they speak them faster. In other words, the speed was already in the scene filmed, and not in the way it was put on film. Andrew Sarris can sometimes be a perceptive commentator on the visual style of films, as can be seen from his comment that Wellman's '...images tend to recede from the foreground to the background...', which is illustrated by the Scale of Shot distribution here for *The Public Enemy*, but the indulgence of his prejudices and his reliance on screenings alone can lead him to make serious mistakes, despite his worthy attempts to use a comparative method.

I find that even after a lot of experience with the methods of analysis I am using here, I am still often unable to anticipate exactly how the statistical results will come out after one viewing of a film, and I am still being surprised by the large scale trends that emerge. I also find that further incidental benefits are gained from my approach to film style analysis, in the way that all sorts of detailed points about film construction emerge while I am actually analysing a film on a viewing

machine. To give just one example, when comparing *Boudu* and *le Million*, which are both pretty much static camera films, I became aware that without sound *le Million* is a rather boring film to watch, but the other two are not. The statistical results partly indicate why this is so: it is because Renoir and Vidor get the camera closer to the actors. But the points that only become apparent on the bench are that in cross-cutting between parallel actions, Renoir cuts while the actors are still moving, rather than between points of repose, and also that in *le Million* there are a number of unnecessary cuts: shots that could have been continued from the chosen camera position are cut short, and the scene continued with only a small change in camera position, such a change being too small to add any dynamic impulse to the film.

Patterns in Shot Lengths

In my search for variables that might characterize different films, I initially looked at the shot lengths in a number of films. I had expected that the numbers of shots of different lengths in a film would give a distribution that would differ in shape from one film to the next in much the same kind of way that the Scale of Shot distributions differ. After obtaining more than twenty of these shot length distributions, for both sound and silent films, I was surprised to discover that films with roughly the same Average Shot Length have roughly the same shot length distributions, no matter who made them, and further than that, the distributions all had the same general kind of shape, as you can see illustrated here for *The Adventures of Robin Hood* and *Une Femme Mariée*. For the further investigation of the nature of these shot length distributions I was fortunate to have the advice and help of Laurence Baxter and Valerie Isham, and Wai Ling Chan made a careful numerical study of some of these distributions under the supervision of Dr. Isham. As a result of all this work, I have drawn the following conclusions.

For those films having Average Shot Lengths up to about 20 seconds or a little beyond, (which includes the vast bulk of ordinary commercial movies), the distribution of numbers of shots with different lengths conforms at least approximately, and very well for films with a short ASL, to a standard statistical distribution, the Lognormal distribution. This distribution is found to apply to many varied phenomena, one example of which is the numbers of insurance claims for different amounts of money as a result of damage to motor cars in accidents. But more interestingly, it has also been found to apply in literary statistics, and amongst other things, the numbers of sentences of various given lengths in a stretch of prose conforms to the Lognormal distribution. Theoretically, the Lognormal distribution results when the quantity under consideration, in our case shot length, is determined as a result of the probabilities associated with a large number of factors being multiplied together. In films, what is presumably concerned in determining the length of a shot is the simultaneous interaction of such factors in the scene being filmed as: how the actor moves in the shot with respect to the closeness of the

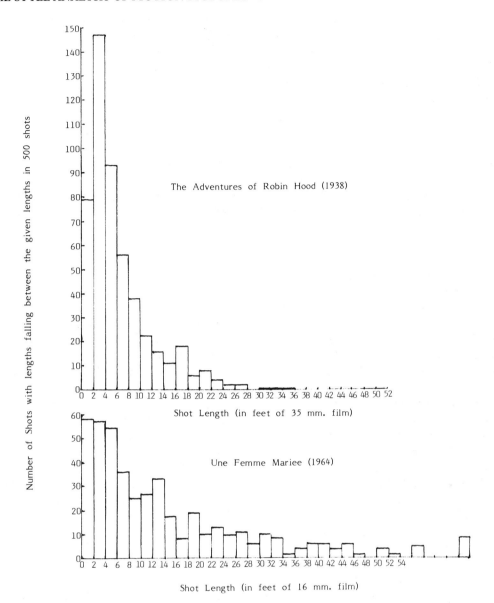

Number of Shots with lengths falling between the given lengths in 500 shots

The Adventures of Robin Hood (1938)

Shot Length (in feet of 35 mm. film)

Une Femme Mariee (1964)

Shot Length (in feet of 16 mm. film)

camera, what lines he speaks, and how the other actors react, and so on. Though there is no way of being certain about this at the moment. For those much rarer films with a very high Average Shot Length of around 30 seconds or more, the nature of the distribution of shot lengths is not at present clear, but the indications are that it will turn out to conform roughly to the Gamma distribution.

The practical result of all this is that, given the Average Shot Length of a film, one can tell roughly how many shots there will be of any given length in it. For instance, if the ASL of a film is 6 seconds, 90% of its shots will be shorter than 12 seconds, and it is unlikely that any of them will be longer than 30 seconds. On the other hand, if the ASL of a film is 21 seconds, only about 40% of its shots will be shorter than 12 seconds, and 12% of its shots will be longer than 30 seconds. And so on.

If we look at the actual lengths of shots as they appear in succession in any particular film, it can be seen that there is a tendency for shorter shots to be grouped together in continuous strings that roughly correspond to scenes and sequences in the film, and the same is true to some extent for the longer shots. To put it another way, there is a fairly high probability that a short shot will be followed by another short shot, and a moderately high probability that a long shot will be followed by another long shot. There is nothing particularly remarkable about this, since it just corresponds to the fairly obvious observation that scenes that are meant to be exciting in one way or another tend to be cut up into a lot of shots, and neutral or romantic scenes are not. There is a statistical measure for the tendency of one shot to be followed by another of roughly the same length, and this is called the autocorrelation coefficient of lag 1. When this is computed it confirms what is visible to the eye, which is that there are a few films which do not conform to the general pattern I have just described of the way the lengths of shots follow one another in most films. In some of Jean-Luc Godard's films the lengths of successive shots are truly distributed at random (within the constraints of the Lognormal distribution), and there is no such expressive organization of their length in relation to the narrative.

To conclude for the moment the discussion of patterns in shot length, I will add that in all films one occasionally sees pairs or triplets of successive shots that have *roughly* the same length, but in sound films at least there are no signs of any tighter metrical patterns.

The Question of Accuracy

The accuracy with which the various parameters I have introduced characterize the work of particular film-makers can be estimated from the results that I have presented themselves, and it is clear that as far as Average Shot Length and Scale of Shot distributions are concerned, differences in quantities have to be well above 10% to be significant for style considerations, and those differences which are below 10% are not. Percentages of reverse-angle cuts and amount of camera movement show wider variations. This means that in the quotation of Average Shot Length, for instance, it is quite sufficient to give it to the nearest second for values over 10 seconds, and to the nearest half second below that.

A related point concerns the estimation of these quantities by sampling sections of a film rather than taking its whole length. In the case of a 16 mm. print of *le Million*, for instance, the first 1000 feet gives an ASL of 5.19 feet, the next 1000 feet an ASL of 5.47 feet, and the remaining 896 feet an ASL of 5.26 feet, all of which stands against an ASL for the whole film of 5.31 feet. Here the deviation of the Average Shot Length from the parts, each about 27 minutes long, to the whole is only a few percent, and this is quite typical in my experience. However this is no longer the case when we are dealing with shorter sections of film, say of the order of 10 minutes. The reason that a thirty minute sample gives an adequate characterization of films as a whole is that once the construction of mainstream narrative films became standardized in the nineteen-twenties, as I have described in Chapter 13, it became the rule that there would be several dramatic climaxes spaced down the length of the film, and the treatment of these in terms of cutting and camera placement was also standardized in a general sort of way.

In my work so far, the Scale of Shot distributions are taken for the whole length of the films under consideration, but most of the figures for Average Shot Length and percentages of reverse-angle cuts are taken from sections of the films in question that are at least 30 minutes in length, and also contain at least 200 shots. If this criterion is not satisfied in both its parts, there is a danger of the error of estimation of the ASL rising above 10%, at which point the value quoted loses its usefulness for comparative purposes. In fact, I found this out the hard way, when in the early stages of my investigations around 1974, I tried taking shorter sections to estimate the overall ASL for the film. In any case, about 400 of the figures for ASL's in my present database *have* been taken from complete films, and the process of obtaining these has given a check on the validity of the approximation by using a sectional sample, in the way described above.

17. FILM STYLE AND TECHNOLOGY IN THE FORTIES

During World War 2 the numbers of films made in all the major film-producing countries fell sharply. However despite this, cinema admissions and box-office takings rose by a good deal in the United States, and something of the same sort of effect occurred in the other combatant countries. This trend continued for a couple of years after the end of the war, but then in 1948 cinema revenues began to fall in the United States. At this date there was still a rather small number of T.V. sets in the U.S., and so it has been suggested that this increasingly rapid fall in box-office returns, which continued into the nineteen-fifties, was due to an increasing movement of the population into the suburbs and a turn to other leisure activities with increasing affluence. Be that as it may, the rise of television probably made some contribution to the reduction of movie income, but it was only during the next decade that the production companies took any positive steps to combat it.

After the end of the war there began to be an increasing tendency to deal with down-beat subject matter in all the major film-making countries, though story construction in such films largely followed traditional lines. An associated trend was an increase in the amount of location filming, mainly of exteriors, but sometimes even interiors. The innovatory films in America include *The House on 92nd. Street* (1946) and *The Naked City*, and this trend emerged before the more famous films from the Italian 'neo-realist' movement had reached the U.S. In fact, if we except Roberto Rossellini's *Paisà* (1946), the style of the Italian 'neo-realist' films was quite continuous with that of Italian films produced both before and during the war, particularly with respect to scripting, dialogue, acting, and the amount of location filming used. (Like all the less wealthy countries, the Italians had always been inclined to use rather more location filming of exteriors than the Americans.) The real, though limited, difference was that the settings and costuming of a number of Italian films at this time were much scruffier than those of other countries, and in a few of them the narrative tone was more unrelievedly grim. In Germany there were also a number of films made dealing with the aftermath of the war – the 'trümmerfilme', but the execution of these was polished in the conventional way, despite the subject matter.

Film Stock and Processing

The only new black and white negative stocks that appeared during the 'forties were Dupont Superior II and III, which had speeds under tungsten light of 100 ASA and 200 ASA respectively. At the introduction of these stocks in 1940 the ASA system of speed rating still did not exist, but it was finally proposed in 1941, and became generally accepted over the next few years. The wide range of film stocks available from this period onwards made the use of exposure meters mandatory on interiors and exteriors, and in 1941 a new instrument joined the small range of meters already available. This was the Norwood exposure meter, which was basically an incident light meter, and the ancestor of the present Spectra and Sekonic meters. Unlike the other incident light meters in use at that time, which simply measured the absolute intensity (in foot-candles) of the light arriving on the scene from one direction, the Norwood meter took a weighted average of the light from all directions, and included a calculating device to give a direct reading of the appropriate exposure. In the 'forties cameramen also continued to use reflected light meters of the already existing Weston type.

The only significant development in film processing was the use of 'latensification', a process which was alleged to have had a vogue with the major studios for some years, starting in 1947. This process involved fogging the negative with an all-over uniform exposure to white light before the film was used in the camera to shoot scenes. This resulted in some increase in the effective speed of the film and a flatter (less contrasty) image. However, such an effect is not particularly obvious in films of the late 'forties as against those made earlier, so it may be that the extent of the use of this process has been exaggerated.

Technicolor

During the nineteen-forties there were no major changes in the three-strip Technicolor process, but in 1943 35 mm. Kodachrome was used for the first time as a camera material to produce a master film from which prints could be made by the Technicolor process. The Kodachrome reversal film could be exposed in any standard 35 mm. camera, and after its development in the usual way at the Eastman Kodak plant, Technicolor then made three black and white negatives corresponding to the three negatives produced by the Technicolor camera, by printing from it with red, green, and blue light in succession. From this point onwards the Technicolor process proceeded exactly as it did normally. Advantage was first taken of the convenience of using this 'Technicolor monopack film' in the filming of sequences in *Dive Bomber* (1941), *Captain of the Clouds* (1941), and *The Forest Rangers* (1942). All the exteriors of *Lassie Come Home* (1943) were shot on 35 mm. Kodakchrome. *Thunderhead, Son of Flicka*, also made in 1944, was the first complete feature to be shot with monopack and printed by the Technicolor process (1944). From this date onwards there continued to be a few Technicolor films made each year using this same monopack process, until Eastmancolor arrived at the beginning of the 'fifties.

The image quality of Technicolor films shot on 35 mm. Kodachrome was substantially inferior to those shot in the standard way with the Technicolor three-strip camera; the definition and colour reproduction were noticeably poor, and the contrast very high, so that shadow areas were rendered as a solid, heavy, featureless black with a blue tinge. This was in fact the typical response of the Kodachrome emulsion of that period, somewhat accentuated by the extra stages of the reproduction process.

The lighting of standard Technicolor usually continued in the general style established at the end of the 'thirties, which was like a simplified version of black and white photography. That is, the angles of application of the lights was roughly the same, but overall the number of lighting units used was reduced, and hence the finer shadings. Also the intensity of the backlights was reduced relative to the key light from the front, and sometimes backlighting was left out altogether. (In black and white filming the intensity of the backlight had always been higher than that of the key light from the front, but this was not usually the case in Technicolor.)

However there were some cases of the black and white type of backlighting being used with Technicolor, and one of the more accessible examples is Ray Rennahan's lighting of the dialogue scenes of *Lady in the Dark* (1944). In this film, as in other Technicolor films of the 'forties, the general level of illumination would be described as high-key or mid-key, with very little strong shadow present in the image, which was always fairly bright all over. Just about the last Technicolor film where a strong-minded director managed to get large amounts of heavy chiaroscuro and simple lighting from one or two sources was Rouben Mamoulian's *Blood and Sand* (1941).

Many cameramen continued the practice, begun in *The Private Lives of Elizabeth and Essex* (1939), of splashing patches of amber light on parts of the backgrounds of interior sets in period films.

Agfacolor

Agfacolor first became available in the 35 mm. negative-positive form in Germany in 1939, and it was almost immediately used for feature production. Agfacolor negative was produced with two different emulsions, one balanced for exposure under tungsten light, and the other for exposure under daylight, and their speeds were approximately 25 ASA These Agfacolor negatives had a three-layer emulsion, the layers being sensitive to red , green, and blue light, with the dye formers that produced the colour being included in the layers and held in place by attached long-chain molecules. This was unlike Kodachrome, in which the dyes had to be introduced into the emulsion layers in a series of complicated steps during processing. The result was that the development of Agfacolor was a relatively simple process, to which ordinary processing machines could be adapted without too much difficulty. The other great advantage of the Agfacolor process was that the negative could be exposed in ordinary cameras,

but it did have its drawbacks as well. The most serious of these was that there were no intermediate duplicating negative and positive stocks provided in the system, so that just as in the early days of black and white, if ordinary camera negative and printing positive were used to make duplicates, then the quality of the final print was noticeably inferior. So fades and dissolves (and also all trick effects), had to be made in the camera, just as in the silent period, and wipes could not be made at all.

(Some early Agfacolor films include what to the casual eye might seem to be wipes, but they are in fact only the illusion of wipes achieved by an ingenious trick. What has been done in these cases is that the negatives of the two shots have been cut straight together, and then the emulsion has been scraped down the length of the film to give a clear diagonal band that moves from one side of the film strip to the other, passing just across the mid-point at the position of the cut. This clear band prints as a black line, and when projected it moves across the frame like a wipe line, readily fooling the eye into seeing the picture moving with it.)

As a result of the impossibility of satisfactorily duplicating Agfacolor, all the scenes had to be shot with three cameras simultaneously, to provide two extra negatives for safety, and to make possible the production of a large number of prints.

The performance of Agfacolor in its earliest stages can be represented by *Münchhausen* (Karel von Baky, 1943), in which the Venice Regatta scenes contain material shot in 1939. This early stock was noticeably inferior to the later material used in the film, with its performance being virtually that of a two-colour system: i.e. giving only reds and blues as well as neutral colours. Even in its final form, Agfacolor did poorly in reproducing bright colours, with bright reds coming out as brick-red. Differentiation of the greens from one another was not good either. The sharpness of the image on the other hand was quite good, particularly in the material produced right at the end of the war, being not much inferior to three-strip Technicolor in this respect. Original prints of Agfacolor films show noticeable unevenness in colour reproduction from scene to scene, and this was due to variations between the batches of film stock used, reinforced by the fact that the dyes used in the positive print stock proved to be extremely fugitive. All these features continued to characterize the films made after the war by the Russians in 'Sovcolor', using the captured Agfa plants, patents, and processes. Even today Russian colour film is incapable of producing an intense red, and the other hues are also slightly muted when compared with Eastmancolor. (Again a word of caution: many Russian prestige productions shown in the West have been printed on one of the Western film stocks, and then the above comments do not apply.)

From a formal point of view, the most interesting German films made in Agfacolor were Veit Harlan's *Opfergang* (1944) and *Immensee* (1943). The handling of colour in these films was bolder than in any Technicolor films made up to that time, with a particular feature of *Opfergang* being the use of large areas of half-light in the interiors, which was something that was avoided in Technicolor, while in *Immensee* there is a ball scene in which there are shots lit entirely by light of various single colours.

Cinecolor

Cinecolor continued to be a two-colour process throughout the 'forties, and a small number of cheap features were made using the system in those years. The process, though essentially the same, had now been considerably improved, with better methods of dye-toning being used at the print stage. In *Gallant Bess* (1946) one can even see a certain amount of differentiation between some greens and some blues, which is quite an achievement for a two-colour process. But inevitably the process could never produce a true red, or strong blues, or any yellows.

Lighting

A survey of light levels used for interior filming at the major studios published in the July 1940 issue of *The American Cinematographer* gave results which can be summarized as follows. Nearly all the negative in use was Eastman Kodak Plus-X, and at Warner Brothers and Paramount the light levels were around 60 foot-candles and the usual camera aperture f2.3. At R.K.O. and M.G.M. the light levels were around 150 foot-candles for an aperture of f2.5, and at Columbia and United Artists the light levels were 40 foot-candles for an aperture of f2.3. The position at Twentieth Century-Fox was quite different, for at that studio it was the rigid policy to photograph everything on interior sets at f3.5 with a light level of 150 foot-candles. These figures show that R.K.O., Fox, and M.G.M. were not concerned about spending three times as much as the other studios on electrical power to secure the particular results they variously wanted. It is also clear from considering the manufacturer's recommendation of an aperture of f2.3 for 100 foot-candles and f3.5 for 250 foot-candles when exposing Plus-X that all the studios except R.K.O. and M.G.M. were underexposing the film and then compensating for this by increased development, while R.K.O. and M.G.M. were overexposing and giving reduced development. The result of these procedures would be that films from the former group of studios would be slightly more contrasty than those from the latter pair, which would tend to have more middle greys in them, and less blacks and whites. However we have also to remember that the general contrastiness of the image is controlled up to a certain point by the lighting ratio between the lit and shadowed parts of the scene, which is arranged at the will of the individual cameraman, though this cannot completely over-ride the effect I am discussing. All the studios except Fox were clearly working at maximum lens aperture, and hence at the position of worst definition for any lens, and even the f3.5. at Twentieth Century-Fox was some way from the aperture of around f5.6 to f8 that gives maximum image sharpness. This whole situation clearly changed with the trend towards greater depth of

field in the late 'forties, but unfortunately no figures are available for that period.

Before leaving this discussion of the trend towards a greyer image in the late 'thirties and early 'forties, it is worth mentioning a particularly fine example of the style, in the work William Daniels did on *New Moon* (1940). Here there is a continuous succession of shots with very finely worked chiaroscuro in grey tones, with the disposition of the grey shadows being controlled in their placement to a degree that no-one ever surpassed, and few equalled. But the influence of *Citizen Kane* was to change all that, despite the initial rejection of Toland's work by many Hollywood cameramen.

Because of the move to faster film stock and lower light levels in the early nineteen-forties, less powerful (and smaller) lighting units were called for, since it was not possible to reduce the number of lights on a particular set to produce these lower light levels, without at the same time changing the style of the lighting. So in 1940 small spotlights with Fresnel lenses and 150 and 300 watt tungsten bulbs as light sources were introduced. They were in fact just miniature versions of the larger incandescent Fresnel-lens spots that had come in a few years before, and like them they focussed from parallel spot beam to medium flood positions. They were colloquially referred to as 'dinky inkies', or just 'dinkies'.

Also in 1940 there appeared what proved to be a passing fancy in the technique of lighting Close Ups. This was the use of fluorescent tube lighting mounted beside, or all around, the camera lens. This did not have too much effect on the style of lighting, as the cameramen concerned still used incandescent floods and spots as well on their Close Ups, and these over-rode any extra softness in the lighting which might have been produced by the fluorescent tubes. In any case the practice was shortly dropped.

But the most significant development in new lighting equipment produced in 1940 proved to be, in the long run, the introduction of photoflood bulbs with reflecting surfaces coated onto the inside of their glass envelopes behind the filament. Developed by General-Electric, these bulbs were just as we know them today, and they produced an even flood-lighting over a spread of about 90 degrees. The light source in them was a tungsten filament that was 'over-run', or operated at a voltage higher than that for which it was really designed, and the result was that a filament consuming 200 to 500 Watts could give far more light than one of the same rating run at its correct voltage. The not very serious drawback to this idea was that the bulbs only had a life of a few hours. Again, some cameramen tried using these bulbs in groups of 4 to give fill light on Close Ups, but their important application began at the end of the decade with the beginning of the move towards filming on location interiors.

This move to location filming was an aesthetic choice, no doubt induced by the experience of all concerned with documentary film in World War 2, and the move was made in the first place with the technical equipment already available in such films as *Roma - città aperta* (1945) and *The Naked City*

(1948). Given that the Italian films concerned were post-synchronized entirely, and the American ones partially, there was no reason why this step could not have been taken in the late 'thirties if the desire to do so had existed. But once the move to location filming was underway, some new lighting equipment appeared in 1949 to help it along. This was the Colortran lighting outfit, which consisted of several 500 Watt and 1 kiloWatt lamps powered through one variable transformer from the A.C. mains current. The lamp-heads, which weighed only a few pounds, contained very large bulbs like overgrown reflecting photoflood bulbs, with their rear internal surfaces shaped and mirror-coated to produce beams of various kinds, both spot and flood. The voltage applied to the lamps, which was again in excess of their design values, could be varied within certain limits, and hence the brightness of the lamps, and also the colour of their light, could be controlled. A 1 kW. Colortran lamp could give roughly the same amount of light as an ordinary 2 kW. film light, although it was several times smaller and lighter. The drawback to these units was that their beams were not as precisely defined, nor could they be as easily controlled, as those in the standard Fresnel spots. Colortran lights were mostly used for the ever-expanding 16 mm. production of the 'fifties, but occasionally they were used on location filming on features.

As far as the style of lighting in these location films of the late 'forties is concerned, we can say that in *The Naked City* there is some simplification of the lighting over what would be expected in a studio film on a similar subject, although in very general terms the approach is the same as regards the types of lights used and the angles from which they were applied. There is some reduction in the amount of backlighting used, but William Daniels still manages to cheat it in on most of the close shots, if not on the Long Shots. And the directions from which the lights come are sometimes not quite as carefully chosen as they would have been in the freedom of the studio. In the case of *Roma - città aperta*, it is important to realize that it contains a number of studio-shot scenes, particularly those in the Gestapo headquarters, and in these the lighting has the polish one would expect from a European film of this vintage, which is slightly less than that in an American film.

The location scenes in *Roma - città aperta* are lit with only a very few lights, but these are still carefully disposed to produce reasonably attractive lighting, though without any backlighting. The roughness in these scenes is in what is lit rather than the way light is applied. But it is in the exteriors, always the crucial test of finesse in applying extra artificial light, that the lighting of this film is crudest. The fill light is just bashed straight on from the front, and in some Long Shots there is none at all, even though they are taken on the kind of overcast day with grubby natural light that is ordinarily avoided, or if not avoided, then sharpened with artificial light. However, it must be noted that these observations are not a judgement on the total aesthetic value of this lighting *in the context of this film*.

Cameras

The only new 35 mm. camera produced in any numbers in America during the 'forties was the Cunningham Combat camera. This lightweight (13 lb.) camera was especially designed for use in World War 2, and it had a three-lens turret, pilot-pin registration, and took 200 foot daylight loading spools in an internal magazine. However it had no reflex viewfinding system, and was much less well suited to its purpose than the Arriflex cameras used by German military cameramen. In fact Bell & Howell 35 mm. Eyemos and 16 mm. Filmos were the cameras most used in action by the Americans, and after the war the Cunningham camera vanished from the scene. British Army cameramen used De Vry, Newman-Sinclair, and Bell & Howell cameras, all of which dated back to the 'twenties. They also had the specially produced and much-despised 'Normandy' clockwork drive camera made by Vinten for the end of the war.

Although the German Arriflex camera was introduced in 1937, it was hardly used in fiction film-making until after the war. Even in Germany documentary cameramen filming sports footage were still using the older Askania (i.e. Debrie) cameras in 1938. The initial form of the Arriflex was identical to the present simplest form of 35 mm. Arriflex for 'wild' filming, though at first it only had a 200 foot magazine, and all the cameras were painted smooth grey rather than matt black as now. The continuous through-the-lens viewfinding system by means of a mirror surfaced-shutter set at 45 degrees to the lens axis was the same as in all 35 mm. Arriflex cameras now, and so was the film movement with its simple single claw driven by an equally simple double-cam gear. The small electric motor powered by rechargeable batteries was set vertically under the small body of the camera, and the detachable magazines incorporated the sprocket drive which was pre-threaded when the camera was loaded. The film transport arrangements meant that the magazines of the Arriflex could be changed very quickly in the heat of the moment, and taking into account its light weight (12 lb.) it was ideally suited to its wartime use as a combat camera. Captured Arriflexes were in use in Hollywood soon after the war, and by 1947 this camera was again being made by Arnold and Richter in West Germany. The first notable use of the hand-held possibilities of the Arriflex was in the subjective camera opening sequences of Delmer Daves' *Dark Passage* (1947), but in general application of this camera was very limited in Hollywood. However in Italy, where post-synchronization of dialogue was the rule, the Arriflex became the major production camera in the nineteen-fifties.

In 1948 a close competitor for the Arriflex appeared in France. This was the Eclair Cameflex, which like the Arriflex had continuous through-the-lens viewing by way of a mirror-reflex shutter, though in this case the axis of rotation of the mirror-surfaced shutter was set at 45 degrees to the lens from below it, rather than to one side, as in the Arriflex. The Cameflex had a 400 foot displacement-type magazine with the film sprocket drive included in the magazine, and a weight of 13 lb. unloaded. This camera had two slight advantages over the Arriflex: firstly, that its different shape permitted the back of the camera to be rested on the shoulder when hand-held, so making hand-held takes slightly steadier, and secondly, that the magazines could be changed in two seconds while the camera motor was still running, since the film loops and the back pressure-plate of the film gate were included in the magazine. The first of these features had some effect on some of the 'Nouvelle Vague' films of a decade later, but the immediate effect of this camera on French production was zero. What we have here is another clear-cut case of the dominance of aesthetic considerations over technical possibilities as far as the form of films is concerned.

During World War 2 a considerable amount of 16 mm. footage was blown up to 35 mm. for use in feature films, and from this point onwards the 16 mm. cameras that were available became important for feature film production. The first relatively quiet 16 mm. camera suitable for synchronous sound filming appeared in 1940. This was the Berndt-Maurer Pro camera, but it was quickly displaced by its descendant, the Auricon single-system sound camera that became available in 1942. This latter camera in its original form weighed 37 lb., had a three-lens turret, and an arrangement for through-the-lens viewing when not shooting by displacing the film gate and sliding a ground glass screen behind the lens. The film was pulled through the gate by a simple long curved claw that would only run forwards, and there was no registration-pin system. Sound could be recorded directly onto the edge of the film in the correct soundtrack position simultaneously with the picture being taken. At this stage in the camera's development only 200 foot magazines of the usual American configuration were fitted, but in 1947 some modifications, including larger magazines, were made to give the Pro model of the Auricon camera which can still be found in some odd corners today.

Camera Supports and the Long Take

As has previously been mentioned, in 1939 there was just beginning to emerge a movement towards the use of longer takes on the part of some directors, led by George Cukor. By 1940 Howard Hawks had definitely joined in with *His Girl Friday* having an Average Shot Length of 13 seconds, and so had William Wyler, with an ASL of 18 seconds for *The Letter*. Prior to this both directors had been working with lower Average Shot Lengths. Other notable contributors to the trend included Henry King, George Marshall, and Edmund Goulding. The net result of all this was that the mean ASL for a large sample of Hollywood production went up from 8.5 seconds in the late 'thirties, to 9.5 seconds in the period 1940-1945, and finally to 10.5 seconds in the period 1946-1950.

In 1940 these longer takes were achieved with conventional dispositions of the actors within the shot, with standard lenses, and without a greatly increased amount of tracking around, though Hawks' method was to use more panning shots than

the average. But already in the famous long take of over 4 minutes in *The Letter*, the lens used is 35 mm. or a bit shorter, and the playing is between actors in Medium Close Shot and Long Shot respectively. This kind of approach was to become important shortly, and will be dealt with below.

Another approach to even greater take lengths involved increased camera mobility, and here the leading figure was Vincente Minnelli, and the key work concerned was *The Clock* made in 1945. With an ASL of 19 seconds, this film naturally has many takes that are minutes long, and these are mostly covered with camera movement, even including the use of a crane to this end, possibly for the first time in a non-musical film.

Up to this point I have been treating of situations that could be dealt with using the equipment already available, but as new directors, including notably Otto Preminger, joined the trend, the demand for the ultimate manoeuverability of camera dollies produced the 'crab dolly'. (A crab dolly can be steered by all four wheels interconnected to turn together, as well as by the usual two wheel steering. Hence it can be instantaneously turned from a movement tracking straight forwards to a 'crabbing' movement sideways at 90 degrees to the original path.) The first crab dollies produced were the Houston crab dolly in 1946 and the Selznick crab dolly in 1948. Both of these dollies had mechanically rising centre posts on which the geared head and camera were mounted, but a crab dolly with hydraulic rise was produced in 1950. In the same year a really small crab dolly was introduced in the Italian studios, the predecessor of the present-day Elemack Octopus crab dolly, and this was capable of passing through ordinary-sized doorways and passages. The result of its use can be seen in Rossellini's *Europa '51*, in the opening party scene.

The introduction of the crab dolly is again a clear-cut case of film technology meeting a purely aesthetic demand.

Given the stylistic developments outlined above, it can be seen that Alfred Hitchcock's *Rope* (1948) and *Under Capricorn* (1949) were not isolated instances that appeared from nowhere, but the culmination of a trend to which Hitchcock did not contribute at first, for it is typical of his early 'forties films that *Saboteur* (1942) and *Shadow of a Doubt* (1943) have ASLs of 9 seconds and 8.5 seconds, which is very close to the norm for that period. But *Under Capricorn*, on the other hand, contains so few shots that the exact value of the Average Shot Length no longer has much significance (though it is in fact about 40 seconds), since the nature of the particular screenplay being filmed with such very long takes begins to dictate the exact ASL in a way that it does not with films that contain a large number of shots. To put it another way, it is only if there are upwards of 200 shots in a film that an averaging effect can take place to produce consistency from one film to the next in the work of a director, regardless of subject matter. And of course the exact Average Shot Length has little significance in the case of a film like *Rope* where there are only four cuts within the whole film.

It should be added that Hitchcock then dropped the whole

idea, and returned to the use of ordinary take-lengths: for instance *Stage Fright* has an ASL of 9 seconds. Later he moved on to even faster cutting.

The Long Take in Europe

In continental Europe long takes had often been used by film-makers right through the 'thirties, and this continued to be the case in the 'forties. As before, these long takes were mostly done with fairly conventional staging of the action, and only a certain amount of camera movement. In England, on the other hand, where nearly all directors had used fast cutting through the 'thirties, the new American fashion for the long take had very little effect. Right at the end of the decade one or two directors such as David Lean briefly flirted with this approach (*The Passionate Friends* has an ASL of 11 seconds, for instance), but after a couple of years they returned to their usual faster cutting. The only British director to pursue an interest in the long take right through the nineteen-forties was Thorold Dickinson, from *Gaslight* to *Secret People* (1950). In his particular case he says the original inspiration came from *Hôtel du Nord* (1938), and other Marcel Carné films, but though these films were highly regarded in England at the end of the 'thirties, there is no other sign of their influence on British cinema.

Lenses

The first zoom lenses of modern design for 16 mm. use became available at the end of the 'forties. These were the American Zoomar lens in 1947, and the French SOM-Berthiot Pan-Cinor in 1950. The former had a maximum aperture of f2.8 and a zoom range from 17 mm. to 51 mm., and the latter a zoom range from 20 mm. to 60 mm., which rather limited their usefulness, and we have to wait till the 'fifties for zoom lens use to become significant. However there are some very rare cases of the use of 35 mm. zoom shots in Hollywood films, for example in Raoul Walsh's *White Heat* (1949), where one is used in a transitional exterior shot establishing a new location, and this was presumably done with one of the old Taylor-Hobson zoom lenses.

The first practical anti-reflective coatings were applied to camera lenses in 1940, and these coatings, which were layers of magnesium fluoride approximately a quarter of a wavelength thick evaporated onto the lens in a vacuum, came into general use from 1941. In an untreated lens there is considerable light loss by reflection backwards of the entering beam of light at each air-glass interface, and the coatings which were applied to the surfaces greatly reduced this loss by an interference effect. In an untreated lens, as well as the loss of light by internal reflection backwards, there is also a general scattering of light in the forwards direction, which produces 'flare', which is a general pale wash of light over the image. Flare is also drastically reduced by the correct lens coatings.

At the time that this happened there were the usual excessive claims from Hollywood cameramen that tend to greet any technical innovation. In *The American Cinematogra-*

pher (p.108, Vol.21, No.3, 1940) William Stull claimed that, on the basis of some simple tests, a coated lens was one stop faster than a similar uncoated lens set at the same aperture. But shortly after this, a group of optical experts and lens designers, including William C. Miller and Dr. Rayton, agreed that on the basis of precise measurements the increase in light transmission after coating was about 40% for a typical lens, which is a speed increase of less than half a stop. Nevertheless the effect of coating was very real, and particularly useful in situations where flare was likely to occur.

Some years after coated lenses became the usual thing, in 1948 in fact, the system of calibrating camera lenses in T-stops as well as f-stops was introduced. The T, or transmission stop, is the aperture setting that passes as much light as the f-stop with the same number would in an ideal lens with no light losses whatever. This transmission stop gives the correct setting of the aperture for the required exposure regardless of the losses in the particular lens being used, and this became important as lenses with a large number of elements in them were introduced, because such lenses have fairly large losses, even when coated. In fact good 18 mm. lenses were just starting to become available from Taylor-Hobson and others at the end of the 'forties, and these inevitably had a large number of elements in them. So the production of these very wide-angle lenses was only made possible by the introduction of lens coating, and likewise the design of zoom lenses with larger zoom ratios in the nineteen-fifties, as these too had a large number of elements in them.

Gregg Toland, Deep Focus, and Wide-Angle Lenses

The first extensive use of coated lenses was in the photography of *Citizen Kane*, but before dealing with this film it is necessary to mention what Gregg Toland had done beforehand. In the films Toland had lit under contract to Goldwyn during the 'thirties there is no sign of any deep focus in the *Citizen Kane* sense, nor is there much sign of the 'Toland-esque' compositions which typify his work in the 'forties. However Toland's films from the 'thirties do show a noticeable simplicity of lighting when compared with the usual lighting set-ups in similar scenes lit by other cameramen. It was really just a matter of Toland using less lighting units than anybody else, and inevitably having a slightly unusual disposition of shadows in his scenes. This is one of the things which enables one to differentiate between the parts of *Come and Get It* (1936) lit by Toland and the parts lit by Rudolph Maté, as I have already discussed. Before leaving Toland's work in the nineteen-thirties, it is worth noting that as well as its distinctive qualities, it also has shortcomings in some areas. For instance, Toland was not particularly good at conventional 'glamour' photography, as is particularly evident in a number of poorly handled Close Ups of Merle Oberon in *Wuthering Heights* (Wyler, 1939), where her slightly difficult face, which was rather flat around the eyes, is not shown to its best advantage.

In 1940 Gregg Toland lit two films for John Ford, *The*

Grapes of Wrath and *The Long Voyage Home*, and in these there are a very few shots where something of his *Citizen Kane* approach becomes evident. In *The Grapes of Wrath* one or two proto-deep focus shots occur accidentally, for reasons I have given in the previous chapter, particularly in the scene in which Tom Joad goes up to the exterior of his family's deserted house, moving past the camera from Close Up to Long Shot, in sharp focus all the way. In *The Long Voyage Home* there are one or two low-angles on the deck of the ship, and some typical Toland compositions in the crew's bunk room, with darker foreground figures massing into roughly triangular areas across one of the lower corners of the frame. There is even one shot in which special measures have been taken to get increased depth of field, probably the use of a split-field dioptre.

Gregg Toland has given a good description of the photography of *Citizen Kane* in *The American Cinematographer* (February, 1941), so only a brief resumé is necessary here before making some additional points about this film. *Citizen Kane* was shot with Super XX negative, and the apertures used throughout were in the range from f8 to f16. Toland claimed that only lenses of 24 mm. and 28 mm. focal length were used, and this means that typical depths of field would have been at one extreme from 2 feet to infinity with the 24 mm. lens at f16, and at the more restricted extreme, from 4 feet to 50 feet with the 28 mm. lens at f8. The second case still carries sharp focus from Close Up to Long Shot, and the first case represents what can now be called true 'deep focus', with sharpness from Big Close Up to Long Shot. However, close examination of the film suggests that other lenses were used as well. The breakfast table scene between Kane and his wife seems to have been shot with something like a 35 mm. lens, as do some of the closer shots of Susan Alexander elsewhere in the film. These latter scenes also get conventional lens diffusion treatment (so-called 'soft focus'), which is otherwise totally absent

in the film. The general absence of lens diffusion throughout the photography of *Citizen Kane* is made more noticeable by the sharp-edged lighting style resulting from using powerful arc floodlights without fill lighting in most of the film.

Lens Diffusion

In this reduction of the use of lens diffusion *Citizen Kane* was in advance of its period, for it was not until the late 'forties that it became usual to limit lens diffusion to a handful of key Close Ups in a film. How important Toland was in causing this trend is not clear to me, for the increasing experience of cameramen with Technicolor filming, in which lens diffusion was never extensively used, may have contributed, as may have the non-photographic concern with 'realism' in the late 'forties. Whatever the cause, one finds that by the end of the 'forties even in romantic melodramas like *Letter From an Unknown Woman* (Max Ophuls, 1948), there is little use of lens diffusion, even on female Close Ups, so that this phenomenon certainly cannot be associated solely with the vague category of so-called *film noir*, as some have tried to do.

Coated Lenses in Citizen Kane

The use of coated lenses made some contribution to the achievement of a smaller aperture with a given light level in the photography of *Citizen Kane*, but not as much as has been claimed. Actually, as I have already indicated, the extra light transmission with coated lenses was only about half a stop, and in fact the use of coated lenses was much more important for securing sharp black and white images in 'against the light' filming situations, such as the scene in the projection room at the beginning of the film. In this scene the figures silhouetted by the strong arc beam from the projection booth would have been turned from crisp black to grey by a wash of flare, and their edges would have been quite blurred, if uncoated lenses had been used.

A female Close Up without lens diffusion in a romantic scene in Letter From an Unknown Woman *(1948). This lighting arrangement, with strong backlight and key-light straight on from a little above eye-level, was consistently used by Fritz Planer for photographing the leading actress in this film.*

A scene in The Keeper of the Flame
*(1943) lit and composed by William
Daniels in a slightly diluted form of the
Gregg Toland style. The main light source
is directly above the centre of the group,
and there is very little fill light relieving the
heavy shadows on the faces.*

Low-Angle Filming

The apertures mentioned as having been used in the photography of *Citizen Kane* could have been achieved by lighting with large arc spotlights of the kind available from the beginning of the 'twenties, by applying them from above the walls of the set in the conventional way, but this would have meant avoiding the kind of low-angle shots used so much in this film. Once the decision had been taken to use low-angle shots, presumably by Gregg Toland, since he had flirted with this approach before, then of course the sets had to have ceilings on them, and this in its turn meant that powerful arc floodlights had to be applied from floor stands if ridiculous lighting patterns were to be avoided. Hence the 'Duarc' floodlights actually used by Toland. These had been available from 1939, and Super XX the year before that, so deep focus in the Toland style had been possible for anyone who wanted to try it from 1939. And true deep focus *without low-angles* was possible long before that. So Toland's creation of 'deep focus' filming was simply an aesthetic decision, without the influence of technological pressures.

Like many features of the photography of *Citizen Kane*, the extensive use of low-angles was adopted by Orson Welles as a feature of his own style when he went on to make films with other cameramen. In *The Magnificent Ambersons* (1942), the use of low-angles is quite relentless, and never before or since have so many been laid end to end.

Wide-Angle Lens Staging

The other aspect of *Citizen Kane* that was to prove most influential through the 'forties and into the 'fifties was the disposition of actors within the field of a wide-angle lens. This followed the pattern already described for some shots in *The Long Voyage Home*, with even stronger emphasis on the triangular areas of foreground mass, and also on the implied diagonal of interest between the foreground figure placed towards a lower corner and the head of the background figure towards the opposite top corner. This sort of composition and staging in depth was gradually taken up by many film-makers, although they usually did not bother about the deep focus element of it, but often let the foreground figures go slightly out of focus. The heavy and broad chiaroscuro of *Citizen Kane* was also not taken up in general.

One of the first films where the influences of *Kane* were visible in the way described was *The Maltese Falcon* (John Huston, 1941), where an even wider angle lens of 21 mm. focal length was used to get some of the shots. The most direct imitation of *Citizen Kane*, both in screenplay and lighting, was Cukor's *The Keeper of the Flame* (1943). For this film William Daniels used a number of low angles in the Toland manner, and also a fair amount of heavy chiaroscuro, but with far softer-edged shadows and a greater complexity of disposition of the same. And naturally Toland took his ideas with him to the films he subsequently photographed for William Wyler, though he dropped the heaviness of the *Citizen Kane* chiaroscuro. Finally, on *The Best Years of Our Lives* (1946), by increasing the light levels even further and stopping down to f22, he managed to get deep focus in some shots made with a 50 mm. lens.

The Long Take with Wide-Angle Lens Staging

Citizen Kane is not very exceptional for its period as regards take length, as its ASL is only 12 seconds, and it only contains a couple of takes that get up around 2 minutes. But the method of staging within the field of view of a wide-angle lens already described in *Citizen Kane* proved to be important for the subsequent development of another current in long take filming. This method of long take filming mostly avoids the use of tracking shots, and as well as using the careful staging in depth as in *Citizen Kane*, it keeps the takes going with pans if actor movement makes this appropriate. This path proved congenial to some older directors as well as to newcomers, and a prime example of this is Henry King. He took up wide-angle lens staging tentatively in *The Song of Bernadette* (1944), and very definitely in 1950 in *Twelve O'Clock High* and *The Gunfighter*, which have ASLs around 12 seconds. Another well-known director who took to this method was Billy Wilder, for whom a good example would be the way many of the dialogue scenes are covered in *Double Indemnity* (1944), which has an ASL of 15 seconds. As a result of these practices involving the frequent use of wide-angle lenses, it was noted in *The American Cinematographer* for September 1950 that in many of the studios a 35 mm. lens was coming to be regarded as a standard lens, instead of the 50 or 40 mm. as formerly.

Wide-Angle Lens Staging in Europe

There had always been a slightly greater tendency to use wide-angle lenses occasionally in European films, and the new American fashion increased this tendency at the very end of the nineteen-forties. Wide-angle lens staging was not necessarily associated with long takes, and one of the more extreme examples of their use, Helmut Käutner's *Der Apfel ist ab* (1948), has an ASL of only 9.5 seconds. This is, I think, the first film to include extensive use of an 18 mm. lens, and the use of this very wide-angle lens is made very conspicuous by fast tilts and tracks. So *Der Apfel ist ab* is a good place to study the slightly disturbing visual effect of this conjunction of wide-angle lens and fast camera movement.

The Third Way

The two ways of filming with longer takes already described, that is, using a very mobile camera with standard lenses, or alternatively using wide-angle lenses and staging in depth, were to a large extent separate, for the extensive use of combined tracking and panning with a wide-angle lens is visually disturbing because of the way the various planes in the image shift with respect to each other as the camera moves. Particularly in the case of rapid movements of a wide-angle lens, objects in the foreground seem to be detached from those in the background and 'swim' past them, unless a certain awkward special measure is taken. This involves shifting the camera back on the supporting head so that the centre of the lens is over the pivot point, and in any case it is doubtful if this not completely satisfactory solution was known at this date. Straight parallel tracking following the actors, and small slow pans are however quite acceptable with a wide-angle lens. Directors using either of these two mutually exclusive methods of long-take filming also did some of their scenes with fairly conventional staging, and still managed to keep the shots going longer. There was also a third stream in the longer take trend as it developed, involving directors both old and new who were perhaps less filmically imaginative, who used nothing but perfectly conventional stagings and standard lens photography, but who still made films with longer takes in

the late 'forties. Directors who spring to mind include George Marshall with films like *The Blue Dahlia* (1946) with an ASL of 17 seconds, and Joseph Mankiewicz with *The Ghost and Mrs. Muir* (1947) with an ASL of 13 seconds, not to mention the founder of the school, George Cukor.

And finally a great many directors ignored all this, and went right on doing what they and the others had been doing in the 'thirties, fast cutting and all.

Dutch Tilts

Dutch tilts or off-angles – shots with the sides of the frame skew to the vertical – had a brief run of popularity with a few European directors at the end of the 'forties. They were usually associated with the extensive use of low-angle shooting, but they were not one of those things that were used to any extent in *Citizen Kane*. The source of this passing fashion was probably Wolfgang Staudte's *Die Mörder sind unter uns* (1946), and it was taken up in the first place in other German 'trümmerfilme'. The shots using dutch tilts were closely associated with the dramatic events in the ruins that gave these films their name, and by 1947 it was possible to parody the style in *Film ohne Titel* (Rudolf Jugert). (This last film is also very interesting for its narrative structure. It opens with the ostensible makers of the film discussing what to put into it, and after several different beginnings are represented, one basic story is followed through, though with three different endings in three different styles being shown and discussed by the 'makers' of the film.)

But the peak of the fashion for the use of dutch tilts was reached outside Germany, in Carol Reed's *The Third Man* (1949). In this film the greater proportion of the shots are framed skew, and when this style reaches this extreme it imposes severe demands on the director's grasp of the scene dissection he is using. It had always been usual when a string of dutch tilts occurred in a montage sequence or the like to make sure that successive shots were tilted in opposite directions to the vertical, and this in turn meant that if a large number were used consecutively in ordinary dramatic scenes the director had to keep in mind which shots were going to be next to each other in the finished film when they were shot out of sequence, as was often the case. Carol Reed was able to get this 'right' most of the time in *The Third Man*, but the same was not true for other directors involved with this fashion.

Amongst the others who picked up the fashion might be mentioned Max Ophuls, but the style made no headway at all in the United States, and as the 'fifties and wide-screen wore on it vanished except in remote corners such as Russia (*Devyat dnei odnovo goda*, Mikhail Romm, 1960) and Argentina (*La casa del angel*, L. Torre-Nilsson, 1957).

Optical Effects and Shot Transitions

If we except the development of a travelling matte system for use exclusively with the Technicolor process (*The Thief of Baghdad*, 1940), there were no major advances in optical effects during the 'forties. The introduction of the Acme-Dunn automatic optical printer in 1943 did no more than increase the efficiency of the basic machine by allowing the exposure of a series of frames to take place automatically from instructions punched into paper tape. This increase in efficiency could only have had a visible outcome in an increase in the number of optical effects used in films, and it is quite easy to think of reasons why this did not happen.

As far as shot transitions in general are concerned, the innovation for Hollywood was the use of a few jump cuts in *Citizen Kane*, though Orson Welles referred to them at the time as 'lightning mixes'. In this film the jump cuts are mostly in fact 'shock cuts' accompanied by purposefully conspicuous sound cuts, which indicates how they had been arrived at by derivation from Welles' radio play techniques. It is not very likely that the small previous use of jump cuts and shock cuts in European films had registered in Hollywood, and in any case, their use in *Citizen Kane* did not make them popular there. In Europe, as indicated in the previous chapter, they continued to be used sometimes, particularly in England, where the major figure most given to the occasional use of the shock cut was Michael Powell in his films made in the late 'forties, from *I Know Where I'm Going* (1945) on to a climax in *The Elusive Pimpernel* (1950).

The wipe continued to be widely used to indicate a short time lapse, particularly in action subjects or sequences at most studios, and on all subjects at Warner Brothers. The Warner editing department used a whole range of simple lateral wipes with edges of varying softness, all the way from an almost hard-edged wipe to a wipe with the edge so fuzzy and broad that it covered the whole frame and was almost indistinguishable from a dissolve. The truly hard- or sharp-edged wipe was no longer used on feature films in the 'forties.

There was still no sign of the use of the wipe freeing the dissolve to be used for some purpose other than indicating a time-lapse, but an interesting isolated case of an alternative meaning being attached to dissolves occurs in *Waterloo Bridge* (Mervyn Le Roy, 1940). In this film, during a romantic scene in which the hero and heroine dance to a small orchestra, the transitions between the shots of the couple and the shots of the musicians are done with a series of dissolves, although the preservation of strict time-continuity is indicated by all concerned keeping time to the continuously synchronous music. Elsewhere in this film dissolves are used conventionally to indicate short time lapses, and as might be expected in an M.G.M. film, no wipes are used. This 'lyrical' use of the dissolve as a form of softer cut seems not to have reappeared till the 'fifties, and not to have become standard practice till the nineteen-sixties.

Sound Recording

There were no major developments in sound recording in Hollywood in the nineteen-forties except for the introduction of magnetic recording in 1949, and since this had no great use until the 'fifties, it is best considered with respect to that period. Otherwise there continued to be a few slight improvements in the various stages of sound-on-film recording, but these had no effects on film form. The Disney studio's Fantasound stereophonic sound system was installed in a limited number of major American cinemas for the first run of *Fantasia*, and thereafter dropped completely, and in any case it was not intimately connected with the nature of that film, so it is best ignored in this survey.

There were some advances in microphone design which should be mentioned for completeness, though they had no formal effects. In 1939 Western Electric introduced an improved type of condenser microphone, the 640A, which had an extended and flat frequency response up to 10 kHz., but moving-coil and ribbon microphones continued to be preferred for film recording in America, though improved condenser microphones held on rather more in Europe. The most favoured moving-coil microphone was still the Western Electric 630 (the 'ball and biscuit'), but directional microphones with a cardioid pattern of sound pick-up gradually began to displace it as the decade wore on. The two major types of these were the Western Electric 639 and the R.C.A. MI-3043, both of which contained ribbon diaphragms. The first also had a moving-coil element in the same housing to produce the cardioid response by the combination of the two signals, and the second had acoustic damping chambers behind the ribbon to alter its response from the figure-of-eight pattern to the cardioid pattern. These microphones dated from 1941 and 1939 respectively. The ribbon elements in both of them were very sensitive to mechanical vibrations as always, and so there were very limited possibilities of movement if they were used on a microphone boom. Nevertheless, they tended to be used whenever possible, because the fact that they picked up sound in the forward direction only meant that they could get clean sound without much background noise further away from the actors than was possible with omni-directional microphones such as the Western Electric 630. Their other advantage was that they had a much more extended and flatter frequency response than earlier microphones.

Reverse-Angle Cutting

The 'forties are a good point from which to survey the development of reverse-angle cutting in mainstream American cinema, for it was not until this period that this stylistic figure reached its peak exploitation. And it really is just a figure of style, for the use of this kind of cutting varies from director to director, and from period to period, as will be shown. Reverse-angle cutting is taken to include all cuts within a scene which change the camera angle by more than 90 degrees. In the adjoining shots on either side of a reverse-angle cut the camera can be either behind, or in front of the shoulders of the two people interacting, but pairs of shots where the camera is placed very far back from *all* the participants are excluded from this category. Cuts between a watcher and his Point of View may be included within this category, provided the camera directions satisfy the criteria, but the two categories are definitely not co-extensive. Usually Watcher-POV cuts (and vice-versa) form only a small proportion of the reverse-angle cuts used in a film, though there is definitely some variation from director to director in this. For instance, it seems that Alfred Hitchcock used the Point of View shot far more than other directors, even those making the same type of film, and in fact such cuts make up about half of his rather high proportion of reverse-angle cuts. For instance, *Strangers on a Train* (1951) has about 50% reverse-angle cuts, and *Family Plot* (1976) has 49%, and in both cases about half of these are Watcher-POV cuts. That is, about a quarter of the cuts in these films are between a watcher and his POV. The high proportion of POV shots in Hitchcock's films can obviously be related to the voyeuristic strain in his personality which is quite evident in his interviews, not to mention the fact that this device is simply a good way of securing audience involvement, and so it is really in need of no further explanation.

The quickest way to treat this matter more fully is to quote a list of the percentages of reverse-angle cuts between shots out of the total number of shot transitions in various films, and then to proceed to an interpretation of the results. It should be noted that the figures quoted are approximate, and subject to several percent error, since they were arrived at by sampling 30 minute sections of the films involved, but this uncertainty is not enough to invalidate the general conclusions that I will draw. The number of films checked for this quantity is now approaching 1000.

It can be seen from the figures, and also from the far larger number not quoted, that some sort of consistency can be detected in the use of reverse-angles by some directors; note the figures for Anthony Mann, John Stahl, King Vidor, Howard Hawks, and Raoul Walsh. However, these percentages are far from showing the consistency through a director's work that other stylistic parameters such as Average Shot

The Phantom of the Opera	1925	R. Julian et al.	10%
The Cradle Snatchers	1927	Howard Hawks	30%
The Crowd	1928	King Vidor	24%
A Girl in Every Port	1928	Howard Hawks	28%
The Champ	1931	King Vidor	23%
Bad Sister	1931	Hobart Henley	21%
The Mad Genius	1931	Michael Curtiz	51%
Red Dust	1932	V. Fleming	29%
Back Street	1932	John Stahl	25%
Dr. Jekyll and Mr. Hyde	1932	R. Mamoulian	41%
Counsellor at Law	1933	William Wyler	17%
It Happened One Night	1934	Frank Capra	18%
Now and Forever	1934	H. Hathaway	29%
Fury	1935	Fritz Lang	29%
The Devil is a Woman	1935	J. von Sternberg	33%
Show Boat	1936	James Whale	25%
Dodsworth	1936	William Wyler	32%
The Road to Glory	1936	Howard Hawks	28%
Ceiling Zero	1936	Howard Hawks	28%
Holiday	1938	George Cukor	21%
Suez	1938	Allan Dwan	10%
Rebecca of Sunnybrook Farm	1938	Allan Dwan	19%
Midnight	1939	Mitchell Leisen	23%
When Tomorrow Comes	1939	John Stahl	32%
The Wizard of Oz	1939	V. Fleming	40%
They Drive by Night	1940	Raoul Walsh	31%
Dark Command	1940	Raoul Walsh	40%
Waterloo Bridge	1940	Mervyn Le Roy	43%
I Love You Again	1940	W.S. Van Dyke	38%
H.M. Pulham, Esq.	1941	King Vidor	23%
Manpower	1941	Raoul Walsh	55%
The Strawberry Blonde	1941	Raoul Walsh	40%
Unfinished Business	1941	G. La Cava	38%
Gentleman Jim	1942	Raoul Walsh	36%
Casablanca	1942	Michael Curtiz	50%

The Purple Heart	1944	L. Milestone	18%
Objective Burma	1945	Raoul Walsh	24%
The Adventures of Don Juan	1948	Vincent Sherman	62%
Key Largo	1948	John Huston	45%
White Heat	1949	Raoul Walsh	33%
All the King's Men	1949	Robert Rossen	15%
The Gunfighter	1950	Henry King	20%
Lady Without a Passport	1950	Joseph H. Lewis	21%
Broken Arrow	1950	Delmer Daves	53%
All About Eve	1950	J. Mankiewicz	65%
Winchester '73	1950	Anthony Mann	28%
On Dangerous Ground	1951	Nicholas Ray	56%
Moulin Rouge	1952	John Huston	33%
Bend of the River	1952	Anthony Mann	33%
El	1953	Luis Buñuel	28%
From Here to Eternity	1953	F. Zinneman	34%
On the Waterfront	1954	Elia Kazan	63%
The Far Country	1955	Anthony Mann	25%
Man Without a Star	1955	King Vidor	25%
War and Peace	1956	King Vidor	32%
Lust for Life	1956	V. Minnelli	33%
The Searchers	1956	John Ford	18%
Un Homme et une femme	1965	Claude Lelouch	4%
Arizona Bushwackers	1967	L. Selander	72%
Barquero	1970	Gordon Douglas	22%
Cry of the Banshee	1970	Gordon Hessler	24%

Length and Scale of Shot have been found to have. As far as Hawks is concerned, it is important to know that his silent films are mostly shot in very different styles, and that it would be difficult for the unprimed viewer to guess that they were all made by the same person. In fact from a formal point of view his style did not begin to settle into a consistent pattern until the 'thirties.

Another anomaly is apparent in the figures for Raoul Walsh's films of the very early 'forties, but this was a period when higher-than-average percentages of reverse-angle cuts began to appear in the work of other directors, and Walsh may have been temporarily responding to the new trend. The highest figures of all seem to be restricted to some of the directors who started to make films in the 'forties or later such as Kazan, Sherman, and Mankiewicz. (Nothing above 60% reverse-angle cuts has so far been found for any director who started his career before the nineteen-forties and continued on through this period.)

It will be remembered that the early history of the use of this device really began in the work of Ralph Ince from 1913 to 1915, for he was the first to get an appreciable number of reverse-angle cuts into his films. In the early 'twenties it was usual for American films to have about 20% reverse-angle cuts, though the figure was usually far lower in European films at that time. In the later nineteen-twenties the Hollywood figure was usually in the 20 to 30% range, and as can be seen from the figures quoted, the norm kept going slowly up through the 'thirties. The figure of 51% reverse-angle cuts for

The Mad Genius (Michael Curtiz, 1931) is quite exceptional for the period as far as I know. On the other hand, note the remarkably low figure for Allan Dwan's *Suez* (1938), a film which I think would certainly be considered a typical 'classical Hollywood movie' by any viewer. In this case what we are seeing is an example of the difficulty film directors often have in moving too far away from the style holding when they started directing, and the same effect is visible as regards the device under consideration in the work of King Vidor and others.

Not very surprisingly, there is some correlation of low-ish percentages of reverse-angle cuts with the films of directors inclined to use long takes, and particularly with films using wide-angle lens staging of the kind described earlier in this chapter. (*All the King's Men*, *Lady Without a Passport*, and *The Gunfighter* all use wide-angle lens staging.)

The figures at the end of the table for four fairly recent films give an indication of the way that the fullest range of percentages of reverse-angle cuts still continues to occur, and this observation is supported by a large number of other 'sixties films which have been checked, but not quoted. Nevertheless these values happen to be extreme ones, and the bulk of films continue to have between 30 and 40% reverse-angle cuts, as they have had since the nineteen-thirties. It is also interesting to note the low figure for *Un Homme et une femme*, which shows, just as did D.W. Griffith's films long ago, that a film can have great success with audiences even though it contains very few reverse-angle cuts. In fact the figure for *Un*

Homme et une femme may be even lower, since I am not certain that all of the mere 25 reverse-angle cuts recorded in the whole length of this film should truly qualify under the definition.

All these results show once more that there was always a large amount of stylistic diversity, not to mention stylistic changes, present in what often seems to be regarded as the stylistically monolithic 'classical cinema'. Although those who make much play with this term are always careful not to define exactly what they mean by it seems that they are usually referring to Hollywood films of the 'thirties and 'forties in general. Recently it has been claimed by Daniel Dayan in *Film Quarterly* (Vol.28, No.1, 1974) that the majority of cuts in 'classical cinema' are reverse-angle cuts, and that this is the result of the exploitation of powerful psychoanalytic processes at work in the audience's minds. Apart from the fact that in the vast majority of films such cuts form the smaller part, there is no doubt that films almost without them such as *Birth of a Nation* can work powerfully on an audience. And further, if the device is so powerful, why is it not pushed to the maximum of around 70% reverse-angle cuts in all commercial films, rather than just a few? In any case, deep explanations are unnecessary, since there has always been a direct explanation for the use of the reverse-angle device. This is that the expression on a person's face is far easier to read from the front than the side, so actors communicate more when shown from the frontal direction. Further than this, the device simply involves the spectator through putting him almost in the position of the characters in the film.

If one wants a deeper explanation of the reverse-angle device beyond the direct ones I have just given, then scientific psychology (as opposed to the baseless fantasies of psychoanalysis) is in a position to supply one in terms of optimum cortical arousal levels in brain functioning. This in its turn relates to current neurophysiological investigation in a close way, as can be studied in *Aesthetic Judgement and Arousal: An Experimental Contribution to Psycho-aesthetics* (G. Smets, Leuven University Press, 1973). The point involved here is that the organism requires sufficiently varied external stimuli (in this case visual stimuli) for its well-being and satisfaction: not too much and not too little, leaving a certain amount of room for intermediate variation. As far as film is concerned, this means that audience satisfaction is most easily produced by presenting sufficiently varied views sufficiently quickly one

way or another, either by angle changes, or by cutting to entirely different scenes, or by camera movement.

The other important neurophysiological factor relates to the use of Close Ups rather than reverse-angles, for the example of the D.W. Griffith films as well as others that were successful with audiences, despite having very few reverse-angle cuts, suggests that the frontal Close Up as such, regardless of what is on either side of it, is the important device. This must be because the perception of the human face seen closely from the front makes use of basic neural connections, and so has a more powerful effect than the sideways and more distant view of the human figure. (The fact that the response to the frontal face shape is inborn – or wired into the brain before birth – is demonstrated by the experiments by C.C. Gorent and collaborators in which new-born babies track a white disc with a schematic face on it far better than they do to a white disc with jumbled-up or inverted facial features.)

Incidentally, the claim that Dayan and others make that there was a taboo on an actor looking directly into the lens was not completely true even for the 'thirties and 'forties, and before and after that not true at all. In the silent period close shots of actors looking straight into the lens were quite common in Griffith's films, and European films in general. All the large number of close shots in Hitchcock's 1928 films *Champagne* and *The Manxman* look straight into the lens, and when we move into the 'thirties it is still possible to find Hollywood films where many of the Close Ups have actors looking straight at the camera, such as *Dr. Jekyll and Mr. Hyde* (1931) and *Of Human Bondage* (1934), while in the 'forties the same is true of Chaplin's *Monsieur Verdoux* (1947). And at the beginning of the 'forties Raoul Walsh made a number of dramas in which characters turn to the camera and address a line to it. And of course in comedies address to the camera had always been possible.

Conclusion

The major formal development in American film-making during the nineteen-forties, the emergence of a trend towards long take filming, can be graphically illustrated with the histograms on this and the next page showing the numbers of films with different Average Shot Lengths in samples of about one hundred and fifty films from each of the six year periods 1940-1945 and 1946-1951. When compared to the 1934-39

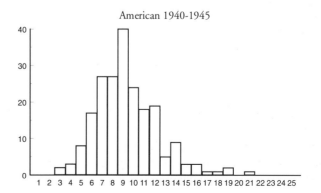

American 1946-1951

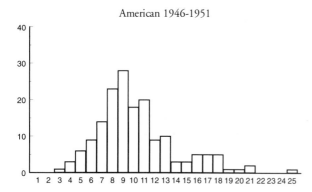

period, we can see that the distributions are becoming more asymmetrical, and developing a lumpy tail to the right, made up of an increased number of films with higher ASLs in the region above 13 seconds. The peak number of films with high ASLs in this tail was actually achived in the 'fifties, and after that it declines period by period. In the late 'fifties another new and rather surprising development began, but I will come to that in a later chapter. Notice also that though the mean value of the ASL keeps increasing from the late 'thirties into the early 'fifties, the modal value still stays the same at 9 seconds. This unchanging modal value corresponds to the persistence of the majority of the directors in shooting films

in the same manner as always.

Although some of the directors who helped to consolidate the trend towards longer takes had come into films from the theatre fairly recently, there were others involved who had been in Hollywood for decades, particularly amongst those who began the movement in 1940, so the cause of this development cannot be the influence of the theatre. I feel that the likeliest explanation is that directors were becoming bored with having to shoot film after film totally within the walls of the studio, which was a situation that had not existed before the latter part of the nineteen-thirties, and so were inclined to welcome a different method of scene dissection once they had noticed it in *Holiday* (1938), and other subsequent films made by George Cukor. Long take filming also had the advantage of preventing the ever more obtrusive producers from interfering with the editing of a film. (According to Leo Rosten in *Hollywood: the Movie Colony, the Movie Makers,* in 1927 there were 34 producers or supervisors involved in the production of 743 feature films in Hollywood. In 1937 220 producers worked on 484 movies. The number of directors working at those two dates hardly changed, going from 246 in 1927 to 234 in 1937.) The next steps from this last piece of information take us onto ground that has been well trodden in writing about films since the nineteen-thirties.

18. FILM STYLE AND TECHNOLOGY IN THE FIFTIES

The commercial decline of the American cinema continued throughout the nineteen-fifties, with rapidly decreasing financial returns to the major studios, and a decreasing number of films being produced each year. 'Double feature' programmes were eliminated as a standard means of exhibition, and most of the minor studios closed. A new feature of the scene was the increasing number of films made by independent producers, though these were mostly released through the major companies. In a bid to retain the decreasing cinema audiences various novel methods of film projection were introduced, and more and more American films had larger and larger parts of them shot on location, particularly in exotic locales. All of these trends, though present, were less marked in the cinema of other countries.

Film Stock

Although the principal thrust of film stock development in the 'fifties was into colour processes, nevertheless Kodak and Dupont produced still faster black and white negative materials. These were Tri-X from Eastman Kodak with a speed of 200 ASA under tungsten light in 1954, and Superior 4 from Dupont in 1956 with a speed of 250 ASA. These new stocks had little importance for feature film production, but they were needed for television news and documentary production, which often had to be done under low available light levels. The increased amount of location filming on feature films continued to be handled with the older stocks such as Superior 2, Super XX, and even Plus-X. Plus-X retained its position as the most popular black and white negative, helped by the substitution of an improved emulsion in 1956, but the use of Super XX continued to increase.

Agfacolor and its Derivatives

After World War 2 the Agfacolor patents were considered as the spoils of war, and colour films based on them were manufactured from the early 'fifties onwards by the Fuji company of Japan, Ferrania in Italy, and Gevaert in Belgium, not to mention the continuation of the original Agfacolor in West Germany. In America, General Aniline and Film, the now completely separate daughter company of I.G. Farben, had already produced an Agfa-type reversal film in 1947, and this was first used for feature film production in 1949 in shooting *The Man on the Eiffel Tower*. This stock was considerably slower than the original German Agfacolor, having a speed of 12 ASA, but when the change to a negative-positive process was made in 1951, the accuracy of the colour reproduction with Anscocolor became better than it had been with Agfacolor, though still lacking the colour saturation obtainable with Technicolor, or even Eastman Color. Much the

same could be said of the other Agfacolor derivatives, excluding Sovcolor, which was worse than the German original.

The M.G.M. studio's Metrocolor process was carried out with Ansco negative and positive stock until 1955, after which date Eastman Color was used. This was the end of all use of Anscocolor in feature films, but 16 mm. Anscochrome reversal stock continued to be produced, and it was joined in 1957 by Super Anscochrome with a speed of 100 ASA. Besides its importance for colour television news and documentary work, this stock was needed for use in the high speed cameras of the missile development programs. (Very high speed cameras have very short exposure times per frame, and cannot be used in daylight without high speed film.)

Another derivative of Agfacolor that was important for a few years was a positive colour print stock made by Dupont from 1949. This was used by Consolidated Film Laboratories to produce Trucolor prints from Eastman color camera negative until 1958. The well-known peculiarities of the Trucolor process, which were poor definition, high contrast, and restriction of the gamut of hues to rather saturated primaries and orangey-brown neutral colours, as in *Johnny Guitar* (1954), were probably due not so much to the deficiencies of Dupont print stock as to unsatisfactory intermediate positive and negative stages between the initial negative and the final print, a problem that had been solved elsewhere by Eastman Kodak from 1953.

Eastman Color

The first feature films shot and printed on Eastman Color positive and negative stock appeared in 1951 (e.g *Sword of Monte Cristo*), though the SuperCinecolor label attached by the processing laboratory concealed the process's true identity. In these newly developed integral tripack materials the dye formers were incorporated in the three primary colour-sensitive layers in the emulsion after the Agfacolor pattern, but the dyes used were different to those in Agfacolor, and the Eastman Color negative layers also incorporated a 'colour mask', which was responsible for the all-over orange colour of Eastman negatives. This colour mask corrected certain of the deficiencies inevitably present in the colour response of *all* colour negative systems; deficiencies which prevented the bright and distinct reproduction of greens and blues in particular. Eventually the Agfacolor derivatives did acquire colour masking systems, but by then Eastman Color had established its dominance. The other advantage that Eastman Color had in the earlier stages was that the system included intermediate duplicating negative and positive stocks, whereas other systems had to go through either black and white separation positives, or simply use the Eastman intermediate materials. The colour response of Eastman Color was thus superior to that of its competitors, as was its definition and speed, which was 16 ASA under daylight, although it was still inferior in this respect to the Technicolor three-strip camera process. However in 1953 the Eastman Color process was improved in every way, with new intermediate negative and positive stocks, as well as a new camera negative now balanced for tungsten light exposure, with better definition and the improved speed of 24 ASA. This was followed by a yet again improved Eastman Color negative Type 5250 in 1959, with a speed of 50 ASA, and this colour negative decisively established the dominance since maintained in this field by Kodak, and also completely eliminated competition in the U.S.A. by its superiority.

Kodak also replied to Ansco's challenge in the 16 mm. colour reversal field by introducing Ektachrome Commercial (25 ASA for tungsten light) in 1958, and in 1959 two high speed Ektachrome E.R. stocks for use under tungsten light and daylight with speeds of 125 ASA and 160 ASA respectively. These were all low contrast reversal stocks intended to be used as master material for making reversal prints, rather than for direct projection of the original, as was the case with the already existing 16 mm. Kodachrome. From 1955 Eastman Kodak had produced a reversal print stock to go with their camera reversal materials, Type 5269.

Technicolor

In 1950 Technicolor improved their three-strip camera process yet again, making the emulsions more sensitive, and also balancing them for filming under tungsten light without a filter, rather than the previous daylight balance. This was because the speed was now equivalent to somewhere between 50 and 100 ASA, and arc lighting (which has a 'white' spectral balance like daylight) was no longer necessary to give the required light level of about 100 foot-candles. From 1951 Eastman Color negative began to displace 35 mm. Kodachrome as the monopack camera material sometimes used for Technicolor production, despite its inferior performance to the three-strip camera material. The contrast between the two possible camera sources of Technicolor prints can be seen within *Rancho Notorious* (1952), where the bulk of the film was shot on monopack in a conventional camera, and only the two big Inserts of the stolen brooch shot with the Technicolor three-strip camera. These Inserts are far sharper than the rest of the film, at least when seen on an original 35 mm. print.

When the improved Eastman Color appeared in 1953, the use of the three-strip camera was phased out as a negative source for Technicolor films. The diminished advantages of that form of Technicolor production no longer counted against the convenience of shooting a single negative in a smaller conventional camera. So from 1955 onwards the name Technicolor only represents a laboratory carrying out a unique printing process which was, as before, printing by dye transfer via three positive relief matrices held in contact with a 'blank' emulsion on three successive register pin belt ma-

chines, one for each of the positive colours. The three positive relief matrices were now made in succession from the single Eastman Color negative printed through three appropriately coloured filters, rather than one-against-one from the three separate negatives from the three-strip camera. The dye transfer printing process was also sufficiently modified and improved in 1953 to finally dispense with the faint black silver 'key' image that had been photographically printed into the not-quite-blank positive emulsion from 1934.

Because Technicolor was now being shot with monopack film in a conventional camera, it was now possible to use any lens desired on that camera, and in particular it was finally possible to use good wide-angle lenses for Technicolor filming. In fact not a great deal of advantage was taken of this possibility, though one film that did was John Huston's *Moby Dick* (1956). This film is also interesting for the special nature of the Technicolor prints that were made for it. To get something of the effect of old coloured engravings in the image, extra black was added to the final print by double printing the three relief matrices with a black and white intermediate negative made from the original colour negative. Actually the principal effect of this process was to desaturate the colours, though where there was already black in the image, it was spread and intensified slightly. John Huston and his cameraman had previously taken another approach to colour control in *Moulin Rouge* (1953). In that case the desaturation of colours in the image was achieved partly by the colours used in the set design, and partly by using moderately heavy artificial fog on the sets, supplemented by the extensive use of fog filters. Although this kind of approach became popular in the 'seventies, it was not particularly taken up by other film-makers at the time.

So from 1956 onwards all American 35 mm. colour films for theatrical exhibition were shot with Eastman Color negative, and with the exceptions already noted of Technicolor and Trucolor, printed onto Eastman print stock. The labels Warnercolor, DeLuxe Color, etc. never signified anything more than the laboratory or studio carrying out the Eastman Color process.

The processing of Eastman Color was fairly simply carried out in any laboratory by the addition of a few extra tanks to the existing type of developing machines, and its printing was made more efficient and easier by the introduction in 1956 of the Bell & Howell additive colour printer, which had automatic control of the light regulation for each shot from instructions on punched paper tape. The accuracy of colour control in the grading (U.S. 'timing') of individual shots was greatly improved by the use of the Hazeltine colour analyzer from 1959 onwards by those laboratories that could afford it. In this machine colour negative is scanned by a colour television camera, and the complementary colours and tones are produced electronically to give a positive colour image on a T.V. screen. Calibrated adjustment of the three colours is provided to give a read-out of the exact corrections to the negative needed to give accurate colour reproduction when the printing stage is later carried out. This is necessary because the orange mask on the negative, plus the necessity of adjusting three colours, make direct visual guessing of the correct printing exposure for each shot immensely more difficult with colour negative than is the case for black and white negative. In fact it is almost impossible, so that prior to the introduction of the Hazeltine analyzer and its later competitors, the correct printing exposure for colour films had been arrived at by making repeated trial prints, and then gradually correcting the errors.

Film Lighting

The only innovation in lighting equipment during the 'fifties was the introduction of 'cone lights' in 1951. These were really called forth by the demands of the television lighting of that time for a general even overall wash of non-directional light applied from above to permit simultaneous multi-camera shooting from all directions. The unit consisted of a large tungsten bulb of up to 10 kiloWatts power inside a large conical reflector painted matt white, with the bulb shielded from casting direct light by a matt-white painted baffle. Cone lights produced so-called 'shadowless' light like present-day 'soft lights' or 'north lights', but as far as standard film-making was concerned, they were only used at a considerable distance from the actors, either suspended overhead on some large sets to provide part of the general lighting, or on floor stands to provide a general fill light. The major part of the lighting of the actors was still done with spots and floods as usual. So cone lights had no great effect on the appearance of film lighting.

The general trend in film lighting continued in the already established direction of simplification, particularly in colour films. The backlighting of the figures, which was already reduced from that in the black and white filming of the previous decade, was now often eliminated altogether, and the number of lighting units used to light the more distant shots from the front and sides was also reduced. (There was not much room for reduction of the number of lights used to light Close Ups.) This trend reached the point where many of the shots were lit with only a handful of lights, so that the result is extremely crude if reduced to monochrome either by printing or T.V. transmission, whereas the lighting in 'forties colour films still looks quite attractive if reduced to black and white.

In this period the lighting for black and white film was not simplified quite so far, but it was being pushed in the same direction, in part because of the vastly increased number of colour films that cameramen practised upon, and also in part by the continuing experience of location filming in black and white. Location filming of interiors still took place on only a few films, but studio interiors were more and more being built to the same dimensions as real interiors, rather than to the much larger scale that had been used before. In either the case of real interiors or correct scale sets, it is difficult to get a large number of lights in, but this restriction fitted in quite well with the continuing movement towards greater naturalism in lighting, as in other things. Prime examples of this process in operation as far as lighting is concerned are given by Boris Kaufman's work on *On the Waterfront* (1954), and James Wong Howe's lighting of *The Sweet Smell of Success* (1957), and both films also show the reduction or elimination of supplementary lighting on daylight exteriors, which was another new development as far as America was concerned.

Cameras

Apart from the special cameras made for exclusive use with the various wide screen processes, which will be considered separately, there were no significant new 35 mm. cameras produced in this decade. For 16 mm. filming the Arriflex 16s became available in America during these years, though without having any great impact even on documentary film-making. The Arriflex 16s was similar to the older 35 mm. Arriflex camera in general configuration, with a mirror-reflex shutter providing continuous through-the- lens viewing, but its basic form took only 100 foot daylight loading spools of film in an internal magazine. It was also possible to use supplementary 400 foot film magazines attached to the top of the camera in the same way as on the 35 mm. Arriflex, but these 16 mm. magazines did not include the sprocket drive, which was inside the camera body. The film movement was also different in the 16 mm. Arriflex, with the pull-down claw entering the film from the front rather than the back, and the mechanism also included a register-pin system, which was not available in the 35 mm. camera. Small interchangeable electric motors, which could be either battery driven or mains driven, were fixed onto the side of the camera, rather than underneath as in the 35mm. Arriflex.

The development that proved to be more important immediately was the adaptation of Auricon Cine-Voice cameras for hand-held filming in 1957, and then their further adaptation by the Leacock-Pennebaker group in 1959 to operate in synchronism with light-weight tape recorders without any connecting cable. The Cine-Voice camera, which was a small form of the Auricon Pro with only a 100 foot internal magazine, was altered to take 400 foot magazines, and to rest on the cameraman's shoulder while he viewed the action directly through a beam-splitting view-finder built into the zoom lens which had also been adapted to fit on this camera. All of this, in combination with the developments in sound recording detailed below, made possible the filming of the first 'direct cinema' films, starting with *Primary* in 1960.

Cameras and Ideology

At the beginning of the nineteen-forties the Russians had got hold of at least one Mitchell BNC, and this was used in shooting Eisenstein's *Ivan Grozny*, amongst other films, while in the 'fifties they produced a design of their own, the Moskva EC 32, which was closely based on the Mitchell. A new lightweight Russian camera, the Kohbac, which also appeared around this time, was likewise closely based on the Cameflex.

When we note that the Communist Chinese film industry of this period used old Mitchell NC's, the only conclusion can be that political ideology has no connection with film technology, whatever some Western Marxists say. Much the same could be said about the forms of mainstream cinema, which are very similar everywhere. As for ideology in its more general sense, which I take to be manner and systems of thinking, then film technology is certainly closely determined by the universal system of rational, causal, empirical thinking that has created the industrialized world, but since the cinema could not exist without this, there is nothing more to be said about this question. The sole achievement of Marxism and socialism in this area is to make the invention of any technology nearly impossible, just as it has prevented new aesthetic forms appearing when it has been rigidly applied.

Lenses

Even wider-angle lenses than had been available before appeared in the nineteen- fifties: a 9.5 mm. lens for 16 mm. cameras in 1953, and then in 1958 a 5.7 mm. lens for 16 mm. cameras that covered a horizontal field of 108 degrees. For 35 mm. cameras a 14 mm. lens became available in 1959. There was also a new ultra-wide-aperture lens produced for 16 mm. cameras in 1956, no doubt in response to the demands of television filming in low-level available light situations. This lens was of 25 mm. focal length, and had a maximum aperture of f0.95. There had been lenses with apertures this large before, but their quality had always been poor, which was not the case with this Angénieux lens. With this lens, and the fastest black and white film, it was possible to get a picture under just about any lighting conditions.

The most important lens developments of the 'fifties centred on the new zoom lenses that became available, and just like the wide-angle lenses their construction incorporated a large number of elements, so that their design had only been made possible by the use of the newly available high speed computers. In 1954 the Zoomar Corporation introduced a lens for 35 mm. cameras similar to the one they already made for 16 mm. cameras. Since this only had a zoom ratio of 3 to 1 it was really no great improvement over the old Taylor-Hobson Varo lens of the 'thirties, except that the focus could be varied. There were only isolated instances of its use, for instance in *Apache* (1954) and *The Incredible Shrinking Man* (1957). The zoom lenses that really made an appreciable difference to film style, though not immediately, appeared in 1956. These were made by SOM-Berthiot of France, who gave them their trade name of Pan-Cinor, and they had a zoom ratio of 4 to 1. The lens for 16 mm. cameras had a focal length range of 17.5 mm. to 70 mm. with a maximum aperture of f2.8, and the lens for 35 mm. cameras had a range from 38.5 mm. to 150 mm., and a maximum aperture of f3.5. Two years later the Angénieux company produced a similar pair of lenses.

In America these new zoom lenses were taken up immediately only for television documentary work, but in continental Europe they were used in some feature films. For instance, Rolf Thiele's *Das Mädchen Rosemarie* (1958), contains many zoom shots, some in combination with panning during extended takes, and occasional use of the zoom can be seen in other German films of the period. However, the most notable early use of the zoom lens was in Roberto Rossellini's *Era notte a Roma* (1960) and *Viva l'Italia* (1960). In *Era notte a Roma* the extensive use of zoom shots in combination with tracking and panning formed a rather dizzying combination, and after that Rossellini was a little more restrained in his use of the zoom.

Magnetic Recording

Although the first 1/4 inch. tape recorders appeared in America a year or two after the war, it was not until 1949 that magnetic recording came to be used for film purposes. In that year recorders that recorded sound onto 17.5 mm. film that was perforated down one edge (i.e. 35 mm. film split down the middle) and coated with magnetic iron oxide came into use in Hollywood studios, replacing the optical sound recording cameras as the first stage of studio recording. In this initial stage of the introduction of magnetic recording, sound tracks were then transferred from these magnetic recordings to optical tracks for editing in the usual way, but from the end of 1949 a changeover was made to editing with magnetic recordings on full-width coated 35 mm. film, as is still done today. The adaptation of existing moviolas to work with magnetic film was extremely simple and cheap, and despite many initial complaints from editors that they could no longer recognize the exact positions of words as they had in the past by their visible traces on the optical soundtrack, the efficiency of the editing process was in no way changed. The real advantage of magnetic recording over optical recording was in the possibility of instant playback on the set, and more importantly in improved recording quality, particularly as regards frequency range and the lowering of background noise. Though by the time the recording got back onto the optical track of the finished film prints for theatrical projection most of this advantage had been lost again.

1/4 inch. tape recorders that produced a recording synchronized with the camera filming the scene were available from 1950, and they gradually displaced the magnetic recorders using perforated film. These synchronous recorders worked by recording a regular synchronizing pulse on a second parallel track on the same 1/4 inch. tape at the same time as the sound signal. The new synchronous recorders, though smaller than anything previously used for recording film sound, were far from portable in the sense of it being possible to carry them around in the hand, so they made no appreciable difference to film style. It was only in 1959 that the first truly portable synchronous 1/4 inch. tape recorders were produced in Europe, and since they only had an effect on film form from 1960 onwards, they will be described in the next chapter.

Magnetic sound recording was also important for the multi-track 'stereophonic' recordings used in the new CinemaScope and 70 mm. film processes. In these processes narrow stripes of the usual magnetic recording medium were coated down the edge of the final show prints, and the multiple soundtracks were magnetically recorded onto these stripes individually for each print made. It was fairly simple to modify the projectors in the cinemas to play these magnetic tracks by adding a set of magnetic replay heads above the film gate. Although some improvement over the sound from optical tracks, these magnetic recordings initially fell far short of present-day ideas of 'high fidelity sound'

Special Forms of Projection

All the special forms of cinematography and projection that were introduced into commercial film-making in the 'fifties had been demonstrated in the nineteen-twenties – all the forms of stereoscopic cinematography at the beginning of the decade, and multiscreen films, wide films, and anamorphic cinematography at the end of it – but none had proved to be commercially viable.

Cinerama

This special form of cinematography and projection involved filming scenes with a special triple camera which was made up of three 35 mm. cameras with 27 mm. lenses, arranged so that their fields joined side by side, with 2 degrees overlap at the edges, to cover a broad panorama. The combined field covered by this multiple camera was 146 degrees horizontally and 55.5 degrees vertically. Although ordinary 35 mm. film was used in these cameras, the height of the frame extended over 6 sprocket holes rather than the usual 4, and in the early years of the process they were run at 26 frames per second rather than the usual 24 frames per second. For projection three projectors were used electrically locked in synchronism to reconstruct the image on a screen that was deeply curved in the horizontal plane around the front part of the auditorium. The screen also had to be constructed in the form of a series of louvered slats to reduce image degradation through light scatter, so because of this, and also because of the other special arrangements, which included multi-track sound reproduction from a separate sound deck locked to the projectors, Cinerama was only exhibited in a small number of special theatres in the largest cities in the world. At first the films made in the process and shown exclusively in these theatres were all documentary and travelogue combinations, but finally two fictional films were made in the process. These were *How the West Was Won* (1962) and *The Wonderful World of the Brothers Grimm* (1963), and after this the films made by the Cinerama Corporation were shot on 70 mm. film with a single camera, and the Cinerama theatres were adapted to projection with a single 70 mm. projector, though still on the deeply curved screen. The only really special characteristic of films made in the original three-camera Cinerama was that the stagings made some effort to avoid having the actors stand in positions where the join between the frames passed, as the

image was blurred down these two narrow vertical strips. A subsidiary restriction on filming in three-camera Cinerama was that the lens axis had to be kept as near horizontal as possible, and yet another minor restriction was that the very wide field of view made it difficult to get good lighting while keeping the lights outs of shot. In the 'sixties fictional films made by other companies in UltraPanavision came to be shown in Cinerama theatres, and finally even ordinary 70 mm. films. At this point the process could be considered to be defunct.

Stereoscopic Films

The brief enthusiasm for stereoscopic feature films that lasted from 1952 to 1954 was entirely carried out by using variants of the anaglyph process, which involved two film strips being shot by two synchronized cameras with their lenses effectively set apart by the eye-separation distance, and then projected by synchronized projectors to give two superimposed images on a single screen. The images corresponding to the left and right eye views were visually separated by either projecting them through oppositely polarizing filters on the two lenses, and then having the audience view the screen with corresponding polarizing filters over each eye, or in the case of films in black and white, by carrying out the same process with red and green filters over the projector lenses and the audience's eyes. This ensured that each eye only received the image from the camera in the position corresponding to the eye. Although strictly speaking both the red-green monochrome process and the polarized light processes were anaglyph processes, in the vernacular only the first was referred to as such.

The cameras used in these processes were either Cameflexes, Arriflexes, or Mitchell NC's, and for sync. filming the pair of cameras were enclosed in a common large blimp. Most ordinarily pairs of Mitchell NC's were used, and in this case the combination was very large and heavy indeed, weighing over 200 lbs.. This factor, as well as the nature of the stereoscopic effect in itself, considerably restricted the amount of camera movement in stereoscopic films. Another drawback to the process was that it was most effective when the photography used as much depth of field as possible, and with the slow colour film of those years this made very high light levels necessary on the set.

Apart from the well-known use of movement towards the camera in stereoscopic films, the only other point worth making about visual style in this connection is to point to Douglas Sirk's *Taza, Son of Cochise* (1954), and Hitchcock's *Dial M for Murder* (1954) as containing some attempts to create novel compositions in three dimensions. *Dial M for Murder* was unusual amongst stereoscopic films in that it contained quite a number of set-ups in which the foreground objects were out of focus, which was usually avoided as much as possible with this technique.

CinemaScope

In 1953 the anamorphic process devised by Henri Chrétien in 1928 was revived by Twentieth Century-Fox in exactly the same form, with a supplementary lens incorporating a cylindrical element placed in front of an ordinary camera lens. This produced an image on the film that included twice the horizontal field which would have been included without it, while leaving the vertical field unchanged. When the image was projected with a similar supplementary lens in front of the ordinary projector lens, the result was an image twice the usual width on the screen, with an aspect ratio of height to width of 1:2.66. The supplementary lens on the camera had to be focussed separately from the prime lens, and the prime lens on the camera could only be a 50 mm. lens in the initial form of the process. For the first couple of films made in the CinemaScope process, *The Robe* and *How to Marry a Millionaire*, there was no soundtrack on the projected print, and the image occupied the full width between the perforations, as well as covering what used to be the thick black bar between the frames. In fact the image on the film was the same size as the old silent image. The sound was run separately in synchronism with the projector on 35 mm. magnetic film on a reproducing deck, and it was made up of 4 tracks which played 'stereophonically' through right, left, and centre loudspeakers behind the screen, and also through a linked set of 'surround' speakers round the back of the auditorium. To create these four sound tracks giving an illusion of sound directionality corresponding to the nominal sources in the image, the original synchronous sound was recorded during the filming in the usual way onto a single track, and then the four 'stereophonic' tracks were created synthetically during the sound track mixing sessions by gradually switching the single track recording from track to track to match the movement of the supposed source of sound in the image.

By 1954 the four soundtracks had been transferred to four magnetic stripes on the picture film, with two of the tracks on each side of the frame. Of these two tracks one was outside the sprocket holes, and the other inside them. This lost some of the width of the image, and the projected aspect ratio on the screen became 1:2.35. Finally alternative prints came to be made with a single monophonic optical soundtrack down one side of the film in the usual place, and this has continued to be the case down to the present day. Because of the synthetic nature of the 'stereophonic' sound for CinemaScope-type films, the sound is never completely convincingly realistic throughout the length of the film, and its defects in this direction are more noticeable than those of ordinary monophonic soundtracks. The synchronous recording of true stereophonic sound with multiple microphones into multiple sound tracks on the set proved to be too difficult to be worth pursuing at this time.

The visual performance of the original CinemaScope system left a lot to be desired; the squeeze ratio (proportion of lateral compression) of the image on the film varied a little depending on the distance of the object photographed from the camera, and in particular faces in Close Up were widened when projected. Because initially only a 50 mm. lens could be used, and also because the film stock was always the very slow colour emulsion of this period, the depth of field tended to be more restricted than usual, and this hindered the use of staging in depth as a mode of scene dissection. However the Cinema-Scope system could be very satisfactorily used by those directors engaged in long take filming with camera movement, and indeed in their 1954 films Preminger and Minnelli pushed on to even longer takes than they had used before. (*Carmen Jones* has an ASL of 43 seconds, and *Brigadoon* an ASL of 26 seconds.)

CinemaScope and Take Length

It is commonly supposed that the introduction of CinemaScope suddenly increased the length of the shots in films that used the process, but in fact the effect was quite small. As I have already shown, take lengths kept on increasing throughout the 'forties and into the early 'fifties, and CinemaScope entered just at the peak of this process. If we consider a group of 21 CinemaScope films made between 1952 and 1957, we find that their mean Average Shot Length is 13 seconds, whereas in the same six year period a fairly random sample of about 100 films of all kinds had a mean ASL of 11 seconds. So it seems there *was* a small tendency for 'Scope films to have longer takes, and particularly so in 1953-54, if we look at the results in detail. But after only a small number of Cinema-Scope films had been made, Robert Aldrich demonstrated that it was possible to cut fast in CinemaScope in *Vera Cruz* (1954), which has an ASL of 5 seconds. And William Wellman had gone back to something like his usual cutting rate in *Track of the Cat* (1954) with an ASL of 7.5 seconds, after making *The High and the Mighty* (ASL of 12.5 sec.) earlier in the year. Another 'fast cutter' who returned to his old ways after his first 'Scope film was Henry Hathaway. And when one looks at the next six year period of 1958-1963, one finds that for a group of 24 'Scope films the mean ASL has gone down to 11 seconds. My reading of the situation is that although the full range of ASLs were used with 'Scope film-making after the first year, there was a tendency for those directors who already preferred long takes to use 'Scope in preference to shooting with non-anamorphic film. Amongst the established 'long take' directors who worked almost exclusively with 'Scope, besides those already mentioned, one can name Henry King, George Cukor, and George Marshall. These last three continued to use normal staging rather than excessive camera movement, while of course the use of long takes with wide-angle lens staging was completely impossible with Cinema-Scope.

Composition and CinemaScope

The initial attitude to composition with CinemaScope was to keep the camera back from the actors and line up as many of them as possible across the frame, as in *The Robe* (1953) and *How to Marry a Millionaire* (1953). The occasional frieze-like processions in the former film were only slightly more imaginative. A rather more subtle approach was visible in Cukor's *A Star is Born* (1955), where he created a kind of variable masking by filling side areas of the frame with heavy black shadows in some of the shots. Nicholas Ray made occasional use of compositions with bi-lateral symmetry in *Rebel Without a Cause* (1955), but mostly everyone shooting 'Scope used conventional ideas about giving compositions lateral balance, including the use of the standard compositional ratios for the lateral divisions between objects of interest and the edges of the screen. The use of the strong diagonal compositions that had been so popular in the previous decade was out of the question with the new screen shape. There were also a number of visually unimaginative directors who just kept everything of interest in the central area of the frame and let the sides go hang. These range from Henry Levin to, I regret to say, Elia Kazan in *Wild River*, but Delmer Daves' claim to have done this on purpose in *Demetrius and the Gladiators* (1954) is false. His eye got the better of his intentions, and a number of the compositions and groupings in that film make full compositional use of the CinemaScope frame.

Composition in the ordinary sense was inevitably not so important for directors such as Preminger who used long takes with mobile camera, but of this group Minnelli had always had a tendency to break his long takes down into sections where the camera was static, interleaved with sections where it moved with the actors to the next resting point. Minnelli did some rather interesting things with some of his 'Scope compositions in *The Cobweb* (1955), using the small bright patch of colour of a bunch of flowers or a lamp at one end of a fairly neutrally coloured frame to balance the actor at the other end.

Superscope

The one process with 'scope' in its title that was not essentially identical to CinemaScope was Superscope. This was used on a few low-budget films like *Riot in Cell Block 11* made around 1954. This process was carried out by filming on ordinary 35 mm. film with the part of the image to be used falling within an area excluding the top and bottom of the frame, so that its aspect ratio was 2:1. Prints were made in an optical printer which applied vertical anamorphic expansion to this area so that it filled the full height of the positive frame, but left narrow strips at each side blank. These prints were projected in the same manner as CinemaScope through an anamorphic projection lens. In a way this was a partial anticipation of the Techniscope system which became important in the next decade, but it did not catch on in this form.

Todd-AO and Other 70 mm. Film Systems

In 1955 a new wide-film process using negative 65 mm. wide and print stock 70 mm. wide was introduced. This was Todd-AO, and although various wide films had been unsuccessfully tried before around 1930, some of them even using 70 mm. film, this new version was compatible with none of its predecessors, as the position of the perforations was different, and the frame was 5 perforations high, with an aspect ratio of 1:2.2. The extra 2.5 mm. of width on each side of the positive film outside the perforations accommodated four magnetic soundtracks, with a further two running between the perforations and the outer edges of the frame. Five of these tracks fed five separate loudspeakers behind and across the width of the screen, and the sixth track fed sound to a set of surround speakers around the back of the auditorium. The 'stereophonic' sound was synthesized from monophonic tracks in the mixing studio, just as for CinemaScope sound. The first Todd-AO films were shot and projected at 30 frames per second, and shown only in special cinemas equipped with very large and deeply curved screens, on the pattern of Cinerama. Since these screens occupied a visual angle of about 90 degrees for much of the audience, the use of the widest-angle lens in the system, which had a horizontal acceptance angle of 128 degrees, did not produce as much 'wide-angle' perspective distortion as might be expected. The longest focal length lens for Todd-AO had a horizontal acceptance angle of 37 degrees, but this was only used for the infrequent Close Ups of actors.

The first films made in Todd-AO tended to use very long takes, just like the first CinemaScope films, but as the use of 70 mm. spread, with other identical but differently named versions such as Super Panavision appearing from 1958, and as ordinary cinemas came to use 70 mm. projection on ordinary screens, faster cutting rates were used in 70 mm. films. Films shot in 70 mm. were also reduced in optical printers to give 35 mm. anamorphic prints that were identical to ordinary CinemaScope prints as far as projection was concerned, though they had far better definition, and lost only the finest sliver of the image from the top and bottom of the original 70 mm. frame. The only two films made in the short-lived CinemaScope 55 process, which involved shooting an exactly double width frame on 55 mm. film in a special camera, were also optically reduced in the same way to give ordinary CinemaScope prints for distribution.

Other Wide-Screen Systems

All the wide-screen systems not involving anamorphic compression or the use of special wide film were identical as far as projection was concerned, and also identical with respect to the requirements of image composition. They all involved projecting standard 35 mm. film with a wider-angle lens than usual, and simultaneously masking off the top and bottom of the image in the projector gate aperture. The result was an image that filled the usual screen height, but whose sides were further out than had previously been the case with the 1:1.35 of the Academy frame, and this changed the aspect ratio (height to width) of the image on the screen to either 1:1.66 or 1:1.75 or 1:1.85. Initially, in May 1953, amongst the major production companies Paramount chose a wide-screen ratio of 1:1.66, M.G.M. one of 1:1.75, and Universal and Columbia 1:1.85, but after a few shifts of policy all ratios were used indiscriminately, though 1:1.75 was eventually little favoured in America, but much favoured in Britain. Some American producers occasionally masked off the picture area slightly at the top and the bottom of the frame *in the camera* to a ratio of 1:1.5, but there was no consistency about this not very common practice. It must be made quite clear that *all* American commercial features made from 1954 onwards have had their images composed by their cameramen to be projected in one of the wide-screen ratios, and not in the old 1:1.35 Academy ratio, even though the image on the film is of Academy proportions. When non-anamorphic American films made after 1954 are printed down to 16 mm. this image in Academy aperture proportions is retained, and since no 16 mm. projectors have any provision for masking the frame to wide screen, the result on the screen is not what was intended or originally seen when the film was first shown. However it must be mentioned that there were a very few old directors with a very strong visual sense who seem to have ignored these requirements for image composition, apart from keeping the actors' faces out of the very top bit of the frame, and their films made after 1954 look better when the full Academy aperture is projected. The most important exhibits here are Fritz Lang's films, but others to whom this applies to a lesser extent are King Vidor and Douglas Sirk. When wide-screen projection became usual in Europe a year or two after 1954, many non-anamorphic films made there had their images masked to the correct wide-screen ratio *on the print*, so making it impossible to project the films in the old (and wrong) ratio.

The result of wide screen projection was that true wide-angle lens photography was effectively no longer possible. This was because with wide-screen projection the full vertical angle of the taking lens was no longer represented in the screen image, and since the sides of the screen had also been moved out to encompass a wider visual angle for the audience, the same impression of normal perspective that had previously been obtained with a lens of focal length 35 to 40 mm. now required a lens with focal length of approximately 25 mm.. Compared to this, an 18 mm. lens, which was the widest available in the 'fifties, no longer gave the extreme 'wide-angle' impression that it had given before, and so the visual effect of the 'wide-angle lens' style was lost. And because of the shape of the image as projected, the possibility of arranging strong diagonal compositions in one way or another was also lost. However depth of focus and the possibility of staging in depth had not been lost if short focal length lenses were used, but since their distinctiveness and noticeability had now gone, interest in using them receded.

VistaVision

The sole peculiarity of Paramount's VistaVision process as it was *actually* worked, apart from in a few showcase cinemas, was that the image was photographed on a double-sized frame 8 sprocket holes long on ordinary 35 mm. film running horizontally sideways behind the lens in a special camera. Although the image was of the same size and proportions as that of a 35 mm. still camera, being 24 mm. high and 36 mm.

long (i.e. 1:1.5 aspect ratio), the left and right extremities were not used in any way, and only an 'Academy ratio' portion of it 24 mm. by 32 mm. was reduced onto 35 mm. positive prints in an optical printer that also turned the image through 90 degrees to give the correct orientation for ordinary projection. The viewfinder of the VistaVision camera had markings on the ground glass indicating the composition areas for the usual wide-screen ratios. The sole advantage of this process over ordinary non-anamorphic wide-screen photography was that the larger area on the negative produced a sharper image in the final print. This is because most of the loss in image sharpness occurs at the negative stage, since the negative emulsion is always far grainier than the positive emulsion. The principal drawback to the process was that it used twice as much negative film as ordinary cinematography, and also that the special camera was heavier and bulkier than an ordinary 35 mm. camera. In fact it weighed 105 lb. in the unblimped form, and it was supplied with a range of lenses from 21 mm. to 152 mm., which corresponds for the frame size in question to a range from true wide-angle to a slightly long focal length, taking into account the angles of view actually seen on the screen. So with VistaVision it would have been possible to continue the 'staging in depth with wide-angle lens' style of filming that had become popular with some directors in the previous decade, but in fact the people using the process did not seem to be interested in doing that. With the appearance of yet sharper Eastman Color negative (Type 5250) in 1959, the extra definition of the VistaVision process was no longer considered important, and the process was abandoned. In more recent times the VistaVision cameras have found a little use for shooting high definition background plates for special effects.

Super Technirama

This process operated by the Technicolor company simply consisted of putting a supplementary anamorphic lens with a squeeze ratio of 1:1.5 in front of the lens of a VistaVision-type camera, and then optically printing the resulting negative onto 35 mm. film with the usual CinemaScope squeeze ratio of 1:2 including all the image as shot, or alternatively printing onto 70 mm. film, when the process was known as Super Technirama 70. The supplementary anamorphoser lens restricted the possible focal lengths of the prime lenses on the camera to 50 mm., 75 mm., and 100 mm.

Travelling Mattes

In the 'forties combinations of foreground and background action which had been shot separately were sometimes made in the Technicolor process by filming the foreground action in front of a bright blue screen, and using the blue film record from the three-strip Technicolor camera to generate high contrast travelling mattes and counter-mattes to make the required effects. In the 'fifties the same approach was used with Eastman Color monopack film, with the black and white matte films being printed from the Eastman Color negative with pure blue light. In this system bright blue colours in the clothing of the actors had to be avoided, and there was also a tendency to print-through of the background image, as can be seen in some 'fifties films such as *The Ladykillers* (1955), so it was not used any more than could be helped.

For black and white cinematography a new form of travelling matte system using a Technicolor-type beam-splitter camera was invented in Britain at the beginning of the decade. In this case the actors performed the foreground action in front of a brilliant yellow screen illuminated by monochromatic yellow light from sodium vapour lamps, and the actors themselves were illuminated with incandescent light from which the wavelengths corresponding to the sodium light were removed with special filters. Corresponding filters were used in the beam-splitter camera so that only light from the actors went through to the film in one gate of the camera, while only sodium light from the background was deviated by the prism into the other gate which contained another film. When this second film was given high contrast development it gave a perfect counter-matte to the actors. Other slightly inferior variants of this process were developed later, but more importantly, the sodium light process was straightforwardly transferred to use with colour film at the end of the decade.

Editing and Scene Dissection

A new trend now appeared in the cutting rate of Hollywood films: a trend towards scene dissection into shorter shots which was the reverse of the long take trend of the nineteen-forties. Although, as always, some long established Hollywood directors moved with this trend, the change was primarily associated with new, younger directors who started making films at the end of the 'forties or the beginning of the 'fifties. Robert Aldrich was one of these, and he has already been mentioned as using fast cutting on a CinemaScope film of 1954, *Vera Cruz*, which has an Average Shot Length of 5 seconds. Other films by Aldrich include *Apache* (1954) with an ASL of 6 seconds, and *The Angry Hills* (1959) with an ASL of 5.5 seconds, and other new directors who contributed to the movement included Byron Haskin, Robert Parrish, and Delmer Daves, all of whom worked with Average Shot Lengths in the range 6 to 7 seconds. And there were a number of less well-known names. The fact that these individual directors just named do exemplify a general trend is shown by considering the mean Average Shot Lengths for samples of more than 100 films for the six-year periods 1952-1957 and 1958-1963, which are 11 seconds and 9.3 seconds respectively. The Average Shot Length distribution for the 1946-1951 period is illustrated again for comparison, and a close resemblance can be seen with the distribution for 1952-1956. Then during the 'fifties the modal (most common) value for Average Shot Length fell from 9 seconds, where it had stayed for the past 25 years, to 6 seconds. All of this corresponds to the fact that hardly any new directors were now going in for long-take filming.

The Life and Times of the Jump Cut – Part 2

It was during the nineteen-fifties that the jump cut began to come into its full glory. As I have already noted, in 1950 Michael Powell's *The Elusive Pimpernel* contained a fairly large number, and in 1952 Luis Berlanga made *Bienvenida Mr. Marshall* in Spain using jump cuts and shock cuts exclusively to advance from one scene to the next. This film by Berlanga together with his subsequent films, and those directed by his scriptwriting collaborator Juan Antonio Bardem, seem to have been the main influence in promoting the use of the jump cut in Europe. In Robert Wise's *Somebody Up There Likes Me* (1956), many of the space-time transitions were made with straight cuts, though without consistency, since wipes, dissolves, and fades were also used for this purpose in this film, but Wise did not pursue this style in his subsequent films, nor did any other American directors take it up at this time. The use of jump cuts or shock cuts had never been popular with French directors before, but at this point the style finally began to catch on, and *le Ballon rouge* (Pierre

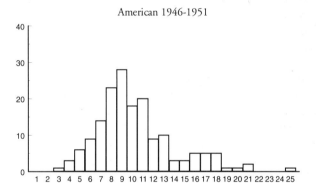

American 1946-1951

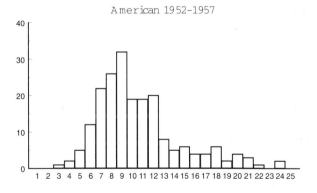

American 1952-1957

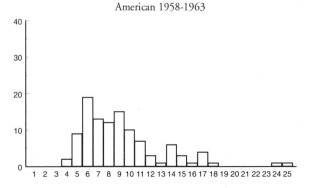

American 1958-1963

Lamorisse, 1956), which is jump cut throughout, was the prelude to the better-known practices of the subsequent Nouvelle Vague. One of the curiosities of the adoption of the jump cut by the Nouvelle Vague directors was that Truffaut and Godard had roundly abused Bardem and Berlanga's use of

shock cuts and jump cuts when they were still film critics, just as they did J. Lee-Thomson's *Woman in a Dressing Gown*, and yet this last film undoubtedly gave rise to Truffaut's mannerism in his early films of showing gigantic and gratuitous Inserts of a hand turning a key or a finger pushing a button.

19. FILM STYLE AND TECHNOLOGY IN THE SIXTIES

Ah!, the swinging 'sixties, when anything and everything seemed possible! This may have had something to do with the change in the film audience, for the continuing decline in total admissions really reflected the loss of the older part of the audience: those over thirty. This change had some effect on the subject matter of Hollywood films, and also helped a number of young film-makers to get a chance to direct feature films. Like the nineteen-twenties, the 'sixties was a period when European film-making had a considerable influence on American cinema, but in this case the major innovations in film form came from France rather than Germany, and they were partly transmitted indirectly by way of British films of the middle 'sixties. It was also a period when more of what were essentially American productions were filmed overseas than ever before, and if we add in the activities of expatriates like Joseph Losey, the concept of 'national cinemas' becomes uselessly vague. The other obvious feature of the decade was the increasing dominance and influence of television over the older medium.

Film Stock and Laboratory Methods

The advent of colour television in America must have encouraged the introduction of new faster colour film stocks, though this would undoubtedly have eventually happened in any case, just as it had done in the past with black and white stocks, through the self-propelling dynamics of competition, research, and development. Eastman Kodak retained their lead in this field with yet another new Eastman Color negative (Type 5251) introduced in 1962, which had the same speed of 50 ASA, but improved definition and colour rendition. The equivalent 16 mm. stock (Type 7251) was only available to special order in the United States before 1967, but in England, where the practice in 16 mm. filming had mostly been to use negative rather than reversal stock, (which was the opposite of American practice), the new 7251 negative became available from Kodak as a standard item at the same time as the new 35 mm. stock, Type 5251.

Improvements in reversal stocks continued apace, with Kodak replacing Ektachrome E.R. in 1965 with Ektachrome E.F. Type 7242 (125 ASA for use under tungsten light) and Type 7241 (160 ASA for daylight use). These new Ektachromes had much better colour rendition, and a marked reduction in grain size, and hence better definition, and in fact the improvement in these stocks, together with that of Eastman Color in 1959, represented the largest jump in quality so far made in the history of three-colour processes. The new Ektachromes were designed to be processed in a modified developing system running faster than usual and at higher temperatures, and they were also suitable for forced (or ex-

tended) development. This enabled them to be exposed with less light than was correct for their normal rating, and meant that the ASA rating of Type 7242 could be increased by one, two, or three stops from the normal 125 ASA to 250 ASA, or 500 ASA, or even 1000 ASA. The deterioration of image quality caused by extended development of one stop was barely perceptible, but when pushed to 1000 ASA the saturation and correctness of the hues was very noticeably reduced, and there was a great increase in granularity and loss in definition. Nevertheless this feature of Ektachrome E.F. was extensively used in documentary work from 1965 onwards, not to mention in television news filming. 35 mm. Ektachrome E.F. was available to special order, and was used on very rare occasions in feature film-making, as in Peter Brook's *Tell Me Lies* (1967), in which a night street scene was shot with available light using this stock, and then copied onto internegative, and interpolated into the film which was otherwise shot on 35 mm. Eastman Color.

In fact forced development had occasionally been used with the earlier High Speed Ektachrome E.R. in documentary work, and Robert Altman had made a telefilm in 1964, *Once Upon a Savage Night*, which was entirely shot on 35 mm. Ektachrome E.R.. This film included night street scenes shot with available light, and with the stock pushed to 500 ASA. In this case the image quality must certainly have been very poor.

The higher temperature developing baths introduced for processing Ektachrome were in part a response for television's need to get news footage onto the screen faster, but it also had economic advantages for the film laboratories, as did the slightly earlier use of the same technique for processing of 35 mm. release prints. In the latter case the ostensible reason was the changing demands of film release patterns at the beginning of the decade, which called for larger numbers of prints of any particular subject. In 1950 the original developing process for Eastman Color positive film had called for 45 minutes of wet time at 70 F. in the developing machine, but film laboratories had begun to reduce this to 28 minutes at 75, and then, finally with Kodak collaboration, to 20 minutes at 80 F. in 1966.

Encouraged by these developments, cameramen began underexposing 35 mm. Eastman Color negative, and giving it forced development to increase its speed. The first notable instance of this was in *You're a Big Boy Now* (Francis Coppola, 1967), in which the stock was pushed three stops to an effective speed of 400 ASA to get shots of the interior of a big department store under available light. From this point onwards increasing resource was had to this technique for the occasional scene in colour feature films, though usually with only one stop forced development.

An associated technique which also produces a speed increase, and de-saturates the colours as well, was used for the first time on *The Deadly Affair* (Sidney Lumet, 1966). This was a matter of pre-fogging the unexposed negative, before its use in shooting the scene proper, by controlled exposure to white light in a printer, in just the same way as for the 'latensification' process used in the late nineteen-forties. In the particular case of *The Deadly Affair* the intention was to use the de-saturation of the colour for expressive purposes.

A very original idea, which proceeded in the opposite direction, was developed by Conrad Hall, starting with *Hell in the Pacific* (1968). this was a matter of over-exposing the film, developing it normally to give a very dense negative, and then having the over-exposure corrected in the printing. The idea was to change the saturation of the colours, and in the fully developed form of the technique, as used by Hall in *Butch Cassidy and the Sundance Kid* 1970 V51 n5 p434 the over-exposure was two stops. The net result was that colours were considerably desaturated, and this was accentuated in this film by the use of fairly heavy Fog filters throughout.

There were also other essays in colour control in *The Taming of the Shrew* and *Reflections in a Golden Eye* in 1967. The colours in the initial run of prints of these films were restricted largely to browns and reds (i.e. the greens and blues were mostly suppressed) by using additional stages of dye transfer printing with extra matrices derived from the green and blue records which had been given an extra exposure to a black and white negative derived from the original colour negative. *Reflections in a Golden Eye* was shown hardly anywhere in this form, and the general run of distribution took place with prints made in the conventional way. This special technique, applicable only to the Technicolor dye transfer printing process, though hardly used subsequently, was capable of a number of other finely controlled colour variations.

Another simpler form of colour modification practised with Technicolor printing involved the interchange of the three matrices that printed each of the three primary colours, which resulted in false colours in the objects in the film shots undergoing this treatment. This process was first used in *2001: A Space Odyssey* (Stanley Kubrick, 1968), in the 'trip through space and time' sequence towards the end, and also subsequently in one or two other films. It is also possible to use this technique of colour modification with ordinary methods of colour printing, but in that case it can no longer be done simply and directly, but involves an extra stage of duplication going through colour separation inter-positives before returning to the final colour print.

A superficially rather similar result was also achieved in 1968 in *Girl on a Motor-Cycle* by Jack Cardiff, only here the images from the original standard colour negative were transferred to videotape, and then the colours were transformed electronically before the video image was refilmed. This too has become standard practice, though it is not frequently used.

Returning to the developments in colour stock, Ansco responded to the challenge from Eastman Kodak by making a new range of 16 mm. and 35 mm. colour reversal materials available in 1963: as well as two Anscochromes with speeds of 100 ASA for use under daylight and tungsten light respectively, they also produced a faster material with a speed of 200 ASA for daylight filming. All of these stocks, like those they replaced, were of higher contrast than the Kodak reversal films, and were intended solely for use of the original by direct projection, rather than as a master for making reversal prints. For this reason they were hardly used even in documentary production. In 1964 Ansco added a 50 ASA stock balanced for daylight to their range, and Kodak also produced a similar 64 ASA stock, but both of these were unsuitable as master material for reversal print making, and again irrelevant to my concerns.

The final major development in colour during the 'sixties was the replacement in 1968 of Eastman Color negative Type 5251 by a new emulsion, Type 5254, which was one stop faster at 100 ASA. There was no marked improvement in colour rendition or image sharpness with this new stock, but the increase in speed was quite important, in the same way as the developments in forced processing just described, in helping to cope with the continuing move all through the decade towards shooting more and more interiors on location. Even the conventional middle of the mainstream of film-making joined in this trend, and although in these cases the location interiors were substantially lit with extra artificial light, there were physical limitations to how much the light level could be raised on real interiors, so faster colour negative had become essential.

In 1968 Kodak produced a new improved colour internegative, and far more importantly, a Colour Reversal Intermediate (CRI) stock. This latter material, which had not existed before, gave a duplicate negative from an original camera negative in one stage, rather than having to go through an extra interpositive film as well, as had previously been the case. Because this new material produced no increase in contrast, and hardly any loss in definition and colour, the duplicate negative so produced was virtually indistinguishable from the original. Not only did this improve the quality of final show prints in general, but it also meant that the sudden loss in quality just before, and during, fades and dissolves in Eastman Color prints no longer took place. Prior to the introduction of Eastman CRI stock the attentive viewer could always see a fade or dissolve coming just before it actually happened in Eastman Color films.

The use of CRI stock was associated with another technical development in laboratory work. This was the increasing use of 'liquid gate' printing, both for contact printing and optical printing. In a liquid gate printer, the negative film in the gate of the printer is completely immersed in a transparent liquid of very nearly the same refractive index as the clear emulsion and acetate base of the film while light is passing through it on its way to produce an exposure in the print stock. This liquid fills any small scratches in the negative, and to some extent stops them being photographically reproduced on the positive image. Although the idea had been developed by Eastman Kodak in the 'twenties, it was not taken up seriously till the nineteen-fifties, when Kodak, Disney, and Technicolor did more work on it, with Kodak publishing a list of liquids suitable for the purpose. In the 'sixties there began to be more films blown up from 16 mm. to 35 mm. for theatrical distribution, and liquid gate printing to using an optical printer became important for this purpose. One of the first feature films for which this was done was Russ Meyer's *The Immoral Mr. Teas* in 1959. With the introduction of Eastman Color Reversal Intermediate Stock in 1968, it became common to use this in conjunction with liquid gate printing for such blow-ups.

Black and White Stock

Despite the rapidly decreasing importance of filming in black and white, new camera stocks of increasing speed continued to be introduced in the nineteen-sixties. Ilford in England put a negative film faster than any there had been before on the market at the beginning of the decade. This was HPS with a speed of 400 ASA, and then in 1962 Ansco put out Hypan (200 ASA), and in 1964 Kodak caught up with 4X, which had a speed of 400 ASA. The availability of Ilford HPS had actually been anticipated by Raoul Coutard in the filming of Jean-Luc Godard's *A bout de souffle* in 1959. He took 18 metre lengths of HPS which were already being sold for use in 35 mm. still cameras, and cemented them together to make 120 metre rolls which he used in a Cameflex movie camera in the shooting of that film. Coutard also gave this Ilford HPS negative special development which increased its speed to 800 ASA, for Godard wanted to film all the scenes of the film on location with available light. This was something that had never been done before on a fictional film. Admittedly the same thing could have been done by using one of the existing film stocks, such as Tri-X, and giving it two stops of forced development, but the visual effect would have been quite different, with a rather contrasty and grainy image. Apart from Godard's subsequent *Alphaville*, it is doubtful if there were any other feature films shot entirely with available light, although Ilford HPS and Kodak 4X were used on a number of later films in which the interiors were lit with added lights to a greater or lesser extent.

The other film manufacturers also updated their black and white stocks in the middle speed range, but this was of rapidly decreasing importance, except that Ilford had a considerable success with their new Mark V negative, introduced in 1965. This was preferred by many cameramen to the other competing 200 ASA stocks because it was considered to have slightly finer grain. Ilford achieved this trick with this stock, as they did with their HPS also, by increasing the red light sensitivity of the emulsion to a greater extent than usual, but this produced no *visible* change in the colour response.

Lighting

For most of the 'sixties Hollywood lighting practice was much the same as it had been in the previous decade, which was still a somewhat simplified version of 'forties lighting. But in Europe new trends were just beginning that eventually, towards the end of the 'sixties, began to have their first effects on American lighting. The central figure in these radical changes was Raoul Coutard, not only in his work for Jean-Luc Godard, but also in the lighting he did for François Truffaut and other 'Nouvelle Vague' directors. One of the styles of interior lighting Coutard developed began with Godard's next film after *À bout de souffle*, which was *le Petit soldat* made in 1960. In this film Coutard introduced the practice of bouncing light off the ceiling from rows of photoflood reflector bulbs fastened above the tops of window and door frames, and pointing upwards at the ceiling. This type of lighting mimics and boosts the natural light coming through the windows, etc., to a point where filming is possible with super-fast stock *without* giving it forced development. Also, because of the rather non-directional nature of this light, it permits filming from all directions during a long take without the lighting units getting into the shot. Advantage was taken of this in *Le Petit soldat*, sometimes in conjunction with hand-held moving camera. The drawback to this approach to lighting is that it only works well in all-white rooms, particularly in colour filming, and also that it tends to leave the eyes of the actors slightly shadowed. Associated with this last point is an absence of 'catch lights' showing in the actors' eye-balls, which are those tiny reflections of the light sources which are conventionally considered to give 'life' to the actor's expression in close shots. Bounce lighting is also a very inefficient method of lighting, owing to the large light losses on reflection, and two to four times the wattage is needed to achieve the same light level on the set as with ordinary direct lighting.

Given the slowness of colour stock for most of the 'sixties, this last point made bounce lighting in its pure form difficult to use – in fact it could only be done with colour by putting a large number of lighting units on 'pole-cats' below the ceiling. (Pole-cats are extensible tubes which can be wedged between opposite walls just below the ceiling to carry small lighting units clamped to them.) Such an arrangement produces the unfortunate result that the upper parts of the walls which are visible in shot just below the lighting units and the top of the frame are brighter than the lower parts of the walls, and this looks rather unnatural. This effect can be studied in Truffaut's *la Mariée était en noir* (1968). If a set filmed with bounce light contains substantial areas of strong colour, all the surfaces, including the actors' faces, will be suffused with a weak wash of light of that colour, and this kind of 'colour cast' is impossible to remove completely by colour correction at the printing stage. This flaw can be seen in some scenes of Hitchcock's *Torn Curtain* (1966), in which most of the interiors were lit by bounce light, this being yet another of the instances in which Hitchcock seized on a new technical development and applied it to his films in modified form. The interiors of *Torn Curtain* were shot entirely in the studio on sets which had no ceilings, so the Coutard style of bounce lighting was out of the question. Instead, the horizontal beams of very large spotlights outside the walls of the sets were diffused downwards into the sets by bouncing them from large flats painted matt white and suspended at 45 degrees to the walls and above them. This rather elaborate procedure was never repeated, but it marks the beginning of the Hollywood interest in recent European cinematographic techniques.

When Coutard began shooting colour with Godard on *Une Femme est une femme* (1961), he dropped the bounce lighting approach, and used ordinary direct lighting on the sets and figures, though done very simply in the European manner. However in this film, and in subsequent Godard films shot in white rooms or on white sets with ceilings, direct lighting produces a large amount of stray light bouncing about the set, and so produces a softer effect in a way that does not happen on studio sets without ceilings when direct light is applied to them. While I am discussing Coutard's work on Godard's films, I should mention that from *le Mépris* onwards, he made further variations in the relative amounts of bounce lighting and direct lighting applied to the various room locations: with more bounce and less direct used on *Pierrot le fou* (1965), and very little bounce and lots of direct on *Deux ou trois choses que je sais d'elle* (1966). All this work was done with the older existing types of lighting units, but in America at the end of the decade the first use of other forms of indirect soft lighting involved new types of lighting units that had just been developed.

Lighting Units

In 1960 a new system of lighting units based on large 500 watt reflector bulbs was designed by Ross Lowel. These units used a lamp socket attached by a small universal joint to a flat aluminium plate a few inches in size. These plates and the lamps they carried could be attached to any flat surface by strips of broad adhesive tape ('gaffer tape') since they only weighed ten ounces, or alternatively the units could be attached to the tops of lightweight telescopic lamp stands by a small chain. Small lightweight 'barn doors' could be attached to the front of the reflector bulb by a spring harness, and the whole unit was small enough to be hidden out of shot in corners or near the ceiling of actual rooms on location. The universal joint on the holder enabled the light to be directed where desired, and the standard kit of three units was enough to light a small room when the fastest film stock was used. These Lowellight kits were extensively used for news and documentary filming over the next few years, along with the already existing Colortran lighting system, to which they were nicely complementary. (A new and more powerful floodlight, the Super 80, which consumed 1.5 kW. of power was added to the Colortran system in 1962).

However, another type of lighting unit began to displace the Colortran boosted-voltage system for small-scale location filming from 1964 onwards. This was also manufactured by the Colortran company amongst others, but it was colloquially referred to as the Quartz-Iodine Multibeam. It was the principal one of a number of new lighting units designed around the new small quartz-iodine (or tungsten-halogen) lamp bulbs. Multibeam lights consisted of a cylindrical housing 6 inches in diameter by 8 inches long weighing only a couple of pounds, and containing a 650 or 1000 watt quartz-iodine bulb which could be moved in front of a rough-surfaced parabolic mirror to give a beam focussing between 'flood', with a spread of 60 degrees, and 'medium spot', with a spread of 30 degrees. The light they gave was slightly harder (i.e. it cast sharper shadows) than that from conventional Fresnel lens spotlights, and also from units containing reflector bulbs of one sort or another, and there was no sharp fall-off in the light intensity past the edge of the main beam of light. All of these features were slightly less than ideal for most feature film purposes, but the small size and light weight for relatively high light levels ensured that these Multibeam units came to dominate news and documentary filming almost immediately. They were often used to give bounce lighting off the ceiling of small locations by cameramen who had plenty of them available, and who were in no hurry. Lowellighting produced their own improved version of this type of unit in 1967 called the Lowel-Quartz system, and the lighting units in this could, though they were much larger than the earlier Lowel system, be taped (just) to walls, etc. by cameramen who had lots of gaffer tape and lots of nerve.

Other forms of standard lighting unit such as simple flood-lights (broads) and so on gradually came to be fitted with large Quartz-Iodine bulbs, rather than the earlier tungsten bulbs, from the late 'sixties onwards, but this made no difference to the quality of light they gave.

Another quite new type of lighting unit introduced in 1968 was the Minibrute, colloquially called a 'nine light' or 'niner', because it was made up of three groups of three 650 watt sealed-beam quartz-iodine reflector spotlight bulbs mounted on three adjustable panels, with the whole unit measuring altogether about two feet by two feet. These sealed-beam spotlight bulbs had a rather narrow beam of only several degrees spread, so the unit could be used as a less powerful replacement for the vastly larger and heavier Brute arc spotlights, in their function of providing figure lighting for actors on exteriors when the lights had to be some distance away. A slight drawback to the use of this lighting unit was that it cast multiple shadows if the actors happened to be close to a wall, but nevertheless it was immediately used a great deal on the exterior shooting of feature films.

Soft Lighting

'Soft lighting' or 'north lighting' is correctly used to describe the kind of light that comes into a room in daytime through a large north-facing window, or some arrangement that produces an identical effect with artificial means. This kind of light results in extremely soft-edged shadows being cast by the protuberances of the face on itself, and is sometimes wrongly called 'shadowless' lighting, despite the fact that under it figures *do* cast shadows, though very tenuous and blurred ones. Although vaguely like the lighting used in film interiors before 1914, it is certainly not identical, since that early form of lighting was produced in *south-facing* studios by direct sunlight diffused by cotton blinds and translucent glass, supplemented by Cooper-Hewitts and arcs applied from a number of angles. In fact such early lighting came from a far greater range of angles than modern 'soft light'.

The modern lighting unit called a 'soft light' or 'north light' came into use for film lighting in 1967, prompted in part by the European use of bounce lighting, and in part by recent fashions in the lighting for commercial still photography. These soft lights were first marketed by Colortran in the form of a large sheet-metal box about three feet square on the open side, and with a very irregular interior surface painted matt white. Long quartz-iodine lamp tubes shone onto this surface from behind a narrow baffle that stopped them radiating light directly forward, and after a number of reflections from the white walls, the light emerged from the front opening of the box as a non-directional glow: indeed very like the light emerging through a north-facing window of rather small size. Different powers were available, from 1.25 kW. to 5 kW., and these lights quickly came to be widely used, but mainly in non-theatrical film-making. On feature films they tended to be used for general fill lighting rather than as key lights producing the main illumination on actors' faces, but European cameramen were rather more inclined to use them as the principal light sources for a scene – e.g. Freddie Young on *Ryan's Daughter* (1969).

An alternative kind of soft-lighting unit, also taken over from still photography, where it had made a come-back after sixty years in limbo, was the 'umbrella light'. The reflector of this unit was, as at the start of the century in still photography, a large white umbrella which had one to four quartz-iodine lights attached to the handle and shining into the cove of it. The first cameraman to make use of this light in feature films

was Haskell Wexler on *The Thomas Crown Affair* (1968), but its use thereafter on features was very limited, as most cameramen preferred to use other forms of soft lighting.

Yet another method of generating large-area soft lighting was also taken over from still photography and television commercials by David Watkin in his lighting of Peter Brook's *The Marat/Sade* (1967). This technique did not involve any new lighting units, but was done by shining a bank of powerful conventional lights from fairly close range onto a large vertical sheet of translucent material, which could be tracing paper or spun glass, and then using the diffuse light that struggled through it and emerged on the other side as the sole light source on the scene. In *The Marat/Sade* this source formed a whole glowing wall about thirty feet square just out of shot at one side of the set. A similar method was used to light a conference room set in *2001: A Space Odyssey*, but after that the method tended to be restricted to window-sized areas in ordinary room sets.

Black and White Lighting in England

Towards the middle of the nineteen-sixties a distinctive trend in the lighting of black and white films, which were still fairly common in England, emerged amongst the younger cameramen such as Walter Lassaly and Ken Higgins. This was to light in a fairly high key even in ordinary scenes in dramatic films, with rather flat lighting on the figures, and very frequently no backlight. This was done by using direct light with a low ratio between the key- and fill-light.

Cameras

The major development in cine cameras during the nineteen-sixties was the proliferation of light-weight silenced cameras for 16 mm. sync. sound filming. The first step in this direction was not taken by camera manufacturers but by film cameramen who had earlier decided that they wanted to shoot

Lighting of a scene in Darling *(1965), with only hard frontal light, and no backlight.*

documentary scenes with sound as they actually happened, rather than restaging them for the camera as had almost invariably been the case up to this point in history. The cameras most used for shooting synchronized sound were the Auricon range, but of these the Pro 600 and Pro 1200 were too large and unwieldy for hand-holding, and the Cine-Voice only accepted 100 foot spools of film running for 2 min. 45 seconds. The men who changed all this were the documentary cameramen Richard Leacock and Donn Alan Pennebaker. In the years immediately prior to 1959 they had moved towards what they came to call 'direct cinema', by shooting documentary films containing unrehearsed scenes with hand-held lightweight cameras and simultaneously taking *unsynchronized* dialogue recordings with portable tape recorders, and then fudging the picture and sound records into approximate synchronism by editing. To further this approach, which was aimed at the television market, in 1959 they adapted an Auricon Cine-Voice camera for shoulder holding by modifying the viewfinder, replacing the internal 100 foot magazine with a changeable 400 foot external magazine, and replacing the drive motor with a battery powered motor whose speed was governed to very high accuracy by control from the tuning fork oscillator from a Bulova Accutron electric watch. The speed of the tape recorder synchronizing pulse was determined by an identical watch oscillator, and so film and sound synchronism could be maintained without any direct connection between the camera and recorder, in an exactly analogous manner to present-day arrangements using crystal oscillators on camera and recorder. Leacock and Pennebaker's films were shot by one or more two-man teams of cameraman and recordist following impromptu action wherever it led, without the intervention of either a director or assistants. The first film in which they managed to get this technique to work properly, at least some of the time, was *Primary*, made in 1959, but subsequently they applied it to a number of television documentaries over the next several years. Others who were associated with them such as the Maysles brothers, and also outsiders, took up these methods of documentary production. Though nearly all concerned applied this approach to intrinsically dramatic material such as an appeal against a death sentence, as in *The Chair* (1963), or the dealings of a big film producer in *Showman* (David and Albert Maysles, 1962), the results were never popular with the major television networks, however influential they were with other film-makers.

Parallel developments in France, where the equivalent of 'direct cinema' was called 'cinéma vérité', led to the design of a silent camera by Michel Coutant, the man who designed the Cameflex for the Eclair camera company. One of his prototypes, which was very different to the final design, was used in filming part of Rouch and Morin's *Chronique d'un été* (1961). This first design weighed only 8 lb., and was definitely not completely silent, so that it had to be used inside a barney (soft padded cover), and all in all it was not much of an improvement on a Bolex Reflex with electric motor drive. Coutant's final design, called the Eclair NPR, weighed 19 lb.

and was specially designed so that a large part of this weight was transferred to the cameraman's shoulder through the bottom of the magazine, which was directly behind the rest of the works in the fashion of the Cameflex. The 400 foot feed and take-up film compartments were arranged side by side coaxially, and just as in the Cameflex, the film drive sprockets and film loops were contained in the magazine rather than in the body of the camera. The film emerged from a light-tight slit in the front of the magazine to run down between the back pressure plate fixed to the front of the magazine, and the front of the gate which was on the back of the front part of the camera. Both the claw, which was the usual Cameflex spring-loaded type, and the register pin, entered the film perforations from this front assembly. It was possible to change magazines in this camera without stopping the camera, just as in the Cameflex. A mirror-reflex shutter gave continuous through-the-lens viewing through an eyepiece that could be oriented in any direction over 360 degrees, which enabled the cameraman to film backwards over his shoulder if necessary. The Eclair NPR had a rotating lens turret with places for two lenses, and almost invariably one of these was an Angénieux 12 mm. to 120 mm. zoom. If the other lens in the turret was a 10 mm. wide-angle lens, it was necessary to remove the zoom lens from the other port before using it, as the zoom protruded into the wide-angle field of view. This camera became available from 1963, and immediately came into wide use, particularly in Europe. From the beginning it was supplied with an optional crystal oscillator controlled motor, so that it could be used for 'cordless' synchronization with a portable tape recorder similarly fitted with a crystal oscillator. One of the first notable films on which this camera was used was Chris Marker's *le Joli Mai* (1963). This film, along with *Chronique d'un été*, was blown up from 16 mm. to 35 mm. for theatrical exhibition, as also happened with some of the American 'direct cinema' films shot in 16 mm. colour in the later 'sixties.

The other major 16 mm. camera that became available in the 'sixties for sync. sound filming was the Arriflex 16 BL. Unlike the Eclair NPR, this was not a completely new design, but was simply a version of the already existing Arriflex 16 M with an extra sound deadening casing and quieter plastic gearing in its mechanism. A sound-proof casing was also provided around the lens of the camera, which now fitted into a single fixed port in the front of the camera, rather than into a turret with ports for three lenses, as in the earlier model. The film movement was the same as in the previous Arriflex 16 mm. cameras, as was the mirror-reflex shutter viewfinding system. However the viewfinder was supplied with a modified eyepiece which could be attached to move the eye position forward, so that the cameraman could rest the back of the camera on his shoulder, although unfortunately it was not very comfortable in this position, and most cameramen who specialized in hand-held 'cinéma vérité' work continued to prefer to use the Eclair NPR when the Arriflex 16 BL became available in 1965. The 16 BL was not completely silent any more than the Eclair NPR, but in the average location interior their running noise was swallowed in the general background noise, given careful use of the microphones in recording. The residual noise of the mechanism of both cameras made them unsuitable for genuine studio film-making without applying further sound deadening material to them, but although both gave the same measured residual noise level when running, the noise of the Eclair had the advantage of having less of an intermittent 25 frame per second component, and so was less noticeable. On the other hand, the Arriflex 16 BL had the advantage of being more robust and less temperamental, and so tended to appeal to large television organizations.

The other lightweight cameras designed for 16 mm. synch. sound shooting that appeared in the 'sixties – the Debrie Sinmor, the Bolex Pro 16, and the Beckmann and Whitley – were all unsuccessful to a greater or lesser extent, and provided no competition to the Arriflex, the Eclair, and the older Auricons which were still being used.

35 mm. Cameras

There were no major new developments in 35 mm. cameras during the 'sixties, for all new types were closely modelled on proven designs. Both the new Mitchell Mark II and the various Panavision cameras used the standard Mitchell movement including the usual film gate, pull-down and register pins, and they were also similar to the old Mitchells in their basic shutter design and also that of the film magazines, though this was not always apparent to the casual glance.

The one of these new cameras that was most nearly original was the Mitchell Mark II or R-35, which was available from 1963. All the usual Mitchell works were enclosed in a smaller, though still substantial, body, and a mirror-reflex shutter was added in front of the ordinary shutter with its variable blades. This was in contradistinction to the European reflex cameras, where a single shutter performed both functions, and it hardly counts as inspired design. There was a three lens rotating turret in front of the reflex shutter, following the Arriflex pattern. The magazine, of the usual Mitchell type, could be mounted in a couple of unorthodox positions slant-wise at the back of the camera, feeding the film into the body of the camera through a long throat. Both erect and inverted mountings of the magazine could be used, with the latter position putting the 400 foot capacity magazine half underneath the camera body so that it could form a shoulder rest if the camera was used for hand-held filming. Since the loaded camera weighed over 40 lb. it was never used in this way to my knowledge, as cameramen naturally preferred to stick to the far, far lighter Arriflex or Cameflex for hand-holding. The Mitchell Mark II was not a silent camera, since it made about as much noise as the old Mitchell NC, and for sync. shooting it had to be enclosed in a blimp, which pretty well negated any advantage it had over the Mitchell BNC, particularly since reflex versions of that camera were being made from 1962 onwards. The only areas of film production where the Mitchell Mark II found much use were in the making of television commercials, where a totally steady pin-registered image was desirable for combination with super-imposed titles and other optical effects and sync. sound was usually not required, and in the production of expensive films in Italy and other countries where total post-synchronization of dialogue was the norm.

The first 50 Mitchell R-35 cameras had a design defect, so were recalled, fixed, and reissued as System 35, R-35 Mark II. Subsequent slight modification to the design were the S35R, which could take a magazine in the traditional position directly on top of the body, as well as in the rear slant positions, and the S35RB, which had a single BNCR lens mount on a fixed front rather than the turret mounts of the initial design.

As just remarked, independent companies started to make reflex modifications of the Mitchell BNC by introducing a beam-splitting prism or a semi-reflecting pellicle mirror into the mount behind the lens from 1962 onwards, as the increasing use of zoom and long focal length lenses for ordinary feature film-making came to demand such a modification. It was not until 1968 that the Mitchell Camera Corporation produced their own standard production modification of the BNC to reflex viewing by adding another reflex mirror shutter in front of the ordinary shutter, just as in the Mark II Mitchell. This version of the BNC was called the BNCR.

Camera Supports

The increasing use of long focal length lenses to follow action that only began to become a marked trend towards the end of the 'sixties was anticipated at the beginning of the decade by the provision of tripod heads with built-in hydraulic fluid damping to their movements. The O'Connor 100 fluid head, which could take cameras as heavy as the Mitchell BNC, was available from 1960, and towards the end of the decade the Miller head for lightweight cameras was joined by models from Sachtler and Wolf, Ronford, and other makers. Fluid heads are preferred under cameras fitted with long focal length lenses, because when a panning shot is made with a focal length longer than 200 mm. (100 mm. in 16 mm. filming) fitted to a camera mounted on an ordinary tripod head with friction joints, small jerks are invariably observed in the movement of the image across the frame due to tiny stickings and releases between the friction surfaces. These tiny jerks in the panning movement of the image across the screen also exist when ordinary lenses are used on a friction head, but in that case they are too small to be apparent to the eye. The already existing geared heads used for studio shooting also give smooth movement with long focal length lenses, but they make it more difficult to follow slight unforeseen changes in the action in such a shot. Geared heads are also heavier than is convenient for 'wild' shooting on location.

The continuing trend towards more location filming called forth other lighter-weight crab dollys to join the Moviola crab dolly, which nevertheless remained the principal one used on American feature film shooting on location. Its size, weight, and fairly large pneumatic balloon tyres meant that it gave smooth and steady motion underneath the camera even on city roads and pavements, whereas its principal competitors among the new crab dollys could not be used in this way. These were the Colortran and the Elemack Spyder dollys, which both became available in the United States in 1966, though the Elemack was introduced in Europe in 1962. It was designed in Italy by Sante Zella, who had previously produced other hydraulic dollys. The Colortran crab dolly was the smallest of its kind, and it had a hydraulic centre column that could raise and lower the camera during the shot. Its width was only 27 inches, which meant that it could be tracked through normal-sized doorways in location interiors. This was not the case with the Moviola crab dolly. The Colortran dolly only weighed 222 lb., which meant that it could be carried up narrow stairs into difficult locations, but it was limited in its usefulness by the fact that it had small wheels with hard rubber tyres which only gave good travel on smooth surfaces, and even more by the fact that it was not perfectly stable. A heavy camera on a Colortran dolly wobbles very slightly when it is tracked.

This was not the case with the Elemack Spyder dolly (sometimes also referred to as the Octopus dolly), which had an equally low weight (210 lb.) and minimum size, but which had a camera column that could not be lowered and raised during the shot. Despite this slight drawback, the Elemack Spyder immediately became the other major location crab dolly for feature film production, since its characteristics were nicely complementary to those of the Moviola crab dolly. The solid rubber tyres that the Elemack was fitted with could be quickly replaced by flanged bogey wheels for running on tubular tracking laid down over rough surfaces. It should be emphasized here that all crab dollys can be steered by two wheels only when it is desired to do so, as well as having the four-wheel steering for crabbing. Inevitably it was in European films that the most visible use was made of the crabbing facility of the Elemack Spyder. Notable examples occur in Truffaut's *Fahrenheit 451* (1966), and Miklós Jancsó's *Szegénylegények* (1965): in the former following people from room to room, and in the latter much more conspicuously tracking in a square round a static group. *Szegénylegények* was a leader in a small trend that developed in European art cinema towards the use of complex tracking shots around quasi-static scenes in conjunction with *extremely* long takes. This tendency had no effect on the American cinema, even its new 'art film' wing.

Helicopter Mounts and Anti-Vibration Devices

In 1964 the increasing inclination of directors on major feature films to use elaborate helicopter shots produced the Tyler camera mount for helicopter filming. Vibration from the camera vehicle causes image blurring with long focal length lenses, and this the Tyler mount overcame to some extent. It was used straight away on such films as *Four for Texas* (Robert Aldrich, 1964), but a more striking application followed in *This Property is Condemned* (Sydney Pollack, 1966), which opens with a helicopter tracking shot of a passenger at

a train window taken at the long focal length end of a zoom lens, which goes into a continuous zoom out and a rise up and away by the helicopter-borne camera to give a very distant shot of the whole train.

Even with the Tyler mount there was a certain amount of vibration that got through to the camera, and this was finally removed by the Dynalens in 1965. This device was effectively a section of a flexible prism with a very narrow angle between the two faces which could be altered at high speed electro-magnetically, and this deviated the image passing through it to the lens by exactly the tiny amount required to compensate for the vibration movements of the lens in the opposite direction, at the very moment they happened. This development was one of the increasing number of instances of the use of very advanced technology in film-making. The Dynalens was not used in film production till 1968 in the documentary film of the Olympic Games, and in 1969 for aerial shots in the feature films *Darling Lili* and *Catch-22*.

Lenses

The major lens development in the nineteen-sixties was the introduction in 1963 by Angénieux of zoom lenses with a zoom range of 10 to 1. The version for 16 mm. cameras had a range of focal lengths from 12 mm. to 120 mm., which is a range from true wide-angle to telephoto, and a maximum aperture of f2.3., and the version for 35 mm. cameras had an equivalent range from 25 mm. to 250 mm., with a maximum aperture of f3.2.. Like all zoom lenses they were best suited to cameras with reflex viewfinding systems, but they were also made available in versions with a reflex viewfinding system built into the lens itself, and in this form they were used with such cameras as the Mitchell BNC and the Auricon. In the latter case they became the standard lens fitted to that camera. The 16 mm. Angénieux zoom lens may be the most successful lens of all time, for vast numbers are still being used 20 years later, as they had been supplied as a standard fitting on thousands of new Eclair NPR and Arriflex 16 BL cameras. The fact that the image definition of this lens was just noticeably inferior to that of ordinary fixed focal length lenses mattered little against its convenience for 16 mm. documentary and news work, particularly since in this application the entire film was usually shot with it, which allowed audiences no standard of comparison. When used for just the occasional shot, as Angénieux 25 to 250 mm. zooms mostly were in American 35 mm. feature films, the drop in definition can be rather noticeable, particularly at the extremes of their range where their performance was worst.

In the early 'sixties the use of zoom lenses even for just the occasional shot was still largely restricted to European cinema (e.g. *Billy Liar*, John Schlesinger, 1963), but when the 'swinging' and post-Nouvelle Vague cinema finally attracted attention in the United States with films like *Darling* (J. Schlesinger, 1965) and *Un Homme et une femme* (Claude Lelouch, 1965), some Hollywood films began to use conspicuous zoom shots, as in *The Professionals* (Richard Brooks,

1966). There was however considerable resistance to this in Hollywood, and the use of a slow zoom as a cheap substitute for a tracking shot, which also happens a couple of times in *Un Homme et une femme*, was confined to T.V. film-making until the nineteen-seventies.

Digression: What Lelouch Did

Although Lelouch's photography of *Un Homme et une femme*, like other aspects of that film, had a large and fast influence, this was to some extent through a misunderstanding of how it was carried out. For instance, though it fairly certainly encouraged the use of heavy lens diffusion applied indiscriminately throughout subsequent films, in *Un Homme et une femme* itself there is no use of lens diffusion whatever. But it *does* contain noticeably poor definition in many shots resulting from the inadequacies of telephoto lenses, and more particularly of zoom lenses used in the telephoto position and shooting at full aperture, often against the light. There is at least one well-known occasion, involving a dog on the beach, when the shot is right out of focus as well. Shooting against the light, in the sense of having a strong light source *directly* behind the figures, had been rigorously avoided in films before the 'sixties, since the resulting flare of light bouncing round in the lens not only puts a wash of white over the whole image, but also seriously impairs definition. Shooting directly against the light in this way had begun to appear occasionally in Nouvelle Vague films from the beginning of the decade, but in the late 'sixties Hollywood cameramen were content to approximate the effect by using heavy lens diffusion on standard lenses, since this also produces a loss of definition and a scattering of white light over the whole image. They may also have been encouraged in this practice by an increasing use of heavy diffusion in the filming of television commercials, though the detailed chronology of this process is by no means clear to me. I did not see any television in the early 'sixties, and in a sample of a twenty or so television commercials from 1962 to 1964 that is all I have been able to examine from this period, there is no heavy lens diffusion (except for the concluding 'pack shots'), in all but one of the commercials. It is only in the late nineteen-sixties that one can see this kind of heavy lens diffusion appearing on general shots in a few Hollywood movies such as *The Graduate* (Mike Nichols, 1968) and *Goodbye Columbus* (Larry Peerce, 1969).

There were however other aspects of Lelouch's photography that were not imitated in commercial film-making, and these included his practice of shooting just before and just after sunset without any special colour compensating filters, so that the shots immediately before sunset have a very strong orange cast all over them, and those just after sunset have a very strong blue cast. His more or less random use, with little narrative connection, of a mixture of black and white and colour stock also had little effect on large scale commercial cinema, which preferred to retain some expressive connection with the story when this was done, though it seems likely that Lindsay Anderson was following Lelouch in a muted way

in *If* (1969).

Finally, I must mention that the increasing use in the late 'sixties of very long focal length lenses to cover staged dramatic action was undoubtedly encouraged by the commercial success of *Un Homme et une femme*. In America this was mostly confined to the new 'art cinema' section of production, as in Brian de Palma's *Greetings* (1968), but there were eventually some conspicuous examples in ordinary features, such as *Butch Cassidy and the Sundance Kid* (1969). In the latter case a zoom lens was used at its maximum focal length of 500 mm. to cover some of the 'Super Posse' scenes, and also the bicycle-riding scene. Here the long focal length lens coverage was used in the most common way, which was to follow a single point of interest in the shot with continuous adjustment of focus. The more flashy mode of staging with a long lens, naturally rarer, is to be seen in *Greetings*, and this consists of pulling (or 'racking') focus from a foreground object to a background object, and vice versa, within the length of a shot.

The Image of Michelangelo Antonioni

Michelangelo Antonioni was another film-maker important for his early use of long focal length lenses in *Il deserto rosso* (1964). In his case he was interested in them as a means of producing near-abstract compositions of hard-edged areas of flat colour, and a large proportion of *Il deserto rosso* was shot with lenses of focal length from 100 mm. upwards. As far back as *La notte* (1961), Antonioni had been creating compositions influenced by the school of 'hard-edged' abstract painting descended from Barnett Newman (an Italian representative was Bruno Marani), though initially he had done this with standard-lens cinematography. This was the first time since the nineteen-twenties that the advanced painting of the recent past had an influence on film image composition. Antonioni's style of image composition had relatively little influence in Europe, though other aspects of his films did, and none at all in America, though it is just possible that John Boorman's *Point Blank* (1967) has some trace of it along with echoes of Alain Resnais' methods of film construction.

Other Specialized Lenses

The first 'fish-eye' lens including the full 180 degree field in front of the camera, which was produced by Kinoptik in 1961, would only just cover the 16 mm. frame size, and if applied to a 35 mm. camera produced a circular image of 17 mm. diameter in the middle of the frame surrounded by a black vignette. But 4 or 5 years later 'fish-eye' lenses that could cover the full 35 mm. frame became available, though they were hardly used in feature film work except for the rare subjective effect in drug trip sequences and the like, as in *Easy Rider* (Dennis Hopper, 1969).

It was only in 1968 that an ultra-wide aperture f0.95 lens of 50 mm. focal length was adapted for normal filming in 35 mm., although such lenses had been used for a decade in 16 mm.. At this date this f0.95 lens was only used on an Eyemo camera for available light location filming on *The Incident* and

The Thomas Crown Affair, because the rear elements of the lens went so far back towards the film plane that it could not be used on any camera with a reflex view-finding system. In fact there was very little demand for shooting at such a wide aperture in feature film work, because under these conditions the depth of field is less than three feet even for a Medium Shot, and this places excessively severe restrictions on the placing of the actors within the shot. There is of course more depth of field with the equivalent 25 mm. lens at f0.95 in 16 mm. work, but it is worth noting that when one is working at this aperture with very fast film under a few foot-candles of available light, it is very difficult to see anything clearly through a reflex viewfinder, and indeed very difficult to focus correctly in an impromptu situation.

The Panavision Systems

The Panavision company got its start in 1954 making anamorphic attachments to go on the front of ordinary projection lenses for the showing of CinemaScope films. These were in great demand at the time, and Robert E. Gottschalk, the founder of Panavision, got his hands on a superior design, which used prisms rather than the usual cylindrical elements to produce the unsqueezing effect. One of the beauties of a prism anamorphoser is that it is easy to design it with a variable squeeze ratio, and this led to Panavision being commissioned to produce an anamorphic attachment for the large camera lenses used in MGM's Camera 65 system. The Camera 65 system involved photography on 65 mm. film plus an extra anamorphic compression of 1.33:1, and it was used for the first time on *Raintree County* in 1957. This system was then further developed by Panavision as UltraPanavision.

UltraPanavision

In 1959 the UltraPanavison system was introduced using the same film (65 mm. negative, 70 mm. positive) as the other 70 mm. processes, but with lenses that gave an anamorphic compression in the horizontal direction of 1:1.25. Very few films were made in this system since it required special anamorphic lenses on the 70 mm. projectors used for exhibition, and also a further sideways extension of the cinema screen, as the aspect ratio of the height to width of the projected image was 1:2.7. The cost involved in all this ensured that all that happened was that the small number of Cinerama theatres using the three-projector Cinerama system changed over to this projection format. But by the late 'sixties the UltraPanavision process had been abandoned, and the Cinerama theatres were reduced to screening ordinary 70 mm. films on their deeply curved screens, which were now reduced in width to accommodate the 1:2.2 aspect ratio of such films. The only notable film made in UltraPanavision was *The Greatest Story Ever Told* (George Stevens, 1964), and only a very limited range of lenses were used in this process, with focal lengths from 57 mm. to 230 mm., which does not cover the wide-angle and telephoto region for the 70 mm. film image. But this was hardly a drawback for a process that was only intended to be projected on large, deeply curved screens half surrounding the audience.

SuperPanavision

It was only after this beginning that Panavision had its own ordinary, non-anamorphic lenses designed for straight filming in 65 mm., and they called the system using them SuperPanavision. Quite a number of films were shot in this process, starting with *Exodus* and *West Side Story* in 1960. All these forms of Panavision lenses and cameras were only available as complete systems rented direct from the Panavision Corporation, unlike all ordinary cameras, which were sold outright, and then perhaps rented out by independent film equipment hire companies. As well as the direct hire charges, people using Panavision equipment had to contract to pay a royalty on the finished film prints of productions using the process. This approach was possible because of the marked superiority of the Panavision lenses.

The Development of Anamorphic Cinematography

In the 'sixties CinemaScope-type films came increasingly to be shot with the anamorphic lenses made by the Panavision Corporation rather than with the lenses which had been originally produced for the process by Bausch and Lomb. These so-called 'block' anamorphic lenses had the cylindrical-surfaced elements producing the lateral image compression designed as an integral part of the complete lens, and so they did not require separate focussing. Their performance was greatly improved over the original CinemaScope lenses, particularly with regard to constancy of squeeze ratio with focussing distance, and in the 'sixties they, together with the cameras rented with them by the Panavision Corporation, came to oust all competition in the English-speaking world. In Europe, and also to some extent elsewhere, there were for some years a number of anamorphic processes identical to CinemaScope which had names such as Dyaliscope, or this-Scope or that-Scope, but they were only used by those who could not get their hands on Panavision.

Panavision obtained the 35 mm. cameras which they rented out in conjunction with their lenses by buying up second-hand Mitchell BNCs, and rebuilding them with a true reflex viewing system, at first with a semi-reflecting pellicle beam-splitter in front of the film aperture, as the Panavision PSR camera. They had the opportunity to buy many used Mitchell BNC cameras because there was a change from shooting television programs on film to recording them on videotape at the beginning of the 'sixties in the United States. Later they produced the Panavision Super R-200 with a mirror shutter viewfinding system like that of the Arriflex built onto the Mitchell BNC bodies. In all cases the outer sound proof casing of the BNC was replaced with a newly designed one, which made the Panavision cameras appear more of an original creation than they were.

Between 1960 and 1963 the range of Panavision block anamorphic lenses for 35 mm. use was built up to fully cover the range from a really wide-angle 25 mm. lens to a 360 mm. telephoto lens by way of a large number of lenses of intermediate focal length. This range included an ultra-wide aperture 50 mm. standard lens which had a maximum aperture of f1, and so was faster than any lens available for standard cinematography in 1960. Up to 1964 the range of Panavision zooms was much more restricted, as none had a zoom range of much more than 3 to 1: from 50 mm. to 150 mm., for instance. A couple of years later this was remedied by the availability of 10 to 1 ratio zooms. Over the same period roughly the same range of lenses became available for SuperPanavision, a 70 mm. film system using ordinary spherical lenses rather than anamorphic lenses.

In the nineteen-sixties most of the filming in standard Panavision in Europe, and a good deal of it in America, was done with Mitchell and Arriflex cameras which had their lens mounts adapted to take Panavision lenses, as well as having a couple of other minor alterations to the film aperture and the view-finding system. The sole original Panavision designs were for the Panaflex hand-held cameras, the first of which was one for use with 65 mm. film introduced in 1960. This had a basic resemblance to the 35 mm. Arriflex, with a slant-mount 500 foot magazine towards the back, and a mirror-reflex shutter at one side, but the small body housed the usual Mitchell type of movement with pin registration, rather than the simple single cam-driven claw of the Arriflex, and it was far heavier at 24 lb.. Since only a part of the weight rested on the shoulder it had to be supported with a brace resting on the camera operator's waist for hand-held work. It was not a silent camera, and was only suitable for 'wild' shooting. The same was true of a similar 35 mm. Panaflex that became available in 1963, but both cameras saw quite a lot of use with the increasing trend towards slipping a few hand-held shots into Hollywood movies where they would not be too conspicuous, in crowd scenes and subjective shots, as in *Grand Prix* (J. Frankenheimer, 1966). (This 1963 model Panaflex was not the same as the present-day Panaflex, which is a silent self-blimped camera, whereas the original Panaflex was used only for 'wild' filming, since it was definitely not silent.)

The economic history of the Panavision Corporation is a particularly clear cut example of a company being built up from great initial success in a 'niche' market, in this case the supply of projection lenses for CinemaScope, and after that by the recognition of further opportunities for business in wider and wider related fields within the industry, until the natural limit of this method of expansion is reached.

Forms and Characteristics of 70 mm. Films

In most formal respects 70 mm. films were equivalent to 35 mm. 'Scope films, but there was a difference with regard to the average depth of field on interiors. Because the standard lens for 70 mm. which gave the impression of normal perspective on the screen had a focal length a little longer than that for CinemaScope, the depth of field was somewhat reduced, and taken in conjunction with the much higher image defini-

tion in 70 mm., this tended to draw attention to any areas in the image which were out of focus, in a way that did not happen with the smaller gauge. Because of the nature of the subjects filmed in 70 mm. there were rather less interior scenes than usual, and the camera tended to be well back most of the time, but this defect does show up in the rare intimate scene filmed with low light levels.

Splitting Up the Screen

The only movie to begin to develop a new form out of the special properties of 70 mm. film was Jacques Tati's *Playtime* (1968). Tati made use of the very high definition given by the large 70 mm. image area to stage most scenes in Very Long Shot, with separate actions involving small groups of people taking place in different parts of the frame simultaneously, and yet still with everything they were doing being clearly visible. Despite the claims made by Noël Burch and Jonathan Rosenbaum that these separate actions in different parts of the frame actually involve different simultaneous comedy interests, calm viewing of the film shows that this is not so, and that there is only one point of any real narrative or comedy interest going on at any one instant, within just one area of the frame. The rest of the action is really just background distraction which makes it a little difficult to find where the main point of interest lies.

The idea of simultaneous actions in different areas of the frame was really only fully developed in a number of films using various split screen effects to give multiple images printed onto different areas of the 70 mm. or 'Scope frame in the late 'sixties. The first examples were *The Boston Strangler* (Richard Fleischer) and *Charly* (Ralph Nelson) made in 1968, which used a screen divided vertically into two parts or more parts for some sequences, mostly involving parallel action. There were occasionally other examples in later years, the most famous example being *Woodstock* (Michael Wadleigh, 1970), which had 16 mm. documentary footage printed into different areas of a 70 mm. frame. The inspiration for all these developments was probably the various forms of special multiple projection systems shown at the International Exposition in Montreal in 1967.

Techniscope

In 1960 the Italian Technicolor laboratories invented a new wide-screen system which was called Techniscope. This involved shooting 35 mm. film in a camera with an ordinary lens, and with the film transport system and claw movement modified to pull down the film by two perforations for each exposure, rather than the usual four. The masking of the film aperture was restricted so that the image height corresponded to the halved pull-down distance, and the result was an image on the film whose actual dimensions corresponded to the aspect ratio that CinemaScope had *on the screen*, namely 1:2.35. The other result of this reduction of the image height on the negative was that there were twice as many images on a given length of negative. When a print was made from this negative it was done in an optical step printer which had an anamorphic lens between the negative and positive which doubled the height of the image while leaving the horizontal dimension exactly the same. The final result on the print was an image of exactly the same kind as CinemaScope and Panavision print images, with anamorphic compression in the usual 1:2 ratio, and which could be projected in exactly the same way with the same anamorphic projection lens. Unlike CinemaScope, ordinary lenses (which are now referred to as spherical lenses to make the distinction) were used on the camera, but to get the same field of view as the corresponding 'Scope lens, they had to be of half the focal length. The result of using shorter focal length lenses was greatly increased depth of field, and this was put to good use by a few directors, most notably Sergio Leone in his *Per un pugno di dollari* (1964) and subsequent films. The other main attraction of the process was that since it used only half the usual amount of negative for the same running time, it was slightly cheaper than other modes of 35 mm. filming. This was of very little significance for the ordinary budgeted Hollywood film with an ordinary shooting ratio, and the result was that when the process was made available in America in 1963, it was only used for cheap films of no particular interest.

The image definition of Techniscope was inevitably inferior to that of Panavision, since the negative image was much smaller, but it was not so very inferior to ordinary 35 mm. film when the latter was projected in the wide-screen format.

Process Work and Special Effects

The major forms of process cinematography at the beginning of the nineteen-sixties continued to be straightforward background projection, and also the system of blue-screen travelling mattes established in the previous decade. In the early 'sixties the blue screen travelling matte process was developed into an improved form that could cope with semi-transparent objects in front of the background scene, but the process was still quite likely to leave 'minuses' round the figures. In 1964 the sodium light travelling matte process using a Technicolor beam-splitter camera that had been developed in England in the 'fifties was imported into Hollywood by the Disney studios for *Mary Poppins*, and this process gave the best results of any travelling matte system there has ever been, particularly after the introduction of Eastman Color Reversal Intermediate stock in 1968.

The major innovation in this decade was the first use of front projection in feature films. The practicability of this system had been demonstrated experimentally as early as 1949, and it depended on the new 'Scotchlite' reflective material which had just become available then, but for some unknown reason the process was not used in actual films till the 'sixties. Scotchlite has the unique property that light falling on it from any particular direction is all reflected back exactly in that direction, and *no other*. No previous directionally reflective coating had this property, for all such materials

reflected light in directions other than that in which it was incident. The arrangement used for carrying out front projection was that the actors performed, lit in the usual way, in front of a large screen made of Scotchlite, and they were filmed by a camera with a semi-reflecting mirror in front of it set at 45 degrees to the lens. The background scene to be combined with the foreground action was projected at exactly 90 degrees to this lens axis onto the front of the semi-reflecting mirror, and reflected by it onto the Scotchlite screen. Assuming that the alignment of camera, mirror, and projector was perfectly adjusted, the light forming the background image was all reflected back from the Scotchlite screen exactly into the camera lens. Those parts of the background image falling on the actors' bodies were invisible from the lens position, as they were completely washed out by the brightness of the lights illuminating the actors. To put it another way, from the lens position the Scotchlite screen was a 200 times better reflector for the projected image than the actors were. As with back projection, the success or otherwise of the combination of background and foreground live action could be seen as the scene was being shot. The drawback to the method, as it was initially worked, was that camera movements were impossible, and the precise alignment of the projector, semi-reflecting mirror, and camera was a time-consuming but vital affair. Although in principle front projection can be used with moving backgrounds projected from a motion-picture projector, in fact it seems only to have been used with the projection of still backgrounds up to 1969. Such was the case when front projection was first used in a feature film in *2001: A Space Odyssey* (1969), in which the backgrounds for the 'Dawn of Man' sequence and some other later sequences were front projected from large 10 inch by 8 inch transparencies.

Special Effects in 2001

Without going into the matter in detail, since literature on the production of *2001: A Space Odyssey* is readily available, it can be said that the special effects used in making this film were mostly remarkably simple. The travelling mattes were mostly made by rotoscoping the action, and then painting the mattes by hand for every frame where areas of combined action were to be matted in. In other words this was a reversion to the way travelling mattes had been made at the beginning of the 'twenties. Some parts of the 'trip through space and time' sequence were done by interchanging the Technicolor printing matrices to produce unnatural colours in the low-level aerial footage used, and some parts were done by macro-photography of coloured oil and water mixtures. The rest of this sequence was generated by the 'slit scan' technique created specially for this picture which I do not propose to discuss, since this was a less efficient way of doing what can be more easily done by means of computer generated graphics. Other than this, most of the effectiveness of *2001* was due to building the sets and models *big*, and then shooting the models with great depth of field.

Sound Recording

In the 'sixties there were a number of new developments in sound recording procedures in Europe, particularly with respect to microphones and tape recorders, and these eventually had an effect on the American scene.

Microphones

In this decade American film recording practice continued to favour moving-coil dynamic microphones, principally the Electrovoice 668, which was directional with a cardiod pick-up pattern. In Europe the AKG 25 cardioid moving-coil microphone was more common until later in the decade when moving-coil microphones began to be displaced by the new condenser (capacitor) microphones introduced by Sennheiser and AKG. As with most of these new developments in these years, television and documentary film-makers led the way in the acceptance of the new technology, which was then taken over into location work on feature films, and finally into the film studio.

Sennheiser, the brand leader in capacitor microphones, introduced a small cardioid-response capacitor microphone, the MHK 405, in 1963. This was about seven inches long and 3/4 inch in diameter, and had a far more extended frequency response than any moving-coil microphone. Like all capacitor microphones it had to have a power supply source and pre-amplifier, but this could now be very small and distant from the actual microphone through the use of transistor circuitry. The MHK 405 and other subsequent capacitor microphones were small and light enough to be swung from a hand-held boom for location recording in a way that the heavier moving-coil microphones could not, particularly on a long take. In 1966 Sennheiser produced an ultra-directional capacitor microphone, the 804 (or 805), and this had a long slotted tube in front of the actual transducer unit, with a total length of about 18 inches. This tube produced the extra directionality in the response through multiple resonance effects on the sound waves coming from the forward direction, but as with all such microphones, some sound was picked up from the side, particularly at the lower frequencies. The Sennheiser 405 and 805 immediately became the major microphones for documentary and location work in Europe, but they were more slowly accepted in America, in part because Electrovoice had earlier produced an ultra-directional microphone on the same principal as the 805 in 1964, but with a large and heavy moving-coil unit at the transducer end. Most interested parties in the United States had already acquired this for location recording, and presumably they were reluctant to write off their investment so quickly, even though the Sennheiser was superior in every way. One must also keep in mind that the upper limits of the frequency response of film soundtracks and theatre sound systems were far lower than those of the latest capacitor microphones, which were level up to 20 kHz. In 1968 AKG produced a multi-purpose capacitor microphone, the C-45 IE. This could be changed from omni-directional, to cardioid, to ultradirectional response patterns by screwing

slotted tubes of different length on the front of the transducer unit, but it made hardly any impression during the 'sixties.

The other approach to separating out the desired sound from background noise in location recording, besides the use of ultra-directional microphones, was the use of lavalier (or chest) microphones. These small moving-coil microphones were slung by a cord round the neck and hidden under the clothing of the actors, and had come into extensive use in television studios in the 'fifties. The favoured types were the Electrovoice 646 and the R.C.A. BK/6B. They had an omni-directional pick-up pattern, but relied on their closeness to the mouth to separate voice from background. Their frequency response was modified to allow for the greater emphasis on bass notes found near the chest, and they were also tunable to a certain extent to allow for variations in this bass emphasis. For close shots they could be directly connected by wire to the recorder by taking a lead down through the clothing, but to be used in Long Shots they had to be connected to a miniature radio transmitter concealed in the actor's costume, and then the signal from this was picked up by a radio receiver connected to the mixer and tape recorder. This use of radio-connected microphones had been introduced into television studios in the nineteen-fifties, but it was very slow to be taken up in film recording, principally because the radio link between microphone and recorder was prone to failure, and also liable to be upset by electrical interference on location. Nevertheless, radio mikes, as the combination of neck microphone and miniature radio transmitter was called, were occasionally used in the recording of scenes in American films, from *The Outrage* (1964) onwards. But their extensive use in a way that made it possible to devise new ways of staging and filming scenes had to wait until they became more reliable in the 'seventies.

Tape Recorders

At the beginning of the 'sixties a good number of the sound recordings in film studios in the United States were still being made on recorders using magnetic coated film with standard sprocket holes, of either 16 mm., 17.5 mm., or 35 mm. gauge. This situation gradually changed until only 1/4 inch synchronous tape recorders of one type or another were used for film recording.

Two European-made tape recorders became available in 1959 which for the first time permitted synchronous recordings to be made on a truly portable machine. Both these recorders achieved this by recording a synchronizing pulse onto the 1/4 inch tape along with the sound signal, this pulse being derived either from a pulse generator attached to the camera mechanism, or from a quartz crystal oscillator attached to the recorder. The Nagra III made by Kudelski in Switzerland proved to be the more successful of these two recorders, and by the end of the decade it was easily the most used film recorder in the world. It weighed 14 lb., measured 12 in. by 9 in. by 4 in., and could be carried slung by a strap from the recordist's shoulder. 5 inch reels of tape could be accommodated with the lid closed for carrying, and the tape speeds possible were 15 inches per second, 7.5 in. per sec., and 3.75 in. per sec.. The first of these speeds was used for feature film work, and gave a recorded frequency range from 20 Hz. to 18 kHz., while the 7.5 in. per second speed gave more than adequate results for 16 mm. filming. The Nagra III had controls for all the usual monitoring and playback functions, and a small accessory mixing panel that could combine the inputs from 3 microphones was also available to go with it.

The other portable recorder that became available in 1959 was the French-made Perfectone, which was rather similar to the Nagra III, but a couple of inches larger in length and width, and weighing 16 lb.. It only had one tape speed, 7.5 inches per second. Partly because of these characteristics, but also because it did not have the servo-feedback control of the speed of the tape drive that the Nagra had, the Perfectone ran a bad second to the Nagra in sales, though the fact that it was cheaper recommended it to some television organizations.

These two recorders were those used by European exponents of Cinéma Vérité, but as already described, the American Direct Cinema film-makers turned ordinary non-synchronous portable recorders into synchronous ones by their own individual adaptations. Amongst the other less important synchronous tape recorders were the Stellavox which was rather similar to the Nagra, but smaller and lighter at 6 lb. The big disadvantage of this machine was that it cost a lot more than the Nagra, and lacked some of the Nagra's facilities. The Uher 1000 Report model with Pilot-tone synchronizing pulse that appeared in 1967 was about the same size and weight as the Nagra, and though much inferior to that machine, it was judged just adequate to serve for low-grade television synchronous filming, such as news reporting.

Single System Sound Cameras

Although all the major 16 mm. camera manufacturers such as Arriflex and Eclair produced models of their silent cameras that would record sound in the camera on a magnetic stripe down the edge of the film simultaneously with the taking of the pictures, these 'single system' sound cameras never became widely used, even for television news filming. The reason for this was that for the maximum quality in recording it is necessary to have a second person manipulating the microphone and regulating the sound levels, so he might as well be carrying and operating a portable recorder, since this gives better recording quality than that from an edge stripe on the film. Another minor point counting against them is that single system cameras take longer to thread with film after the contents of each film magazine has been shot.

Sound Dubbing or Re-mixing

At the beginning of the 'sixties it was becoming usual in 16 mm. sound mixing or dubbing studios to use what was called 'rock and roll' or 'roll-back' mixing, in which the projector showing the cutting copy of the film could be stopped and run backwards, without losing the interlock

between it and the decks transporting the separate soundtracks on magnetic film which were being mixed. In some systems it was even possible to do this at double speed. This facility made mixing the separate soundtracks into the final combined track much more efficient than the old system of having to realign all the tracks from the beginning if they were stopped because of a mistake or an otherwise unsatisfactory mixing run. Towards the end of the decade this facility was becoming generally available in 35 mm. sound mixing studios as well.

Editing Machines

During the 'sixties there was a major transformation in the type of machine used for viewing the separate picture and sound tracks during the editing process, particularly in Europe. Up to this point in America the Hollywood Moviola or similar machines had been used almost exclusively, but this kind of machine was not particularly convenient for the very long-running shots that were becoming usual in television work, particularly in 16 mm. documentary films. Also, when an editor is using a Hollywood Moviola he needs an assistant present nearly all the time to rewind the shots for him and so on, and this was an expense that the lower television budgets could do without. (There *are* assistant editors in television editing, but they are occupied with other absolutely essential tasks such as synchronizing rushes and editing sound tracks.)

As it happens, there had been a tradition in continental Europe from the 'thirties onwards of using another type of editing machine for feature film work which was designed to work with large rolls of film which were left on the machine while working, rather than continuously putting different shorter lengths through the machine as with the Hollywood Moviola. These machines, which were referred to as editing tables, or 'flat-plate machines', or simply by the maker's name in recent times, carried the feed and take-up rolls of film and soundtrack lying flat on rotating discs, which fed them continuously, not intermittently, past the picture gate and sound head. To produce a stationary image without the film being held stationary for each frame, as was the done in Moviola-type machines, the frame was scanned through a multi-sided polygonal prism with parallel opposite faces, rotating between the film and the lens in such a way that the image displacement produced by the path of the light through the prism exactly compensated for the continuous displacement of the film frame. As the next frame came along the next pair of faces of the prism took over the same function. (A pre-war version of this general type of editing machine made by Zeiss used a moving mirror rather than a rotating prism.) Earlier versions of these machines, the most popular of which at the beginning of the 'sixties was made by the Italian firm of Prevost, projected the image through a series of mirrors onto a screen several inches across fixed to the far side of the table. This arrangement allowed several people to see the picture simultaneously, which was also a great convenience on occasion, as was the fact that such machines could easily be adapted to project an anamorphic image in unsqueezed form. The Prevost machines and their subsequent competitors were produced in a variety of models, either running a single picture track, or picture track together with one, or two, or three sound tracks, and most could be converted from 16 mm. to 35 mm. gauge by the simple substitution of a central module.

In British television film editing from the late 'fifties onwards, a closely related type of editing table, the Acmade Mark II, which ran the picture and sound track continuously from *vertical* rolls at either side, was extensively used as it was smaller and cheaper than the Prevost and similar machines. About 1965 what proved to be the most successful of these table editing machines, the Steenbeck, became available in Europe from its German manufacturers. This was again similar to the Prevost, with the only major difference being that the image was back-projected onto a large ground glass screen for viewing. A further advantage of these editing tables was that the models with multiple soundtracks could give an impression of what the finished film would be like with the final mixed soundtracks by setting the volume controls for each track at the appropriate level.

All of these machines had hardly any impact on American feature film-making during the 'sixties, and very little on that in Britain, but in documentary film-making in Europe they came to dominate the scene by the end of the 'sixties.

The Picture-Synchronizer

In 1965 the Acmade company in Britain produced a very cheap alternative to the editing tables just described. Called a picture synchronizer, or colloquially a pic-sync (now the CompEditor in the U.S.), this was essentially a 4 track 16 mm. sound synchronizer with the front sprocket-drum carrying the picture track modified to include inside it a small rotating polygonal prism block of the same kind and function as those described above in editing tables. This prism block, which produced a stationary image on a small ground glass screen on the front of the machine, was driven at the correct speed by a train of gears inside the front sprocket drum, and the whole device was driven in its turn by a crank handle mounted on the usual large knob on the front of the main shaft of the synchronizer. The picture synchronizer was used on an editing bench in the same way as an ordinary sound synchronizer without the picture head, with the picture and sound tracks being fed through it from split spools mounted on winders on either end of the bench. A motor driven version of the pic-sync became available almost immediately, and in this form the device was almost equivalent to a flat plate editing machine at one tenth of the price. In fact a picture synchronizer together with a double-headed projector was all that was necessary to edit with speed and efficiency, and the swing to such combinations was immediate in Great Britain, although owing to supply problems this device did not really penetrate the United States market till over a decade after its invention. American editors working on low budgets made do with the *ad hoc* but inferior arrangement of a cheap 16 mm. movie

viewer fixed in line with the rear drum of an ordinary sound synchronizer through which the picture passed after passing through the viewer.

The C.I.R. Tape Splicer

In 1964 a new form of butt splicer for 16 and 35 mm. film was produced in Italy. The butt splicers previously available had used transparent adhesive tape of the same width as the film being joined with sprocket holes already punched in the tape, which was laid over the butt join between two pieces of film aligned on a jig with pins through the sprocket holes of the film. It was a fiddly business to get the tape in the right place with these splicers, but with the C.I.R. splicer unperforated polyester tape was laid *across* the butt join, and then a combined guillotine and punch was pushed down to cut through the tape along the edges of the film, at the same time perforating it where it overlaid the sprocket holes of the film. If desired the film could then be flipped over and a second tape layer applied to the other side of the join. This was much more efficient than the previous type of tape splicer, and since the C.I.R. splicer was a butt splicer cutting through the middle of the frame line, splices made with it could be undone and then remade, without having lost any frames, if the editing of a scene had to be changed on the work print. Given these advantages, the C.I.R. tape splicer immediately became standard in European editing rooms, but yet again its penetration of the American industry was slow.

Editing Patterns in the 'Sixties

The innovations in editing equipment described above had no influence on trends in the way film scenes were dissected. Although the flat plate editing machines made the handling of large quantities of lengthy sync. shots easier, the trend towards the use of very long takes in *cinéma vérité* and Direct Cinema had already started before the new equipment became available, and in feature film-making people had always managed to handle the editing of long take films with the older equipment when necessary. In fact the trend during the nineteen-sixties in the scene dissection of fictional films was in quite the opposite direction, and this trend had started in the late 'fifties.

If one looks at the histograms showing the distribution of Average Shot Lengths for American films made during the six year periods 1958-1963 and 1964-1969, based as usual on a sample of more than a hundred films for each period, and then compares them with those for the earlier six year periods, one can easily see the way the general cutting rate speeded up as the 'sixties wore on. The mean value of ASL for the sample had already come down from 11 seconds to 9.3 seconds in 1958-1963, and in the next six years it had fallen even further to 7.7 seconds, its lowest value since the silent period. It must be emphasized that this increase in the number of shots used to film a scene is not immediately obvious to the casual viewer, and indeed has not even been noticed by people writing about films, largely because it has been achieved with the use of

American 1958-1963

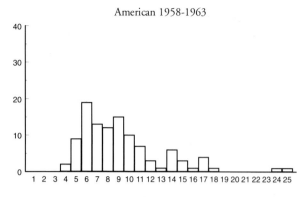

American 1964-1969

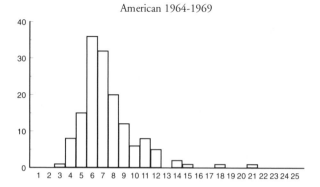

British 1964-1969

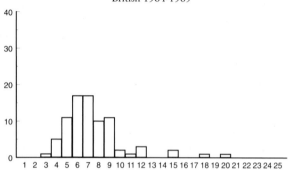

Continental 1964-1969

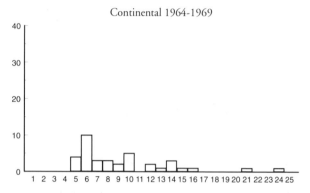

continuity cutting in the conventional manner. My total sample includes a film with ASL of only 3.5 seconds, a figure that was barely exceeded in the late silent period.

The cause of this increase in the cutting rate is so far obscure. It seems fairly certain that the trend was not led from methods of scene dissection being used in television production, for a sample of 18 American television programs of all kinds – dramas, Western series, comedy shows – made around 1960 all have ASLs in the range 7 to 40 seconds, with a mean of 13 seconds. This sample of programmes includes both productions shot on film in the studio, and kinescope recordings of live shows. On the other hand the trend does not seem to have been led from Europe either, because its beginning at the end of the nineteen-fifties predates the renewed American interest in European film developments. British production had never really joined the trend towards the long take in the 'forties, and so it did not move much from the fastish cutting style established there in the nineteen-thirties. In fact the mean ASL for the sample of British films from 1964-1969 which is illustrated is 7.7 seconds, which is just the same as that for the American sample. The sample of films from continental Europe is only mad up of 39 films, which is not large enough to be completely confident about what is going on there, but it is made up of quite a high proportion of films with ASLs longer than 10 seconds, and the mean ASL is 10.7 seconds. This suggests that things had changed little in Europe in this respect, but certainly the young European makers of 'art films' used even longer takes than their older predecessors. In fact the best generalization that I can make about the use of long takes is that they now largely came to be associated with high artistic ambition in feature films from

any country. To cite just two examples from among many, Jean-Luc Godard's *À bout de souffle* has an ASL of 15 seconds, and Joseph Losey's *The Servant* (1964), which I count as a British film, has an ASL of 20 seconds. When the United States finally acquired a definite 'art film' sector of production at the end of the 'sixties, the films from the directors who formed part of it such as Bob Rafaelson also mostly used long takes. It must be added at this point that the increasing tendency to use a large proportion of jump cuts for shot transitions in the art films of all countries probably tends to conceal the great length of most of the shots, by increasing the number of 'noticeable' cuts when compared to ordinary commercial films of the same period.

The Life and Times of the Jump Cut – Part 3.

The limited increase in the use of the simpler kind of jump cut which I have briefly indicated in the previous chapter as taking place during the 'fifties continued into the early 'sixties in European art films. The simpler and softer kind of jump cut makes a simultaneous time and space transition from a character (or characters) seen in one location to the same character seen in another place at a later time, and just how soft (i.e unnoticeable) this kind of jump cut is felt to be depends on how much explanatory and preparatory information has been provided before the cut. To take an obvious example, if we have already seen a series of shots of an actor running down different streets, another cut to a shot of him running down yet another street will be seen as a fairly soft kind of jump cut. Other factors involved in the softness or hardness of the jump cut are the relative positions and movements of the actor in the frames on either side of the cut. In the example just mentioned, if the cut is made with a good action match it will be even softer, while if the cut changes the actor's direction of movement to the opposite direction in the frame it will be a harder jump cut, just as is the case for ordinary cuts. As such jump cuts slowly diffused into mainstream film-making, the tendency was to use them in a conventionally expressive way, as in *The L-Shaped Room* (Bryan Forbes, 1962), where just such a progress through the streets as that described above takes place, and these jump cuts in this film were intended to indicate the heroine's agitation, according to a statement by the film's editor.

The harder type of jump cut, in which the same actor is shown in different positions in the *same* location on either side of the cut, probably first appeared in Godard's *À bout de souffle* (1959). In this film there is a continuous sequence of shots of the female lead sitting in the front seat of an open car while she is driven around Paris. The shots are taken from a fixed camera position in the car, and joined by cuts across which her position in the seat and the frame change suddenly, as does the background behind her. In subsequent films by Nouvelle Vague directors, including Godard himself, there was a tendency to naturalize, and hence slightly soften, this hardest form of the jump cut. For instance, in Godard's *le Petit soldat* (1961), a similar series of jump cuts on Close Ups of the female lead are established as Point of View shots of a photographer through being preceded by a general shot of the scene showing him photographing her. Thus although the Close Ups are in live action, they can be taken to correspond to his succession of photographs. However the hardest form of the jump cut did continue to be a possibility, as can be seen in *Prima della rivoluzione* (B. Bertolucci, 1962).

The two categories of jump cut just described – space-time jumps, and time jumps – just about exhaust the possible varieties of jump cuts, since a cut that shows a different person or group in another place will always be taken to be a cut to parallel action, or at least a continuity cut, unless the second shot contains immediate evidence to the contrary. The 'shock cut' variety of jump cut in which there is a great discrepancy in sound as well as image across the cut came to be less used in the 'sixties.

As interest in the jump cut mode of shot transition grew in the United States, some directors there consciously took up the challenge of making films in which cuts form the only kind of shot transition used. Early examples of this that spring to mind include *The Hanged Man* (Don Siegel,1964), and *Hurry Sundown* (Otto Preminger, 1966).

Ambiguities of the Cut

Dissolves and other special forms of shot transition had always been the site of ambiguity of meaning, so when films came to be made with cuts as the only form of shot transition there was an increase in the potential ambiguity of the cut. Use was made of this ambiguity in *L'Année dernière à Marienbad* (Alain Resnais, 1961) and some other subsequent films, with the intention of presenting the audience with a puzzle as

to the correct temporal order of the scenes in the film, which might, or might not, be soluble. This new ambiguity of the cut was only a potential ambiguity, as it was quite possible, if desired, to give a definite indication of the temporal relation of successive shots by the things, actions, or words included in the filmed scenes represented in those shots.

Ambiguities of the Scene

It was only at the beginning of the nineteen-sixties, with the film *L'avventura* in particular, that the increasing use of '*temps mort*' became widely noticed in European art cinema. *L'avventura* (M. Antonioni, 1960) contains a number of scenes which appear to have no obvious function in advancing the plot or illuminating the characters, and when they were combined with the enigma that was the centre of that film's narrative, they had much more impact than the episodes of irrelevant fooling around that had already appeared in the previous couple of years in the first works of the French Nouvelle Vague. In fact it seems that it had been Antonioni's intention for nearly a decade to use such scenes to give some insight into his character's psychology, but it also seems that this was not effective with most audiences, and that the actual effect was one of pronounced uncertainty as to the character's internal states. This aspect of Antonioni's films had some influence on the European art films of the 'sixties, as in Patroni-Griffi's *Il mare* and others.

The Nouvelle Vague kind of *temps mort* with its lighter fooling around proved rather more assimilable into mainstream cinema, particularly as strained through the British cinema of the 'swinging London' period, from such 1963 films as Ken Russell's *French Dressing* and Tony Richardson's *Tom Jones* onwards. What we are dealing with here is really more in the nature of entertaining digressions irrelevant to the plot than *temps mort* in its full sense.

The Newest Naturalism

The main seat of a move towards an even greater naturalism in incident and acting than had ever been achieved before in film was in the Czech cinema, particularly in the films of Milos Forman (*Cerny Petr*, 1963), Ivan Passer (*Intimi osvetleni*, 1966), and Jiri Menzel (*Ostre sledovane vlaky*, 1966), but this had little impact in ordinary commercial film-making in the rest of the world in the nineteen-sixties. There were some small parallel developments in England and America; in the former country inspired perhaps by new developments in television drama that were now taken over into the cinema by their creators, as in *Poor Cow* (Ken Loach, 1967). In the United States the new naturalism was almost the personal property of John Cassavetes, who began it with the first entry in the development of the American art film, *Shadows* (1960). (The other main participants in this movement, which they called the New American Cinema, were Adolfas Mekas and Shirley Clark, with *Hallelujah the Hills* (1963) and *The Connection* (1960). However *Hallelujah the Hills* was much closer in style to the Nouvelle Vague, which had inspired the movement in the first place.)

Improvisation

Cassavetes' *Shadows* was original in that it was created largely through guided group improvisation, and Cassavetes continued to use the idea in his low-budget films for some time, but such use of improvisation has remained very rare in mainstream cinema for obvious reasons. Limited use of improvisation also had its place in Peter Brooks' *Lord of the Flies* (1962). Those Nouvelle Vague films which at first glance appear to be improvised were in fact more or less scripted, though some had the lines given to the actors just before the scene was shot, and a few had the lines fed to them during the shooting of what were to be post-synchronized scenes. However Nouvelle Vague directors, and in particular Jean-Luc Godard, often altered their scripts according to the inspiration of the day of shooting, and they also used unforeseen moves by the actors that were dictated by the particular location chosen, as well as actual accidents such as slips and falls that happened during the shot.

Large-Scale Film Construction

Apart from the large-scale constructional features already mentioned, another innovation due again to Godard was the presentation of a film in a number of discrete sections preceded by descriptive intertitles, as in *Vivre sa vie* (1962).

The effect of this was not so very far away from the type of construction used in many early films before the advent of dialogue titles. This device was imitated directly by others, mainly in comedy films, as in Billy Wilder's *The Fortune Cookie* (1966). This was also true of the related weaker form, which was the simple use of the occasional silent-style intertitle, as opposed to the complete division of the film by intertitles. These joky intertitles penetrated down to even the more banal levels of film-making in the later nineteen-sixties. The use of the freeze frame as a concluding device, or indeed elsewhere in serious films, began to appear in a certain number of movies, most famously at the end of Truffaut's *les Quatre cent coups* (1959). Like other Nouvelle Vague tricks, this took up a device which had been promoted elsewhere earlier in the 'fifties, in this case in *All About Eve* (1954), a film well known to Truffaut. However, the way the device was used in *les Quatre cent coups* represented a real development in its relation to film narration, in that the story of the film was cut short at this point, when what might happen next to the protagonist was a matter of real interest and uncertainty. This was not the case in an earlier example like *All About Eve*.

The other obvious feature of much of the new international Art Cinema, partly connected with some of the constructional features I have just discussed, is a disregard of some of the rules of traditional script construction, in particular causality in character motivation and dramatic progression.

20. FILM STYLE AND TECHNOLOGY IN THE SEVENTIES

In the 'seventies I began to feel a certain lack of interest in the subject matter and attitudes of most of mainstream cinema. The source of this disaffection is probably the fact that most of the movies are now written, produced, and directed by people younger than myself, and mostly aimed at audiences young enough to be my grand-children. This is a new situation, and not just for me. Even though the bulk of the cinema audience has always been young, there was once a substantial older component that was taken into account by film-makers. This older component hardly exists any longer, and in any case the relative youth of those on the production side is quite a new situation. As a result, I have not been following developments quite as closely as I used to, and so I may have missed some significant trends. Developments in avant-garde cinema are quite another matter, since avant-garde cinema is always mostly concerned with kinetic visual processes, and in fact quite a lot of interesting work continued to be done in the 'seventies, both in the U.S. and in other countries.

Besides a marked increase in the introduction of new technology, the nineteen-seventies also saw an increase in the amount and depth of technicalities discussed in the journals associated with the film industry, in books, and elsewhere. This was in marked contrast to the high Hollywood period of the 'twenties to the 'forties, when film technicians quite intentionally kept much of their art and mystery to themselves and their chosen associates. I feel this excuses me from giving extra space to all the details of these new techniques, since they can be read in *The American Cinematographer* and other magazines by anyone really interested. However, I will continue to summarize the main trends, as before, particularly since such a summary of trends is not available elsewhere. A certain caution about all the extra technical detail being published nowadays is also quite necessary. To give an example, in an interview reply on page 137 in *Masters of Light* by Denis Schaefer and Larry Salvato, William Fraker says that when filming *1941*, "...we tried not to put anything in front of the lens.", and implies that he was aiming at a very sharp negative. However, in an *American Cinematographer* interview (Vol. 60, No 12., p.1208), Fraker says that he used a No.2 Fog filter plus a 1/2 Coral filter right throughout the production, and indeed the use of a heavy Fog filter is very evident when viewing prints of the actual film. Although *Masters of Light* and other recent and similar books are some improvement on most of the interview material published in previous decades, the film industry interviewees are still being allowed to get away with quite bit of wild talk, much of it as misleading as the example I have just cited.

Film Stock

This decade saw the first occasion when American cinematographers decisively rejected a new film stock introduced by Eastman Kodak. In 1974 Kodak produced the colour negative type 5247, which was intended as a replacement for the existing Eastman Color Type 5254. Although the new emulsion was rated at the same speed as Type 5254, i.e. 100 ASA, it needed a new development process similar to the ME-4 process used for the Kodak high speed reversal stocks of the previous decade, with higher temperature development balanced by a faster speed through the developing bath. Amongst other results this new developing process made it possible to increase the throughput of film laboratories. The new 5247 stock for 35 mm. (and the 7247 for 16 mm.) also had sharply improved definition, and most significantly, greater saturation of the colours. The change in the hues of the dyes was allegedly the problem for the cameramen, but I suspect that the increase in their saturation was the real source of objection. As it happens, the 5247 emulsion produced in England at the Kodak Harrow plant from 1975 onwards was not identical to the American emulsion, and was accepted more or less immediately by British cameramen, who photographed many feature films using it during 1975. On the other hand, in the U.S. none at all used the American version of the stock. Eventually, in 1976 Eastman Kodak in the U.S. replaced the first 5247 emulsion with a modified emulsion rather similar to that from the British plant, calling it '5247 Series 600', and American cameramen immediately began to use this on feature productions.

Slightly before Kodak introduced its new negative, the Fuji company of Japan, already a large manufacturer of colour still camera film using the Agfa methods of anchoring the dye formers, introduced a professional motion picture negative which had the same speed as the Kodak material (100 ASA), but which was to be developed in the bath used for the old Kodak 5254 negative. This Fuji stock was little used for feature production in the United States, though it was extensively used for TV filming there, purely because it was cheaper than Kodak stock. A few American feature cameramen at the time of the 5247 débacle did say that they would have liked to use Fuji negative because it was 'softer' (i.e. the colours were less saturated), but it was only in Europe that Fuji negative was taken up to a limited extent, for use in some low-budget feature films. It was generally agreed by cameramen that the colour reproduction of the Fuji stock was not quite as faithful to reality as that of Eastman material, and also that it was more contrasty than Eastmancolor 5254, being more like the previous 5251 negative in this respect. In 1976 Agfa-Gevaert also introduced a new colour negative using the same development process as the old Kodak film. This had the designation T6.80, but just like the Fuji negative, it was not greatly used for feature film work, though Claude Lelouch did shoot *le Chat et le souris* with it.

The nineteen-seventies were also the period when 16 mm. negative finally began to be used regularly for documentary, industrial, and television production in the United States. Up to this point, Ektachrome Commercial (ECO) 16 mm. reversal stock was the preferred medium for these applications, and it was frequently pushed one or two stops to 50 ASA or 100 ASA by American cameramen, rather than use Eastmancolor Negative. To cater for this preference, in 1970 Eastman Kodak introduced a new improved version of Ektachrome Commercial, type 7252, which had the same speed, but slightly improved colour rendition and sharpness. It needed a new higher temperature developing process like that used for High Speed Ektachrome 7242. The previous High Speed Ektachrome EF was replaced by Eastman Video News Film, types 7240 and 7241, still with the same speed of 125 ASA under tungsten and daylight, but with noticeable decrease in graininess, more detail in shadows, better whites, and generally warmer colour response. Agfa-Gevaert also introduced new Gevachrome 16 mm. reversal stocks in 1970, Types 6.00 and 6.05, with speeds of 50 ASA and 125 ASA under tungsten light respectively. These were replaced in 1975 with Gevachrome II types 710 (125 ASA tungsten) and type 720 (125 ASA daylight).

Eastern European Practices

Although film stock based on the Agfa patents continued to be produced in the Soviet Union, and also in East Germany under the Orwo label, film-makers preferred to use imported Eastman Kodak negative, if they could get it. And in fact limited quantities of Kodak negative were made available by the authorities in the Communist Block countries for what they considered would be the more prestigious productions. Examples range from things like the Bondarchuk *Voina i mir* to Tarkovsky's *Solaris* and *Zerkalo*, and in some cases the important export prints of such films would also be printed on Eastman print stock. However, it seems that prints for internal distribution were usually made on locally produced stock, which continued to be inferior to Western products, with the usual characteristic lack of saturation in the colours, poor differentiation in the greens, and a slight orange tinge to the reds. These deficiencies in Soviet film stocks were put to effective use in Tarkovsky's *Stalker*, which mixed sequences in black and white with others in colour, as had his previous *Zerkalo*. In *Stalker* in particular, the black and white sections printed onto Soviet stock had an oily quality, with a faintly greenish cast to the blacks, that blended nicely with the restricted range of tones in the colour sections. Tarkovsky's use of the contrast of colour against black and white may have been encouraged by the continuing practice in Eastern Europe of editing colour films using a black and white work print, as

well as by the restrictions on the amount of good Western colour stock available.

Laboratory Procedures

The greatest resistance to the use of 16 mm. colour negative actually came from American film laboratories rather than from cameramen, presumably because they would have to exercise greater care in handling it to keep it free from dirt and scratches, and even more importantly, because they would have to buy new developing machines to process it. However, the fact that European television companies, and in particular the BBC, had been using Eastmancolor negative as standard for all TV production (except news reporting) for some time began to be noticed by American cameramen, and they began to publicly register scepticism about the laboratory managements' claims about the difficulty of handling 16 mm. negative.

In film photography the use of pre-flashing of camera negative to reduce its contrast and lower the saturation of the colours had now become quite common, with the variations on this technique being given special proprietary names. One process which may have been slightly different from the others was the 'Chem-tone' process developed by TVC Laboratories in New York. It was suggested this was a matter of a special pre-development chemical bath rather than exposing the negative to light, though the firm was very secretive about it. 'Chem-tone' was said to bring out the shadow detail and produce speed increases up to 500 ASA, with no degradation of definition and colour at 250 ASA, and it proved to be quite popular with cameramen; early examples of its use being on *Rancho Deluxe*, and *Harry and Tonto*.

The use of forced development of camera negative to effectively increase its speed continued to increase. For shooting night exteriors on location this had long been standard, but the exact choices and combinations of flashing the negative and special development beyond that was a matter of individual preference by particular cameramen, tempered by the nature of the story being filmed. These practices were continued with the new Eastmancolor negative in the latter part of the 'seventies, though this stock did not respond well to extended development beyond that required to give a one stop increase in speed.

As always, there were a few special tricks carried out in the laboratory to get unusual qualities in the image. For the catacomb scene in Francesco Rosi's *Cadaveri eccellenti*, the negative was given a preliminary development in the sound negative developing bath first to produce high contrast colour, while in John Boorman's *Deliverance*, the desaturating method was similar to that used on *Moby Dick* to desaturate the colours. This process involved printing with a second B&W negative derived from the original colour negative. In the particular case of *Deliverance*, the colours of things appearing in the original scenes were also controlled to eliminate bright colours, and the effect was reinforced by only shooting on overcast days where possible.

In 1978 Eastman Kodak introduced a new intermediate stock, Eastmancolor Internegative II (5243/7243). Unusually, this could be used as both interpositive and internegative successively in the duplicating process. When this was done, it was claimed that the combination was almost as good as Eastman CRI in producing a duplicate print. However, the real need for improved interpositive and negative was for special purposes such as making film titles.

The continuing pressure for increased productivity in the making of release prints led to Kodak introducing new print stocks 5383/7383 in 1974, together with a new high temperature developing process for them, in the style of the 16 mm. reversal processes used since the 'sixties. This process was called ECP-2, and had a bath temperature of 98F, which reduced the wet time to 10 minutes. The new colour print stocks had a ten-fold increase in resistance to fading, and made the previous low fade stock type 7387 unnecessary. (Producers hadn't been using that stock, as it cost 10% more than ordinary release print stock.)

Lighting Units

During this decade more and more feature films were made entirely on location throughout the Western world, sometimes with a new production approach, which consisted of using a large rented interior space of some kind on location as an improvised studio in which sets could be built. There was also a tendency to build interior sets, both under these circumstances, and even when the film was shot in the old Hollywood studios, with solid ceilings and complete walls. Notable examples of this include *Network*, where the office sets were built by installing new solid walls within one floor of a skyscraper office building, and *All the President's Men*, where a total solid reproduction of the interior of the Washington Post offices was built in the studio, but there were many other examples as well. All this was in part to avoid the large fixed studio charges in Hollywood, but even so labour costs continued to escalate on these all-location productions. ('Runaway' productions in American parlance). A partial solution to all these financial pressures was to use smaller and lighter, but more powerful, lighting units, and these were forthcoming.

Two new kinds of light source, the enclosed xenon arc and the enclosed metal halide arc, were part of the technological response. The first of these was an electric arc enclosed inside a quartz envelope containing a high pressure atmosphere of xenon gas. This light, which produced a daylight-type light of colour temperature 6,000 Kelvin, had been developed and produced initially for searchlights for American Army tanks, but it was adapted for use as a spotlight for other purposes by Xenotech, Inc. The Xenon arc was marketed in 1970 as the 'Sunbrute', which weighed about 30 lbs., and gave almost as much light as an ordinary 'Brute' arc spotlight, while consuming only 4000 watts of power from a 30 volt D.C. source. Although these new lights were put into use immediately for daylight fill lighting when shooting location exterior scenes, they had the drawback that the bulb containing the arc was sometimes liable to explode dangerously when handled.

The metal halide arc came in two varieties, both developed in Europe with television application in mind; the CSI bulb originated by Thorn in the U.K., and the Osram HMI bulb made in Germany, and the latter proved to be the more popular for film purposes. These two patented devices differed in the rare earth metals inside the bulb which were ionized by an initial high voltage current, and which then emitted light in an arc between the electrodes powered by the ordinary A.C. mains voltage of 240 or 120 Volts, as the case might be. The CSI bulb had no strict colour temperature, as it was not a black body source, but the HMI bulb gave 5,500 K light, and hence needed no correction for daylight use. Like the Xenon arc, these lamps gave 2 to 3 times more light than ordinary lighting units for the same power consumed. A slight disadvantage to their use was that the bulbs broke easily and became opaque prematurely, and also had poor colour consistency at first.

A more important disadvantage was that their brightness fluctuated in time with the mains voltage frequency on which they operated. This was no problem if the lamps were used in conjunction with video cameras, but there could be problems with 'strobing' or 'flicker' when using a film camera under their light, just as had been the case with A.C. arc lights when they were introduced in the early days before World War I. (In this context 'strobing' or 'flicker' is the fluctuation in brightness of the film image at a low frequency which is the difference between the frequency of the opening and closing of the camera shutter, and the frequency of the light source.) In Europe the problem did not exist for filming at 25 frames per second, which was now completely standard for 16 mm. film shot for TV, but at the 24 frame per second feature film rate the flicker would be at 1 Hz, while in the U.S. with 60 Hz mains current and 24 f.p.s. filming for all purposes, the flicker was at 6 Hz. However, this flicker could be eliminated by choosing a suitable non-standard camera shutter opening, which was 172.8 for a 50 Hz electricity supply, and 144 for 60 Hz., as long as the camera speed and mains supply were kept very constant.

An alternative solution to the flicker problem was to generate A.C. power for the lights and camera from a special frequency-regulated generator, and this eventually became the most popular solution in the United States, where the light weight of HMI lights made them very attractive for location lighting, when compared to the giant old-style arc lights previously used. Not to mention the fact that they could be run without an electrician always standing by them to adjust them, as the big old arc spotlights required.

Another general solution to the flicker problem was to modify the ballast unit, which produced the initial high voltage to strike the arc when the lamp was switched on, smoothed out small variations in mains voltage, and held voltage current relationship constant as the electrodes slowly burnt away during the 200 hour life of the lamp, so increasing the gap. The modification required was to include circuitry to that changed the sinusoidal A.C. voltage into a square wave voltage, but this was only possible for lamp powers up to 1200 watts. The Thorn CSI lights in the Lee Electric 2k 'Twinhead' housing had some use in England, on *The Slipper and the Rose*, *Superman* and other films, despite this lamp housing being less flexible than the standard type used for the HMI metal halide lights.

When metal halide lighting was first made available in 1974, the major European lighting equipment manufacturers produced Fresnel lens spotlight units in a number of sizes matched to all the available bulb powers from 200 watts up to 4 kW in fairly even steps. The most prominent makers of these HMI units were Ianiro in Italy and LTM in France, shortly followed by Arri in Germany. Eventually Mole-Richardson in the U.S. also produced a range of HMI lamp units.

For small-scale location lighting, Ross Lowel and his associates in New York continued their innovations, the most important of which during this period was the Tota-light system, which centered on a new type of very small flood light. The Tota-light incorporated the novel idea of having reflecting barn doors on a very small trough containing a 1000 watt Quartz halide bulb (800 watt for 240 Volt use), all of which folded up when not in use to a package 12"x3"x2". The unit gave 150 foot candles at 10 feet, and was part of a complete modular 'Lowellink' system including reflecting umbrellas, flags, clamps, stands, and extensible mounting poles. At the end of the decade Lowel added to this system a new type of unit, the Omni-light, which took a 1000 watt metal halide bulb in a reflector with a double parabolic curved surface. This made a change from narrow spot to wide flood accompanied by an 11 to 1 brightness change possible for the first time. Lowel and others also produced new designs of smaller lightweight 'soft lights' ('north lights') early in the decade. For instance the Lowel design of soft light only weighed 7 lb., and folded up into a small space, while the Berkey Colortran unit weighed 8.5 lb.

A novel lighting unit introduced towards the end of the decade in England was David Watkin's 'Wendy' light. This was made up of 4 large square grids, each carrying 44 PAR type reflector bulbs, all pointing forwards. The sections were loosely hinged together, enabling them to be inclined at a small angle to each other, so that there could be a crude focussing or spreading effect of their combined beams. It was hoisted on a large crane for night shots, and gave 10 foot-candles over a wide area from 300 yards distance.

General Trends in Cinematography

In film photography, the major trend was the destruction of the ever-higher image definition and colour reproduction made possible by the improvements in film stocks and lenses. The use of heavy lens diffusion throughout whole films, on Long Shots as well as closer shots, continued to increase, and the use of artificial smoke on film sets, without much regard for plausibility, intensified the result. The interaction of these techniques with the lighting produced quite a new look in the film image.

As far as reducing image sharpness by putting things in front of the lens other than the standard diffusion filters and nets was concerned, there was now frequent use throughout whole films of the heaviest kind of glass diffusion filters, called 'fog filters'. These were originally designed to produce the effect of a mist or fog when a mist or a fog was not actually present, and they created a moderately convincing fuzzy effect to this end, as long as the lighting was right, and the camera didn't move. But by the beginning of the decade even the heaviest kind of fog filter (No. 4) was being used on action movies shot outdoors in sunlight, and also on scenes indoors under fairly ordinary lighting as well. One of the most notable cases of this was *Butch Cassidy and the Sundance Kid*, but there were large numbers of others as the decade wore on.

Various other ways of deforming the natural response of the negative were also used, starting with the incorrect exposure of the stock. That is, it was frequently underexposed, either with extra development to compensate for this, or sometimes just given ordinary development to produce a 'thin' (low density) negative, which was then corrected at the printing stage. Of course, underexposure had always been used occasionally when there was not sufficient light, followed by forced processing to compensate, but with the ever-increasing trend to location filming, this became standard for night exteriors. However, some cinematographers, led by Gordon Willis and Vittorio Storaro, specified normal development even though they were underexposing the film. When the resulting thin negative was printed, the result was inevitably slightly reduced definition of the image, while at the same time the saturation of the colours was slightly increased. That is, the image was both fuzzed and brightened. Willis started this on the *The Landlord* in 1970, but the really important film in this connection was *The Godfather*, shot in 1971. For the latter, he exposed Eastman Color 5254 as 250 ASA, but only had it forced one stop in development. This meant that the negative was still about a 1/2 stop underexposed. The intention was expressive, and referring to the New York scenes in the film, Willis said "... the film should be brown and black in feeling, and occasionally hanging on the edge from the standpoint of what you see and what you don't see. A lot of cameramen work to increase the quality of the image, but in this specific case I'm working to decrease it." (*American Cinematographer*, Vol. 52, No. 6, Feb. 1971, p. 568). Another cameraman using this idea was Owen Roizman on *The French Connection* (1971). He said he wanted "...a rough, almost documentary look." and "I wanted the images to have a dismal dreary look." (*American Cinematographer* Vol.53, No.2, Feb. 1972, p.158)

The cameramen Vittorio Storaro, working for the director Bernardo Bertolucci in Italy, also arrived at a rather similar effect, though not as a conscious expressive device, but more under the pressure of lighting low budget films on location, when it is difficult to get enough light into an interior. The films in question were *Strategia del ragno* (1969) and *Il conformista* (1970). Storaro's basic idea, which must have been supported by Bertolucci's fine visual sense, was to let the light from a diffuse source out of shot, well away from the centre of action at one side of the set, fight its way through to light the actors, bouncing off the walls of the set on its way. This approach, which only appeared tentatively in *Il conformista* (1970), tends to leave the image in low-key, with only small areas at full exposure level, and it also means that the light picks up the major colour of the walls of the set, as can be seen in *Last Tango in Paris* (1972), where all the interiors are lit in this way. Both Gordon Willis's and Vittorio Storaro's approach had in common the look resulting from a large-area soft-light moderately remote from the main part of the scene, however it was actually achieved. By the end of the decade this style was beginning to spread, with the result was that the interiors in a number of ordinary dramatic films were now continuously photographed in low-key, which was something that had never happened before. Perhaps the most graphic demonstration of the rise of the fashion for general low key lighting is given by the photography of the *Star Wars* series of films. The first of these has in general the ordinary kind of mid-key lighting that one would expect for a children's adventure film, but by *The Empire Strikes Back* (1980) the lighting is fairly consistently low key, even on daylight exteriors such as the 'Ewok' scenes. Such an approach *does* have the virtue of concealing the matte lines in the many process shots in the film, although I don't believe that this was the reason for it.

The developments just described were mostly associated with a concept of increasing importance in American cameramen's minds; namely 'source lighting'. This meant producing a closer approximation to the appearance of the lighting in a real room that was just like the film set that they were lighting, with the direction of light apparently coming from its nominal sources within the scene. Although good cameramen had always made some effort to roughly mimic the effect of the fall of light in a real room, these attempts had usually been very partial, except in low-key situations. (Bad camera-

men didn't bother at all about relating their lighting to reality when lighting in mid- or high-key on the typical film set.) This new trend was of course following the direction set by some European cameramen working in the previous decade, most importantly Raoul Coutard and other Europeans who were influenced by him in their turn. Some of the most notable of these, such as Sven Nykvist, Nestor Almendros, and Vittorio Storaro, lit American films during the nineteen-seventies.

Nykvist took the 'source lighting' idea to its natural conclusion on *One Day in the Life of Ivan Denisovitch* (1972), filming this story of life in a Soviet Arctic prison camp completely with available light. In consequence, many of the dawn, dusk, and lamplit scenes had a very muddy image quality in conventional terms, but this could be considered to go with the subject in an expressive way. Almendros went almost as far on *Days of Heaven*, though under more favourable conditions, since this subject was mostly shot under higher levels of natural daylight. In this film many interiors had no supplementary lighting at all, and on firelit scenes the Close Ups were lit by the flames from propane burners. Quite a number of the scenes in this film were shot in the last glow of day, using a T1.1 lens to get an exposure. For the closer shots of exterior scenes under full daylight Almendros exposed for the shadow areas without fill light, so the sky burnt out. This was an extreme case, and a more typical piece of Almendros' work was *Going South* (1979), which was also shot on location, but boosting natural light slightly, and sometimes using some soft fill on exteriors.

Stanley Kubrick continued to encourage his cameramen towards new ideas. For *Barry Lyndon*, the daytime interiors in location interiors were basically lit with translucent plastic sheets over the windows, and with mini-brutes shining onto them from outside. This technique had been common in the lighting of television commercials for several years, but had not been extensively used for feature films before. The resulting lighting in the rooms mimicked the fall of natural light fairly well, but at the higher levels required by film photo-

A location interior scene in Stanley Kubrick's Barry Lyndon *(1975) basically lit by light through the windows. This synthetic window light is produced by powerful spots diffused by translucent sheets over the windows.*

graphy. Some extra fill light was supplied from inside the rooms with Lowelllights directed into white umbrella reflectors. Kubrick had been using these since *A Clockwork Orange* (1971).

Cameramen, like other film-makers, were becoming much more aesthetically self-conscious about what they were doing as the result of increasing interest in their work outside the film industry, and this accelerated the speed of change in fashions in lighting style. For instance, by the end of the decade there was already beginning to be a reaction against the general use of heavy lens diffusion of various kinds. To quote one example amongst a number in which the cinematographer's intentions are recorded, Laszlo Kovacs did not use lens diffusion on *F.I.S.T.*, which was set in the 'thirties, in conscious reaction to other films using this on period subjects. He also used direct light, not soft light, but the art direction of the film *did* limit the tones of the sets and locations to earth colours.

Another of the leading young cameramen, Bill Butler, shot *Grease* with no lens filters at all, and also used direct (though diffused) lighting throughout, except for the fantasy sequence, which had soft lighting. Yet another example of the way cameramen more readily varied their approach to lighting from film to film is given by Conrad Hall. He dropped his very original idea of overexposing and underdeveloping, which he had previously worked out from *Hell in the Pacific* through to *Butch Cassidy and the Sundance Kid*, when he lit *The Day of the Locust* and *Smile* in 1975. In fact on the latter film he did the reverse, underexposing even on the exteriors, and then restoring the density in printing.

Colouring Colour Films

What was really a new kind of 'flashing' process was invented by Gerald Turpin, a British cameraman, and used on *Young Winston* in 1973 to give a different overall colour bias to scenes taking place in different locations. This was at first called the 'Turpin Colorflex' system, and it was carried out by reflecting light from fairly small sources behind a coloured filter into the camera lens with a half silvered optical flat placed in front of it at 45 to the optical axis. Turpin claimed that this treatment did not affect face colours or the whites in the scene, but this was visibly not true. It could also be used with white light, when its effect was very like other forms of flashing the film, producing desaturation of the colours and some speed increase. Under the new name of the 'Lightflex' system, the fully developed version of this device was taken up for use on quite a number of films in the following years.

It now became fairly common to add a greater overall colour bias for films set in the past. When this was done, it was almost always an overall warm tone, which was added with coloured filters on the lens, or alternatively after shooting at the printing stage. Amongst numerous examples of added colour tinting there were — amber added in printing to *The Runner Stumbles* and *The Day of the Locust*, brown gauze filters

on *Fiddler on the Roof*, brown-beige added in printing to *Chinatown*, pink chiffon net behind the lens for *Caddie*, and yellow net in front of the lens on *Picnic at Hanging Rock*. And, as just mentioned, *Young Winston* was tinted in many varied colours depending on the location. Just to show that film-makers were not going to succumb to any mindless conformism on this issue, all the footage of *The Hindenburg* was printed slightly blue for the release prints, and in any case, some period films were not given any overall colour bias at all. Obvious examples include *The Wild Party*, *MacArthur*, and *Days of Heaven*.

Films in Black & White

A small return to filming in black and white was initiated by *The Last Picture Show* (1971) shot by Robert Surtees entirely on location exteriors and interiors. Curiously enough, this production approach was apparently combined with some sort of Orson Welles influence in the mind of the director, Peter Bogdanovitch. The light level was high, with apertures in the f8 to f10 range, and a 28 mm. lens was used throughout. This inevitably gave *Citizen Kane*-type deep focus, and there was also some staging in depth to go with this, though nowhere near as much as in *Kane*. But the result was bound to be different, because *The Last Picture Show* was framed in wide-screen, and in this format a 28 mm. lens gives an effect of normal perspective in the screen image, rather than the forced perspective effect apparent in an Academy ratio image shot with this lens. Robert Surtees lit with old-style direct light, mostly from floor stands, and he also consciously avoided the use of back light, except when justified by the practical lighting visible in shot. In my opinion the result was rather on the crude side in a lot of the scenes, and I don't care that the photography of *The Last Picture Show* won an Academy Award. However, Robert Surtee's black and white photography improved with practice, and *Lenny* (1974) is a lot better, basically because it moves more consistently in the direction of the available light look.

Filming in black & white was also used for filming period parodies, as in *Young Frankenstein* (1974), where Gerald Hirschfeld used heavy backlight and made Eastman XX contrasty by pushing it to 500 ASA (2 stops). This was not enough to accurately recreate the look of 'thirties lighting.

From the late 'seventies onwards, Woody Allen used black and white most often of any American director, and the various cameramen handling the lighting for him also used more conventional modern location lighting, with softer sources used in a rather more naturalistic way.

Coloured Lighting

Yet another new trend in lighting that began to emerge during these years was the use of different coloured light in different areas of the film scene. My interpretation of this development is that it largely began accidentally, due to an increasing acceptance of the natural situation in location filming. In the contemporary world there are two things that naturally produce light of different colours within filmed scenes, one being the presence of daylight and tungsten light in different areas of the picture, and the other being the contrasts between the different sorts of electric lighting in the contemporary world – tungsten bulbs, different types of fluorescents, sodium vapour lights, etc. In the past it had been the practice to eliminate these colour differences by various means when location filming, such as putting colour correcting filters over windows, or by swamping the light from fluorescents with extra film lights of the correct colour temperature, but in the 'seventies it became increasingly common not to bother with such correction. This trend can be seen increasing through such films as *The French Connection* (1971). In this case, railway station and train fluorescents were left as they were; some warm, others cold. For *The Exorcist* (1973), *The Sugarland Express* (1974) and *Taxi Driver* (1976), most location scenes with fluorescent lights were left uncorrected. In the last of these films there are some scenes in which the light through windows is left blue, and this contrast between blue daylight and orange tungsten light within the scene is developed in *The Deer Hunter* (1978). For the steel town scenes in this film Vilmos Zsigmond shot the exteriors early and late in the day, and also had them printed a bit on the blue side. (It was actually summer, and exterior vegetation was defoliated and browned.) For interiors, the light was kept warm, and what was visible of the outside through open windows and doors was allowed to go blue, without 85 filters over windows. The further development of this trend, with coloured light played onto scenes from film lights with coloured gels over them, begins with *The Exorcist II – The Heretic* lit by William Fraker. Here the desert scenes were shot in the studio, and stylized with orange and blue light emphasized beyond the natural.

Cameras

This was the most active period there has ever been for the development of new cameras, with the most innovative designs continuing to come from Europe. In 1971 the Eclair company of France made its final contribution with the extremely lightweight 16 mm. ACL camera, which continued the concept of their NPR camera in a reduced size. It had similar pre-threaded coaxial magazines that could be instantly clipped onto the front part of the camera containing the shutter and drive mechanism. In the process of reducing the size of camera, the shutter was changed from a rotating one to a single small mirrored blade which oscillated backwards and forwards in front of the film aperture, and more significantly for 16 mm. camera design, the tiny driving motor used semi-conductor technology and the Hall effect for power. This meant that it could run off a nickel-cadmium battery weighing only 1 lb., which could be easily slipped into the cameraman's pocket. This motor also initiated a trend for the motors for new camera designs to have quartz crystal oscillator speed control built into them, so that they could be used in conjunction with recorders with built-in crystal oscillators for

'cordless' synchronization. Unlike the Eclair NPR, the ACL did not have a register pin, which meant that it was rather sensitive to the correctness of the film threading in the magazine. All the new features just mentioned made the ACL noticeably quieter than the NPR, and indeed quieter than any other 16 mm. camera available at the time. It was initially sold in 1971 with 200 foot magazines, in which form it weighed 8.5 lbs. Although it produced a remarkable sense of freedom when hand-held, it has to be said that a camera of this weight is on the edge of being too light for its inertia to iron out the tiny jiggles that can occur in the cameraman's hands. A 400 foot magazine was quickly made available, and in this form the ACL also marked the move towards designing lightweight cameras so that they could be carried with their centre of gravity directly above the shoulder when hand-held.

Arnold and Richter in Germany now dropped their previous design approach, and took up some of the Eclair concepts for their new Arri cameras. Their new self-blimped 35 mm. camera, the Arriflex 35 BL, had the same general lay-out as the Eclair NPR, with a magazine with coaxial feed and take-up compartments directly behind the lens, shutter, gate and drive unit. It also had its rotating mirror shutter below the lens like the Eclair cameras, rather than at the side in the previous Arriflex style. The claw movement was still basically like that of the original 35 mm. Arriflex, but the newly added register pins were driven by another separate cam from behind the film gate. At about 15 lbs. without film it was light enough to be comfortably shoulder held, and prototypes were made available in 1972. This was the first production camera to fully realize the concept of being completely balanced when hand-held on the cameraman's shoulder, which was inserted into a notch between the lens, mirror shutter, viewfinder, and gate unit in front, and the magazine behind. Of course it could also be used on a tripod head in the standard way. One of the prototypes was used to shoot *Across 110th Street* entirely on location interiors and exteriors in New York, with much hand-held footage, but initially this design was a little too noisy for studio use, since it produced about 33 dB at 3 feet. Various small design changes, such as making the body castings from heavier aluminium rather than magnesium, putting the lens in a blimp, and redesigning the pull-down claw, reduced the noise level to about 28 dB for the series manufactured models from 1973, though when a zoom lens was used on it the noise went up to 33 dB again. Finally in 1980 the Mark III version of the 35 BL, which had further modifications to the movement mechanism, achieved a noise level of about 25 dBA without the necessity for even a lens blimp, by which point it was quite suitable for studio shooting.

The 16 mm. equivalent of this design from Arnold & Richter was the Arri 16 SR, available from early in 1975. Although the general layout of the major parts of the camera was like that of the Arri 35 BL, and even more like the Eclair NPR, the claw and register pin mechanism was rather different. But the register pin did enter the film from the front, just like the Eclair NPR. The Arri 16 SR also had a rotating mirror shutter with 180° opening below the lens and film gate, and weighed 11 lbs. with a 200 ft. coaxial magazine. The viewfinder was orientable and could be swung to either side of the camera body, to allow for left-eyed cameramen.   A built-in through-the-lens exposure meter was fitted, and the Zeiss 10-100 mm. zoom lens was fitted as standard. It had a 24-25 fps crystal controlled motor, and the speed could be varied continuously from 8-40 frames per second with an accessory control.

Panavision cameras were now definitely the preferred choice for the productions of the major American film companies, and this was sealed by the introduction of a series of ordinary spherical lenses made by Panavision for their cameras. At the beginning of the 'seventies the Panavision company had been making do with a special fibre-glass blimp around a modified Arriflex 2C for use on the shoulder to satisfy the increasing demand for hand-held sync. sound filming, but they were also working on an original design for a new silent reflex camera. This appeared in 1973, and was called the Panaflex, though it was different to the earlier camera with the same name. The new Panaflex mechanism was still based on the Mitchell movement, but in a slightly smaller and more refined form, and the camera as a whole was much smaller and lighter. In part this was achieved through the use of modern electric motor technology, in part by simplifying the drive gears, and in part by going to a simplified mirror reflex shutter technology along the lines of the European cameras. The new Panaflex weighed 25 lbs with a 250 ft. magazine, and 34 lbs with a loaded 500 ft. magazine. The noise level was about 27 dB. It had a 200 shutter, and the motor could run from at any speed from 6 to 32 fps, with crystal control on 24 and 25 fps. By changing the movement the camera could be used at 100 fps. It had an orientable viewfinder in short and long lengths, with a built in de-ana-morphoser.

The first Panaflex was used on *The Sugarland Express* by Steven Spielberg, where he shot scenes that were previously impossible in 35 mm., such as hand-held sync. dialogue shots inside a moving car.

The old American camera making companies began to fade from the scene in the nineteen-seventies. The Mitchell Camera Corporation made a number of efforts to produce new designs that imitated the foreign-led innovations, such as a Mitchell Mark III, and also made two attempts at lightweight hand- held 16 mm. sync. cameras, but these got nowhere in the market, being too late, too heavy, and too expensive. The ossification of the Mitchell company's thinking was strongly underlined by Edmund DiGiuglio, who had worked there from 1963 to 1967, and who then left to set up Cinema Products in 1968, at first specializing in the conversion of Mitchell BNC's to true reflex cameras by putting a partially reflecting 45 pellicle mirror in front of the shutter. Within a few years most of the BNC's still in use in the United States had been given this treatment, by Cinema Products or somebody else, and then in 1971 DiGiuglio's company intro-

duced a new lightweight (15 lbs.) sync. sound 16 mm. camera, the CP-16. Although built from scratch, this was in essence a reduced size version of the old Auricon cameras, but with a modern crystal controlled battery-powered motor drive. It did not have a built-in reflex system, but relied on having the model of the Angénieux 10 to 1 zoom lens that included its own beam-splitter viewing system and tube being permanently mounted on the camera. In fact it was essentially a polished-up version of the home-made Auricon conversions of the Leacock-Pennebaker team a decade before. The beauty of this camera was that it was cheap compared to the imported Eclair and Arriflex cameras, particularly given the weakness of the dollar during the 'seventies. American TV stations, 64% of which were still using Auricons in 1973, re-equipped principally with the CP-16, and Cinema Products had sold 2,000 CP-16 and CP-16R's by 1975. The CP-16R was a version of the CP-16 with integral mirror reflex shutter that was introduced in 1973, and this version was able to compete successfully for use in TV news shooting even in the European market. The final contribution of Cinema Products in 16 mm. cameras was the GSMO, introduced in 1976. This was a smaller and lighter quiet mirror shutter reflex camera, much more like the Arriflex 16SR in layout, with the magazine behind the body.

In 1973 Cinema Products also succeeded with a new 35 mm. camera where the Mitchell Company was now failing, when it introduced the X35R. Again, this was in fact just a refined version of the Mitchell camera, designed with an integral mirror reflex shutter, and weighing 93 lbs. without lens and film. It had a single lens mount of the BNCR pattern, which meant that all those old Mitchell lenses could be still used, and its noise level at 27 dB was just suitable for studio use. The improvements made to the design by Cinema Products included a shutter which stopped closed, and a new stroke length and entry adjustment for the claw. There was still a market for a suitably priced modern studio camera in the United States and elsewhere because many producers did not wish to meet the requirements of the Panavision Company when its equipment was used on a film. (Remember that Panavision did not sell its equipment, but only hired it out, and also required a footage royalty on the number of release prints finally struck of any film made with Panavision cameras.) One of the first Cinema Products X35Rs was used in shooting *Apocalypse Now*, with anamorphic lenses produced by the new Italian Technovision company. These lenses were actually made for the Technovision company by Rank Taylor-Hobson, and quickly acquired a reputation for superior definition. Cinema Products even bought the design rights to the Bell & Howell Filmo and Eyemo cameras, when that company finally abandoned the camera business entirely.

Apart from the Panaflex, the most successful of the new cameras using the Mitchell movement was the Moviecam 3N. This was made in Austria to a design by Fritz G. Bauer, and weighed only 27 lbs. when loaded with 500 ft. of film. It was the most silent of all 35 mm. cameras, registering less than 18 dBA at 3 feet. It also had the highest degree of electronic control of any camera produced up to this point. There was a built in digislate which printed the scene number onto the negative, and the speed could be varied during shot with a linked lens aperture change. There was a plug-in time coding module, and also a phase-shifter module available. A fitting for the addition of video assist was also standard. The motor ran from 1 to 50 frames per second, and the shutter could be adjusted from 0 to 176 f.p.s.

The Photosonics company, which had long been a major maker of very high-speed cameras for special purposes, produced a camera which had a somewhat wider use in the United States during this period. This camera was the 1PD, which could film at all speeds from 16 to 200 frames per second in its standard form, with an alternative version which could manage 500 frames per second, even though it had pin registration. This was a first in this area. Viewing was through a beam splitting arrangement behind the lens, and the camera came to be particularly popular for sports filming.

As a result of take-over and re-organizational manoeuvers involving the Eclair company and the older French Debrie company and others, the team led by J-P. Beauviala which had designed the ACL camera left Eclair, and then set up a company which produced the new Aäton 16 mm. camera in 1974. This was similar to the Arri 16SR in general layout, though a bit heavier at 16.5 lb. Its noise level of 30 dB at 1 metre was not especially remarkable either. The intermittent mechanism was a remarkable return to the basic conception of the Williamson camera movement from the beginning of the century. High claims, at least partly justified, were made for the image steadiness of this simple arrangement, despite the camera not having a register pin. Part of the reason for the extra weight was the inclusion of a small video tube as a standard part of the viewfinder system, which could produce a signal for an external TV monitor if desired. The Aäton was moderately successful, but did not stop the Arri 16SR from becoming the new standard 16 mm. camera.

Although video monitor systems for filming had been used in the 'sixties, the imperfections of small lightweight vidicon tubes that had to be used on the movie camera to produce the video image had restricted their appeal. Now that these small vidicon tubes had improved, video monitor systems became popular with more film-makers, as a way for the director to see exactly what he was getting on the film without waiting for the rushes on the next day. At first, the video camera was just attached to the film camera with some kind of arrangement that reduced the parallax between them to a minimum, but eventually systems were devised which took the video image through the film camera lens with some kind of beam-splitting arrangement in the film camera viewfinding system.

Super-16

At the beginning of the decade a completely new film format was introduced. This was 'Super-16', and it was ef-fected by using a 16 mm. camera which had been specially adapted by having the film aperture in the gate filed out at one side so that the negative was exposed right out to the edge of the film, over what would be the sound track area on an ordinary finished 16 mm. married print. Since ordinary 16 mm. lenses were constructed to just cover the area of the ordinary 16 mm. frame with the highest possible definition, and their optical performance usually declined outside that area, it was necessary to re-centre the position of the lens mount by moving it 1 mm. to the side, and also to use lenses designed for television cameras, or in some cases, lenses for 35 mm. cameras. The first feature shot in Super-16 was *Lycklige Skitar* (1970), photographed by Rune Ericsson. He shot it on Eastman Color 7254 using an Eclair NPR with Canon Vidicon lenses. The Eclair NPR proved to be the most popular camera for conversion to Super-16, as its viewfinder showed lots of space at the sides beyond the ordinary 16 mm. frame, and this could easily accommodate the extension of the Super-16 image. In fact, the new format was not greatly taken up for feature film-making, as its use did not save much money for an ordinary feature film production. Although Super-16 reduced the cost of the film used through to the cutting stage, the saving was very small compared to the average feature film budget, and also, despite the improvement in image quality over the ordinary 16 mm. image when projected onto a big cinema screen, the Super-16 image was in its turn still inferior to the image originated on 35 mm. negative. For very low budget feature film production, on the other hand, the cost of the CRI intermediate necessary for producing a final print in 35 mm. was quite high, so Super-16 was not really a lot of help there either. Nevertheless, there were some other less notable films shot in Super-16 during the decade, both in America and Europe.

Stereoscopic Cinema

A small revival of interest in 3-D films had begun at the end of the 'sixties with Arch Oboler's *The Bubble*, shot in 'Spacevision', and this continued into the new decade before guttering out again. 'Spacevision' was the invention of Colonel Robert Bernier, and involved the images from two laterally separated lenses being placed by prism systems in the upper and lower halves of the 'Scope frame area on 35 mm. film in 'Scope proportions. Thus the layout on the film itself looked rather like that on Techniscope negative when inspected directly, though the process did not actually involve anamorphic lenses at any point. Projection reversed this process, with a special double prism and lens system replacing the lens on an ordinary projector. There were Polaroid filters over the two projection lenses with their polarization axes crossed, and the audience had to wear glasses with Polaroid filters on them as usual. The more expensive productions in this new ripple of 3-D such as *Flesh for Frankenstein* (1974) used the 'Spacevision' system, but older, cruder equipment was resurrected for other really cheap productions, most of them sex films.

Camera Mounts, etc.

During the nineteen-seventies there were a number of important developments in ways of mounting moving cameras to get various kinds of control over their motion. Attempts to use a computer to control the detail of all the movements of a camera mounted on some kind of dolly or small crane in a reproducible way started early in the decade. Apart from the computer, the other basic part of the new technology needed for this was the 'stepping motor', now a standard electrical product. This was a small electric motor in which the drive shaft could be controlled electronically to turn through an exact fraction of a revolution in either direction, rather than just rotating continuously in one direction. Such motors could be attached to gears to drive the wheels of a dolly, or to move the arm of a small camera crane in response to signals recorded on a computer disk, and such a series of signals could be changed gradually through a series of trials to get the motion desired, which could then be repeated precisely as often as needed. This was something no human operator could do.

The first important step towards a remotely controlled camera mount was the Louma crane. This was a French invention that was developed into a practical system with the support of Samuelson Film Services in London. The Louma crane was rather like a more sophisticated, and bigger than usual, microphone boom. A tubular extensible arm with a reach of 23ft. 8 in. all the way out was pivoted at its balance point on a stand, and could be rotated in any direction. At the end of the boom the camera was suspended from a pan and tilt mount whose movements could be controlled by stepping motors. The camera was of course fitted with a remote video viewing system, which enabled the operator to see the effect of his movement of the remote pan, tilt, and focus controls. The point of the device was to enable camera moves that were otherwise impossible, such as forward and backward tracks through very narrow spaces, and this is the way it was used occasionally in films in Britain from 1976, and in the U.S. from 1978.

Working on a cruder level, but very effective for all that, were various devices to make the movement of a camera while hand-held easier and smoother. The first of these was the Fleximount, of which 200 had been sold by the middle of 1973. This mount supported the camera in front of the operator on a cross-piece at one end of two bars which were balanced across the operator's shoulders, while being weighed down at their ends behind him by the camera battery, supplemented by springs pulling down to fastenings on the back of a waist belt. This gadget was supplanted by another which may have been partly inspired by it, Garrett Brown's 'Steadicam'. After some years of development by its cameraman inventor, this was put on sale by Cinema Products in 1976. The Steadicam had two main parts. One was a flexed folding arm mounted at the cameraman's waist on a joint fixed to a chest and waist harness that he wore. The arm contained internal springs acting like those in the well-known 'Angle-

poise' desk lamp to support the object at its outer end, though in this case they had to be much stronger to carry about 10 Kg. of camera, etc. On the end of this arm there was a gimbal joint, through which passed a vertical rod capable of rotating in every direction about this joint. On the top end of the rod, several inches above the joint, was the camera, and at the bottom end, about a foot below the joint, was the camera battery. In the prototype system the camera, which was an Arriflex 2C modified to have its magazine on a gooseneck behind it, and also a video tube inserted in the viewing system, was permanently fastened to the mount, and it had a very small high intensity video monitor mounted above it. This part of the device was probably inspired by the now fairly standard construction of helicopter camera mounts such as the Tyler mount, or the late Albert Lamorisse's 'Helivision' mount. The leverage of the spring system in the arm was adjusted to compensate for all but a pound or two of the weight of the camera, leaving this last fraction of the weight supported and controlled by the cameraman's own arm grasping a handgrip on the rod below the gimbal joint. Through the joints on the arm system the camera could be moved up and down across in front of the cameraman's body, and also out to the side, while the gimbal permitted it to be tilted and turned in any direction. With the Steadicam, it was possible not only to get a smooth flat motion while the cameraman walked around, which could already be done by a skilled operator doing ordinary hand-holding, but even to run with the camera without any up and down bounce being visible. Indeed what was possible with the device used by a skilled operator was quite remarkable. The drawback to the Steadicam was that it required not only quite a bit of training to use it well, but also quite a lot of strength to support it for any length of time, as the arm and harness weighed about 12 lb., and the camera, etc. mounted on it about 30 lb. The first films the Steadicam was used on were *Bound for Glory*, *Marathon Man*, and *Rocky*, and Brown did most of the operating of the device on these. *Bound for Glory* included a number of clever tricks, which have since become standard, such as starting a shot with the operator carrying the camera on a crane platform, which is then lowered to the ground, and having him walk off it and around and about through the scene, filming all the time.

A universal model of the Steadicam, which did not have the camera built onto it, and could take any camera weighing up to about 20 lb., was produced almost immediately for sale or rental by Cinema Products. This had the framing monitor in the battery base unit, with its screen inclined upwards, though the high monitor on the earlier version was much better for framing control by the operator. In fact, even with the earlier version, framing while in motion could not be as precise as that done by a cameraman with his eye to the reflex viewfinding system of an ordinary handheld camera. In use, the Steadicam tends to feel as though it has a life of its own, which is the reason for the training in its use being necessary, and shots including slowish sideways movements tend to have a slight look of 'balloon-like' motion to them. A whole style was created round this movement quality of the Steadicam by John Carpenter in his film *Halloween* (1978), by establishing at the beginning of it that this kind of movement of the camera was associated with the POV of the mad sex killer, and then repeatedly tricking the cinema audience by revealing that sometimes it was just a purely objective shot. This notion proved to have quite an appeal to immature sensibilities, and hence a long life afterwards in the commercial cinema of recent times.

Another novel camera support system was the Wesscam. This was conceived by the Istec Corporation of Canada for use in taking helicopter shots, where there was a restriction on camera pans and tilts, because of the necessity for the mount to be inside the aircraft, with the camera shooting out through an open door. The actual design was done by the American Westinghouse company, and involved a camera housed inside a fibreglass sphere 117 cm. in diameter, with its panning and tilting remotely controlled by servo motors, and monitored on a TV screen. The whole apparatus weighed 81 Kg., and was suspended outside the helicopter in its initial application. It was found that it removed all vibration even with a 250 mm. camera lens, and was then taken up for use in other situations, for instance suspended on a car in filming the 1976 Montreal Olympics. For feature films it was also suspended from a crane, and used to get the maze shots in *Sleuth* (1972). Its most famous accomplishment was the final shot of Antonioni's *Reporter* (1975).

Lenses

In this period the vast, ever-expanding world television industry had a strong indirect influence on the new lenses produced for film cameras. For some time, television cameras had been equipped only with permanently mounted zoom lenses, and this meant that the market for new fixed focal length lenses for film cameras was relatively minor, particularly since it was often the practice to adapt good older lenses for mounting on the new film camera designs. As a result of this, the venerable Taylor-Hobson company in England stopped making fixed focal length lenses altogether, and concentrated its efforts on zoom lens manufacture, where a television camera lens design could be fairly easily reworked for film use. And they had a good success with their Cooke Varotal 5 to 1 (20-100mm) zoom introduced in 1970. This had a T3.2 maximum aperture, and focussed as close as 0.34 m. One of the most interesting aspects was that it was not focused by rotating the front of the lens, as had been necessary with all previous zoom lenses, but by twisting a ring further down the lens barrel. This feature was almost essential for use on broadcast type video cameras, and was also much more convenient for film use.

In 1975 Taylor-Hobson made a similar lens for 16 mm. cameras, the Cooke Varotal 9-50 mm. zoom. Its maximum aperture was T2.5 and it focussed as close as 9 inches. It also had a fixed front element, which was even more helpful to

cinéma vérité and news cameramen who pulled focus for themselves without an assistant.

Canon, the major Japanese manufacturer of lenses for still cameras, now entered the film lens market in collaboration with the large American equipment hire firms, producing sets of lenses to their specification. Like Taylor-Hobson, and likewise in the interest of getting the highest possible optical resolution, Canon did not try to make zooms covering a focal length change of 10 to 1, but were satisfied with a zoom ratio of around 5 to 1. In 1971 they produced a 25-120 mm. zoom with a maximum aperture of T2.8, and anamorphic zooms of focal length ranges 40-135 mm. and 79-200 mm., both with maximum aperture of T4.5. A little later there was a Canon zoom for 16 mm. with a focal length range of 12.5-75 mm. and maximum aperture of T2.1. All these Canon zooms had a so-called Macro facility of the kind now familiar to still camera enthusiasts, so that by a twist of a ring on the lens it could be set to focus very close to the front element, even as close as 3.125' in the case of the 16 mm. zoom. This permitted great magnification of any tiny object being filmed. The special features of these Canon lenses was in part made possible by the replacement of some glass elements by internal elements made of synthetic fluorite crystal, which has a much higher refractive index than any glass. Although this was a well-known theoretical possibility, it had been avoided because fluorite absorbs water vapour and swells under some conditions. However, Canon apparently worked out a way round this problem. In 1974 they also produced a series of fixed focal length lenses of high resolution and higher speed than usual, and here the trick was to use elements with 'aspheric' surfaces. (Unlike ordinary lens elements, in which all surfaces are sections of a sphere, these were ground with computer calculated curves that helped reduce the aberrations of the total lens further than had been possible before.) The maximum apertures of these lenses was mostly T1.4. And all had multiple layers of anti-flare coatings on their surfaces, instead of the single layer that had been standard for film lenses up to this point, which reduced even further than usual the light flare which can degrade the image.

Also in 1974, Zeiss produced a very similar series of fixed focal length lenses using the same techniques, but with the extra innovation of having 'floating' internal elements which moved relative to the outer groups of elements when the focus was changed, rather in the way that zoom lenses have moving internal elements to change the focal length. Zeiss also made a similar set for 16 mm. photography, though in this case the maximum aperture was T1.3. These new Zeiss lenses were generally referred to as the SuperSpeed range, and proved very successful. Zeiss also produced a zoom lens for 16 mm., the Vario Sonnar, which was likewise popular, with a range of 10-100 mm. and maximum aperture of f2.8.

One crucial point in zoom lens specification from a cameraman's point of view, both in 16 mm. and 35 mm.. is to have a shortest focal length of about 10 mm. or 20 mm., depending on the gauge of film. This means that a location scene in a small space could be covered without having to replace the zoom lens with a wider angle fixed focus lens. Another point is to have the maximum possible aperture available on the same lens for filming under low light conditions. Taylor-Hobson and Zeiss zooms satisfied the best combination of these requirements in general.

The French Angénieux company continued to bring out new models of zoom lenses, working in the same direction as the newer entrants to the competition, which was to reduce the zoom range and increase the maximum aperture and optical performance. However, Angénieux stayed with older design techniques, and so began to lose their commanding position. However, they did retain their lead in lenses with ever greater zoom ranges. They produced a zoom lens with a 20 to 1 zoom ratio of 25-500 mm. especially for the Samuelsons film equipment rental company in London in 1970, and in 1974 a 15 to 1 (10-150 mm.) zoom with a maximum aperture of T3.2 for 16 mm. cameras. And Cinema Products in Los Angeles had another 20 to 1 zoom (24-480 mm.) made out of Angénieux parts at the request of Stanley Kubrick. This lens can be seen used in *Barry Lyndon*, doing quite slow zooms straight in and out on exterior scenes in the beautifully landscaped grounds of English country mansions, which forms an important part of the style of that film. Finally, Angénieux put on sale a 25 to 1 ratio zoom (25-625 mm.) for 35 mm. photography in 1980. This had a maximum aperture of T8.

Following the lead of Haskell Wexler in the previous decade, Stanley Kubrick had two Zeiss 50 mm. f0.7 still camera lenses originally made for NASA adapted for movie camera mounting for his production of *Barry Lyndon*. One was kept as a 50 mm. lens, and the other was converted into a 35 mm. lens with an adaptor. Because the rear element of these lenses had to be very close to the film, they could only be mounted on a specially adapted old non-reflex BNC Mitchell camera. By forcing the Eastman Color negative one stop to 200 ASA, with these lenses it was possible to photograph interior scenes lit only by candles, in fact with light at a measured level of 3 foot-candles. The resulting shots were of very poor definition, and in the finished film they were left with the inevitable strong orange bias of low temperature light, but it could be argued that they served their function in the overall film. Since the field of sharp focus at f0.7 is only inches deep, focus changes to accommodate actor movement had to be judged by a special video system reproducing the scene as seen from the side on a monitor with a distance graticule on its face. This part of the operation was an idea with no future.

The Technovision anamorphic lenses made by Rank Taylor-Hobson for the Italian company of that name were made available for rental in U.S. from 1977, and could be used on any of the standard cameras as desired.

A small-scale trend in film photography during the 'seventies was the use by some directors of very wide-angle lenses, with focal lengths in the range from 10 mm. to 15 mm, for the photography of a large proportion of the ordinary scenes in their films. A good example of this is provided by Fred Perry's *Rancho DeLuxe* (1974), but other films in which such very wide-angle lenses were used some of the time include *Charley Varrick* (Don Siegel, 1973), and *Death Wish* (Michael Winner, 1974). *Patton* gives an example of this in 70 mm., with much of the film shot with the 28 mm. Todd-AO lens. Unlike the trend towards the use of wide-angle lenses in the nineteen-forties, in which their use was associated with the staging of the action in depth, between actors near the camera and others in the background, this new trend merely used these very wide-angle lenses with ordinary staging of the scenes, even though they gave greater depth of field. The inspiration for this use of very wide-angle lenses may have come from a fashion for their use in still photography a few years before, where they had been taken up as soon as they became available for still cameras. Although lenses with focal lengths of 9.8 mm. and 14 mm. were available for cinematography from before 1965, they had hardly ever been used on feature films. A rather similar situation had arisen previously in the 'sixties with the use of long focal-length lenses, which although always available for film cameras, were only used to film ordinary scenes after they had become fashionable in still photography at the beginning of that decade.

The general trend towards filming on location and the use of low light levels continued to militate against the use of deep focus, but there was still some interest in staging in depth, occasionally under the even more unsuitable conditions of photography using 'Scope as well. To achieve depth of field when 'Scope filming, resort was had to the use of split field dioptres – supplementary lenses which covered only part of the lens field. Examples of this include scenes in *The Andromeda Strain* and *I Walk the Line*, on which David M. Walsh used two dioptres simultaneously in front of the two sides of the lens to get 3 separate areas of the scene having different depths in focus at the same time. Non- 'Scope films which strove to obtain even greater depth of field with the use of split dioptres, even though they were already being shot at f4.5, included *All the President's Men* and *The Iceman Cometh*.

Sound

The major new film sound recorder in this period was the tiny Nagra SN recorder produced by Kudelski in 1971. The dimensions of this were only 5.75' x 4' x 1', and its weight 1lb. 1oz. To achieve this size, it recorded on 150 mil tape of the same width as that used in amateur cassette recorders, but the quality of the recording was quite good enough for film purposes, and it could also give crystal synchronization. It was used sometimes connected to a chest microphone and carried in an actor's pocket in situations where a radio microphone link would not work, but its principal application was in the kind of documentary filming which was physically awkward for a sound recordist, such as filming mountain climbing with sync. sound. Although such things were mostly a concern of non-fiction filming, the device was also useful for filming parts of some features, such as *The Eiger Sanction*.

The Kudelski company was unsuccessful with its other innovation of the 'seventies, the Nagra IS-D recorder. Roughly speaking, this had the same facilities as the old Nagra III, but in a smaller and lighter unit (10 lbs.). In fact it was rather similar in size and weight to the Stellavox recorder. But the Nagra IS-D was only 20% less in price than the Nagra IV, while lacking the capacity for the extra internal features such as crystal sync. unit and transfer resolver that the latter had. The Nagra IV was now also available in a stereo sound version, which used a different incompatible sync. pulse system to the original Nagra Pilotone. Towards the end of the period the stereo Nagra IV SL came to be increasingly used for film recording, not to record stereo sound directly, but as a two channel recorder, taking the signals from two microphones on different parts of the set, so that the balance of their sound could be readjusted later at leisure. Nagra recorders continued to be used for nearly all feature film recording world-wide, including Russia and Eastern Europe.

Sennheiser microphones did not have quite the same dominance, for although older microphones of other makes were continually being replaced, new condenser microphones from Schoeps in the United States and AKG in Austria took some of the business, basically because they were cheaper in the U.S. and European market respectively than the Sennheiser microphones, and not that much inferior to them as well. All were available in models that gave omni-directional, or cardioid, or ultra-directional sound pick-up. The AKG models used the new idea of having just one basic diaphragm unit, onto which were screwed interchangeable slotted tubes of various lengths to get the appropriate degree of directionality. Sennheiser introduced a new condenser microphone into its range in 1971, the 415. This had a spatial response pattern intermediate between the cardioid 405 and the ultra-directional 805, combined with a frequency response virtually as flat as the 405, and eventually it proved to be the most popular of all with film sound recordists, replacing the 405 as the preferred option in most situations.

Another general development was the use of the 'electret' type of microphone for film purposes. These were a type of capacitor microphone in which the electric charge on the diaphragm was applied permanently during manufacture, rather than by power supplied from batteries or the recorder during use. Although electret microphones are in general far cheaper than powered capacitor microphones, their performance is also slightly inferior, and it is possible to destroy them with a sharp very loud sound which drives the diaphragm onto the back plate of the capacitor, so discharging the device. Nevertheless, Sennheiser and others produced ranges of electret mikes, but they had little use in professional film-making, except as neck-microphones or lapel microphones, which were now so small they could even be pinned to the outside of performer's clothing fairly inconspicuously.

On the technological side, the major developments was the increasing use of radio microphones, now that these were finally reliable for location use. One of the new tricks to ensure reliability was the use of two separate receivers for the signals from the transmitters on the actors, so eliminating any 'dead spots' in reception in location filming situations.

Robert Altman's Methods

It seems to me that the only American director who has created a truly distinctive formal style during the 'seventies was Robert Altman, and he was also the director who has made most use of the new technological developments just mentioned. Already in 1969, in *That Cold Day in the Park*, he was beginning to develop a special way of using camera movements in combination with zooms and actor movement. At first, in *M.A.S.H.* (1971), the result was to keep the actors roughly the same size in the frame while they traced out a complex path on the set, but by *The Long Goodbye* (1973) some of the zooming in and out was being applied in a random way to nearly stationary actors, and this trend has since continued in Altman's work.

Simultaneously with these developments on the visual side, Altman also pushed the use of overlapping dialogue beyond earlier models, which had restricted themselves to the overlapping of the beginning and ends of lines of dialogue spoken by different actors. Altman used whole sentences spoken simultaneously, and initially this was done by post-synchronizing the extra layers of speech, but he quickly moved on to make use of the improved radio microphones in combination with a multi-track recorder to record the dialogue from several actors separately, for later adjustment in the mixing. This idea was introduced in *California Split* to overcome the staging restrictions Altman had experienced while making *McCabe and Mrs. Miller*, and also to allow improvisation and overlapping of on-screen dialogue, as well as the incorporation of off-screen dialogue into direct recordings.

Altman used a recorder designed for music recording, which was a Stevens Electronics 8 track 1" machine running at 15 inches per sec., and in this application one track was used to record a sync. pulse, and the other seven for the different microphones that might be needed. A quartz crystal sync. pulse generator, resolver, and V.S.O. (speed varier) were added to the standard machine. Altman had several of these recorders, with two 8 input, 4 output channel mixers for each recorder, and two such recorders were used interlocked for the recording of *A Wedding*. In general, Sony ECM-50 electret lavalier mikes and Artech radio links were used for each performer, but some fixed mikes were also used on the sets. It was, of course, impossible to balance all these properly during the initial recording. These individual microphone tracks were transferred to three track recordings on 35 mm. sprocketed magnetic film, which produced two or more of these magnetic films, and the editing was done on a six plate KEM editing table, with a special added 9 channel amplifier. Altman also had two portable projectors with triple head double head facility, which could be interlocked to an extra 35 mm. magnetic film deck. After editing, the tracks were separated back to single track 35 mm. magnetic films for the final mixing session in a conventional dubbing theatre.

This multi-track recording system was subsequently used on all Altman films and also on Alan Rudolph's *Welcome to L.A.*. In the case of Altman's *Nashville* (1975) the separate dialogue tracks were mixed to give the usual fairly realistic sound perspective, but by the time of *A Wedding* (1978) Altman was no longer bothering with this, and left most of the dialogue tracks at the same level in an unnatural way. What one is to make of this, and also the random zooming in Altman's later films I do not know. In any case, Altman's methods in their fullest form did not catch on with anyone else, in part because the sound quality from neck microphones fell short of the highest standards. However, it did become increasingly common for sound recordists to take two-track recordings when using more than one microphone simultaneously, quite often by using the two tracks of a stereo Nagra independently for this purpose.

A quite opposite approach to the treatment of sound was followed over this same period by John Boorman. In his case all of his films were post-synchronized throughout, using a sync. guide track taken at the time of shooting.

Sensurround

Sensurround was introduced by Universal Studios as a special feature for presentations of *Earthquake* (1974). It involved the installation of special loudspeakers and horns in cinemas which relayed very low frequency sound, mostly below audibility. this low frequency sound was generated electronically in special units when they were triggered by signals on the optical sound track of the film, and then amplified by special 1000 watt amplifiers. Some actual low frequency recorded sounds, such as that of rushing floodwater, were also taken from the optical track and fed into these extra amplifiers and speakers to accompany appropriate scenes in the film. The system was also used on *Midway* (1976) and *Rollercoaster* (1977), but on the latter it was simplified, with the required very low frequency sound, down to 15 Hz, being recorded on the optical track, and simply amplified for playback through the special extra amplifiers and low frequency speakers in the theatres, rather than being synthesized on receipt of a coded signal. After this the idea was swept away by the developments in the Dolby system of film sound recording.

Dolby System Recording

The Dolby noise reduction process was first used for film purposes in the professional Dolby A form for the sound mixing stages of *Clockwork Orange* (1971). The Dolby process was then applied to the optical recording of monaural film sound tracks and theatre systems on some films made from 1974 to 1977, starting with *Steppenwolf* (1974) and *Stardust* (1974). Dolby recording was also applied to the stereo magnetic film track recording and also the reproduction in theatres for *The Little Prince* (1974) and *Nashville* (1975). At the same time, from 1973 Eastman Kodak and RCA had been develo-

ping a simple stereo optical track system, and they quickly brought Dolby Labs into the project. (A system with more than two tracks would have created a number of problems, including compatibility with mono tracks.) The Dolby theatre system synthesized a signal for the centre speaker behind the screen from the difference between the two recorded tracks, and the two basic tracks were reproduced through the standard left and right theatre speakers. *Tommy* (1975) was released in Europe using this system in 1975, and *A Star is Born* in 1976 in the U.S.A. Sound for the surround speakers already installed for CinemaScope could be reproduced by the Sansui matrix (QS) system encoding onto the two recorded tracks. It was decided to use this last refinement of the system on *Star Wars* before the production on that film was started in 1975. For *Star Wars* Dolby encoding was used on the original recordings onto 1/4' tape, without limiting and equalization, and also with no high frequency boost. The final mix was to four tracks – left, right, centre, and surround, and these were remixed to 6 tracks for the 70mm. magnetic sound prints. When production on *Star Wars* started, it was anticipated that more than 50% of the first wave release theatres would be Dolby equipped.

Editing

During the 'seventies flat-bed editing machines continued to gain in popularity, even invading feature film-editing in the United States. The most popular make continued to be the Steenbeck, but the market was so big that various other companies kept trying to get some of the business, mostly without much success. A new entrant that had some success was the KEM machine, also from Germany, despite the fact that its price was much higher than the Steenbeck. Part of its attraction was its modular construction, so that it was possible to create various combinations within its four track form. I.e. you could have one picture head and three sound tracks locked together, or run two pictures and two sound tracks simultaneously, or three pictures and one sound-track. Such facilities were particularly useful for films which were shot with multiple cameras.

The venerable Moviola company finally produced a successful American flatbed machine in 1971, and this was known colloquially as the Magnasync Moviola. The layout of this machine was very similar to that of the Steenbeck, but the technology was more advanced, with independent electric motors driving each of the take-up and feed plates, as well as each of the drive sprockets. The optics of the machine were also an improvement on those of the Steenbeck, with specially ground facets on the rotating prism that made the transition from one frame to the next on the screen quite invisible, no matter how slowly the film was advanced.

Time Code Systems

Starting in 1973, the broadcasting companies making up the European Broadcasting Union (EBU) collaborated to develop a system that encoded synchronizing signals con-

American 1970-1975

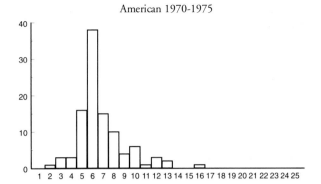

American 1976-1981

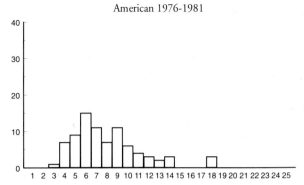

taining the exact instant of shooting down the whole length of both the sound and picture track recordings. In the case of the sound track the signals were recorded on a specially adapted recorder as an extra track on the 1/4 inch tape, while in the camera there was an array of light emitting diodes (LEDs) that imprinted a type of bar code at intervals down the length of the edge of the negative. The timing signals were generated by oscillators in small solid state electronic units included in both the recorder and camera. These were synchronized by making a connection from a master generator to them at the beginning of the day's shoot, after which the time code generators would hold the synchronism in the signals they produced for some hours. Inevitably, a competing system appeared in 1976 from the Aäton camera company which was basically similar, but which identified the instant of filming with small Arabic numerals down the edge of the film. The EBU system was used from 1976 for television purposes, but neither system was used for ordinary feature film-making. The main use of time code systems proved to be for multiple camera filming

General Editing Trends

The trend in cutting rates towards faster and faster cutting that was underway in the previous decade continued and reached a peak, with by far the most common Average Shot Length being about 6 seconds. Average Shot Lengths of 4 seconds or less were now fairly common, and hardly any ordinary commercial American films had ASLs longer than 13 seconds, as can be seen from the graphs showing the distributions for this quantity. Long Average Shot Lengths were now

almost exclusively associated with high artistic ambition, as such rare American examples as *Being There* (Hal Ashby, 1980) and *American Gigolo* (Paul Schrader, 1979) indicate. For a sample of 101 American films made in the six year period from 1970 to 1975, the mean ASL was 7.0 seconds, but when we look at 75 American films made during the next six-year period 1976 to 1981, we find that the mean ASL has gone up to 8.4 seconds, though the modal ASL is still about 6 seconds. In other words, the 1976-1981 sample includes rather more films with a long ASL than samples from the previous six year periods. Whether this result is just a result of the rather small, and possibly skewed, sample for the second period I am not sure. Certainly I would feel a lot happier if I had counted a group of twice the size for 1976-1981.

And of course the long take continued to be the standard mode in European art movies; in fact, the higher the pretensions, the longer the take.

It seems that the break-down of the studio system and the long apprenticeship of editors associated with it meant that knowledge of what I called 'the dialogue cutting point', when writing about editing in the 'thirties, was lost. Well-known films made in the 'seventies which contain dialogue scenes in which the cuts from one speaker to another are made almost at random include *The Long Goodbye, The Godfather II*, and *New York, New York*. Another trend in cutting style was that the use of nothing but jump cuts to progress from one scene to the next was largely abandoned, and mixtures of jump cuts, dissolves, and fades used at will became the usual thing. The use of wipes remained very rare, and this continued into the next decade.

21. FILM STYLE AND TECHNOLOGY IN EIGHTIES

During the nineteen-eighties, film-makers working on ordinary commercial features and made-for-television films in the United States and Britain came under increasing pressure to complete shooting as quickly as possible. This had a noticeable effect on production procedures, and even some slight effect on the forms of cinema. Because of the increasing cost of using Hollywood studios, and also because the number of these available for feature film-making decreased, the established trend towards shooting more and more American features away from Hollywood continued. Any sets needed were usually built in improvised studios near the locations being used, but studios around Vancouver in Canada, and the big Churubusco studios near Mexico City were also used more and more. However, by the end of the decade, the cost of shooting in the Vancouver studios was approaching that of shooting in Los Angeles, and the construction of a brand new studio complex in the latter city was begun. In Europe, the television financing of feature films became even more important.

There was also a lot of activity on the technical side of film-making during the decade, only partly connected with the pursuit of the perfect illusion in special effects.

New Production Procedures

The use of storyboards on quite a number of ordinary dramatic films, as opposed to films dependent on special effects, continued throughout the decade. Brian de Palma's variant of the technique used photographic images of the projected shots taken with stand-ins on location, rather than hand-drawn images.

Also during the 'eighties, Francis Coppola went one better on Robert Altman's conception of movie-making as a technical circus of which the director was the ring-master. The first stage of his vision of what he called 'the electronic cinema' was realized with the filming of *One From the Heart* in 1982. After the script for this film was storyboarded in the standard way there were actor rehearsals which were recorded on sound. This sound was combined with music and effects, and transferred as an accompaniment track to the storyboard drawings recorded on videotape. After viewing this videotape, or 'electronic storyboard', the script was modified. Then the actors were taken to Las Vegas, and their performance of the script was videorecorded, and then roughly edited. This footage was edited into the 'electronic storyboard', replacing the corresponding storyboard drawings. Next the studio sets were built as accurate reproductions of the original Las Vegas locations. On the actual shoot, the Technovision cameras had video taps, and Coppola watched what was being shot on a monitor in his control vehicle while communicating by radio with the studio stage. The tapes from the video assist cameras were woven into the electronic storyboard, and Coppola then viewed an edited version of previous day's shooting with music and effects. The final editing of the film was also done on video.

The claim was made at the time about this method that:- "Remarkably cost efficient, the 'electronic cinema' allows the film-makers to continually preview the film. This advance opportunity to 'see' the film leads to tightening of the script and elimination of unnecessary scenes and sets, further cutting the cost of the movie." (*American Cinematographer* January 1982 V.63 n.1 p.22) In this particular case this was certainly not true, because not only was the film very costly for what it was, but it was also very unsuccessful at the box office. The unsurprising result was that nobody else took up Coppola's ideas about production methods, and he himself quickly retreated from them. For his next film, *Rumblefish*, he was still using a reduced form of electronic storyboarding using material from video-recorded rehearsals done on location, plus other rehearsals shot against a blue screen in the studio. But the actual editing of the film was completely conventional. By 1987 and *Gardens of Stone*, all that was left of Coppola's 'electronic cinema' was two weeks of videotaped rehearsals.

A simpler (and actually successful) method of increasing production efficiency was the greater use of multi-camera filming. This had always been standard for the shooting of mass action scenes, and was also quite often used for filming musical numbers, but rarely before this period for filming ordinary scenes. Towards the end of the 'eighties it became much more common, led by the way it had been used in previous years for filming scenes with extremely expensive and lazy actors like Marlon Brando. Some of the directors who used multi-camera filming, such as Michael Cimino, obviously did not have any clear idea how the shots in their films would be put together, and used it as protection, while others, such as Walter Hill, who worked with very short Average Shot Lengths, needed it to double or treble the number of set-ups they could get in a given length of time. There was another very small group of British directors, with a strong visual sense and training, who had got their start making advertising films, who also at first used two camera filming. When they started feature film-making, Adrian Lyne and Ridley Scott insisted on having a second camera that they could be allowed to operate themselves, to get just exactly the compositions they wanted, rather than those the official camera operator would give them. However, by the end of the decade, most directors with a strong idea of the kind of images they wanted settled for the help of the increasingly used video assist in getting their ideal pictures.

Film Stock

During the 'eighties, the near total dominance of Eastman Kodak film stocks in professional film-making weakened for the first time. There were two factors at work here. One was the fact that the Fuji and Agfa companies were prepared to undercut Kodak prices slightly in search of a larger share of the market, and the other was that Kodak was slow in introducing a very fast colour negative. This latter point gave Fuji, and to some extent Agfa-Gevaert, a chance to supply something which was increasingly needed by film-makers who were shooting more and more on location, and in particular in location interiors.

The first of these new fast negative stocks was Fuji A250 (Type 8518), introduced at the end of 1980, which had a speed of 250 ASA. It was most used in Europe, where a small saving on stock costs was important, but it was also used on a number of American features for filming night scenes. A year later, at the end of 1981, Eastman Kodak responded with their own equally fast 250 ASA negatives, 5293 and 7293, for 35 mm. and 16 mm. respectively. But the important point was they were not *first* with a fast colour stock. (Prior to this, many American cameramen had solved the problem of filming under low light levels by forcing Eastman Color 5247 up to 400 ASA.) Agfa-Gevaert also introduced a fast colour negative, type 722, but this was of less significance.

Kodak now entered a period of almost continuous improvement in the negative stocks they manufactured. Film speeds, which had previously been described in terms of either the American Standards Association (ASA) system, or alternatively by the Deutsche Industrie Normen (DIN) or Scheiner system in continental Europe, were now described by the consolidation of these various systems into ISO numbers regulated by the International Standards Organization. These ISO numbers were in fact the continuation of the previous systems in one combined number. For example, the new Eastman Color 5294, which replaced 5293 at the beginning of 1984, was officially ISO 400/27. But to confuse the issue further, Kodak replaced the ISO tag with the term 'Exposure Index' (EI, for short), and in America Eastman Color 5294 came to be referred to simply as being of speed EI 400. Inevitably, most cameramen in England and the United States continued to refer to film speeds in terms of ASA numbers for the rest of the decade, though in practice this did not create any confusion. I shall use the designation Exposure Index or EI for the rest of this history. At this same time, Eastman Kodak took the opportunity to re-rate the speed of their standard professional negative 5247 from ASA 100 to EI 125. In 16 mm., the new fast Kodak stock was 7294, with an Exposure Index (EI) of 320 under tungsten light.

Fuji Film also improved their negative films in 1983, with Fujicolor AX (Type 8518) becoming the new fast stock with an increased speed of EI 320, and Fujicolor A the normal speed stock with a speed of EI 125 under tungsten light. In 1985 Fuji got their nose in front again with AX 8514 and AX 8524 for 35 mm. and 16 mm. respectively, which both had

an EI of 500. These stocks, like their predecessors, had quite prominent grain, and hence a noticeable lack of definition, and compared to the fast Kodak stocks the colours they produced were quite markedly desaturated. Fuji claimed that these desaturated colours were an aesthetic choice, but *I* think that it was more a matter of what they could achieve practically. Nevertheless, the fast Fuji stocks saw quite a lot of use for location night scenes, more particularly in Europe, but even to some extent in the United States. Fuji film of various kinds was most used in the USA on films shot for television, where the slightly lower price compared to that for Eastman materials was an important consideration.

Control of the Agfa-Gevaert company had been bought by the German chemical company Bayer in 1978, and in the 'eighties the Gevaert name was gradually dropped, and the film stocks produced by this company came to be referred to simply as Agfa films. In the early nineteen-eighties the new camera negatives from this company were Agfa XT125 and Agfa XT320, with Exposure Indices corresponding to the included numbers. These stocks were finally made available in the USA in 1985. This seems to be because some English cameramen, particularly Chris Menges and David Watkin, used them on big films with American stars released during that year. David Watkin gave as his reason for favouring Agfa XT320 that it had greater latitude than Eastman 5294. Watkin had taken a very idiosyncratic approach to film photography since the 'sixties, and in the case of *Out of Africa* (1986), he used the fast Agfa XT320 for the day exteriors, and the slower Eastman 5274 for interiors, so reversing the usual procedure. He also let the brighter background parts of the daylight scenes; those not inhabited by the principal actors, 'burn out' (i.e. become overexposed), which was also against the traditions still holding for Hollywood films in the nineteen-eighties.

Another reason for the eventual popularity of Agfa XT320 was that it reproduced the greens of foliage as a lighter hue than the more accurate Kodak stocks. The problem, to which this was a solution, is that most of the greenery in the real world makes a rather dull mass if reproduced in its true colours in outdoor daylight scenes, and so cameramen prefer an artificially lighter colour to help in composing a more 'artistic' picture, following the various conventional ideas on this point. (At any rate, that is my interpretation of the matter.)

The major development at the end of the decade was Kodak's gradual introduction of a negative emulsion containing a new type of silver halide crystal. These crystals had a tabular form, being thin plates, rather than the irregular chunky crystals into which the silver halides naturally crystallize, and which everyone had used up to this point. Kodak called these 'T-grains', and they made it possible to coat the emulsion into much thinner layers for the same sensitivity to light. This increased sensitivity for smaller emulsion volume was aided by the tendency of the T-grains to tessellate when the emulsion containing them was coated onto the base material. That is, the edges of the adjoining grains tended to line up like tiles within the one plane, leaving no empty space between the grains for light photons to get through without hitting and activating a halide crystal.

T-grain emulsion had been first used in 1983 by Eastman Kodak in their Kodacolor VR 1000 negative made for still photography, but for film purposes this technology was first used in the high speed 16 mm. negative 7292 released in 1986 to replace the previous 7294 negative. T-grain halides were only used in some of the colour responsive layers in 7292, as was also the case when they were first applied to 35 mm. negative in the fast 5295 stock which replaced 5294 in 1987. Finally, in 1989 and 1990, a range of new camera negatives using T-grain material completely throughout was built up under the designation of 'EXR' stocks. Those introduced in 1989 were Type 5296 with EI 500 Tungsten and 5245 with EI 50 Daylight for 35 mm., and 7248 with EI 100 Tungsten and 7245 with EI 50 Daylight for 16 mm. They were specially designed to record truer colours under fluorescent light, which was an ever more important consideration, as more and more scenes were being filmed on location interiors. In 1990 Kodak added the medium speed negative EXR 5248 with EI 100 Tungsten for 35 mm., and the fast EXR 7296 with EI 500 tungsten for 16 mm. filming.

Another innovation with these Kodak negative stocks was that the traditional edge numbers which were printed into the film every foot on manufacture (or half-foot in the case of 16 mm.), were supplemented with a kind of bar code imprint every 6 frames, which identified the exact length of film to that point. Every 24 frames there was also a barcode identifying the serial roll number in the order that the film was produced by Kodak. This system was trade-marked as 'Keycode', and may prove to be important in the future, though the traditional latent image Arabic edge numbers were still provided to give equivalent information.

Fuji Film's response to Kodak's major innovation in photographic emulsion technique was what they called 'double structure' grains, which were first used in motion picture negative in 1988. The new stocks were Fujicolor Negative film F-64 for tungsten light, and the F-500 negative was renamed to high speed film AX-500. There were also F-64 D for daylight, F-125 for tungsten light, and moderately fast F-250 tungsten. Fuji did not publicize the exact nature of the grain structure of these new silver halide materials, but the visible result on the screen came nowhere near the perfection in colour response, latitude, and definition of the Kodak EXR materials.

During this decade there was some development in print stocks as well. At the beginning of the 'eighties a certain amount of justified fuss was made about the fading of old colour films by a number of people, most notably Martin Scorsese. This helped to prod the film stock makers into introducing new print materials containing dyes that were much more resistant to fading. The chemistry for doing this had existed for some time, and indeed for many years Kodak had been making available a low-fade 16 mm. print stock

alongside its normal material, but this low-fade stock was little used, in part because its price was higher than the standard print stock. So when Fuji introduced new positive print materials Types 8816 and 8826 in 1983, which were claimed to match the colour response of the standard Kodak print materials, they emphasised their low-fade properties as well. Kodak in their turn then drew attention to the long-lasting dyes in their new low contrast print stocks introduced in 1984 especially for making prints for television transmission, which were types 5380 and 7380.

Laboratory Work and Special Treatment Techniques

The kinds of special treatment of film introduced in the previous couple of decades such as pre- and post-flashing of negative continued to be used when judged appropriate. Panavision introduced a way for the cameraman to do this himself in the camera with their 'Panaflasher' device. This fitted onto the magazine port of the camera, and it exposed the film to a weak controlled light as it passed either on its way to the gate of the camera, or on its way back into the magazine. An increasingly popular alternative for in-camera flashing was the Lightflex device, described in the previous chapter. In 1985 the rights to this were bought by Arnold & Richter, and in a slightly redesigned form it became the Arri Lightflex. Then Arri completely redesigned it as the Arri VariCon, a much smaller device that was used from 1990 onwards on a number of films. In this form it was an optical flat held perpendicularly in front of the lens, with light injected into it through its edges. The amount of light was controlled by variable apertures, and its colour by filters as before.

Another enthusiasm of this period was a new kind of treatment applied to positive release prints of some films. The first form of this was developed in Italy, following on from the special treatment given to part of *Cadaveri eccellenti* mentioned in the previous chapter, and it was now called the ENR process. It was a form of secondary development of the film, by passing it through another developing bath after the initial one. Vittorio Storaro used it on the prints of *Reds* (1981) for better integration of the black and white footage with the colour material making up the main body of the film. Eventually it became available in the United States as 'Colour Contrast Enhancement' or CCE, but seems to have been little used. It is not clear whether this was the same as the process used for the release prints of *Top Gun*, which were passed through the developer a second time to enrich the blacks with more silver. In this case, the general effect was to make the film look more contrasty. A more interesting variant of the idea was used in France on *Un dimanche à la campagne*. The release prints of this film were developed without the bleach bath to give far denser blacks in the image. The idea of the makers was to give this story, which was set in 1912, the look of the Lumière Autochrome colour process for still photography, which had just come into use at that date. But the result did not really look all that similar to an Autochrome picture, and because of the highly increased contrast in the images, special make-up was needed to compensate for the whitened faces of the actors. Another feature of the photography of *Un dimanche à la campagne*, also part of the striving for a period effect, was that it was photographed on fast Eastman 5293, and lit to a sufficient level to get apertures of T5.6 indoors and T11 outdoors, so giving a fairly large depth of field.

Lighting

The major development in lighting equipment was the increasing use of metal halide arc (HMI) lights, which now became available in more and more powerful forms. The major manufacturers – LTM, Arri, Ianiro, and Mole-Richardson – introduced 6 kW units in 1981, 12 kW units in 1984-85, and finally 18 kW units from 1989. Although the manufacturers claimed that the 12 kW lamp units were as powerful as old style 'Brute' arc spotlights, this was not quite true, and only became so when units with 18 kW bulbs appeared. Nevertheless, even before 1989, Brutes were being used less and less for large area fill light on bright sunlit exteriors, and likewise for night exteriors.

HMI bulbs also came to be used in soft light or north light units from 1981, when LTM put their Soft-Daylight lamps on the market, with wattages from 575 to 1200, in single and dual units. The main solution to the possibility of stroboscopic flicker in the image generated by the difference between the frequency of the camera shutter and that of the AC current driving the lights was the use of power generators whose frequency was accurately controlled to match that of the camera shutter. Lee Lighting continued to develop square wave ballast units that also eliminated the problem, but although they produced a model that would handle the current for a 12 kW HMI, such ballasts were large and heavy, and only the smaller models came to be used for small HMI lights.

The other major lighting unit developed with HMI lights in the United States was the Musco Mobile light, which was really a more sophisticated version of David Watkin's 'Wendy' light, by now known in America as well as Britain. The Musco mobile light was made up of 15 light-weight lamp heads, each containing a 6 kW HMI bulb, and fixed on a grid on top of a large mobile construction crane, which had a generator added to its chassis. In the initial 1983 form of the device, the angle and direction of the whole grid of lights could be remotely controlled, but on the improved 1985 model each lamp head could be directed independently from the ground after it was raised. Because of the speed with which it could be set up, the Musco mobile light became a popular solution to the rapid lighting of large-scale night location exteriors.

Another new lighting method was the use of racks of fluorescent light tubes as supplementary fill lighting, when filming location scenes that were mainly lit by existing fluorescent light fixtures. If possible, the fluorescent tubes in the existing fixtures on location interiors were replaced with tubes, specially made for film purposes, which had better suppression of the intense blue-green lines in the mercury spectrum, and which also had better general colour balance as well. Tubes from the Kinoflo company were favoured, particularly as some of these gave a higher intensity light than usual, and also could be dimmed to some extent. An example in point was *The Color of Money*, in which the pool table scenes were lit by fluorescents in the fixtures over the tables, and fill light was often supplied from outside the film frame by extra racks of fluorescents in the way mentioned. This practice became one of the standard ways of dealing with fluorescent lighting on location. The older method, which continued to have its adherents, was to over-ride the light level from the existing fluorescent fixtures with extra light of approximately the right colour from ordinary film tungsten lighting units.

Photographic Style

During the nineteen-eighties a great range of lighting styles co-existed in the American cinema. For example, an irredeemably old-fashioned item like *The Living Daylights* (1987) was lit by Alec Mills with direct light, and with diffusion on the lights, though not on the lens. On the other hand, Don Peterman used backlighting whenever possible on *Cocoon* (1985), though with soft lights providing the key light. Probably the largest group of cameramen believed in 'source lighting', but modified this as necessary with light from non-realistic directions when it was desired to get a more attractive image. A few insisted on using no lens diffusion, but then lit almost entirely with soft light, so that the resulting images still had enough softness to satisfy conventional ideas of attractiveness. The use of really hard lighting and clear lenses continued to be unknown, except for such a very idiosyncratic project as *Pink Floyd - The Wall*, which had the live action scenes lit with arcs with clear glass, and no lens filters. This fitted with the general unrealistic nature of the film, and in particular with the grotesque imagery of the animation sequences.

The great and innovative individualist Nestor Almendros continued with his minimalist approach, even on fairly straightforward commercial subjects, such a *Kramer vs. Kramer*. For *The Blue Lagoon* he returned to the improvised simplicity of his beginnings on *la Collectionneuse*. *The Blue Lagoon* was entirely filmed on location, and on the exteriors only fill light from the sun bounced off reflectors was used. The scenes inside the children's hut were done in a specially built hut that was partly open at the top, with diffusing silk over it, so that no artificial lighting was needed for the daytime scenes. The night scenes were shot with black fabric draped over the hut, but with open cracks to let in bits of daylight that registered as a blue night effect, because the scene was shot without the 85 conversion filter on the lens. However, some artificial light was used to reinforce the flame light in scenes involving a fire. On the other hand, for *Heartburn* he shot the main interior scenes on a studio set lit to a high level to give apertures of f5.6-f8 and deep focus. Nevertheless, this lighting was still applied as though coming from the apparent sources.

In 1987 Almendros turned against some of the trends he had initiated when he lit *Places in the Heart* with white light, and avoided sunsets and shooting at the 'magic hour'. It is worth pointing out that Almendros' techniques did require that he have quite a lot of control over stagings and scene dissection. For instance, on *Nadine* he had the positions of things in the scene changed, and in one scene he had a glass brick wall put into the set for a better lighting effect. Although Almendros much preferred to follow the Continental tradition of the lighting cameraman operating as well, in the United States he had to make do with the use of video monitoring of the viewfinder image to control what the camera operator was doing.

In general, a major theme of the decade was the greater use of coloured light in film photography. This had been developing at the end of the previous decade, but it had not gone much further than using the wrong colour imparted by existing light sources in location scenes. Now this effect came to be pushed much further in many films. A notable example of this trend was *Gremlins* (1984), for which John Hora used much coloured light, unjustified by any existing visible sources within the scenes. The bright colours were apparently the idea of the director, Joe Dante. There was a repeat performance, with even more exaggeration, in *Gremlins 2 - the New Batch* (1990), and the idea was much imitated. Whether this too is a passing trend remains to be seen.

As far as more serious subjects were concerned, coloured light was increasingly used as part of the more and more elaborate expressive schemes that some film-makers developed to go with the narratives of their films. The main influence here was Vittorio Storaro, who had begun to put forward such expressive programs to go with the lighting of the films he did for Bernardo Bertolucci in the previous decade. Such a Storaro programme for *One From the Heart*, with its would-be philosophical underpinnings, can be read in *The American Cinematographer* (Volume 63, No.1, p.22), and his most elaborate scheme so far was for *The Last Emperor*. In this film he claimed to be using as dominant colours for each scene the whole spectral range in succession, starting with red, and going through orange, yellow, etc. to violet, as the film wore on. Just where the art director's choices of colours for the sets and accessories of these films came into the matter has not so far been satisfactorily explained.

The low budget independent sector of American film-making was particularly fond of the use of striking and somewhat unrealistic colour schemes in both the lighting and the set design, and this was another source of the trend I have been describing. In particular, the very low budget features that were made by people associated with the New York 'New Wave' music and art scene tended to be in what they thought of as *film noir* style, plus a certain amount of alienation technique. A few of the personnel crossed over from one area to the other, such as the cameraman Ed Lachman, who lit *Union City* in 1979 for Mark Reichert. For this film Lachman

used coloured gels on the lights, on sets which were already unnaturally brightly coloured. Some years later on *Desperately Seeking Susan*, he collaborated in a highly designed colour presentation with the director, who herself had art training. The basic scheme was soft light and colours plus static camera for the suburban housewife's world, and primary colours with a more chiaroscuro feel plus moving camera for the punk's world. This latter effect was further emphasized by shooting on Eastman 5294 overexposed about one stop to give more saturated colours. Further than this, the designer and director had worked out designs with two distinct colour areas in a number of scenes. Lachman lit pink rooms with pink light, green with green, but left white light areas in the frame as well. The existing fluorescents in the locations were exaggerated with green gels on the film lights. I have described the principles consciously used by the film-makers in their lighting schemes in this film, but it seems to me that in this, and a number of other similar cases, the colour schemes used for the set design make a much stronger effect than the colour of the light played upon them.

Someone else who crossed over into more standard film-making from the New York independent scene was Johanna Heer. She had already lit Amos Poe's *Subway Riders* using unnatural coloured lighting, and then she was engaged to photograph Percy Adlon's 1986 *Sugarbaby*, on which she used gels and filters on nearly every shot. The first section of this film was in cooler greens and blues, which then moved to reds, oranges, and magentas as the heroine gets closer to THE MAN. The camera movements were also integrated with the narrative development.

In basic mainstream film-making, the expressive connotations of lighting were much more conventional, and indeed banal. For instance, in *Wall Street* (1987), as the aspiring young man who wants to get seriously wealthy becomes more involved with the big money man he admires, the light seen in the background on the windows becomes more golden. This was done by increasing the colour of the gels on the windows from to to full Wratten 85 filter material, but with daylight-balanced light inside. In scenes when money was involved, the camera made off-balance moves, and the shots were connected with hard cuts. In opposition to this, the scenes with the protagonist's morally upright father were shot with static frames and low angles.

By 1987 the idea of overexposing by to 1 stops to get better colour saturation and grain structure had become quite popular with the more adventurous directors of photography, particularly those working from New York. Lachman, Ballhaus, Judith Irola, Willis, and Dickerson were amongst those involved. Lachman also used polarizers and graduated filters to accentuate the saturated look on David Byrne's *True Stories*. Slightly more subtle was *Married to the Mob* (1988). Here cameraman Tak Fujimoto and director Jonathan Demme used red colour for the Mafia scenes, and blue light for those where the heroine was away from the Mob, with a progression from one to the other, and green and blue at the end of the film. They did not use No. 85 colour correcting filters on the windows for the Long Island scenes, allegedly to suggest the divided the nature of the heroine. The film also used yet another expressive device, which was making a small comeback in these years, namely Dutch tilts for suggesting tension in the scene.

Many other films with less detailed expressive programs in the use of lighting and lenses and camera placement included *Born on the Fourth of July, The Hot Spot, Frances, Heathers,* and *The Bonfire of the Vanities.*

The Dark Side of Science

The 'eighties were also notable for the application of low-key lighting to subjects for which it had previously been considered unsuitable. The first of these was science fiction. The fashion was probably set by *Alien* (1979), and it showed its power in the way it affected the photography of the *Star Wars* series of films. The first of these had the ordinary kind of mid-key lighting in general that one would expect on a children's adventure film, but in *The Empire Strikes Back* (1980) the lighting becomes fairly consistently low key, even on daylight exteriors such as the 'Ewok' scenes. Such an approach does have the virtue of concealing the matte lines in the many process shots in the film, although I don't believe that this was the reason for it. Another example from 1980 was the Disney Studio's *The Black Hole,* for which an overall low-key look was chosen at the design stage, and carried through with the photography following the designs carefully. Amongst other subsequent examples of this trend, the third in the Star Wars series, *The Return of the Jedi* was even darker throughout, and then there was *Bladerunner,* for which Ridley Scott naturally followed the style he had so successfully set in *Alien.* Although there were yet more followers, the automatic application of low-key lighting to science fiction films showed some signs of weakening by the end of the decade.

A New Angle on Comedy

Even stranger was the use of low-key lighting for some comedy subjects, giving a literal meaning to the phrase 'black comedy'. This appeared near the end of the decade with the first directorial effort of the actor Danny De Vito, *Throw Mama From the Train* (1988). Barry Sonnenfeld lit this with soft light without fill from bay lights, and kept the light off the walls, which were dark green and red. About half the shots were done with the new Panavision Primo 21 mm. lens, including close shots of Vito, but not the close shots of the other leads. There was quite possibly an influence here from his cameraman, Barry Sonnenfeld, who had made his name working with Joel and Ethan Coen on *Blood Simple* and *Raising Arizona* (1987), for which the brothers continually wanted to know if Sonnenfeld was making the shot look 'wacky enough'. The filming of *Raising Arizona* certainly did not pursue the idea of low-key photography to any great length, though it did use a lot of wide-angle lens shots from extreme positions.

In his subsequent comedy films Danny De Vito retreated a little from the low-key idea, but persisted with the use of wide angle lenses. Other films which applied low-key lighting to comedy subjects included *We're No Angels* (1990) and *I Love You to Death* (1990). All of these comedy films were not particularly big successes at the box-office, but it is impossible to say whether a lighting style which had previously been considered to be inappropriate for comedy had anything to do with this.

Other Wacky Ideas about Style

By now, it was not uncommon for films to consciously refer to earlier films in one way or another, and in the process some slightly off-centre ideas about the distinguishing stylistic features of old-time movies surfaced. For instance, Matt Leonetti claimed that his lighting of *Eyewitness* was in 'forties style because it had shadows on the walls. Other odd notions included John Bailey's claim that his photography of *The Accidental Tourist* was inspired by Egon Schiele, but he was more down-to-earth and believable in his claim that *American Gigolo* was shot with hard concentrated light without diffusion to get the look of French and Italian fashion photography. Stephen H. Burum was also more rational in supposing that the period feel of *The Untouchables* might be conveyed by looser framing with more space around the people, and the use of shorter focal length lenses without lens diffusion, except on Close Ups. He also avoided the use of an overall colour bias in his images for this film.

But the feather-brain award goes to Adrian Lyne for his belief that one of the things that will set his *Flashdance* apart from other contemporary masterworks such as *All That Jazz* and *Saturday Night Fever* was that '...one specific dance number was inspired by a Maxell tape commercial'.

Expressive Lens Use

As well as using non-standard lighting arrangements for expressive purposes, a number of directors, in collaboration with their cameramen, used different focal length lenses in different sections of their films with the intention of communicating the appropriate feelings to the cinema audience. For instance, in *Ordinary People,* which centered on the psychoanalysis of a disturbed youngster, the analysis sessions were filmed with a progression from 29 and 35 mm. to 75 to 100 mm. lenses as the film wore on. As usual, this was combined with lighting changes, which were naturalistically justified by the time of day. The last night meeting scene was shot with 150 to 200 mm. lenses, and an overhead 'coffin box' light plus a little bounce. Another example of an expressive scheme depending on focal length control was *Lost in America* (1985). This was shot with a 29 mm. lens until the dramatic turning point in the middle of the film, which was shot with a 1000 mm. lens, and then a zoom lens was used for the final New York scenes. An almost contrary approach to the possible expressive meaning of lens focal length was given by *Cocoon,* which was shot with colder lighting and wide angle lenses at first, and then shifted to warmer lighting and longer lenses when the rejuvenated old people began to feel better.

A Change of Speed

An expressive device which had been much used in the silent period, filming at non-standard speeds, was now extended into new areas. In a neat reversal, Barry Levinson's *Avalon* (1990), which had a frame story set in 1948-51, and flashbacks to 1914, 1926, and 1939, plus a flashforward to the 'sixties, had the silent period sequences shot at 16 fps. and then stretch-printed to 24 fps. A more technical development was to shoot sync. sound scenes in some films at speeds other than 24 fps. For *Top Gun* some scenes were shot at 28 fps., and all of *Deepstar Six* (1989) was shot at 22 fps to get feeling of frenetic activity. For these last two films the voice recordings were 'harmonized'; that is, the recording was varied to exactly match 24 fps., and then the pitch of the voices was altered electronically back to that of the originals. Such a trick depended on newly available electronic devices that could accomplish this.

Filming in Black and White

A minor trend to shooting a whole film in monochrome, which had just begun at the end of the previous decade, continued into the early 'eighties. For ordinary commercial projects this option was only available to film-makers of considerable standing. The notable instances of this were mostly Woody Allen films: *Stardust Memories, Manhattan, Zelig*, and *Broadway Danny Rose*. The other outstanding examples were Scorsese's *Raging Bull* and Coppola's *Rumblefish*. On the first of these the use of monochrome was due in part to Scorsese's worry at that time about the permanence of colour film stock, coupled with a justification because of the period setting of the film, while on the second the use was more purely wilful. The visual treatment of *Rumblefish* was also distinctive in that the Plus-X and XX negative was pushed into greater contrast in development, and most of the film was shot with wide-angle lenses, sometimes even a 9.8 mm. Shadows were sometimes painted onto the sets.

At the truly low budget end of feature film-making, there was much less to stop a director choosing to film in black and white, though this was no longer a way of making a cheaper film in the United States. By the end of the decade, shooting in black and white didn't really save much money in other Western countries either. But there continued to be intermittent examples of this, such as *Stranger Than Paradise* and *Last Night at the Alamo*. The director of the latter film in particular pretended that the incompetence of the lighting was a stylistic choice. (Its lighting left the figures darker than the background, and in general its photography was muddy in exactly the way that every other film made by absolute beginners manages without trying at all.) As for *Stranger Than Paradise*, some of the look of this film was due to it being shot with old short ends of film stock left over from Wim Wender's *Lightning Over Water*, which were then processed badly. As well as

that, it was also shot with fairly wide angle lenses of 18 and 25 mm. focal length, but since the camera height was mostly up around eye level, the general look of it was nothing like the old-style *Citizen Kane* wide-angle lens stagings.

Cameras

Around the beginning of the decade, the French Aäton company made a clever strategic alliance with the American Panavision company. The Aäton cameras filled a gap for lightweight cameras where Panavision had nothing, and in return Panavision promoted the Aäton time-code system in the United States. The Aäton 35 mm. camera, the 8-35, as it was now known, eventually came to be used by a few people other than J-L. Godard, when it became available from 1982 as a production model. In this final(?) form it weighed 7 kg, and had a noise level of 32 dB at one metre, as long as it was enclosed in a soft blimp. It was first used on a Hollywood film in *Triumph of the Spirit* (1990), for some scenes which required hand-held sync. sound, as this was the only good reason for using it. As might be expected from its quoted noise level, the Aäton 8-35 proved to be not as silent as might be desired. The 16 mm. Aäton camera continued its successful career all over the world, and in particular it was the camera most used for filming in Super-16, in part because its standard version was now built so that it could be immediately adapted for this process. Although Panavision themselves finally produced a 16 mm. camera in 1984, the Panaflex-16, they clearly did this just because they felt they had to protect themselves, in case filming in 16 mm. became generally accepted for American TV production. Actually the Panaflex-16 made no impression in the 16 mm. field, but for the record I note that it was essentially the same as the 35 mm. Panaflex.

Arnold & Richter continued to make detailed improvements in their Arriflex range. The 35BL passed through a series of models; the 35BL-III in 1980, and the 35BL-4 in 1988, by which time they claimed to have got the noise level down under 20 dBA, and then finally the Arriflex 535. Although this last was still in essence the same camera, it had redesigned body castings, and more built-in electronics. The most important of the electronics was an electrical interlinking of the variable shutter and the aperture diaphragm, so that changes in either one of these during the course of the shot would change the other to keep the exposure automatically constant. The Arriflex 535 also had a built-in SMPTE time code and Kodak Keycode generator. Its other new feature was a modification to the view-finder system so that it could be swung over from the left to the right side of the camera if desired. The viewfinder also included a set of illuminated frame markings on the ground glass viewing screen, which made it much easier for the camera operator to see what he was including in the picture under low light levels. In fact these improvements were designed to keep the Arri 35 mm. sync. sound camera competitive with the Panaflex camera, for these two companies, together with Moviecam, were the only major ones left in the competition to sell new professional

35 mm. cameras.

Of course various other companies tried to produce new 35 mm. cameras, mostly based on the Mitchell movement, particularly in the United States, but none of these made any lasting impression, whether they were from Cinema Products (the CP 35), Continental Camera (the Feathercam CM35), or anyone else.

There was even more activity in 65 mm. camera design, in part because of the demand for cameras to take special effects shots for later optical combination, and in part because of excitement about special projection systems such as Douglas Trumbull's 'Showscan' process. This last was essentially just the existing 70 mm. process, but shot and projected at 60 frames per second. In 1987 Cinema Products produced a 65 mm. camera specially for the Showscan company, the CP-65, which was claimed to be the first self-blimped 65 mm. camera with mirror reflex shutter ever made. (The earlier quiet cameras for 65 mm. were of the old Mitchell type, with rackover viewing system, and no reflex shutter.) Todd-AO also made a rather crude 'new' 65 mm. camera by putting mirror shutters on old Mitchell AP 65 mm. cameras, but despite all this effort, the Showscan system did not catch on. In 1989, just in case, Arri also produced a brand new 70 mm. camera based on their 35 BL, called the 765, which naturally was also self-blimped, and had a mirror reflex viewfinding system, and was a lot smaller and handier than the rest, to boot. All of these cameras had crystal controlled motors with fixed speeds of 24, 30, and 60 frames per second, so they could be used for ordinary filming and television filming, as well as for Showscan. The Arri 765 also had continuously variable speeds from 2 frames per second up to 100 frames per second, and was available with a complete set of new Zeiss lenses, which should be altogether conclusive in this competition.

There were also a number of individually hand-made Vistavision cameras produced during the decade, basically for the benefit of the independent special effects companies.

Lenses

There was a certain amount of improvement in lens construction during the decade, mostly centering on the use of new types of glass for some elements of the lens. These special glasses, which were mostly of the fluophosphate type, had higher refractive indices than had been practicable before. Such glass made it possible to design lens combinations which were nearer the theoretical ideal, and of course there continued to be improvements in the computerized design systems that the lens manufacturers used. The dominant companies specializing in professional movie camera lenses were now Zeiss, Rank Taylor-Hobson, and Angénieux, with the latter two specializing in zoom lenses, and Zeiss making very successful fixed focal length lenses as well as zoom lenses. Rank Taylor-Hobson continued to make anamorphic lenses for the Technovision system, which was available in Britain and the United States, as well as in Italy. Panavision had its own lenses, both anamorphic and spherical, made for it by the Canadian Leitz company, and a new range of spherical lenses called the Primo range were introduced in 1987. These had maximum apertures of about T1.4, clearly intended to compete with the Zeiss Superspeed range which had been available for several years, and as usual these Primo lenses were only available for hire as part of the whole Panavision royalty-payment camera package.

On the zoom lens side, the new Angénieux designs adopted the Taylor-Hobson practice of having the front element of the lens fixed and non-rotating, though they were unable to produce a design that would also focus at distances closer than 80 cm., as most cameramen prefer. There continued to be quite a bit of small-scale activity in converting Canon and Nikon still camera lenses for use on movie cameras. To serve well in this way, these lenses had to be rebuilt with new stronger barrels, as the construction of still camera lenses is too flimsy to stand up to film use. Zoom lenses which were converted also had to be realigned, as they were prone to image drift during a change in focal length. This does not matter for still photography, but is fatal for film purposes. Those still camera lenses that were converted had focal lengths in special ranges, like the Canon 20 to 35 mm. zoom, which was adapted to get a really lightweight variable focal length lens for Steadicam use.

Camera Supports

As far as moving cameras about in space goes, there were both major and minor developments. To start at the less significant end, the Italian Elemack company, which had acquired a major part of the market for relatively lightweight location dolly equipment long ago with its Spyder (or Octopus) crab dolly, produced an improved version in the Cricket dolly. This was essentially the same as the Spyder, but with the hydraulic rise and fall of the centre column carrying the camera head powered by an electric pump, rather than relying on manually, or rather pedally, created pressure. This meant that the camera could be raised and lowered during the shot, rather than it being a somewhat jerky operation that had to take place between shots. In 1983 the German Panther company introduced a dolly with that name, which was very similar to the Elemack, but with the rise and fall of the camera support column powered directly by an electric motor. The Panther dolly had its wheels set to the same width as those of the Elemack dollies, so that it could run on what had become the standard tracking, and just like the Elemack, its bogie wheels could be changed from rimmed wheels for use on tracks to rubber wheels for use on tracking boards, or indeed on other existing smooth hard flat surfaces. The Panther had quite a lot of success.

The Dutch Egripment company was also very successful with lightweight camera supports. The standard camera cranes made by Chapman and others were excessively large and heavy for the kind of equipment now used in this period, which had to be moved faster and faster from one location to another. The old-style cranes usually had built-in motors to power them during tracking shots, and to move them from place to place. This was not really necessary for the medium size cranes supporting the newer lighter cameras, and because of improvements in materials, it was now possible to build lattice girder jib arms lighter, but with sufficient strength. This is where Egriment scored with its 'Tulip' crane, introduced at the beginning of the 'eighties, and they built on this with an improved model, the 'Piccolo', at the end of the decade. These cranes had a total rise and fall of about 15 feet, and fitted on to a fairly small dolly. In theory they could carry the camera operator and focus-puller as well as the camera on the platform on the end of the jib arm, but their stability was not particularly good when used for complicated crane movements loaded with two people in this way. This was not a serious objection, given the increasing use of video viewfinders and remote focus control.

Remote control

The idea of using remote control of the panning and tilting movements of cameras gained more and more ground during this decade. The Louma crane, which had been used on a number of films for several years previously, was joined by various other devices incorporating electric motors driving a pan and tilt head that could be attached to any standard camera support system. These came to be called generically 'hot heads', and the first of them was the Nettman Cam-Remote system, which became available from 1984. Fairly inevitably its facility for rotating the camera through 360 was straightaway used by Francis Coppola on *Cotton Club*. Other very similar devices appearing in the next few years included the Power Pod head and the Technovision Sputnik. These devices allied themselves naturally with the ever-expanding use of motion control, which got more sophisticated as the decade progressed, and as computer power for the controlling of the motion became more sophisticated and cheaper. In 1980 the major special effects companies such as Industrial Light and Magic were still using mini-computer systems for motion control, with the control data stored on tape drives, but by the end of the 'eighties ordinary microcomputers could easily do the job. For instance, the Ultimatte Memory Head was produced as a standard product in 1988. It had the feel of fluid head, and it recorded moves and zooms and focus pulls onto 3.5 inch diskettes, after which it could then repeat them exactly.

There were also more elaborate combinations of devices, such as putting motion control heads together with specially modified dollies into a package that could be used on location, rather than only in a specially built studio environment, as had been the case in the previous decade. One such combination was Industrial Light and Magic's 'Tondreau dolly' or 'Vista-glide', built in 1989. This was essentially a Panther dolly with extra wheels attached to measured its position along its path, and then feeding the data to the motion control computer, which in turn controlled the motors driving the wheels. This motion-controlled dolly was used on *Back to the Future - Part*

II to produce split-screen effects for the doubling of characters, not only on interiors, but also when they were walking around outside followed by a tracking camera. Although the use of split-screen double exposure to let the same actor act with himself or herself had been accomplished during panning shots in ancient times, doing it while simultaneously tracking had been impossible up to this point. The same effect was also achieved in *Dead Ringers*, with a similar system.

The use of the Steadicam camera support device increased throughout the decade, and in particular it was used more and more as a substitute for standard tracking shots in general, and not just because physical cirumstances made the use of tracks and a dolly impossible. This trend occurred because of the production pressures mentioned at the beginning of this chapter. (Laying tracks for a tracking shot takes quite a while, not to mention the number of rehearsals needed to co-ordinate the efforts of the dolly-pushing grips, camera operator and focus-puller.) A novel intermediate strategy to increase production speed in this area was to have a Steadicam operator riding a pneumatic-tyred dolly over a rough surface, instead of attempting to get a smooth dolly movement by laying levelled tracks in the old way. Other devices were invented which attempted to mimic some of the virtues of the Steadicam, the most notable and noticeable of which was the 'Shakicam'. This was a crude hand-made improvisation invented by the cameraman Caleb Deschanel for the film *More American Graffiti*, and it consisted of a 12 foot length of 2' by 2' timber, with cross pieces used as carrying handles at each end. A wild Arriflex with a very wide angle lens (usually 9.8 mm.) was fixed to the centre of the beam at right angles to it, and the contraption was used to get a high speed tracking shot close to the ground, by having it carried forwards at running speed by two grips who held each end of the beam. The flexibility of the beam acted as a spring smoothing out the joggling caused by the irregularity in the running motion of its carriers. It was subsequently applied for shock effects in a number of cheap films made by such people as the Coen brothers and Sam Raimi.

Garrett Brown himself attempted to top his Steadicam with the ultimate remote camera movement device, which he called the Skycam. This had a camera mounted at the bottom of a vertical shaft with a counterweight at the other end, the shaft being suspended by a gimbal joint near its centre, just like that of the Steadicam when it was used in the underslung position. The directional control which the cameraman's hand provided for the Steadicam was here supplied by electric motors driving sector gears on the vertical shaft at the gimbal fulcrum point. The whole device was suspended in mid-air by four lines coming through pulleys at the top of four tall towers set up at the corners of the area to be covered by the general horizontal movement of the camera. This movement in the horizontal plane was accomplished by the four support wires being paid out and/or reeled in at differential rates from four electrically driven winch drums at the base of the support pillars. All the motors involved were under computer control, regulated by positional feed-back to the control program. Brown got this very complicated device to work more or less properly in 1984, when it was used for one shot in *Birdy*. It was also used briefly on *The Slugger's Wife*, but although commercially available since then, the device is obviously not very practical for ordinary film production.

Special Wide Screen Systems

Filming in Super-16 continued to be used in a small way on some low budget films during the nineteen-eighties, particularly in Sweden, where Rune Ericsson, one of its originators, now ran a film laboratory, and energetically promoted the system. To some extent its use was a matter of fashion. For instance, a group of films backed by the British Film Institute Production Board in the early 'eighties, starting with Peter Greenaway's *The Draughtsman's Contract*, were shot in Super-16, but this institutional promotion died out, and certainly Greenaway preferred to have his subsequent films shot in ordinary 35 mm. Although a number of low budget American films also used the process at the beginning of the decade, most notably Robert Altman's *Come Back to the Five and Dime, Jimmy Dean, Jimmy Dean* (1982), the enthusiasm for Super-16 tended to die down there as well. At the same time, other well known directors in the 'independent' sector, such as John Sayles, were perfectly happy to use ordinary 16 mm. film, and then blow that up to 35 mm. for wide-screen projection in the standard way. The truth of the matter is that even with the best of the negative stocks, Eastman Color 7247, the quality of a Super-16 blow-up to 35 mm. was still visibly inferior to ordinary 35 mm., and the use of the process did not save that much money, even on a low budget film.

Eventually, someone had the idea of applying similar concepts to 35 mm. film, and 'Super 35 mm.', and other new 'Supers', were born. All of these new filming processes involved letting the picture image extend into the area of the camera negative reserved for the future sound track on the final print; or in other words, returning to the use of the full silent aperture for recording the picture. This was possible with most of the major professional cameras, just by replacing the film aperture plate in the gate of the camera. The first of the various alternatives now taken up was SuperTechniscope. This involved shooting with ordinary spherical lenses, and composing for an image of 'Scope shape which extended across the top of the full silent aperture, and down the frame to a little below the half-way mark. The negative was then printed with a near 2:1 vertical anamorphic expansion on an optical printer. This was almost the same as the Technicolor company's previous Techniscope system, and the same optical printers could be used with a slight adjustment. The differences from Techniscope were firstly that the same footage of negative was used as in ordinary filming, instead of half the amount as with the old Techniscope system, and secondly that there was a slight improvement in definition over the old Techniscope, as a result of the slightly greater negative area used.

One of the first films made using the SuperTechniscope system was *Greystoke* (1984), and in this case the bottom of the frame was masked off in the gate of the camera during exposure to give a 1:1.85 aspect ratio negative image. The process was not worked this way in general, so that the bottom strip of the exposed image that was not used for the 'Scope prints for theatrical exhibition could be recovered for video and television exhibition. It turned out that, unlike the original Techniscope, Technicolor could not patent this variant process, so other laboratories could use it as well, as they did under the general title of Super 35. Yet another slight variant was Super 1.85. In this case the full silent aperture was exposed, but the essential action was kept within what was roughly the top 2/3 of the frame, in an area with the aspect ratio of 1:1.85. In this case too, the full height of the aperture be used to generate the TV and video copies if desired, as long as nothing unwanted had crept into the bottom of the full frame. Of course, to make the theatrical release prints, the top 1:1.85 wide-screen part of the negative image had to be reduced slightly, and also displaced to one side to fall within the usual Academy aperture area, so leaving the sound track area free. This process was said to have been invented by Jim Dickson for the TV series *Counsellor*.

A filming system which was related to these ideas was that of using a three perforation pull-down in 35 mm. filming, rather than the standard film advance of 4 perforations for each exposure. This process naturally gives a wide screen image of aspect ratio almost 1:1.85, if the full width of the film between the sprocket holes is used. Because this idea had been suggested at various times in the past, no-one could patent the idea, though Rune Ericsson, in alliance with Panavision, did manage to copyright the *name* 'Three- perf.' for the process. This did not get them anywhere, since anybody could still talk about and advertise 'three-perf*oration*' filming. It was fairly easy to adjust most cameras to give a three perforation pull-down, and by the end of the decade the facility was being built into the newest model cameras from the major makers. The idea proved quite popular with American television production companies, for whom the 25% reduction in negative stock costs was important, even though for present television purposes they did not need to use the full width of the image, but only the central part of it, to give a picture with the usual TV aspect ratio. But it did give them protection for future exploitation of their product in widescreen 'High Definition Television' (HDTV). Given the continual improvement in the definition of negative stocks, it is probable that some form of Super 35 has a very good future for feature film-making, as it enables ordinary spherical lenses to be used, and so the depth of field problems with anamorphic lenses can be avoided.

As might be expected, given the involvement of Rune Ericsson, 'Three-perf.' is used quite a bit in Swedish film-making. Another money-saving Swedish trick used in recent times is to reduce film shot on 35 mm. to 16 mm. for editing, and then to conform the 35 mm. negative to the cutting copy of the final prints. These things are not usually done in other European countries.

3-D

There was yet another brief burst of interest in stereoscopic filming in 1982. Nearly all the features produced used what were now described as the 'under-over' processes. These took left and right eye images in 'Scope proportions, and shifted them with a special prism system into the area of one ordinary 35 mm. frame, where they appeared like two Techniscope frames one above the other. The final print was made by contact printing from this negative, and another special prism and lens system on the projector put them into superimposition on the cinema screen, after they had passed through the usual Polaroid filters. The audience viewed through glasses with Polaroid lenses as usual too. The most popular stereoscopic system of this type was now Arrivision, though another called Depix did quite well while the craze lasted. The films themselves were all from the exploitation end of American production, though some had more money spent on them than others. One of the main intentions was to give a bit of a lift to the third repetition of series items like *Jaws 3-D*, *Amityville 3-D*, and *Friday 13th - Part 3*.

Special Effects

The major innovations in special effects technique during this period revolved around the use of motion control, which I have already dealt with. The blue screen travelling matte process continued to be the major means of producing composite images, and even the Disney studios dropped the sodium light process for *The Black Hole* and subsequent films. The main process competing with blue screen for producing composite images was front projection, with rear projection running third. A minor new idea in travelling mattes was the 'reverse blue screen' process. This was only applicable to combining shots of moving models with other moving images, and involved photographing the model against a totally black ground, and then coating it with a transparent paint that phosphoresced under ultra-violet light. A second pass was filmed with the model illuminated by ultra-violet light, and repeating its movements exactly under motion control, so generating the matte that would hold back the background image where the model was. The point about this was that it was possible to reproduce objects with shiny surfaces and recessed areas without partial print-through of the background scene. The first film this process was used on was *Firefox* (1982), and it reappeared thereafter on appropriate occasions.

Another minor innovation in the increasing use of moving puppets in fantasy films was what was called 'go-motion'. When object animation is done in the conventional way, the puppet or other object is moved only between the exposure of each individual frame. But for what are meant to be seen as fast moving objects, this produces a jerky, flickery effect, since in the real world fast-moving objects produce a streaked-

out image on each frame when filmed conventionally. In 'go motion' animation the model is moved by remote control while the shutter is open to get this more realistic effect. It was first used on *Dragonslayer*, and subsequently on *Young Sherlock Holmes* and other films.

Computer Animation

Almost as soon as computer animation was developed to a reasonably high level it was used to create scenes for movies. In *Tron* (1982) it was only used to a limited extent, despite the fact that most of the story of this fantasy took place inside a computer, where more or less anything might be considered acceptable. Contrary to appearances, most of the film was done with conventional animation; the only exception being the Long Shots of the imaginary futuristic vehicles doing this and that. A higher level of realism was achieved in the space scenes in *The Last Starfighter* (1984), in which 230 scenes were created with computer graphics; i.e. about 20 minutes running time in total. Part of the reason for this script being made was that John Whitney Jr. had been looking for something to show off the computer animation which his firm was able to produce, using the most powerful supercomputer available at the time. The computer images were produced to a resolution of about 2000 lines, but even so, the definition of the computer-generated pictures was appreciably inferior to that of the live action parts of the film. Since 1984 Kodak has moved the goalposts again, with the increased resolution of its latest stocks.

Video for Film

Given the money the Sony Corporation was prepared to put into promoting its high definition television system (HDTV), it was inevitable that someone would be persuaded to shoot a production on HDTV that was at least partly intended for ordinary theatrical release in cinemas. In 1987 *Julia and Julia* (also known as *Borderlines*) was shot on Sony HDTV in Italy, and then transferred to film in Japan. The film prints were given the ENR treatment using an extra black and white developing bath to add silver to the blacks. The next year a feature length pop music film, *Do It Up*, was shot on HDTV. Both these films didn't get anywhere much as far as theatrical release was concerned. Again, the definition offered after transfer from HDTV to film was noticeably inferior to that of straight 35 mm. film, and in any case broadcast HDTV is still far from being established.

There were also isolated attempts to use video techniques for producing film special effects, of which the most prominent was in *Flash Gordon* (1983). For this film six matte shots were composited in an electronic optical printer at 3,300 lines resolution, which in theory is about equal to ordinary 35 mm. film resolution, and then transferred back from video to film for the final print. Despite the very high video resolution used, there was still some slight loss in definition compared to travelling matte shots done in the conventional film way, probably due to imperfections in the video to film transfer process, so nothing more was heard of the idea.

Sound

There were only detailed improvements in the established means of recording film sound during the decade, and the microphones and recorders used stayed essentially the same as before. Although digital tape recording became standard in the music recording industry, its application to film was limited. This was basically because digital tape recorders remained bulky and expensive, and because the extra fidelity obtainable in this way was likely to be lost on the reproduction of a film sound track in even the best equipped cinema. However, starting around the middle of the decade, the background music for some Disney Studio films was digitally recorded, and the digital recording was retained through the mixing stages. Examples include *Something Wicked This Way Comes*, *Splash*, and *Country*.

Another dubbing studio idea from the television industry was also tried out in a limited way. This was the mixing of ordinary analogue sound-tracks on 2 inch multi-track sound tape synchronized to a video copy of the picture track. This approach was particularly relevant to a few films for which the sound effects were synthesized electronically, such as *Tron*. The creation of synthesized effects was almost entirely confined to some science fiction films, such as *Star Trek* and *The Final Countdown*. In all of these cases the final mix with the voice tracks was done using conventional film dubbing equipment, with the sound tracks on 35 mm. perforated magnetic film, and with the film being projected in sync. in the old way.

Total use of digital recording all through the various stages of film production and exhibition is sure to come eventually, and it has already appeared in the final stage of film sound reproduction, with the first use of the Cinema Digital Sound system in 1990. This system was the result of a collaboration between Kodak and Optical Radiation Corporation. It involves the digital recording of dots representing binary digits across and down the sound track area, with 6 separate sound channels and 2 control tracks encoded on both 35mm. and 70 mm.prints of a film. The way it is done is that sound for each of the eight tracks is encoded digitally, and then interleaved into a single digital stream. This stream is subdivided into 180 parallel streams and these are recorded down the sound track area of special very fine grain negative, using a row of LEDs to give 180 tracks of microscopic width made up of a succession of microscopic black and white dots, which represent digital zeros and ones. The final print is made by printing this special sound track negative and the picture negative in succession in the conventional way. Under a microscope the sound track area looks rather like a long crossword puzzle that hasn't been filled in. The sound is recorded in advance of the picture, just like the standard film magnetic sound track used to be on CinemaScope prints, and it is read by a CCD sensor above the projector gate near the position of the conventional magnetic track heads. The CCD sensor has a row of 512 light sensitive spots across the track

width, and no matter how the track weaves about, all the 180 individual tracks are picked up. The encoding is to the same standard as ordinary domestic compact discs, with 16-bit words streaming at 44.1 kHz.

The Cinema Digital Sound system has already been used on *Dick Tracy* and *Days of Thunder* in 70 mm. form. However, Dolby Laboratories has demonstrated another similar system, in which a digital track is recorded in blocks between the sprocket holes of the print, and since this new Dolby system enables the print to retain an ordinary conventional analogue sound track as well, the odds are that this will become the standard in the 'nineties.

There were minor improvements in the control of the post-synchronization of film sound in dubbing theatres, all centering on the application of computer control. The most generally applied methods were called Automatic Dialogue Replacement (ADR), but this name gives a much-exaggerated idea of what was basically a system of automatic control of exactly when the sounds to replaced the guide track are brought up in relation to the picture. There are also patented systems, such as 'Wordfit', which do actually seek out the synchronism point between the sounds on the guide track and those produced for the re-recorded track, and electronically mould the latter to fit, without human intervention, but they have not yet become generally used.

New Editing Systems

The major developments affecting editing were time code systems, and the related methods for editing film using a videotape transfer of the original rushes. In most Western countries there was some use of time coding from 1984 onwards for music films shot with multiple cameras, but otherwise its use was restricted to some television programmes made on film. In the United States the Aäton system, which conformed to the SMPTE standard for time coding, was promoted by Panavision, and its first use in 35 mm. was for the *Star Trek* TV series in 1987. There was also use of the earlier EBU system in 16 mm. in Europe. After fairly careful trials, there was a strong feeling in the United States that the use of time coded rushes offered absolutely no advantage if the editing was done on the old-style 'Hollywood' moviolas, which many editors still preferred.

The other new development of some significance was the use of video systems for editing material shot and finally released on film. As I have noted in the **Production Procedures** section of this chapter, Francis Coppola tried out a specially constructed video editing system on his 1982 film *One From the Heart*, but he subsequently abandoned this part of his production methods. As the decade wore on, a similar system called Ediflex became increasingly accepted for the production of television series in the United States, and to a limited extent elsewhere. This worked by making multiple video copies of the rushes onto 1/2 inch cassettes from the developed negative, using a standard telecine, which applied *television* time coding to them. The uncut shots were organ-

American 1976-1981

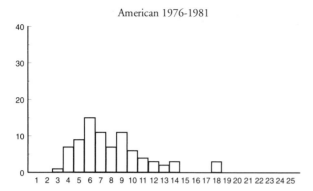

American 1982-1987

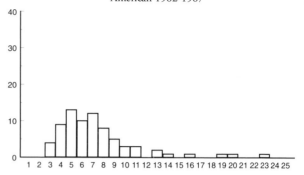

ized into groups on the videocassettes according to the scenes they were to fall into in the finished film. These video cassettes were run simultaneously on banks of videocassette players under computer control, so that experimental cuts from one shot to another could be tried out very quickly using a videotape editing system. The editing points chosen were then recorded on the computer system so that a 1/2 inch videotape edited version could be automatically assembled and studied as the editing process continued. Two other variants of this idea were attempted under the trade names of Montage and Editdroid, the latter being a joint venture of Convergence Corporation and George Lucas. These two systems, which used the slightly more sophisticated idea of intermediate video recordings onto large capacity magnetic disks, encountered various financial and technical problems on the way to market, though they were functioning by the end of the 'eighties. By this time there finally came to be a few feature films edited on videotape, including Bertolucci's *The Sheltering Sky*.

Editing

The indications are that the small retreat by some American directors from a very fast cutting rate that had begun at the end of the 'seventies continued into this decade. A sample of 75 films from the six year period 1982-1987 (inclusive) gives a mean value for the ASL of 8.4 seconds, which is the same as that for the previous six year period, and the distribution of ASLs across the range looks pretty much the same. Nevertheless, the most popular values continue to be around 6 seconds, and this is still also the point around which most of the more commercial films lie. The greater spread in values for this variable reflects the fact that some directors such as Martin Scorsese slowed down in the cutting rates they used over

the decade.

It was now rare to have a mainstream film that used nothing but jump cuts for transitions between scenes, and much more usual to see the use of a mixture of old-style dissolves and fades for the scene transitions, spiced up with just a few jump cuts. (e.g. *The Postman Always Rings Twice.*) Some directors dropped the use of jump cuts altogether.

There was a very definite trend, as part of the ever-increasing increasing self-consciousness of American movie directors, towards breaking the 'rules' of scene dissection. Scorsese is an obvious example again here, and is reported by his regular editor Thelma Schoonmaker as making cuts 'unsmooth' on purpose, and this can readily be observed in such films as *The Color of Money*. This trend reached the point where even Clint Eastwood sometimes 'crossed the eyeline' on purpose in his films. The intention was always of course expressive, though I must remind the reader again that the extent to which this is effective with the average audience is questionable.

And a New Trend in Movie Construction?

As we enter the nineteen-nineties, there are some signs that the conventional wisdom about the best sort of script construction to use for box-office success may be wrong. There have begun to appear extremely successful films, such as *Total Recall*, which do not have the traditional alternation of types of dramatic scene, but are almost totally made up of tense action scenes. Some of these films are also lacking in dramatic logic as well, but this does not seem to harm them in the least at the box-office. It will be interesting to see if this is just a temporary anomaly, or whether it portends a truly new trend in film construction.

22. STYLISTIC ANALYSIS OF THE FILMS OF MAX OPHULS

The analytic tools and ideas that I have put forward can now be applied to the discussion of the work of one individual film-maker, and even extended further in the process. In a way, this is an attempt to bridge the gap between the work in the earlier part of this book and something like ordinary film criticism. As always, the analysis is to be conducted in terms of how the films concerned were put together, which is an approach that has been neglected in ordinary critical writing in favour of treating films in terms of how a particular member of the audience sees them. There is also usually the further assumption that everyone sees the films in the same way as the critic. The advantage of making an analysis in terms of how a film was constructed is that if one gets it right, the analysis will always be correct, since the relation of a film to its makers is fixed for all time, whereas the way members of an audience perceive a film varies from one person to another, and even more from one period of time to another, depending on both subjective factors and also on passing intellectual fashions. If you need to be convinced of this, think about how little you value most of the comment written about films a few decades ago. And this process is even more apparent in the older arts. I am not saying here that critical comment which is shot through with subjectivity in the usual way does not have its uses, either as entertainment, or even in giving a hint as to which films might be worth seeing, given that we have some experience of how the subjective responses of a particular critic chime with our own. And it can sometimes, but not always, turn out that subjective criticism is correct by more objective standards. At this point I must say once more that objectivity is not an absolute quantity, but something that one can have more or less of, and when dealing with subjects of great complexity such as art there is no point in pursuing it beyond reason. Since few have even set out on this hunt, it is something just to have begun it.

In my discussion a number of aspects of Max Ophuls' films will be analysed more carefully than they have been before, and they will be related to their context in a way that has also been neglected. Amongst other things that will emerge is that Ophuls' style varied more than is usually supposed. Only after this analysis, which has been kept as free of value judgements as possible, will the question of the excellence of Ophuls' films

be considered, using the results of the analysis in combination with a set of criteria that are the most objective possible. I will also make some comments on the interpretation of Max Ophuls' films using what we know of their maker as a check for validity.

The basic information about Ophuls and his films contained in *Max Ophuls - An Index* by Richard Roud (British Film Institute, 1958) is complementary to my analysis.

Beginnings

Max Ophuls' first films derive their style directly from features already common in German films of the years 1930-32, and most particularly from the now almost forgotten musicals of those years. Indeed, Ophuls' first work in film was as dialogue director on one of those German musicals made in 1930, *Nie wieder Liebe*, and although in that year the Germans, unlike the Americans, had not got their cameras moving again, the position was radically changed by 1931. This is very apparent from the figures for camera movement in *Kameradschaft* (Pabst, 1931), *Der Kongress tanzt* (Erik Charell, 1931), and *Ich bei Tag und Du bei Nacht* (Ludwig Berger, 1932) which are quoted in the table on the next page. Ophuls' first films do not have such extensive camera movement, and in fact it only begins to appear in his films with *Die verkaufte Braut* (1932) and *Liebelei* (1933), and even then it does not surpass its source, as can be seen from the figures quoted. The massive success of *Der Kongress tanzt*, even on the international scale, proved a shining example, and Ophuls' early films are attempts to convert the material he had in hand to something as much like it as possible. The camera movement in *Der Kongress tanzt* was used to follow people about at a ball, on staircases, and travelling in a carriage in a way that has come to be regarded as uniquely Ophuls, though Ophuls' way was not fully established until after World War 2, as the tabulation of camera movement clearly shows. Besides this major source for the style of Ophuls' films, one can also recognize specific individual features that derive from the work of other film-makers, in particular from René Clair's *A nous la liberté* (1931), and von Sternberg's *Die blaue Engel* (1930) and *Morocco* (1930).

We can also see from the histograms of Scale of Shot

	Pan	Tilt	Pan with Tilt	Track	Track with Pan	Track with Pan & Tilt	Crane
Die lachenden Erben	17	1	3	15	6	1	0
Die verliebte Firma	27	1	6	5	4	4	0
Die verkaufte Braut	41	2	5	14	7	5	1
Liebelei	100	0	15	17	17	3	0
La signora di tutti	42	4	7	59	31	14	1
Komedie om geld	17	1	10	25	15	16	1
la Tendre ennemie	22	6	1	32	22	3	0
Yoshiwara	28	6	6	27	10	4	2
Werther	68	0	5	17	31	5	0
Sans lendemain	39	0	5	12	30	5	1
De Mayerling à Sarajevo	48	4	4	18	15	4	2
The Exile	29	1	17	19	37	22	17
Letter from an Unknown Woman	67	2	14	22	59	10	10
Caught	23	2	12	30	65	25	0
The Reckless Moment	92	2	21	24	62	11	3
la Ronde	49	5	9	26	39	24	5
le Plaisir	87	4	28	17	72	42	31
Madame de ...	64	4	18	13	77	39	3
Lola Montès	52	8	19	19	62	54	9
Der Kongress tanzt	50	3	13	59	55	20	8
Kameradschaft	53	7	13	23	42	3	7
Ich bei Tag und Du bei Nacht	34	9	28	33	49	29	1
Madame Bovary (1949)	49	2	5	50	37	12	4
Back Street (1941)	13	0	6	12	19	5	2

Number of Shots with Given Kinds of Camera Movement per 500 Shots for the Named Films

distributions on the next page that *Kameradschaft* has a Scale of Shot distribution almost identical with one that was to be characteristic of *Liebelei* and some subsequent Ophuls' films, though this is not particularly remarkable, since such distributions with emphasis on the use of Medium Shots and more distant shots commonly occur in long take filming of all periods, though most markedly so at the beginning of the 'thirties. And the films we are concerned with here *are* long take films, containing many takes minutes long, as is indicated by the Average Shot lengths, which for both *Liebelei* and *Der*

Kongress tanzt are 17 seconds, and for *Kameradschaft* 12 seconds.

What *was* unusual and innovative in Max Ophuls' approach from *Liebelei* onwards was to apply features which were characteristic of early German musicals to films that were not musicals. At this point in his career, as later, the use of mood music (commonly called background music) was important to Ophuls' strategy, though in most other dramatic films made before 1933 only 'featured' music (i.e. music whose source is visible in the filmed scene) is used. In one

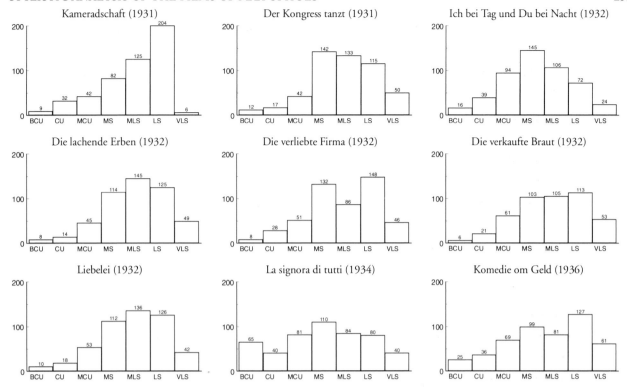

Number of Shots with Given Scale of Shot per 500 Shots for the Named Films

instance in *Liebelei* featured music from the opera house orchestra is turned into mood music by carrying it on beneath succeeding scenes.

Die lachenden Erben

It might seem at first sight that Ophuls' first long film, *Die lachenden Erben* (1931), is an exception to what I have said in a previous chapter about the difficulties of mixing mood music with dialogue at that date, since it has background music running almost continuously under whole sequences. But in fact this film was not released till 1933, and it seems that the producers took advantage of the improvement that had then taken place in sound re-recording to lay in the music track to salvage a work of doubtful commercial potential. Given this modification of the film, it is not surprising that the mood music has no relation to the movement within the scenes, except in one instance. In a sequence on a pleasure steamer on the Rhine the featured music from an orchestra and chorus accompanies a short section of film containing rhythmical movements by waiters, crew, and passengers, but this is in no way superior to similar things in previous musicals from German directors. The same sequence indicates a real weakness in Ophuls' technique, for scenic shots of the passing Rhine landscape are cut bang on the first beat of every eight bars of the song. The same defect is apparent in his later filming of Brailowsky playing Chopin's 'Grande Valse Brillante' in the film of that name (1937), and it indicates that Ophuls took the right course in relying on a loose combination between the music and movement within the frame to

get his effects in later films, rather than on matching musical rhythms to the visual rhythms created by cutting.

The static nature of *Die lachenden Erben* is sufficiently indicated by the figures for camera movement, though after a very stiff opening indeed there is a slight increase in this through the course of the film.

Die verliebte Firma

Die verliebte Firma (1931) is the first of Ophuls' films, as he himself remarked, in which he succeeded in imposing a rhythm throughout, and this is not very surprising, since unlike *Die lachenden Erben*, it is a true musical. It is also heavily indebted to its musical predecessors by Lubitsch (*The Love Parade*, 1929, *Monte Carlo* 1930), and Wilhelm Thiele (*Die Privatsekretärin*, 1931). This is noticeable in particular in the comedy business with people on either side of doors, and in the way songs are worked into the conduct of long-distance communication and office routine. There are also a number of specific references to von Sternberg's *Die blaue Engel* and *Morocco*, though most of these can be taken to be satire and parody – the soubrette lead does a Dietrich chair pose, and is later shown in a shot reproducing (very crudely) a Dietrich dressing room with tat on the walls and a net curtain before. These sorts of things are deftly placed, and even though the acting is broad to the edge of acceptability, the overall effect is altogether the best comedy Ophuls ever put on film. However, this film also contains the first sign of the weakness in plot construction that was to plague most of his European films. The point, which is admittedly of small importance in this particular case, is that the ingénue lead is not presented in a way that justifies and makes plausible the fact that the film company who are the subject of this film should see any talent in her and sign her on, so setting the plot in motion. The momentum of events and the accompanying music just manage to over-ride this consideration, as they do similar plot short-comings in *Die verkaufte Braut*, but when Ophuls turned away from making musicals this was no longer the case.

As one can see from the tabulation, the quantitative amount of camera movement is no greater than in *Die lachenden Erben*, though with more emphasis on pans than on tracks, but the impression of movement in *Die verliebte Firma* is much greater, in part because in *Die lachenden Erben* a number of the tracks are on quasi-static scenes, and in part because in *Die verliebte Firma* the characters do more rushing around while they are followed by the panning shots I have recorded. The way the tracking shots are handled in relation to the actors and decor, particularly in the scene of the company's departure from the railway station, suggests very strongly the influence of Sternberg's use of tracks in *Morocco*.

The Closeness of Shot throughout this film is not too dissimilar to that in Ophuls' previous film, and for that matter to other German films from the early 'thirties, but it is even closer to that of a number of subsequent films by Ophuls which have the same relative avoidance of the use of Medium Long Shot: to be specific *la Tendre ennemie*, *Sarajevo*, *Caught*, and *The Reckless Moment*. It is in fact one of the two main characteristic patterns in this dimension in Ophuls' films prior to 1950.

Towards the end of *Die verliebte Firma*, Ophuls for the first time achieves a powerful effect that he was to repeat in some of his other films, by cutting or pulling the camera back to Long Shot or further at a point of emotional intensity, and keeping it there. In this particular case, the heroine is returning home by train miserable and defeated in her hopes. The camera cuts back to outside the windows of the compartment, leaving her crouched in the corner and small in the frame, and the shot is held, and held. Of course something like this had been a standard tactic for a long time in films, applied particularly to burial scenes, for instance, and as a matter of fact in *Der Kongress tanzt* in a somewhat similar context to *Die verliebte Firma*, but the originality in Ophuls' use of it is to hold the shot long after anyone else would have cut. This device can only be used effectively if the camera is not being set far back most of the time, and so it was one of the things Ophuls' denied himself in his last films.

As far as cutting rate is concerned, this film, like *Die lachenden Erben*, is very close to the norm for the period, since both have an Average Shot length of 10 seconds, and hence no really long takes. In this *Die verliebte Firma* differs from other contemporary musicals, which nearly all have an ASL appreciably longer than the norm for films of all types taken together. This cutting rate may well result from a pursuit of greater speed of movement at any cost, which is certainly

the case in Ophuls' next film.

Die verkaufte Braut

Only some of the best known numbers from Smetana's opera were used in Ophuls' film of *Die verkaufte Braut* (1932), and in fact the handling of the subject was such as to make it as much like the previous German film musicals as possible, with spoken dialogue and reprises of the most popular music. The 'ducats' duet, which happens to have a trotting rhythm in the refrain, was cleverly adapted to a horse and coach drive after the now standard *Der Kongress tanzt* pattern, and the marriage broker's big number, which has a near-*parlando* line in the original opera, was simply spoken over the music. The plot was slightly reduced and altered, though only in favour of incidental filmic elaborations that mostly involve the characters rushing hither and yon in a way that was to be better integrated into the narrative in later Ophuls films. The stuttering brother-in-law who was the hero's rival was handled more sympathetically in the film, which is not surprising, since his infatuation with a show and its performers against the wishes of his parents almost exactly matched Ophuls' own initial involvement with the theatre.

When he made *Die verkaufte Braut*, Ophuls had still not fully found his own style, and this is apparent in a number of different ways. For one thing, there are still scenes taken over intact from other directors' films, which was something Ophuls was never to do again. The most obvious instance is that in which the heroine, crossed in love, hurls herself around her room, from one wall to another, in a way that exactly copies the behaviour of the heroine of Dovshenko's *Zemlya* (1930) when she was bereft of her lover. The ballad-singer character from Pabst's *Die Dreigroschenoper* (1931) was also inserted bodily into *Die verkaufte Braut*, and given a specially written song to sing in the same style. Another Russian-derived feature in this film is the fast cutting throughout, but especially in the dance scenes, and this fast cutting is reflected in the shorter Average Shot length of 8 seconds. Although the Scale of Shot distribution is already very close to that of many subsequent Ophuls' films, from *Liebelei* onwards, the amount of camera movement is not, being quite small compared to that of later films. Ophuls had quite clearly not yet decided to make camera movement a major feature of his style. There are a few tracking shots following people about in what was to become his usual way, but quite a number of the other tracking shots are on quasi-static scenes done in a way that he was quickly to abandon in later films.

Another visual feature that is present to an even greater degree than in most subsequent Ophuls films is the often gratuitous interposition of foreground objects between the camera and the action: foliage particularly, but also window frames and other things, usually out of focus. This foreground detail which provides a 'natural' decorative frame for some of the images is nearly always well lit in Ophuls' films, unlike say von Sternberg's use of foreground nets and tracery to fill dead space (as he put it), in which case the objects are always in focus and silhouette, so contributing to the overall chiaroscuro. In 1932, as later, there is some use of chiaroscuro in Ophuls' films, but only in situations in which it would occur in anybody's films.

An early prefiguration of that favourite Ophuls scene which shows a pair of lovers 'travelling' through an artificial world of one kind or another occurs in this film when the hero and heroine visit a fairground side-show containing a miniature reconstruction of a famous battle, and their shadows slide over the terrain in a way that chimes in with the showman's spiel.

The presence of Karl Valentin and Liesl Karlstadt in this Munich-made film signals a possible connection with their silent short *Karl Valentin und Liesl Karlstadt zu das München Oktoberfest* which includes, amongst other fairground fooling, a feature in common with *Die verkaufte Braut*. This is a comic scene involving a photographer's booth, though the Ophuls version is more elaborate, and in fact contains one of his rare truly funny gags.

Another formal feature of *Die verkaufte Braut* that was part of a passing fashion at the time is the use of whip pans amongst the relatively limited number of camera movements.

It is very noticeable that a large proportion of the numerous cuts in this film have poor position-matching of the actors across them, and also that the continuity is in general rough in a way that was never again to be the case in later films by Ophuls; indeed his mastery of this technical matter quickly came to be excellent. It seems likely to me that the choppy continuity from shot to shot within scenes in *Die verkaufte Braut* resulted from the problems of fudging the shots involving singing on to a pre-recorded music track with inadequate facilities, perhaps because the film was shot without proper synchronization to music play-back on the location sets. (Previous German musical films which do not suffer from this largely avoided location shooting.)

Liebelei

Like many *auteur*-rated directors, Max Ophuls seems to have stumbled on to what are now regarded as some of his characteristic themes, for not all of these are evident in his films before *Liebelei* (1933), the subject of which was suggested to him by a producer who was not finally involved in the production. Ophuls' description of Schnitzler's play as "a bit dusty" seems strange until one realizes that he is referring to the detail in the dialogue and the action that very specifically belong to the Vienna of 1895. Although a lot of this detail, particularly the dialect, would be out of place in a German commercial film of 1933, the fact is that despite setting many of his films in pre-World War 1 Vienna, Ophuls had not the slightest interest in, or knowledge of, that actual time and place, but merely found that it gave a convenient and tenuous background to his interests. Despite the changes and additional scenes already commented on by Richard Roud in his book, the film retains a very simple structure, and the dialogue is severely pared down from the original.

For detailed analysis, the action of *Liebelei* can be broken down into 38 consecutive sections of equal length, each corresponding to 200 feet of 35 mm. film, or 2 minutes 13 seconds running time. These sections happen to roughly correspond to scenes in the following way:

1. Fritz and Theo attend the opera, as do the Baron and his wife, who is Fritz's mistress.
2. The Emperor arrives, Christine and Mizi drop their opera glasses from the gallery, and the overture begins.
3. Fritz and the Baroness leave independently to meet secretly at her house.
4. The Baron returns home early and Fritz hides from him.
5. Fritz manages to evade the suspicious Baron, while back at the opera Theo, who has picked up the opera glasses, meets Christine and Mizi.
6. Theo invites the girls to a café, and Christine's father, who plays in the orchestra, leaves the opera-house separately with a colleague.
7. Theo and the girls talk in a café.
8. Fritz arrives at the café and makes arrangements with Theo.
9. Fritz is introduced to Christine, and all four leave the café.
10. Christine's father talks with his colleague at home. Theo smuggles Mizi into his flat.
11. Fritz and Christine walk through the snowy night streets.
12. Fritz and Christine arrive at her home, where she talks to her father inside.
13. At the barracks Fritz is found to have left his officer's cap with Christine. He and Theo go out on manoeuvres.
14. Christine visits Mizi at the glove shop where she works.
15. Back at the barracks, Fritz receives a letter from the Baroness.
16. The Junior officers are inspected, and in the Officer's Mess, in the Baron's presence, insinuations are made about Fritz's affair with the Baron's wife.
17. The two young couples meet at a café and dance together.
18. Fritz and Christine continue dancing not noticing that Theo and Mizi have slipped away.
19. Fritz dances at a ball with the Baroness.
20. The Baron's suspicions are further aroused.
21. Fritz and Christine go for a sleigh ride through the snowy woods.
22. Fritz visits the Baroness at home and breaks off his relationship with her. A friend of the Baron tells him of his wife's affair.
23. The Baron accuses his wife of infidelity. Mizi and Theo put up Christmas decorations at the men's flat.
24. Fritz returns to the flat, and everyone fools around.
25. The Baron appears at the flat and accuses Fritz.

26. The Baron challenges Fritz to a duel. The arrangements for it are discussed.

27. In the flat, not knowing of the duel, Christine tells Theo that she has gained an audition for the opera. At the station, the Baron sends his wife away to the country.

28. Alone together, Christine tells Fritz of her dreams for their future together.

29. Arrangements for the duel are made according to the army duelling code.

30. The arrangements continue, and Theo pleads with the commanding officer to forbid the duel.

31. When he is refused, Theo resigns his commission.

32. Christine's father discusses her future with his colleague, and then with her at home.

33. Christine's successful audition for the opera.

34. Fritz is killed in the duel.

35. Theo and Mizi bring the news to Christine's father who is rehearsing at the opera.

36. All return to Christine who is waiting at the men's flat.

37. Christine is told that Fritz is dead.

38. Christine jumps to her death from the window. The empty forest where the sleigh ride had taken place.

The tabulation of the shot distributions for these 38 equal sections enables one readily to see the variations in cutting rate throughout the length of the film, and also the inflections in Scale of Shot from scene to scene. To make these changes clear, the numbers of shots of each kind which might be expected in a 200 foot section, if the scenes were shot in just the same way as the average for the whole film inside each section, are given at the beginning and end of the tabulation. That is, there would be eight shots in each section since the Average Shot length is 25 feet (17 seconds), and these shots would be expected to be very nearly one Medium Close Shot, two Medium Shots, two Medium Long Shots, and one Very Long Shot. There would also be an expectation of the fractional presence of a Close Up or Big Close Up, so this means that the presence of zero or one Close Up in a section is not a significant deviation from the overall norm, but the presence of two or more Close Ups is a significant inflection.

Expressive Variations

Keeping the above information in mind, and looking at the sectional tabulation for the film, one can see that the overall large-scale formal movement of *Liebelei* falls into several fairly well defined segments. The first of these comprises Sections 1 to 5 in which the cutting is faster than average, and in which there are on the whole more very close shots and very distant shots than there are overall. This corresponds to the excitement surrounding the opera performance, the necessity to introduce the principal characters, and also to the fact that rather more plot is got through in this 1000 feet of film than elsewhere in the same length. Then in Sections 6 to 19 the

cutting slows down to the average rate or less as the scenes here involve less emotional tension. The deviations from the overall Scale of Shot distribution are not so marked as in the previous segment, though there *are* smaller significant fluctuations from scene to scene. (The Big Close Up in Section 15 is a letter Insert.) From Section 20 onwards the cutting rate increases again as the Baron becomes more suspicious, the challenge is issued, the preparations for the duel are made, and Theo tries to prevent it. There is also a general movement towards using closer and closer shots as the tension rises to Section 31, which roughly corresponds to the scene of the military committee arranging the duel. In context the handling of this scene through a series of relatively fast-cut Medium Close Shots might be considered excessive, a case of technical overkill, as what takes place in the scene is a pre-determined ritual, and not inherently tense. The general formal movement from Section 20 to Section 31 that has just been described is briefly interrupted by a slowing down of the cutting for the relaxed scene with Mizi and Theo in the flat in Section 24, and also by the unknowingly final scene together of Fritz and Christine in Section 29. At this point the method of dissection I am using partially conceals a very slow track from Long Shot into Medium Close Shot on Fritz and Christine that lasts about two minutes. This device was used a couple of times elsewhere in this film, but not in Ophuls' later films. From Section 32 onwards to the end the cutting rate again slows down very markedly, and also the scenes are shot further back as the end is approached, but there is a small speed-up in the cutting rate from below normal to near normal for the scene of Christine's frenzy on hearing of the death of Fritz in Section 36.

There is more that could be said along these lines about individual sections, but I hope that the usefulness of this approach for showing how the large scale movements in the formal treatment relate to the content is now clear. A more obvious variant of this method will be used later for analysing *Letter from an Unknown Woman.* Incidentally, it should be remarked that very large scale formal patterns that are as clear cut as those in *Liebelei* will not necessarily be found in all films. If such patterns exist, some care is necessary in choosing the best equal-section intervals to show them off. At the moment the indications are that it is best to start with something like one minute or 100 foot intervals with 35 mm. film, and if appropriate condense them into larger sections, which is what I did in this particular case.

I did not judge it worthwhile to include the types of camera movement in the sectional breakdown, but this might yield insights in some cases. In *Liebelei* the work of following the characters around the scenes is mostly done with panning shots, and it was only later in Ophuls' career that this function was transferred to tracking shots. The way that these panning shots are used in one particular scene, that of the dance in the café (Sections 17 and 18) needs discussion, but this is rather difficult to carry out in written form. Suffice it to say that the striking quality of this scene does not reside in using a series

	BCU	CU	MCU	MS	MLS	LS	VLS
Norm->	0	0	1	2	2	2	1
Section							
1	3			3		2	1
2	1		3	5	6	9	5
3		1		6	3	3	
4		1		3	2		
5			3	6	7	4	1
6				1	3		1
7				1		1	
8				4		1	
9				1	5	2	
10				1	1		
11				2	2	4	
12				1		2	
13				1	2	2	1
14					1		1
15	1	1		2	3	3	
16				2	1		
17			1		3	2	
18				2	2	3	
19				1	3		
20			2	4	4	2	2
21			1	5		6	4
22				2	1	4	
23			1	8		6	1
24				3			
25				4			
26			2	3	2	1	
27			1	1	4	1	2
28				2	1		
29				5			
30		1	7	3	3		
31		2	4	3	2	1	
32				3	2		
33			1	1	1	2	1
34			1				4
35				1	2	4	
36				2	3	4	1
37		1					
38				1	2	3	3
Norm ->	0	0	1	2	2	2	1

Numbers of Shots with the given Scale of Shot within a series of 200 foot sections of Liebelei. *The number of shots expected on the average for a 200 foot section, given the Scale of Shot distribution for the whole film, is entered at the top and bottom of the table.*

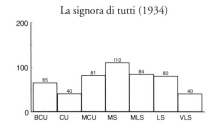

La signora di tutti (1934)

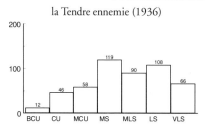

la Tendre ennemie (1936)

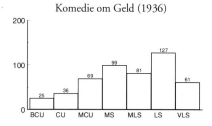

Komedie om Geld (1936)

of panning shots to follow a dancing couple, which was quite banal by 1933, but in the rhythmic way the couple is lost behind a wall, etc. from one shot, and picked up by a cut to the next pan following them. Detailed points like this are most easily brought out on an editing table by pointing to exactly what happens, and ideally in comparison with another director's treatment of the same sort of scene to lend greater objectivity to the demonstration.

La signora di tutti

By the time Max Ophuls had shot *Liebelei* the stakes in the German musical camera movement game had been raised. Ludwig Berger's *Ich bei Tag und Du bei Nacht* (1932) contains far more fast camera movement shot from close in to the actors than ever before, and this was the lead Ophuls followed when a producer commissioned him to make *La signora di tutti* in Italy in 1934. For this film Ophuls had the use of a camera crane for the first time, and the result of all this can be seen in the tabulation of camera movement. This is the first time that crane shots up and down staircases make their appearance in Max Ophuls' films, though their use does not go much beyond their model in *Der Kongress tanzt*, but the general technical flashiness extends to a 360 degree pan that then retraces its course in the reverse direction as a whip pan. (*Der Kongress tanzt* only contains pans covering most of the circle.) The justification for this device at this point in the film is 'expression' of the characters dizziness, and indeed most of the obvious technique is integrated into *La signora di tutti* in this sort of way, though a few very striking effects do exist independently of obvious meaning. I am thinking here of such things as a pair of intercut tracking shots, both moving with the Point of View of two characters, one of whom is in a motor car driving through a series of arbours, and the other paddling a boat parallel to the road in a lake alongside.

The Scale of Shot distribution exaggerates the impression of the actual closeness of the camera with respect to the actors, since most of the Big Close Ups are in fact Inserts of objects and letters, a lot of them in montage sequences. This is not usually the case in Ophuls' films, though it does happen again in *De Mayerling à Sarajevo* and *Caught*. The really heavy emphasis is on Medium Shot, and from this film onwards this emphasis on Medium Shot in many of Ophuls' films seems to correspond to a wish to build up a particular actress because that was where the money was in the film, to the extent of the leading lady being married to the producer. Though Ophuls pronounced himself satisfied with the films he made in which this was the case, perhaps deep down it rankled a little, and

the resentment finally peeped through in *Lola Montès*.

Another major feature appearing in Ophuls' work for the first time in this film was the flashback structure, which even extends at one point to a flashback inside a flashback. Such things were uncommon in the early 'thirties. A less satisfactory aspect of the film is the acting, which is all of a remarkably bad broadness. Now it *is* possible, though rare, to have exaggerated acting that is not bad because it shows original thought in the invention of its detail, but the acting in *La signora di tutti* merely consists of the most ancient clichés of melodrama.

As far as the story is concerned, this shows the beginning of that absence of rational causality which later increased in Ophuls' films. We are not shown any reasonable way in which the financier lover of the female lead could have lost all his money through his infatuation with her, nor how she suddenly becomes a film star, though these points are to some extent concealed in the speed of the movement, the *confusione*, and the incessant surging background music. The important point for future reference is that she *chooses* to become an actress, and the indications given early in the film are that this is because of her vanity, and her love of glamour and luxurious living.

Divine

The eponymous heroine of *Divine* (1935) also chooses to become an actress without the slightest necessity to do so, though she is unusual amongst Ophuls' heroines in rejecting the profession after having tried it. The story of this film is an unskilful cobbling together of bits and pieces of Colette's music hall anecdotes, and in general the way it is shot represents the beginning of Ophuls' retreat to conventional film-making in the later part of the nineteen-thirties. There is a sharp reduction in the amount of camera movement, as is partly indicated by the reduction of the Average Shot length from the 13 seconds of *La signora di tutti* to 10 seconds.

la Tendre ennemie

la Tendre ennemie also conforms to the trend away from the long take that was taking place everywhere, and though it contains a fair number of tracking and panning shots, most of these are fairly limited in extent, and would not be out of place in an American film of the same date. The Scale of Shot distribution is close to that of Ophuls' post-war American films, particularly *The Reckless Moment*, but also *Letter from an Unknown Woman* and *Caught*. The large number of Very Long Shots is due to the recurring presence of an aeroplane in the story.

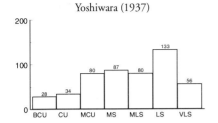

Yoshiwara (1937)

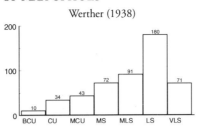

Werther (1938)

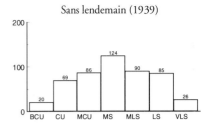

Sans lendemain (1939)

An interesting feature of *la Tendre ennemie* is the striking way the flashbacks are handled. The scenes set in the past are distinguished by having very stylized sets, consisting of not much more than furniture and props in front of a blank background onto which is projected a dappled pattern of abstract light and shade continuously streaming from one side to another. These flashbacks were also marked off from the rest of the film by being tinted pink and lavender.

Much more importantly, *la Tendre ennemie* introduced the Ophuls woman in the extreme form: vain, spoilt, and selfish, and directly responsible for the death of one lover and another admirer also. She is the enemy of the film's title, and it seems likely to me that Ophuls regarded her tenderly, though the author of the original play did not, just because she is pretty and charming. We shall meet her again, particularly in *Madame de ...*, but also elsewhere.

Komedie om Geld

This film is more distinctive than most of the films Ophuls made in this period, and is the only one with a fully original screenplay, in which he himself had a large hand. Not surprisingly it is the worst constructed from the narrative point of view, with a quite pointless idyll for a pair of totally unnecessary young lovers shoved into the middle of the film, and a total and very apparent lack of logic in the resolution of the difficulties of the hero in the second half. The pacing in the later stages is also noticeably sluggish. These faults are not in the least overcome by the Brechtian presentation of the story by a clown compère in a circus set who comments in song at the beginning, middle, and end. The Brechtian elements, which are included more baldly than in any prior film, are nevertheless partly anticipated and wholly inspired by *Die Dreigroschenoper* and René Clair's *A nous la Liberté* (1932). Apart from the sung commentary that plays a minor part in both earlier films, *Komedie om Geld* also takes from Clair's film the explicit and crude parody of the workings of capitalism amongst very similar palatial *moderne* sets. A feature of the photography was the extensive use of wide-angle lenses of focal length around 25 mm. to exaggerate the grandeur of the interiors. There were far more high and low-angle shots used in this film than ever before, or indeed after, in Ophuls' films. Such a stylistic feature is of course incompatible with the extensive use of long takes with mobile camera, and the amount of camera movement in this film is indeed very low for Ophuls. The high- and low-angles are partly used in what had come to be a conventionally 'expressive' way at the beginning of the 'thirties, with low angles used to increase the

awe-inspiring stature of authority figures. Compositions with the authority figures filling the frame and pushing the dominated character into a corner are also used.

Yoshiwara

The only thing of any interest in *Yoshiwara* (1937) is another stylized fantasy journey, in this case to the opera and back again in an imaginary sleigh, but this is missing from some prints of this film.

Werther

The Scale of Shot distribution for *Werther* (1938) shows clearly what I take to be the natural inclination of Max Ophuls in the handling of this dimension when he has no need to favour the female lead. Both *Yoshiwara* and *Komedie om Geld* have a very similar Scale of Shot distribution to *Werther*, with the same heavier emphasis going towards the more distant shots, and so do *The Exile* and *le Plaisir* after the war. Such a heavy emphasis on Long Shot puts a lot of weight on the design and decor of the film sets, and only the very best designers stand a chance of carrying so much. What is particularly important here is that Ophuls' own static pictorial sense was no more than fairly good, and of the kind that would use the good conventional arrangements provided for him by the designer and cameraman. However, a succession of conventionally composed Long Shots of this nature possesses no inherent dynamic when the cutting rate is not very fast, and *Werther* only has an ASL of 12 seconds. To make the point clearer by comparison, the films of von Sternberg also rely on pictorial composition with slowish cutting, but in that case there is a continuous change of Scale of Shot from shot to shot, with a fairly equal distribution from Close Up to Long Shot. It is also just possible to get away with restriction to Long Shot by using a fast cutting rate, as in sections of Eisenstein's *Oktyabr*, or alternatively by using a good deal of camera movement, as Ophuls himself did in *le Plaisir*, or yet again by sheer non-filmic dramatic interest, as in some early cinema. It is my judgement that *Werther* is on the verge of succeeding in this last way, but really I think that Ophuls was more interested in scoring some anti-Nazi points in a version of a German literary classic. However worthy and understandable they were at the time, these points are forced in without regard for plausibility. In one scene Werther is told that Rousseau's *Contrat Social* is '...subversive literature, forbidden in the Grand Duke's territory.', but the issue is confused by having Werther's partner in radicalism suddenly become, for no reason other than sexual jealousy, an extreme conservative

De Mayerling à Sarajevo (1940)

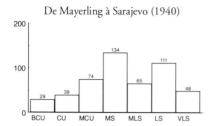

The Exile (1948)

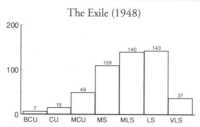

Letter From an Unknown Woman (1948)

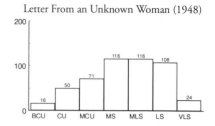

condemning Werther in the name of society and the family, and effectively executing him by giving him pistols when it is clear that he intends suicide. Though I suppose there *may* be an audience these days eager to believe that Fascist monsters are created by sexual jealousy.

Sans lendemain

Sans lendemain (1939) is nothing but a star vehicle for Edwige Feuillère, and as such is entirely constructed of clichés, from her performance downwards. The percentage of reverse-angle cuts is up to 34% from Ophuls' usual 20-25%, and the ASL is down to 8 seconds, and there is no way of telling that it was made by Max, apart from his name on the front.

De Mayerling à Sarajevo

Another Feuillère vehicle, though on this particular occasion there are just three small moments that indicate that someone with talent might have been in charge, and these all derive their force from holding the camera back in Long Shot when the average director would not have ben able to resist going in closer. I refer to the rendezvous on horseback in the woods, the interior of the carriage of the Royal train rushing through the night to Sarajevo, and the assassination itself. Not a lot.

The Exile

When Ophuls finally returned to film-making in America in 1947, the stylistic context had radically changed. Long takes had become an accepted part of the scene again, and extensive camera movement had been used by Minnelli and Preminger and others from 1945 onwards. Skilled grips were on hand to operate cranes and the new crab dollies, and these had not been available to Ophuls before when he was in Europe. The immediate outcome was the increase in take length and in tracking and craning visible in the camera movement figures for *The Exile* (1947). Despite this, a number of episodes of violent physical action which were done with fast cutting, and without camera movement, keep the Average Shot length down to 11.5 seconds, near Ophuls' old figure for most of the 'thirties. In *The Exile* the extremely heavy emphasis on more distant camera placement is there to show off Douglas Fairbanks Jr.'s imitation of the movement style of his father; an imitation that is fairly accurate, but unfortunately lacking in force.

The excellence of the set design in this film is the only major factor in its favour.

Letter from an Unknown Woman

Letter from an Unknown Woman (1948) was conceived as a star vehicle for Joan Fontaine using Stefan Zweig's short story of the same name. In its original form this story, which was written in 1931 and had a contemporary setting, was quite close to the 'mother love' genre popular in Hollywood films of the early 'thirties; those films in which Constance Bennet or Ruth Chatterton or some other had to prostitute herself to support her child. The best-known example, though rather late in the cycle, is von Sternberg's *Blonde Venus* (1932). It was not possible to film such a story in Hollywood after 1933, and in any case Ophuls had a fairly free hand to adapt it in the way he preferred, which was to make it as much as possible like his biggest successes so far, *Liebelei* and *La signora di tutti*. And *Letter from an Unknown Woman* does indeed combine important elements from both films; the double death combined with duel set in 1900's Vienna from *Liebelei*, and the flashback structure, and also the way events happen independent of any logical relation with society, as in *La signora di tutti*.

The Scale of Shot distribution for *Letter from an Unknown Woman* is very close to that for *Liebelei*, and the Average Shot length is rather longer at 16 seconds. For comparison with other possible approaches to the romantic melodrama I have included tabulations of Scale of Shot and camera movement for *Back Street* (Robert Stevenson, 1940) and *Madame Bovary* (Vincente Minnelli, 1949). The scene dissection of *Back Street* is of a kind that was quite common in the 'High Hollywood' period of the late 'thirties and early 'forties, though far from universal even then, and other examples of this kind of concentration on closer shots can be seen in statistics quoted elsewhere in this book. Often the Close Ups in *Back Street* are used to end a scene, and sometimes to start one as well, as happens quite frequently in Hollywood films. The idea has got around recently that the usual way that scenes in Hollywood films are broken down into shots is by starting with a general shot of the scene, and then cutting in closer and closer towards the central part of the scene, and finally reversing the process to bring the scene to an end in a more distant shot again. And hence that a director using a different approach is a 'modernist' film-maker, as claimed for Ozu by Edward Branigan in *Screen* Vol.17, No.2 ('The Space of *Equinox Flower*'). This mistaken idea about scene dissection seems to have been culled from 'How to ...' books, which are never written by feature film-makers, and it has been advanced without bothering to check it against the films themselves. In fact in mainstream films made by anyone except the worst hacks, the scenes are broken down in quite varied ways, and one can often get films like Michael Curtiz's *The Sea Hawk* where successive scenes tend to start and end on Close Ups, often of objects. Or does this make Curtiz a 'modernist' film-maker too? Anyway, like most directors who favour the more distant shot, Ophuls very rarely used this form of construction, though *The Exile* is an exception to this, where perhaps he engaged in some idle flourishes because his attention was not fully engaged by the subject, or perhaps because he was using Curtiz's films as models of the swashbuckler genre.

In a more general way comparison with *Back Street* provides a useful check on the over-interpretation of *Letter from an Unknown Woman* in particular, and Ophuls' films in general. Some of the features that Robin Wood in *Personal Views* (1976) supposes to characterize Max Ophuls' films are, to use his itemization: No.2 Staircases, and meetings on them, No.3 Places of transition such as doorways and entrances, No.5 Stations, trains, and scenes of arrival and departure, No.6 Carriages, No.7 Dances, No.10 Theatres and places of entertainment, and No.15 Framing the heroine in mirrors, but in fact these features are all common to virtually every example of the genre of romantic melodrama, and in no way specific to Ophuls. As might be expected, all of these features also occur in Minnelli's *Madame Bovary*, plus long takes (ASL=15 seconds.) and plenty of camera movement. What then is the difference between the style of this film and that of *Letter from an Unknown Woman*? If we look carefully at the table of camera movements quoted, we notice that Minnelli has an excess of tracking shots without panning over that in any Ophuls film, including *Letter from an Unknown Woman*. A large number of these are tracks straight into and out from a scene, and this kind of track does not usually occur in Ophuls' work, which is thus the principal point of formal difference.

A noticeable indication of the better facilities available for dolly shots in Hollywood at this time is that many of the tracking shots in *Letter*, and also in the other films, take place around interior sets that are much smaller and more obstructed with furniture than in Ophuls' pre-war films. Another feature unique to the camera movement in these Hollywood films is the numerous small adjustments in dolly position, usually accompanied by small panning movements to reframe at various points within the duration of a longish take that also contains large scale camera movements with a number of camera holds. (Small frames and tilts to keep the actors well framed when they move slightly are not counted as camera movements in my analytical tabulations, since they have been made automatically by cameramen from the beginning of the 'twenties.) These frequent extra small dolly movements give the American films an extra 'life' that is missing from the later, as well as the earlier European films by Max Ophuls.

Turning to the detailed analysis of *Letter from an Unknown*

Woman, and given that my preferred approach is through the way the film was put together, then the obvious unit of narrative analysis is the script scene, which is determined by its absolute unity of time, place, and location. The looser unit of 'sequence' is only a secondary form, and just re-naming sequences 'syntagms' gets one no further forward. So the beginning of *Letter* is here analysed scene by scene in terms of Scale of Shot. The brief outline of the action in the first 24 scenes is as follows:

1. Stefan Brand arrives outside his flat in a carriage with a friend. He has just been challenged to a duel.

2. Inside his flat, he is given a letter by his mute servant. He starts to read it.

3. *Flashback* The letter tells how the adolescent Lisa was intrigued by the belongings of a pianist which were being moved into the flat above that in which she and her mother lived.

4. The hands of the pianist playing.

5. Later the pianist, Stefan Brand, practises, while Lisa listens to him from the courtyard and simultaneously her girl friend talks coarsely of love.

6. Lisa meets Stefan for the first time at the entrance to the house.

7. Scenes in which Lisa prepares herself to be worthy of Stefan by studying music, dancing, etc.

8. Lisa sees Stefan bringing one of many women home to his flat.

9. On a later night Lisa creeps out from her bed to listen to his playing.

10. Lisa is cleaning carpets in the courtyard and helps carry one into Stefan's flat.

11. She prowls around his flat until found by his servant.

12. leaving the flat, she comes upon her mother with an admirer on the stairs.

13. In their own flat, her mother tells Lisa that she intends to remarry.

14. At the railway station, as her new step-father is taking them to live in Linz, Lisa runs away, back to their former home.

15. She tries to get into Stefan's flat but no-one is there.

16. From the stairs, she sees Stefan bring a woman into his flat.

17. *Present* Stefan continues to read the letter.

18. *Flashback* It tells how, some years later in Linz, Liza promenades to church with her mother and step-father.

19. After church Lisa rejects the proposal of a young Lieutenant whom her parents expect her to marry.

20. *Present* Stefan continues to read the letter.

21. *Flashback* It tells now how Lisa returned to Vienna and got a job modelling in a dress shop.

22. She waits, as always, outside Stefan Brand's house. This night he appears for the first time, and, not recognizing her, picks her up.

	Scene	BCU	CU	MCU	MS	MLS	LS	VLS	Expected no. of shots in scene
Norm for 10 shots->		0.5	1	1.5	2	2	2	0.5	10
Footage									
127	1	1		1		1	1		5
349	2	1	1	1	2	2			9
523	3				1	1	2		7
536	4		1						1
710	5				6	3	4		7
808	6		1	1	3		4		4
918	7				2	3			5
974	8					1			2
1145	9				1	2			7
1263	10					1			1
1452	11			1	2	3	2		8
1491	12					4	1		2
1652	13				1	3	2		6
1811	14			1		4			7
1971	15			1			5		7
2083	16					1	1		5
2105	17			1					1
2286	18			1			2		8
2599	19		1		3	3	6		13
2630	20			1					1
2790	21				1	3	2		7
2987	22		1	4	2	1	3	1	8
3154	23				2	6	2		6
3382	24		5	1	3				5
Norm for 10 shots->		0.5	1	1.5	2	2	2	0.5	10

Number of shots with given Scale of Shot in successive scenes of Letter from an Unknown Woman. *The 35 mm. footage at which each scene ends is noted in the left-most column, and the number of shots in each scene in the right-most column. The normal number of each Scale for 10 shots, derived from the overall Scale of Shot distribution for the whole film, is given above.*

23. He takes her to a café where he surreptitiously cancels an appointment with another woman.
24. Stefan wines and dines Lisa in a private room in a restaurant.

In this break-down there a few cases of what are strictly separate script scenes that I have combined into one scene for convenience, particularly in Nos.7 and 21, but also in No.5, in which a series of shots of Stefan playing are cut into the exterior scene showing Lisa and her girl-friend listening in the courtyard. These condensations are irrelevant to the particular points I want to make.

It can be seen in the table above that in this film there are no very obvious large-scale movements in the Scale of Shot distribution and cutting rate that show up in the scene by scene breakdown, but some idea of the smaller scale fluctuations of the cutting rate can be obtained by noting the deviations from the expected number of shots in each scene that would apply if all the shots in the film were of the same length. The magnitude of this quantity has been entered in the tabulation for each scene, and the total of shots actually occurring can easily be added up for the scene in question, and hence one can decide if the cutting rate is faster or slower than the overall norm at that point. For instance, in scene No.1 five shots would be expected if the cutting were even throughout everym part of the film, but in fact there are only 3 shots. Contrariwise, in scene No.5, while only seven shots would be expected, there are actually fourteen.

Proceeding in the same way, the distribution of Scale of Shot which would hold if the film was shot with the average distribution even over the small length of ten successive shots is also shown at the beginning and end of the tabulation. Thus the deviations from this can also be seen, though with rather more difficulty in calculation. For instance, in scene No.7 it would be expected that only 2 out of 10 (or 1 out of 5) of the shots would be Long Shots, but in fact 3 shots out of 5 are Long Shots, whereas the expected 1 out of the 5 shots in this scene which should be a Medium Shot is missing. And so on. Because the number of shots involved is so small at the scene level, only large deviations from the norm can be considered significant, as is indeed the case for the excess of Long Shots in scene No.7, and also for those I shall single out for comment. I am afraid that this may seem a little involved, but the alternative is a tabulation using positive and negative fractional numbers for Scale of Shot distributions within scenes. In fact it was because of this difficulty in making the results leap to the eye that I chose to use regular length sections rather than strict scene divisions in my analysis of *Liebelei*

Taken scene by scene, the major deviations from the norm are pretty much what might conventionally be expected. For instance, the cutting rate is a lot faster than normal when Lisa hears Stefan playing, and then meets him for the first time in Scenes 5 and 6, and also when he picks her up and takes her for a meal in Scenes 22 and 24. The scene in which Lisa discovers her mother with her mother's new admirer and husband-to-be is the only other fast-cut scene in the first 35 minutes of the film. On the other hand, Ophuls gets in his longest takes in the most emotionally neutral scenes, such as

the promenade before church at Linz, which is Scene 18 in my dissection. The scene at the station (No.14) as Lisa's step-father takes the family off to Linz might be considered anomalous in this respect, as it is the locus for considerable tension in our heroine, but it is nevertheless shot with long takes from far back. Indeed it could be argued that this scene could be presented with more force with either more cutting, or with different staging to keep Lisa's reactions more before us while the scene lasts.

As far as Scale of Shot is concerned, the only strongly marked deviation from the norm from scene to scene occurs when Stefan picks Lisa up and has dinner with her in Scenes 22 and 24. In fact in this film it is just possible to see beginning to emerge that lack of variation in Scale of Shot which was to be such an important feature of Ophuls' last films.

At the next more detailed level of analysis one deals with the individual shot in relation to the scene as a whole, and here I do not have any particularly original proposals beyond the kind of thing that has been done in critical writing in the past, though I would insist that such detailed interpretation be compatible with what might have been the film-maker's likely intention in constructing the shot.

Turning to more general aspects of *Letter from an Unknown Woman*, a comparison with *Back Street*, as well as with most other previous 'weepies', shows that what is missing from *Letter* is the external pressures of society, and even most people other than the central couple. In virtually all romantic melodramas the things that keep the lovers absolutely apart are events like the marriage of one of them, natural disasters, the intentional or unintentional intervention of third parties, wars, and so on, but in *Letter* nothing prevents the union of Stefan and Lisa except the shallowness of the first and the perversity of the second. These features are fairly certainly the reason for the lack of commercial success of *Letter from an Unknown Woman*, whereas *Back Street* and other 'weepies' are still in distribution without the benefit of financial subsidy organized by a pressure group of film culturists.

The flashback reprise showing a montage of precious moments of love in *Letter from an Unknown Woman* is preceded by numerous similar examples in *Back Street* and other films, and in fact in this form it was an old cliché already. Whereas in *Liebelei* Ophuls found a new form for the same device by showing the scene of past happiness, but with the lovers gone. To put it simply, quality mostly resides in the exact way something is done in a film. Minnelli's crane work in *Madame Bovary* is banal, and even descends to the use of a

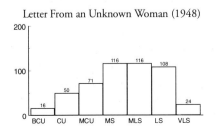

Letter From an Unknown Woman (1948)

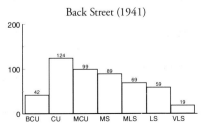

Back Street (1941)

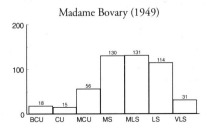

Madame Bovary (1949)

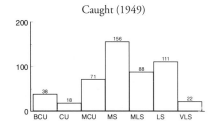

Caught (1949)

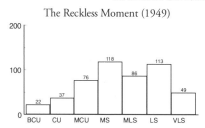

The Reckless Moment (1949)

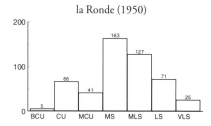

la Ronde (1950)

crane down from a chandelier to the dancers below, which was a device with long grey whiskers on it, but on the other hand, he had a truly New Idea for covering a waltzing couple in the same ball scene. After following them waltzing in one direction with a pan in the ordinary way, he had them reverse, and then he followed them back with a pan in the opposite direction, still in the same shot without cutting. The force of this has to be seen to be appreciated.

Banality of character conception is present in *Letter from an Unknown Woman*, not for the first or last time in Ophuls' films, particularly in the presentation of Lisa's mother and step-father. *Letter from an Unknown Woman* also contains easily the highest proportion of reverse-angles in any Ophuls film, and this must come under the heading of more star tribute.

Caught

Caught (1948), on the other hand, has a much more typical proportion of reverse-angle cuts for an Ophuls film at 21%, and also a quite typical ASL of 17 seconds. The Scale of Shot distribution resembles that of *Sarajevo*, and in particular the relatively large number of Big Close Ups again represent Inserts in montage sequences. The amount of camera movement is rather down in general, and there are no crane shots at all, even though one of the sets contains a nice big staircase. There is more depth of field than is usual in an Ophuls film, and this is done with moderately wide-angle lens shooting, though it does not go all the way to true 'deep focus', and some use is made of this depth of field in some of the stagings. The photography is also on the low-key side throughout, and this is again unusual for an Ophuls film, so it does look as though all this represents a half-hearted flirtation with the post-*Citizen Kane* style under the influence of Lee Garmes, who was on camera for the film.

Caught is the first Max Ophuls film in which there is a very definite reduction in the amount of variation in Scale of Shot and cutting rate from scene to scene, and this becomes very apparent if a breakdown into 100 foot sections is made on a 35 mm. print. After the point in the film at which Leonora has married Smith-Ohlrig and been left alone in his mansion, we have for the next half-hour of screen time very little departure from the average Scale of Shot distribution, and the cutting rate is also very steady for lengths of several minutes at a time, despite the occurrence of scenes of a quite varied dramatic nature. It is only in the last 12 minutes of the film, when the most dramatic twitches of the plot take place, that there are any strong deviations from the norms.

The satirical presentation of the world of an aspirant model in *Caught* represents some of the few truly amusing scenes in Max Ophuls' work, for despite his claim that he was celebrated for his handling of comedy in the theatre, most of his rare filmic attempts in this direction are not very successful. Ophuls has also said that he found the conclusion of the script he had to shoot unsatisfactory, and given his favourite films one can easily imagine another ending in which Leonora dies in childbirth, and Larry Quinada is condemned to death for killing Smith-Ohlrig, leaving him with memories of his happiness with Leonora in his last hours. Or something similar. But really the flaw in the story is quite fundamental, as the connection between the world of the possessive tycoon and that of the poor doctor is completely forced and unconvincing. Such is not the case with Ophuls' next film.

The Reckless Moment

In *The Reckless Moment* (1950) the relation between the small-time criminal world and that of suburban domesticity is of the essence, and the transitions between these two worlds form a major element of the film. The rushes the mother makes from one to the other – from the house to the city, or from the house to the boat-house with the blackmailer in it – are very present visually as well as thematically. *The Reckless Moment* is in fact an original combination of at least two sub-genres, namely the 'lady in a jam' type of thriller, and the 'mother coping in husband's absence' domestic drama which was common during World War 2.

Formally speaking the Scale of Shot distribution returns towards the *Liebelei* type, and the camera movement and Average Shot length (15.5 seconds) are much as before. More importantly, there is a return towards more conventional inflection of the Scale of Shot and of cutting rate from scene to scene. There is more movement of the cast about the room sets, which are realistically sized and cluttered, than there had been in the previous two films, and this is covered with the excess of panning shots present. A fair number of these shots are through doorways and windows, and this had never happened to this extent before in Max Ophuls' films, though it was to reappear in *le Plaisir*.

One might ask why Ophuls' stylistic approach attracted some comment at the time these films were made, given that other directors were also going in for extensive camera movement. The answer would seem to be that there *was* a general resistance to this trend, particularly from cameramen who liked to produce a series of static pictures beautifully lit, and producers who liked to have a lot of shots to re-edit, but also

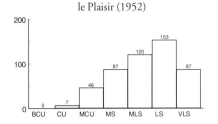

le Plaisir (1952)

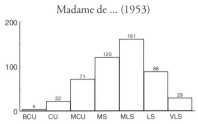

Madame de ... (1953)

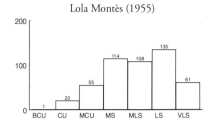

Lola Montès (1955)

because Ophuls went that little bit further. For instance he had tracks laid on a beach front when a minor scene there could have been covered in a series of pans, and a staircase set built with a 'wild' (i.e removable) wall, which complicates set construction, so that he could follow a scene with a crane in one take, when it could have been covered in more than one shot from the open side of the staircase.

Given the extra complexities of attitudes and behaviour of the principal characters in *The Reckless Moment*, and also taking into account some of the points dealt with above, not to mention other touches of imaginative detail, such as the way a dead man's teeth are drawn back from his lips like those of a shot rabbit, it is not surprising that this film was the most successful of Ophuls' American productions.

la Ronde

When Max Ophuls returned to France, the public for his work substantially changed, with an 'art cinema' audience in France and elsewhere now forming a prominent part of it. A subject such as Schnitzler's play *Reigen* now became possible, and many of the critics in France were interested in films that were different from the general run. As a result, features that had only appeared in embryo came to dominate Ophuls' work.

The Scale of Shot distributions for Ophuls' last films are very different to those in most other sound films, though one can notice resemblances to some early sound films and some early silent films. The very strong concentration on a single camera distance, which happens to be Medium Shot in the case of *la Ronde* (1950), corresponds to a sharp reduction in the inflection of Scale of Shot from scene to scene, and even more so within scenes. *la Ronde* starts with 16 script-scenes covering the first seven minutes of the action, and all but one are 'one shot scenes'. These are scattered over the Medium to Long Shot range, but with the scene between The Young Man and The Chambermaid we get, after the first 11 shots, long strings of up to 10 shots each with the same camera distance in every shot. Most of these are also in the Medium or Medium Long Shot scale, and the film continues in the same manner after this scene. At one point there is a string of 15 consecutive Close Ups, which is the sort of thing that just did not happen in other people's films in the sound period, as a little checking will show. It should also be added that only 19 of the 294 shots in *la Ronde* contain large changes of scale within their length, and none of these occurs amidst the strings of shots mentioned. Incidentally, the scene between The Young Man and The Chambermaid just mentioned is

shot throughout with 'dutch tilt' framing, which follows a fashion that had arisen in the late 'forties in Europe. In this particular instance it could fairly be claimed to heighten the erotic tension in the scene.

The take lengths are only slightly longer than before, with an ASL of 18 seconds, and the camera movement has decreased because the original play is a series of static duologues, and hence the amount of movement that could be introduced into it was limited. Indeed the desire to have as much camera movement as possible was probably one of the motives for introducing the 'Master of Ceremonies' form of presentation into the film adaptation. This presentation, with the Master of Ceremonies' asides to the audience, his intervention in the action, starting a scene by operating a clapperboard, cutting out sex in the editing room, etc. was fairly novel in the 'art film' at the time, though not of course in general if one includes American comedy films such as the '*Road to ...*' series and *Hellzapoppin'*.

le Plaisir

Emboldened perhaps by the commercial success of *la Ronde*, with *le Plaisir* (1951) Max Ophuls went to new extremes in his formal procedures. The takes lengthened even more, with the ASL going up to 21 seconds, the camera movement increased beyond anything he had done before, and the film was shot from very far back indeed. Ophuls had reached the commercially dangerous point of relying almost entirely on the visual interest thrown up by camera movement and what was in the filmed scene itself to carry the film.

Strictly speaking, *le Plaisir* is an omnibus film made up of three separate Maupassant stories, and reflects a fashion for that sort of construction, complete with voice-over narrator to hold the stories together, that had developed in the previous couple of years with *Quartet* (1948), etc. There are some differences in the way the three parts of *le Plaisir* are filmed.

In *The Mask* the dancing is covered with camera movement of unprecedented speed, and this generates a lot of excitement, but the remoteness of the camera makes it difficult to see what is happening to the masked dancer who has collapsed, who he is, and even that he is wearing a mask.

The general treatment of the longest story, *La Maison Tellier*, is of an 'Ooh-la-la' Frenchiness fairly exactly indicated by the casting of Madeleine Renaud and Danielle Darrieux as the madame and prostitute of a provincial brothel, and this clichéd quality was apparent to sophisticated viewers even when the film was made. This story again suffers in its earlier stages from an unvaryingly remote camera, with the extensive tracking and craning not adding anything because they do not interact with the actor movement, which had not been the case in earlier Ophuls films. In the second half of the story, with the prostitutes arrived in the country, on the farm, and at the first communion of the madame's niece, closer shots are mixed in a little, a number of the images are interesting in themselves, and the relatively reduced amount of camera movement is integrated with the action.

The final story, *The Model*, has the general characteristics of the film to the greatest degree, with the takes even longer than in the other sections, and the camera consistently far back. It is here that it is most apparent that a lot of the moves the actors make, even from room to room, have no motivation, but only take place so that there can be an accompanying camera movement. The distant camera also throws more weight on to the decor, and Jean d'Eaubonne's design, which tends to have a sameness of approach anyway, is here at its weakest ever. This is not helped by Agostini's lighting, which is flatter than that of Christian Matras who did the rest of the film.

A large proportion of the shots in *le Plaisir* are 'dutch tilts', more so than in any previous film, but they do not seem to be distributed with any expressive intent.

Madame De ...

In *Madame de ...* (1953), Ophuls retreated slightly from the extreme stylistic position he had reached, as is readily apparent from the camera movement and Scale of Shot distributions. The Average Shot length is also back near the Ophulsian norm at 16 seconds. But the Medium Long Shot on which the film concentrates is still rather distant from the actors, and when combined with the attenuated and audience-alienating narrative, commercial failure was assured. The film is just the story of how a spoilt, vain, stupid, and selfish woman is reduced to nothing by those very qualities: qualities over which she had no control. Danielle Darrieux incarnates Madame de ... perfectly, but the casting of the husband and lover should have been reversed if Ophuls had wanted the audience to care more for the fate of the latter. Again, in this film one is given plenty of time to contemplate the fact that Jean d'Eaubonne's style of set design depends on one gimmick; the splashing of lengths of vastly inflated and simplified Rococo-type moulding here and there on mirrors, walls, etc. There are quite a number of jump cuts in this film, advancing what was an embryonic fashion in 1953.

Lola Montès

As you can see from the Scale of Shot distribution, which is quite close to that of *le Plaisir*, in *Lola Montès* (1955) Ophuls was continuing on his commercially dangerous course of using very long takes (ASL=18 sec.) shot from far back, with just a little emphasis on Medium Shot as a small gesture to his supposed 'star'.

Ophuls and his producers showed a great lack of perception in not noticing that Martine Carol's fame was solely due to her willingness to appear naked in her previous films, and that she was devoid of any personality and acting ability. Even worse for the portrayal of someone who made her way as a dancer, Martine Carol had absolutely no dancing ability whatever, as is quite evident in this film, and to top the whole folly, no effort was made to display her body, as the actual Lola had been only too eager to do in the pursuit of fame and fortune. In the film no real reason for her career is shown, either in her circumstances or in her personality as depicted, other than a desire to spite her mother, which is hardly adequate. There are some compensations for these lacks, and they are of course achieved with a combination of the movements of camera, actors, and even the decor. The opening eight minutes establishing the circus setting are undoubtedly the peak of Ophuls' achievement in this direction, but with the first flashback we get the stale *marivaudage* of Lola's dialogue with Franz Lizst, which is shot with a mechanical alternation of identical reverse-angles in the manner of the duologue scenes in *la Ronde*. Jacques Natanson was not Schnitzler, as a quotation demonstrates:

Liszt: Do you never dream of a caprice that never ends?

Lola Montès: Oh ... dreams! Dreams are personal, you cannot share them with somebody else, but sometimes they are very embarrassing.

Liszt: Embarrassing! Why? Because they do not last?

Lola: Perhaps!

Liszt: Because there is an awakening? It is enough to hold on to them, to live them before it is too late, isn't that so?

Lola: Life for me is .... a movement.

Liszt: You are tired by the journey.

Lola: No, a little sad.... But if the inn is charming ... A nice dinner and it will pass.

These lines receive a performance that matches them in quality – a pair of bad actors' idea of 'sophisticated' acting.

A curious feature of *Lola Montès*, particularly given Ophuls' comments on the use of CinemaScope before he started work on it, is how little he used the 'Scope frame in composition. Very nearly all the action in the whole film falls within an Academy aspect ratio frame area, as when a 'Scope print is scanned for T.V. transmission. The only exception to this is the scene in a theatre box in which Lola's mother tries to betrothe her to a rich man. In fact for an appreciable part of the film Ophuls has the frame physically masked in to Academy proportions, which is a defeatist attitude to composition when the new format had made a whole new approach possible. If the intention was to use the contrast between the sections that have the masked-in frame, and the sections that have the full 'Scope frame, the answer is that this does not work in this film, because the outer edges of the full 'Scope image are just filled with bits of decoration that are compositionally connected very weakly, if at all, with the central area. There are just one or two novel ideas for 'Scope framing in the inn scene with Franz Liszt, but this is not much for such a long film. Rather better use is made of dutch tilts, which still crop up occasionally in this film, with the tilt slowly developing during the course of the shot.

The second half of *Lola Montès* is devoted to her liaison with the King of Bavaria, and here all the scenes are protracted far beyond what their substance will bear, mostly without any compensating visual interest whatever being supplied. This is also the section where the bad acting in subsidiary parts, usually hovering round the edges of Ophuls' films, becomes most obtrusive. To love actors too much is a doubtful asset in directing them.

After the catastrophic failure at the box-office of *Lola Montès*, and when it became clear that Max Ophuls was not going to get any more work because of this, his admirers put forward the claim that *Lola Montès* was an avant-garde masterpiece, and hence too good for the understanding of the general public. This is clearly untrue of the film in the form in which Ophuls considered it finished, for it contains too much material that is crashingly conventional, as I have briefly indicated above, and it was certainly made with the intention of making a profit, which is never the case with true avant-garde films.

The Evaluation of Max Ophuls' Films

Summarizing Max Ophuls' stylistic progression, it can be said that he moved from a work, *Die verliebte Firma*, that was solidly within the norms for its kind, time, and place, to *Die verkaufte Braut*, in which he attempted to combine features drawn from widely disparate sources, and also showed signs of wanting to outdo the best German musicals of the time in bravura. In this he was partially successful, though at some cost in craftsmanship and coherence. This last objection could not be made against *La signora di tutti*, in which camera movement was pushed into new regions, and other minor flashiness was well integrated. So both *Die verkaufte Braut* and *La signora di tutti* score well on my first evaluative criterion, which is that of originality, but *Liebelei* is not outstanding in this respect except for such lesser features as the use of music and the ending. As other directors retreated from the 'long take with mobile camera' style as the 'thirties wore on, so did Ophuls, and retreat towards conventionality, in this as in other features, reduces the value of some of his late 'thirties films. I consider unvaried repetition of a style once established to lessen the value of any film-maker's work, and my attitude on this point is very different to that of the strict *auteur* theory, according to which all that matters is the successful expression of the maker's personality, and that all the films in which this

happens are equally valuable, no matter how similar they may be.

In any case, amongst the films from the later nineteen-thirties *la Tendre ennemie* is distinguished by some features previously commented upon, including a fresh way of handling flashbacks, even though it declines into banality in its later stages. *Komedie om Geld* also has something to be said for it on the score of originality, as it contains the most extreme form of Brechtian presentation recorded on film up to that date, but Max Ophuls' other pre-war films offer little in this respect.

There is some improvement in his American films, with his return to an increased use of camera movement, though since he was entering an established trend, the distinction rests in exactly how that camera movement was used to follow people around, rather than in its amount. The post-1950 films push into new territory from a formal point of view, mostly in terms of unvarying and remote camera distance, and in the case of *le Plaisir* and *Lola Montès*, in terms of camera movement. Obviously the framing presentation of *la Ronde* and *Lola Montès* are also extremely important in terms of originality.

The Influence of the Films of Max Ophuls

As far as I can tell, the films Ophuls made before 1950 had no influence whatever on any other film-maker. However the films of his second French period fairly certainly had a considerable effect on the Nouvelle Vague directors, particularly Jean-Luc Godard and Jacques Demy, and this was explicitly acknowledged by the latter. Godard's fondness for having the participants in a conversation wandering round the room, or even from room to room for no necessary reason probably comes from Ophuls, as may his use of a consistently remote camera. There is also an inclination towards pointless actor mobility in early Chabrol. The use of audience distancing devices in narration was presumably encouraged by *la Ronde* and *Lola Montès*, and Godard's use of artificial colour filtration by the latter. Stanley Kubrick has also spoken of his debt to Ophuls with regard to the use of camera movement. Since my influence criterion is weighted more heavily for influence on good films rather than bad films, all Ophuls' post-1950 films score heavily in this respect.

Success in Realizing the Maker's Intentions

This criterion is obviously the most complex and difficult to evaluate, but at least the difficulties are out in the open where they can be discussed objectively, which is more than can be said for other approaches to aesthetic evaluation. To judge by his autobiography and interviews, Ophuls accepted the conventional attitudes of mainstream directors of his time towards the film-making task, at any rate until his return to France. In *Max Ophuls par Max Ophuls* he says it was his desire to "... obtain for each scene what seemed to me the ideal expression of the content.", and his other relatively few specific comments on aesthetic points chime with conventional attitudes. It will be readily apparent that my knowledge of this attitude of his has underlain my analysis of his films earlier in this chapter. Because of Ophuls' acceptance of the conventional film-maker's attitudes, features in his films made before 1950 that could be guaranteed to alienate the general audience can reasonably be considered to be faults. This mostly applies to the pre-war films, and mostly involves irrationality and non-sequiturs in the narrative construction of some of them, particularly *Komedie om Geld* and *Yoshiwara*, but also to some extent *Divine* and *Sans lendemain*. The American films are largely free from this failing, except for *letter from an Unknown Woman*.

But when Ophuls returned to France there came to be change in his attitude under the influence of those French critics who praised his work in the most hyperbolic terms. In articles and interviews by Ophuls in *Cahiers du Cinéma*, mostly from after the *Lola Montès* disaster, this change in attitude is clearly visible. In a dialogue written by Ophuls in *Cahiers du Cinéma* No.81, he imagines a conversation between himself and a potential backer which goes in part as follows:

Financier. And who guarantees me that what gives you pleasure will give the spectators pleasure?
Director. Well, one believes that one has a heart that beats for them, insights that see for them, in short, finally, a nose.
Financier. Aside from that, there are other guarantees?
Director. None.

And later in this particular piece Ophuls sees himself in company with artists and poets, and says that he will take his time over shooting a film if he feels it appropriate. There are no signs of such attitudes in his earlier statements. The quotation above also shows a certain lack of contact with reality, since the box-office failure of his last two films clearly indicated that Ophuls did not have the empathy with the audience that he continued to imagine he had.

Other comments in these last interviews suggest that Ophuls was indeed moving in an inconsistent way towards the truly avant-garde attitude that commercial success did not matter to him. For this reason some of the usual limits that are placed on formal deviations by the necessity of appealing to the general audience can no longer be considered to apply to his post-1950 films, and such things as the continuously distant camera of *Madame de ...* cannot be considered a fault. Since Ophuls made no admissions of failure with his last two films, though he did for some of the earlier ones, I have to give him the benefit of the doubt and take it that he exactly realized his intentions in this case. This is also the appropriate point to remind the reader that I place the least weight on my intentionality criterion, and the most weight on my originality criterion.

So all in all, using my three criteria for aesthetic evaluation, Max Ophuls' last French films must be rated very highly indeed, followed by the somewhat less valuable *Liebelei* and

La signora di tutti, and then some of the American films for the perfection of their craftsmanship. Of these there is no way that *Letter from an Unknown Woman* can be rated more highly than *The Reckless Moment* according to the criteria being used, since the themes and structure are no more original, and it did badly at the box-office as well. (This judgement may cause some people to wish to reject the evaluative methods being used here out of hand. Let them reflect that their strong personal preference for *Letter* may depend on personality factors which cannot be expected to be the same for everybody else. My purpose is to eliminate these subjective elements as far as possible, and I believe I have succeeded, since if I were proceeding by my own feelings alone I would rate the last three Ophuls films rather low.) Of the remaining films from the earlier period there are one or two that are lifted slightly above the level of good craftsmanship by a few specific features that I have previously mentioned, though some of them such as *Divine* and *Sans lendemain* do not have even that.

Interpretations

The general meanings that have been read from (or into) Max Ophuls' films mostly derive from French critical writing of the nineteen-fifties, and one major source can be studied in Claude Beylie's *Max Ophuls* (Club du Livre de Cinéma, Brussels, 1958). The basically Catholic nature of this and other French interpretations can be rejected out of hand as a classic case of the particular spectator seeing what he wants to see in a complex object, a process as mired in subjectivity as picking out images of objects from the cracks and patches on an old wall, and hence of no lasting interest. The justification for my rejection of the religious interpretation is that Ophuls never showed the slightest sign of religious feeling or interest in his autobiography or interviews, and his films contain no explicit signs of religion beyond a few minor features demanded by the works from which they were adapted.

The better-known comments on Max Ophuls in Andrew Sarris' *The American Cinema* (E.P. Dutton, 1968) are largely an ingenious secularization of Claude Beylie's interpretations. The one aspect of Sarris' interpretations that I find convincing, and then only in relation to the last French films, is a feeling of the hollowness of life, tinged with despair. This interpretation is convincing because it can be related to the bad heart Ophuls suffered from in the latter part of his life.

In fact Ophuls himself has explicitly indicated a central feature of his films, in his expressed preference for people who are like 'big children' (in *Mon Expérience* in *Cahiers du Cinéma* No.81, March 1958), and also in his repeated strong expressions of liking for actors. This excessive fondness for actors must be responsible for the less than ideal performances and casting in a number of his films. In any case, 'big children' accurately describes the protagonists of what are usually regarded as his most characteristic films, and this interest can be traced all the way back to his first film, a fantasy which has children taking the place of adults in the social world. Such a central preoccupation is no drawback in the light of my criteria for aesthetic evaluation, but it surely raises an obstacle for those who require that a work of art presents or promotes 'maturity' or other 'finer' moral qualities.

The temper of our times forces me unwillingly to write down the connection between the shallowness of many of the heroines of Max Ophuls' films and the philandering side of his personality which is smugly implied in his autobiography and interviews, and made explicit in Howard Koch's reminiscences in *Film Comment* Vol.6, No.4. To say it simply, Ophuls believed in, and acted on, the 'double standard'. As the hero of *Die verliebte Firma* put it to the would-be actress to whom he was proposing marriage and domesticity: the dizzy, amusing film stars were people he could have a good time with during part of the day, but then he would like to come home to a wife and home comforts. There is no sign of Ophuls' acceptance of the possibility of any kind of inverse situation in his films or his life.

It is important to note that the heroines of most of Ophuls' films *choose* to put themselves on display in one way or another; the particular profession is not forced on them, as was also the case for the real actresses who fascinated Ophuls himself. He was also obsessed to an exceptional degree with the theatre, and the way this too is directly represented in his films is unique in the medium. Other minor disconnected themes that surface a few times in a few of his movies are oppressive parents and leftish political attitudes, but both of these are, with the exception of *Komedie om Geld*, just stuck into the film rather than being an integral part of its structure, in the way that a leftish political attitude was a fundamental part of Renoir's 'thirties films. One of the more amusing sights of the last decade has been the neglect by Marxist film 'theorists' of genuinely left directors like Ophuls and Renoir in favour of less talented directors like Douglas Sirk, who was at best an opportunist liberal, both in his life and in his films.

I see no way that Ophuls' use of the moving camera can be associated exclusively with the themes of mortality and the loss of love, as Andrew Sarris would have it, since his pre-war films are shot much more conventionally, including those films like *Sans lendemain* which deal specifically with the standard theme of 'weepies'; the loss of love. In fact Ophuls applied the long take with moving camera indiscriminately, as the 'Maison Tellier' episode of *le Plaisir* demonstrates.

The really distinctive thing about Max Ophuls' films is that there is nothing underneath the superficially present concerns already mentioned, which is not the case with some other major directors, where at least some of the deeper interpretations made of their work can find plausible circumstantial support. One could make an interesting case, if it mattered, that Ophuls' cinema is one of immaturity rather than the reverse. After all, songs about the loss of love are at least as much favoured by the young as by the old.

The Ophuls problem is that his few major and minor themes, his motifs and his forms, do not really connect with each other, and only in some of his films do some of them integrate properly with the story. When he was not working from a strongly constructed pre-existing narrative, he was left with his own major interests in theatre and women, but these interests had no real causal relation with anything else in the world at large that he wanted to put into his films, and so tended to produce an invertebrate lack of structure. He did make some attempts to compensate for this with formal repetitions and mirrorings, particularly in *Lola Montès*, but these were insufficient to hold together films that were deficient in other respects.

At the end of his career Ophuls claimed that he would have liked to work in the fairy-tale mode, but here he was probably deluding himself, for both real and synthetic fairy-tales demand well-established connections between their events if they are to be compelling, even if those connections are unnatural. One might cite Cocteau's *la Belle et la Bête* (1946). Fantasies by Frank Capra and Michael Powell were also successful in the post-war years, but this genre demands a belief by its creators in powerful forces below appearances. All the indications are that Ophuls was not equipped to handle either of these modes. However there is a fascinating indication in his radio script *Gedanken über den Film* of 1956 that he could have taken part in the Nouvelle Vague developments if he had lived. This radio feature keeps changing freely between sections that are straightforward dramatizations, or are readings of quotations from literary classics, or first-person reflections by the author, or musical quotations, or interjections, and so on, in a way that fairly closely anticipates what Jean-Luc Godard was to do in films after 1960. But as things stand Ophuls did nothing like it himself in the cinema.

23. AFTERWORD

Here I conclude for the moment my demonstration that, with the right sort of approach, a good deal of progress can be made in dealing with some aspects of film analysis and film history. Although the kind of methods I use have already been succesful in musicology and art history, they are particularly suitable to the analysis of mainstream cinema because films are in general synthetic group creations resulting from the not quite completely co-ordinated efforts of a number of people. Virtually all ordinary commercial films are inherently superficial if seen from the standpoint of high literature, and one of the reasons for this is that there are hardly any movies whose every aspect and detail has been controlled and considered at length by one person, in the way that we suppose that the interrelationships of every word and sound have been considered at length by a poet in the composition of a good poem. (Though the extent to which this is really true is something that I suspect literary types do not really want to investigate).

In my approach, the films themselves form the basic material for research and reference, with other contextual material being subsidiary to the inspection of as large a number of the films as possible. With more work it would be possible to expand each of the preceding chapters into a whole book, and in the process one would do the work that neither I (nor anyone else), has done, such as inspecting the records of film equipment manufacturing companies and film studios for exact information on the introduction of film technology. Frequently all that can be found in the trade and technical journals is the announcement that a particular piece of equipment is about to become available, and there is subsequently no indication in such places when it was first actually used.

Worse than that, what information there is in the trade journals is very often incomplete, and it is impossible to understand its significance without a great deal of background knowledge. For instance, there is very little significant information on the mechanical details of the early versions of the Mitchell camera that was published at the time, or indeed later. From the first of these descriptions, in the *American Cinematographer* (Vol.2, no.18, p.13), it is impossible to understand exactly how the film transport mechanism worked, unless one is familiar with the camera (or its descendants) itself, and this and subsequent sources carefully avoid showing any picture of the gate mechanism. This is quite typical of the situation, and for this reason nothing is to be gained by giving precise references to the line in a trade journal where I picked up an isolated scrap of information from which I then made a set of deductions about availability and use, by combining this information with other scraps of information, and then taking all this in conjunction with my knowledge of the film equipment of more recent times. Since the first edition of this book there has been a practical demonstration of the pitfalls for the uninformed trying to do this kind of work, in Bordwell and Thompson's *The Classical Hollywood Cinema* (Routledge, 1985). Here the authors repeatedly miss key points, or get them wrong because of their incompetence in film technique, aided by their conceit that a Ph.D. in Film Studies, combined with as many footnotes as possible, is all you need to produce useful knowledge. In any case, written sources alone should not be trusted, as I have illustrated at one or two points along the way.

The book you have just read also conclusively demonstrates at various points throughout its length that the search, so dear to Marxists, for a few simple overarching principles that will explain the development of film technology or film style – whether these principles be ideas like standardization, efficiency, or class advantage – is futile, and only the ignorant and self-deluding could believe they have discovered them.

Nevertheless, there is much more that can be done in the way of detailed rational explanation for what happened in the development of cinema, and there is lots of room in this field for more work, though only if done by well-informed people. Although during recent years there has been an increasing interest in doing research on the early years of the cinema to find out what actually happened, rather than what has been copied from one history book to the next, I am afraid most people in film studies are still quite satisfied with creating their own feeble fantasies of interpretation of the 'meaning' of films.

24. BIBLIOGRAPHY

The basic research for the technology aspect of this book was done by going through complete runs of *The Journal of the Society of Motion Picture and Television Engineers* (originally *The Transactions of the Society of Motion Picture Engineers*) from 1916 to 1970, and *The American Cinematographer* from 1921 to 1992, and then by checking all the other old books on film technique and technology available in England. Apart from what I already knew about film-making from sources I have now mostly forgotten, I list below those other books which provided some extra items of information.

AGFA *Kinehandbuch* (ca.1927).

Alton, John *Painting with Light* (Macmillan, 1949).

anon. *Encyclopédie par l'image. Le cinéma* (Hachette, 1925).

Bennet, Colin N. *The Handbook of Cinematography* (E.T. Heron & Co., 1911).

Cameron, James R. *Cameron's Encyclopaedia of Sound Motion Pictures* (Cameron Publishing Co., 1930 & 1945).

Cameron, James R. *Sound Motion Picture Recording and Reproducing* (Cameron Publishing Co., 1930).

Clarke, Charles G. *Professional Cinematography* (American Society of Cinematographers, 1964).

Clyne, Adrian Cornwell- *Colour Cinematography* (Chapman & Hall, 1951).

Combined Intelligence Objectives Sub-Comittee *Investigation of Film Production and Methods at AGFA* (H.M.S.O., 1945).

Cowan, Lester *Recording Sound for Motion Pictures* 9McGraw-Hill, 1931).

Ducom, Jacques *Le Cinématographe muet, sonore, parlant* (193?).

Franklin, Harold B. *Sound Motion Pictures* (Doubleday & Doran, 1929).

Gregory, Carl Louis (editor) *A Condensed Course in Motion Picture Photography* (Falk Publishing Co., 1920).

Hall, Hal (editor) *The Cinematographic Annual. Vol.1* (American Society of Cinematographers, 1930).

Hall, Hal (editor) *The Cinematographic Annual. Vol.2* (American Society of Cinematographers, 1931).

Hepworth, Cecil M. *Animated Photography* (Hazell, Watson, & Viney, 1899).

Hulfish, David S. *Cyclopaedia of Motion Picture Work* (American Technical Society, 1911).

Hulfish, David S. *Motion Picture Work* (American School of Correspondence, 1913 & 1915).

Jones, Bernard E. *The Cinematograph Book* (Cassel, 1919).

Klein, Adrian Bernard *Colour Cinematography* (1st. & 2nd. editions) (Chapman & Hall, 1936 & 1939).

Lehmann, H. *Die Kinematographie* (Teubner, 1911).

Lescarboura, Austin C. *The Cinema Handbook* (Sampson Low, Marston & Co., 1921).

Liesegang, F. Paul *Handbuch der praktischen Kinematographie* (Verlag M. Eger, 1918).

Lipp, H. and Felix, F. *Führer durch das Wesen der Kinematographie. 2nd. Ed.* (Gustav Kühn, 1921).

MacBean, L.C. *Kinematograph Studio Technique* (Pitman, 1922).

McKay, Herbert C. *Handbook of Motion Picture Photography* (Falk Publishing Co., 1927).

Mascelli, Joseph V. *The Five C's of Cinematography* (Cine/Grafic Publications, 1965).

Pathé-Cinéma *Le film vierge Pathé* (, Pathé, 1926).

Pfeiffer, H. (ed.) *Das Deutsche Lichtbildbuch* (Deutschen Lichtbild Gesellschaft, ca.1925).

Robinson, Jack Fay *Bell & Howell Company: A 75 Year History* (Bell & Howell Company, 1982)

Rolle, Johannes *Kinotechnisches Jahrbuch* (Guido Hackebeil A-G., 1924).

Schmidt, R. & Kochs, A. *Farbfilmtechnik* (Max Hesses Verlag, 1943).

Talbot, I.A. *Moving Pictures: How they are made and worked* (Heinemann, 1912).

Thomas, D.B. *The First Colour Motion Pictures* (Her Majesty's Stationery Office, 1969).

Thun, R. *Der Film in der Technik* (V.D.I. Verlag, 1925).

Wheeler, Leslie J. *The Principles of Cinematography* (1953).

Other books which provide useful background information for readers of this book, including more pictures of film equipment than I can afford, and which in a few cases have also provided one or two pieces of information that I have used, include the following:

Abel, Richard *French Cinema: The First Wave 1915-1929* (Princeton University Press, 1984).

Abel, Richard *French Film Theory and Criticism: a history/anthology 1907-1939* (Princeton University Press, 1988)

Balio, Tino (ed.) *The American Film Industry* (University of Wisconsin Press, 1976).

Balshofer, Fred J. & Miller, A. *One Reel a Week* (University of California Press, 1967).

Barnes, John *The Beginnings of the Cinema in England* (David & Charles, 1976).

Barnes, John *The Rise of the Cinema in Great Britain* (Bishopsgate Press, 1983).

Barnes, John *Pioneers of the British Film* (Bishopsgate Press, 1988).

Barnes, John *Filming the Boer War* (Bishopsgate Press, 1992).

Bowser, Eileen *The Transformation of Cinema: 1907-1915* (Charles Scribner's Sons, 1990).

Brown, Karl *Adventures with D.W. Griffith* 9Secker & Warburg, 1973).

Brownlow, Kevin *The Parade's Gone By* (Secker & Warburg, 1968).

Brownlow, Kevin & Kobal, John *Hollywood -- The Pioneers* (Collins, 1979).

Carr, R.E., and R.M. Hayes. *Wide Screen Movies: A History and Filmography* (McFarland & Co., 1988).

Dmytryk, Edward *On Film Making* (Focal Press, 1986).

Eisner, Lotte H. *The Haunted Screen* (Thames & Hudson, 1969).

Elsaesser, T. (ed.) *Early Cinema: space - frame - narrative* (BFI Publishing, 1990).

Fell, John L. (ed.) *Film Before Griffith* (University of California Press, 1983).

Fell, John L. *Film and the Narrative Tradition* (University of Oklahoma Press, 1974).

Gaudreault, André *Cinema 1900-1906 (Vol.2 Analytical Filmography)* (Fédération Internationale des Archives du Film, 1982).

Gunning, Tom *D. W. Griffith and the Origin of the American Narrative Film* (University of Illinois Press, 1991).

Higham, Charles *Hollywood Cameramen* (Thames & Hudson, 1971).

Holman, Roger (ed.) *Cinema 1900-1906 (Vol.1 Symposium)* (Fédération Internationale des Archives du Film, 1982).

Hull, D.S. *Film in the Third Reich* (University of California Press, 1969).

Koszarski, Richard *An Evening's Entertainment: the Age of the Silent Feature Picture* (Charles Scribner's Sons, 1990).

Low, Rachel & Manvell, Roger *The History of the British Film: 1896-1906 Vol.1* (Allen & Unwin, 1948).

Low, Rachel *The History of the British Film: 1907-1913 Vol.2* (Allen & Unwin 1949).

Low, Rachel *The History of the British Film: 1914-1918* (Allen & Unwin, 1950).

Low, Rachel *The History of the British Film: 1918-1929* (Allen & Unwin, 1971).

Mayersberg, Paul *Hollywood, The Haunted House* (Allen Lane, 1967).

Musser, Charles *The Emergence of Cinema: The American Screen to 1907* (Charles Scribner's Sons, 1990).

Perkins, Victor F. *Film as Film* (Penguin Books, 1972).

Pratt, George C. *Spellbound in Darkness* (New York Graphic Society, 1973).

Prolo, Maria Adriana *Storia del cinema muto Italiano, Vol.1* (Poligono, 1951).

Renzi, Renzo (ed.) *Sperduto nel buio* (Capelli editore, 1991).

Rosten, Leo C. *Hollywood: The Movie Colony, The Movie Makers* (Harcourt, Brace 1941).

Sadoul, Georges *Histoire Générale du Cinéma (3rd. Ed.)* (Denoël, 1973).

Schaefer, Dennis & Salvato, Larry *Masters of Light* (University of California Press, 1984).

Smith, Albert E. *Two Reels and a Crank* (Doubleday, 1952).

Spehr, Paul C. *The Movies Begin* (The Newark Museum, 1977).

Taylor, R. & Christie, I. (eds.) *The Film Factory: Russian and Soviet Cinema in Documents, 1896-1939* (Routledge, 1988).

Taylor, R. & Christie, I. (eds.) *Inside the The Film Factory: New Approaches to Russian and Soviet Cinema* (Routledge, 1991).

Tsivian, Yuri & Usai, Paolo Cherchi *Silent Witnesses: Russian Films 1908-1919* (Edizioni Biblioteca dell'Immagine, 1989).

Usai, Paolo Cherchi & Codelli, Lorenzo (eds.) *Before Caligari* (Edizioni Biblioteca dell'Imagine, 1990)

Usai, Paolo Cherchi (ed.) *Vitagraph Co. of America* (Edizioni Studio Tesi, 1987)

Walker, Alexander *The Shattered Silents* (Elm Tree Books, 1978).

Weis, E. & Belton, J. (eds.) *Theory and Practice of Film Sound* (Columbia University Press, 1985).

Werner, Gösta *Mauritz Stiller och hans Filmer* (Norstedt & Söhner, 1971).

Another important part of the background to this book is the ideas that film-makers have had about what they were doing, and a quick round-up of their statements about this can be found in:

Leyda, Jay *Voices of Film Experience: 1894 to the present* (Collier Macmillan, 1977).

Koszarski, Richard *Hollywood Directors 1914-1940* (Oxford University Press, 1976).

Koszarski, Richard *Hollywood Directors 1941-1976* (Oxford University Press, 1977).

To get the most value from the present work the reader should have a fair familiarity with present-day film technology, but failing this, some work such as Bernard L. Happé's *Basic Motion Picture Technology* (Focal Press, 1978), should be consulted.

Many of the key films made before 1909 that are referred to in the early chapters of this history can now be bought on video-cassettes from the British Film Institute.

25. TECHNICAL GLOSSARY AND INDEX

Additive Colour Printer A printing machine for colour film that controls the colour balance of the print automatically by the independent control of red, blue, and green light beams shining through it. The current standard type of machine, 242.

American Foreground (Obsolete) Framing with the actors playing up to a line nine feet from the camera. Roughly equivalent to the modern Medium Shot, 87, 90

Anamorphic 1. Having a noticeably distorted shape. 2. The special case of this, more usual in terms of film practice, of an image being distorted by compression purely in the horizontal direction, 260, 265, 293.

Anamorphic Lens Lens which produces compression of the film image in one direction only. 247, 248, 261, 262, 291

Anamorphosis The production of an image of noticeably distorted shape, 132, 166, 167.

Animation Producing the illusion of filmed action by shooting each frame separately, while changing the ojects in the scene in front of the lens between each exposure, 48, 80, 83.

Aperture:(Film) The rectangular opening cut in the metal plate immediately in front of the film in the camera that delimits the area of film receiving the image for each exposure, 138.

Aperture:(Lens) The variable opening in the iris diaphragm built into the middle of camera lenses that regulates the amount of light passing through the lens, 31, 84, 85, 127-9, 154, 160-3, 182, 185, 196, 202, 207, 229, 232, 277, 279, 287.

Aperture:(Projector) The rectangular opening cut in the metal plate (the aperture plate) immediately in front of the film passing through a projector that delimits the extent of the image on the film that is actually projected onto the cinema screen, 211.

Apotheotic Shot (Neologism) A shot whose nature is modelled on the theatrical apotheosis as used in the nineteenth century and earlier, 55.

Arc Floodlight Floodlight (q.v.) whose source is an electrical arc, 32, 43, 44, 64, 67, 69, 71, 73, 74, 75, 76, 116, 118, 119, 120, 122, 123, 124, 152, 153, 182, 234.

Arc Light Light whose source is the flame created by the electrical spark between two carbon poles. The earliest form of electrical lighting, and hence sometimes referred to up to the early years of this century as "the electric light". See **Arc Floodlight** and **Arc Spotlight**, 41, 42, 66, 70, 77, 133, 255.

Arc Spotlight Spotlight (q.v.) whose source is an electrical arc, 115, 116, 151, 254, 271, 287.

Art Titles Intertitles incorporating illustrations, 136.

Aspect Ratio The ratio of the vertical to horizontal dimensions of the screen image, 209, 211, 246, 247, 260, 262, 293.

Atmospheric Insert (Neologism) A shot of a location in which actors do not appear, 133, 139, 174, 175.

Available Light The light ordinarily present in a location used for filming, without the addition of special film lighting, 43, 44, 68, 69, 179

Average Shot Length or **ASL** The length or running time of a film, excluding the front and end titles, divided by the number of shots, including intertitles, in it. Also the quantity arrived at in the same way for parts of a film, 144 and very frequently thereafter.

Background Music Music on the film soundtrack for which there is no source indicated in the film. (See **Mood Music**), 213, 299

Background Plate The film that is shot to provide the background image for Background Projection (q.v.) or Travelling Mattes (q.v.), 195

Back Angle Sometimes used for **Reverse angle** (q.v.).

Core Lighting Term used in modern still photography to describe figure lighting with equal lights sets straight out at each side shining towards the figure, and so leaving a dark unilluminated band down the centre of the face and body. A variety of **double cross back lighting** , 154

Counter-Matte A **Matte** (q.v.) which reveals exactly what its complementary Matte obscures of the image, and vice-versa, 83.

Crabbing Tracking movement with respect to a fixed scene at right angles to the camera lens axis.

Crab Dolly A **Dolly**, all four of whose wheels may be instantaneously rotated through 90 degrees to change its motion from a forwards to a sideways **Crabbing** movement, 231, 258, 291, 306.

Cross-cutting (between parallel actions) Use of shots alternately showing parts of two actions which are understood to be taking place simultaneously, 57, 60, 98-101, 136, 139-141, 172, 224.

Crystal Synchronization Usually abbreviated to **Crystal Sync.**, this refers to synchronous sound filming with a camera and recorder kept in synchronization by the pulses generated by a pair of matched crystal-controlled oscillators attached to each of them. 331.

Cut The direct transition from one film shot to the next film shot without use of a fade, dissolve, or wipe, 49, 50, 52-57, 59, 91, 93, 97, 98, 138, 249, 300.

Cutting Copy A print made directly from the original negative of the film shots, and used for the editing process. See also **Work Print**.

Cutting on Action Making the cut to another angle on a scene in the middle of an actors movement, 60.

Cutting in the Camera Method of shooting a film that produces only those shots that the director knows he will use in the finished film, with no alternative angles shot of the same action in any scene.

Cylindrical Lens Lens which has at least one surface formed by an axial segment of cylinder, as opposed to the segments of a sphere which form the surfaces of ordinary lenses.

Day for Night Cinematography The filming of a scene in the daytime with special exposure and filtration to give the impression that it is taking place at night, 148.

Deep Focus A popular term for cinematography with great **Depth of Field** (q.v.), 163, 202, 208, 232, 233, 234, 274, 287, 310.

Depth of Field The distance along the lens axis in front of the camera over which filmed objects appear to be in sharp focus when the film is projected on the cinema screen, 90, 127, 161, 162, 163, 182, 185, 208, 233, 246, 261, 280, 287.

Desaturation Reducing the intensity of the colours in a scene in a colour film, 31, 195, 196, 229, 242, 251, 269, 271, 286.

Developing Chemical treatment to turn the invisible latent image in an exposed film into a visible image, 31, 63, 195, 196, 229, 242, 251, 269-271, 286.

Dialogue Titles Intertitles which reproduce words understood to be spoken by a character in the adjoining shot, 59, 107, 108, 135, 136.

Diffusing Screen A sheet of translucent material, for instance "ripple" glass, placed in front of the opening of a lighting unit to soften the light that it emits, 32, 118, 120, 129, 153.

Diffusion Filter Filter placed in front of a camera lens to reduce or soften the definition of the image that the lens produces. See **Lens Diffusion**.

Dioptre An optical measure (related to the reciprocal of the focal length) which is used colloquially to denote a supplementary lens which is placed in front of the prime camera lens to reduce its focus to those distances close to it which are normally inacessible.

Direct Lighting Film lighting falling direcy onto the scene without being bounced off a reflector, 254.

Directional Continuity Getting the directions of entrance and exit of actors, and of their glances, correct according to standard film conventions, 97, 171.

Direct Cinema The original American term for **Cinéma vérité** (q.v.), 256, 265.

Dissolve The gradual fading out of one film shot simultaneously with the fading in of a second shot which replaces it on the film, 34, 52-59, 84, 85, 101, 130, 140, 147, 156, 157, 165, 166, 176, 180, 195, 200, 228, 236, 249, 252, 253, 283, 296.

Documentary Montage Sequence (Neologism) Montage sequence containing documentary-type material not involving the actors in the film, 175.

Dolly Wheeled vehicle specially made to carry a camera for making **Tracking Shots**, 184, 206, 278, 292, 307.

Down-Angle Sometimes used for **High-Angle**.

Dunning Process Early **travelling matte process**, 186, 187, 209, 210

Duplicating Negative and **Duplicating Positive** Special film stocks intended to produce copies of negative and positive film with the minimum possible loss of quality, 180, 210, 228, 280.

Duplitized Print Stock (Obsolete) Special print stock use with two-colour colour processes, and having emulsion coated on both sides of the transparent base material, 198.

Dutch Tilt Shot in which the top and bottom of the frame are at an angle to the horizontal lines in the image. See also **Off Angle**, 159, 206, 207, 235, 289, 311, 312.

Dynamic Microphone See **Moving Coil Microphone**, 212.

Edge Numbers Small numbers incorporated in film stock during manufacture at one foot intervals (or half foot intervals on modern 16 mm. stock), and increasing serially throughout the length of the roll, 286.

Effect Lighting Lighting intended to suggest some unusual light source in the scene, and other than that for conventional illumination of the set, 43, 44.

Emblematic Shot (neologism) Extra shot attached to the beginning or end of a film which does not contain any of the action of the narrative, but indicates by its contents the general nature of the film, 54, 55, 89, 90.

Exposure Meter Device for determining the correct exposure of a scene, 181, 227.

Extended Development see **Forced Development**, 251

Eyeline The notional line (and its extensions) joining the eyes of a person in a film scene to what they are looking at, 94, 171, 172.

Eyeline Match A cut to another camera position within a scene which stays on the same side of the **Eyeline** as it had been established in the previous shot. (Also referred to as "not crossing the eyeline".), 170, 171, 296

Fade Gradual darkening of the film image to complete blackness (Fade-out), or conversely gradual appearance of the film image at correct density from complete blackness (Fade-in), 53, 57, 84, 102, 127, 141, 147, 156, 157, 165, 200, 228, 249, 252, 253, 283, 296.

Featured Music Music accompanying a film scene which is ostensibly produced by a source within the scene. Also called **Source Music**, 298.

Fill Light Light producing the subsidiary lighting of the actors which has been applied from a frontal direction other than that of the **Key Light** (q.v.), 73, 77, 117, 121, 123, 152, 154, 256, 287

Filter Glass or plastic plate coloured or coated with dye, or with irregular surface, which is placed in front of, or behind, a lens to produce some change in the image-forming light passing through it, 124, 259, 269, 274, 288.

Fish-eye Lens Lens which includes the full 180 degree field in front of the camera, 259, 260.

Flashback A scene taking place earlier inserted amongst scenes taking place in the present time of the film story, 84, 100-102, 139, 140, 165, 172, 218, 290, 304, 309, 312.

Flashforward A scene that takes place later than the events in the framing story, 101, 290.

Flashing Exposing the negative briefly to weak white light before or after exposure in the camera, to change its photographic response. See also **Fogging the negative** and **Latensification**, 270, 286.

Floodlight Type of lighting unit which emits a fairly even intensity of light over 90 degrees or more in the horizontal and vertical directions, 65, 70, 117, 197, 199, 203, 205, 254, 272.

Fluid Head Pivot system placed between the camera and its support (tripod, etc.) in which irregularities in the camera rotations are smoothed out by hydraulic damping, 257.

Focal Length The distance from the optical centre of a lens to the plane behind it at which an infinitely distant object produces the sharpest possible image.

Focus-Pull (or **Pull-Focus**) A change in the focus of a lens during the course of a shot, 57, 204, 292.

Fog filter A filter put in front of the camera lens that produces a very fuzzy image, something like a scene observed in a fog, 269, 272.

Fogging the negative See **Flashing**, 227, 252.

Foot-Candle A measure of the intensity of light.

Forced Development The development of film stock for an appreciably greater length of time than that recommended by its manufacturer, 179, 251, 252, 270.

Frame Refers to both an individual image on the film strip and to the edge of the film image.

Framing Movement A small pan or tilt (approximately, less than 30 degrees) made by the camera operator upon the movement of an actor to keep him or her well framed, 82, 126, 307.

Freeze Frame The image in a single film frame rendered stationary on the screen through the reproduction of many copies of it down the length of the film by means of **Optical Printing** , 168, 268

French Foreground (Obs.) Framing with the actors playing up to a line four metres from the camera, 90.

Fresnel Lens Large diameter lens without excessive thickness at its centre, which is effectively made up of a series of concentric thin annular lenses. Used to produce an efficient lens for **Fresnel Lens Spotlights**, 202, 203.

Friction Head Arrangement of simple pivots fastened to the top of a tripod to permit rotations of the camera in various directions, 184, 258.

Front Projection Method of combining studio-staged action in the foreground with separately shot film for the background using projection of the latter onto a special highly reflective screen placed behind the actors, 262.

Gauzing The placing of screens of gauze, usually dark in colour, in front of the camera lens to reduce the definition of the image, 163, 164.

Geared Head Mechanical arrangement fastened to the top of a tripod involving gears turned by crank handles that rotates the camera fastened to it in various directions, 258.

Glass Matte Shot Technique for combining action confined to one part of the frame with painted backgrounds which occupy the rest of the film frame, 83, 134, 135, 149

Hand-held camera Filming with a camera supported by the operator's body rather than a fixed camera support, 183, 230, 253, 275, 276, 278, 290.

Hard Cut A cut which produces a marked discontinuity in actor position across itself, 177.

Helicopter Shots Shots taken from a helicopter, 258, 279.

High-Angle Shot or **High Angle** A shot in which the camera is pointed markedly downwards from the horizontal, 54, 85-7, 126, 193, 206, 305.

High-key Lighting Form of lighting of a film shot which produces an image which is made up of mostly light tones. (N.B. This effect is impossible to produce if the sets and costumes are predominantly dark in tone.), 152, 165, 204, 228, 273

Hot Head A motorized pan and tilt head controlled remotely by the operator, 292.

Image Diffusion Reduction of the definition of the film image by the use of a special lens, or by **Gauzing** (q.v.), or by use of a **Diffusion Filter** (q.v.), or by throwing the lens out of focus, or some other means.

Optical Printing Printing of a film positive from a film negative in a special printer which forms the image from one film onto another by a lens system between them. See also **Projection Printer**, 47, 150, 168, 180, 209, 210, 236, 247, 253, 262, 293.

Orthochromatic Film Film whose emulsion responds strongly only to blue and green light, slightly to yellow light, and not at all to red and orange light, 63, 79, 148, 179, 182, 197.

Overcranking Running the camera faster than normal to produce an effect of **Slow Motion** (q.v.), 159

Pack Shot The static shot of the product alone which concludes a cinema or television commercial, 259.

Panchromatic Film Film whose emulsion responds almost equally to all wavelengths of visible light.

Panning Rotation of the camera about a vertical axis while it is taking a shot, 46, 47, 60, 81, 82, 126, 127, 155, 156, 157, 171, 184, 185, 205, 223, 231, 235, 244, 257, 298, 302, 307, 309.

Panoramas Early name that included both **panning shots** and **Phantom Rides**, 32, 33

Parallel Tracking Shot A **Tracking Shot** in which the camera moves at a roughly fixed distance from moving actors, but separately from them, 126.

Phantom Ride Early name for a shot taken from the front or back of a moving train, 32, 37, 38.

Photoflood Bulbs Bulbs of roughly the size of domestic lighting bulbs which give a far brighter light in exchange for a shorter working life of a few hours, 229, 230, 253.

Picture Synchronizer (**Comp-Editor** in the U.S.) A small machine that can sit on an editing bench and show a small film image in sychronism with several magnetic sound tracks for editing purposes, 265.

Plan Américain French name for the **American foreground**, 90.

Point of View Shot or **P.O.V. Shot** A shot taken with the lens pointing along the direction of view of a character shown in the previous or subsequent shot, 49, 51, 60, 61, 85, 94, 95, 96, 97, 126, 132, 138, 139, 147, 158, 167, 193, 237, 267.

Polarizing Filter A transparent sheet of glass and plastic which only permits light polarized in one direction to pass, 245, 288, 294.

Pole-cat Telescopic tube wedged between walls of room or between floor and ceiling to support lights when filming on location, 253.

Post-Synchronization Process of recording sound after the film has been shot in such a manner as to give the illusion that the sound was taken synchronously with the picture, 188, 189, 212, 213, 230, 268, 282, 295.

Projection Printing See **Optical Printing**, 47.

Projection Speeds Speed of film through projector in frames per second, or feet per minute, 146, 158, 211.

Pull-Focus See **Focus-Pull**, 259.

Pushed in developing Another term for **Forced Processing** or **Extended Development**, 252, 290

Quartz-Iodine Lights Lighting units whose source is a form of small incandescent bulb with tungsten filament in a silica envelope containing iodine vapour. Often referred to as **Tungsten-Halogen Lights**, 254

Radio Microphone or **Radio Mike** A small microphone whose signal is transmitted to the sound recorder by a very small radio transmitter attached to it and concealed in an actor's clothes, 263

Reflector fill-light Figure lighting on exteriors produced by reflecting the sunlight shining from behind the actors back onto their shadow side from a sheet or other large surface, 74, 182, 183, 287.

Reflector Photofloods These are **Photoflood Bulbs** (q.v.) which include a parabolic mirror reflecting surface built into their envelopes so that they give a directed flood or spot beam without the usual subsidiary attachments.

Reflector Spotlight Large spotlight in which the beam was formed solely by a large parabolic reflector behind the light source. Colloquially called a 'Sunlight Arc' in the 'twenties.

26. INDEX OF FILM-MAKERS AND COMPANIES

27. INDEX OF FILM TITLES